西安

XI'AN STATISTICAL YEARBOOK

统计年鉴

2019

中英文对照 Chinese/English

中国统计出版社
China Statistics Press

西安市统计局
XI'AN MUNICIPAL BUREAU OF STATISTICS
国家统计局西安调查队
NBS SURVEY OFFICE IN XI'AN

©中国统计出版社有限公司 2019
版权所有。未经许可，本书的任何部分不得以任何方式在世界任何地区以任何文字翻印、拷贝、仿制或转载。

©2019 China Statistics Press Co.,Ltd.
All rights reserved. No part of the publication may be reproduced or transmitted in any form or by any means, electronic or mechanical, including photocopying, recording, or any information storage and retrieval system, without written permission from the publisher.

图书在版编目（CIP）数据

西安统计年鉴. 2019 / 西安市统计局, 国家统计局西安调查队编. -- 北京 : 中国统计出版社, 2019.9
ISBN 978-7-5037-8930-4

Ⅰ. ①西… Ⅱ. ①西… ②国… Ⅲ. ①统计资料—西安—2019—年鉴 Ⅳ. ①C832.411-54

中国版本图书馆CIP数据核字(2019)第182155号

西安统计年鉴—2019

作　　者/ 西安市统计局 国家统计局西安调查队
责任编辑/ 钟 钰
装帧设计/ 西安乐成品牌策划设计有限公司
出版发行/ 中国统计出版社有限公司
地　　址/ 北京市丰台区西三环南路甲6号
邮政编码/ 100073
电　　话/ 邮购（010）63376909 书店（010）68783171
网　　址/ http://csp.stats.gov.cn
印　　刷/ 西安第一印刷厂
经　　销/ 新华书店
开　　本/ 890mm×1240mm 1/16
字　　数/ 1563千字
印　　张/ 44
版　　别/ 2019年9月第1版
版　　次/ 2019年9月第1次印刷
定　　价/ 260元

如有印装差错，由本社发行部调换。

《西安统计年鉴—2019》编辑部

总编辑：张民伟　程海营

副总编辑：秦来生　赵群洁　李　红　陈瑾瑜　谷晓春　朱　强　陈立民
焦卫冬　董　军　张　敏

主编：赵群洁

副主编：刘　婷　李　芬

编辑：（以姓氏笔划为序）
丁抗玲　马建华　马　琰　王义龙　王子明　王金桂　冯军魁
边可为　刘栋婷　安海军　张利民　张　欣　李　娜　李　航
连　鹏　陈　英　罗朝晖　赵　剑　赵　晖　郝　静　席锋旭
栾立森　贾薪萼　高小琴　高　唯　曹　华　黄小丹　黄雪冰
曾文元　雷麦鸽　薛　丰

责任编辑：康　敏　侯计平　罗延庆　罗　茜　赵　博　孟　刚　张　熠

英文翻译：董　骋

XI'AN STATISTICAL YEARBOOK-2019
EDITORLAL STAFF

Editor-in-chief: Zhang Minwei Cheng Haiying

Associate Editors-in-chief: Qin Laisheng Zhao Qunjie L Hong Chen Jinyu Gu Xiaochun Zhu Qiang
Chen Limin Jiao Weidong Dong Jur Zhang Min

Editor-in-Chief: Zhao Qunjie

Deputy Editors-in-Chief: Liu Ting Li Fen

Editorial Staff: Ding Kangling Ma Jianhua Ma Yan Wang Yilong Wang Ziming Wang Jingui
Feng Junkui Bian Kewei Liu Dongting An Haijun Zhang Limin Zhang Xin Li Na
Li Hang Lian Peng Chen Ying Luo Zhaohui Zhao Jian Zhao Hui Hao jing
Xi Fengxu Luan Lisen Jia Xinrong Gao Xiaoqin Gao Wei Cao Hua Huang Xiaodan
Huang Xuebing Zeng Wenyuan Lei Maige Xue Feng

Coordinators: Kang Min Hou Jiping Luo Yanqing Luo Qian Zhao Bo Meng Gang Zhang Yi

English Translater: Dong Cheng

编者说明

一、《西安统计年鉴—2019》系统收录了全市、区县及开发区2018年经济、社会各方面统计数据，以及重要历史年份主要统计数据，是一部全面记载西安市国民经济和社会发展情况的大型连续性统计文献资料和重要工具书。

二、本年鉴正文内容分为二十二个篇章：（一）综合；（二）基本单位；（三）国民经济核算；（四）人口、从业人员与职工工资；（五）固定资产投资；（六）财政；（七）物价指数；（八）人民生活；（九）城市公用事业；（十）环境保护；（十一）农业；（十二）工业；（十三）能源；（十四）建筑业；（十五）运输、邮电和信息化；（十六）国内贸易；（十七）对外经济贸易和旅游；（十八）服务业；（十九）金融业；（二十）教育和科技；（二十一）文化、体育、卫生、社会福利和其他；（二十二）企业调查。同时，为方便读者使用，各篇章前设有简要说明和主要统计指标，对本篇章的主要内容、资料来源以及历史变动情况予以简要概述，篇末附有《主要统计指标解释》。

三、本年鉴统计资料的统计标准，按当时国家统计制度执行，有关指标的涵义、口径、范围、计算方法等，在不同时期可能有所不同，使用时请注意。如，国民经济行业分类按GB/T4754—2017标准执行。

四、为便于国内外读者查阅，本年鉴全部内容均采用中英文对照编辑。

五、本年鉴中国民经济核算部分的2013年数据为全国第三次经济普查数据，2009-2012年数据为依据第三次经济普查修订数据，2017年及以后GDP核算包含研发支出新增GDP数据，2018年第一产业增加值为三农普修订数据；工业部分的2013年数据为第三次经济普查数据；国内贸易部分的2009-2013年为依据第三次经济普查调整后数据；农业部分的2007-2017年农林牧渔业总产值、产量等和2013-2017年畜产品等为依据第三次农业普查调整后数据；城镇居民和农村居民人均可支配收入2017年为依据新口径修订数据；固定资产投资部分主要为增长速度等相对指标数据；科技部分（除部门数据）为2017年数据。

六、数据口径：本年鉴中2017年起全市数据中，基本单位、国民经济核算、农业(除个别指标)、工业、建筑业、国内贸易、服务业、能源、固定资产投资、常住人口、从业人员和职工工资、信息化、企业调查、城市公用事业（除城市公共交通部分等）、财政、教育、文化、卫生、社会福利和行政区划等指标数据包含西咸新区；2018年人民生活、利用外资等指标包含西咸新区。物价指数（除部分指标）、运输邮电、环境保护、对外贸易和旅游(除部分指标)、金融、体育、户籍人口、土地面积、气象等指标数据为西安原口径或不包含西咸新区（不含西咸新区指不包含西咸西安片区和咸阳片区）数据，具体情况见表下附注。

七、本年鉴中的部分指标合计数或相对数由于单位取舍不同产生的计算误差均未作机械调整。

八、本年鉴所使用的计量单位均依据2018年相关统计报表制度。

九、本年鉴使用的符号说明："空白"表示该项统计指标无数据或数据不详；"#"表示其中项；"*"表示另有注解。

感谢社会各界长期以来对《西安统计年鉴》的广泛关注和大力支持。为进一步做好工作，更好地为广大读者服务，希望社会各界提出宝贵意见。

PREFACE

I. Xi'an Statistical Yearbook 2019 is a periodical statistic yearbook which record economic and social development of Xi'an all-around in 2018 and some selected data series in historical important years. With its features of comprehensive and intensive information, this practically provides data covering the situation of social and economic developments in Xi'an.

II. The book contains twenty-two parts, 1.General Survey; 2.Basic Unit; 3.National Economic Account; 4.Population, Employment and Wages; 5.Investment in Fixed Assets; 6.Government Finance; 7.Price Indices; 8.People's Livelihood; 9.Urban Public Utilities; 10.Environmental Protection; 11.Agriculture; 12.Industry; 13.Energy; 14.Construction; 15.Transportation, Post and Informatization; 16.Domestic Trade; 17.Foreign Trade; 18. Service Industry; 19.Financial Intermediation; 20.Education, Science and Technology; 21.Culture, Sports, Public Health, Social Welfare and Other Social Activities; 22.Enterprises Investigation. Meanwhile, for the convenience of the reader, a brief explanation and major statistical indicators are provided before each chapter, the main contents, sources and historical changes of this chapter are briefly summarized. The final part is accompanied by the interpretation of major statistical indicators.

III. The data of various years in conformity to the statistical standards prescribed by national statistical system of the time. The meaning, scope and calculating method of indicators may have some difference in different periods, which readers must pay attention to. For example, national industries classification is carried out according to standard GB/T4754 -2017. For the sake of comparison of the old and new industry standards, we edit the division's data in some major indicators according to standard GB/T4754 -2017.

IV. For the convenience of being consulted by foreigners, the book is Chinese-English bilingual edition.

V. In this yearbook the data of 2013 at the part of National Economic Accounting and Industry is the results of Third National Economic Census, the data from 2009 to 2012 at the part of National Economic Account have adjusted by Third National Economic Census, GDP calculations for 2017 and beyond include new GDP data for R&D expenditures, The value added of the primary industry in 2018 is revised data for San Nongpu; the data in 2013 for the industrial segment is the third economic census data; the domestic trade part of 2009-2013 is based on the adjusted data of the third economic census. The agricultural output, the total output value, output of agriculture, forestry, animal husbandry and fishery in 2007-2017 and the livestock products and in 2013-2017 are based on the adjusted data of the third agricultural census. The per capita disposable income of urban residents and rural residents is revised based on the new caliber in 2017; Fixed asset investment data are mainly relative indicator data such as growth rate;2018 technology(except departmental data)is the previous year's data.

VI. Statistical scope: in this yearbook, the data from 2017 about the basic unit, the national economic accounting, agriculture, industry, construction industry, domestic trade, services, energy, investment in fixed assets, labor wages, informatization, enterprise survey, urban public utilities, finance, education, culture, health and social welfare contains Xi Xian New Area; in 2018, indicators such as people's living and utilization of foreign capital include Xixian New District. The price index (except for individual indicators), transportation, post and telecommunications, environmental protection, foreign trade and tourism (except for some indicators), finance, sports, household registration, land area, meteorological and other indicators are Xi'an original caliber or does not include data in Xixian New Area(Does not include Xixian New Area, meaning that it does not include some are of Xi'an and xianyang in Xixian). See the notes under the table for details.

VII .Statistical discrepancies due to rounding are not adjusted automatically in this yearbook.

VIII. Unit of measurement is used in this yearbook according to 2018 statistics system.

Ⅸ.Explanations on symbols used in this yearbook:

(Blank) indicates the data not available;

# indicates the items of the total.

* indicates some other explanatory note.

Here we would like to express our sincere thanks to the people for their concerning and support to the Xi'an statistical yearbook. In order to do better and provide better service to readers, we hope that the whole society fields can propose constructive advices.

生产总值（亿元）

Gross Domestic Product (100 million yuan)

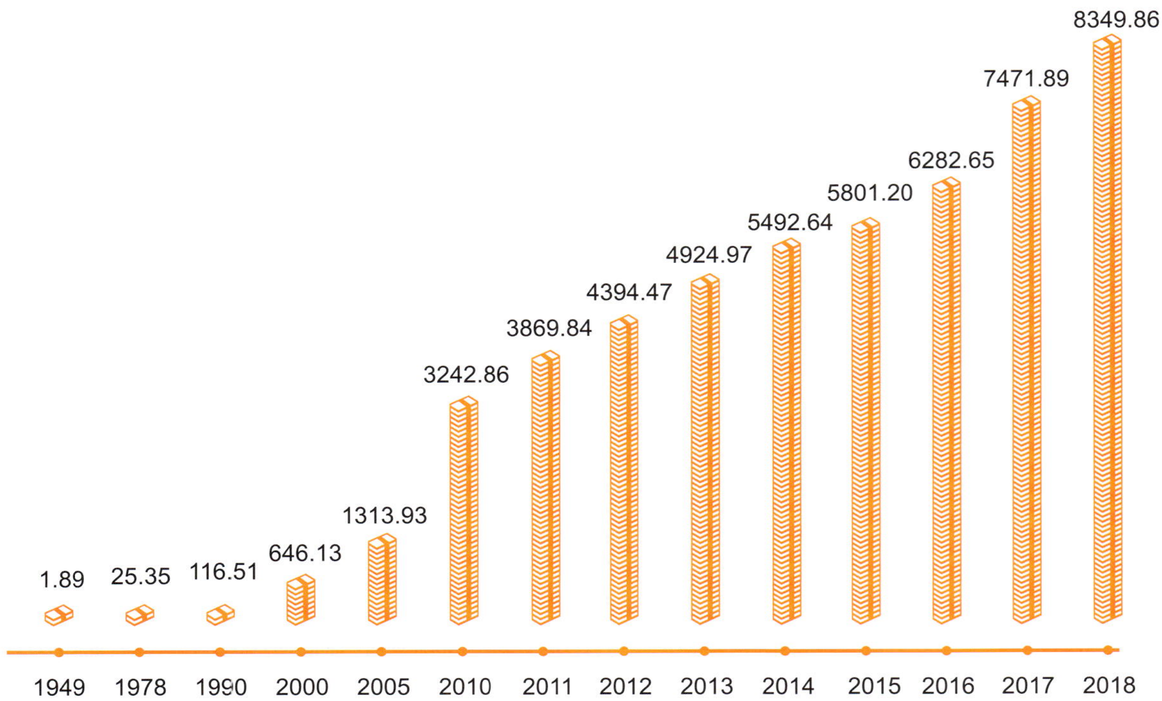

生产总值指数（以上年为100）

Indices of Gross Domestic Product (preceding year = 100)

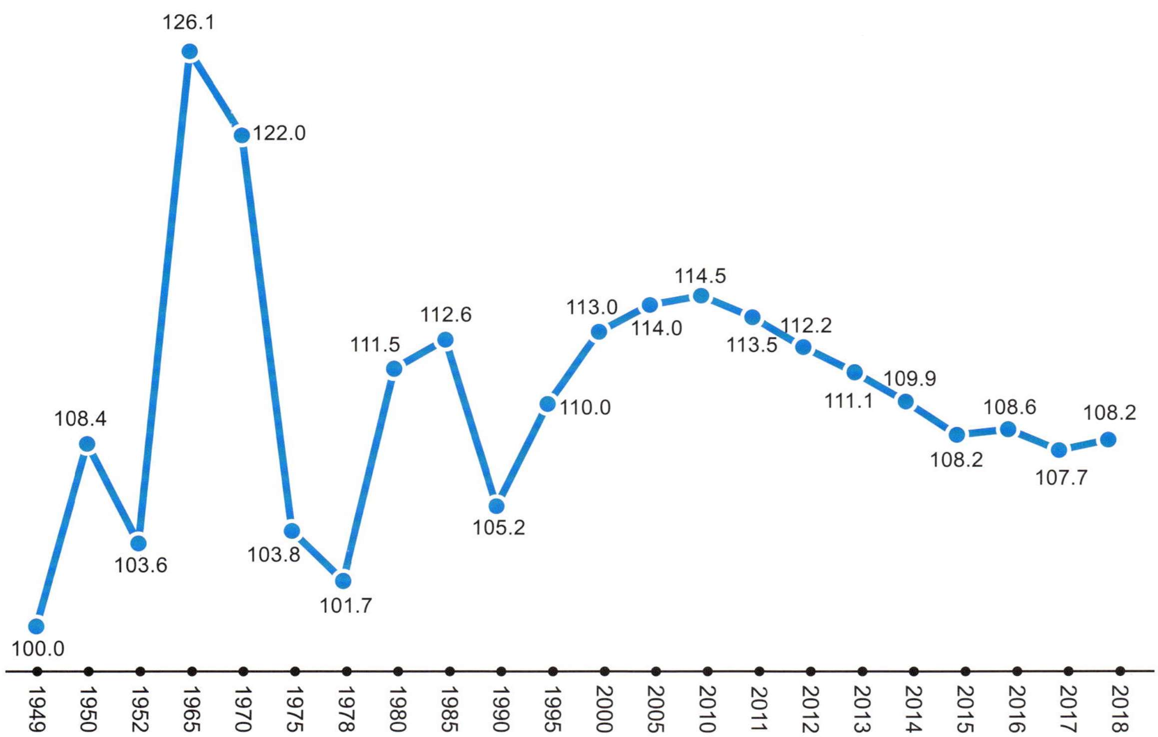

生产总值构成（%）

Composition of Gross Domestic Product (%)

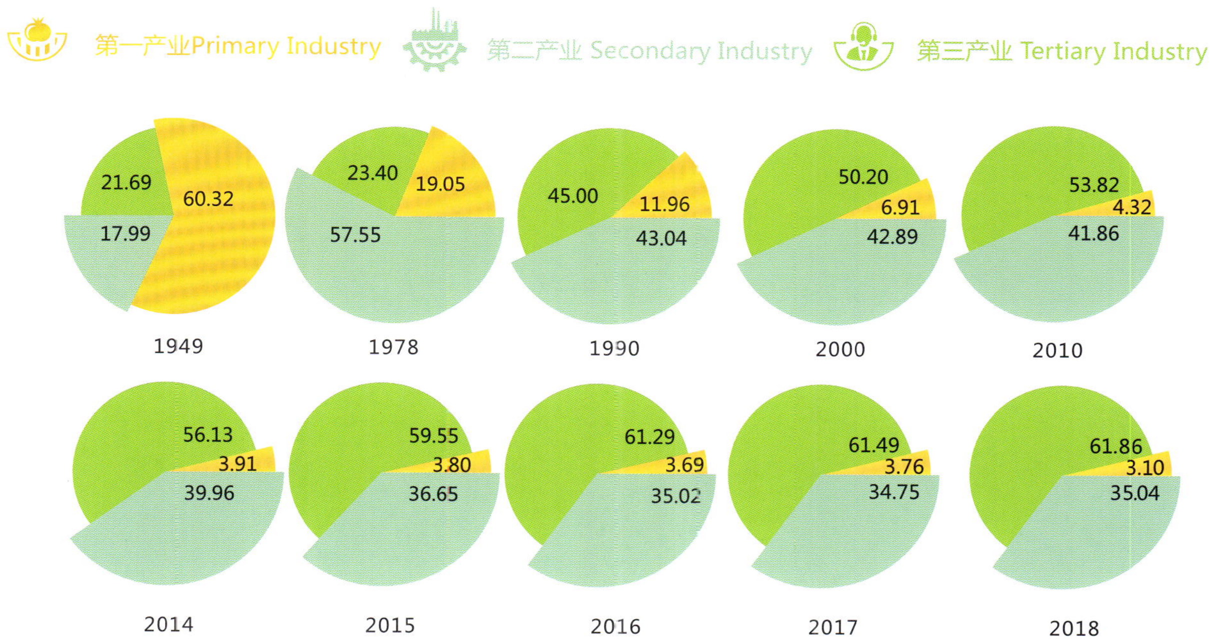

人均GDP（元/人）

Per Capita GDP(yuan/person)

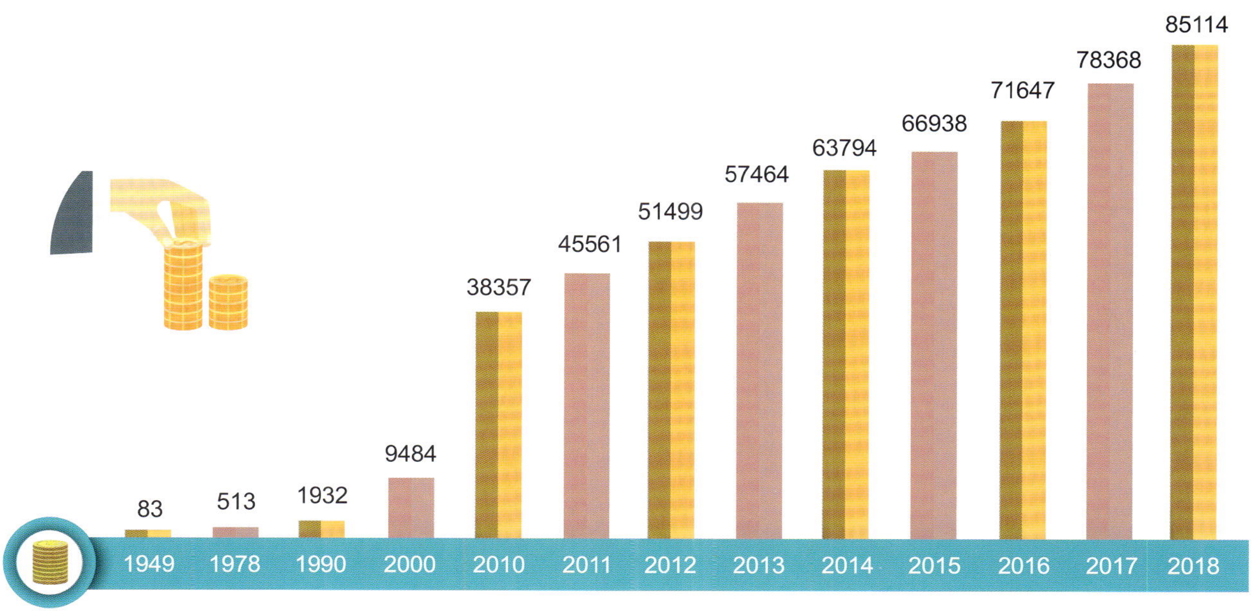

年末常住人口（万人）

Year-end Permanent Population(10000 persons)

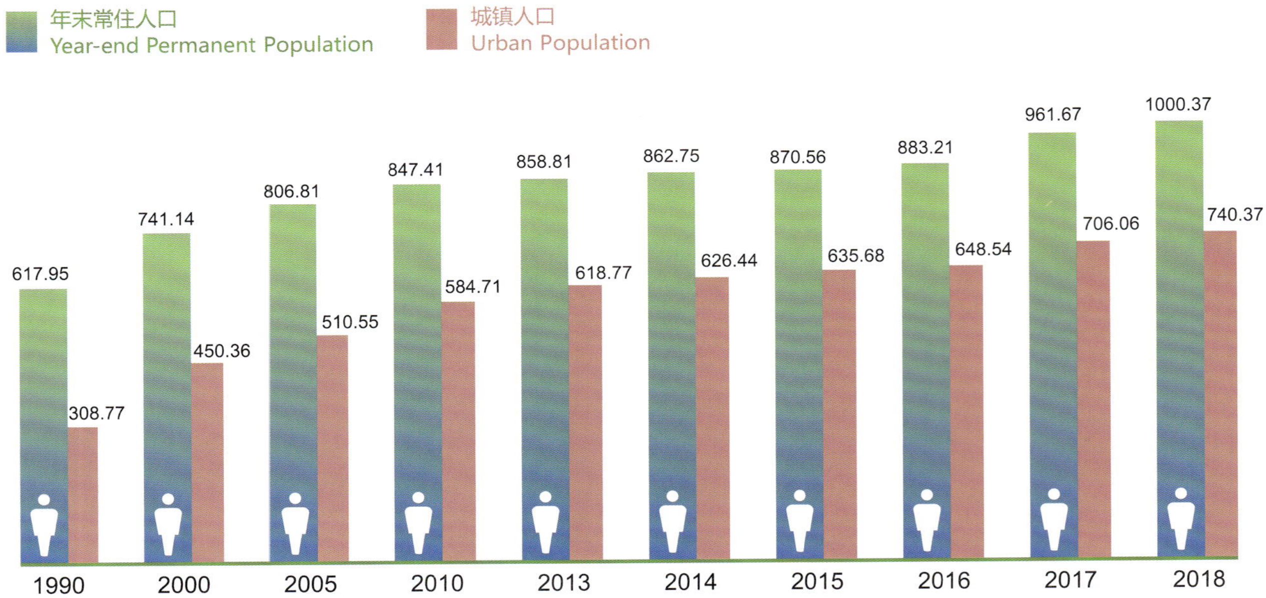

社会从业人数（万人）

Social Workers(10000 persons)

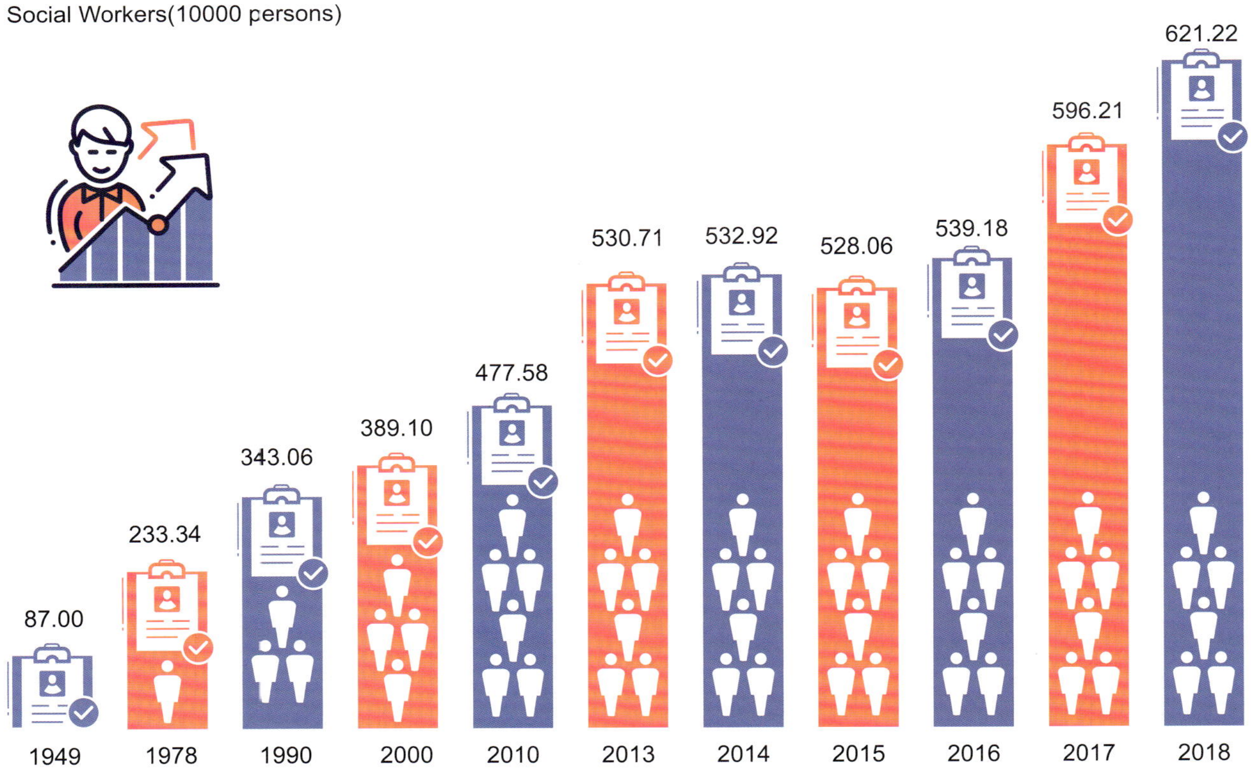

固定资产投资增长速度（%）

Growth Rates of Investment in Fixed Assets（%）

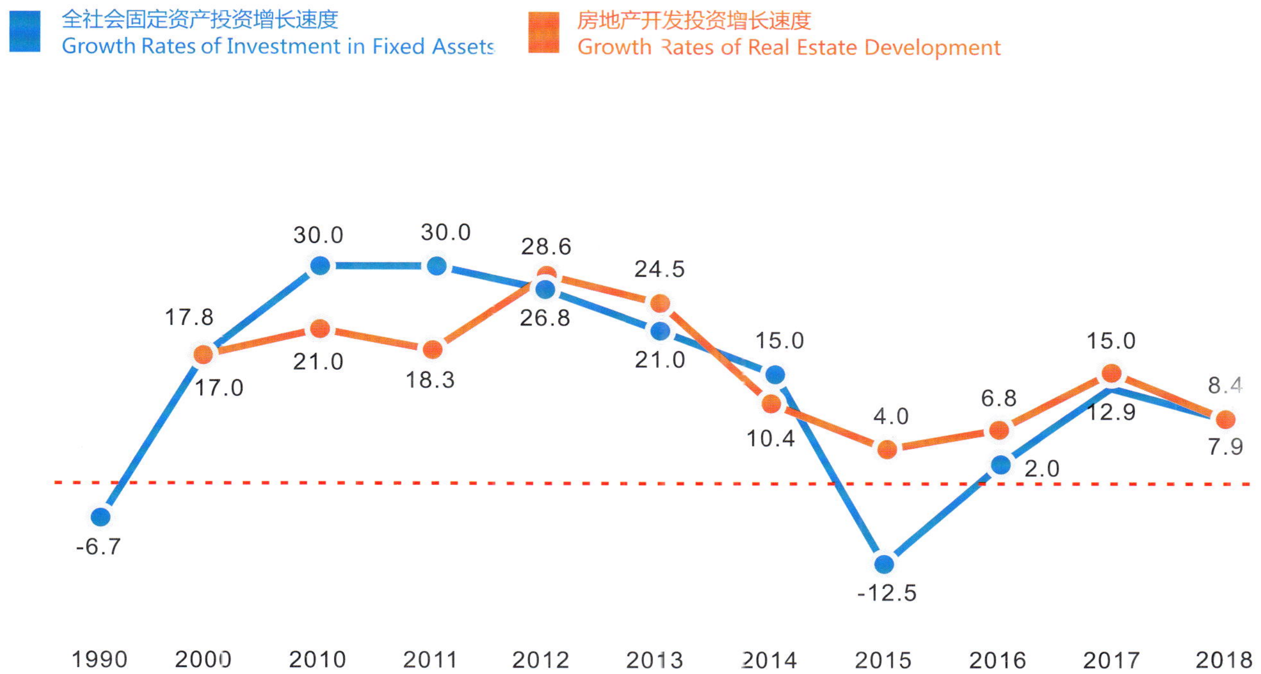

商品房销售面积（万平方米）

Floor Space of Commercialized Buildings Sold（10000sq.m）

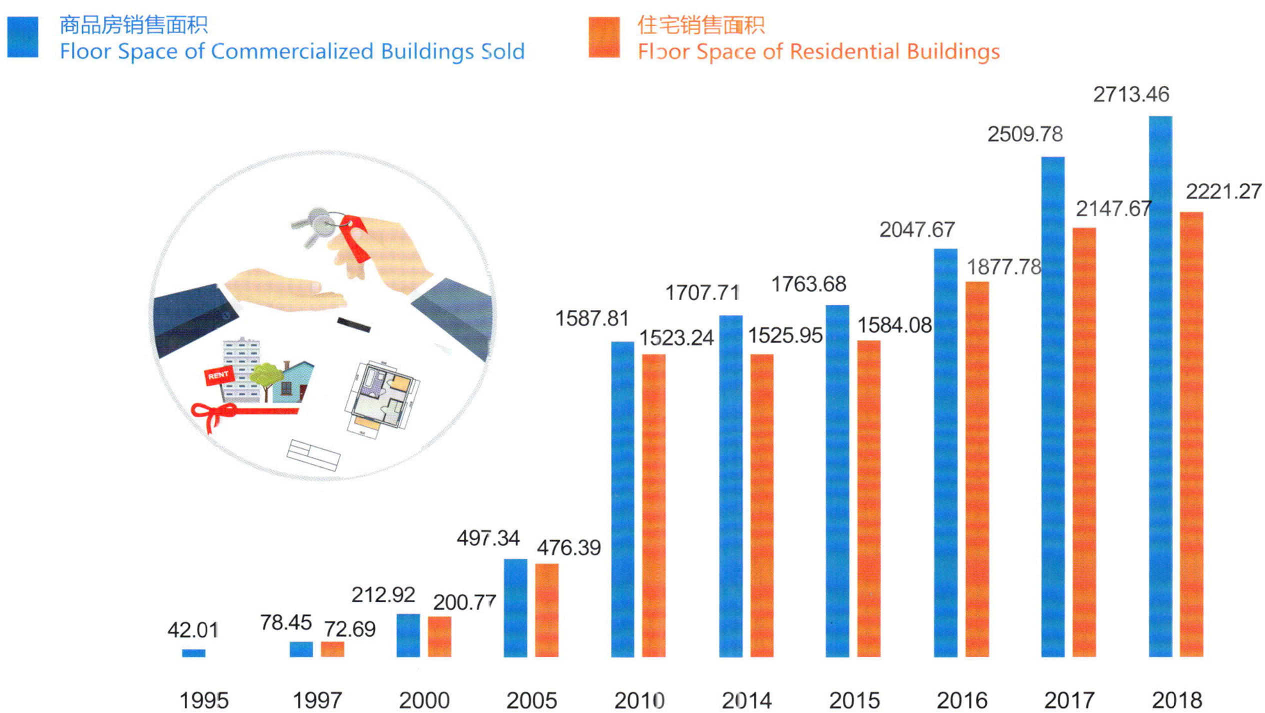

农林牧渔业总产值（亿元）

Gross Output Value of Farming,Forestry,
Animal Husbandry and Fishery (100 million yuan)

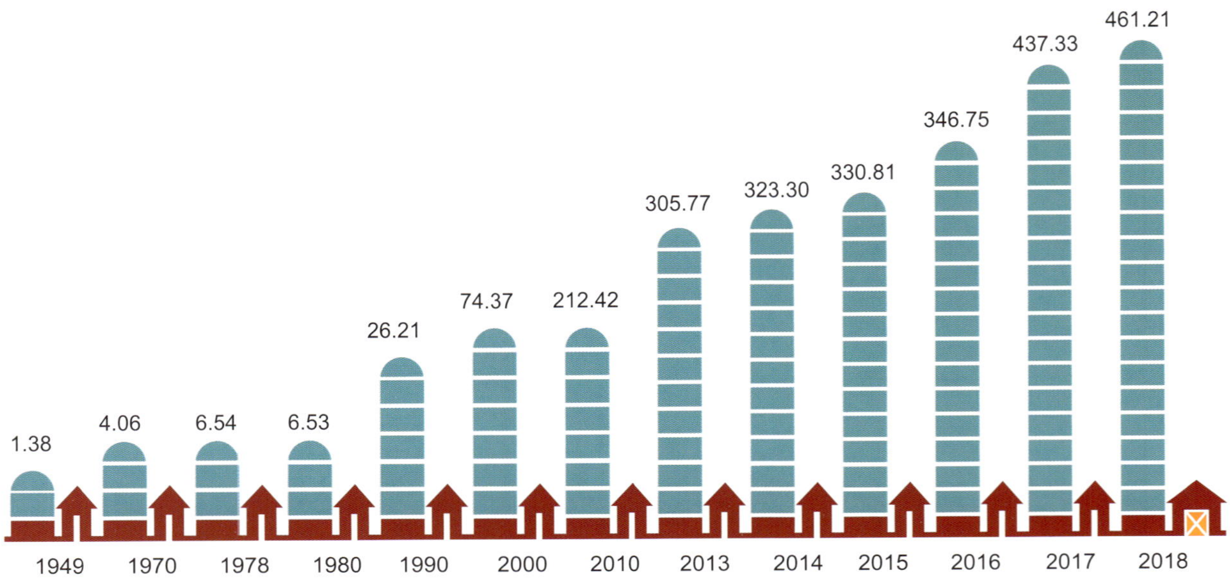

粮食产量（万吨）

Grain Product(10000 tons)

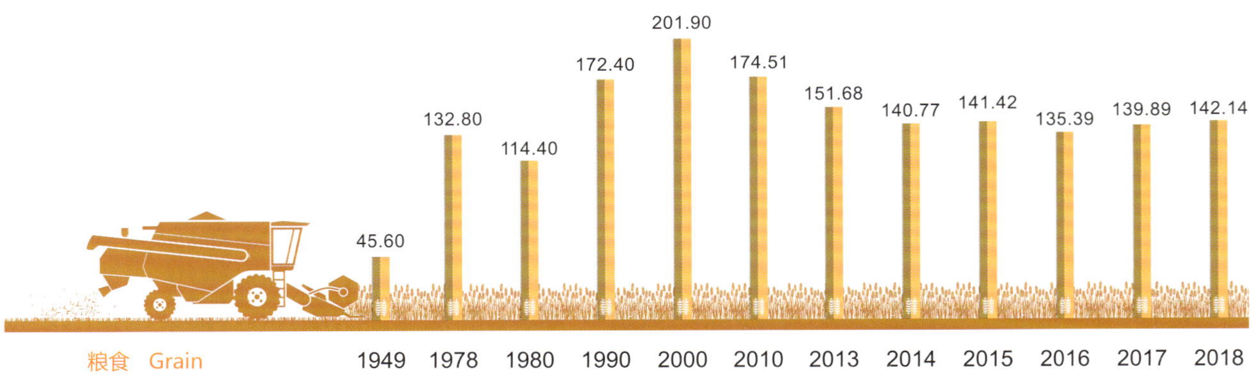

蔬菜产量（万吨）

Vegetables Product(10000 tons)

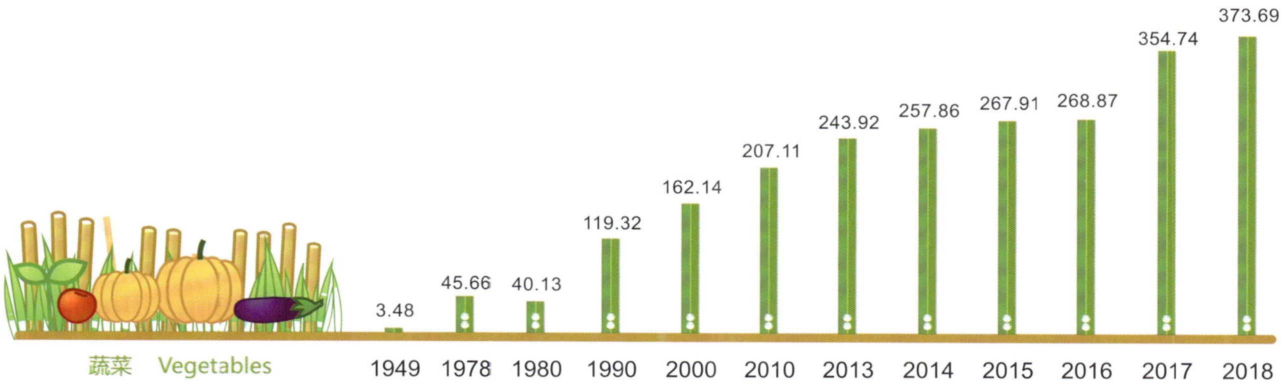

规模以上工业企业主要产品产量

Output of Major Industrial Products Of Enterprises Above Designated Size

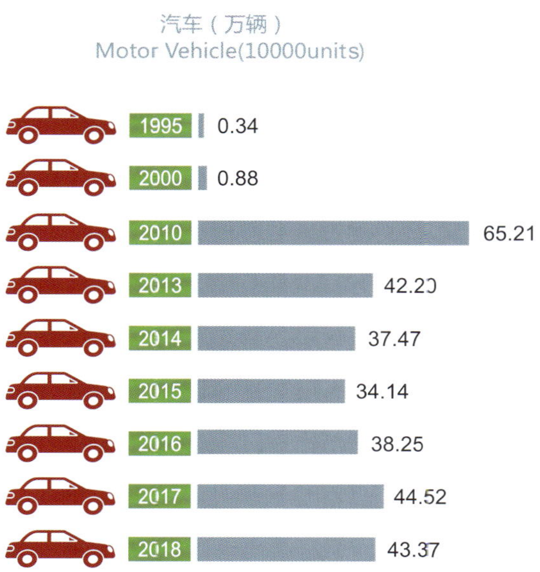

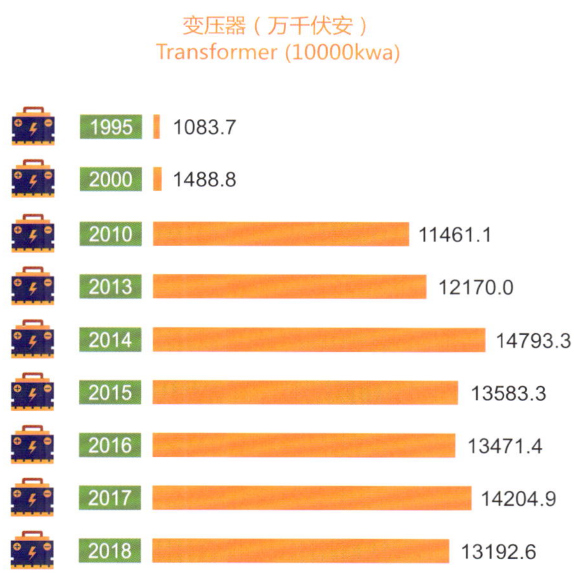

交通
Traffic

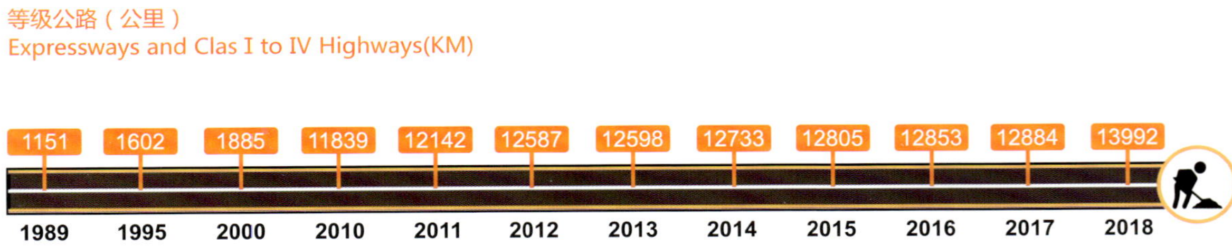

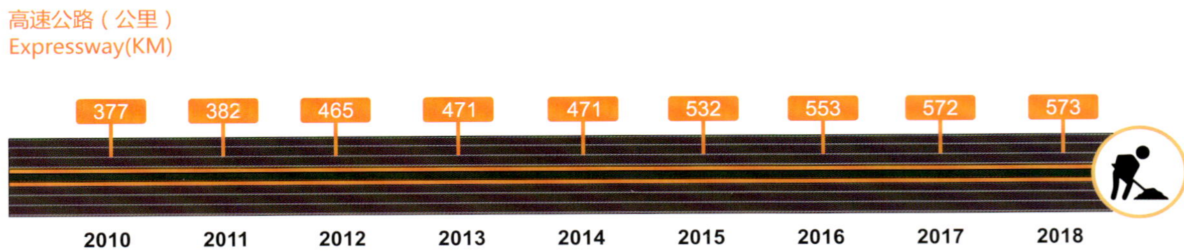

全社会车辆数（万辆）
Possession of Civil Vehicles(10000 units)

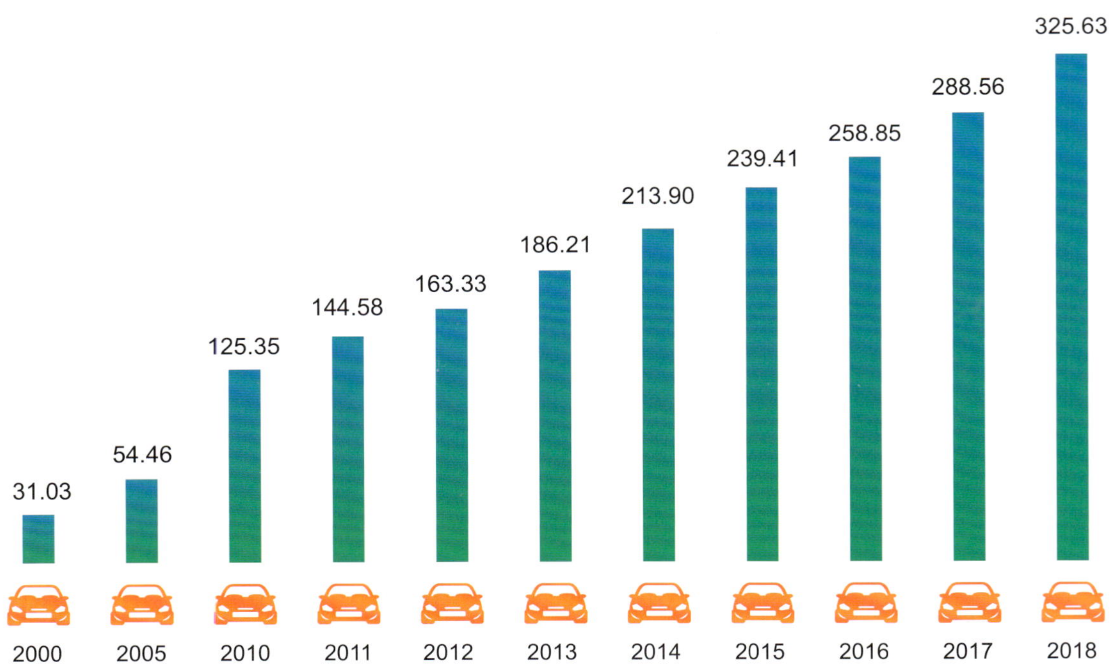

社会消费品零售总额（亿元）

Total Retail Sales of Consumer Goods(100 million yuan)

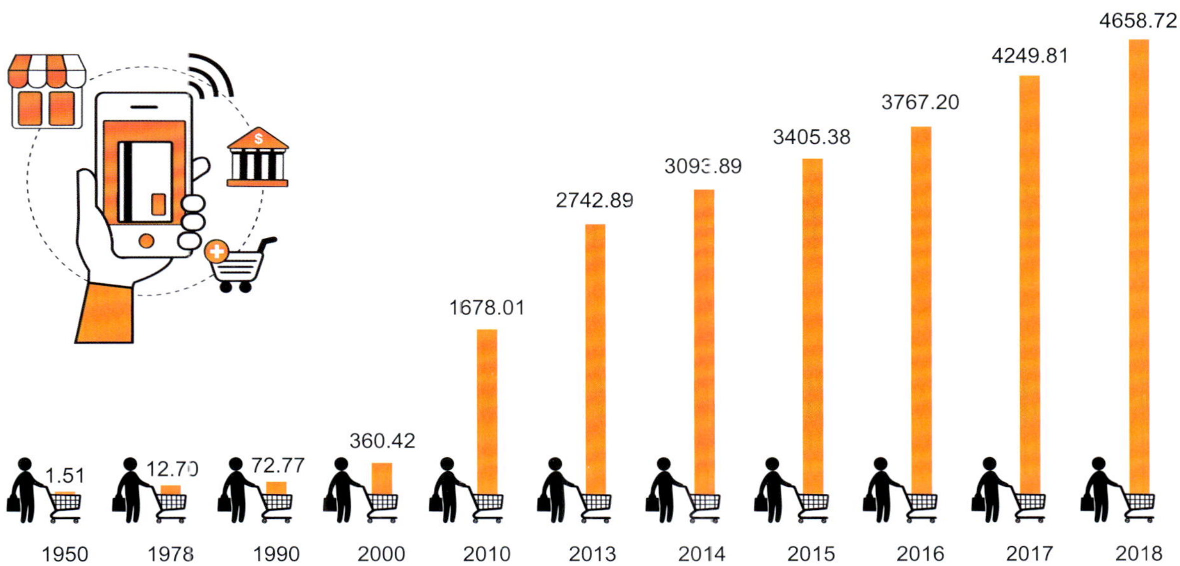

实际利用外商直接投资额（亿美元）

Foreign Direct Investment(USD 100 million)

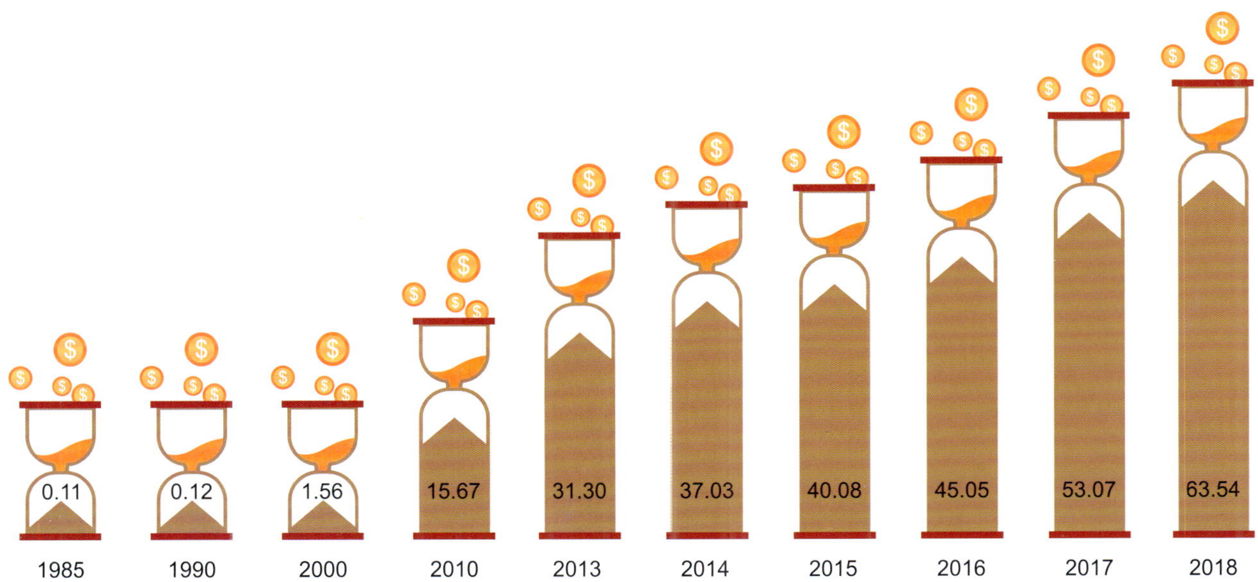

进出口总值（亿美元）

Total Value of Imports and Exports(USD 100 million)

	1987	1990	2000	2010	2011	2012	2013
进出口总值	1.36	3.82	17.37	103.92	126.02	130.14	179.85
出口总值	0.75	2.83	10.61	53.17	58.27	72.99	84.78
进口总值	0.61	0.99	6.76	50.75	67.75	57.16	95.07

	2014	2015	2016	2017	2018
进出口总值	1532.15	1761.69	1829.95	2545.08	3303.24
出口总值	734.68	819.88	947.31	1552.22	1957.17
进口总值	797.47	941.81	882.64	992.86	1346.07

注：2014年起单位为人民币亿元

旅游人数及收入

Number of Tourists and Tourism Income

接待旅游者人数（万人次）
Number of Tourists （10000 person-times)

旅游总收入（亿元）
Total Tourism Earnings(100 million yuan)

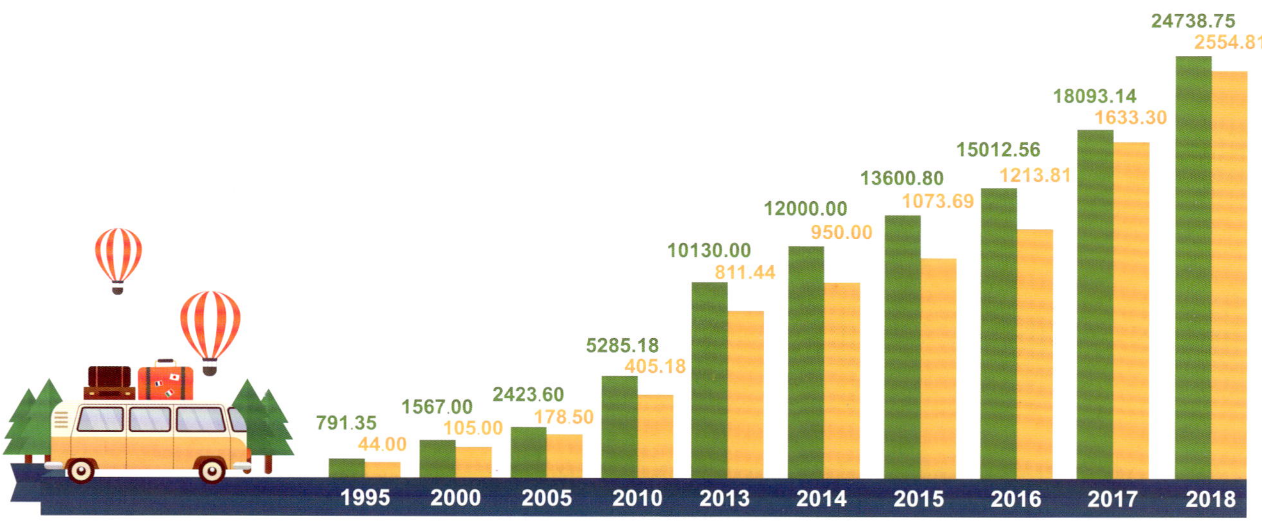

财政收支（亿元）

Govement Revenue and Expenditure(100 million yuan)

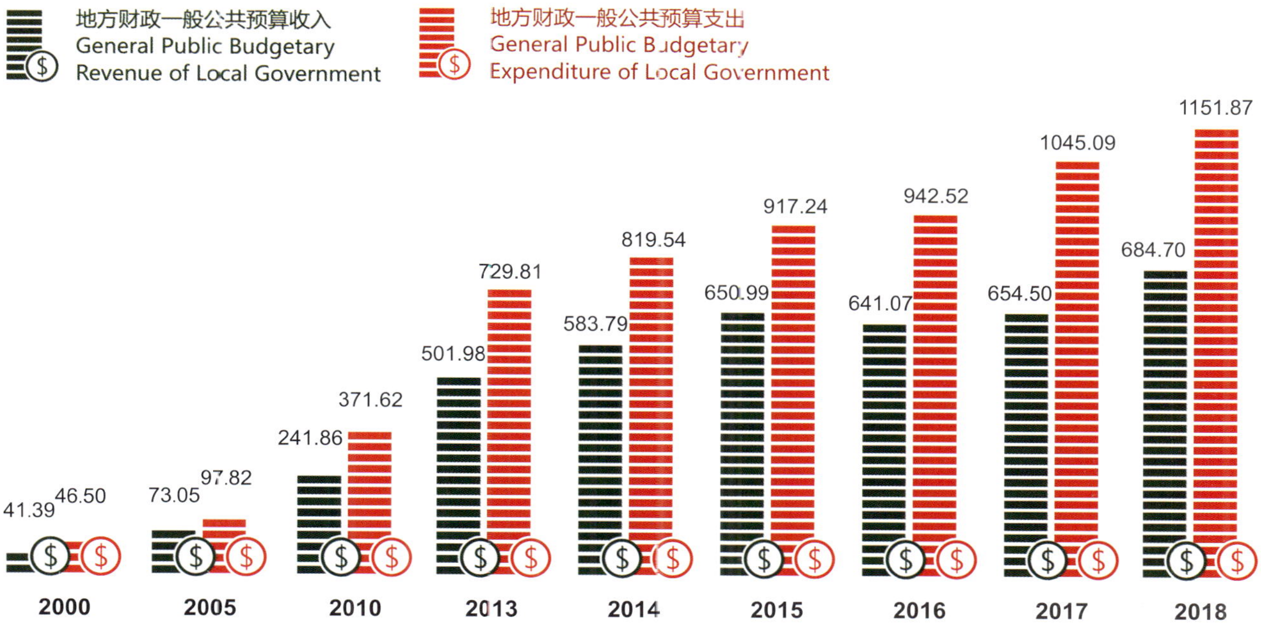

金融机构人民币存贷款年末余额（亿元）

Year-end Deposit and Loans in Financial Institutions (100 million yuan)

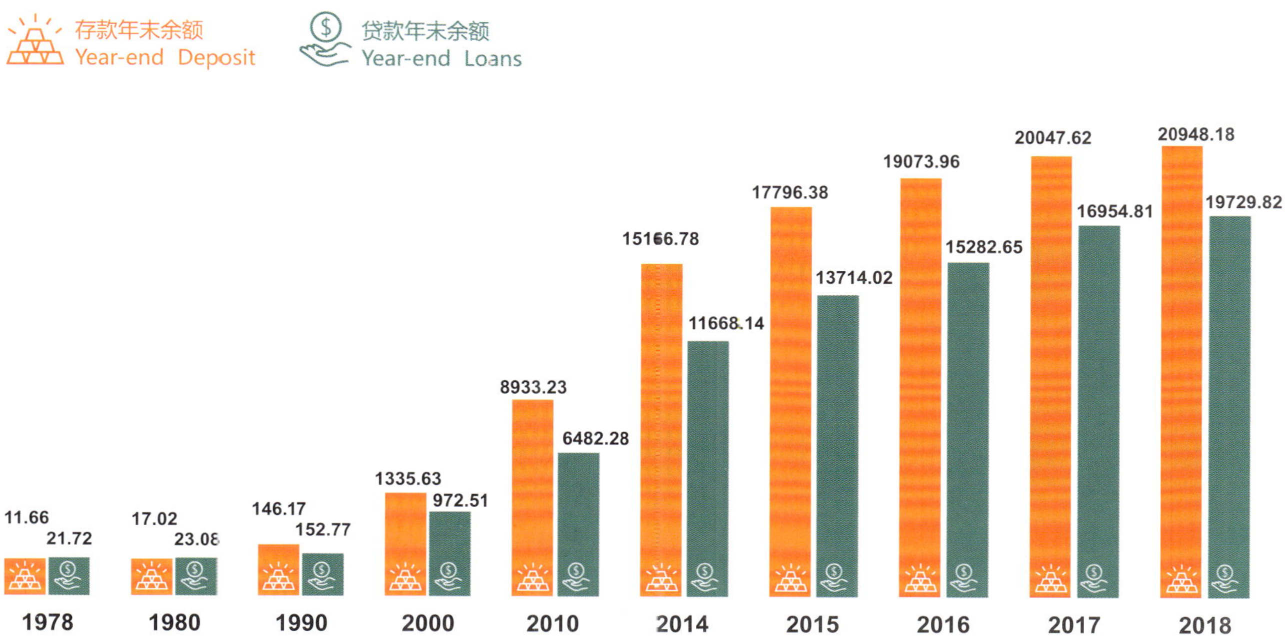

建成区面积（平方公里）

Area of Regions Built-up(sq.km)

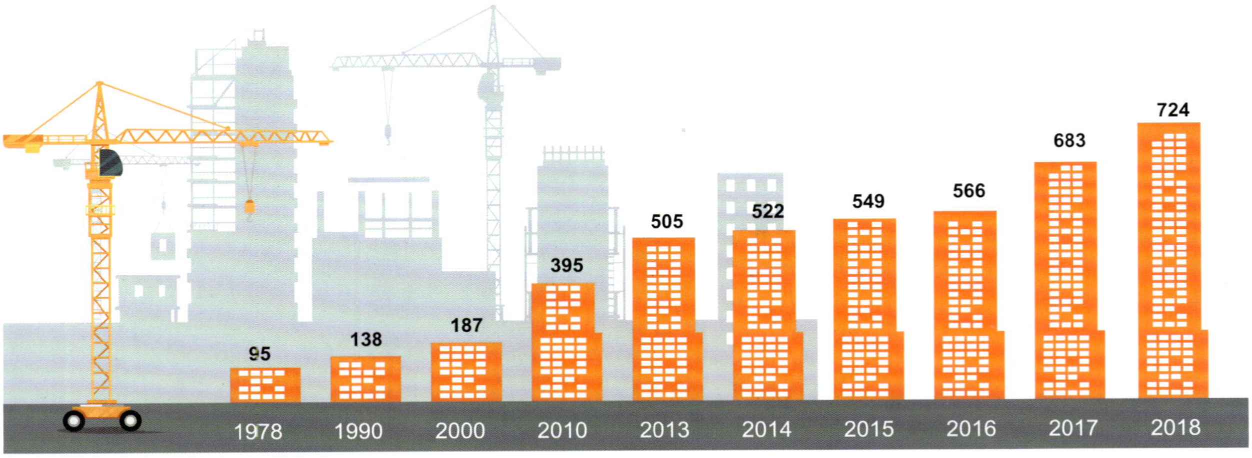

城市公共运营车辆（辆）

City Operating Vehicles(unit)

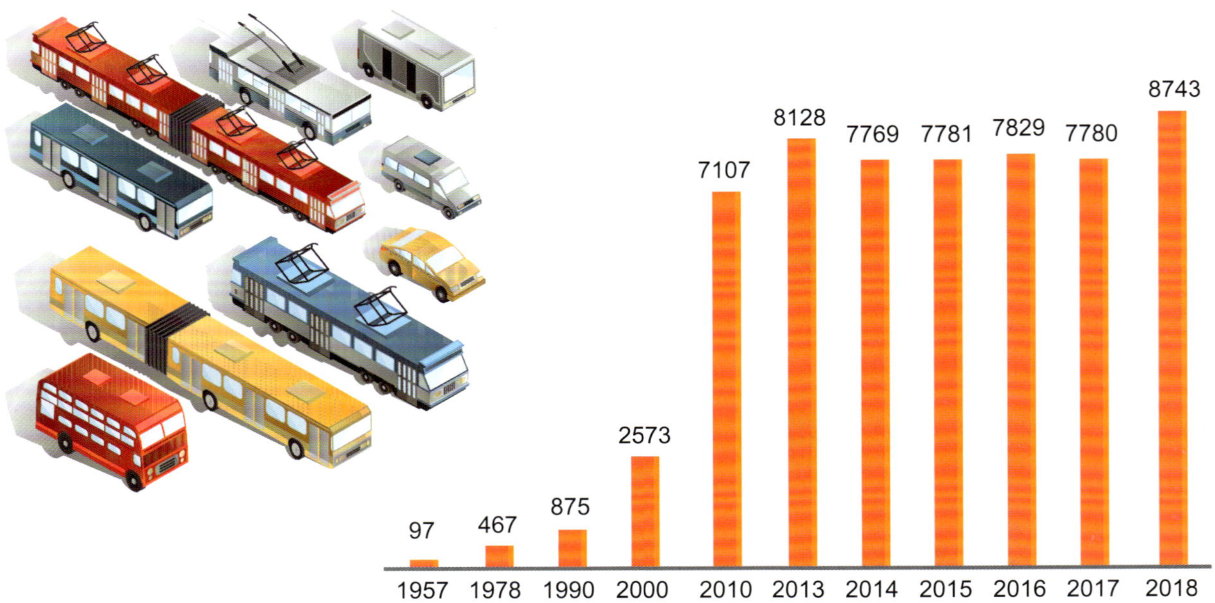

天然气供气总量（万立方米）

Total Natural Gas Supply(10000 cu.m)

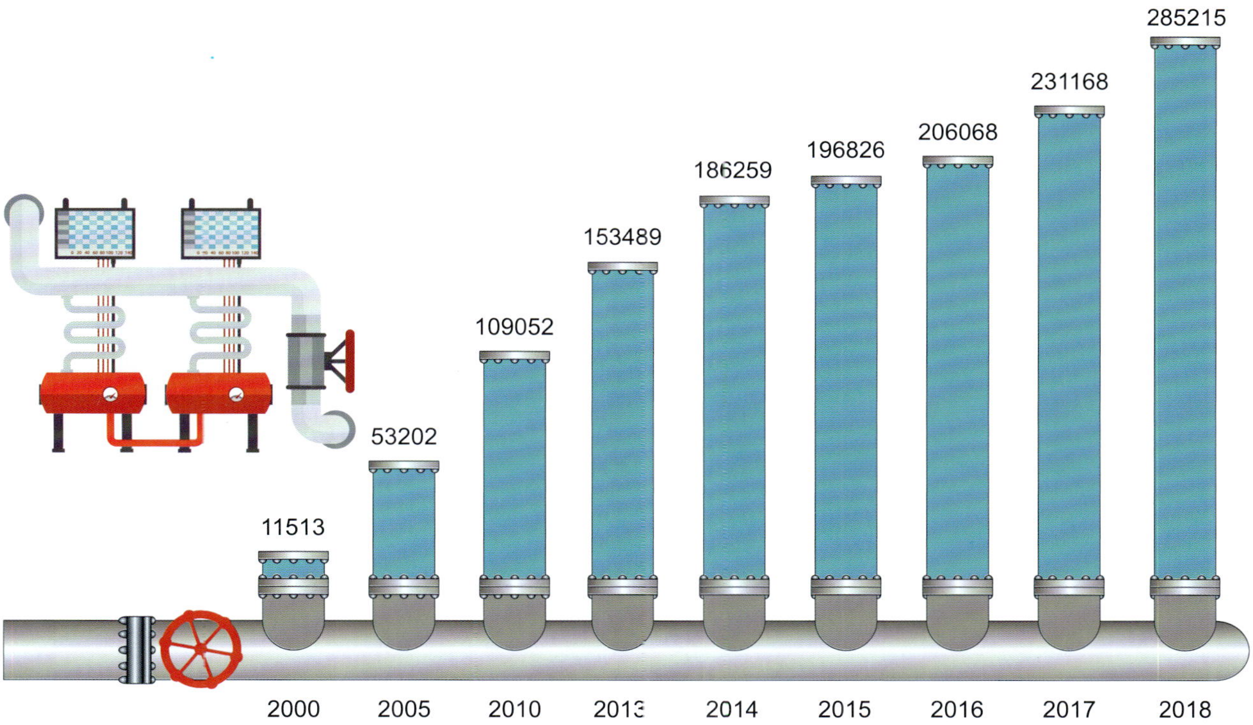

园林绿地面积（公顷）

Total Area of Park，Gardens and Green Area（hectare）

普通教育在校学生（万人）

Total Enrollment of Regular Education（10000 persons）

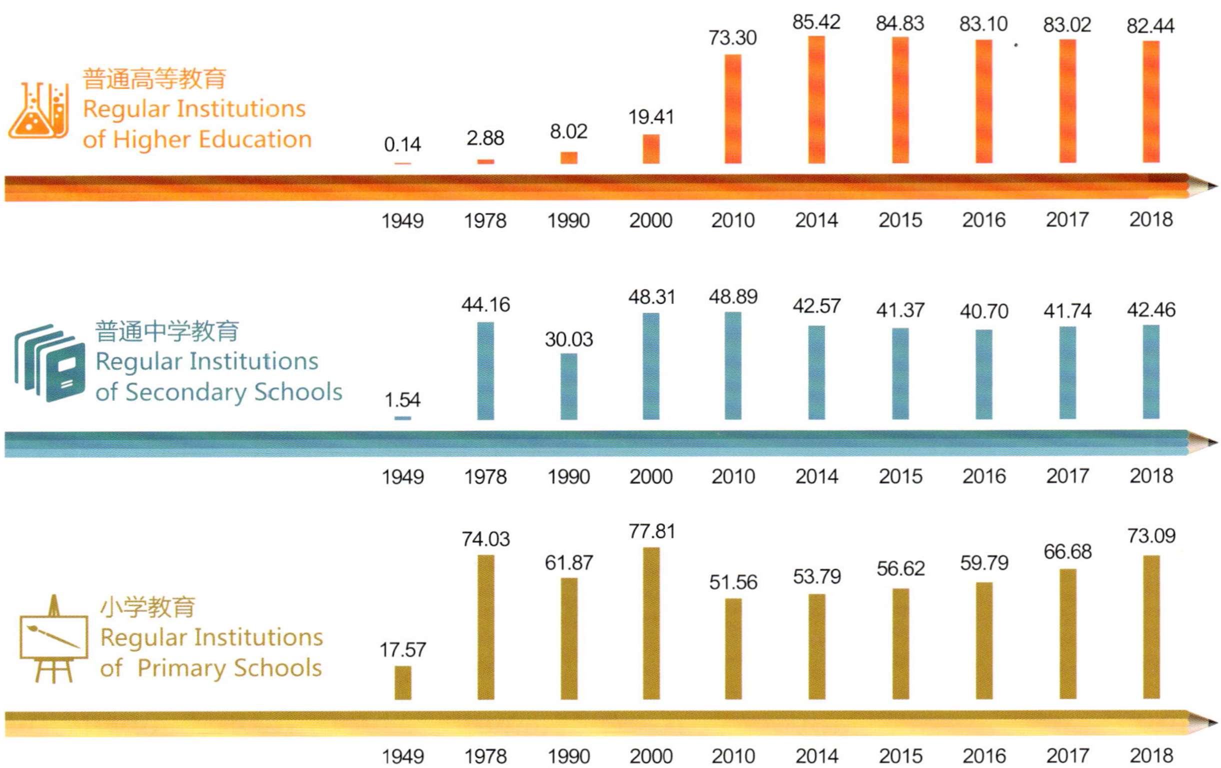

专任教师(万人）

Full-time Teachers (10000 persons)

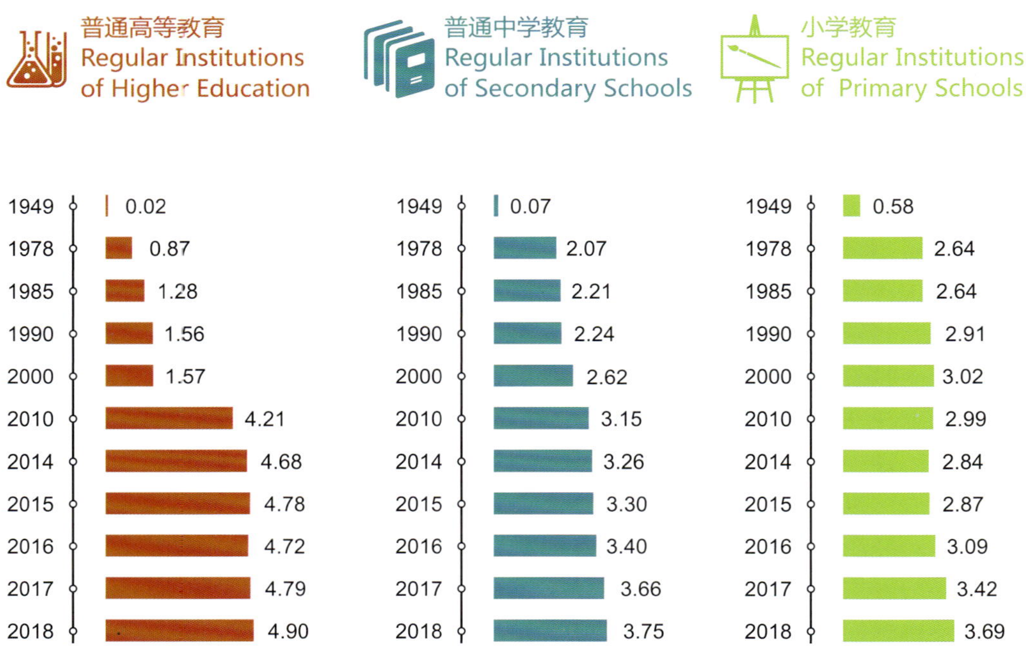

城乡居民收入（元）

The Income of Urban and Rural Residents(yuan)

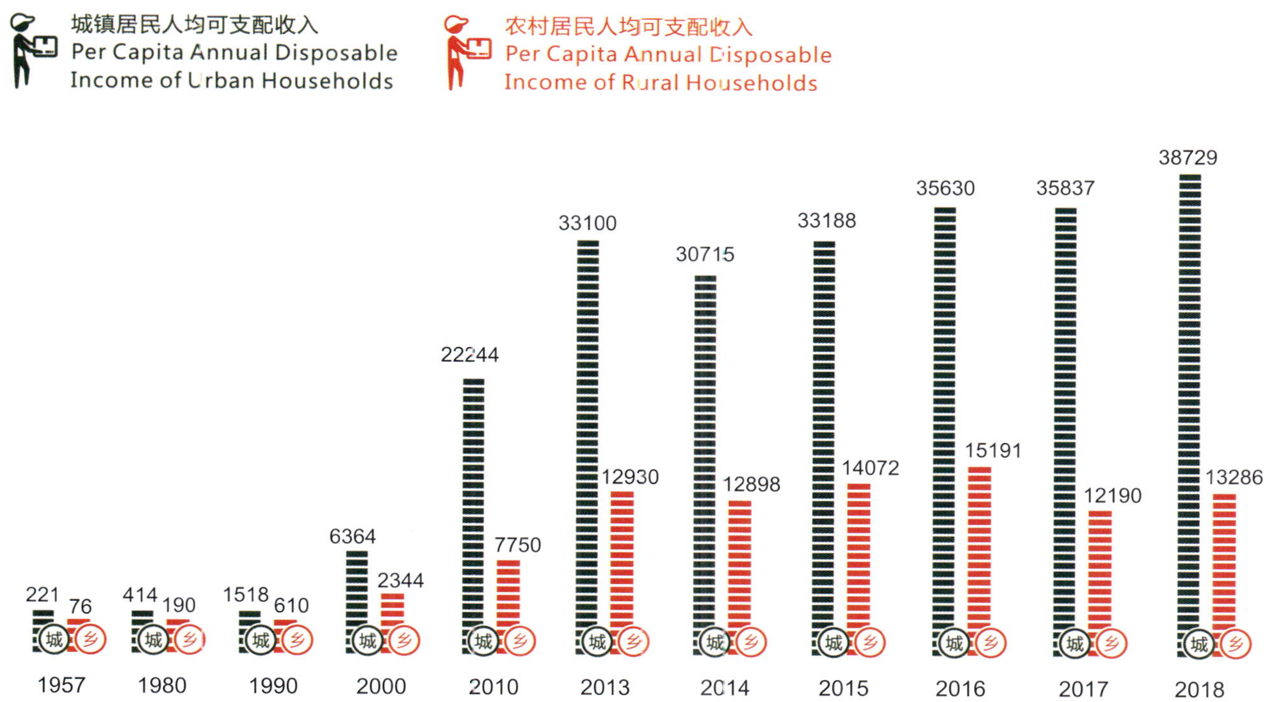

注：2013年前"农村居民人均可支配收入"为"农村居民人均纯收入"。

价格指数（以上年价格为100）

Price Indices(the price of preceding year=100)

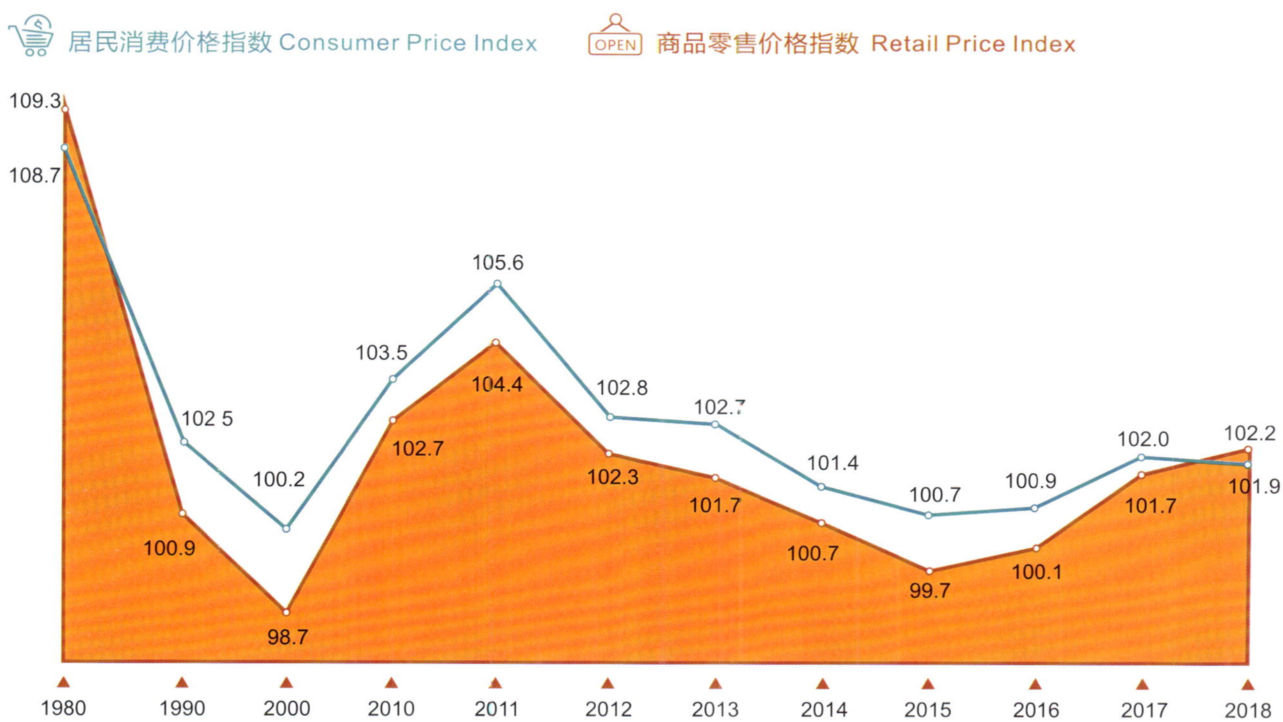

目　　录

CONTENTS

一、综　　合

GENERAL SURVEY

二、基本单位

BASIC UNIT

三、国民经济核算

NATIONAL ECONOMIC ACCOUNTS

四、人口、从业人员与职工工资

POPULATION, EMPLOYMENT AND WAGES

五、固定资产投资

INVESTMENT IN FIXED ASSETS

六、财　政
GOVERNMENT FINANCE

七、物价指数
PRICE INDICES

八、人民生活

PEOPLE'S LIVELIHOOD

九、城市公用事业

URBAN PUBLIC UTILITIES

十、环境保护

ENVIRONMENT PROTECTION

十一、农　业
AGRICULTURE

十二、工　业

INDUSTRY

十三、能　　源

ENERGY

十四、建筑业

CONSTRUCTION

十五、运输邮电和信息化

TRANSPORT，POSTAL TELECOMMUNICATION SERVICE AND INFORMATIZATION

十六、国内贸易

DOMESTIC TRADE

十七、对外经济贸易和旅游

FOREIGN TRADE AND ECONOMIC COOPERATION TOURISM

十八、规模以上服务业

SERVICE INDUSTRY OBOVE DESIGNATED SIZE

十九、金融业

FINANCIAL INTERMEDIATION

二十、教育和科技

EDUCATION，SCIENCE AND TECHNOLOGY

二十一、文化、体育、卫生、社会福利和其他
CULTURE, SPORTS, PUBLIC HEALTH, SOCIAL WELFARE INSTITUTIONS AND OTHER SOCIAL ACTIVITIES

二十二、企业调查

ENTERPRISES INVESTIGATION

西安市2018年国民经济和社会发展统计公报[1]

西安市统计局　国家统计局西安调查队

2019年3月17日

2018年，全市上下坚持以习近平新时代中国特色社会主义思想为指引，深入贯彻落实党的十九大精神，紧扣追赶超越定位和“五个扎实”要求，围绕“五新战略”和“聚焦三六九、振兴大西安”奋斗目标，以“三个年”为抓手，锐意进取、攻坚克难，经济运行稳中向好，经济结构继续优化，发展质量不断提高，民生福祉持续增进，社会事业获得新进步，实现了经济平稳健康发展与社会和谐稳定，大西安发展稳步推进，国家中心城市建设精彩开局。

一、综合

初步核算，全年地区生产总值[2]（GDP）8349.86亿元，比上年增长8.2%。其中，第一产业增加值258.82亿元，增长3.3%；第二产业增加值2925.61亿元，增长8.5%；第三产业增加值5165.43亿元，增长8.3%。三次产业构成为3.1:35.0:61.9。按常住人口计算，全年人均生产总值85114元，比上年增长5.2%。

全年非公有制经济增加值4459.64亿元，占生产总值的比重为53.4%，比上年提高0.4个百分点。

图1：2014-2018年地区生产总值及其增长速度

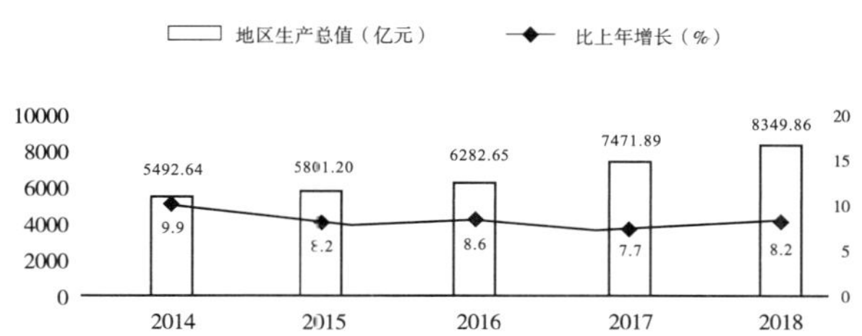

图2：2014-2018年三次产业增加值占地区生产总值比重（%）

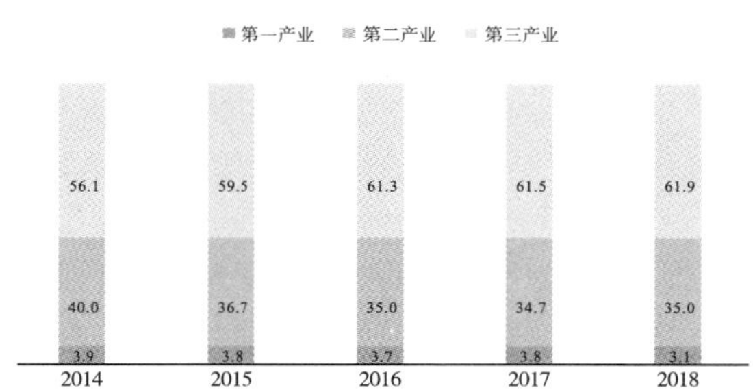

全年居民消费价格比上年上涨1.9%，其中，食品烟酒价格上涨2.2%。商品零售价格上涨2.2%。工业生产者出厂价格上涨1.1%，工业生产者购进价格上涨2.7%。固定资产投资价格上涨4.7%。新建商品住宅销售价格上涨14.6%。

图3：2018年居民消费价格月度涨跌幅度（%）

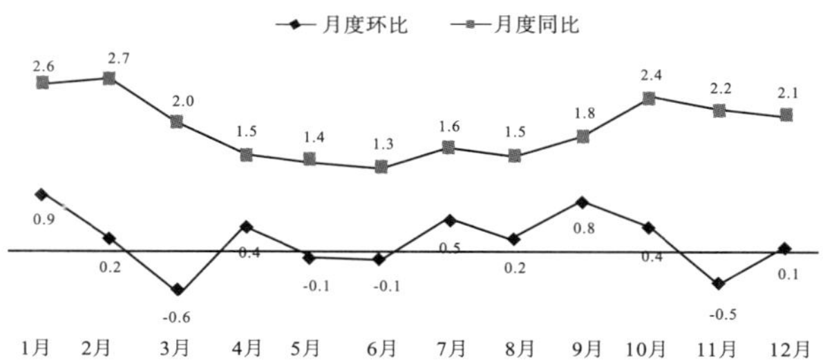

表1：2018年居民消费价格比上年涨跌幅度（%）

指　标	涨跌幅度（%）
居民消费价格	1.9
食品烟酒	2.2
衣着	0.9
居　住	1.7
生活用品及服务	2.8
交通和通信	0.7
教育文化和娱乐	1.6
医疗保健	4.3
其他用品和服务	0.1

全年新增城镇就业14.39万人，城镇失业人员再就业6.25万人。年末城镇登记失业率为3.26%。引进产业发展与科技创新类人才36.64万人，培养实用型人才6.07万人。

全年新登记各类市场主体54.30万户，比上年增长91.7%。其中，新登记企业12.65万户，增长36.5%；新登记个体工商户41.54万户，增长1.2倍。

全年地方财政一般公共预算收入684.71亿元，比上年增长10.8%，其中，税收收入556.58亿元，增长24.0%。全年地方财政一般公共预算支出1151.61亿元，比上年增长10.2%。

二、农业[3]

全年粮食种植面积419.56万亩，比上年下降1.1%；蔬菜种植面积107.74万亩，增长3.0%；瓜果种植面积14.92万亩，增长1.0%；油料种植面积4.61万亩，增长7.5%；棉花种植面积0.09万亩，下降0.3%。

全年粮食产量142.14万吨，比上年增长1.6%，其中，夏粮74.27万吨，秋粮67.86万吨。蔬菜产量373.69万吨，增长5.3%；水果产量89.15万吨，下降0.7%。

表2：2018年主要农产品产量及其增长速度

产品名称	单位	产量	比上年增长（%）
粮食	万吨	142.14	1.6
蔬菜	万吨	373.69	5.3
水果	万吨	89.15	-0.7
肉类	万吨	5.45	-7.2
#猪肉	万吨	3.59	-2.6
奶类	万吨	11.33	-2.7
禽蛋	万吨	5.26	-0.3
猪年末存栏数	万头	31.29	-6.8
牛年末存栏数	万头	5.06	-0.7
羊年末存栏数	万只	7.42	-1.3
家禽年末存栏数	万只	625.83	-2.6

三、工业和建筑业

全年全部工业增加值 1874.36亿元，比上年增长9.0%。规模以上工业增加值增长9.4%。在规模以上工业中，轻工业增加值增长8.4%，重工业增加值增长9.6%。

图4：2017-2018年规模以上工业增加值增长速度（%）

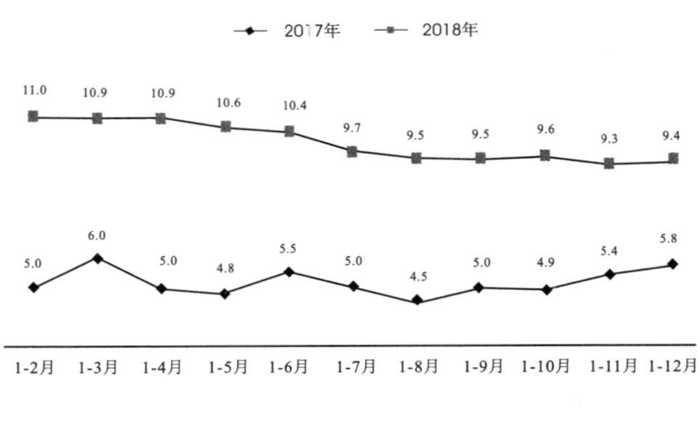

全年规模以上工业中，装备制造业[4]增加值增长11.1%，占规模以上工业增加值的比重为60.2%。其中，铁路、船舶、航空航天和其他运输设备制造业增长11.7%，计算机、通信和其他电子设备制造业增长14.8%，电气机械和器材制造业增长10.5%，汽车制造业增长7.1%。六大高耗能行业[5]增加值增长6.0%，其中，非金属矿物制品业增长16.6%，有色金属冶炼和压延加工业下降2.7%，黑色金属冶炼和压延加工业增长13.6%，石油加工、炼焦和核燃料加工业下降1.2%，化学原料和化学制品制造业增长1.0%，电力、热力生产和供应业增长8.2%。

表3：2018年10大行业增加值增长速度及占规模以上工业比重

行业名称	比上年增长（%）	占比（%）
规模以上工业增加值	9.4	100.0
10个行业合计	10.5	74.3
通用设备制造业	13.8	2.4
专用设备制造业	0.7	3.6
汽车制造业	7.1	15.3
铁路、船舶、航空航天和其他运输设备制造业	11.7	4.0
电气机械和器材制造业	10.5	9.8
计算机、通信和其他电子设备制造业	14.8	21.4
仪器仪表制造和金属制品业	18.7	3.8
食品制造业	12.0	3.1
医药制造业	4.9	5.1
电力、热力生产和供应业	8.2	5.9

全年规模以上工业中，战略性新兴产业[6]总产值比上年增长9.7%，占规模以上工业比重为39.8%；高技术制造业[7]总产值增长8.5%，占规模以上工业比重为24.4%，其中，电子及通信设备制造业总产值增长5.4%，占高技术制造业的比重为54.2%，信息化学品制造业增长9.2%，航空、航天器及设备制造业增长17.0%，计算机及办公设备制造业增长35.0%。

工业新产品产量快速增长。单晶硅2038.32万千克，比上年增长25.1%；新能源汽车13.85万辆，增长70.0%；光纤801.48万千米，增长51.3%；锂离子电池1504.00万只，增长202.0%；光缆716.10万芯千米，增长22.1%；光电子器件152.20万只，增长328.7%。

表4：2018年主要工业产品产量及其增长速度

产品名称	单位	产量	比上年增长（%）
发电量	亿千瓦小时	172.76	-4.1
饮料	万吨	174.23	-8.8
小麦粉	万吨	55.57	8.2
饲料	万吨	77.33	-10.8
乳制品	万吨	74.86	13.1
中成药	万吨	1.06	56.5
交流电动机	万千瓦	260.10	31.4
变压器	万千伏安	13192.59	-7.1
汽车	万辆	43.37	-2.6
其中：载货汽车	万辆	18.32	-3.1
轿车	万辆	18.08	-0.3
运动型多用途乘用车(SUV)	万辆	6.94	-5.7
新能源汽车	万辆	13.85	70.0
单晶硅	万千克	2038.32	25.1
电力电缆	万千米	13.28	11.8
光纤	万千米	801.48	51.3
光缆	万芯千米	716.10	22.1
锂离子电池	万只	1504.00	202.0
光电子器件	万只	152.20	328.7
电子元件	亿只	4.37	1.8
集成电路圆片	万片	150.00	-1.1

规模以上工业企业主营业务收入5215.00亿元，比上年增长9.9%。实现利润总额352.40亿元，增长6.7%。

全年全社会建筑业增加值1073.12亿元，比上年增长7.9%。全市具有资质等级的总承包和专业承包建筑业企业实现建筑业总产值3898.37亿元，增长15.8%，其中，国有及国有控股企业产值3026.19亿元，增长14.1%。所有资质等级企业签订合同额10120.16亿元，增长9.1%。

图5：2014-2018年建筑业增加值及其增长速度

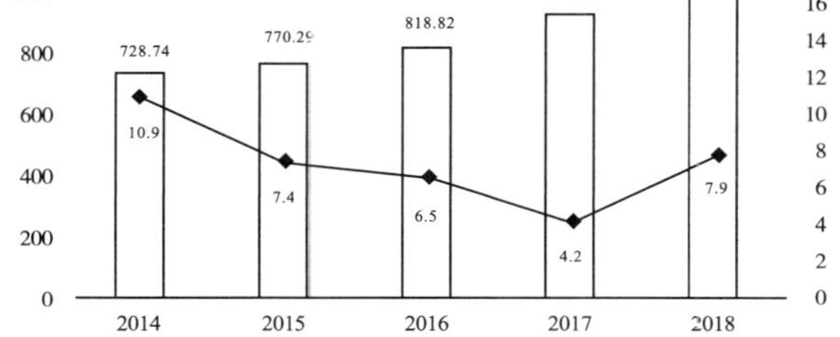

四、服务业

全年批发和零售业增加值842.06亿元，比上年增长7.0%；交通运输、仓储和邮政业增加值357.49亿元，增长6.3%；住宿和餐饮业增加值204.85亿元，增长5.8%；金融业增加值874.91亿元，增长5.3%；房地产业增加值643.18亿元，增长5.8%；营利性服务业增加值964.58亿元，增长22.9%；非营利性服务业增加值1229.13亿元，增长3.0%。全年规模以上服务业企业营业收入2414.84亿元，比上年增长17.3%。

图6：2014-2018年服务业增加值及其增长速度

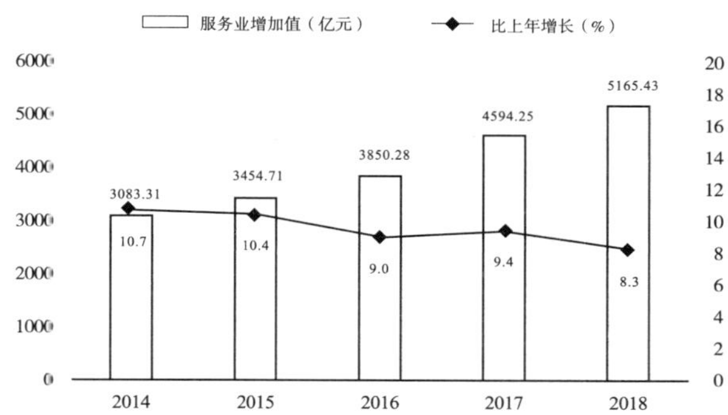

全年货物运输总量2.62亿吨，比上年增长5.2%；货物运输周转量518.90亿吨公里，增长10.0%。旅客运输总量2.61亿人次，增长6.4%；旅客运输周转量362.42亿人公里，增长12.3%。国际航线64条，境外航班通航架次20004架。年末全市机动车保有量325.63万辆，比上年末增长12.8%。私人汽车保有量279.52万辆，增长13.3%。

全年邮政业务总收入61.68亿元,比上年增长13.3%。电信业务总收入150.21亿元，增长1.7%。年末全市固定电话用户259.94万户，移动电话用户1858.09万户，固定互联网宽带接入用户[8]393.47万户。

五、固定资产投资

全年全社会固定资产投资比上年增长8.4%。其中，固定资产投资（不含农户）增长8.5%。

图7：2018年固定资产投资（不含农户）增长速度（%）

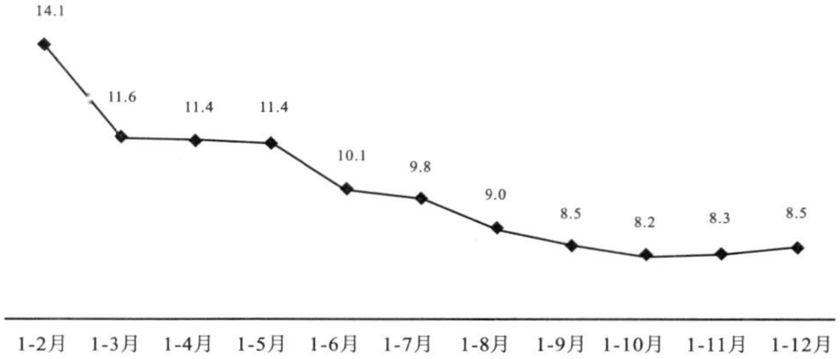

在固定资产投资（不含农户）中，第一产业投资

比上年增长20.8%；第二产业投资增长28.6%，其中，工业投资增长28.7%；第三产业投资增长5.4%。民间固定资产投资[9]比上年增长20.3%，占固定资产投资（不含农户）的比重为45.8%。

表5：2018年分行业固定资产投资（不含农户）增长速度（%）

行业	比上年增长	行业	比上年增长
固定资产投资（不含农户）	8.5	金融业	-50.3
农、林、牧、渔业	18.1	房地产业[10]	5.7
采矿业	21.0	租赁和商务服务业	-6.6
制造业	31.8	科学研究和技术服务业	-12.1
电力、热力、燃气及水的生产和供应业	17.0	水利、环境和公共设施管理业	7.1
建筑业	-62.7	居民服务和其他服务业	-15.7
批发和零售业	-16.6	教育	-38.6
交通运输、仓储和邮政业	17.6	卫生和社会工作	22.4
住宿和餐饮业	133.3	文化、体育和娱乐业	19.4
信息传输、软件和信息技术服务业	15.4	公共管理和社会组织	10.7

全年房地产开发投资比上年增长7.9%。其中，住宅投资增长5.7%，办公楼投资下降5.9%，商业营业用房投资下降2.2%。房屋施工面积16044.57万平方米，增长1.3%；房屋竣工面积977.28万平方米，下降40.2%。

表6：2018年房地产开发和销售主要指标及其增长速度

指标	绝对数（万平方米）	比上年增长（%）
房屋施工面积	16044.57	1.3
其中：住宅	11208.59	0.7
房屋竣工面积	977.28	-40.2
其中：住宅	623.40	-51.4
商品房销售面积	2713.46	8.1
其中：住宅	2221.27	3.4
商品房待售面积	240.04	-36.8
其中：住宅	59.98	-66.1

六、国内贸易

全年社会消费品零售总额4658.72亿元，比上年增长9.6%。其中，限额以上企业（单位）消费品零售额2973.14亿元,增长9.3%。按经营地统计，城镇消费品零售额4489.78亿元，增长9.6%；乡村消费品零售额168.94亿元，增长11.3%。按消费形态统计，商品零售额4286.21亿元，增长9.5%；餐饮收入372.51亿元，增长11.5%。

图8：2014-2018年社会消费品零售总额及其增长速度

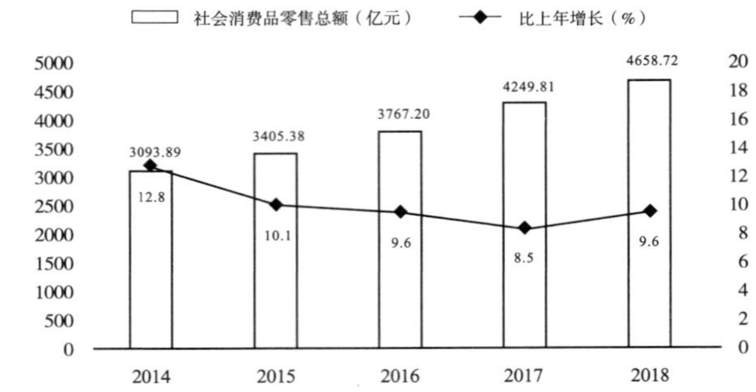

限额以上企业（单位）消费品零售额中，网上商品零售额[11] 341.57亿元，占限额以上消费品零售额的11.5%，比上年提高3.2个百分点；比上年增长33.7%，增速高于限额以上消费品零售额24.4个百分点。

在限额以上企业（单位）商品零售额中，粮油、食品类零售额比上年增长20.0%，服装、鞋帽、针、纺织品类增长13.5%，化妆品类增长20.9%，金银珠宝类下降14.4%，日用品类增长27.7%，体育、娱乐用品类增长9.2%，电子出版物及音像制品类下降47.3%，家用电器和音像器材类增长4.4%，通讯器材类增长14.2%，家具类下降0.4%，石油及制品类增长19.6%，建筑及装潢材料类增长27.6%，汽车类增长3.1%。

七、对外经济

全年进出口总值3303.87亿元，比上年增长29.6%。其中，出口1957.49亿元，增长26.1%；进口1346.38亿元，增长35.0%。

图9：2014-2018年进出口总值及其增长速度

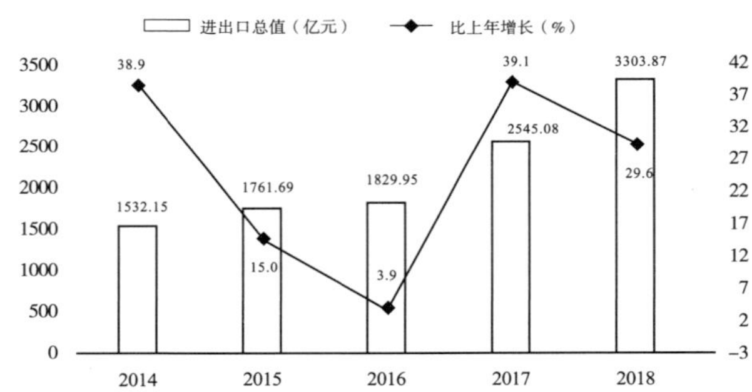

在进出口总值中，加工贸易进出口2201.30亿元，增长28.5%，占进出口总值的66.6%；一般贸易进出口603.85亿元，增长13.3%，占进出口总值的18.3%。

主要进口商品有，机电产品进口1097.95亿元，增长37.2%；精炼铜进口53.74亿元，增长130.0%；矿砂进口43.81亿元，下降19.4%；医药品进口23.31亿元，增长25.8%。主要出口商品有，机电产品出口1809.89亿元，增长29.1%；单晶硅片出口24.18亿元，下降13.4%；农产品出口24.77亿元，下降6.1%；有机化学品出口17.67亿元，增长19.1%。

全年实际利用外商直接投资63.54亿美元，比上年增长14.9%。

八、金融

年末全市金融机构本外币存款余额21266.72亿元，比上年末增长4.4%。人民币存款余额20948.18亿元，增长4.5%，其中，住户存款余额8360.33亿元，增长11.5%。金融机构本外币贷款余额19891.60亿元，增长16.0%。人民币贷款余额19729.82亿元，增长16.4%。

表7：2018年末金融机构本外币存贷款余额及其增长速度

指 标	年末数（亿元）	比上年增长（%）
期末金融机构存款余额	21266.72	4.4
#住户存款	8465.50	11.4
非金融企业存款	8318.31	-1.1
广义政府存款	3725.07	3.0
非银行业金融机构存款	732.87	0.6
期末金融机构贷款余额	19891.60	16.0
#住户贷款	5209.41	29.6
非金融企业及机关团体贷款	14661.39	11.7
非银行业金融机构贷款	0.19	-5.0

全年证券市场各类证券交易总额32892.35亿元，比上年下降29.7%。年末全市拥有上市股份公司34家，上市总股本550.02亿股，总市值3838.09亿元。

年末全市共有保险公司62家，其中，财产险30家，人寿险32家。保险专业中介机构123家。全年保费收入478.56亿元，比上年增长13.7%。其中，财产险保费收入112.56亿元，增长8.5%；人身险保费收入365.99亿元，增长15.3%。全年支付各类赔款给付130.82亿元，比上年增长10.2%。其中，财产险业务55.36亿元，增长13.1%；人身险业务75.46亿元，增长8.2%。

九、教育、科技、文化旅游和体育

全市普通高校63所，在校学生[12]127.13万人，毕业生27.26万人；普通中学456所，在校学生42.46万人，毕业生13.50万人；小学1130所，在校学生73.09万人，毕业生9.32万人。

全年实施市级科技计划项目178项。国家级高新技术企业数2139家，比上年增加300家。全年技术市场合同交易额1028.33亿元。全年专利申请量71250件，其中，发明专利申请量26625件。全市众创空间1156个，比上年增加734个；众创空间面积3281万平方米，比上年增加1892万平方米。

全市博物馆134座，各级别文物保护单位424处。公共图书馆13个，群众艺术馆2个，文化馆14个，文化站186个。地市广播电视台2座，县级广播电视台6座。电视及广播人口覆盖率均达到100%。全年举办各类会展活动230个，其中，举办国际性会展活动62个；全年参展参会人数322万人次。

全年接待国内外游客24738.75万人次，比上年增长36.7%；旅游业总收入2554.81亿元，增长56.4%。

全年举办各类群众体育展示表演和竞赛活动共计300项次，体育社团举办和承办体育赛事300项次，其中，国际性和全国性赛事117项次。新建和更新社区全民健身路径60个。全市新增社会体育指导员1738名。我市培养输送运动员参加国际、国内各项比赛获得金牌70枚、银牌52枚、铜牌65枚。

十、卫生健康和社会服务

年末全市共有各类卫生机构6638个，其中，医院343个，社区卫生服务中心（站）222个，卫生院119个。各类卫生技术人员10.15万人，其中，执业（含助理）医师3.38万人。各类卫生机构床位6.90万张。

全市提供住宿的法定社会服务机构156个，床位2.82万张，年末收养人数18940人。年末城市低保对象1.7万户、2.6万人，发放低保金2.4亿元；农村低保对象2.5万户、7.2万人，发放低保金3.9亿元。6383人享受农村特困人员救助供养，发放供养金5478.2万元。全年民政部门直接医疗救助6.4万人次。

十一、人口、人民生活和社会保障

年末全市常住人口1000.37万人，比上年末净增加38.70万人，其中，男性人口511.79万人，占51.2%；女性人口488.58万人，占48.8%，性别比为104.75（以女性为100，男性对女性的比例）。全年出生人口12.23万人，出生率为12.47‰；死亡人口5.38万人，死亡率为5.48‰；自然增长率为6.99‰。城镇人口740.37万人，占常住人口比重（常住人口城镇化率）74.01%；乡村人口260.00万人，占25.99%。年末全市户籍总人口986.87万人，比上年增长9.0%。

全年全市居民人均可支配收入比上年增长8.7%，其中，城镇常住居民人均可支配收入增长8.1%，农村常住居民人均可支配收入增长9.0%。

年末全市城镇基本医疗保险参保人数527.00万人，城镇企业职工养老保险参保人数417.57万人，失业保险参保人数167.54万人，工伤保险参保人数229.00万人，职工生育保险参保人数213.01万人。年末农村新型合作医疗参保人数438.10万人，实际参合率99.44%。

十二、城市建设、环境和应急管理

全年完成市政公用设施投资773.60亿元。新建人行天桥及地下通道2座，新建改造绿地广场62个。新建道路面积10291.72万平方米。年末建成区面积700.27平方公里，市区人均公园绿地面积11.92平方米，建成区绿化覆盖率41.6%。年末城市污水处理厂日处理能力310.10万立方米，比上年末增长11.7%。

全年空气质量优良天数188天。二氧化硫年平均浓度为15微克/标立方米，二氧化氮年平均浓度为55微克/标立方米。颗粒物（PM10）年平均浓度为122微克/标立方米，颗粒物（PM2.5）年平均浓度为63微克/标立方米。全市集中式饮用水源地的水质达标率为99.7%。区域环境噪声等效声级均值为56.1分贝，道路交通噪声等效声级均值为69.8分贝。

全年发生各类生产安全事故417起，死亡196人；其中，生产经营性道路交通事故380起，死亡153人；工矿商贸事故33起，死亡41人。

注释：

[1]本公报中2018年数据为初步统计数，2017年及以前年份数据为年报数；部分数据因四舍五入的原因，存在着分项与合计不等的情况。

[2]生产总值、各行业增加值和人均生产总值绝对数按现价计算，增长速度按可比价格计算。根据第三次全国农业普查结果，对2018年地区生产总值、三次产业增加值比重等数据进行了修订。

[3]农业数据根据第三次全国农业普查结果进行了修订。

[4]装备制造业包括金属制品业，通用设备制造业，专用设备制造业，汽车制造业，铁路、船舶、航空航天和其他运输设备制造业，电气机械和器材制造业，计算机、通信和其他电子设备制造业，仪器仪表制造业。

[5]六大高耗能行业包括石油加工、炼焦和核燃料加工业，化学原料和化学制品制造业，非金属矿物制品业，黑色金属冶炼和压延加工业，有色金属冶炼和压延加工业，电力、热力生产和供应业。

[6]工业战略性新兴产业包括节能环保产业，新一代信息技术产业，生物产业，高端装备制造产业，新能源产业，新材料产业，新能源汽车产业等七大产业中的工业相关行业。

[7]高技术制造业包括医药制造业，航空、航天器及设备制造业，电子及通信设备制造业，计算机及办公设备制造业，医疗仪器设备及仪器仪表制造业，信息化学品制造业。

[8]固定互联网宽带接入用户是指报告期末在电信企业登记注册，通过xDSL、FTTx+LAN、FTTH/0以及其他宽带接入方式和普通专线接入公众互联网的用户。

[9]民间固定资产投资是指具有集体、私营、个人性质的内资企事业单位以及由其控股（包括绝对控股和相对控股）的企业单位建造或购置固定资产的投资。

[10]房地产业投资除房地产开发投资外，还包括建设单位自建房屋以及物业管理、中介服务和其他房地产投资。

[11]网上商品零售额是指通过公共网络交易平台（主要从事实物商品交易的网上平台，包括自建网站和第三方平台）实现的商品零售额。

[12]普通高校在校学生数由于口径变化与往年不可比，2018年数据在普通本专科基础上增加了成人本专科、网络本专科以及研究生。

数据口径：本公报中2018年进出口、交通运输、邮政电信、环境监测等指标数据为西安原口径数据，居民人均可支配收入、就业与引进人才、市场主体、财政、利用外资、金融证券和保险、会展、旅游、教育、体育、博物馆、文化、卫生、社会服务、低保、农村特困人员救助供养、人口、城市建设、安全生产、生产总值、农业、工业、建筑业、固定资产投资、国内贸易等指标数据为包含西咸新区数据。物价数据中，2018年居民消费价格、商品零售价格、固定资产投资价格、新建商品住宅销售价格为西安原口径数据，工业生产者出厂价格、工业生产者购进价格为包含西咸新区数据。科技数据中，科技计划项目、高新技术企业、技术市场合同交易额和专利数据为西安原口径数据，众创空间为包含西咸新区数据。社会保障数据中，城镇企业职工养老保险参保人数为西安原口径数据，城镇基本医疗保险、失业保险、工伤保险和职工生育保险参保人数、农村新型合作医疗参保人数、参合率为包含西咸新区数据。

资料来源：本公报中物价、居民人均可支配收入数据来自国家统计局西安调查队；城镇新增就业、登记失业率、引进人才、社会保障数据来自西安市人力资源和社会保障局；市场主体数据来自市工商局；财政数据来自市财政局；进出口数据来自西安海关；利用外资数据来自市投资合作局；旅游数据来自市文化旅游局；铁路运输数据来自西安铁路局；公路运输数据来自市交通局；民航运输数据来自西安咸阳国际机场；机动车数据来自市车管所；邮政业务数据来自市邮政管理局；电信业务数据来自中国移动西安分公司、中国电信西安分公司、中国联通西安分公司；货币金融数据来自中国人民银行西安分行营业管理部；证券数据、保险业数据来自市金融办；教育数据来自市教育局；科技数据来自市科技局；博物馆数据来自市文物局；艺术表演团体、公共图书馆、文化馆、广播、电视数据来自市文化广电新闻出版局；会展数据来自市会展办；体育数据来自市体育局；卫生、新农合数据来自市卫生和健康委员会；社会服务、低保、农村特困人员救助供养数据来自市民政局；户籍人口数据来自市公安局；城市建设数据来自市住房和城乡建设局；环境监测数据来自市生态环境局；安全生产数据来自市应急管理局；其他数据均来自市统计局。

Statistical Communique of Xi'an City On 2018 National Economic and Social Development[1]

Xi'an Municipal Bureau of Statistics and NBS Survey Office in Xi'an

Mar.17th，2019

In 2018, the whole city earnestly studied and implemented the spirit of the 19th Party Congress, guided by Xi Jinping's new era of socialism with chinese characteristics, and closely focused on the "five new strategies" and the goal of "gathering 369 and revitalizing the great Xi'an." Adhere to the general tone of steady progress, strive to promote steady growth, promote reform, adjust structure, protect people's livelihood, prevent risks, achieve stable and healthy economic development and social harmony and stability, and open a new pattern of construction in Xi'an.

I. General Outlook

Based on the preliminary calculation, the gross domestic product[2] (GDP) preliminarily estimated was 834.986 billion yuan, up by 8.2% against the previous year. Analyzed by different industries, the value added of the primary industry was 258.82 billion yuan, up by 3.3%; the value added of the secondary industry was 292.561 billion yuan, a rise of 8.5%; and the value added of the tertiary industry was 5165.43 billion yuan, up by 8.3%. The composition of the three industries is 3.1:35.0:61.9. According to the resident population calculation, the per capita GDP of the year was 85.114 thousand yuan, up by 5.2% against the previous year.

The value added of non-public sectors of the economy is 445.964 billion yuan, accounted for the proportion of GDP is 53.4%, an increase of 0.4 percentage points over the previous year.

Table 1 The GDP and its Growth Rate 2014–2018

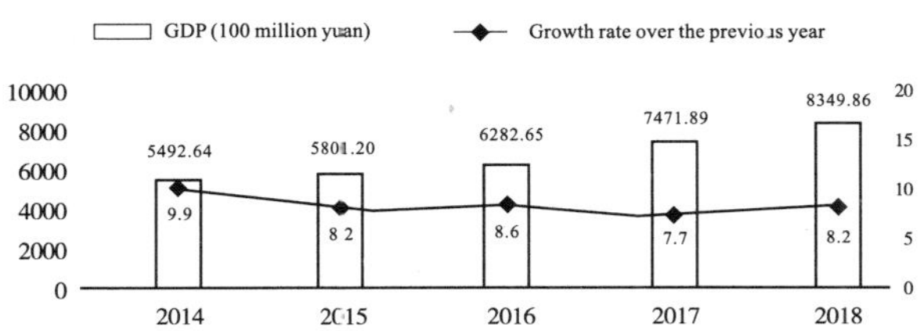

Table 2 Composition of Gross Domestic Product 2014–2018

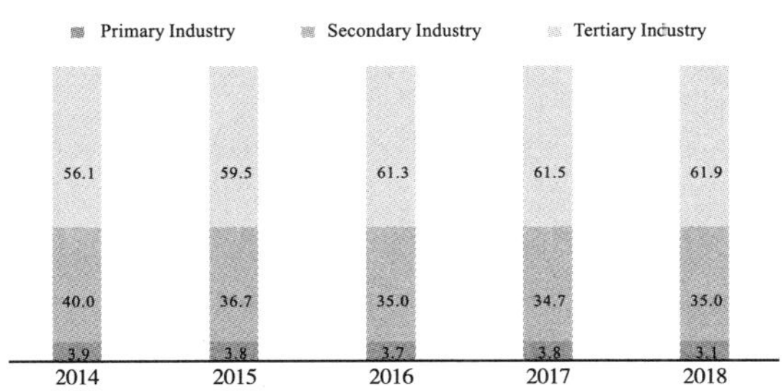

The general level of consumer prices in Xi'an was up by 1.9% against the previous year. Of this total, the prices of food, tobacco and liquor went up by 2.2%. The retail prices of commodities went up by 2.2%. The producer prices of manufactured goods went up by 1.1%. The purchasing prices of manufactured goods went up by 2.7%. The fixed asset investment price went up 5.4% and the price of newly founded house increased by 14.6%.

Table 3 The Rate of Increase and Decrease of CPI in 2018(%)

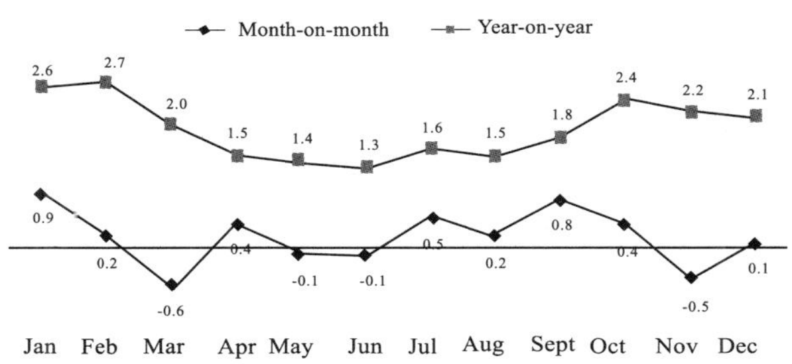

Sheet 1 Up and Fall Extent of Residents Consumer Price Indices against Previous Year (2018)

Item	2018 (%)
Consumer Price Index	1.9
Food, tobacco and liquor	2.2
Clothing	0.9
Residence	1.7
Household facilities and maintaining services	2.8
Transportation and Communication	0.7
Recreation, Education and Cultural articles and Services	1.6
Medical Health and Personal Articles	4.3
Other supplies and services	0.1

In 2018, the number of newly increased employees in urban areas in Xi'an was 143.9 thousand, the number of reemployment of laid-off workers was 62.5 thousand, the urban unemployment rate through unemployment registration was 3.26% at the end of 2018. Introduced 366.4 thousand in industrial development and scientific and technological innovation, trained practical talents 60.7 thousand.

The city registered new market entities of various types 543.0 thousand, an increase of 91.7% compared with the previous year; of this, the number of newly registered enterprises reached 126.5 thousand, an increase of 36.5%. The number of newly registered individual industrial and commercial households increased by 1.2 times to 415.4 thousand.

The General Budget Revenue of Regional Finance reached 68.471 billion yuan, up by 10.8%. Of this, tax revenue was 55.658 billion yuan, an increase of 24.0% compared with the previous year. The General Budget Expenditure of Regional Finance totaled 115.161 billion yuan, up by 10.2%. II. Agriculture[3]

In 2018, the sown area of grain was 4195.6 thousand mu, a decrease of 1.1% compared with the previous year; the sown area of vegetables was 1077.4 thousand mu, an increase of 3.0%; The planting area of melon and fruit was 149.2 thousand mu, an increase of 1.0%; the sown area of oil-bearing crops was 46.1 thousand mu, a decrease of 7.5%; the sown area of cotton was 0. 9 thousand mu, a decrease of 0.3%. The total output of grain in 2018 was 1.4214 million tons, a decrease of 1.6%. Of this, the output of summer crops was 0.7427 million tons, and that of the autumn grain was 0.6786 million tons. Vegetable production was 3.7369 million tons, an increase of 5.3%. Fruit production was 0.8915 million tons, a decrease of 0.7%.

Sheet 2 The Main Product of Agriculture Production in 2018

Name of Product	Units	Output	Increase over the last year(%)
Grain	10,000 tons	142.14	1.6
Vegetable	10,000 tons	373.69	5.3
Fruit	10,000 tons	89.15	-0.7
Meat	10,000 tons	5.45	-7.2
#Pork	10,000 tons	3.59	-2.6
Milk	10,000 tons	11.33	-2.7
Poultry eggs	10,000 tons	5.26	-0.3
Year-end Pig on hand	10,000 head	31.29	-6.8
Year-end Ox on hand	10,000 head	5.06	-0.7
Year-end Sheep on hand	10,000 head	7.42	-1.3
Year-end Fowl on hand	10,000 head	625.83	-2.6

III. Industry and Construction

In 2018, the value added by the industrial sectors was 187.436 billion yuan, up by 9.4% over the previous year. The value added of industrial enterprises above the designated size increased up by 9.4%. Of this, the value added of the light industry increased up by 8.4%; that of the heavy industry increased up by 9.6%.

Table 4 The Growth of Above-Scale Industrial added Value 2017–2018 (%)

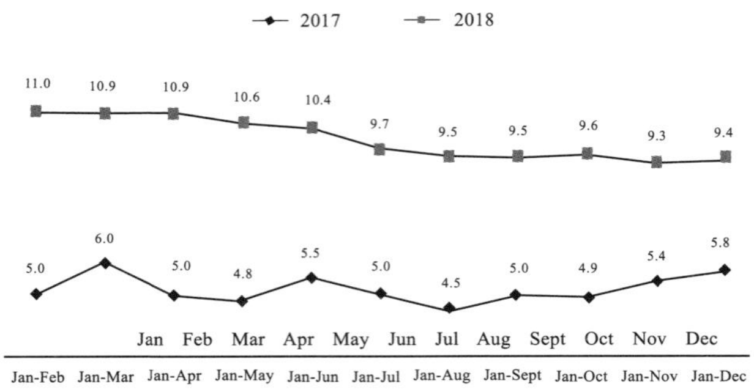

In 2018 of the industrial enterprises above designated size, the growth of value added for equipment manufacturing industry[4] was up by 11.1%, accounted for 60.2% of the added value of industrial enterprises above designated size. Of this, manufacturing of railways, ships, aerospace and other transportation equipment increased by 11.7%, the growth of value added for manufacture of computer, communication and other electrical devices was up by 14.8% over the previous year, manufacturing of electrical machinery and equipment increased by 10.5%. The growth of the value added for the major six high energy consuming industries[5] was increased by 6.0%, of which, that of the manufacture of raw chemical materials and chemical products up by 16.6%, smelting and pressing of non-ferrous metals down by 2.7%, smelting and pressing of ferrous metals up by 13.6% and 1.2% decrease for processing of petroleum, coking, processing of nuclear fuel, manufacture of raw chemical materials and chemical products up by 1.0%, production and supply of electric power and heat power up by 8.2%.

Sheet 3 The Growth of 10 Major Industrial added Value and Their Proportion to Industrial Enterprises above Designated Size in 2018

Item	Increase over the last year(%)	Proportion (%)
Growth of Industrial added Value above Designated Size	9.4	100.0
Total: 10 Major Industrial Enterprises	10.5	74.3
Manufacture of General Purpose Machinery	13.8	2.4
Manufacture of Special Purpose Machinery	0.7	3.6
Manufacture of Automobiles	7.1	15.3
Manufacture of Railway, Ship, Aerospace and Other Transport Equipments	11.7	4.0
Manufacture of Electrical Machinery and Apparatus	10.5	9.8
Manufacture of Computers, Communication and Other Electronic Equipment	14.8	21.4

Item	Increase over the last year(%)	Proportion (%)
Manufacture of Metal Products, Measuring Instruments and Machinery	18.7	3.8
Manufacture of Foods	12.0	3.1
Manufacture of Medicines	4.9	5.1
Production and Supply of Electric Power and Heat Power	8.2	5.9

In 2018, the output of strategic emerging industries[6] soared by nearly 9.7% compared with last year, accounted for 39.8% of the value for industrial enterprises above designated size. The gross output value of high technology industry industrial manufacturing enterprises above designated size[7] soared by nearly 8.5% compared with last year, accounted for 24.4% of the value for industrial enterprises above designated size. Of which, the gross output value of the electronic and communication equipment manufacturing up by 5.4% compared with last year, accounted for 54.2% of the value for high technology industry. The information chemicals manufacturing industry up by 9.2%, the aviation, spacecraft and equipment manufacturing industry up by 17.0%, and the computer and office equipment manufacturing industry up by 35.0%.

In 2018, the output of new industrial products increased rapidly. Single crystal silicon 20.3832 million kilograms, an increase of 25.1%; the number of the new energy vehicle was 138.5 thousand, up by 70.0% over the previous year; the length of the optical fiber was 8.0148 million kilometers, up by 51.3% over the previous year; the number of the lithium ion battery was 15.0400 million, up by 202.0% over the previous year; the length of the optical cable was 7.1610 million core kilometers, up by 22.1% over the previous year; the number of the optoelectronic devices was 1.5220 million, up by 328.7% over the previous year.

Sheet 4 Output of Major Industrial Products above Designated Size in Xi'an (2018)

Name of Product	Units	Output	Increase over the last year(%)
Electricity	100 million kilo watt-hour	172.76	-4.1
Soft Drink	10,000 tons	174.23	-8.8
Wheat Meal	10,000 tons	55.57	8.2
Feed	10,000 tons	77.33	-10.8
Dairy	10,000 tons	74.86	13.1
Chinese Patent Medicine	10,000 tons	1.06	56.5
AC Motors	10,000 Kilowatt	260.10	31.4
Transformer	10,000 kilovolt amperes	13192.59	-7.1
Motor Vehicle	10,000 units	43.37	-2.6
Truck	10,000 units	18.32	-3.1
Car	10,000 units	18.08	-0.3
Sports Utility Vehicle	10,000 units	6.94	-5.7
New Energy Vehicle	10,000 units	13.85	70.0
Monocrystalline Silicon	10,000 kg	2038.32	25.1
Electric Cable	10,000 km	13.28	11.8
Optical Fiber	10,000 km	801.48	51.3
Optical Cable	10,000 core kilometers	716.10	22.1
Lithium Ion Battery	10,000 units	1504.00	202.0
Optoelectronic Devices	10,000 units	152.20	328.7
Electronic Component	100 million units	4.37	1.8
Integrated Circuit Chip	10,000 chips	150.00	-1.1

The main business income of the industrial enterprises above designated size is 521.500 billion yuan, up by 9.9% over the previous year. The profit was 35.240 billion yuan, up by 6.7%. In 2018, the added value of construction sectors was 107.312 billion yuan, increased by 7.9% over the previous year. The total output value created by qualified contractors and professional building contractor companies was 389.837 billion yuan, increased by 15.8%. Of it, the output of state-owned and state holding corporations was 302.619 billion yuan, increased by 14.1%; Contracts signed by all qualified enterprises amounted to 1012.016 billion yuan, increased by 9.1%.

Table 5 The Added Value of Construction and Growth Rate 2014–2018

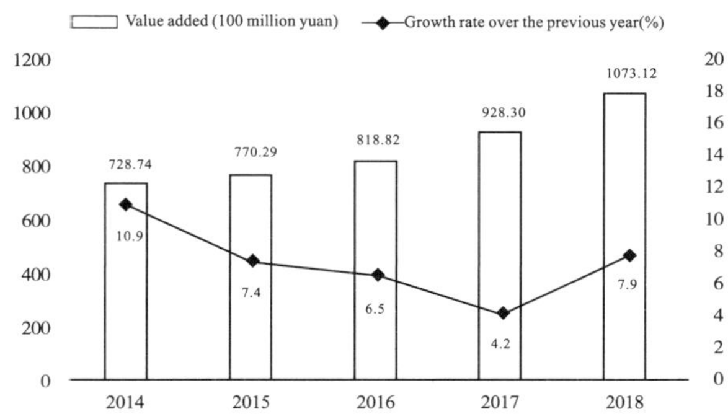

IV. Service Sector

In 2018, the value added of wholesale and retail trades was 84.206 billion yuan, up by 7.0% over the previous year; that of transport, storage and post was 35.749 billion yuan, up by 6.3%; that of hotels and catering services was 20.485 billion yuan, up by 5.8%; that of financial intermediation was 87.491 billion yuan, up by 5.3%; that of real estate was 64.318 billion yuan, up by 5.8%; that of for-profit service industry was 96.458 billion yuan, up by 22.9%; that of non-profit service industry was

122.913 billion yuan, up by 3.0%. In 2018, the business revenue of service enterprises above the designated size was 241.484 billion, grew by 17.3% over the previous year.

Table 6 The Added Value of Service Sector and Growth Rate 2014–2018

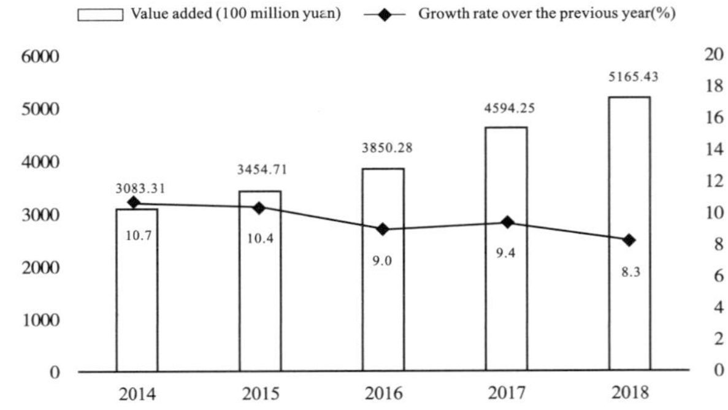

The total freight traffic in 2018 reached 0.262 billion tons, up by 5.2% over 2017. The freight flows were 51.890 billion ton-kilometers, up by 10%. The total passenger traffic reached 0.261 billion person-times, up by 6.4%, and the passenger flows were 36.242 billion person-kilometers, up by 12.3%. The total number of international aviation routes was 64, and the total number of international aviation flights was 20004. The total number of motor vehicles reached 3.2563 million by the end of 2018, up by 12.8% over that at the end of 2017, of which the privately-owned vehicles numbered 2.7952 million, up by 13.3%. The revenue of post services totaled 6.18 billion yuan, up by 13.3% over the previous year. The revenue of telecommunication services totaled 15.021 billion yuan, up by 1.7% over the previous year. By the end of 2018, there were 2.5994 million fixed phone users and 18.5809 million mobile phone users. The number of fixed broadband internet users [8] reached 3.9347 million. V. Investment in Fixed Assets

The total investment in fixed assets of the city in 2018 was up by 8.4% over the previous year. Of the total investment, the investment in fixed assets (excluding by rural households) was up by 8.5%.

Table 7 Investment in Fixed Assets(excluding by rural households) Growth Rate in 2018 (%)

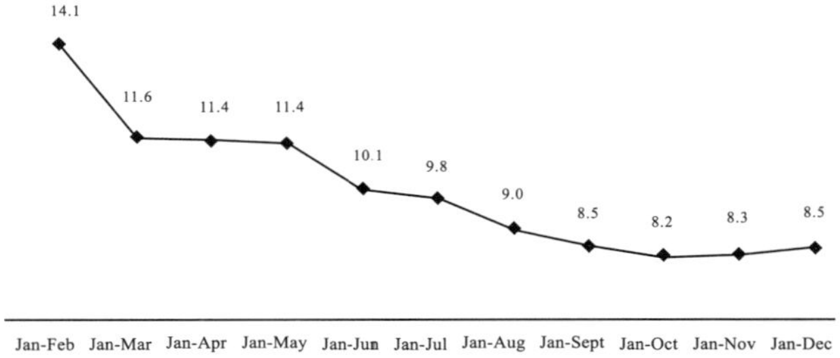

In the investment in fixed assets (excluding by rural households), the investment in the primary industry was up by 20.8%; that in the secondary industry was up by 28.6%, of which industrial investment was up by 28.7%; and that in the tertiary industry was up by 5.4%. The private investment in fixed assets[9] was up by 20.3%, accounting for 45.8% of the investment in fixed assets (excluding by rural households).

Sheet 5 The Investment in Fixed Assets and Growth Rate in Main Industries in 2018

Industries	Growth rate(%)
Investment in Fixed Assets (excluding by rural households)	8.5
Agriculture, Forestry, Animal Husbandry and Fishery	18.1
Mining Industry	21.0
Manufacturing	31.8
Electricity, Heat, Gas and Water Production and Supply Industry	17.0
Construction Industry	-62.7
Wholesale and Retail Trade	-15.6
Transportation, Storage and Postal Services	17.6
Hotels and catering services	133.3
Information Transmission, Computer Services and Software Industry	15.4
Finance	-50.3
Real Estate Industry[10]	5.7
Leasing and Business Services	-6.6
Scientific Research and Technical Service	-12.1
Water Conservancy, Environment and Public Facilities Administration Industry	7.1
Residential Services and Other Services	-15.7
Education	-38.6
Sanitations, Social Security and Social Welfare	22.4
Culture, Sports and Entertainment	19.4
Public Administration and Social Organizations	10.7

In 2018, the investment in real estate development was up by 7.9%. Of this total, the investment in residential buildings was up by 5.7%, that in office buildings was down by 5.9%, and that in buildings for commercial business was down by 2.2%. Floor space under construction was 160.4457 million square meters, up by 1.3%; floor space completed was 9.7728 million square meters, down by 40.2%.

Sheet 6 The Main Indicators of Real Estate Development and Sales in 2018

Item	Units	Absolute Number	Increase over the last year(%)
Floor Space of Buildings under Construction	10,000 sq.m	16044.57	1.3
# Residential Building	10,000 sq.m	11208.59	0.7
Floor Space of Buildings Completed	10,000 sq.m	977.28	-40.2
# Residential Building	10,000 sq.m	623.40	-51.4
Floor Space of Commercialized Buildings Sold	10,000 sq.m	2713.46	8.1
# Residential Building	10,000 sq.m	2221.27	3.4
Floor Space of Commercialized Buildings for Sale	10,000 sq.m	240.04	-36.8
# Residential Building	10,000 sq.m	59.98	-66.1

VI. Domestic Trade

In 2018, the total retail sales of consumer goods reached 465.872 billion yuan, a growth of 9.6% over the previous year. Of this, the total retail sales by wholesale and retail enterprises above designated size was 297.314 billion yuan, up by 9.3%. An analysis on different areas showed that the retail sales of consumer goods in urban areas stood at 448.978 billion yuan, up by 9.6%, and that in rural areas reached 16.894 billion yuan, up by 11.3%. Grouped by consumption patterns, the retail sales of commodities was 428.621 billion yuan, up by 9.5%, and that of catering industry was 37.251 billion yuan, up by 11.5%.

Table 8 The Total Retail Sales of Social Consumer Goods and its Growth Rate 2014–2018

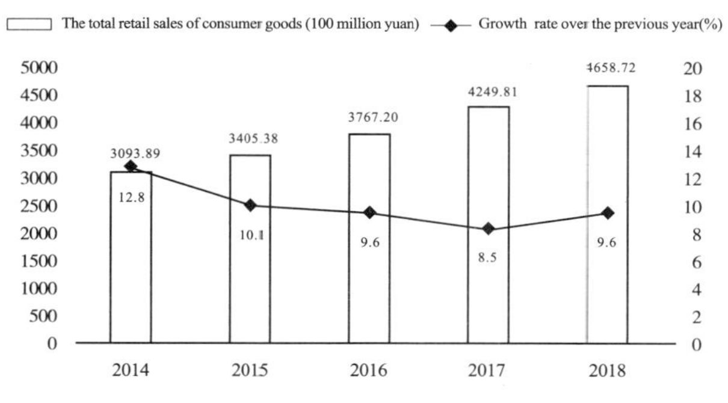

Of the total retail sales of consumer goods by wholesale and retail enterprises above designated size, the online sales[11] was 34.157 billion yuan, accounted for 11.5% of retail sales of consumer goods above designated size, and increase 3.2 percentage points the previous year, with year-on-year growth of 33.7%, 24.4 percentage points higher than the retail sales of consumer goods above designated size.

Of the total retail sales of commodities by wholesale and retail enterprises above designated size, the year-on-year growth of sales for grain, oil and food went up by 20.0%; clothes, shoes, hats and textiles up by 13.5% ; cosmetics up by 20.9%; gold, silver and jewelry down by 14.4%; daily necessities up by 27.7%; sports-recreation up by 9.2%; electronic appliances and audio-video productions down by 47.3%, household appliances and audio-video equipment up by 4.4%; telecommunication equipment up by 14.2%; furniture down by 0.4%; oil and oil products up by 19.6%; building decoration materials down by 27.6% and motor vehicles up by 3.1%.

VII. Foreign Economic Relation

In 2018, the total value of imports and exports reached 330.387 billion yuan, up by 29.6% over the previous year. Of this, the value of exports was 195.749 billion yuan, up by 26.1%, and that of imports was 134.638 billion yuan, up by 35.0%.

Table 9: Total Value of Import and Export of Goods and the Growth Rates 2014–2018

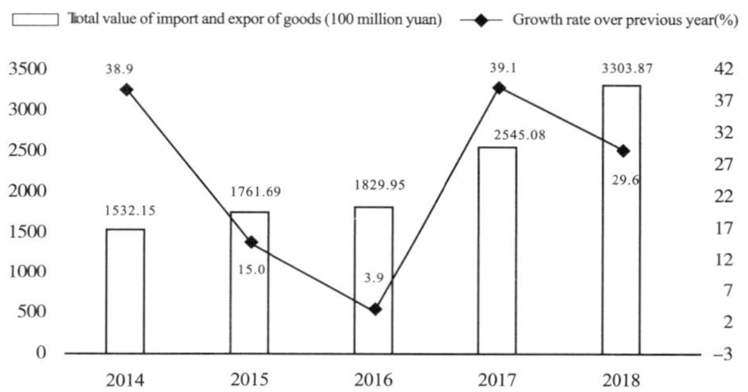

In total imports and exports, the value of processing trade was 220.130 billion yuan, up by 28.5%, accounted for 66.6% of import and export whole value of Xi'an region. The value of imports and exports of general trade was 60.385 billion yuan, increased by 13.3%, accounted for 18.3% of total import and export whole value of Xi'an region.

Among the main import commodities, the value of imports of electromechanical products was 109.795 billion yuan, up by 37.2%, the value of imports of refined copper was 5.374 billion yuan, up by 130.0%; the value of imports of ore sand was 4.381 billion yuan, down by 19.4%; the value of imports of medical products was 2.331 billion yuan, up by 25.8%. Among the main export commodities, the value of exports of electromechanical products was 180.989 billion yuan, up by 29.1%; the value of exports of monocrystalline silicon was 2.418 billion yuan, down by 13.4%; the value of exports of agricultural product was 2.477 billion yuan, down by 6.1%; the organic chemicals was 1.767 billion yuan, up by 19.1%.

In 2018, the realized foreign direct investment was 6.354 billion US dollars, up by 14.9%.

VIII. Finance

Savings deposit in RMB and foreign currencies in all items of financial institutions totaled 2126.672 billion yuan at the end of 2018, an increase of 4.5% compared with the end of the previous year. The savings deposit in RMB stood at 2094.818 billion yuan, an increase of 4.5%, of which the household deposit was 836.033 billion yuan, up by 11.5%. Loans in all items of financial institutions in RMB and foreign currencies reached 1989.160 billion yuan, an increase of 16.0% as compared with the end of the previous year. The loans in RMB stood at 1972.982 billion yuan, an increase of 16.4%.

Sheet 7 Savings Deposit and Loans in RMB and Foreign Currencies in All Financial Institutions and the Growth Rates at the End of 2018

Item	Year–end figure (100 million yuan)	Increase over 2017 (%)
Total Deposits	21266.72	4.4
# Households Deposits	8465.50	11.4
Non-Financial Enterprise Deposits	8318.31	-1.1
Broad Government Deposit	3725.07	3.0
Non-bank Financial Institution Deposits	732.87	0.6
Total Loans	19891.60	16.0
# Households Loans	5209.41	29.6
Non-Financial Enterprise and Organizations and Communities Loans	14661.39	11.7
Non-bank Financial Institution Loans	0.19	-5.0

The trading volume of stock exchange market was 3289.235 billion yuan in 2018, a decrease of 29.7% compared with the previous year. There were 34 listed companies in Xi'an at the end of 2018 of which the total capital stock was 55.002 billion shares, and the total market value was 383.809 billion yuan.

By the end of 2018, there were 62 insurance institutions, of which the number of property insurance was 30, and that of life insurance was 32. There were 123 intermediary organs of insurance. The received by the insurance companies totaled 47.856 billion yuan in 2018, up by 13.7%. Of this, the revenue from property insurance was 11.256 billion yuan, up by 8.5%; that from life insurance was 36.599 billion yuan, up by 15.3%. In total, insurance companies paid an indemnity worth of 13.082 billion yuan, up by 10.2% over the previous year, of which the property insurance was 5.536 billion yuan, up by 13.1%; the personal insurance business was 7.546 billion yuan, up by 8.2%.

IX. Education、Science & Technology、Culture and Sports

There were 63 general universities and colleges, with 1271.3 thousand general tertiary education enrollments [12], including 272.6 thousand graduates. There were 456 general middle schools and high schools, with 424.6 thousand junior high education enrollments and 135.0 thousand graduates; there were 1130 primary schools, with 730.9 thousand primary education enrollments and 93.2 thousand graduates.

178 science and technology projects were carried out in 2018. The number of state-level high-tech enterprises was 2139, an increase of 300 over the previous year. The turnover in technology market reached 102.833 billion yuan, and the number of annual patent applications was 71,250. Among them, the number of invention patent applications was 26,625. There are 1156 space creations in the city, an increase of 734 over the previous year. The space area of the creation is 32.81 million square meters, an increase of 18.92 million square meters over the previous year.

By the end of 2018, there were 134 museums, 424 cultural relics protection units at all levels, 13 public libraries, 2 mass art museum, 14 cultural centers, 186 culture stations. There were 2 city radio and television stations and 6 county radio and television stations. Radio broadcasting and television broadcasting coverage rates both reached 100 percent. There were 230 various exhibitions held throughout the year, including 62 international exhibitions; the number of participants in the year was 3.22 million.

The annual domestic and foreign tourists count was 247.3875 million person-times, up by 36.7%. The revenue from tourism totaled 255.481 billion yuan, up by 56.4%. 300 mass sports performances and competition activities were organized in 2018, and 300 sports competition were organized and host by sports associations, including 119 international and national sports competition. In 2018, there were 60 public national fitness paths of community built. The number of social sports instructors had increased 1,738. In 2018, the delegation of Xi' an won 70 gold medals, 52 silver medals and 65 bronze medal in the National and international Games.

X. Health and Public Service

At the end of 2018, there were 6,638 health institutions in Xi' an, including 343 general hospitals, 222 community health centers, and 119 health centers. There were all 101.5 thousand health care workers, including 33.8 thousand practicing (assistant) doctors. General health centers in Xi' an possessed 69.0 thousand beds.

There were 156 social welfare adoption class units, with a total of 28.2 thousand beds, and 18,940 people adopted at the end of 2018. There were 17 thousand of urban low-income households, with 26 thousand people, and 240 million yuan were distributed to them. There were 25 thousand of rural low-income households, with 72 thousand people, and 390 million yuan were distributed to them. 6383 rural residents living in extreme poverty received relief and assistance and 54.782 million yuan were distributed. 64 thousand people gained medical relief directly from civil affairs departments in 2018.

XI. Population, Living Conditions and Social Security

At the end of 2018, the total permanent resident population of the city was 10.0037 million people, an increase of 387.0 thousand people over the previous year. Among them, the male population was 5.1179 million, accounting for 51.2%, the female population was 4.8858 million, accounting for 48.8%, and the sex ratio was 104.75 (take female as 100, male to female ratio). The year 2018 saw 122.3 thousand births, a crude birth rate of 12.47‰ and 53.8 thousand deaths, a crude death rate of 5.48‰. The natural growth rate was 6.99‰. Urban residents numbered 7.4037 million, accounting for 74.01% of the total population (the urbanization rate of permanent residents). Rural residents numbered 2.6000 million, accounting for 25.99%. At the end of the year, the total registered population of the city was 9.8687 million people, up by 9.0%.

In 2018, the annual per capita disposable income of all the city residents in Xi' an has a growth of 8.7% over the previous year. That of urban households grew 8.1% over the previous year. And that of rural households grew 9.0% over the previous year. By the end of 2018, a total of 5.2700 million people participated in urban basic health insurance program; a total of 4.1757 million people participated in basic pension program for staff and workers of enterprises; a total of 1.6754 million people participated in unemployment insurance programs; a total of 2.2900 million people participated in work accident insurance; a total of 2.1301 million people participated in maternity insurance programs for staff and workers. The number of farmers taking part in the new cooperative medical care system in rural areas reached 4.3810 million, with a participation rate of 99.44% covered.

XII. Urban Construction, Environment and Work Safety

The total investment of municipal utilities was 77.360 billion yuan. 2 new pedestrian bridges, and underground passages were built. 52 new green squares were built. The newly built road area was 102.9172 million square meters. By the end of the year, the built-up area was 700.27 square kilometers, and the per capita green space of the city was 11.92 square meters, with a green coverage rate of 41.6% in the built-up area. At the end of the year, the municipal wastewater treatment plant has a daily capacity of 3.110 million tons, an increase of 11.7% over the previous year. In 2018, there were 188 days with air quality better than standard Grade II. The annual average sulfur dioxide concentration of 15 micrograms/m^3, the annual average concentration of nitrogen dioxide was 55 micrograms/m^3, PM10 average concentration of 122 micrograms/m^3. PM2.5 average concentration of 63 micrograms/m^3. The water quality compliance rate of centralized drinking water sources in the city was 99.7%. The average equivalent level of regional environmental noise is 56.1 decibels, and the average equivalent noise level of road traffic noise is 69.8 decibels. In 2018, various kinds of work accidents amounted to 417, death of 196 people. Of this, there were 380 road traffic accidents in production and operation, 153 deaths; 33 industrial and mining accidents and 41 deaths.

Notes:

[1] All figures in this Communique are preliminary statistics. Due to the rounding-off reasons, the subentries may not add up to the aggregate totals.

[2] Gross domestic product (GDP), value added, per capita GDP and gross national income (GNI) as quoted in this Communiqué are calculated at current prices whereas their growth rates are at comparable prices. GDP, shares of three industries' value added of GDP, the overall labor productivity and other historical data have been revised based on the results of the third national agricultural census.

[3] Historical data of agriculture have been revised based on the results of the third national agricultural census.

[4] Equipment manufacturing industry includes metal products industry, general equipment manufacturing industry, special equipment manufacturing industry, automobile manufacturing, railway, marine, aerospace and other transportation equipment manufacturing, electrical machinery and equipment manufacturing, computer, communications and other electronic equipment manufacturing, measuring instruments and machinery manufacturing.

[5] Six highly energy-consuming industries are: manufacture of raw chemical materials and chemical products, manufacture of non-metallic mineral products, smelting and pressing of ferrous metals, smelting and pressing of non-ferrous metals oil processing, coking and nuclear fuel processing, and production and supply of electricity and heat.

[6] Industrial strategic emerging industries, including energy conservation, environmental protection industry, a new generation of information technology industry, biology industry, high-end equipment manufacturing industry, new energy industry, new material industry, new energy automotive industry and so on seven big industry in the industrial industry.

[7] High tech manufacturing industry includes pharmaceutical manufacturing, aviation, aerospace and equipment manufacturing industry, electronics and communications equipment manufacturing, computer and office equipment manufacturing, medical equipment and instrument

manufacturing, chemicals manufacturing information.

[8] Fixed Internet broadband access users are people who have the registration of Telecom Enterprises at the end of the reporting period and access to the public Internet by xDSL、FTTx+LAN、FTTH/0 or other broadband access ways and common line access.

[9] Private investment in fixed assets is the construction or purchase of fixed assets investment by collective, private and individual domestic enterprises or institutions and enterprise units by its holdings (including absolute holdings and relative holdings).

[10] The real estate investment, in addition to investment in real estate development, also includes the construction of self-built housing units, as well as property management, intermediary services and other real estate investment.

[11] Online retail sales of goods refers to the retail sales of goods through the public website trading platform (the online platform mainly engaged in physical goods trading, including the self-established website and the third-party platform).

[12] The statistical caliber of general tertiary education enrollments was changed in 2018. Data are added to undergraduates in regular HEIS, including undergraduates in adult HEIS, web-based undergraduates and postgraduates.

The Data Size:

In this bulletin in 2018 import and export, transportation, postal telecommunications, environmental monitoring index data were for Xi'an the original diameter. Such as the per capita disposable income, employment and the introduction of talent, market main body, finance, external use of foreign capital, finance, securities and insurance, exhibition, tourism, education, sports, museums, cultural, health, social services, and rural strands personnel assistance support, rural residents living in extreme poverty received relief and assistance, population, urban construction, production safety, gross domestic product, agriculture, industry, construction industry, investment in fixed assets, domestic trade index data were to include Xi Xian new area. In the data of 2018 prices, consumer price index, retail price index, price index for investment in fixed assets, sales price index of new residential buildings were the original data of Xi'an. Producer price index for industrial products, purchasing price index for industrial products were to include Xi Xian new area. In the data of science and technology, the volume of contract transaction and patent data of 2018 science and technology plan project, high-tech enterprise, technology market were the original data of Xi'an, and the crowd-creation space was to include Xi Xian new area. In the data of Social security, the basic pension program for staff and workers of enterprises number was the original data of Xi'an. Urban basic medical insurance, unemployment insurance, employment injury insurance and worker bears insurance, the new rural cooperative medical care system participation number and the new rural cooperative medical care system participation ratio were to include Xi Xian new area.

Data Sources:

In this communiqué, data of price are from NBS Survey Office in Xi'an; data of newly increased employed people, unemployment rate through unemployment registration, the introduction of talent and social security are from the Xi'an Municipal Bureau of Human Resources and Social Security; The main market data comes from the Industrial and Commercial Bureau; financial data are from the Xi'an Municipal Bureau of Finance; data of imports and exports are from the Xi'an Customs; data on the utilization of foreign capital came from the Municipal Investment Commission; tourism data from the city Tourism Commission; data of railway transportation are from the Xi'an Municipal Bureau of Railways; data of highway transportation are from the Xi'an Municipal Bureau of Transport; data of air transport are from the Xi'an- Xian yang International Airport; data of motor vehicles for civilian use are from the Xi'an vehicle administration; data of post services are from the Xi'an Municipal Bureau of post; data of telecommunications are from Xi'an branch of China Mobile、China Unicom、China Telecom, and Shaanxi CTT; data of monetary and financial are from business management department for Xi'an branch of the People's Bank of China; data of listed companies and insurance are from Xi'an Municipal Finance Office; data of education are from the Xi'an Municipal Bureau of Education; data of technology are from Xi'an Municipal Bureau of Technology; data of museum are from Xi'an Municipal Bureau of Heritage; data of art-performing groups, public libraries, culture centers, radio and television are from the Xi'an Municipal Bureau of Culture, Radio, Press and Publication; the exhibition data comes from the Municipal Exhibition Office; data of sports are from the Xi'an Municipal Bureau of Sport; data of health and new cooperative medical care system in rural areas are from the Xi'an Municipal Bureau of Health; data on social services, subsistence allowances for the poor and the rural poor came from the Civil Affairs Bureau; the household registration data came from the Municipal Public Security Bureau; data of urban construction are from Urban and Rural Construction Commission; data of environment monitoring are from the Xi'an Ecology and Environment Bureau; data of work safety are from the Xi'an Bureau of Emergency Management; all the other data are from Xi'an Municipal Bureau of Statistics.

1 综　合

GENERAL SURVEY

资料整理：李　芬
Data management：Li Fen
数据审核：刘　婷
Data audit：Liu Ting

第一部分　综合

一、简要说明

本章资料主要包括西安市行政区划、自然地理、自然资源、气象、国民经济和社会发展等综合资料，由西安市统计局综合处根据局内各专业处及有关部门统计资料进行整理和编辑。

二、主要指标

生产总值（亿元）	8349.86	比上年增长	8.2%
农林牧渔业总产值（亿元）	461.21	比上年增长	3.5%
全部工业总产值（亿元）	6759.43	比上年增长	7.5%
全社会固定资产投资额（亿元）	–	比上年增长	8.4%
社会消费品零售总额（亿元）	4658.72	比上年增长	9.6%
财政一般公共预算收入（亿元）	684.70	比上年增长	10.8%
财政一般公共预算支出（亿元）	1151.87	比上年增长	10.2%
进出口总值（亿元）	3303.24	比上年增长	29.6%
城镇居民人均可支配收入（元）	38729	比上年增长	8.1%
农村居民人均可支配收入（元）	13286	比上年增长	9.0%

1　GENERAL SURVEY

Ⅰ.Brief Introduction

This chapter consists of mainly unified data of administrative divisions, natural geography, natural resources, meteorology, national economy and social development of Xi'an city. It is compiled by Integration Division according to the reported data from other divisions of the Xi'an Bureau of Statistics and other departments of the municipal government.

Ⅱ. Major Indicators

		Increase over Preceding Year
Gross Domestic Product (100 mil. Yuan)	8349.86	8.2%
Gross Output Value of Farming, Forestry, Animal, Husbandry and Fishery (100 mil. Yuan)	461.21	3.5%
Gross Output Value of Industry (100 mil. Yuan)	6759.43	7.5%
Total Investment In Fixed Assets (100 mil. Yuan)	–	8.4%
Total Retail Sales of Consumer Goods (100 mil. Yuan)	4658.72	9.6%
Government General Public Budgetary Revenue (100 mil. Yuan)	684.70	10.8%
Government General Public Budgetary Expenditures (100 mil. Yuan)	1151.87	10.2%
Total Value of Imports and Exports (RMB 100 mil.Yuan)	3303.24	29.6%
Per Capita Annual Disposable Income of Urban Households (Yuan)	38729	8.1%
Per Capita Annual Disposable Income of Rural Households (Yuan)	13286	9.0%

1-1 行政区划（2018年）

Administrative Division（2018）

单位：个 (unit)

地 区	Region	乡镇及街道办 Township and Urban Subdistrict Office	镇数 Town	街道办事处 Urban Subdistrict Office	村民委员会 Villagers' Committee	社区居委会 Neighbourhood Committee
西安市	**Xi'an**	**137**	**48**	**139**	**2074**	**1047**
新城区	Xincheng	9		9		101
碑林区	Beilin	8		8		98
莲湖区	Lianhu	9		9		131
灞桥区	Baqiao	9		9	113	69
未央区	Weiyang	10		10	52	141
雁塔区	Yanta	10		10	61	168
阎良区	Yanliang	7		7	73	24
临潼区	Lintong	23		23	226	42
长安区	Chang'an	21		21	294	115
高陵区	Gaoling	7		7	86	17
鄠邑区	Huyi	13	6	7	245	20
蓝田县	Lantian	19	18	1	337	9
周至县	Zhouzhi	20	19	1	264	16
西咸新区	Xixian	22	5	17	323	96

注：本表数据来源市民政局。

1–2 土地面积和常住人口密度（2018年）

Statistics on Land Area and Density of Permanent Population（2018）

地 区	Region	土地面积 Area 绝对数（平方公里）Absolute Value (sq.km)	比重（%）Proportion (%)	常住人口（万人）Total of Permanent Population (10 000 persons)	常住人口密度（人/平方公里）Density of Permanent Population (person/sq.km)
西安市	**Xi 'an**	**10096.81**	**100.0**	**1000.37**	
市区	**Urban**	**5145.66**	**51.0**	**784.96**	
新城区	Xincheng	30.13	0.3	64.13	21286
碑林区	Beilin	23.37	0.2	67.97	22560
莲湖区	Lianhu	38.32	0.4	76.86	25511
灞桥区	Baqiao	324.50	3.2	67.73	22481
未央区	Weiyang	264.41	2.6	77.74	
雁塔区	Yanta	151.44	1.5	134.32	44583
阎良区	Yanliang	244.55	2.4	30.12	9997
临潼区	Lintong	915.97	9.1	69.69	23131
长安区	Chang'an	1588.53	15.7	104.28	
高陵区	Gaoling	285.03	2.8	36.26	12035
鄠邑区	Huyi	1279.42	12.7	55.86	
二县	**Two Counties**	**4951.15**	**49.0**	**113.09**	**37537**
蓝田县	Lantian	2005.95	19.9	53.68	17817
周至县	Zhouzhi	2945.20	29.2	59.41	19719
西咸新区	Xixian				

注：1.本表土地面积数据来源市自然资源和规划局，为西安原口径数据。
2.全市常住人口数据包含西咸新区。
3.由于全市、市区及相关区县常住人口包含西咸新区，土地面积为原口径，暂不计算人口密度。

1-3 自然状况和资源（2018年）

Nature Conditions and Resources（2018）

指　标	Item	2018
一、自然状况	**Nature Conditions**	
土地总面积（平方公里）	Total Land Area (sq.km)	10096.81
#市区面积	Urban Area	5145.66
气候（市区）	Climate (Urban)	
年平均气温（℃）	Average Annual Temperature (℃)	15.5
年降水量（毫米）	Total Annual Precipitation (mm)	459.1
日照总时数（小时）	Total Sunshine Time (hour)	2087.7
平均风速（米/秒）	Average Wind-speed (m/sec.)	2.3
二、自然资源	**Natural Resources**	
年末常用耕地面积（千公顷）	Cultivated Area Year-end (1 000 hectare)	245.07
林业用地面积（千公顷）	Area of Forestry (1 000 hectare)	508.39
全市水面面积（千公顷）	Whole Water Area (1 000 hectare)	4.23
水资源总量（亿立方米）	Total Water Resource (0.1 billion cu.m)	21.90
#天然地表水资源总量	Total Savageness Surface Water Resource	17.99
地下水资源总量（亿立方米）	Total Underground Water Resource (0.1 billion cu.m)	11.19

注：1. 全市水面面积包括湖泊、水库、鱼塘、城市沿河流面积等。
2. 本表数据来源市气象局、自然资源和规划局、水务局等。
3. 本表年末常用耕地面积含西咸新区，其他指标数据均为西安原口径数据。

1-4 气象情况（2018年）

Climate Condition（2018）

地　区	Region	平均气温（℃）Average Temperature（℃）	日照时数（小时）Sunshine Time (hour)	降水天数（天）Raining days (day)	年降水量（毫米）Total Annual Precipitation (mm)	平均风速（米/秒）Average Wind-speed (m/second)
市　区	Urban	15.5	2087.7	83.0	459.1	2.3
临潼区	Lintong	15.0	2384.7	90.0	568.8	1.9
长安区	Chang'an	13.9	1815.4	102.0	682.5	1.3
高陵区	Gaoling	14.7	2288.8	89.0	437.0	1.6
鄠邑区	Huyi	14.6	2236.4	131.0	607.8	1.7
蓝田县	Lantian	13.7	1679.9	102.0	736.7	1.6
周至县	Zhouzhi	14.1	1899.6	124.0	618.5	1.6

注：本表数据来源市气象局，为西安原口径数据。

1-5 市区及远郊区县各月平均气温（2018年）

Average Temperature of Xi'an and the Districts and Outer Suburban of Each Month（2018）

单位：℃　　　　(℃)

月　份	Month	市区 Urban	临潼区 Lintong	长安区 Chang'an	高陵区 Gaoling	鄠邑区 Huyi	蓝田县 Lantian	周至县 Zhouzhi
一月	January	-0.9	-1.2	-1.9	-1.8	-1.5	-2.7	-1.6
二月	February	4.5	3.9	2.8	3.3	3.7	1.7	3.5
三月	March	13.2	12.7	12.0	12.2	12.4	11.6	12.2
四月	April	17.8	17.3	16.1	16.9	16.8	15.9	16.8
五月	May	21.8	21.3	19.8	21.3	20.8	19.9	20.2
六月	June	26.6	26.3	24.6	26.4	25.4	25.0	24.7
七月	July	28.4	27.9	27.0	28.8	27.3	27.5	26.7
八月	August	29.1	28.6	27.3	28.8	28.0	27.6	27.4
九月	September	20.7	20.1	19.2	20.2	19.9	19.3	19.2
十月	October	15.3	14.9	13.3	14.1	14.4	12.8	13.0
十一月	November	7.9	7.5	6.6	6.9	7.2	6.4	6.5
十二月	December	1.7	1.2	0.5	0.6	1.3	-0.4	0.9

注：本表数据来源市气象局，为西安原口径数据。

1-6 市区及远郊区县各月日照时数（2018年）

Sunshine Duration of Xi'an and the Districts and Outer Suburban of Each Month（2018）

单位：小时 (hour)

月份	Month	市区 Urban	临潼区 Lintong	长安区 Chang'an	高陵区 Gaoling	鄠邑区 Huyi	蓝田县 Lantian	周至县 Zhouzhi
一月	January	92.0	124.9	105.6	113.6	109.4	75.8	118.5
二月	February	185.5	212.1	174.2	202.6	189.7	148.6	172.8
三月	March	196.7	230.0	124.6	207.7	201.3	169.3	178.9
四月	April	196.8	231.5	201.5	214.9	208.6	184.6	207.6
五月	May	185.5	198.4	163.8	195.3	191.8	150.1	184.0
六月	June	203.2	257.7	213.4	236.9	224.5	182.4	189.9
七月	July	184.8	238.1	145.0	232.0	221.8	134.5	148.5
八月	August	284.3	313.1	214.1	297.4	307.3	231.3	227.5
九月	September	148.4	157.9	122.4	159.6	152.0	119.5	119.8
十月	October	202.2	213.7	184.2	206.5	213.6	151.0	156.4
十一月	November	118.1	98.6	99.2	122.6	110.2	71.9	110.4
十二月	December	90.2	108.7	67.4	99.7	106.2	60.9	85.3

注：本表数据来源市气象局，为西安原口径数据。

1-7 市区及远郊区县各月降水天数（2018年）

Precipitation Days of Xi'an and the Districts and Outer Suburan of Each Month（2018）

单位：天 (day)

月份	Month	市区 Urban	临潼区 Lintong	长安区 Chang'an	高陵区 Gaoling	鄠邑区 Huyi	蓝田县 Lantian	周至县 Zhouzhi
一月	January	8	7	8	8	12	9	11
二月	February	3	4	4	3	5	4	4
三月	March	7	6	8	8	9	5	11
四月	April	7	11	10	8	10	10	9
五月	May	8	9	13	8	12	11	14
六月	June	7	10	9	9	15	9	13
七月	July	8	13	13	10	17	15	12
八月	August	4	3	8	4	9	9	8
九月	September	14	13	12	14	16	13	14
十月	October	5	4	5	7	7	5	9
十一月	November	9	7	7	7	9	7	11
十二月	December	3	3	5	3	10	5	8

注：本表数据来源市气象局，为西安原口径数据。

1-8 市区及远郊区县各月降水量（2018年）

Amountof Precipitation of Xi'an and the Districts and Outer Suburan of Each Month（2018）

单位：毫米 (mm)

月份	Month	市区 Urban	临潼区 Lintong	长安区 Chang'an	高陵区 Gaoling	鄠邑区 Huyi	蓝田县 Lantian	周至县 Zhouzhi
一月	January	22.0	20.6	29.9	21.1	24.2	23.6	21.8
二月	February	3.6	9.4	22.9	5.3	12.8	13.4	10.5
三月	March	21.2	27.0	39.4	27.8	27.9	36.6	24.1
四月	April	36.4	61.5	76.4	23.2	64.7	74.8	85.4
五月	May	25.7	47.6	53.7	24.7	37.3	61.9	34.1
六月	June	50.7	70.5	88.6	48.0	101.9	100.8	102.4
七月	July	114.1	141.4	149.9	114.1	148.6	188.4	118.1
八月	August	71.7	38.9	84.3	59.8	70.5	61.4	104.8
九月	September	73.7	103.5	95.4	82.6	70.7	119.0	76.2
十月	October	8.9	7.8	7.7	5.4	4.9	9.7	6.1
十一月	November	28.6	34.2	25.0	23.8	37.3	42.1	21.8
十二月	December	2.5	1.9	9.3	1.2	7.0	5.0	13.2

注：本表数据来源市气象局，为西安原口径数据。

1-9 市区及远郊区县各月平均风速（2018年）

Average Wind Velocity of Xi'an and the Districts and Outer Suburban Districts（2018）

单位：米/秒 (m/s)

月份	Month	市区 Urban	临潼区 Lintong	长安区 Chang'an	高陵区 Gaoling	鄠邑区 Huyi	蓝田县 Lantian	周至县 Zhouzhi
一月	January	2.4	1.8	1.4	2.0	1.6	1.2	1.4
二月	February	1.9	1.6	1.5	1.7	1.7	1.5	1.7
三月	March	2.5	1.9	1.5	2.3	1.7	1.7	1.7
四月	April	2.5	2.1	1.3	2.3	2.0	1.8	2.1
五月	May	2.5	2.1	1.4	2.4	1.9	1.8	1.9
六月	June	2.3	2.0	1.2	2.2	1.9	1.6	1.8
七月	July	2.8	2.2	1.3	2.6	1.8	1.7	1.6
八月	August	2.8	2.0	1.2	2.3	1.6	1.6	1.7
九月	September	2.4	1.8	1.2	2.0	1.7	1.5	1.4
十月	October	2.1	1.8	1.2	1.9	1.7	1.6	1.5
十一月	November	1.7	1.5	1.3	1.6	1.5	1.3	1.3
十二月	December	2.1	1.8	1.2	1.8	1.5	1.4	1.4

注：本表数据来源市气象局，为西安原口径数据。

1-10 主要年份国有土地使用权出让、划拨情况

The Transfer and Allocation of State-Owned Land Use Right in Representative Years

项目	Item	2010	2011	2012	2013	2014	2015	2016	2017	2018
国有土地使用权出让	**Lease of the Use Right of State-owned Land**									
出让地块(宗)	Land leased (item)	386	474	581	550	506	416	457	397	387
协议	Agreement	173	133	80	90	109	72	82	69	79
招标	Invitation for Bid	3								
拍卖	Auction	11							25	203
挂牌交易	Listed Transaction	199	341	500	460	397	344	375	303	105
出让面积（公顷）	Area of Totally Leased Land (hectare)	1364	1386	1853	2195	1789	1294	1599	1736	1623
土地使用权出让总收入（万元）	**Total Revenue from Leasing of the Use Right(10 000 yuan)**	**358098**	**334069**	**218817**	**292945**	**183901**	**109116**	**2832632**	**3988818**	**5738433**
国有土地使用权划拨	**Administrative Allocation of the Use Right of State-owned Land**									
划拨地块（宗）	Land Allocated (item)	108	253	154	234	152	141	132	130	116
划拨面积（公顷）	Area of Land Allocated(hectare)	1027	1426	1617	1986	1739	1209	1135	1411	3099

注：1.本表数据来自市自然资源和规划局，为西安原口径数据。
2.2016年起土地使用权出让总收入，包括协议出让和招拍挂出让收入。

1-11 主要年份国民经济和社会发展总量与速度指标

指 标	Item	总量指标 Total quantity index			
		1995	2000	2005	2010
人口与就业	**Population and Employment**				
人口	**Population**				
年底户籍总人口（万人）	Population at the Year-end （10 000 persons）	648.21	688.01	741.73	782.73
城镇人口	Urban Population	255.71	285.79	333.14	374.64
乡村人口	Rural Population	392.50	402.22	408.59	408.09
男性人口	Male Population	334.75	355.18	382.02	398.80
女性人口	Female Population	313.46	332.83	359.71	383.93
就业	**Employment**				
全社会从业人员数（万人）	Employment（10 000 persons）	372.60	389.10	415.83	477.58
#全部单位在岗职工人数	Number of Employed Staff and Workers	141.17	109.62	119.73	130.70
城镇登记失业人数（万人）	Registered Unemployed in Urban Areas（10 000 persons）	5.92	3.85	8.45	10.46
宏观经济	**Macroeconomic Indicator**				
国民经济核算	**National Accounts**				
生产总值（亿元）	Gross Domestic Product（100 mil. yuan）	330.35	646.13	1313.93	3242.86
第一产业	Primary Industry	41.40	44.65	66.01	140.06
第二产业	Secondary Industry	135.33	277.13	540.50	1357.53
第三产业	Tertiary Industry	153.62	324.35	707.42	1745.27
工业	Industry	112.50	218.44	420.00	954.38
建筑业	Construction			120.50	403.15
在生产总值中：最终消费	Total Consumption	239.64	413.43	766.62	1598.51
资本形成总额	Total Investment	151.55	287.82	839.01	2835.42
固定资产投资	**Investment in Fixed Assets**				
全社会固定资产投资总额（亿元）	Total Investment in Fixed Assets（100 mil. yuan）	103.42	232.37	835.10	3250.56
按类别分：	By classification:				
固定资产投资（不含农户）	Investment in Fixed Assets （excluding farmers）	88.50	203.01	776.33	3104.92
#房地产开发投资	Real Estate Investment	21.65	51.85	225.23	842.34
农户投资	Farmer Investment	14.92	29.36	58.77	145.64
按经济成分划分:	By Economic Component				
国有单位	State-owned	69.08	159.60	373.70	1348.76
集体单位	Collective-Owned	9.78	14.65	59.23	326.44
个体经济	Self-employed Individual	11.13	24.40	79.04	54.73
其他经济	Other	13.43	33.72	323.13	1520.63
财政	**Public Finance**				
地方财政一般公共预算收入（亿元）	General Public Budgetary Revenue of Local Government （100 mil. yuan）	18.21	41.39	73.05	241.86
地方财政一般公共预算支出（亿元）	General Public Budgetary Expenditure of Local Government （100 mil. yuan）	18.42	46.50	97.82	371.62
物价指数（上年=100）	**Price Indices（preceding year=100）**				
商品零售价格指数	Retail Price Index	114.6	98.7	99.7	102.7
居民消费价格指数	Consumer Price Index	117.0	100.2	100.3	103.5
工业生产者出厂价格指数	Producer Price Indices （PPI） for Manufactured Goods	110.8	99.4	103.9	102.3
利用外资	**Utilization of Foreign Capital**				
利用外资签定协议额（万美元）	Amount of Foreign Capital for Utilization Through Signed Contracts or Agreements（USD 10 000）	28956	54123	121499	119689
外商实际直接投资额（万美元）	Amount of Foreign Capital Actually Utilized （USD 10 000）	18653	15633	57113	156653

注：1.国民经济核算2004—2008年为全国第二次经济普查修订数据。2009—2012年为三经普修订数据，2013年为全国第三次经济普查数据。2014—2015年为年报最终核实数。2017年起GDP核算包括研发支出新增GDP数据。2018年第一产业增加值为三农普修订数据。
2.2009年及以前年份财政收支为一般预算收支与基金预算收支之和。部分历史年份数据有所修订。
3.由于2010年固定资产投资起报点的变化，指数和平均增长速度为可比口径计算。
4.2015年，市公安局提供户籍人口分类为“城镇人口”和“乡村人口”，2015年之前，分类为“非农业人口”和“农业人口”。
5.2015年，国家取消了城乡投资分组，“农户投资”2014年之前为原来的“农村投资”。
6.由于2017年部分指标包含有西咸新区数据,速度指标为同口径计算数据。
7.本表数据2018年数据口径情况详见总说明和相关章节表下注释。
8.农业部分数据依据三农普数据对2007-2017进行了修订。畜牧业数据2013-2017年为三农普修订数据。下同。
9.投资有关数据2018年为相对数据，与2018年投资总量相关的指标，暂不计算。下同。

Total and Speed Index of National Economy and Social Development in Representative Years

				速度指标 （%）				Indices and Growth Rates（%）		
				指数（2018比以下各年）（2018 as percentage of the following years）				平均增长速度 Average Annual Growth Rate		
2015	2016	2017	2018	2005	2010	2015	2017	2006-2010	2011-2015	2016-2018
815.66	824.93	845.09	922.82	124.4	117.7	113.0	109.2	1.1	0.8	4.2
545.95	552.21	567.26	639.62	192.0	170.7	117.1	112.8	2.4	7.8	5.4
269.71	272.72	277.83	283.20	69.3	59.4	105.0	101.9	-0.02	-7.9	1.6
412.23	416.54	424.98	461.51	120.8	115.7	111.9	108.6	0.9	0.7	3.8
403.43	408.39	420.11	461.31	128.2	120.2	114.3	109.8	1.3	1.0	4.6
528.06	539.18	596.21	621.22	138.4	120.5	109.0	104.2	2.8	2.0	2.9
181.86	184.93	188.42	181.76	149.7	137.1	98.5	96.5	1.8	6.8	-0.5
10.74	11.29	11.51	12.48	147.5	119.2	116.1	108.4	4.4	0.5	5.1
5801.20	6282.65	7471.89	8349.86	427.9	212.9	126.6	108.2	15.0	11.0	8.2
220.20	232.01	281.12	258.82	200.5	146.6	112.2	103.3	6.5	5.5	3.9
2126.29	2200.36	2596.52	2925.61	407.4	204.7	124.0	108.5	14.8	10.6	7.4
3454.71	3850.28	4594.25	5165.43	467.6	224.6	129.1	108.3	15.8	11.7	8.9
1376.72	1397.25	1684.02	1874.36	389.6	207.2	125.9	109.0	13.4	10.5	8.0
770.29	818.32	928.30	1073.12	476.7	200.2	119.8	107.9	19.0	10.8	6.2
5165.98	5191.36	7556.47		975.1	250.5	124.9	108.4	31.2	14.9	7.7
5086.93	5097.00	7463.31		1062.3	265.6	126.7	108.5	31.9	15.9	8.2
1831.67	1955.82	2333.34		1077.8	288.2	132.5	107.9	30.2	16.8	9.8
79.05	78.65	93.16		144.3	58.2	107.2	102.1	19.9	-11.5	2.3
1826.62	2332.08	4127.66		829.1	229.8	134.4	97.1	29.3	11.3	10.4
158.14	152.05	153.36		114.0	20.7	33.8	45.5	40.7	-9.4	-30.3
80.47	81.68	93.94		0.0	0.0	0.0	0.0	-7.1	13.2	-100.0
3100.75	2625.55	3181.51		1309.1	278.2	108.4	108.6	36.6	20.7	2.7
650.99	641.07	654.50	684.70	1267.1	379.5	135.2	110.8	27.3	22.9	10.6
917.24	942.52	1045.09	1151.87	1148.2	301.9	121.3	110.2	30.6	20.0	6.6
99.7	100.1	101.7	102.2					2.5	1.7	1.3
100.7	100.9	102.0	101.9					3.1	2.6	1.6
98.5	97.8	100.3	101.1					2.2	0.1	-0.3
193684	102103	464954	475508	195.1	198.1	122.4	51.0	-0.3	10.1	7.0
400833	450466	530680	635370	1067.7	389.3	152.1	114.9	22.4	20.7	15.0

1-11 续表1

指 标	Item	总量指标 Total quantity index 1995	2000	2005	2010
产 业	**Industry**				
农业	**Agriculture**				
耕地面积（万亩）	Cultivated Areas（10 000 hectares）	463.97	443.37	400.17	383.32
农林牧渔业总产值 （亿元）	Gross Output Value of Farming，Forestry, Animal Husbandry and Fishery（100 mil yuan）	75.46	74.37	106.54	212.42
主要农产品产量（万吨）	Output of Major Farm Products（10 000 tons）				
粮 食	Grain	175.30	201.90	205.50	174.51
奶 类	Milk				
蔬 菜	Vegetables	133.60	162.14	195.70	207.11
水 果	Fruits	24.10	34.36	51.29	66.11
肉 类	Meat				
水产品	Aquatic Products	0.85	1.14	0.94	1.19
工业	**Industry**				
全部工业总产值（亿元）	Gross Industrial Output Value（100 mil. yuan）	405.90	639.48	1308.56	3562.88
规模以上工业企业主要经济指标（亿元）	Main Economic Indicators of Industrial Enterprises above Designated Size				
资产总计	Total Assets		958.05	1503.85	3592.13
主营业务收入	Revenue from Principal Business		420.42	980.97	3011.19
利润总额	Profits		16.11	28.72	245.37
从业人员年平均人数 （万人）	Annual Average Employees（10 000 persons）		43.25	37.92	47.11
主要工业产品产量	Output of Major Industrial Products				
布（亿米）	Cloth（100 mil.m）	3.03	2.48	2.70	2.38
机制纸及纸板（万吨）	Machine-Made Paper（10 000ton）	36.44	5.47	22.19	49.60
发电量（亿千瓦时）	Electricity（100 million kwh）	22.00	19.00	48.00	96.94
钢材（万吨）	Steel Products（10 000ton）	31.44	10.00	24.02	110.77
汽车（万辆）	Motor Vehicle （10 000 units）	0.30	0.90	4.10	65.21
建筑业	**Construction**				
建筑业企业从业人数（人）	Number of Employed Persons（person）		136718	158311	539000
建筑业总产值（亿元）	Gross Output Value（100 mil. yuan）	42.55	105.93	326.65	1334.00
房屋建筑施工面积 （万平方米）	Floor Space of Buildings under Construction （10 000 sq.m）	601.70	793.30	1801.20	4592.57
房屋建筑竣工面积 （万平方米）	Floor Space of Buildings Completed （10 000 sq.m）	177.15	336.80	569.01	1391.91

注：规模以上工业2013年为全国第三次经济普查数据。以前年份未做修订。
由于2010年规模以上工业起报点的变化，指数和平均增长速度为可比口径计算。

continued 1

2015	2016	2017	2018	速度指标（%） Indices and Growth Rates（%）						
				指数（2018比以下各年）（2018 as percentage of the following years）				平均增长速度 Average Annual Growth Rate		
				2005	2010	2015	2017	2006-2010	2011-2015	2016-2018
356.89	346.80	374.45	367.61	83.3	86.9	93.4	98.2	-9.0	-1.4	-2.3
330.81	346.75	437.33	461.21	206.6	147.9	113.0	103.5	6.8	5.5	4.2
141.42	135.39	139.89	142.14	82.9	76.9	94.2	101.6	1.5	-4.0	-2.0
7.68	7.93	11.65	11.52	116.8	77.8	77.3	98.9	8.5	0.1	-8.2
267.91	268.87	354.74	373.69	190.3	147.2	111.9	105.3	5.3	5.6	3.8
73.33	75.53	89.80	89.15	216.7	131.2	105.7	99.3	10.6	4.4	1.9
7.21	6.87	5.87	5.45	82.7	110.2	93.4	92.8	-5.6	3.4	-2.3
1.42	1.34	1.38	1.35	143.6	113.4	95.1	97.8	5.7	3.6	-1.7
5159.91	5462.43	6285.34	6759.43	496.3	190.1	131.0	107.5	21.2	7.7	9.4
6740.26	7473.07	7862.59	8294.07	562.7	235.5	125.5	105.5	19.0	13.4	7.9
4374.11	5028.28	5710.70	6021.12	579.9	189.0	130.1	105.4	25.1	7.8	9.2
206.88	290.96	367.77	402.44	1208.8	141.5	167.8	109.4	53.6	-3.4	18.8
50.59	49.55	51.11	51.40	124.5	100.2	93.4	100.6	4.4	1.4	-2.3
1.04	1.22	1.27	1.28	47.0	53.4	122.2	100.3	-2.5	-15.3	6.9
12.22	13.44	18.62	15.39	47.2	21.1	85.6	84.6	17.5	-24.4	-5.1
158.68	161.00	176.74	172.76	309.3	153.2	93.5	95.9	15.1	10.4	-2.2
37.03	43.92	54.91	33.40	200.5	43.5	130.1	115.3	35.8	-19.7	9.2
34.14	38.25	44.52	43.37	1057.3	56.5	127.0	97.4	73.9	-12.1	8.3
596245	588418	703169	740351	461.8	135.7	122.7	105.3	27.8	2.0	7.1
2650.41	2897.55	3304.54	3925.72	1198.0	293.4	147.7	118.8	41.0	14.7	13.9
11979.16	11945.73	13491.49	15855.39	864.8	339.1	130.1	117.5	20.6	21.1	9.2
2712.01	2233.20	2553.10	2755.17	454.0	135.6	95.3	107.9	19.6	14.3	-1.6

1-11 续表2

指 标	Item	总量指标 Total quantity index 1995	2000	2005	2010
交通运输	**Transportation**				
货运量（万吨）	Freight Traffic（10 000 tons）	9590	6999	12051	34323
铁 路	Railways	3317	3101	540	706
公 路	Highways	6268	3890	11505	33610
民用航空	Civil Aviation	5	8	6	7
客运量（万人次）	Passenger Traffic（10 000 persons-times）	9069	8068	10479	30294
铁 路	Railways	2678	2130	1796	2781
公 路	Highways	6128	5578	8294	26536
民用航空	Civil Aviation	263	360	389	977
邮电通信业	**Post and Telecommunication Services**				
邮电业务总量（亿元）	Total Business Revenue（100 mil. yuan）	7.65	46.16	132.04	323.11
函 件（万件）	Number of Letters Delivered（10 000 pieces）	14647	8230	9526	8176
本地电话局用交换机容量（万门）	Capacity of Local Office Telephone Exchanges（10 000 line）	58.30	204.80	457.30	449.00
本地电话年末用户（万户）	Local fixed telephone end users （million）	29.95	124.26	321.48	261.77
城市电话用户	Urban Telephone Subscribers	29.11	107.24	271.40	228.26
乡村电话用户	Rural Telephone Subscribers	0.84	17.02	50.08	33.50
移动电话用户（万户）	Number of Mobile Telephone Subscribers（10 000 subscribers）		73.10	419.96	1423.08
互联网年末宽带用户（万户）	Number of Subscribers of Intemet Services（10 000 subscribers）			33.93	146.18
国内贸易	**Domestic Trade**				
社会消费品零售总额（亿元）	Total Retail Sales of Consumer Goods（100 mil. yuan）	186.60	360.42	670.56	1678.01
对外经济贸易	**Foreign Trade**				
进出口总值（万美元）	Total Value of Exports and Imports（USD 10 000）	137510	173696	390146	1039273
出口总值	Exports	110163	106062	263441	531729
进口总值	Imports	27347	67634	126705	507544
旅游	**Tourism**				
旅游者人数（万人次）	Number of Tourists（10 000 persons）	791.35	1567.00	2423.60	5285.18
旅游总收入（亿元）	Earnings from Tourism （10 000yuan）	44.00	105.00	178.50	405.18
金融业	**Financial Intermediation**				
金融机构（不含外资）人民币存款余额（亿元）	Balance of Deposits in Domestic Funded Financial Institutions （100 mil. yuan）	359.51	1335.63	3599.70	8863.36
金融机构（不含外资）人民币贷款余额（亿元）	Balance of Loans in Domestic Funded Financial Institutions （100 mil. yuan）	334.50	972.52	2158.10	6420.72
保险公司保费收入（亿元）	Insurance premium income （100 million Yuan）	4.70	13.58	44.94	129.38
保险公司赔款及付给金额（亿元）	Indemnity Insurance and Amount Paid（100 million yuan）	1.70	1.39	9.50	26.39

注：1.2006年铁路数据按新口径统计；
2.2006年国际互联网络用户改为互联网宽带用户。
3.2009—2013年社会消费品零售总额为全国第三次经济普查修订数据。2016年社会消费品零售总额数据依据第三次农业普查和相关制定进行了修订。
4.2014年起，海关不发布美元口径数据，为了数据可持续性，使用年均汇率折算为美元口径。

continued 2

2015	2016	2017	2018	速度指标 （%） Indices and Growth Rates（%）						
				指数（2018比以下各年）（2018 as percentage of the following years）				平均增长速度 Average Annual Growth Rate		
				2005	2010	2015	2017	2006-2010	2011-2015	2016-2018
46270	23888	25497	26892				105.5	23.3		
848	854	994	1170				117.7	5.5		
45401	23011	24477	25691				105.0	23.9		
21	23	26	31				119.2	3.1		
26904	23671	24287	25543				105.2	23.7		
3982	4199	4500	5523				122.7	9.1		
19625	15773	15601	15555				99.7	26.2		
3297	3699	4186	4465				106.7	20.2		
331.53	383.11	439.85	739.53	560.3	229.0	223.1	168.1	19.6	0.5	30.7
1707	1367	1360	1081	11.3	13.2	63.4	79.5	-3.0	-26.9	-14.1
145.10	75.92							-0.4	-20.2	
292.08	284.33	273.22	262.28	81.6	100.2	89.8	96.0	-4.0	2.2	-3.5
261.44	252.88	243.81	237.78	87.5	104.0	90.9	97.5	-3.4	2.8	-3.1
30.63	31.45	29.41	24.50	49.0	73.1	80.0	83.3	-7.7	-1.8	-7.2
1767.00	1739.50	1854.21	1858.09	442.3	130.6	105.1	100.2	27.6	4.4	1.7
289.97	335.83	346.79	392.48	1157.2	268.6	135.4	113.2	33.9	14.7	10.6
3405.38	3767.20	4249.81	4658.72	661.8	264.5	130.3	109.6	19.5	15.2	9.2
2828479	2754991	3769490	4991748	1279.1	480.2	176.4	132.4	21.6	39.6	20.8
1316350	1426175	2298972	2957605	1121.9	555.9	224.5	128.6	15.1	35.3	30.9
1512129	1328816	1470518	2034142	1605.9	400.9	134.6	138.3	32.0	43.9	10.4
13600.80	15012.56	18093.14	24738.75	1020.6	467.9	181.8	136.7	21.6	37.0	22.0
1073.69	1213.81	1633.30	2554.81	1432.2	630.9	238.0	156.4	15.1	38.4	33.5
17682.94	18957.55	19943.41	20811.95	578.4	234.9	117.8	104.4	19.7	14.8	5.6
13604.89	15159.40	16831.48	19610.88	908.2	305.3	144.1	116.5	24.4	16.2	13.0
263.02	345.85	421.10	478.56	1065.0	369.9	182.0	113.6	23.6	15.2	22.1
87.62	115.91	118.71	130.82	1376.9	495.6	149.3	110.2	24.8	27.1	14.3

1-11 续表3

指 标	Item	总量指标 Total quantity index			
		1995	2000	2005	2010
教育、科技、文化	**Education, Science and Technology and Culture**				
教育	**Education**				
专任教师数（人）	Full-time Teachers（person）				
#普通高等学校	Institutions of Higher Education	15914	15679	29498	42098
普通中等专业学校	Regular Specialized Secondary Schools	2533	3172	2130	1845
普通中学	Regular Middle Schools	21984	26230	31094	31506
小 学	Primary Schools	30270	30215	29647	29944
在校学生数（万人）	Students Enrollment（10 000 person）				
#普通高等学校	Institutions of Higher Education	11.67	19.41	53.06	73.30
普通中等专业学校	Regular Specialized Secondary Schools	3.74	6.02	6.16	6.75
普通中学	Regular Schools	32.32	48.31	55.74	48.89
小 学	Primary Schools	79.36	77.81	60.47	51.56
科技	**Science and Technology**				
国家级高新技术企业数（个）	Hi-tech Enterprises （unit）				827
企事业单位累计授权专利数（件）	Accumulated patents awarded（unit）	3164	6139	11670	31999
文化	**Cultural**				
图书馆总藏量（千册件）	Total Collections in Library （1000 Volume-time）	2830	3214	3671	4465
文化馆、站（个）	Cultural Centers or Stations （unit）	201	251	192	197
电视节目制作时间（小时）	Time for TV Programs Production（hour）	5738	11871	27377	29626
家庭、生活、环境	**Family, People's Livelihood and Environment**				
家庭	**Family**				
家庭总户数（户籍人口）（万户）	Total Number of Households（10 000 household）	171.25	187.08	203.04	226.71
城镇常住居民平均每户家庭人口（人）	Average Household Size in Urban Areas（person）	3.88	2.99	2.93	2.81
农村常住居民平均每户家庭人口（人）	Average Household Size in Rural Areas（person）	4.60	4.30	4.22	3.94
婚姻	**Marriages and Divorces**				
结婚（对）	Number of Marriages（couple）	47236	46415	49962	83645
离婚（对）	Number of Divorces（couple）	4296	5161	12747	19060
居住	**Housing**				
城镇居民人均现住房建筑面积（平方米）	Per Capita Building Area of Urban Residents （sq.m）	13.05	14.82	16.38	28.70
农村居民人均现住房建筑面积（平方米）	Per Capita Building Area of Rural Residents（sq.m）	21.77	28.31	36.73	66.73

注：1.2008年及以前图书馆总藏量为图书馆藏书量。
2.2005年以前城镇居民人均现住房总建筑面积为城镇人均住房使用面积。
3.2014年城乡居民人均住房面积为城乡住户调查一体化改革后新口径数据，与往年不可比。
4.结婚和离婚对数2018年数据含西咸新区与往年不可比，增速暂不计算。

continued 3

2015	2016	2017	2018	速度指标 （%）				Indices and Growth Rates（%）		
				指数（2018比以下各年）（2018 as percentage of the following years）				平均增长速度 Average Annual Growth Rate		
				2005	2010	2015	2017	2006-2010	2011-2015	2016-2018
47768	47158	47917	49018	166.1	116.4	102.6	102.3	7.4	2.6	0.9
1228	1210	998	958	45.0	51.9	78.0	96.0	-2.8	-7.8	-7.9
33014	33962	36565	37539	113.6	112.0	106.9	102.7	0.3	0.9	2.2
28748	30941	34163	36878	114.7	113.5	119.7	107.9	0.2	-1.1	6.2
84.83	83.10	83.02	82.44	155.4	112.5	97.2	99.3	6.7	3.0	-0.9
3.47	3.11	2.74	2.48	40.2	36.7	71.4	90.5	1.9	-12.5	-10.6
41.37	40.70	41.74	42.46	73.3	83.6	98.9	101.7	-2.6	-3.3	-0.4
56.62	59.79	66.68	73.09	114.3	134.2	122.2	109.6	-3.1	1.9	6.9
1316	1506	1839	2620		316.6	199.1	142.5		9.7	25.8
103910	150021	175063	206703	1772.0	646.2	199.0	118.1	22.4	26.6	25.8
6522	6957	7340	7711	210.2	172.9	118.3	105.1	4.0	7.9	5.8
199	190	202	202	94.7	92.4	91.5	100.0	0.6	0.2	-2.9
43563	54200	49001	45731	166.9	154.2	105.0	93.3	1.6	8.0	1.6
253.13	256.65	267.68	290.41	143.0	128.2	114.8	108.5	2.2	2.2	4.7
2.80	2.80	2.80	2.80	95.6	99.6	100.0	100.0	-0.8	-0.1	0.0
3.60	3.60	3.60	3.70	87.7	94.0	102.8	102.8	-1.6	-1.8	0.9
80790	77371	70954	93007					10.9	-0.7	
22748	25448	28811	42034					8.4	3.6	
32.10	33.40	33.70	34.40			107.2	102.1	11.9		2.3
50.70	51.70	52.40	51.40			101.4	98.1	12.7		0.5

1-11 续表4

指　标	Item	总量指标 Total quantity index			
		1995	2000	2005	2010
生活	**People's Livelihood**				
城镇居民人均可支配收入（元）	Per Capita Annual Disposable Income of Urban Households （yuan）	4153	6364	9628	22244
农村居民人均可支配收入（元）	Per Capita Annual Disposable Income of Rural Residents（yuan）	1353	2344	3460	7750
住户存款(亿元)	Household deposits（100 mil. yuan）	291.46	675.83	1716.76	3641.09
工资	**Wages**				
在岗职工工资总额（亿元）	The Gross Salary of Workers （100 mil. yuan）	67.23	101.68	211.14	501.76
城镇非私营单位从业人员年平均工资（元）	Aunual Average Wage of Stuff and Workers in Urban Non-privite Enterprises（yuan）	4763	9179	17728	37870
卫生	**Health Care**				
医院、卫生院（个）	Number of Hospitals（unit）	368	426	479	412
执业（助理）医师（人）	Licensed （Assistant） Doctors （person）	18846	18750	17730	18763
医院、卫生院床位数（张）	Number of Hospital Beds（unit）	28265	28697	30087	36796
市政建设	**City Construction**				
自来水供应量（万立方米）	Volume of Tap Water Supply（10 000 cu.m）	35885	30273	35776	41089
自来水供水管道长度（公里）	Length of Water Supply Pipelines（km）	1066	2237	2315	2416
城市天然气供气总量 （万立方米）	Volume of Natural Gas Supply in Urban Areas （10 000 cu.m）	8419	11513	53202	109052
城市公共运营车辆（辆）	Total Number of Public Buses and Trolley Buses（unit）	977	2573	4762	7107
道路长度（公里）	Length of Paved Roads（km）	835	975	1382	2662
绿地面积（公顷）	Areas of Green Land（hectare）	5603	4116	4867	12140
环境、灾害	**Environment and Disaster**				
工业废水排放量（万吨）	Volume of Waste Water up to the Standard for Discharge（10 000 tons）	12479	9145	16969	13840
火灾发生数（起）	Number of Fire Disasters（case）	426	1040	2664	1825
火灾事故损失额（万元）	Fire Loss（10 000 yuan）	742	472	1566	2224
交通事故发生数（起）	Number of Traffic Accidents（case）	3065	4099	4903	2323
交通事故损失额（万元）	Loss of Traffic Accidents（10 000 yuan）	1103	1116	2024	737

注：1.城镇非私营单位从业人员年平均工资2012年前为城镇非私营单位在岗职工年平均工资。
2.2014年及以后城乡居民人均收入为新口径数据。2013年及以前“农村居民人均可支配收入”为“农村居民人均纯收入”。依据2018年新口径对2017年城乡居民收入进行了衔接，其他年份不可比。
3.部门对住户存款部分历史年代数据进行了修订。2015年之前住户存款为储蓄存款。
4.市政建设大部分指标2017年起包含西咸新区，与以前年份不可比，故不计算相关增速指标。

continued 4

				速度指标 （%） Indices and Growth Rates（%）						
2015	2016	2017	2018	指数（2018比以下各年）（2018 as percentage of the following years）				平均增长速度 Average Annual Growth Rate		
				2005	2010	2015	2017	2006-2010	2011-2015	2016-2018
33188	35630	35837	38729	508.9	220.3	125.6	108.1	18.2	15.1	7.9
14072	15191	12190	13286	584.0	250.8	128.1	109.0	17.5	15.3	8.6
6571.18	7035.81	7497.30	8360.33	487.4	229.8	127.3	111.5	13.3	12.5	8.4
1202.01	1309.59	1488.71	1622.72	742.6	312.6	130.5	109.0	18.9	19.1	9.3
60557	67205	75262	83821	475.2	222.5	139.1	111.4	16.4	9.8	11.6
395	392	448	462	86.5	100.6	105.0	103.1	-3.0	-0.8	1.6
26626	27854	30820	33776	183.9	173.7	122.4	109.6	1.1	7.3	7.0
51345	53008	60513	65552	208.2	170.1	121.9	108.3	4.1	6.9	6.8
56055	59953	89216	90394				101.3	2.8	6.4	
4371	4522	4900	4960				101.2	0.9	12.6	
196826	206058	231168	285215				123.4	15.4	12.5	
7781	7829	7780	8743	183.7	123.1	112.4	112.4	8.3	1.8	4.0
3571	3683	4399	4712				107.1	14.0	6.1	
20582	22503	30704	31681				103.2	20.1	11.1	
5204	4030	4248	4163	25.8	31.5	83.7	98.0	-4.0	-17.8	-5.8
2590	3434	2353	2066	77.5	113.2	79.7	87.8	-7.3	7.3	-7.3
2402	1901	1659	1783	114.1	80.2	74.3	107.5	7.3	1.5	-9.4
2392	2943	2858	3153	64.3	135.7	131.7	110.3	-13.9	0.6	9.6
1470	1654	1777	2191	108.3	297.6	149.1	123.3	-18.3	14.8	14.2

1-12 主要年份国民经济和社会发展结构指标

单位: %

指标	Item	1995	2000	2005
人口与就业	**Population and Employment**			
人口	**Population**			
城乡结构	Structure			
城镇人口	Urban Population	39.45	41.54	44.91
乡村人口	Rural Population	60.55	58.46	55.09
性别结构	Sexual Structure			
男	Male	51.64	51.62	51.50
女	Female	48.36	48.38	48.50
就业	**Employment**			
全社会从业人员产业结构	Industrial Structure of the Whole Society			
第一产业	Primary Industry	41.17	37.78	32.78
第二产业	Secondary Industry	29.43	27.57	27.46
第三产业	Tertiary Industry	29.40	34.65	39.76
宏观经济	**Macro Economy**			
国民经济核算	**National Accounting**			
生产总值产业结构	Industrial Structure			
第一产业	Primary Industry	12.53	6.91	5.02
第二产业	Secondary Industry	40.97	42.89	41.14
第三产业	Tertiary Industry	46.50	50.20	53.84
生产总值支出结构	Structure of Gross Domestic by Expenditures			
最终消费	Total Consumption	72.54	63.99	58.35
资本形成总额	Total Investment	45.88	44.55	63.85
货物和服务净出口	Net Export of Goods and Services	18.42	8.54	22.20
投资	**Investment**			
全社会固定资产投资结构	Structure of Total Investment in Fixed Assets			
报表种类结构	By classification			
固定资产投资（不含农户）	Investment in Fixed Assets (excluding farmers)	85.57	87.36	92.96
#房地产开发投资	Real Estate Investment	20.93	22.31	27.00
农户投资	Farmer Investment	14.43	12.64	7.04
经济成分结构	Registion Status Composition			
国有经济	State-owned Enterprises Investment	66.79	68.68	44.75
集体经济	Collective-owned Enterprises Investment	9.46	6.30	7.09
个体经济	Self-employed Individual	10.76	10.50	9.46
其他经济	Other	12.99	14.51	38.69

注：2015年，市公安局提供户籍人口分类为“城镇人口”和“乡村人口”，2015年之前，分类为“非农业人口”和“农业人口”。

Structural Indicators of National Economic and Social Development in Representative Years

(%)

2010	2011	2012	2013	2014	2015	2016	2017	2018
47.86	49.42	50.05	50.79	51.29	66.93	66.94	67.12	69.31
52.14	50.58	49.95	49.21	48.71	33.07	33.06	32.88	30.69
50.95	50.83	50.75	50.66	50.59	50.54	50.49	50.29	50.01
49.05	49.17	49.25	49.34	49.41	49.46	49.51	49.71	49.99
25.65	24.41	22.33	20.81	19.71	20.39	19.50	18.98	16.30
29.65	30.51	31.55	28.55	28.49	24.53	23.72	22.73	24.79
44.70	45.08	46.12	50.64	51.80	55.08	56.78	58.29	58.91
4.32	4.47	4.45	4.07	3.91	3.80	3.69	3.76	3.10
41.86	40.91	40.53	40.59	39.96	36.65	35.02	34.75	35.04
53.82	54.62	55.02	55.34	56.13	59.55	61.29	61.49	61.86
49.31	48.07	47.93						
87.47	84.52	86.65						
36.78	32.60	34.58						
95.52	95.87	96.80	97.03	96.25	98.47	98.18	98.77	
25.91	29.79	30.21	31.08	29.84	35.46	37.67	30.88	
4.48	4.13	3.20	2.97	3.75	1.53	1.52	1.23	
41.49	36.00	39.15	34.49	32.46	35.36	44.92	54.62	
10.04	7.71	4.59	4.28	3.44	3.06	2.93	2.03	
1.68	2.23	1.95	1.64	1.41	1.56	1.57	1.24	
46.78	54.05	54.31	59.58	62.69	60.02	50.58	42.10	

1–12 续表1

单位: %

指　　标	Item	1995	2000	2005
财 政	**Government Finance**			
财政收入结构	Structure of Government Revenue			
中　央	Central Government		31.94	58.30
地　方	Local Governments		68.06	41.70
产　业	**Industry**			
农　业	**Agriculture**			
农林牧渔业总产值结构	Structure of Gross Output Value of Farming, Forestry,Animal Husbandry and Fishery			
农　业	Farming	68.03	69.23	61.69
林　业	Forestry	0.96	1.14	1.23
牧　业	Animal Husbandry	30.29	28.58	30.96
渔　业	Fishery	0.72	1.05	0.69
农林牧渔专业及辅助性活动	Farming,Forestry,Animal Husbandry and Fishery			5.43
工 业	**Industry**			
工业总产值经济类型结构	Structure of Gross Output Value of Industry by Registion Status			
国有经济	State-owned Enterprises	51.04	43.00	45.21
集体经济	Collective-owned Enterprises	40.98	32.76	5.16
其他经济类型	Others	7.98	24.24	49.63
工业总产值轻重结构	Structure of Gross Output Value of Industry by Light Industry and Heavy Industry			
轻工业	Light Industry	40.31	48.81	31.17
重工业	Heavy Industry	59.69	51.19	68.83
工业总产值规模结构	Structure of Gross Output Value of Industry by Size of Enterprises			
大型企业	Large Enterprises	38.80	36.29	35.46
中型企业	Medium-sized Enterprises	9.14	5.14	24.67
小型企业	Small Enterprises	52.06	58.57	39.87

注：本表2008年以后财政收入结构中地方指地方财政一般公共预算收入。

continued 1

(%)

2010	2011	2012	2013	2014	2015	2016	2017	2018
37.28	35.78	32.37	30.80	29.61	28.94	31.68	35.63	39.86
47.36	49.02	52.71	55.60	57.25	58.39	56.45	47.96	46.88
65.40	66.02	65.61	66.66	67.95	68.06	68.00	68.81	70.04
1.26	1.38	2.24	2.62	2.69	2.96	2.95	3.10	3.67
25.35	24.67	23.09	21.22	19.60	18.54	17.93	16.67	14.74
0.60	0.59	0.71	0.74	0.74	0.59	0.57	0.52	0.57
7.39	7.35	8.34	8.75	9.02	9.85	10.56	10.90	10.98
51.52	50.46	52.20	50.29	48.32	48.47	44.85	45.74	45.29
1.22	0.92	0.81	0.64	0.59	0.31	0.25	0.32	0.82
47.26	48.62	46.99	49.07	51.09	51.22	54.90	53.94	53.89
22.01	21.97	21.95	18.44	18.32	19.55	17.89	17.48	18.43
77.99	78.03	78.05	81.56	81.68	80.45	82.11	82.52	81.57
42.11	41.15	48.46	34.49	43.95	51.33	52.36	54.82	52.81
23.96	15.17	13.41	14.42	15.47	16.34	14.78	15.99	16.59
33.93	43.68	38.13	51.09	40.58	32.33	32.86	29.19	30.60

1–12 续表2

单位: %

指　　标	Item	1995	2000	2005
建筑业	**Construction**			
建筑业总产值结构	Structure of Gross Output Value of Construction Industry			
房屋建筑业	Building Construction	12.84	9.28	34.05
土木工程建筑业	Civil Engineering Construction	86.27	88.50	56.59
建筑安装业	Installation of Construction			
建筑装饰和其他建筑业	Decoration and others	0.89	2.22	9.36
交通运输业	**Transportation**			
客运量结构	Structure of Passenger Traffic			
铁　路	Railways	29.53	26.40	17.14
公　路	Highways	67.57	69.14	79.15
民　航	Civil Aviation	2.90	4.46	3.71
货运量结构	Structure of Freight Traffic			
铁　路	Railways	34.59	44.30	26.92
公　路	Highways	65.36	55.58	73.04
民　航	Civil Aviation	0.05	0.12	0.04
国内贸易	**Domestic Trade**			
社会消费品零售总额结构	Composition of Retail Sales of Consumer Goods			
城　镇	Urban Area	88.95	87.99	90.17
农　村	Rural Area	11.05	12.01	9.83
国际旅游	**International Tourism**			
国际旅游人数结构	Structure of Tourists			
外国人	Foreigners	89.76	84.03	84.91
华侨及港澳台同胞	Overseas Chinese and Compatriots form Hong Kong, Macao and Taiwan	10.24	15.97	15.09
教育文化、卫生、人民生活	**Education and Culture，Health Care，People's Livelihood**			
教　育	**Education**			
在校学生结构	Structure of Student Enrollment			
#普通高等学校	Institutions of Higher Education	8.81	12.44	28.48
普通中等专业学校	Regular Specialized Secondary Schools	2.84	3.84	3.33
普通中学	Regular Schools	24.55	30.93	29.89
小　学	Primary Schools	59.91	49.89	32.45

continued 2

(%)

2010	2011	2012	2013	2014	2015	2016	2017	2018
24.63	36.81	43.03	43.03	41.58	38.41	36.69	36.64	37.73
68.61	53.75	47.57	47.86	49.43	51.84	53.63	54.13	54.84
4.39	6.70	6.49	5.86	5.32	5.91	6.61	6.30	4.88
2.37	2.74	2.91	3.25	3.67	3.84	3.07	2.93	2.55
9.18	8.57	8.07	8.02	13.65	14.80	17.74	18.53	21.62
87.59	87.96	85.45	85.18	74.97	72.95	66.63	64.24	60.90
3.23	3.46	6.48	6.80	11.38	12.25	15.63	17.24	17.48
2.06	2.10	1.84	1.71	2.14	1.83	3.58	3.90	4.35
97.92	97.88	98.13	98.25	97.81	98.12	96.32	96.00	95.53
0.02	0.02	0.04	0.04	0.05	0.05	0.10	0.10	0.12
96.00	96.53	96.92	96.89	96.85	96.69	96.46	96.43	96.37
4.00	3.47	3.08	3.11	3.15	3.31	3.54	3.57	3.63
86.97	88.43	87.91	88.26					
13.03	11.58	12.08	11.74					
32.60	29.74	31.00	33.09	33.16	32.78	31.38	29.13	27.52
3.02	2.37	2.08	1.84	1.58	1.34	1.17	0.96	0.83
21.74	18.32	17.40	17.26	16.53	16.00	15.37	14.65	14.18
22.95	19.95	19.52	20.51	20.88	21.88	22.58	23.40	24.40

1-12 续表3

单位: %

指　　标	Item	1995	2000	2005
专任教师结构	Structure of Full-time Teachers			
#普通高等学校	Institutions of Higher Education	21.25	19.89	29.93
普通中等专业学校	Regular Specialized Secondary Schools	3.38	4.02	2.16
普通中学	Regular Middle Schools	29.37	33.21	31.55
小 学	Primary Schools	40.41	38.34	30.08
人民生活	**People's Livelihood**			
城镇居民消费结构	Consumption Structure of Urban Residents			
食品烟酒	Food,Tobacco and Alcohol	44.68	36.46	37.04
衣 着	Clothing	12.67	8.13	9.03
居 住	Residence	6.49	11.23	9.10
生活用品及服务	Living Articles and Services	13.75	11.33	4.73
交通和通信	Transport and Communication Services	5.58	6.93	9.67
教育文化娱乐	Recreation, Education and Culture Services	9.05	13.74	17.18
医疗保健	Medical and Health Care Services	3.27	7.23	9.45
其他用品和服务	Other Commodities and Services	4.51	4.95	3.80
农村居民消费结构	Consumption Structure of Rural Residents			
食品烟酒	Food,Tobacco and Alcohol	50.31	36.63	36.34
衣 着	Clothing	8.39	6.65	6.11
居 住	Residence	5.92	21.41	17.76
生活用品及服务	Living Articles and Services	5.17	5.47	5.11
交通和通信	Transport and Communication Services	8.09	4.21	8.19
教育文化娱乐	Recreation, Education and Culture Services	18.53	14.49	16.15
医疗保健	Medical and Health Care Services	1.78	6.93	8.19
其他用品和服务	Other Commodities and Services	1.81	4.21	2.15
卫　生	**Health Care**			
卫生技术人员结构	Medical Technical Personnel by Types			
执业（助理）医师	Licensed（Assistant） Doctors	45.42	44.82	41.96
注册护士	Registered Nurses	32.68	34.29	33.14
药　师	Junior Paramedics	8.78	8.31	7.30
技　师	Technicians	5.21	5.21	5.33
其　他	Others	7.91	7.37	12.27

注：2014年及以后为城乡住户调查一体化改革后数据，居民消费结构与2014年之前不可比。

continued 3

(%)

2010	2011	2012	2013	2014	2015	2016	2017	2018
32.47	31.97	32.96	33.91	33.87	34.52	32.63	30.90	30.74
1.42	1.29	1.18	1.08	0.97	0.89	0.84	0.64	0.60
24.30	23.70	23.36	22.95	23.62	23.86	23.50	23.58	23.54
23.10	22.37	21.97	21.49	20.57	20.52	21.41	22.03	23.13
31.29	31.29	32.48	32.44	29.21	29.59	29.26	29.44	27.08
11.11	12.27	12.17	12.02	9.09	8.78	8.22	8.12	7.91
9.33	8.26	8.47	7.82	17.89	17.78	17.87	17.84	20.01
7.56	8.11	7.87	7.80	7.21	7.42	7.59	7.57	7.86
12.06	12.81	14.26	14.01	14.16	13.31	13.67	13.00	11.74
14.66	14.27	14.33	14.17	12.60	12.48	12.29	12.61	13.93
9.50	9.00	8.52	7.99	7.32	7.92	8.14	8.28	8.97
4.49	4.00	1.91	3.76	2.53	2.72	2.96	3.15	2.50
32.54	31.89	33.83	32.96	29.93	28.18	26.86	27.27	24.43
6.55	7.20	7.42	7.87	7.44	7.12	6.65	6.50	5.94
24.41	23.92	21.91	19.82	21.99	23.28	23.38	23.54	23.60
6.53	7.10	7.46	7.76	6.97	6.60	7.59	7.85	7.67
8.45	9.01	10.19	9.86	10.66	10.70	10.76	10.69	11.71
11.20	10.43	10.20	10.56	10.26	11.68	11.86	11.90	13.26
8.54	8.65	8.85	8.41	11.07	10.68	11.17	10.47	12.05
1.78	1.80	0.14	2.77	1.68	1.76	1.73	1.79	1.34
33.16	35.17	34.46	33.58	32.66	32.69	32.30	32.71	33.28
40.01	40.87	41.61	42.13	42.28	42.74	43.50	44.15	45.77
5.36	5.10	5.05	4.99	4.88	4.86	4.72	4.54	4.36
8.11	5.91	5.91	5.75	5.63	5.76	5.86	5.94	5.95
13.36	12.95	12.97	13.55	14.56	13.97	13.62	12.66	10.64

1-13 主要年份国民经济和社会发展比例和效益指标

指　　标	Item	1995
人口与就业	**Population and Employment**	
人口	**Population**	
出生率(‰)	Birth Rate (‰)	11.95
死亡率(‰)	Death Rate (‰)	4.98
自然增长率(‰)	Natural Growth Rate (‰)	6.79
就业	**Employment**	
就业者负担人口	Dependency Ratio	1.7
三次产业就业者比例	Employment Ratio by Type of Industry	
(以第一产业为100)	(Employment in primary industry=100)	
第一产业	Primary Industry	100
第二产业	Secondary Industry	71.5
第三产业	Tertiary Industry	71.4
城镇登记失业率(%)	Unemployment Rate in Urban Areas(%)	3.1
宏观经济	**Macro Economy**	
国民经济核算	**National Accounting**	
三次产业增加值比例	Ratio of Value-added by Type of Industry	
(以第一产业为100)	(Employment in primary industry=100)	
第一产业	Primary Industry	100
第二产业	Secondary Industry	326.9
第三产业	Tertiary Industry	371.1
全社会劳动生产率(元／人)	Overall Labor Productivity(yuan/person)	8963
第一产业	Primary Industry	2698
第二产业	Secondary Industry	12404
第三产业	Tertiary Industry	14488
人均生产总值(元)	Per Capita GDP(yuan)	5131
固定资产投资	**Investment in Fixed Assets**	
全社会固定资产投资相当于生产总值比例(%)	Proportion of Investment in fixed Assets to GDP(%)	31.3
房屋建筑面积竣工率(%)	Rate of Floor Space of Buildings Completed in Construction(%)	33.4
固定资产交付使用率(%)	Rate of Fixed Assets Completed in Capital Construction and Put into Use(%)	70.7
建设项目建成投产率(%)	Rate of Projects Completed in Capital Construction and Put into Use(%)	43.7
财政	**Finance**	
财政总收入相当于生产总值比例(%)	Proportion of Government Revenue to GDP(%)	5.5
一般公共预算支出相当于生产总值比例(%)	Proportion of Government General Public Budgeary Expenditures to GDP(%)	5.6
利用外资	**Utilization of Foreign Capital**	
外商实际直接投资额相当于利用外资协议金额比例(%)	Proportion of Foreign Capital Actually Used to Total Amount of Foreign Capital for Utilization by Signed Contracts or Agreements (%)	64.4

注：本表财政收入数据2009年及以前为一般预算财政收入和基金收入之和。依据部门历史年份修订结果对财政相关数据进行了重新计算。

Proportions of National Economic and Social Development and Benefit Index in Representative Years

2000	2005	2010	2011	2012	2013	2014	2015	2016	2017	2018
13.07	9.58	9.73	9.71	10.13	9.57	10.11	10.15	11.54	12.62	12.47
5.96	5.16	5.34	5.38	5.57	5.37	5.47	5.51	5.40	5.42	5.48
7.11	4.42	4.39	4.33	4.56	4.20	4.64	4.64	6.14	7.20	6.99
1.8	1.8	1.8	1.7	1.7	1.6	1.6	1.6	1.6	1.6	1.6
100	100	100	100	100	100	100	100	100	100	100
73.0	83.8	124.0	125.0	141.3	137.2	144.6	120.3	121.7	119.7	152.1
91.7	121.3	183.3	184.7	206.5	243.3	262.9	270.1	291.3	307.1	361.4
3.4	4.3	4.2	3.9	3.5	3.4	3.4	3.4	3.3	3.3	3.3
100	100	100	100	100	100	100	100	100	100	100
620.7	818.8	969.3	914.4	910.6	997.2	1023.0	965.6	948.4	923.6	1130.4
726.4	1071.7	1246.1	1220.7	1236.2	1359.8	1437.1	1568.9	1659.5	1634.3	1995.8
16367	31837	68990	79498	86971	94233	103281	109356	117736	131617	137171
2960	4747	11701	14530	16578	17789	19915	20705	21805	25755	24141
25443	47853	98027	106710	113561	127374	144703	151144	170975	197154	202087
24024	44024	82377	96392	104914	107722	113188	121876	128977	140561	144795
9484	16406	38357	45561	51499	57464	63794	66938	71647	78368	85114
36.0	65.8	100.2	86.5	96.6	104.3	107.5	89.1	82.6	101.1	
42.0	28.1	6.9	10.0	8.7	13.2	11.4	6.8	9.9	11.2	6.4
74.0	52.8	38.4	40.4	42.4	37.1	42.5	40.3	38.3	43.4	26.9
44.2	54.2	53.9	54.9	56.1	56.1	62.5	61.0	64.6	62.4	36.3
9.5	12.5	15.7	16.8	17.1	18.3	18.6	19.2	18.1	18.3	17.5
7.2	7.4	11.5	12.8	13.6	14.8	14.9	15.8	15.0	14.0	13.8
28.9	47.0	130.9	167.0	68.8	124.3	145.0	207.0	441.2	114.1	133.6

1-13 续表1

指　　标	Item	1995
能　　源	**Energy**	
单位生产总值能耗降低率(%)	Decreasing Rate of Energy Consumption per Unit GDP(%)	
产　　业	**Industries**	
农业	**Agriculture**	
农业从业者人均耕地面积(公顷)	Cultivated Land per Agricultural Laborer(hectare)	0.20
每公顷耕地农业机械总动力(千瓦)	Total Power of Agricultural Machinery per Hectare of Cultivated Land(kw)	5.23
每公顷耕地化肥施用量(公斤)	Chemical Fertilizer Consumption per Hectare of Cultivated Land(kg)	536
每公顷耕地生产的农业总产值(元)	Agricultural Output Value per Hectare of Cultivated Land(yuan)	24396
每个农林牧渔业劳动力农产品生产量(公斤)	Output of Farm Products per Farming,Forestry,Animal Husbandry and Fishery Husbandry and Fishery Laborer (kg)	
粮食	Grain	1150
蔬菜	Vegetables	877
禽蛋	Poultry Eggs	
肉类	Meat	
水产品	Aquatic Products	6
每公顷播种面积农产品产量(公斤)	Output of Farm Crops per Hectare of Sown Area(kg)	
粮食	Grain	3806
油料	Oil-bearing Crops	1753
蔬菜	Vegetables	34800
工业	**Industrial**	
规模以上工业企业经济效益	**Economic Benefit of Industrial Enterprises above Designated Size**	
总资产贡献率(%)	Ratio of Total Assets to Industrial Output Value (%)	
资产负债率(%)	Assets-Liability Ratio (%)	
流动资产周转次数（次/年）	Rate of Annual Turnover Working Capitals(times/year)	
成本费用利润率(%)	Ratio of Profits to Cost (%)	
产品销售率(%)	Proportion of Industrial Products Sold(%)	
全员劳动生产率（元/人）	Overall Labor Productivity (yuan/person)	
建筑业	**Construction**	
机械装备率(元／人)	Value of Machinery per Laborer(yuan/person)	5990
产值利润率(%)	Ratio of Per-tax Profits to Gross Output Value (%)	3.5
全员劳动生产率(元／人)(按总产值计算)	Overall Labor Productivity(yuan/person) (in terms of gross output value per employee)	37689
邮电通信业	**Post and Communication Services**	
电话普及率(含移动电话）(部/百人)	Access to Telephones, National(include mobilphone) (set/100 persons)	7.9
移动电话普及率(部/百人)	Access to Mobilphones (set/100 persons)	0.48

continued 1

2000	2005	2010	2011	2012	2013	2014	2015	2016	2017	2018
		2.06	3.56	3.51	3.57	5.89	3.20	3.83	4.61	5.99
0.20	0.22	0.22	0.22	0.22	0.23	0.22	0.23	0.22	0.22	0.25
6.78	8.39	10.48	11.50	12.10	12.73	13.32	13.68	11.31	10.19	9.91
664	794	922	953	987	982	1045	1035	1050	1023	1031
25161	39937	83123	99492	112961	125238	134435	139040	149979	175189	188192
1382	1493	1497	1438	1480	1398	1276	1346	1323	1267	1456
1110	1421	1777	1844	2012	2249	2338	2549	2628	3214	3827
					45	43	49	61	48	54
					61	64	69	67	53	56
8	7	10	10	12	13	13	14	13	13	14
4342	4796	3931	3968	4104	3992	3829	4073	3848	3826	3895
1526	1821	1950	2027	1992	1948	1519	2099	1408	2173	2180
37797	35231	39798	40668	42990	45271	38085	48711	39152	50851	52027
	8.4	12.2	8.6	7.7	8.5	7.4	5.7	6.4	7.2	7.3
65.0	65.0	57.6	57.7	59.4	59.5	59.7	57.3	55.7	53.0	54.5
1.0	1.3	1.7	1.5	1.5	1.5	1.4	1.3	1.3	1.4	1.3
4.2	3.1	8.8	5.2	4.5	5.2	5.2	4.8	6.0	6.6	6.8
97.1	97.5	97.1	97.4	96.7	95.7	94.9	94.5	96.0	97.3	96.2
29496	82815	188483	194105	230032	264324	275288	268182	277240	294393	
6805	13332	9461	28669	12216	10339		12712	14193	10051	10005
3.4	4.8	4.4	4.4	2.8	2.6	2.3	2.3	3.1	2.8	3.0
74347	206337	321340	334172	479232	354419	347000	406962	422421	411690	457700
31.2	100.0	199.0	221.3	247.2	288.7	270.3	236.5	229.1	221.2	212.0
10.62	56.62	168.00	189.58	210.87	251.59	234.75	203.00	197.00	192.80	185.74

1-13 续表2

指　　标	Item	1995
国内贸易	**Domestic Trade**	
人均批发零售和住宿餐饮业消费品零售额(元)	Per Capita Retail Sales of Wholesale,Retail Trade and Accommodation Catering Trade (yuan)	1979
对外经济贸易	**Foreign Trade**	
进出口总值相当于地区生产总值比例(%)	Proportion of Total Imports & Exports to GDP(%)	34.76
旅游	**International Tourism**	
每一游客花费(元)	Expenditure per Tourist (yuan)	556
金融业	**Finance and Insurance**	
金融机构存款相当于生产总值比例(%)	Bank Deposits as Percentage of GDP(%)	108.83
金融机构贷款相当于生产总值比例(%)	Bank Loans as Percentage of GDP(%)	101.26
教育、科技、文化	**Education, Science and Technology and Culture**	
教育	**Education**	
毕业率(%)	Graduation Rate(%)	
小学	Primary Schools	
初中	Junior Schools	
学校教师负担系数	Student-teacher Ratio(in percentage)	
高等学校	Colleges and Universities	6.83
中等学校	Secondary Schools	14.42
小学	Primary Schools	26.22
文化	**Culture (unit)**	
每百万人有艺术表演团体	Number of Troupes per Million Persons	3.39
每百万人有公共图书馆	Number of Public Libraries per Million Persons	2.31
家庭、生活、环境	**Family, People's Livelihood and Environment**	
家庭	**Family**	
城市居民家庭	Urban Households	
平均每一劳动力负担人口（人）	Persons supported by Each Laborer (person)	1.8
农村居民家庭	Rural Households	
平均每一劳动力负担人口（人）	Persons supported by Each Laborer (person)	1.6
卫生	**Health Care**	
每万人医院数（个）	Number of Hospitals per 10 000 Persons(unit)	0.60
每万人医生数(人)	Number of Doctors per 10 000 Persons(person)	29.10
每万人医院床位数(张)	Number of Hospital Beds per 10 000 Persons(unit)	43.60
市政建设	**City Construction**	
城市自来水普及率(%)	Percentage of Households with Access to Tap Water(%)	
城市用气普及率(%)	Percentage of Households with Access to Tap Gas (%)	
人均公园绿地面积(平方米)	Public Green Areas per 10 000 Persons(hectare)	3.80

continued 2

2000	2005	2010	2011	2012	2013	2014	2015	2016	2017	2018
4027	8795	19848	24007	28132	32004	35943	39293	42545	46071	47489
22.25	24.79	21.22	20.52	18.61	22.27	27.89	30.37	29.13	34.06	39.56
645	737	767	797	820	801	792	789	809	903	1033
206.71	283.41	273.32	267.47	274.09	277.48	274.26	304.82	301.74	266.91	249.25
150.51	169.91	198.00	193.71	194.77	201.63	210.76	234.52	241.29	225.26	234.86
		100.4	100.2	100.2	99.8	99.6	99.6	99.8	99.8	100
		99.7	100.6	98.7	99.3	99.9	98.3	98.7	98.3	100
12.38	17.99	17.41	17.92	18.15	18.05	18.27	17.76	17.62	17.33	16.82
17.84	18.47	17.78	16.91	16.43	15.07	14.01	13.88	13.05	12.78	13.10
25.75	20.38	17.22	18.06	17.15	17.66	18.94	19.94	11.98	11.42	11.31
3.20	2.56	1.53	3.52	2.22	2.10	2.09	2.07	2.04	1.87	1.80
2.18	2.02	1.77	1.76	1.75	1.75	1.74	1.49	1.47	1.35	1.30
2.2	2.1	1.9	1.8	1.9	1.8	1.3	1.3	1.3	1.3	1.3
1.6	1.6	1.5	1.5	1.5	1.5	1.4	1.4	1.4	1.4	1.5
0.57	0.59	0.49	0.43	0.44	0.44	0.44	0.45	0.44	0.47	0.46
25.30	21.98	22.14	25.31	26.95	27.81	28.77	30.58	31.55	32.05	33.76
38.72	37.29	43.42	43.77	47.45	51.45	54.56	58.98	60.02	62.92	65.53
98.95	99.00	98.77	99.95	100	100	100	100	100	99.25	97.85
81.51	91.30	97.02	97.46	98.19	98.68	98.71	98.79	98.89	96.07	99.90
5.12	5.63	9.11	9.89	10.22	10.70	11.22	11.47	11.61	12.04	9.97

1-14 主要年份平均每天主要社会经济活动

指　　标	Item	1995	2000
一、每天创造的财富	**Daily Production**		
生产总值（万元）	Gross Domestic Product（10 000 yuan）	9050.7	17702.2
第一产业	Primary Industry	1134.3	1223.3
第二产业	Secondary Industry	3707.7	7592.6
第三产业	Tertiary Industry	4208.8	8886.3
工业	Industry	3082.2	5984.7
建筑业	Construction	625.5	1608.0
批发和零售业	Wholesale and Retail Trade	909.6	1804.7
交通运输、仓储和邮政业	Transport, Storage, Post & Telecommunication Services	674.0	1178.4
住宿和餐饮业	Hotels and Catering Services		505.8
财政总收入（万元）	Total Government Revenue（10 000 yuan）	498.8	1686.8
财政一般公共预算支出（万元）	Government General Public Budgetary Expenditures（10 000 yuan）	504.7	1274.0
粮食（吨）	Grain（ton）	4801	5532
奶类（吨）	Milk（ton）		
蔬菜（吨）	Vegetables（ton）	3660	4442
肉类（吨）	Meat（ton）		
水产品（吨）	Aquatic Products（ton）	23	31
布（万米）	Cloth（10 000 m）	83.0	77.0
发电量（万千瓦小时）	Electricity（10 000 kwh）	610	534
钢材（吨）	Steel（ton）	861	274
汽车（辆）	Motor Vehicle（unit）	8	25
二、每天消费量	**Daily National Consumption**		
社会消费品零售总额（万元）	Total Retail Sales of Consumer Goods （10 000 yuan）	5112.3	9874.5
三、每天其他经济活动	**Other Daily Economic Activities**		
竣工住宅面积（平方米）	Floor Space of Buildings Completed （sq.m）	6927	14930
货运量（万吨）	Freight Traffic（10 000 tons）	26.3	19.2
客运量（万人次）	Passenger Traffic（10 000 person-times）	24.8	22.1
邮电业务总量（万元）	Business Volume of Postal and Telecommunications Services（10 000 yuan）	209.6	1264.7
进出口总值（万美元）	Total Value of Imports and Exports （USD 10 000）	110.2	475.9
出口值	Exports	82.5	290.6
进口值	Imports	27.7	185.3
外商实际直接投资额（万美元）	Foreign Capital Actually Used（USD 10 000）	51.1	42.8
旅游者人数（人次）	Number of Tourists （person-time）	21681	42932
四、每天人口变动和婚姻	**Daily Population Changes and Marriages**		
出　生（人）	Births（person）	211	247
死　亡（人）	Deaths（person）	88	113
结　婚（对）	Marriages（couple）	129	129
离　婚（对）	Divorces（couple）	12	14

注：本表财政收入数据2009年及以前为一般预算财政收入和基金收入之和。依据部门历史年份修订结果对财政相关数据进行了重新计算。

Major Social and Economic Activities Per Day in Representative Years

2005	2010	2011	2012	2013	2014	2015	2016	2017	2018
35998.1	88845.5	106023.0	120396.4	134930.7	150483.3	158937.0	172127.4	204709.3	228763.3
1808.5	3837.3	4743.6	5358.6	5491.8	5878.1	6032.9	6356.4	7701.9	7091.0
14808.2	37192.6	43375.6	48797.0	54762.2	60131.0	58254.5	60283.8	71137.5	80153.7
19381.4	47815.6	57903.8	66240.8	74676.7	84474.2	94649.6	105487.1	125869.9	141518.6
11506.9	26147.7	30095.9	33644.9	37718.9	40767.7	37718.4	38280.8	46137.5	51352.3
3301.4	11045.2	13279.5	15151.8	17596.2	19965.5	21103.8	22433.4	25432.9	29400.5
4032.9	9654.0	12047.9	14053.7	15773.2	17360.3	18301.1	19241.1	21124.4	23070.1
1816.4	3717.8	4525.5	5272.9	5893.4	6454.2	7132.3	8178.6	9151.2	9794.2
1381.9	2816.4	3233.4	3550.1	3714.5	3949.3	4360.0	4675.9	5155.6	5612.3
4489.6	13991.5	17805.0	20632.1	24733.3	27936.7	30547.4	31114.5	37389.3	40010.7
2680.0	10181.4	13550.0	16369.6	19994.8	22453.2	25129.9	25822.5	28632.6	31558.1
5631	4781	4577	4594	4156	3857	3875	3709	3833	3894
				202	222	210	217	319	316
5362	5674	5867	6245	6683	7065	7340	7366	9719	10238
				181	194	198	188	161	149
26	33	32	38	39	39	39	37	38	37
74.0	65.2	44.8	39.1	38.0	33.0	28.5	33.4	34.8	35.1
1316	2656	2603	2726	5055	4920	4347	4411	4842	4733
658	3035	506	857	1488	1175	1015	1203	1504	915
112	1787	1525	1484	1156	1027	935	1048	1220	1188
18371.5	44850.4	53862.5	62023.6	75147.7	84764.1	93298.1	102211.0	116433.0	127636.0
16400	12287	23601	24762	23014	40078	22632	36472	36683	
33.0	94.0	107.5	123.1	137.3	115.2	126.8	65.4	69.9	73.7
28.7	83.0	91.4	99.1	104.9	70.5	73.7	64.9	66.5	70.0
3617.7	8852.3	5494.8	5923.6	6793.0	8016.4	9083.1	10496.2	12050.7	20261.1
1068.9	2847.3	3452.5	3565.6	4927.5	6833.5	7749.3	7547.9	10327.4	13676.0
721.8	1456.8	1596.3	1999.7	2322.8	3276.7	3606.4	3907.3	6298.6	8103.0
347.1	1390.5	1856.2	1565.9	2604.7	3556.8	4142.8	3640.6	4028.8	5573.0
156.5	429.2	549.4	678.9	857.5	1014.5	1098.2	1234.2	1453.9	1740.7
66400	144799	182280	218585	277534	328767	372625	411303	495702	677774
210	225	226	237	225	238	241	277	330	335
63	124	125	130	126	129	131	130	142	147
137	229	259	246	244	250	221	212	194	255
35	52	53	51	56	60	62	70	79	115

1-15 各区县国民经济和社会发展主要指标（2018年）

指 标	Item	新城区 Xincheng	碑林区 Beilin	莲湖区 Lianhu
一、年底总人口（常住人口）（万人）	Population at the Year-end Permanent population(10 000 persons)	64.13	67.97	76.86
二、生产总值（亿元）	Gross Domestic Product(100 mil. yuan)	650.64	965.26	820.73
第一产业	Primary Industry			
第二产业	Secondary Industry	209.86	202.93	255.61
第三产业	Tertiary Industry	440.78	762.33	565.12
三、全社会固定资产投资增长速度（%）	The growth rate of Total Investment in Fixed Assets(%)	-49.1	0.3	3.8
固定资产投资（不含农户）增长速度	The growth rate of Investment in Fixed Assets (excluding farmers)	-49.1	0.3	3.8
#房地产开发投资增长速度	The growth rate of Real Estate	-75.1	-52.1	-1.8
四、财政一般公共预算收入（万元）	General Public Budgetary Revenue(10 000 yuan)	218916	438308	488104
财政一般公共预算支出（万元）	General Public Budgetary Expenditure(10 000 yuan)	220282	320013	401303
五、农林牧渔业总产值（万元）	Gross Output Value of Farming，Forestry Animal Husbandry and Fishery(10 000 yuan)			
主要农产品产量（万吨）	Output of Major Farm Products(10 000 tons)			
粮食	Grain			
蔬菜	Vegetables			
瓜果	Melon and Fruit			
肉类(吨)	Meat (Ton)			
奶类(吨)	Milk (Ton)			
六、规模以上工业总产值（亿元）	Gross industrial Output Value(100 mil. yuan)	248.69	17.60	531.29
七、建筑业	Construction			
房屋建筑施工面积（万平方米）	Floor Space of Buildings under Construction (10 000 sq.m)	1320.08	4511.33	2139.47
房屋建筑竣工面积（万平方米）	Floor Space of Buildings Completed(100 mil. yuan)	366.73	834.92	397.50
八、社会消费品零售总额（亿元）	Total Retail Sales of Consumer Goods (100 mil. yuan)	739.79	670.40	544.95
九、城镇居民人均可支配收入（元）	Per Capita Annual Disposable Income of Urban Households (yuan)	44637	44382	44440
农村居民人均可支配收入（元）	Per Capita Disposable Income of Rural Households (yuan)			
十、医疗机构数（个）	Number of Health Care Institutions(unit)	260	425	392
卫生技术人员（人）	Number of Medical Technical Personnel (person)	12122	13934	12324
床位数（张）	Number of Beds(unit)	7657	9374	8223

Major Indicators of National Economy and Social Development by Region（2018）

灞桥区 Baqiao	未央区 Weiyang	雁塔区 Yanta	阎良区 Yanliang	临潼区 Lintong	长安区 Chang'an	高陵区 Gaoling	鄠邑区 Huyi	蓝田县 Lantian	周至县 Zhouzhi	西咸新区 Xixian
67.73	77.74	134.32	30.12	69.69	104.28	36.26	55.86	53.68	59.41	102.32
480.78	964.83	1757.98	250.10	237.52	909.11	378.45	217.26	151.67	146.27	381.94
18.19	0.40		26.55	32.77	26.89	24.99	25.65	27.17	32.94	43.27
140.93	477.01	403.72	114.56	67.31	481.45	238.93	94.04	40.05	33.68	158.05
321.66	487.42	1354.26	108.99	137.44	400.77	114.53	97.57	84.45	79.65	180.62
20.3	-11.8	4.0	13.8	34.9	38.3	7.9	0.8	21.5	4.6	12.6
20.4	-11.7	4.0	13.9	37.7	39.9	7.9	2.2	23.7	0.3	12.5
32.0	-14.1	2.4	7.2	70.1	9.5	-15.3	-31.5	183.6	-47.1	104.4
484137	196462	354078	96672	134213	243684	124008	117810	30470	26801	519693
347208	330784	340916	217355	436318	569454	340275	430238	387317	458309	872338
311278	8814		446310	601608	455700	482906	447692	494077	589596	774107
2.77	0.01		12.03	32.91	15.62	12.35	19.13	17.04	11.91	18.37
17.93	0.11		69.21	50.44	19.09	58.62	28.51	10.40	22.13	97.26
0.65			26.48	8.57	3.41	1.06	4.90	2.71	0.31	3.04
1394	105		2263	16537	5963	3365	5895	9371	7294	2309
5141	38		21398	44289	4771	14726	6881	12636	3500	1820
123.92	1083.72	663.32	350.69	209.65	1401.03	1214.57	126.00	73.47	44.26	308.08
493.34	2772.67	3628.57	37.95	80.79	252.23	150.58	81.61	110.00	48.70	228.07
21.36	236.06	529.66	15.56	17.72	70.78	73.62	52.48	84.48	15.00	39.30
260.53	615.17	847.50	49.94	107.75	258.60	59.15	86.61	81.10	62.84	274.39
37306	41056	44995	37448	28449	38900	35788	22909	22082	20633	23333
16395			14423	13363	14520	14936	12415	13404	11954	12775
415	422	441	183	507	635	230	461	626	530	710
4449	10456	15201	2542	3172	7560	3071	4092	2483	2862	3447
3129	6795	8992	1605	2799	6692	2202	2946	1706	2353	2644

主要统计指标解释

行政区划 指国家对行政区域的划分。根据有关法规规定，我国的行政区域划分如下：（1）全国分为省、自治区、直辖市；（2）省、自治区分为自治州、县、自治县、市；（3）自治州分为县、自治县、市；（4）县、自治县分为乡、民族乡、镇；（5）直辖市和较大的市分为区、县；（6）国家在必要时设立的特别行政区。

气候 指地球与大气之间长期能量交换与质量交换所形成的一种自然环境状态，它是多种因素综合作用的结果。气候既是人类生活和生产的环境要素之一，又是供给人类生活和生产的重要资源。气温、降水、湿度等气象要素的多年平均值是用来描述一个地区气候状况的主要参数，而各种气象要素某年、某月的平均值（或总量）则可以反映出该时期天气气候状况的重要特征。

自然资源 指人类可以直接从自然界获得，并用于生产和生活的物质资源。自然资源一般可以分成可再生资源和非再生资源两大类。可再生资源指在较短时间内可以再生、可以循环利用的资源，包括土地资源、水资源、气候资源、生物资源和海洋资源等。非再生资源指在使用后不能再生的资源，包括矿产资源和地热能源。

土地资源 土地指陆地的表层部分，它主要由岩石、岩石的风化物和土壤构成。土地资源按利用类型可以分为农用地、建筑用地和未利用地。农用地包括耕地、园地、林地、牧草地和水面。建筑用地包括居民点及工矿用地、交通用地和水利设施用地。未利用地指农用地和建筑用地以外的土地，包括滩涂、荒漠、戈壁、冰川和石山等。

耕地面积 指经过开垦用以种植农作物并经常进行耕耘的土地面积。包括种有作物的土地面积、休闲地、新开荒地和抛荒未满三年的土地面积。

森林面积 指由乔木树种构成，郁闭度0.2以上（含0.2）的林地或冠幅宽度10米以上的林带的面积，即有林地面积。森林面积包括天然起源和人工起源的针叶林面积、阔叶林面积、针阔混交林面积和竹林面积，不包括灌木林地面积和疏林地面积。

林业用地面积 指生长乔木、竹类、灌木、沿海红树林等林木的土地面积，包括有林地、灌木林、疏林地、未成林造林地、迹地、苗圃等。

水资源总量 指评价区内降水形成的地表和地下产水总量，即地表产流量与降水入渗补给地下水量之和，不包括过境水量。

地表水资源量 指评价区内河流、湖泊、冰川等地表水体中可以逐年更新的动态水量，即当地天然河川径流量。

地下水资源量 指评价区内降水和地表水对饱水岩土层的补给量，包括降水入渗补给量和河道、湖库、渠系、渠灌田间等地表水体的入渗补给量。

气温 指空气的温度，我国一般以摄氏度（℃）为单位表示。气象观测的温度表是放在离地面约1.5米处通风良好的百叶箱里测量的，因此，通常说的气温指的是离地面1.5米处百叶箱中的温度。其统计计算方法为：

月平均气温是将全月各日的平均气温相加，除以该月的天数而得。

年平均气温是将12个月的月平均气温累加后除以12而得。

降水量 指从天空降落到地面的液态或固态（经融化后）水，未经蒸发、渗透、流失而在地面上积聚的深度。其统计计算方法为：

月降水量是将全月各日的降水量累加而得。

年降水量是将12个月的月降水量累加而得。

日照时数 指太阳实际照射地面的时间。其统计方法与降水量相同。

平均增长速度 平均增长速度表明社会经济现象在一个较长的时期内逐期平均增长变化的程度，它不能根据各个环比增长速度直接求得，但与平均发展速度之间存在着一定的数量关系：平均增长速度 = 平均发展速度 − 1。

平均发展速度 是一种根据环比发展速度计算的序时平均数,由于各时期对比的基础不同，所以计算平均发展速度不能采用一般的序时平均数的计算方法，计算方法分为水平法和累计法。水平法，又称几何平均法，即将环比发展速度按连乘法用几何平均数公式计算。累计法，也称方程法，根据一段时期内各年发展水平总和与基期水平的关系，列出方程式计算平均发展速度。水平法着重考虑最后一年所达到的发展水平；累计法着重考虑整个时期累计发展水平的总量。

本《年鉴》内所列的平均增长速度，均用“水平法”计算。从某年到某年平均增长速度的年份，均不包括基期年在内。如建国六十年以来的平均增长速度是以1949年为基期计算的，则写为1950–2009年平均增长速度，其余类推。

Explanatory Notes on Main Statistical Indicators

Divisions of Administrative Areas refers to the division of administrative areas by the State. The relative laws stipulate that (1)the whole country is divided into provinces, autonomous regions and municipalities directly under the Central Government;(2)provinces and autonomous regions are further divided into autonomous prefectures, counties, autonomous counties and cities; (3)autonomous prefectures are further divided into counties, autonomous counties and cities; (4)counties and autonomous counties are further divided into townships, ethnic townships and towns; (5)municipalities directly under the Central Government and large cities are divided into districts and counties, (6)the State shall, when necessary, establish special administrative regions.

Climate refers to the natural environmental status formed by the long-term exchange of energy and mass between the earth and the atmosphere, and is the result of interaction of many factors. Climate is both one of the environment factors and also the important resources for living and production activities of the human being. The average values across several years of meteorological factors such as temperature, rainfall and humidity are used as important parameters to describe the climate of a region, while the average values (or total values)of a given year or month of meteorological factors reflect the key characteristics of climate for that period of time.

Natural Resources refer to material resources that could be obtained from the nature by human being and used for production and living. Natural resources in general can be classified as renewable resources and non-renewable resources. Renewable resources refer to resources that could be renewed and recycled during a relatively short period of time, including land resource, water resource, climate resource, biology resource and marine resource. Non-renewable resources include resources that could not be renewed, such as minerals and geothermal resource.

Land Resource Land refers to the surface of the earth, consisting of mainly rocks and its whethering and earth. Land resource can be classified, by its utilization, as land for agriculture, land for construction and unused land. Land for agriculture includes cultivated land, plantation land, forestland, grassland and waters. Land for construction includes land for residential purpose, for manufacturing and mining, for transportation and for water-conservancy projects. Unused land refers to land other than land for agriculture and.construction, including beaches, deserts, Gobi, glaciers and rock mountains.

Area of Cultivated Land refers to area of land reclaimed for the regular cultivation of various farm crops, including crop-cover land, fallow, newly reclaimed land and land laid idle for less than 3 years.

Forest Area refers to the area of trees and bamboo grow with canopy density above 0.2, the area of shrubby tree according to regulations of the government, the area of forest land inside farm land and the area of trees planted by the side of villages, farm houses and along roads and rivers.

Area of Afforested Land refers to area for land for trees bamboo, bushes and mangrove, including forest-covered land, bush-covered land, sparse forest land, land planned for afforestation and nurseries of young trees.

Total Water Resources refers to total volume of water resources measured as run-off for surface water from rainfall and recharge for groundwater in a given area, excluding transit water.

Surface Water Resources refers to total renewable resources which exist in rivers, lakes, glaciers and other collectors from rainfall and are measured as run-off of rivers.

Groundwater Resources refers to replenishment of aquifers with rainfall and surface water.

Temperature refers to the air temperature. China uses centigrade as the unit. The thermometry used for weather observation is put in a breezy shutter, which is 1.5 meters high from the ground. Therefore, the commonly used temperature refers to the temperature in the breezy shutter 1.5 meters away from the ground. The calculation method is as follows:

Monthly average temperature is the summation of average daily temperature of one month divided by the actual days of that particular month.

Annual average temperature is the summation of monthly average of a year divided by 12 months.

Volume of Precipitation refers to the deepness of liquid state or solid state (thawed)water falling from the sky to the ground that has not been evaporated, infiltrated or run off. The calculation method is as follows:

Monthly precipitation is the summation of daily precipitation of a month.

Annual precipitation is the summation of 12 months precipitation of a year.

Sunshine Hours refer to the actual hours of sun irradiating the earth. The calculation method is the same as that of the precipitation.

Average Annual Growth Rate shows the average growth rate of social and economic development during a longer period. It can not be directly calculated by chain based growth rate. The relation is:

Average Annual Growth Rate=Average Speed of Development 1

Average speed of development is the time series average of speed which calculated by chain based.Because the reference bases during the different periods are not same, average speed of development can not be calculated by the general method. Level approach and accumulative approach for calculating average speed of development rate are applied. The "level approach" , or the method of calculating the geometric average, is derived by the formula of geometric average of the chain-based speeds of development, or comparing the level of the last year of the interval with that of the beginning year; the other is called the "accumulative approach" or the "algebraic average" , "equation" method, which is derived by the summation of the actual figure of each year in the interval divided by the figure in the base year. The level approach focuses on the level of the last year, while the accumulative approach emphasizes the aggregate development in the duration.

The average annual growth rates listed in the Yearbook are calculated by the level approach except for the growth rate of investment in fixed assets. The base year is not listed in the duration for which average annual growth rates are computed. For instance, the average annual growth rate of the 60 years since 1949 is shown as the average annual growth rate of 1950-2009 without showing the base year 1949.

2 基本单位

BASIC UNIT

资料整理：张　奇　张　斌
Data management：Zhang Qi　Zhang Bin
数据审核：张利民
Data audit：Zhang Limin

第二部分　基本单位

一、简要说明

本章资料主要包括法人单位、产业活动单位和企业一套表调查单位数等资料，由西安市统计局普查中心提供。本年统计年鉴一套表单位数为年报数，使用时请注意。

二、主要指标

法人单位数（个）	168779	比上年增长	9.7%
产业活动单位数（个）	182420	比上年增长	9.4%
规模以上工业企业数（个）	1441	比上年增长	5.5%
限额以上批发零售住宿餐饮业企业数（个）	2084	比上年增长	7.9%
资质内建筑业企业数（个）	1209	比上年增长	14.6%
房地产开发经营企业数（个）	1129	比上年增长	8.1%
规模以上服务业企业数（个）	1670	比上年增长	7.9%

2　BASIC UNIT

Ⅰ.Brief Introduction

This chapter consists of unified data of enterprises and industrial active unites and investigation unit in "Enterprises Data in One sheet", provided by census center of Xi' an Municipal Bureau of statistics . Data of "Enterprises Data in One Sheet" in this Yearbook is the number of annual reports, please note that when used.

Ⅱ.Major Indicators

		Increase over Preceding Year
Number of Enterprises (unit)	168779	9.7%
Number of Industrial Active Units (unit)	182420	9.4%
Number of Industrial Enterprises above Designed Size (unit)	1441	5.5%
Number of Enterprises about Wholesale、Retail、Accommodation and Catering above Designed Size (unit)	2084	7.9%
Number of Qualified Construction Enterprises (unit)	1209	14.6%
Number of Real Estate Development Enterprises (unit)	1129	8.1%
Number of service Enterprises above Designed Size (unit)	1670	7.9%

2-1 按登记注册类型分法人单位数（2018年）

Impersonal Entities by Status of Registion（2018）

单位：个 (unit)

分 组	Classify	法人单位数 Number of Enterprises	企业 Enterprises
总 计	**Total**	**168779**	**147865**
#非公有制企业法人	Non-public corporate	141589	141589
按登记注册类型分	**Grouped by Status of Registion**		
（一）内资	Domestic Funded Enterprises	167538	146628
国有	State-owned Enterprises	7491	1584
集体	Collective-owned Enterprises	2727	1561
股份合作	Cooperative Enterprises	328	311
联营	Joint Ownership Enterprises	217	176
国有联营	State Joint Ownership Enterprises	24	17
集体联营	Collective Joint Ownership Enterprises	122	113
国有与集体联营	Joint State-collective Ownership Enterprises	13	7
其他联营	Other Joint Ownership Enterprises	58	39
有限责任公司	Limited Liability Corporations	44945	44822
国有独资公司	State Sole Funded Corporations	453	453
其他有限责任公司	Other Limited Liability Corporations	44492	44369
股份有限公司	Share-holding Corporations Limited	1245	1238
私营	Private Enterprises	93218	92917
私营独资企业	Private-funded Enterprises	14230	14031
私营合伙	Private Partnership Enterprises	1745	1703
私营有限责任公司	Private Limited Liability Corporations	75873	75816
私营股份有限公司	Private Share-holding Corporations Ltd.	1370	1367
其他	Other Domestic Funded Enterprises	17367	4019
（二）港、澳、台商投资企业	Enterprises with Funds from Hong Kong, Macau and Taiwan	494	493
与港、澳、台商合资经营	Joint-venture with Funds from Hong Kong,Macau and Taiwan	141	141
与港、澳、台商合作经营	Cooperative Enterprises with Funds from Hong Kong Macau and Taiwan	13	12
港澳台商独资经营	Enterprises with Sole Investment from Hong Kong Macau and Taiwan	191	191
港澳台商投资股份有限公司	Share-holding Corporations Ltd. with funds from Hong Kong, Macau & Taiwan	19	19
其他港澳台商投资	Other Enterprises with Funds from Hong Kong, Macau and Taiwan	130	130
（三）外商投资	Foreign Funded Enterprises	747	744
中外合资经营	Sino-foreign Joint Ventures	242	241
中外合作经营	Sino-Foreign Cooperation Enterprises	14	14
外资企业	Foreign Owned Enterprises	416	415
外商投资股份有限公司	Limited Company Funded by Foreign Investment	43	43
其他外商投资	Other Foreign Funded Enterprises	32	31

2-2 按国民经济行业分法人单位数（2018年）

Impersonal Entities by Industry of the National Economy（2018）

单位：个 (unit)

分 组	Classify	法人单位数 Number of Enterprises	企业 Enterprises
总 计	**Total**	**168779**	**147865**
（一）农、林、牧、渔业	Agriculture,Forestry,Animal Husbandry and Fishery	6997	3396
农业	Farming	3391	1330
林业	Forestry	977	563
畜牧业	Animal Husbandry	1944	1142
渔业	Fishery	113	68
农、林、牧、渔专业及辅助性活动	Agriculture, Forestry, Animal husbandry, Fishery and Auxiliary Activities	572	293
（二）采矿业	Mining	270	270
煤炭开采和洗选业	Mining and Washing of Coal	9	9
石油和天然气开采业	Extraction of Petroleum and Natural Gas	17	17
黑色金属矿采选业	Mining of Ferrous Metal Ores	12	12
有色金属矿采选业	Mining of Non-ferrous Metal Ores	23	23
非金属矿采选业	Mining and Processing of Nonmetal Ores	80	80
开采专业及辅助性活动	Mining Professional and Auxiliary Activities	109	109
其他采矿业	Mining of Other Ores	20	20
（三）制造业	Manufacturing	17623	17584
农副食品加工业	Processing of Food from Agricultural Products	587	568
食品制造业	Manufacture of Foods	596	595
酒、饮料和精制茶制造业	Manufacture of Beverages	238	235
烟草制品业	Manufacture of Tobacco	5	5
纺织业	Manufacture of Textile	188	186
纺织服装、服饰业	Manufacture of Textile Wearing Apparel	170	169
皮革、毛皮、羽毛及其制品和制鞋业	Manufacture of Leather, Fur, Feather and Related Products and Footware	39	36
木材加工和木、竹、藤、棕、草制品业	Timber Processing,Bamboo,Cane, Palm Fiber and Straw Products	301	301
家具制造业	Manufacture of Furniture	552	552
造纸及纸制品业	Manufacture of Paper and Paper Products	402	401
印刷和记录媒介复制业	Printing,Reproduction of Recording Media	653	653
文教、工美、体育和娱乐用品制造业	Manufacture of Articles For Culture, Education and Sport Activities	290	289

2-2 续表1 continued 1

单位：个 (unit)

分组	Classify	法人单位数 Number of Enterprises	企业 Enterprises
石油、煤炭及其他燃料加工业	Processing of Petroleum, Coking, Processing of Nuclear Fuel	80	80
化学原料和化学制品制造业	Manufacture of Raw Chemical Materials and Chemical Products	884	883
医药制造业	Manufacture of Medicines	376	376
化学纤维制造业	Manufacture of Chemical Fibers	21	21
橡胶和塑料制品业	Manufacture of Rubber and Manufacture of Plastics	601	601
非金属矿物制品业	Manufacture of Non-metallic Mineral Products	1751	1750
黑色金属冶炼和压延加工业	Smelting and Pressing of Ferrous Metals	130	130
有色金属冶炼和压延加工业	Smelting and Pressing of Non-ferrous Metals	200	200
金属制品业	Manufacture of Metal Products	1406	1406
通用设备制造业	Manufacture of General Purpose Machinery	2268	2268
专用设备制造业	Manufacture of Special Equipment	1695	1693
汽车制造业	Manufacture of Motor Vehicle	219	219
铁路、船舶、航空航天和其他运输设备制造业	Railways,Shipbuilding,Aerospace and Other Transportation Equipment Manufacturing Industry	383	382
电气机械和器材制造业	Manufacture of Electric Equipment and Machinery	1599	1599
计算机、通信和其他电子设备制造业	Manufacture of Communication Equipment, Computers and other Electronic Equipment	944	944
仪器仪表制造业	Manufacture of Measuring Instruments and Machinery	609	609
其他制造业	Other Manufacturing	122	122
废弃资源综合利用	Recycling and Disposal of Waste	72	71
金属制品、机械和设备修理业	Metal Products,Machinery and Equipment Repair Industry	242	240
（四）电力、热力、燃气及水的生产供应业	Production and Distribution of Electricity,Heat ,Gas and Water	494	488
电力、热力生产和供应业	Production and Supply of Electric Power and Heat Power	315	313
燃气生产和供应业	Gas mining and supplying industry	56	55
水的生产和供应业	Production and Supply of Water	123	120
（五）建筑业	Construction	14810	14809
房屋建筑业	Construction of Building	3042	3042
土木工程建筑业	Civil Engineering	3107	3107
建筑安装业	Architectural Installation	2320	2320
建筑装饰、装修和其他建筑业	Architectural Decoration and Other Construction	6341	6340
（六）批发和零售业	Wholesale and Retail Trades	53946	53305

2-2 续表2 continued 2

单位：个

分 组	Classify	法人单位数 Number of Enterprises	企业 Enterprises
批发业	Wholesale Trade	29365	28852
零售业	Retail Trade	24581	24453
（七）交通运输、仓储和邮政业	Traffic, Transport, Storage and Post	3250	3164
铁路运输业	Transport Via Railway	32	31
道路运输业	Transport Via Road	1917	1880
水上运输业	Water Transport	10	10
航空运输业	Air Transport	80	79
管道运输业	Transport Via Pipeline	3	3
多式联运和运输代理业	Multimodal Transport and Transportation Agency	637	635
装卸搬运和仓储业	Loading,Unloading,portage,storge and management of Land industry	424	379
邮政业	Post	147	147
（八）住宿和餐饮业	Hotels and Catering Services	4450	4432
住宿业	Hotels	1611	1605
餐饮业	Catering Services	2839	2827
（九）信息传输、软件和信息技术服务业	Information Transmission, Computer Services and Software	8544	8525
电信、广播电视和卫星传输服务	Telecom & Other Information Transmission Services	352	347
互联网和相关服务	Internet and Relevant Services	1104	1102
软件和信息技术服务	Software Industry	7088	7076
（十）金融业	Financial Intermediation	966	950
货币金融服务	Monetary and Financial Services	299	293
资本市场服务	Capital Market Services	333	331
保险业	Insurance	180	177
其他金融业	Other Financial Intermediation	154	149
（十一）房地产业	Real Estate	8672	8656
房地产业	Real Estate	8672	8656
（十二） 租赁和商务服务业	Leasing and Business Services	17218	16905
租赁业	Leasing	1448	1443
商务服务业	Business Services	15770	15462
（十三）科学研究和技术服务业	Scientific Research, Technical Sevice	7394	6704
研究与试验发展	Research and Experimental Development	884	799
专业技术服务业	Professional Technical Services	4336	4043

2-2 续表3 continued 3

单位：个 (unit)

分组	Classify	法人单位数 Number of Enterprises	企业 Enterprises
科技推广和应用服务业	Services of Science and Technology Exchanges and Promotion	2174	1862
（十四）水利、环境和公共设施管理业	Management of Water Conservancy, Environment and Public Facilities	1594	1386
水利管理业	Management of Water Conservancy	170	77
生态保护和环境治理业	Environmental Management	153	133
公共设施管理业	Management of Public Facilities	1098	1006
土地管理业	Lang management	173	170
（十五）居民服务、修理和其他服务业	Services to Households and Other Services	3458	3382
居民服务业	Services to Households	1273	1215
机动车、电子产品和日用产品修理业	The Repair Service Industry for Motor Vehicle、Electronic	1559	1556
其他服务业	Other Services	626	611
（十六）教育	Education	4222	628
教育	Education	4222	628
（十七）卫生和社会工作	Health, Social Security	3678	431
卫生	Health	3430	391
社会工作	Social	248	40
（十八）文化、体育和娱乐业	Culture, Sports and Entertainment	3190	2845
新闻和出版业	Journalism and Publishing Activities	183	137
广播、电视、电影和录音制作业	Broadcasting,Movies,Television and Audiovisual Activities	640	620
文化艺术业	Cultural and Art Activities	878	639
体育	Sports Activities	293	264
娱乐业	Entertainment	1196	1185
（十九）公共管理、社会保障和社会组织	Public Management and Social Organizaion	8003	5
中国共产党机关	Organs of Communist Party of China	182	1
国家机构	Government Agencies	2276	
人民政协、民主党派	People's Political Consultative Conference and Democratic Parties	31	
社会保障	Social Security	70	3
群众团体、社会团体和其他成员组织	Mass organizations、Social Groups and other members of the organization	1407	1
基层群众自治组织	Grass-roots Mass Self-Government Organizations	4037	
（二十）国际组织	International Organizations		
国际组织	International Organizations		

2-3　各区县法人单位数（2018年）

Impersonal Entities by Region and Development Zone (2018)

单位：个　　(unit)

区　县	Region	法人单位数 Number of Enterprises	企业 Enterprises
总　计	**Total**	**168779**	**147865**
新城区	Xincheng	8784	7888
碑林区	Beilin	13497	12534
莲湖区	Lianhu	16858	15909
灞桥区	Baqiao	7668	6573
未央区	Weiyang	25240	24350
雁塔区	Yanta	42825	41768
阎良区	Yanliang	3335	2623
临潼区	Lintong	5410	3387
长安区	Chang'an	14031	11797
高陵区	Gaoling	4115	3006
鄠邑区	Huyi	6261	4035
蓝田县	Lantian	5478	3259
周至县	Zhouzhi	4967	2366
西咸新区	Xixian	10310	8370

注：西安市行政区不包含西咸新区单位数，西咸新区单位数按统计局代码汇总。

2-4 按登记注册类型分产业活动单位数（2018年）

Industrial Active Units by Status of Registion（2018）

单位：个 (unit)

分 组	Classify	产业活动单位数 Number of Industrial Active Units	企业 Enterprises
总计	**Total**	**182420**	**158591**
按登记注册类型分	Grouped by Status of Registion		
（一）内资	Domestic Funded Enterprises	180129	156304
国有	State-owned Enterprises	10933	2815
集体	Collective-owned Enterprises	3428	1941
股份合作	Cooperative Enterprises	560	543
联营	Joint Ownership Enterprises	291	244
国有联营	State Joint Ownership Enterprises	44	37
集体联营	Collective Joint Ownership Enterprises	148	135
国有与集体联营	Joint State-collective Ownership Enterprises	20	12
其他联营	Other Joint Ownership Enterprises	79	60
有限责任公司	Limited Liability Corporations	48156	48029
国有独资公司	State Sole Funded Corporations	483	483
其他有限责任公司	Other Limited Liability Corporations	47673	47546
股份有限公司	Share-holding Corporations Limited	2474	2467
私营	Private Enterprises	96331	96017
私营独资企业	Private-funded Enterprises	14655	14449
私营合伙	Private Partnership Enterprises	1830	1785
私营有限责任公司	Private Limited Liability Corporations	78357	78297
私营股份有限公司	Private Share-holding Corporations Ltd.	1489	1486
其他	Other Enterprises	17956	4248

2-4 续表 continued

单位：个 (unit)

分组	Classify	产业活动单位数 Number of Industrial Active Units	企业 Enterprises
（二）港、澳、台商投资企业	Enterprises with Funds from Hong Kong,Macau and Taiwan	728	727
与港、澳、台商合资经营	Joint-venture with Funds from Hong Kong,Macau and Taiwan	166	166
与港、澳、台商合作经营	Cooperative Enterprises with Funds from Hong Kong Macau and Taiwan	24	23
港澳台商独资经营	Enterprises with Sole Investment from Hong Kong Macau and Taiwan	357	357
港澳台商投资股份有限公司	Share-holding Corporations Ltd. with funds from Hong Kong, Macau & Taiwan	26	26
其他港澳台商投资	Other Enterprises with Funds from Hong Kong,Macau and Taiwan	155	155
（三）外商投资	Foreign Funded Enterprises	1563	1560
中外合资经营	Sino-foreign Joint Ventures	358	357
中外合作经营	Sino-Foreign Cooperation Enterprises	24	24
外资企业	Foreign Owned Enterprises	927	926
外商投资股份有限公司	Limited Company Funded by Foreign Investment	149	149
其他外商投资	Other Foreign Funded Enterprises	105	104

2-5 按国民经济行业分产业活动单位数（2018年）

Industrial Active Units by Industry of the National Economy (2018)

单位：个 (unit)

分组	Classify	产业活动单位数 Number of Industrial Active Units	企业 Enterprises
总计	**Total**	**182420**	**158591**
（一）农、林、牧、渔业	Agriculture,Forestry,Animal Husbandry and Fishery	7027	3415
农业	Farming	3400	1338
林业	Forestry	983	565
畜牧业	Animal Husbandry	1950	1148
渔业	Fishery	113	68
农、林、牧、渔专业及辅助性活动	Agriculture, Forestry, Animal Husbandry, Fishery and Auxiliary Activities	581	296
（二）采矿业	Mining	284	284
煤炭开采和洗选业	Mining and Washing of Coal	10	10
石油和天然气开采业	Extraction of Petroleum and Natural Gas	20	20
黑色金属矿采选业	Mining of Ferrous Metal Ores	12	12
有色金属矿采选业	Mining of Non-ferrous Metal Ores	23	23
非金属矿采选业	Mining and Processing of Nonmetal Ores	80	80
开采专业及辅助性活动	Mining Professional and Auxiliary Activities	119	119
其他采矿业	Mining of Other Ores	20	20
（三）制造业	Manufacturing	18024	17985
农副食品加工业	Processing of Food from Agricultural Products	602	583
食品制造业	Manufacture of Foods	615	614
酒、饮料和精制茶制造业	Manufacture of Beverages	249	246
烟草制品业	Manufacture of Tobacco	6	6
纺织业	Manufacture of Textile	189	187
纺织服装、服饰业	Manufacture of Textile Wearing Apparel	173	172
皮革、毛皮、羽毛及其制品和制鞋业	Manufacture of Leather, Fur, Feather and Related Products and Footware	39	36
木材加工和木、竹、藤、棕、草制品业	Timber Processing,Bamboo,Cane, Palm Fiber and Straw Products	308	308
家具制造业	Manufacture of Furniture	561	561
造纸及纸制品业	Manufacture of Paper and Paper Products	405	404
印刷和记录媒介复制业	Printing,Reproduction of Recording Media	672	672
文教、工美、体育和娱乐用品制造业	Manufacture of Articles For Culture, Education and Sport Activities	295	294

2-5 续表1 continued 1

单位：个 (unit)

分 组	Classify	产业活动单位数 Number of Industrial Active Units	企业 Enterprises
石油、煤炭及其他燃料加工业	Processing of Petroleum, Coking, Processing of Nuclear Fuel	80	80
化学原料和化学制品制造业	Manufacture of Raw Chemical Materials and Chemical Products	900	899
医药制造业	Manufacture of Medicines	386	386
化学纤维制造业	Manufacture of Chemical Fibers	21	21
橡胶和塑料制品业	Manufacture of Rubber and Manufacture of Plastics	609	609
非金属矿物制品业	Manufacture of Non-metallic Mineral Products	1791	1790
黑色金属冶炼和压延加工业	Smelting and Pressing of Ferrous Metals	132	132
有色金属冶炼和压延加工业	Smelting and Pressing of Non-ferrous Metals	204	204
金属制品业	Manufacture of Metal Products	1439	1439
通用设备制造业	Manufacture of General Purpose Machinery	2312	2312
专用设备制造业	Manufacture of Special Equipment	1730	1728
汽车制造业	Manufacture of Motor Vehicle	234	234
铁路、船舶、航空航天和其他运输设备制造业	Railways,Shipbuilding,Aerospace and Other Transportation Equipment Manufacturing Industry	392	391
电气机械和器材制造业	Manufacture of Electric Equipment and Machinery	1634	1634
计算机、通信和其他电子设备制造业	Manufacture of Communication Equipment, Computers and other Electronic Equipment	965	965
仪器仪表制造业	Manufacture of Measuring Instruments and Machinery	630	630
其他制造业	Other Manufacturing	127	127
废弃资源综合利用	Recycling and Disposal of Waste	74	73
金属制品、机械和设备修理业	Metal Products,Machinery and Equipment Repair Industry	250	248
（四）电力、热力、燃气及水的生产供应业	Production and Distribution of Electricity,Heat ,Gas and Water	599	588
电力、热力生产和供应业	Production and Supply of Electric Power and Heat Power	408	401
燃气生产和供应业	Gas mining and supplying industry	61	60
水的生产和供应业	Production and Supply of Water	130	127
（五）建筑业	Construction	15480	15479
房屋建筑业	Construction of Building	3372	3372
土木工程建筑业	Civil Engineering	3211	3211
建筑安装业	Architectural Installation	2404	2404
建筑装饰、装修和其他建筑业	Architectural Decoration and Other Construction	6493	6492
（六）批发和零售业	Wholesale and Retail Trades	57932	57291

2-5 续表2 continued 2

单位：个 (unit)

分组	Classify	产业活动单位数 Number of Industrial Active Units	企业 Enterprises
批发业	Wholesale Trade	30113	29600
零售业	Retail Trade	27819	27691
（七）交通运输、仓储和邮政业	Traffic, Transport, Storage and Post	3873	3756
铁路运输业	Transport Via Railway	57	56
道路运输业	Transport Via Road	2098	2041
水上运输业	Water Transport	11	11
航空运输业	Air Transport	91	90
管道运输业	Transport Via Pipeline	7	7
多式联运和运输代理业	Multimodal Transport and Transportation Agency	718	716
装卸搬运和仓储业	Loading,Unloading,portage,storge and management of Land industry	445	400
邮政业	Post	446	435
（八）住宿和餐饮业	Hotels and Catering Services	5246	5225
住宿业	Hotels	1790	1782
餐饮业	Catering Services	3456	3443
（九）信息传输、软件和信息技术服务业	Information Transmission, Computer Services and Software	9043	9010
电信、广播电视和卫星传输服务	Telecom & Other Information Transmission Services	587	571
互联网和相关服务	Internet and Relevant Services	1140	1137
软件和信息技术服务	Software Industry	7316	7302
（十）金融业	Financial Intermediation	2595	2570
货币金融服务	Monetary and Financial Services	1494	1482
资本市场服务	Capital Market Services	394	392
保险业	Insurance	530	525
其他金融业	Other Financial Intermediation	177	171
（十一）房地产业	Real Estate	9106	9087
房地产业	Real Estate	9106	9087
（十二） 租赁和商务服务业	Leasing and Business Services	18107	17722
租赁业	Leasing	1501	1496
商务服务业	Business Services	16606	16226
（十三）科学研究和技术服务业	Scientific Research, Technical Sevice	7748	6986
研究与试验发展	Research and Experimental Development	918	831
专业技术服务业	Professional Technical Services	4555	4240

2-5 续表3 continued 3

单位：个 (unit)

分组	Classify	产业活动单位数 Number of Industrial Active Units	企业 Enterprises
科技推广和应用服务业	Services of Science and Technology Exchanges and Promotion	2275	1915
（十四）水利、环境和公共设施管理业	Management of Water Conservancy, Environment and Public Facilities	1706	1435
水利管理业	Management of Water Conservancy	214	81
生态保护和环境治理业	Environmental Management	157	134
公共设施管理业	Management of Public Facilities	1151	1039
土地管理业	Lang management	184	181
（十五）居民服务、修理和其他服务业	Services to Households and Other Services	3753	3658
居民服务业	Services to Households	1458	1390
机动车、电子产品和日用产品修理业	The Repair Service Industry for Motor Vehicle、Electronic	1644	1641
其他服务业	Other Services	651	627
（十六）教育	Education	4818	701
教育	Education	4818	701
（十七）卫生和社会工作	Health, Social Security	4035	462
卫生	Health	3775	421
社会工作	Social	260	41
（十八）文化、体育和娱乐业	Culture, Sports and Entertainment	3360	2930
新闻和出版业	Journalism and Publishing Activities	196	144
广播、电视、电影和录音制作业	Broadcasting,Movies,Television and Audiovisual Activities	659	636
文化艺术业	Cultural and Art Activities	964	651
体育	Sports Activities	319	289
娱乐业	Entertainment	1222	1210
（十九）公共管理、社会保障和社会组织	Public Management and Social Organizaion	9684	7
中国共产党机关	Organs of Communist Party of China	199	1
国家机构	Government Agencies	3774	
人民政协、民主党派	People's Political Consultative Conference and Democratic Parties	41	
社会保障	Social Security	100	4
群众团体、社会团体和其他成员组织	Mass organizations、Social Groups and other members of the organization	1526	2
基层群众自治组织	Grass-roots Mass Self-Government Organizations	4044	
（二十）国际组织	International Organizations		
国际组织	International Organizations		

2-6 各区县产业活动单位数（2018年）

Industrial Active Units by Region and Development Zone（2018）

单位：个 (unit)

区 县	Region	产业活动单位数 Number of Industrial Active Units	企业 Enterprises
总 计	**Total**	**182420**	**158591**
新城区	Xincheng	9608	8589
碑林区	Beilin	15414	14323
莲湖区	Lianhu	18263	17167
灞桥区	Baqiao	8516	7141
未央区	Weiyang	26449	25442
雁塔区	Yanta	44898	43703
阎良区	Yanliang	3668	2870
临潼区	Lintong	6358	3888
长安区	Chang'an	15051	12724
高陵区	Gaoling	4403	3252
鄠邑区	Huyi	6901	4473
蓝田县	Lantian	6319	3588
周至县	Zhouzhi	5568	2587
西咸新区	Xixian	11004	8844

2-7 按统计机构分企业一套表调查单位数（2018年）

Number of Survey Units by Statistical Agencies of "One Sheet"（2018）

单位：个 (unit)

区县、开发区	Region	合计 Total	规模以上工业 Industrial Enterprises above Designed Size	限额以上批发零售住宿餐饮业 Above wholesale and Retail Accommodation and Catering Industry	资质内建筑业 Qualified Construction Enterprises	房地产开发经营企业 Real Estate Development Enterprises	规模以上服务业 Service Enterprises above Designed Size
全　市	**Total**	**7533**	**1441**	**2084**	**1209**	**1129**	**1670**
新城区	Xincheng	360	9	153	65	38	95
碑林区	Beilin	731	12	287	164	76	192
莲湖区	Lianhu	507	23	160	95	84	145
灞桥区	Baqiao	183	55	32	30	40	26
未央区	Weiyang	321	26	102	78	55	60
雁塔区	Yanta	518	38	150	141	62	127
阎良区	Yanliang	200	69	53	29	27	22
临潼区	Lintong	190	72	40	34	19	25
长安区	Chang'an	233	28	94	31	45	35
高陵区	Gaoling	205	84	44	16	38	23
鄠邑区	Huyi	173	69	48	9	34	13
蓝田县	Lantian	128	51	29	13	18	17
周至县	Zhouzhi	130	32	49	14	20	15
西咸新区	Xixian	614	180	190	55	120	69
高新区	GaoXin	1233	354	210	243	111	315
经开区	JingKai	945	235	258	139	88	225
曲江新区	Qujiang	292		45	18	84	145
航空基地	Aviation Industry Base	74	39	10	3	12	10
航天基地	Aerospace Base	142	38	25	7	49	23
浐灞生态区	Chanba Eco-District	220	6	61	20	90	43
国际港务区	International Trade &Logistic Park	134	21	44	5	19	45

注：由于统计口径不同，一套表调查单位数与各专业有差异。

2-8 各区县企业一套表调查单位数（2018年）

Number of Survey Units of "One Sheet" by Region and Development Zone（2018）

单位：个 (unit)

区 县	Region	合计 Total	规模以上工业 Industrial Enterprises above Designed Size	限额以上批发零售住宿餐饮业 Above wholesale and Retail Accommodation and Catering Industry	资质内建筑业 Qualified Construction Enterprises	房地产开发经营企业 Real Estate Development Enterprises	规模以上服务业 Service Enterprises above Designed Size
全 市	**Total**	**7533**	**1441**	**2084**	**1209**	**1129**	**1670**
新城区	Xincheng	360	9	153	65	39	95
碑林区	Beilin	718	9	287	164	74	194
莲湖区	Lianhu	511	23	160	96	85	146
灞桥区	Baqiao	473	82	124	50	111	105
未央区	Weiyang	1395	210	422	234	216	306
雁塔区	Yanta	1814	253	384	380	232	566
阎良区	Yanliang	275	108	63	32	39	33
临潼区	Lintong	204	72	41	35	28	28
长安区	Chang'an	550	167	139	57	108	75
高陵区	Gaoling	299	161	50	17	42	29
鄠邑区	Huyi	226	107	53	13	41	13
蓝田县	Lantian	128	51	29	13	18	17
周至县	Zhouzhi	154	53	50	15	20	16
西咸新区	Xixian	426	136	129	38	76	47

2-9 按区县和国民经济行业分法人单位数（2018年）

单位：个

区 县	Region	合计 Total	农、林、牧、渔业 Agriculture Forestry Animal Husbandry and Fishery	采矿业 Mining	制造业 Manufacturing	电力、燃气及水的生产和供应业 Production and Distribution of Electricity Gas and Water
全 市	**Total**	**168779**	**6997**	**270**	**17623**	**494**
新城区	Xincheng	8784	5		301	2
碑林区	Beilin	13497		6	220	7
莲湖区	Lianhu	16858	8	3	415	9
灞桥区	Baqiao	7668	246		1168	27
未央区	Weiyang	25240	82	51	1834	41
雁塔区	Yanta	42825	153	89	3348	103
阎良区	Yanliang	3335	285		781	22
临潼区	Lintong	5410	911		715	31
长安区	Chang'an	14031	756	27	2128	43
高陵区	Gaoling	4115	501	11	817	26
鄠邑区	Huyi	6261	854	28	1707	27
蓝田县	Lantian	5478	1206	24	669	72
周至县	Zhouzhi	4967	1117	25	336	32
西咸新区	Xixian	10310	873	6	3184	52

注：1.西安市行政区不包含西咸新区单位数，西咸新区单位数按统计局代码汇总；
2.建筑业房地产专业按照注册地区划汇总。

Impersonal Entities by Region and Development Zone and Industry of the National Economy (2018)

(unit)

建筑业 Construction	批发和零售业 Wholesale and Retail Trades	交通运输、仓储和邮政业 Traffic Transport Storage and Post	住宿和餐饮业 Hotels and Catering Services	信息传输、软件和信息技术服务业 Information Transmission Software and Information Technology Services	金融业 Financial Intermediation
14810	**53946**	**3250**	**4450**	**8544**	**966**
466	4251	263	471	184	43
997	5596	115	646	549	83
1482	7681	375	652	551	126
616	2293	402	154	193	54
2807	12213	622	480	640	101
4386	12650	335	882	5077	331
208	737	102	84	53	18
539	836	119	107	77	12
1482	2708	171	429	932	82
305	745	130	87	38	11
333	635	108	80	75	15
444	685	62	117	44	17
180	1026	132	69	39	8
565	1890	314	192	92	65

2-9 续表

单位：个

区 县	Region	房地产业 Real Estate	租赁和商务服务业 Leasing and Business Services	科学研究和技术服务业 Scientific Research Technical Services	水利、环境和公共设施管理业 Management of Water Conservancy, Environment and Public Facilities
全 市	**Total**	**8672**	**17218**	**7394**	**1594**
新城区	Xincheng	522	687	248	51
碑林区	Beilin	928	1952	769	99
莲湖区	Lianhu	1011	2064	665	161
灞桥区	Baqiao	431	571	277	84
未央区	Weiyang	1305	2242	1107	218
雁塔区	Yanta	2564	6758	2936	289
阎良区	Yanliang	126	209	63	40
临潼区	Lintong	126	342	183	58
长安区	Chang'an	680	1265	594	220
高陵区	Gaoling	208	211	69	45
鄠邑区	Huyi	167	241	164	100
蓝田县	Lantian	94	197	47	49
周至县	Zhouzhi	104	85	110	83
西咸新区	Xixian	406	394	162	97

continiude

(unit)

居民服务、修理和其他服务业 Services to Households Repairs and Other Services	教育 Education	卫生和社会工作 Health and Social Work	文化、体育和娱乐业 Culture Sports and Entertainment	公共管理、社会保障和社会组织 Public Administration Social Security and Social Organizations	国际组织 International Orgnizations
3458	**4222**	**3678**	**3190**	**8003**	
261	204	73	168	584	
341	319	120	305	445	
418	308	152	295	482	
173	285	68	151	475	
430	247	92	213	515	
826	485	178	971	464	
65	102	106	69	265	
84	259	359	133	519	
314	462	456	313	969	
96	202	208	87	318	
76	268	506	107	770	
70	241	563	110	767	
45	385	466	96	629	
259	455	331	172	801	

2-10 按区县和机构类型分法人单位数（2018年）

Impersonal Entities by Agencies Types of Legal Entities Corporate Units and Region and Development Zone（2018）

单位：个 (unit)

区 县	Region	法人单位数 Number of Enterprises	企业法人 Business Entity	事业法人 Institution Entity	机关法人 Government Entity	社会团体 Social Organization	其他 Other
全 市	**Total**	**168779**	**147865**	**5002**	**1315**	**1257**	**13340**
新城区	Xincheng	8784	7888	280	157	220	239
碑林区	Beilin	13497	12534	317	87	199	360
莲湖区	Lianhu	16858	15909	329	93	143	384
灞桥区	Baqiao	7668	6573	240	73	78	704
未央区	Weiyang	25240	24350	278	146	57	409
雁塔区	Yanta	42825	41768	330	94	71	562
阎良区	Yanliang	3335	2623	146	62	46	458
临潼区	Lintong	5410	3387	574	75	63	1311
长安区	Chang'an	14031	11797	655	76	44	1459
高陵区	Gaoling	4115	3006	309	80	25	695
鄠邑区	Huyi	6261	4035	371	71	82	1702
蓝田县	Lantian	5478	3259	223	104	73	1819
周至县	Zhouzhi	4967	2366	384	70	103	2044
西咸新区	Xixian	10310	8370	566	127	53	1194

注：西安市行政区不包含西咸新区单位数，西咸新区单位数按统计局代码汇总。

2-11 按区县和登记注册类型分企业法人单位数（2018年）

The Corporate Units by Types of Corporate Registration and Region and Development Zone（2018）

单位：个 (unit)

区 县 Region	企业单位数 Number of Enterprises	内资企业 Domestic Investment Enterprises	国有企业 State-owned Enterprises	集体企业 Collective-owned Enterprises	股份合作企业 Share-holding Corperative Enterprises	联营企业 Joint Ownership Enterprises
全 市 Total	**147865**	**146628**	**1584**	**1561**	**311**	**176**
新城区 Xincheng	7888	7862	256	282	42	19
碑林区 Beilin	12534	12458	230	119	35	25
莲湖区 Lianhu	15909	15851	254	234	19	23
灞桥区 Baqiao	6573	6507	74	122	15	6
未央区 Weiyang	24350	24183	106	91	33	17
雁塔区 Yanta	41768	41246	161	85	42	17
阎良区 Yanliang	2623	2604	40	48	16	4
临潼区 Lintong	3387	3372	65	85	8	2
长安区 Chang'an	11797	11655	82	95	37	12
高陵区 Gaoling	3006	2982	54	32	16	7
鄠邑区 Huyi	4035	4003	84	108	17	7
蓝田县 Lantian	3259	3240	48	93	10	16
周至县 Zhouzhi	2366	2365	52	30	4	3
西咸新区 Xixian	8370	8300	78	137	17	18

2-11 续表 continued

区 县 Region	有限责任公司 Limited Liability Corporations	股份有限公司 Share-holding Corperation Ltd.	私营企业 Private Enterprises	港、澳、台商投资企业 Enterprises with Funds from Hong Kong, Macao and Taiwan	外商投资企业 Enterprises with Foreign Investment
全 市 Total	**44822**	**1238**	**92917**	**493**	**744**
新城区 Xincheng	4084	100	3020	12	14
碑林区 Beilin	5841	130	5865	33	43
莲湖区 Lianhu	1375	95	12952	28	30
灞桥区 Baqiao	2597	43	3527	38	28
未央区 Weiyang	7483	135	16221	77	90
雁塔区 Yanta	15165	321	25332	182	340
阎良区 Yanliang	829	38	1224	9	10
临潼区 Lintong	218	8	2974	7	8
长安区 Chang'an	2285	133	8271	47	95
高陵区 Gaoling	1008	53	1720	5	19
鄠邑区 Huyi	410	56	3161	17	15
蓝田县 Lantian	373	26	2322	8	11
周至县 Zhouzhi	179	28	1623		1
西咸新区 Xixian	2975	72	4705	30	40

注：西安市行政区不包含西咸新区单位数，西咸新区单位数按统计局代码汇总。

主要统计指标解释

企业（单位）登记注册类型 是以在工商行政管理机关登记注册的各类企业为划分对象，以工商行政管理部门对企业登记注册的类型为依据，将企业登记注册类型分为内资企业、港澳台商投资企业和外商投资企业三大类。内资企业包括国有企业、集体企业、股份合作企业、联营企业、有限责任公司、股份有限公司、私营公司和其他企业；港澳台商投资企业和外商投资企业分别包括合资经营企业、合作经营企业、独资经营企业和股份有限公司。对不在工商行政管理部门进行登记注册的行政机关、事业单位和社会团体，主要按其经费来源和管理方式进行划分。

国有企业 指企业全部资产归国家所有，并按《中华人民共和国企业法人登记管理条例》规定登记注册的非公司制的经济组织。不包括有限责任公司中的国有独资公司。

集体企业 指企业资产归集体所有，并按《中华人民共和国企业法人登记管理条例》规定登记注册的经济组织。

股份合作企业 指以合作制为基础，由企业职工共同出资入股，吸收一定比例的社会资产投资组建，实行自主经营，自负盈亏，共同劳动，民主管理，按劳分配与按股分红相结合的一种集体经济组织。

联营企业 指两个及两个以上相同或不同所有制性质的企业法人或事业单位法人，按自愿、平等、互利的原则，共同投资组成的经济组织。联营企业包括国有联营企业、集体联营企业、国有与集体联营企业和其他联营企业。

有限责任公司 指根据《中华人民共和国公司登记管理条例》规定登记注册，由两个以上、五十个以下的股东共同出资，每个股东以其所认缴的出资额对公司承担有限责任，公司以其全部资产对其债务承担责任的经济组织。有限责任公司包括国有独资公司以及其他有限责任公司。

股份有限公司 指根据《中华人民共和国公司登记管理条例》规定登记注册，其全部注册资本由等额股份构成并通过发行股票筹集资本，股东以其认购的股份对公司承担有限责任，公司以其全部资产对其债务承担责任的经济组织。

私营企业 指由自然人投资设立或由自然人控股，以雇佣劳动为基础的营利性经济组织。包括按照《公司法》、《合伙企业法》、《私营企业暂行条例》规定登记注册的私营有限责任公司、私营股份有限公司、私营合伙企业和私营独资企业。

其他企业 指上述企业之外的其他内资经济组织。

与港澳台商合资经营企业 指港澳台地区投资者与内地企业依照《中华人民共和国中外合资经营企业法》及有关法律的规定，按合同规定的比例投资设立、分享利润和分担风险的企业。

与港澳台商合作经营企业 指港澳台地区投资者与内地企业依照《中华人民共和国中外合作经营企业法》及有关法律的规定，依照合作合同的约定进行投资或提供条件设立、分配利润和分担风险的企业。

港澳台商独资经营企业 指依照《中华人民共和国外资企业法》及有关法律的规定，在内地由港澳台地区投资者全额投资设立的企业。

港澳台商投资股份有限公司 指根据国家有关规定，经原外经贸部依法批准设立，其中港、澳、台商的股本占公司注册资本的比例达25%以上的股份有限公司。凡其中港、澳、台商的股本占公司注册资本的比例小于25%的，属于内资企业中的股份有限公司。

中外合资经营企业 指外国企业或外国人与中国内地企业依照《中华人民共和国中外合资经营企业法》及有关法律的规定，按合同规定的比例投资设立、分享利润和分担风险的企业。

中外合作经营企业 指外国企业或外国人与中国内地企业依照《中华人民共和国中外合作经营企业法》及有关法律的规定，依照合作合同的约定进行投资或提供条件设立、分配利润和分担风险的企业。

外资企业 指依照《中华人民共和国外资企业法》及有关法律的规定，在中国内地由外国投资者全额投资设立的企业。

外商投资股份有限公司 指根据国家有关规定，经原外经贸部依法批准设立，其中外资的股本占公司注册资本的比例达25%以上的股份有限公司。凡其中外资股本占公司注册资本的比例小于25%的，属于内资企业中的股份有限公司。

行政机关、事业单位和社会团体 参照企业登记注册类型，主要按其经费来源和管理方式划分。具体规定如下：

（1）行政机关：包括国家机关和政党机关，原则上均列为“国有”。但有特殊规定的，如供销社等，则列为“集体”。

（2）事业单位：包括经国家机构编制部门和有关业务主管部门批准成立的各类事业单位，不包括实行企业化管理的事业单位。事业单位的划分办法如下：

①由国家财政预算拨款或列入财政预算外资金管理以及经费主要来源于国有主管部门或国有上级单位的事业单位，列为“国有”。

②经费主要来源于集体单位的事业单位，列为“集体”。

③公民个人（或个人合伙）开办的事业单位，列为“私营”。

④上述以外的其他事业单位，如果其经费来源不明确，按管理方式进行归类。

（3）社会团体：包括经民政部门批准成立以及未纳入社会团体管理条例范围的工会、妇联等各类社会团体。社会团体的划分办法如下：

①未纳入民政部社会团体管理条例范围的工会、妇联、共青团、青联、工商联、科协、侨联等社会团体，国家拨款设立的基金会或基金管理组织以及经费主要来源于国有业务主管部门或国有上级单位的社会团体，列为“国有”。

②经费主要来源于集体单位的社会团体，列为“集体”。

③公民个人（或个人合伙）开办的社会团体，划为“私营”。

④上述以外的其他社会团体，如果其经费来源不明确，改按管理方式进行归类。

Explanatory Notes on Main Statistical Indicators

Registration Status of Enterprises Enterprises are classified into 3 categories, namely domestic-funded enterprises, enterprises with investment from Hong Kong, Macau and Taiwan, and enterprises with foreign investment, according to the registration status of an enterprise in industrial and commercial administration agencies. Domestic-funded enterprises include State- owned enterprises, collective-owned enterprises, cooperative enterprises, joint ownership enterprises, limited liability corporations, share-holding corporations Ltd., private enterprises and other enterprises. Included in the enterprises with investment from Hong Kong, Macau and Taiwan and enterprises with foreign investment are joint-venture enterprises, cooperative enterprises, sole investment enterprises and share-holding corporations Ltd. For government agencies, institutions and social organizations which are not registered in industrial and commercial administration agencies, they are classified mainly by their sources of funding and manner of management.

State–owned Enterprises refer to non-corporation economic units where the entire assets are owned by the State and which have been registered in accordance with the Regulation of the People's Republic of China on the Management of Registration of Corporate Enterprises. Not included from this category are solely State-funded corporations in the limited liability corporations.

Collective–owned Enterprises refer to economic units where the assets are owned collectively and which have been registered in accordance with the Regulation of the People's Republic of China on the Management of Registration of Corporate Enterprises.

Cooperative Enterprises refer to a form of collective economic units (enterprises)where capitals come mainly from employees as their shares, with certain proportion of capital from the outside, where production is organized on the basis of independent operation, independent accounting for profits and losses, joint work, democratic management, and a distribution system that integrates remuneration according to work with dividend according to capital share.

Joint Ownership Enterprises refer to economic units established by two or more corporate enterprises or corporate institutions of the same or different ownership, through joint investment on the basis of voluntary participation, equality, and mutual benefits. They include State joint ownership enterprises; collective joint ownership enterprises; joint State-collective enterprises; and other joint ownership enterprises.

Limited Liability Corporations refer to economic units established with investment from 2-50 investors and registered in accordance with the Regulation of the People's Republic of China on the Management of Registration of Corporations, each investor bearing limited liability to the corporation depending on its share of investment, and the corporation bearing liability to its debt to the maximum of its total assets. Limited liability corporations include solely State-funded limited liability corporations and other limited liability corporations.

Share–holding Corporations Ltd. refer to economic units registered in accordance with the Regulation of the People's Republic of China on the Management of Registration of Corporations, with total registered capital divided into equal shares and raised through issuing stocks. Each investor bears limited liability to the corporation depending on the holding of shares, and the corporation bears liability to its debt to the maximum of its total assets.

Private Enterprises refer to profit-making economic units invested and established by natural persons, or controlled by natural persons using employed labour~ Included in this category are private limited liability corporations, private share-holding corporations Ltd., private partnership enterprises and private-funded enterprises registered in accordance with the Company Law, the Law on Partnership Business and Interim Regulations on Private Enterprises.

Other Domestic–funded Enterprises refer to domestic-funded economic units other than those mentioned above.

Joint Venture Enterprises with Funds from Hong Kong, Macau and Taiwan are enterprises established by investors from Hong Kong, Macau and Taiwan with enterprises in the mainland of China in accordance with the Law of the People's Republic of China on Sino-foreign Equity Joint Ventures and other relevant laws, where the establishment of the investment and the sharing of profits and risks are stipulated under joint venture contracts.

Cooperative Enterprises with Funds from Hong Kong, Macan and Taiwan established by investors from Hong Kong, Macau and Taiwan with enterprises in the mainland of China in accordance with the Law of the People's Republic of China on Sino-foreign Contractual Joint Venture and other relevant laws, where the investment or provision of facilities and the sharing of profits and risks are stipulated under cooperative contracts.

Enterprises with Sole (exclusive)Investment from

Hong Kong, Macau and Taiwan refer to enterprises established in the mainland of China with exclusive investment from investors from Hong Kong, Macau and Taiwan in accordance with the Law of the People's Republic of China on Wholly Foreign-owned Enterprises and other relevant laws.

Share–holding Corporations Ltd. with Investment from Hong Kong, Macau and Taiwan refer to share- holding corporations Ltd. established with the approval from the former Ministry of Foreign Trade and Economic Relations in line with relevant State regulations, where the share of investment from Hong Kong, Macau or Taiwan businessmen exceeds 25% of the total registered capital of the corporation. In case the share of investmentfrom Hong Kong, Macau or Taiwan is less than 25% of thetotal registered capital, the enterprise is to be classified as domestic-funded share-holding corporation Ltd.

Joint Venture Enterprises with Foreign Investment refer to enterprises jointly established byforeign enterprises or foreigners with enterprises in themainland of China in accordance with the Law of thePeople's Republic of China on Sino-foreign Equity JointVentures and other relevant laws, where the sharing ofinvestment, profits and risks is stipulated under contract.

Cooperative Enterprises with Foreign Investment refer to enterprises jointly established by foreign enterprises or foreigners with enterprises in the mainland of China in accordance with the Law of the People's Republic of China on Sino-foreign Contractual Joint Venture and other relevant laws, where the investment or provision of facilities and the sharing of profits and risks are stipulated under cooperative contracts.

Enterprises with Sole (exclusive)Foreign Investment refer to enterprises established in the mainland of China with exclusive investment from foreign investors in accordance with the Law of the People's Republic of China on Wholly Foreign-owned Enterprises and other relevant laws.

Share–holding Corporations Ltd. with Foreign Investment refer to share-holding corporations Ltd. established with the approval from the former Ministry of Foreign Trade and Economic Relations in line with relevant State regulations, where the share of investment from foreign investors exceeds 25% of the total registered capital of the corporation. In case the share of foreign investment is less than 25% ofthe total registered capital, the enterprise is to be classified as domestic-funded share-holding corporation Ltd.

Government Agencies, Institutions and Social Organizations are classified into the following categories by source of funds and manner of management taking reference of thc registration status of enterprises:

(1)Government agencies: include State and party agencies, classified in principle as State-owned. There are exceptions, such as supply and marketing cooperatives which are classified as collective-owned.

(2)Institutions: include institutions of various types established with the approval by organization and staffing departments of the government, but exclude institutions where enterprise management system is introduced. Institutions are further classified as follows:

(a)Institutions for which their main budgets are from government budget appropriations or extra-budget funds, or allocated from the budget of their competent government agencies. Such institutions are classified as state-owned.

(b)Institutions for which their budget mainly come from collective units. Such institutions are classified as collective-owned.

(c)Social institutions established by individual or a group of citizens, which are classified as private.

(d)Institutions other than those mentioned above for which their sources of budget are not clear. Such institutions are classified by the manner of management.

(3)Social organizations: include social organizations established with the approval from the Ministry of Civil Affairs, and organizations that are not covered by social organization management regulations such as trade unions, women's federations etc.. Social organizations are further classified as follows:

(a)Social organizations that are not covered by social organization management regulations of the Ministry of Civil Affairs such as trade unions, women federations, communist youth leagues, youth associations, industrial and commerce associations, scientist associations, overseas Chinese associations, etc., foundations and fund management organizations established with funds from the state, and social organizations whose funds mainly come from the budget of their competent government agencies. Such institutions are classified as State-owned.

(b)Social organizations for which their budget mainly come from collective units. Such institutions are classified as collective-owned.

(c)Social organizations established by individual or a group of citizens, which are classified as private.

(d)Social organizations other than those mentioned above for which their sources of budget are not clear. Such organizations are classified by the manner of management.

3 国民经济核算

NATIONAL ECONOMIC ACCOUNTS

资料整理：刘晓敏　李晋贤　张　洁
Data management：Liu Xiaomin Li Jinxian Zhang Jie
数据审核：连　鹏
Data audit：Lian Peng

第三部分　国民经济核算

一、简要说明

1.本章资料反映西安市国民经济核算情况。

2.本章资料包括西安市生产总值、构成和指数，非公有制经济增加值及占比等。生产总值是根据不同产业部门、不同行业的特点和资料来源情况而采用不同方法计算的。非公有制经济增加值测算执行的是《陕西省统计局关于非公有制经济增加值测算的暂行办法（修订版）》。

3.本年鉴公布的国内生产总值以及与之有关的指标数据，如果遇到普查或者重大核算方法改革，在能够获得更详细的基础资料的情况下，国内生产总值的历史数据还会发生变动。

2016年，国家统计局改革研发支出的核算方法，将能够为所有者带来经济利益的研发支出不再作为中间消耗，而是作为固定资本形成处理。根据新的核算方法，本年鉴2017年（含）之后全市和各区县数据包含研发支出新增GDP数据。

2018年数据为初步核算数，其他年份数据为年报最终核实数据。第一产业为第三次农业普查修订结果。

4.2012年，根据国家质检总局和国家标准委颁布的《国民经济行业分类》（GB／T 4754—2011），国家统计局对《三次产业划分规定》进行了修订，将“农、林、牧、渔业”中的“农、林、牧、渔服务业”，“采矿业”中的“开采辅助活动”，“制造业”中的“金属制品、机械和设备修理业”等三个大类一并调入第三产业。2013年（含）之后三次产业分类执行国家统计局2012年制定的新《三次产业划分规定》。

5.2004年（含）之前人均GDP按户籍人口计算，2005年（含）之后按常住人口计算。

6.国民经济核算数据绝对数按当年价格计算，指数按可比价格计算。

二、主要指标

生产总值（亿元）	8349.86	比上年增长	8.2%
第一产业	258.82	比上年增长	3.3%
第二产业	2925.61	比上年增长	8.5%
第三产业	5165.43	比上年增长	8.3%
人均生产总值（元/人）	85114	比上年增长	5.2%

3 NATIONAL ECONOMIC ACCOUNTS

I.Brief introduction

1.Data in this chapter reflects the National Economic accounting situation of Xi' an.

2.Data in this chapter includes Xi' an GDP, composition, index,the added value and the proportion of the non-public sectors of the economy, etc.Data of GDP are based on different approaches in accordance with different features of various sectors, industry and data sources. The estimation of the non-public sectors of the economy is based on Interim Measures of Shaanxi Provincial Bureau on the Estimation of Value Added of the Non-Public Sectors of the Economy (Revised Edition).

3.For data of GDP and related indicators published in the Yearbook, if there are census or reformation of significant accounting method, historical data of GDP may also undergo change under the circumstance that more specific data can be obtained.

In 2016, National Bureau of Statistics reforms the Methodology of Research and Development Expenditure. It regulates that R&D expenditure which will bring economic benefit for the owners should be treated as Fixed Assets instead of Intermediate Consumption. According to new accounting method, data of the whole city and all districts in this Yearbookinclude R&D expenditure since 2017.

Data of 2018 is preliminary accounting data, and data of other year is final revised data.The data of PrimaryIndustry is from the revised result of the third agricultural census.

4.Classification Rules of Three Strata of Industry was adjusted by National Bureau of Statistics of China in accordance with Industrial Classification for National Economic Activities (GB/T 4754-2011) in 2012, which was promulgated by AQSIQ and SAC. Services in support of agriculture, forestry, animal husbandry and fishery, support activities for mining, repair service of metal products, machinery and equipment are categorized into the Tertiary Industry. Industrial classification is based on adjusted Classification Rules of Three Strata of Industry (2012) since 2013.

5.Per capita GDP was calculated by register population before 2005, but since 2005 it is based on permanent resident population.

6.Data on national accounts are calculated at current prices, and the indices are calculated at constant prices.

Ⅱ.Major Indicators

		Increase over Preceding Year
Gross Domestic Product(100 mil. yuan)	8349.86	8.2%
Primary Industry	258.82	3.3%
Secondary Industry	2925.61	8.5%
Tertiary Industry	5165.43	8.3%
Per Capita Gross Domestic Product (yuan/person)	85114	5.2%

3-1 主要年份生产总值

Gross Domestic Product in Representative Years

(本表按当年价格计算)　　(Data in the table are calculated at current prices)

单位：亿元　　(100 million yuan)

年份 Year	生产总值 Gross Domestic Product	第一产业 Primary Industry	第二产业 Secondary Industry	第三产业 Tertiary Industry	人均生产总值 (元/人) Per Capita GDP (yuan/person)
1952	3.37	1.59	0.88	0.90	135
1965	12.76	2.62	7.22	2.92	323
1970	17.76	3.13	10.96	3.67	412
1975	21.33	4.14	12.63	4.56	448
1978	25.35	4.83	14.59	5.93	513
1980	31.66	4.73	18.69	8.24	623
1983	35.89	5.22	20.14	10.53	674
1984	44.14	7.45	24.17	12.52	817
1985	57.58	8.76	30.83	17.99	1049
1986	65.78	9.59	33.86	22.33	1178
1987	80.16	10.73	37.69	31.74	1409
1988	99.22	11.47	46.58	41.17	1711
1989	109.38	12.78	48.91	47.69	1861
1990	116.51	13.94	50.15	52.42	1932
1991	136.14	17.17	57.06	61.91	2224
1992	164.85	18.78	69.22	76.85	2662
1993	229.56	22.58	110.88	96.10	3661
1994	289.82	31.68	128.27	129.87	4563
1995	330.35	41.40	135.33	153.62	5131
1996	406.95	46.94	161.63	198.38	6246
1997	488.82	51.33	197.97	239.52	7424
1998	525.85	51.91	216.32	257.62	7906
1999	577.29	45.53	243.35	288.41	8599
2000	646.13	44.65	277.13	324.35	9484
2001	734.86	45.87	312.90	376.09	10628
2002	826.68	47.77	353.58	425.33	11831
2003	946.66	50.72	407.38	488.56	13341
2004	1102.39	60.21	476.92	565.26	15294
2005	1313.93	66.01	540.50	707.42	16406
2006	1538.94	70.44	645.65	822.85	18890
2007	1856.63	82.51	781.94	992.18	22463
2008	2318.14	103.45	981.58	1233.11	27794
2009	2724.88	110.38	1144.75	1469.75	32420
2010	3242.86	140.06	1357.53	1745.27	38357
2011	3869.84	173.14	1583.21	2113.49	45561
2012	4394.47	195.59	1781.09	2417.79	51499
2013	4924.97	200.45	1998.82	2725.70	57464
2014	5492.64	214.55	2194.78	3083.31	63794
2015	5801.20	220.20	2126.29	3454.71	66938
2016	6282.65	232.01	2200.36	3850.28	71647
2017	7471.89	281.12	2596.52	4594.25	78368
2018	8349.86	258.82	2925.61	5165.43	85114

注：1.2004年（含）之前人均GDP按户籍人口计算，2005年（含）之后按常住人口计算。
2.全市2009年—2012年数据为第三次经济普查修订结果，2013年数据为第三次经济普查结果。
3.2013年（含）之后三次产业分类依据国家统计局2012年制定的新《三次产业划分规定》。
4.2017年开始数据包含研发支出核算改革、西咸新区由西安代管统计范围变化两部分新增GDP，之前年份则不含（下同）。
5.2018年第一产业为第三次农业普查修订结果（下同）。

3-2 主要年份生产总值指数（上年=100）

Indices of Gross Domestic Product in Representative Years(preceding year = 100)

(本表按可比价格计算) (Data in the table are calculated at constant prices)

年份	Year	生产总值 Gross Domestic Product	第一产业 Primary Industry	第二产业 Secondary Industry	第三产业 Tertiary Industry	人均生产总值 Per Capita GDP
1952		103.6	92.2	137.5	123.7	
1965		126.1	134.1	133.0	106.7	
1970		122.0	109.4	140.0	100.1	
1975		103.8	92.6	107.1	107.5	
1978		101.7	101.6	99.4	108.2	
1980		111.5	83.3	119.7	116.5	
1985		112.6	107.5	111.8	116.9	
1986		111.4	107.7	108.4	118.8	
1987		113.6	100.8	109.1	126.6	
1988		111.4	81.2	115.5	114.7	
1989		106.7	103.0	104.5	110.8	
1990		105.2	103.0	102.5	109.6	
1991		109.8	118.6	108.6	108.6	108.2
1992		115.6	109.4	118.1	115.0	114.3
1993		123.9	112.5	142.7	108.4	122.3
1994		110.3	98.4	110.6	113.2	108.8
1995		110.0	104.5	112.1	108.6	108.5
1996		114.9	106.8	118.8	111.7	113.5
1997		114.4	109.1	116.7	112.4	113.2
1998		113.3	106.5	117.5	108.8	112.1
1999		112.2	97.4	115.7	110.1	111.2
2000		113.0	103.5	115.1	111.5	111.4
2001		113.1	102.5	115.3	112.6	111.4
2002		113.3	103.1	115.0	113.0	112.1
2003		113.5	101.8	117.5	111.2	111.7
2004		113.5	106.7	115.9	112.0	111.7
2005		114.0	107.5	112.3	116.3	112.2
2006		114.0	107.1	113.7	114.9	112.9
2007		115.6	104.5	115.7	116.4	113.9
2008		116.3	107.6	116.4	116.9	115.3
2009		114.5	106.3	112.8	116.3	113.7
2010		114.5	106.9	115.2	114.5	113.8
2011		113.5	106.7	112.5	114.9	113.0
2012		112.2	106.0	112.0	112.9	111.7
2013		111.1	104.7	113.6	109.7	110.6
2014		109.9	105.1	109.3	110.7	109.4
2015		108.2	105.0	105.6	110.4	107.5
2016		108.6	103.8	108.5	109.0	107.4
2017		107.7	104.6	105.3	109.4	106.0
2018		108.2	103.3	108.5	108.3	105.2
平均每年增长	**Yearly Average Growth Rates**					
“一五”时期	**The First Five-Year Plan Period**	**15.8**	**5.9**	**37.7**	**16.9**	
“二五”时期	**The Second Five-Year Plan Period**	**2.0**	**-3.7**	**2.5**	**8.4**	
1963--1965年	**Readjust Period**	**14.2**	**16.1**	**23.4**	**0.3**	
“三五”时期	**The Third Five-Year Plan Period**	**7.1**	**0.1**	**11.7**	**5.4**	
“四五”时期	**The Fourth Five-Year Plan Period**	**5.0**	**4.0**	**5.3**	**5.0**	
“五五”时期	**The Fifth Five-Year Plan Period**	**6.0**	**-0.7**	**6.5**	**10.1**	
“六五”时期	**The Sixth Five-Year Plan Period**	**10.7**	**7.9**	**10.4**	**12.9**	
“七五”时期	**The Seventh Five-Year Plan Period**	**9.6**	**-1.3**	**7.9**	**15.9**	
“八五”时期	**The Eighth Five-Year Plan Period**	**13.8**	**8.5**	**17.8**	**10.7**	**12.3**
“九五”时期	**The Ninth Five-Year Plan Period**	**13.6**	**4.6**	**16.8**	**10.9**	**12.3**
“十五”时期	**The Tenth Five-Year Plan Period**	**13.5**	**4.3**	**15.2**	**13.0**	**11.8**
“十一五”时期	**The Eleventh Five-Year Plan Period**	**15.0**	**6.5**	**14.8**	**15.8**	**13.9**
“十二五”时期	**The Twelve Five-Year Plan Period**	**11.0**	**5.5**	**10.6**	**11.7**	**10.4**

3-3 主要年份生产总值指数（1952年=100）

Indices of Gross Domestic Product in Representative Years(1952= 100)

(本表按可比价格计算) (Data in the table are calculated at constant prices)

年 份 Year	生产总值 Gross Domestic Product	第一产业 Primary Industry	第二产业 Secondary Industry	第三产业 Tertiary Industry
1952	100.0	100.0	100.0	100.0
1965	341.6	173.3	1048.3	329.2
1970	481.6	174.3	1821.0	428.6
1975	614.2	211.9	2362.5	547.9
1978	678.7	231.3	2560.8	643.8
1980	821.4	204.2	3237.2	885.2
1983	988.4	222.5	3846.2	1154.4
1984	1213.6	278.2	4748.8	1388.7
1985	1366.8	299.1	5310.6	1632.4
1986	1523.1	322.3	5756.7	1928.9
1987	1730.0	324.9	6280.6	2441.6
1988	1926.3	263.7	7256.6	2801.2
1989	2054.8	271.6	7583.1	3104.6
1990	2162.5	279.7	7772.7	3403.6
1991	2374.4	331.7	8441.2	3696.3
1992	2744.8	362.9	9969.1	4250.7
1993	3400.8	408.2	14225.9	4607.8
1994	3751.1	401.8	15733.8	5216.0
1995	4126.2	419.9	17637.6	5664.6
1996	4741.0	448.5	20953.5	6327.4
1997	5423.7	489.3	24452.7	7112.0
1998	6145.1	521.2	28731.9	7737.9
1999	6894.8	507.6	33242.8	8519.4
2000	7791.1	525.4	38262.5	9499.1
2001	8811.7	538.5	44116.7	10696.0
2002	9983.7	555.2	50734.2	12086.5
2003	11331.5	565.2	59612.7	13440.2
2004	12861.3	603.1	69091.1	15053.0
2005	14661.9	648.3	77589.3	17506.6
2006	16714.6	694.3	88219.0	20115.1
2007	19322.1	725.5	102069.4	23414.0
2008	22471.6	780.6	118808.8	27371.0
2009	25730.0	829.8	134016.3	31832.5
2010	29460.8	887.0	154386.8	36448.2
2011	33438.0	946.5	173685.2	41879.0
2012	37517.5	1003.3	194527.4	47281.3
2013	41681.9	1050.4	220983.1	51867.6
2014	45808.4	1104.0	241534.5	57417.5
2015	49580.4	1158.8	255076.2	63393.7
2016	53863.1	1202.3	276727.1	69125.3
2017	57999.0	1257.7	291436.6	75632.5
2018	62754.9	1299.2	316208.7	81910.0

3-4 主要年份生产总值构成

Composition of Gross Domestic Product in Representative Years

(本表按当年价格计算)　　　　(Data in the table are calculated at current prices)

单位:%　　　　(%)

年　份	Year	生产总值 Gross Domestic Product	第一产业 Primary Industry	第二产业 Secondary Industry	第三产业 Tertiary Industry
1952		100	47.18	26.11	26.71
1965		100	20.53	56.58	22.89
1970		100	17.62	61.71	20.67
1975		100	19.41	59.21	21.38
1978		100	19.05	57.55	23.40
1980		100	14.94	59.03	26.03
1985		100	15.21	53.54	31.25
1986		100	14.58	51.47	33.95
1987		100	13.39	47.02	39.59
1988		100	11.56	46.95	41.49
1989		100	11.68	44.72	43.60
1990		100	11.96	43.04	45.00
1991		100	12.61	41.91	45.48
1992		100	11.39	41.99	46.62
1993		100	9.84	48.30	41.86
1994		100	10.93	44.26	44.81
1995		100	12.53	40.97	46.50
1996		100	11.53	39.72	48.75
1997		100	10.50	40.50	49.00
1998		100	9.87	41.14	48.99
1999		100	7.89	42.15	49.96
2000		100	6.91	42.89	50.20
2001		100	6.24	42.58	51.18
2002		100	5.78	42.77	51.45
2003		100	5.36	43.03	51.61
2004		100	5.46	43.26	51.28
2005		100	5.02	41.14	53.84
2006		100	4.58	41.95	53.47
2007		100	4.44	42.12	53.44
2008		100	4.46	42.34	53.20
2009		100	4.05	42.01	53.94
2010		100	4.32	41.86	53.82
2011		100	4.47	40.91	54.62
2012		100	4.45	40.53	55.02
2013		100	4.07	40.59	55.34
2014		100	3.91	39.96	56.13
2015		100	3.80	36.65	59.55
2016		100	3.69	35.02	61.29
2017		100	3.76	34.75	61.49
2018		100	3.10	35.04	61.86
"一五"时期	**The First Five-Year Plan Period**	**100**	**32.88**	**43.92**	**23.20**
"二五"时期	**The Second Five-Year Period**	**100**	**18.08**	**58.63**	**23.29**
1963--1965年	**Readjust Period**	**100**	**19.36**	**55.38**	**25.26**
"三五"时期	**The Third Five-Year Plan Period**	**100**	**18.60**	**57.33**	**24.07**
"四五"时期	**The Fourth Five-Year Plan Period**	**100**	**20.46**	**59.59**	**19.95**
"五五"时期	**The Fifth Five-Year Plan Period**	**100**	**18.41**	**57.69**	**23.90**
"六五"时期	**The Sixth Five-Year Plan Period**	**100**	**16.03**	**55.01**	**28.96**
"七五"时期	**The Seventh Five-Year Plan Period**	**100**	**12.42**	**46.11**	**41.47**
"八五"时期	**The Eighth Five-Year Plan Period**	**100**	**11.44**	**43.52**	**45.04**
"九五"时期	**The Ninth Five-Year Plan Period**	**100**	**9.09**	**41.45**	**49.46**
"十五"时期	**The Tenth Five-Year Plan Period**	**100**	**5.49**	**42.47**	**52.04**
"十一五"时期	**The Eleventh Five-Year Plan Period**	**100**	**4.34**	**42.04**	**53.62**
"十二五"时期	**The Twelve Five-Year Plan Period**	**100**	**4.10**	**39.55**	**56.35**

3-5 主要年份分行业增加值

The Value added by Industry in Representative Years

单位：亿元 （100 million yuan）

年 份 Year	地区生产总值 Gross Domestic Product	农、林、牧、渔业 Farming Forestry Animal Husbandry Fishery	工业 Industry	建筑业 Construction	批发和零售业 Wholesale and Retail Trades
1992	164.85	18.78	61.33	7.89	18.16
1993	229.56	22.58	98.88	12.00	22.63
1994	289.82	31.68	110.52	17.75	27.83
1995	330.35	41.40	112.50	22.83	33.20
1996	406.95	46.94	132.52	29.11	44.51
1997	488.82	51.33	161.97	36.00	59.31
1998	525.85	51.91	175.00	41.32	64.93
1999	577.29	45.53	194.00	49.35	70.27
2000	646.13	44.65	218.44	58.69	65.87
2001	734.86	45.87	246.90	66.00	78.38
2002	826.68	47.77	280.20	73.38	91.57
2003	946.66	50.72	324.88	82.50	106.82
2004	1102.39	60.21	383.46	93.46	125.12
2005	1313.93	66.01	420.00	120.50	147.20
2006	1538.94	70.44	494.22	151.43	166.72
2007	1856.63	82.51	594.95	186.99	195.51
2008	2318.14	103.45	721.40	260.18	242.91
2009	2724.88	110.38	816.92	327.83	298.29
2010	3242.86	140.06	954.38	403.15	352.37
2011	3869.84	173.14	1098.51	484.70	439.75
2012	4394.47	195.59	1228.05	553.04	512.96
2013	4924.97	217.76	1376.74	642.26	575.72
2014	5492.64	233.61	1488.02	728.74	633.65
2015	5801.20	241.69	1376.72	770.29	667.99
2016	6282.65	256.38	1397.25	818.82	702.30
2017	7471.89	312.46	1684.02	928.30	771.04
2018	8349.86	286.18	1874.36	1073.12	842.06

注：1999年（含）之前，批发和零售业与住宿和餐饮业无法分类，故1999年（含）之前批发和零售业数据为批发和零售业与住宿和餐饮业合计数。

3-5 续表 continued

单位：亿元 (100 million yuan)

年份 Year	交通运输、仓储和邮政业 Transport，Storage and Post	住宿和餐饮业 Accommodation and Catering Trade	金融业 Financial Intermediation	房地产业 Real Estate	其他服务业 Others Services
1992	15.21		16.28	1.58	25.62
1993	18.01		20.59	1.97	32.90
1994	22.02		31.19	3.76	45.07
1995	24.60		35.20	4.90	55.72
1996	32.73		40.15	7.42	73.57
1997	43.02		37.50	8.74	90.95
1998	48.64		32.95	11.95	99.15
1999	55.35		30.37	14.42	118.00
2000	43.01	18.46	33.00	16.96	147.05
2001	45.50	21.97	36.21	21.38	172.65
2002	48.25	25.27	43.48	26.90	189.86
2003	51.37	29.41	50.76	32.42	217.78
2004	55.10	35.89	61.49	39.05	248.61
2005	66.30	50.44	75.00	52.48	316.00
2006	74.08	52.23	96.50	62.32	371.00
2007	84.21	70.09	128.50	75.26	438.61
2008	99.16	85.65	160.84	92.97	551.58
2009	112.02	93.82	197.87	128.18	639.57
2010	135.70	102.80	236.36	186.42	731.62
2011	165.18	118.02	294.44	235.20	860.90
2012	192.46	129.58	359.63	260.53	962.63
2013	215.11	135.58	429.51	292.41	1039.88
2014	235.58	144.15	534.00	326.10	1168.79
2015	260.33	159.14	658.90	398.34	1267.80
2016	298.52	170.67	724.35	459.20	1455.16
2017	334.02	188.18	800.94	550.35	1902.58
2018	357.49	204.85	874.91	643.18	2193.71

3-6 主要年份分行业增加值指数（上年 = 100）

Indices of the Value added by Industry in Representative Years（preceding year = 100）

(本表按可比价格计算) (Data in the table are calculated at constant prices)

年 份 Year	地区生产总值 Gross Domestic Product	农、林、牧、渔业 Farming Forestry Animal Husbandry Fishery	工业 Industry	建筑业 Construction	批发和零售业 Wholesale and Retail Trades
1992	115.6	109.4	118.1	118.2	130.7
1993	123.9	112.5	143.7	135.6	108.0
1994	110.3	98.4	106.8	141.3	103.1
1995	110.0	104.5	108.1	136.6	109.6
1996	114.9	106.8	117.1	126.8	116.0
1997	114.4	109.1	116.4	117.8	124.0
1998	113.3	106.5	116.1	123.4	110.7
1999	112.2	97.4	114.0	122.8	106.4
2000	113.0	103.5	113.8	120.1	111.4
2001	113.1	102.5	116.3	111.8	110.5
2002	113.3	103.1	116.4	109.3	115.3
2003	113.5	101.8	115.7	125.0	110.8
2004	113.5	106.7	115.5	117.3	109.1
2005	114.0	107.5	110.3	120.0	112.7
2006	114.0	107.1	112.3	118.7	112.5
2007	115.6	104.5	114.9	118.4	112.9
2008	116.3	107.6	115.7	118.9	115.0
2009	114.5	106.3	110.1	121.2	121.8
2010	114.5	106.9	114.3	117.6	115.0
2011	113.5	106.7	112.8	111.7	119.5
2012	112.2	106.0	112.7	110.3	114.0
2013	111.1	104.8	114.0	113.9	110.4
2014	109.9	105.1	108.4	110.9	109.3
2015	108.2	105.1	104.8	107.4	105.6
2016	108.6	104.0	109.2	106.5	104.8
2017	107.7	104.7	105.8	104.2	105.6
2018	108.2	103.5	109.0	107.9	107.0

注：1999年（含）之前，批发和零售业与住宿和餐饮业无法分类，故1999年（含）之前批发和零售业数据为批发和零售业与住宿和餐饮业合计数。

3-6 续表 continued

(本表按可比价格计算) (Data in the table are calculated at constant prices)

年 份 Year	交通运输、仓储和邮政业 Transport，Storage and Post	住宿和餐饮业 Accommodation and Catering Trade	金融业 Financial Intermediation	房地产业 Real Estate	其他服务业 Others Services
1992	111.3		107.6	119.5	112.2
1993	102.7		109.7	107.4	111.4
1994	102.5		126.9	160.7	114.8
1995	102.6		103.7	119.7	113.6
1996	115.1		98.7	130.8	114.2
1997	122.4		87.0	109.6	115.1
1998	114.4		88.8	138.3	110.3
1999	111.9		90.6	118.6	117.0
2000	111.7	111.7	107.7	116.6	111.7
2001	111.6	114.2	103.6	123.5	114.2
2002	106.1	116.5	104.6	106.0	116.5
2003	113.6	111.6	107.4	108.8	111.6
2004	115.6	112.9	107.1	110.3	112.9
2005	113.2	136.1	109.3	112.9	117.7
2006	112.3	116.6	107.3	117.5	117.7
2007	110.3	117.3	126.7	119.7	116.3
2008	108.4	111.6	113.6	107.6	122.5
2009	111.0	106.6	123.7	130.8	112.5
2010	119.4	106.6	116.1	128.1	111.9
2011	115.7	108.5	117.9	113.5	112.9
2012	112.6	105.4	124.8	108.8	110.4
2013	108.2	100.7	119.0	111.9	106.1
2014	106.2	102.0	121.1	107.7	110.2
2015	111.3	109.2	119.3	107.9	109.7
2016	109.5	105.7	109.3	113.1	110.7
2017	107.4	105.4	105.7	109.6	113.8
2018	106.3	105.8	105.3	105.8	111.3

3-7 主要年份三次产业贡献率

Three Industries Contribution Rate in Representative Years

(本表按可比价格计算) (Data in the table are calculated at constant prices)

年份 Year	生产总值 Gross Domestic Product	第一产业 Primary Industry	第二产业 Secondary Industry	第三产业 Tertiary Industry
2000	100	1.8	66.9	31.3
2001	100	1.3	50.4	48.3
2002	100	1.5	49.4	49.1
2003	100	0.8	57.7	41.5
2004	100	2.5	54.1	43.4
2005	100	2.6	41.3	56.1
2006	100	2.5	40.2	57.3
2007	100	1.4	41.4	57.2
2008	100	2.0	41.4	56.6
2009	100	1.7	36.5	61.8
2010	100	1.7	42.5	55.8
2011	100	2.1	38.5	59.4
2012	100	2.0	40.7	57.3
2013	100	1.5	50.3	48.2
2014	100	1.7	39.3	59.0
2015	100	1.9	28.4	69.7
2016	100	1.7	36.0	62.3
2017	100	2.4	26.1	71.5
2018	100	1.4	37.5	61.1

3-8 主要年份三次产业拉动率

Three Industries Pulling Rate in Representative Years

(本表按可比价格计算) (Data in the table are calculated at constant prices)

年 份 Year	生产总值 Gross Domestic Product	第一产业 Primary Industry	第二产业 Secondary Industry	第三产业 Tertiary Industry
2000	13.0	0.2	8.7	4.1
2001	13.1	0.2	6.6	6.3
2002	13.3	0.2	6.6	6.5
2003	13.5	0.1	7.8	5.6
2004	13.5	0.3	7.3	5.9
2005	14.0	0.4	5.8	7.8
2006	14.0	0.4	5.7	7.9
2007	15.6	0.2	6.4	9.0
2008	16.3	0.3	6.8	9.2
2009	14.5	0.2	5.3	9.0
2010	14.5	0.3	6.2	8.0
2011	13.5	0.3	5.2	8.0
2012	12.2	0.2	5.0	7.0
2013	11.1	0.2	5.6	5.3
2014	9.9	0.2	3.9	5.8
2015	8.2	0.2	2.3	5.7
2016	8.6	0.1	3.1	5.4
2017	7.7	0.2	2.0	5.5
2018	8.2	0.1	3.1	5.0

3-9 分行业增加值

Value added by Industry

单位：亿元 (100 million yuan)

指 标	Item	增加值 Value Added		指数（上年=100） Index	
		2017	2018	2017	2018
地区生产总值	**Gross Domestic Product**	**7471.89**	**8349.86**	**107.7**	**108.2**
农、林、牧、渔业	Farming Forestry Animal Husbandry Fishery	312.46	286.18	104.7	103.5
工业	Industry	1684.02	1874.36	105.8	109.0
建筑业	Construction	928.30	1073.12	104.2	107.9
批发和零售业	Wholesale and Retail Trades	771.04	842.06	105.6	107.0
交通运输、仓储和邮政业	Transport,Storage and Post	334.02	357.49	107.4	106.3
住宿和餐饮业	Accommodation and Catering Trade	188.18	204.85	105.4	105.8
金融业	Financial Intermediation	800.94	874.91	105.7	105.3
房地产业	Real Estate	550.35	643.18	109.6	105.8
其他服务业	Others Services	1902.58	2193.71	113.8	111.3
第一产业	Primary Industry	281.12	258.82	104.6	103.3
第二产业	Secondary Industry	2596.52	2925.61	105.3	108.5
第三产业	Tertiary Industry	4594.25	5165.43	109.4	108.3

3-10 各区县生产总值（2018年）

Gross Domestic Product by Region（2018）

单位：亿元 （100 million yuan）

指　标	Item	生产总值 Gross Domestic Product	第一产业 Primary Industry	第二产业 Secondary Industry	第三产业 Tertiary Industry	人均生产总值（元） Per Capita GDP (yuan)
全　市	**Total**	**8349.86**	**258.82**	**2925.61**	**5165.43**	**85114**
新城区	Xincheng	650.64		209.86	440.78	103121
碑林区	Beilin	965.26		202.93	762.33	144988
莲湖区	Lianhu	820.73		255.61	565.12	109045
灞桥区	Baqiao	480.78	18.19	140.93	321.66	72962
未央区	Weiyang	964.83	0.40	477.01	487.42	130462
雁塔区	Yanta	1757.98		403.72	1354.26	135328
阎良区	Yanliang	250.10	26.55	114.56	108.99	83940
临潼区	Lintong	237.52	32.77	67.31	137.44	34254
长安区	Chang'an	909.11	26.89	481.45	400.77	88586
高陵区	Gaoling	378.45	24.99	238.93	114.53	105183
鄠邑区	Huyi	217.26	25.65	94.04	97.57	39220
蓝田县	Lantian	151.67	27.17	40.05	84.45	28365
周至县	Zhouzhi	146.27	32.94	33.68	79.65	24718
西咸新区	Xixian	381.94	43.27	158.05	180.62	37985

注：本表区县数据为初步核算数。

3-11 各区县生产总值指数（2018年）（上年＝100）

Indices of Gross Domestic Product by Region（2018）（preceding year = 100）

(本表按可比价格计算) (Data in the table are calculated at constant prices)

指 标	Item	生产总值 Gross Domestic Product	第一产业 Primary Industry	第二产业 Secondary Industry	第三产业 Tertiary Industry	人均生产总值 Per Capita GDP
全 市	**Total**	**108.2**	**103.3**	**108.5**	**108.3**	**105.2**
新城区	Xincheng	107.7		107.5	107.8	105.0
碑林区	Beilin	108.0		113.5	106.6	104.7
莲湖区	Lianhu	107.1		104.6	108.2	103.8
灞桥区	Baqiao	112.1	102.6	106.4	115.7	107.8
未央区	Weiyang	107.3	50.4	107.3	107.3	100.4
雁塔区	Yanta	108.3		109.7	107.8	103.6
阎良区	Yanliang	107.7	105.6	109.1	106.8	105.8
临潼区	Lintong	108.2	101.7	109.0	109.0	107.0
长安区	Chang'an	108.2	100.6	108.8	108.3	105.4
高陵区	Gaoling	108.1	104.8	107.9	109.5	106.4
鄠邑区	Huyi	108.0	104.3	107.2	110.0	106.5
蓝田县	Lantian	108.0	105.7	104.5	110.7	107.2
周至县	Zhouzhi	106.0	102.6	104.1	108.3	105.2
西咸新区	Xixian	113.3	103.8	115.5	114.4	110.4

注：本表区县数据为初步核算数。

3-12 主要年份非公有制经济增加值

The Added Value of Non-public-owned Economic in Representative Years

年 份 Year	非公有制经济增加值（亿元） the Added Value of Non-public-owned Economic (100 million yuan)	第一产业 Primary Industry	第二产业 Secondary Industry	第三产业 Tertiary Industry
2005	568.45	20.86	232.66	314.93
2006	684.66	26.27	279.06	379.33
2007	854.26	25.25	365.24	463.77
2008	1103.96	36.42	468.58	598.96
2009	1327.87	36.32	535.02	756.53
2010	1611.71	42.66	636.73	932.32
2011	1956.41	52.93	761.31	1142.17
2012	2258.95	59.79	831.93	1367.23
2013	2569.20	53.72	970.24	1545.24
2014	2892.90	57.40	1079.59	1755.91
2015	3060.38	58.09	1060.92	1941.37
2016	3314.20	61.42	1071.54	2181.24
2017	3962.95	67.89	1322.16	2572.90
2018	4459.64	48.56	1510.49	2900.59

3-12 续表 continued

年 份 Year	非公有制经济增加值占GDP比重(%) the Added Value of Non-public-owned Economic Percentage to GDP(%)	第一产业 Primary Industry	第二产业 Secondary Industry	第三产业 Tertiary Industry
2005	43.3	31.6	43.1	44.5
2006	44.5	37.3	43.2	46.0
2007	46.0	30.6	46.7	46.7
2008	47.6	35.2	47.7	48.6
2009	48.7	32.9	46.7	51.5
2010	49.7	30.5	46.9	53.4
2011	50.6	30.6	48.1	54.0
2012	51.4	30.6	46.7	56.6
2013	52.2	26.8	48.5	56.7
2014	52.7	26.8	49.2	56.9
2015	52.8	26.4	49.9	56.2
2016	52.8	26.5	48.7	56.7
2017	53.0	24.1	50.9	56.0
2018	53.4	18.8	51.6	56.2

注：1.2009年—2012年数据根据第三次经济普查GDP修订结果相应进行了调整。
2.2013年—2017年数据为年报最终核实数据。
3.2018年数据为初步核算数。

主要统计指标解释

生产总值(GDP) 是按市场价格计算的一个地区(或国家)所有常住单位在一定时期内生产活动的最终成果。生产总值有三种表现形态，即价值形态、收入形态和产品形态。从价值形态看，它是所有常住单位在一定时期内生产的全部货物和服务价值超过同期中间投入的全部非固定资产货物和服务价值的差额，即所有常住单位的增加值之和；从收入形态看，它是所有常住单位在一定时期内创造并分配给常住单位和非常住单位的初次收入分配之和；从产品形态看，它是所有常住单位在一定时期内最终使用的货物和服务价值与货物和服务净出口价值之和。在实际核算中，生产总值有三种计算方法，即生产法、收入法和支出法。三种方法分别从不同的方面反映生产总值及其构成。

人均生产总值 即“人均GDP”，常作为发展经济学中衡量经济发展状况的指标，是最重要的宏观经济指标之一，它是人们了解和把握一个国家或地区的宏观经济运行状况的有效工具。将一个国家核算期内(通常是一年)实现的国内生产总值与这个国家的常住人口(或户籍人口)相比进行计算，得到人均生产总值。

三次产业 指根据社会生产活动历史发展的顺序对产业结构的划分。目前我国的三次产业划分是：

第一产业是指农、林、牧、渔业(不含农、林、牧、渔服务业)。

第二产业是指采矿业(不含开采辅助活动)，制造业(不含金属制品、机械和设备修理业)，电力、热力、燃气及水生产和供应业，建筑业。

第三产业即服务业，是指除第一产业、第二产业以外的其他行业。

劳动者报酬 指劳动者因从事生产活动所获得的全部报酬。包括劳动者获得的各种形式的工资、奖金和津贴，既包括货币形式的，也包括实物形式的，还包括劳动者所享受的公费医疗和医药卫生费、上下班交通补贴、单位支付的社会保险费、住房公积金等。

生产税净额 指生产税减生产补贴后的余额。生产税指政府对生产单位从事生产、销售和经营活动以及因从事生产活动使用某些生产要素(如固定资产、土地、劳动力)所征收的各种税、附加费和规费。生产补贴与生产税相反，指政府对生产单位的单方面转移支出，因此视为负生产税，包括政策亏损补贴、价格补贴等。

固定资产折旧 指一定时期内为弥补固定资产损耗按照规定的固定资产折旧率提取的固定资产折旧，或按国民经济核算统一规定的折旧率虚拟计算的固定资产折旧。它反映了固定资产年当期生产中的转移价值。各类企业和企业化管理的事业单位的固定资产折旧是指实际计提的折旧费；不计提折旧的政府机关、非企业化管理的事业单位和居民住房的固定资产折旧是按照统一规定的折旧率和固定资产原值计算的虚拟折旧。原则上，固定资产折旧应按固定资产当期的重置价值计算，但是目前我国尚不具备对全社会固定资产进行重估价的基础，所以暂时只能采用上述办法。

营业盈余 指常住单位创造的增加值扣除劳动者报酬、生产税净额和固定资产折旧后的余额。它相当于企业的营业利润加上生产补贴，但要扣除从利润中开支的工资和福利等。

三次产业贡献率 各产业不变价增加值增量与不变价GDP增量之比。

三次产业拉动率 GDP增长速度与各产业贡献率之乘积。

非公有制经济 非公有制经济是指国民经济中除国有经济和集体经济以外的部分，对其中的混合制经济要依据实收资本之间的比例，按经济成分对各主要经济总量进行划分。

Explanatory Notes on Main Statistical Indicators

Gross Domestic Product (GDP) refers to the final products at market prices produced by all resident units in a country (or a region) during a certain period of time. Gross domestic product is expressed in three different perspectives, namely value, income, and products respectively. GDP in its value perspective refers to the total value of all goods and services produced by all resident units during a certain period of time, minus the total value of input of goods and services of the nature of non-fixed assets; in other words, it is the sum of the value-added of all resident units. GDP from the perspective of income includes the primary income created by all resident units and distributed to resident and non-resident units. GDP from the perspective of products refers to the value of all goods and services for final demand by all resident units plus the net exports of goods and services during a given period of time. In the practice of national accounting, gross domestic product is calculated from three approaches, namely production approach, income approach and expenditure approach, which reflect gross domestic product and its composition from different angles.For a region, it is called as Gross Regional Product (GRP) or regional GDP.

Per capita gross domestic product: "per capita GDP", often used as a measure of economic development in development economics, it is one of the most important macroeconomic indicators, and people's understanding and grasp of a country or a region effective tool of macroeconomic performance. The gross domestic product (GDP) of a country's accounting period (usually one year) is divided by the country's resident population (or household population), resulting in per capita GDP.

Three Strata of Industry Classification of economic activities into three strata of industry is a common practice in the world, although the grouping varies to some extent from country to country. In China economic activities are categorized into the following three strata of industry:

Primary industry refers to agriculture, forestry, animal husbandry and fishery and services in support of these industries.

Secondary industry refers to mining and quarrying, manufacturing, production and supply of electricity, water and gas, and construction.

Tertiary industry refers to all other economic activities not included in the primary or secondary industries.

Compensation of Employees refers to the total payment of various forms to employees for the productive activities they are engaged in. It includes wages, bonuses and allowances, which the employees earn in cash or in kind. It also includes the free medical services provided to the employees and the medicine expenses, transport subsidies and social insurance, and housing fund paid by the employers.

Net Taxes on Production refers to taxes on production less subsidies on production. The taxes on production refers to the various taxes, extra charges and fees levied on the production units on their production, sale and business activities as well as on the use of some factors of production, such as fixed assets, land and labour in the production activities they are engaged in. In contrast to taxes on production, subsidies on production refer to the unilateral government transfer to the production units and are therefore regarded as negative taxes on production. They include subsidies on the loss due to implementation of government policies, price subsidies, etc.

Depreciation of Fixed Assets refers to the depreciation of fixed assets in a given period, drawn in accordance with the stipulated depreciation rate for the purpose of compensating the wear-and-tear loss of the fixed assets or the depreciation of fixed assets imputed in accordance with the stipulated unified depreciation rate in the national economic accounting system. It reflects the value of transfer of the fixed assets in the production of the current period. The depreciation of fixed assets in various enterprises and institutions managed as enterprises refers to the depreciation expenses actually drawn. In government agencies and institutions not managed as enterprises which do not draw the depreciation expenses, as well as for the houses of residents, the depreciation of fixed assets is the imputed depreciation, which is calculated in accordance with the stipulated unified depreciation rate. In principle, the depreciation of fixed assets should be calculated on the basis of the re-purchased value of the fixed assets. However, currently the conditions in China do not facilitate the revaluation of all the fixed assets. Therefore, only the above-mentioned methods can be adopted at present.

Operating Surplus refers to the balance of the value added created by the resident units after deducting the labourers remuneration, net taxes on production and the depreciation of fixed assets. It is equivalent to the business profit of the enterprises plus subsidies to production, but the wages and welfare expenses paid from the profits should be deducted.

Three Industry Contribution Rate The ratio of all industries incremental value added to GDP increment at constant prices.

Three Industries Pulling Rate The product of GDP growth rate and the contribution rate of each industry.

Non–public Economy It refers to the part of in addition to state-owned economy and collective economy in the national economy,On which the mixed-economy should be divided according to the major economic components of total economic output based on the proportion in paid-in capital.

4 人口、从业人员与职工工资

POPULATION, EMPLOYMENT AND WAGES

资料整理：张　叶　张　磊
Data management: Zhang Ye Zhang Lei
数据审核：冯军魁
Data audit: Feng Junkui

第四部分　人口、从业人员与职工工资

一、简要说明

（一）人口部分反映西安市人口发展变化基本情况。

1.年末常住人口、性别比例、年龄比例、城镇人口比例以及人口出生率、人口死亡率和人口自然增长率等数据，根据人口普查、1%人口抽样调查或年度人口变动情况抽样调查推算所得，2006-2009年年末常住人口根据2010年第六次全国人口普查数据进行了调整。

2. 户籍人口资料数据来源于西安市公安局人口统计年报，为西安原口径数据。

3.人口统计调查方法。目前人口统计调查有：在逢“0”的年份进行全国人口普查；在逢“5”的年份进行全国1%人口抽样调查；其余年份进行人口变动情况抽样调查。

（二）就业部分

1.反映西安市劳动就业与工资的基本情况。主要内容包括全社会从业人员数、城镇非私营单位从业人员数、全社会从业人员工资、城镇非私营单位从业人员工资、城镇登记失业率等。（城镇登记失业人数及失业率资料由市人力资源局提供并整理）

2.统计范围和调查方法

（1）城镇非私营单位是指城镇地区全部非私营法人单位，具体包括国有单位、集体单位、联营经济、股份制经济、外商投资经济、港澳台投资经济等单位。工资统计是统计单位的从业人员，而个体从业人员、自由职业者等非单位从业人员不在工资统计范围内。

根据国家统计局制定的《企业一套表统计调查制度》和《劳动工资统计调查制度》，对城镇非私营法人单位采用全面调查的方法。

（2）城镇私营单位主要是指在内资法人单位中由自然人投资设立或由自然人控股，以雇佣劳动为基础的营利性经济组织，包括按照《公司法》《合伙企业法》《私营企业暂行条例》规定登记注册的私营有限责任公司、私营股份有限公司、私营合伙企业和私营独资企业。

根据国家统计局制定的《企业一套表统计调查制度》和《劳动工资统计调查制度》，对私营单位工资统计采用全面调查和抽样调查相结合的方法。

二、主要指标

年末户籍人口（万人）	922.82	比上年增长	9.2%
人口自然增长率（‰）	6.99	比上年下降	0.21个千分点
常住人口（万人）	1000.37	比上年增长	4.0%
男女性别比（以女性为100）	104.75	比上年下降	0.65个百分点
户籍人口密度（人／平方公里）	914	比上年增加	77人/平方公里
城镇非私营单位在岗职工年平均工资（元）	87125	比上年增长	12.0%

4 POPULATION,EMPLOYMENT AND WAGES

I .Brief Introduction

I. Population part reflects the basic conditions of development and changes of population in Xi' an.

1. Permanent population at the year-end, proportion of population by sex, proportion of population by age, proportion of urban population, birth rate, death rate and natural growth rate of population. The data are estimated by Xi' an Bureau of Statistics on the basis of population censuses, the one percent sample survey on population, or annual sample surveys on population changes. Permanent Population at the Year-end from 2006 to 2009 have been adjusted in accordance with the flash sums of the 6th National Population Census in 2010.

2. The total population with residence registration are obtained from the annual reports of population of Xi' an Public Security Bureau. It is the original caliber data of Xi' an

3. Investigation methods. The statistical surveys on population are as follows:

The national populationcensus is conducted in the year ending with 0; the national 1 percent population sample survey is conducted in the year ending with 5; sample survey on population changes are conducted in the rest of the years.

II. Employment part

1. This part reflects the basic conditions of labour employment and wages of Xi' an, mainly including the number of all employed persons, number of urban non-private units, wages of all employed persons, wages of urban non-private units employed persons, registered urban unemployment rate and etc. (the number of registered urban unemployment and registered urban unemployment rate are obtained from the Xi' an municipal human resources bureau).

2. The statistical coverage and investigation methods.

a) The urban non-private units: are non-private legal units in urban area, including state-owned units, urban collective-owned units, joint ownership units, cooperative units, foreign funded units and units with funds from Hong Kong, Macao & Taiwan etc. Wage of employed persons in urban non-private units are the persons employed in those units, except self-employed and freelancers.

In accordance withA Set of Statistical Survey System for Enterprises and The Survey System on Labour Wageby National Bureau of Statistics of China, the investigation method of non-private legal units in urban area is comprehensive survey.

b) The urban private units: are established by natural person or controlled by natural person in legal units invested by domestic, are for-profit units based on wage-labor, including private limited liability corporations, private share holding corporations Ltd., partnership corporations and private sole proprietorship corporations registered in accordance with the Company Law,Partnership Enterprise Law and Provisional Regulations.

In accordance with A Set of Statistical Survey System for Enterprises and The Survey System on Labour Wageby National Bureau of Statistics of China, the investigation method of wage of employed persons in private legal units is combined with comprehensive survey and sampling survey.

Ⅱ.Major Indicators

		Increase over Preceding Year
Total registered Population of Year-end(10 000 persons)	922.82	9.2%
Natural Growth Rate(‰)	6.99	-0.21per thousand
Permanent Population(10 000 persons)	1000.37	4.0%
Sex Ratio (Female=100)	104.75	-0.65percentage points
Density of Population (person/sq.km)	914	77person/sq.km
Annual Average Wage of Staff and Workers in Urban Non-privite Enterprises(yuan)	87125	12.0%

4-1 主要年份人口数、人口密度和人口发展情况

Population, Population Density and Population Development in Representative Years

单位：万人 (10 000 persons)

年份 Year	总人口 Total Population	市区 Urban Area	女性人口 Number of Female	城镇人口 Urban Population	人口密度（人/平方公里）Density of Population (person/sq.km)	总人口指数（上年为100）Total Population Index (100 for preceding year) 全市 Whole City	市区 Urban Area
1952	252.92	92.42	118.81	57.61	254	102.6	103.1
1965	400.05	179.88	190.72	136.39	401	102.5	103.4
1970	435.12	188.12	210.47	139.12	436	101.9	101.4
1978	498.10	210.15	241.82	159.98	499	101.7	102.7
1980	511.91	221.19	249.26	172.85	513	101.4	102.6
1985	553.11	245.76	268.40	201.90	554	101.6	102.2
1986	563.97	251.80	273.30	205.92	565	102.0	102.5
1987	574.46	257.69	278.12	210.25	575	101.9	102.3
1988	585.85	264.94	283.68	216.99	587	102.0	102.8
1989	597.36	270.80	289.44	222.54	598	102.0	102.2
1990	608.89	275.69	295.29	226.98	610	101.9	101.8
1991	615.48	419.29	298.13	230.85	617	101.1	152.1
1992	623.20	429.54	301.92	236.45	624	101.3	102.4
1993	630.91	435.41	305.30	240.85	632	101.2	101.4
1994	639.45	442.30	309.17	248.35	641	101.4	101.6
1995	648.21	448.65	313.46	255.71	645	101.4	101.4
1996	654.87	454.68	316.60	261.28	653	101.0	101.3
1997	662.06	461.17	320.18	267.52	663	101.1	101.4
1998	668.22	466.31	323.20	271.75	669	100.9	101.1
1999	674.50	463.56	326.12	276.14	676	100.9	99.4
2000	688.01	483.10	332.83	285.79	689	102.0	104.2
2001	694.84	489.88	336.04	292.62	696	101.0	101.4
2002	702.59	497.38	339.51	300.05	704	101.1	101.5
2003	716.58	510.26	346.26	312.88	718	102.0	102.6
2004	725.01	516.30	350.85	318.50	717	101.2	101.2
2005	741.73	533.21	359.71	333.14	734	102.3	103.3
2006	753.11	540.97	365.74	343.78	745	101.5	101.5
2007	764.25	549.19	371.84	353.85	756	101.5	101.5
2008	772.30	554.73	376.76	363.87	764	101.1	101.0
2009	781.67	561.58	382.39	370.66	773	101.2	101.2
2010	782.73	562.65	383.93	374.64	774	100.1	100.2
2011	791.83	568.77	389.31	391.31	783	101.2	101.1
2012	795.98	572.76	392.04	398.40	788	100.5	100.7
2013	806.93	580.60	398.15	409.82	799	101.4	101.4
2014	815.29	587.16	402.83	418.16	807	101.0	101.1
2015	815.66	588.43	403.43	545.95	808	100.0	100.2
2016	824.93	629.24	408.39	552.21	817	101.1	106.9
2017	845.09	649.08	420.11	567.26	837	102.4	103.2
2018	922.82	725.58	461.31	639.62	914	109.2	111.8

注：本表为公安年报数据,系户籍人口。2016年起公安年报调整至11月30日，市区数1991年增加临潼、长安，2016年增加高陵，行政区划面积自2012年发生变更，调整了2012年和2013年户籍人口密度。2015年公安局户籍改革，按统计上城乡划分标准统计城镇与乡村人口。户籍人口为西安原口径数据。

4-2 主要年份人口自然变动情况

Natural Population Movements in Representative Years

单位：万人 (10 000 persons)

年份 Year	出生 Birth 人数 Population	出生率（‰） Birth Rate (‰)	死亡 Death 人数 Population	死亡率（‰） Death Rate (‰)	自然增长率（‰） Natural Growth Rate (‰)	迁入人口 Immigrant Population	迁出人口 Emigrant Population
1985	8.95	16.30	3.01	5.48	10.82	11.60	8.74
1986	10.14	18.15	2.78	4.97	13.18	11.79	8.39
1987	9.76	17.14	2.83	4.97	12.17	12.58	9.26
1988	9.42	16.24	2.89	4.98	11.26	13.54	8.97
1989	11.78	19.92	3.04	5.13	14.79	12.73	10.15
1990	12.40	20.55	3.45	5.72	14.83	11.82	9.86
1991	8.73	14.25	3.26	5.33	8.92	8.98	6.09
1992	8.98	14.49	3.39	5.48	9.01	13.94	9.54
1993	9.25	14.75	3.37	5.38	9.37	11.50	8.33
1994	8.08	12.71	3.16	4.97	7.74	13.40	8.59
1995	7.69	11.95	3.21	4.98	6.97	14.41	8.85
1996	7.26	11.15	3.41	5.24	5.91	11.94	8.88
1997	6.84	10.38	3.12	4.75	5.63	12.58	8.62
1998	6.40	9.62	3.10	4.66	4.96	10.89	8.36
1999	6.19	9.22	3.88	5.78	3.44	12.58	9.23
2000	8.90	13.07	4.06	5.96	7.11	17.12	9.23
2001	5.11	7.39	2.89	4.19	3.20	15.16	10.83
2002	5.34	7.64	3.08	4.41	3.23	13.90	9.41
2003	6.02	8.48	3.32	4.68	3.80	20.60	9.15
2004	6.63	9.19	4.23	5.87	3.32	15.56	10.19
2005	7.67	9.58	4.13	5.16	4.42	22.61	9.46
2006	8.13	9.98	4.45	5.46	4.52	17.23	11.75
2007	8.27	10.00	4.53	5.48	4.52	19.90	14.01
2008	8.47	10.15	4.65	5.57	4.58	18.49	15.04
2009	8.47	10.08	4.73	5.63	4.45	16.84	13.14
2010	8.23	9.73	4.51	5.34	4.39	14.09	13.50
2011	8.25	9.71	4.57	5.38	4.33	14.21	11.74
2012	8.64	10.13	4.75	5.57	4.56	12.55	13.10
2013	8.20	9.57	4.60	5.37	4.20	10.83	8.60
2014	8.70	10.11	4.71	5.47	4.64	9.10	7.61
2015	8.80	10.15	4.78	5.51	4.64	8.08	11.61
2016	10.12	11.54	4.74	5.40	6.14	6.21	4.68
2017	12.03	12.62	5.17	5.42	7.20	25.22	4.94
2018	12.23	12.47	5.38	5.48	6.99	76.53	8.02

注：2004年以前为公安年报数据。迁入人口和迁出人口为公安年报数据。2010年出生、死亡、自然增长率根据第六次人口普查数据推算得出。2005-2009、2011-2017年出生、死亡、自然增长率为人口变动抽样调查推算数据。2017 年起公安数据为西安原口径数据。

4-3 人口年龄构成和抚养比

Population Age Composition and Dependency Ratio

单位：% (%)

年 份 Year	各年龄段人口比重 Proportion of Population of All Ages			总抚养比 Total Dependency Ratio		
	0-14岁 0-14 year old	15-64岁 15-64 year old	65岁及以上 65 year old and above		少年儿童 Children	老年人口 Elderly Population
1990	25.71	69.08	5.21	44.76	37.21	7.55
2000	22.27	71.26	6.47	40.33	31.25	9.08
2010	12.89	78.65	8.46	27.15	16.39	10.76
2011	12.57	78.33	9.10	27.66	16.04	11.62
2012	12.54	78.02	9.44	28.17	16.07	12.10
2013	12.46	77.88	9.66	28.40	16.00	12.40
2014	12.52	77.46	10.02	29.10	16.16	12.94
2015	12.56	76.94	10.50	29.98	16.33	13.65
2016	12.76	76.35	10.89	30.97	16.71	14.26
2017	13.63	75.20	11.17	32.97	18.12	14.85
2018	13.75	74.96	11.29	33.40	18.34	15.06

注：1990、2000、2010年数据根据人口普查数据加工整理，2011-2018年数据根据人口变动抽样调查数据推算，自2017年起为纳入西咸新区咸阳片区后的结构。抚养比指0-14岁、65岁及以上人口占15-64岁人口的比重。

4-4 全市及各区县人口数和户数（2018年）

Population and Households by Region（2018）

单位：万人 (10 000 persons)

区 县	Region	总户数（万户） Number of Households (10 000 households)	总人口 Total Population	城镇人口 Urban Population	按性别划分Grouped by Sex 男 Male	女 Female	迁入人口(人) Immigrant Population (person)	迁出人口(人) Emigrant Population (person)
全 市	**Total**	**290.41**	**922.82**	**639.62**	**461.51**	**461.31**	**765305**	**80196**
新城区	Xincheng	18.07	52.83	52.83	26.26	26.57	44687	4110
碑林区	Beilin	22.74	71.75	71.75	35.68	36.07	63051	10142
莲湖区	Lianhu	25.93	73.18	73.18	36.11	37.07	70489	6187
灞桥区	Baqiao	20.52	62.54	60.18	30.58	31.96	50694	2522
未央区	Weiyang	28.98	89.39	89.39	43.60	45.79	185270	9311
雁塔区	Yanta	37.81	118.37	118.37	58.11	60.26	210040	13655
阎良区	Yanliang	8.48	27.13	12.46	13.59	13.54	5725	1285
临潼区	Lintong	22.31	72.52	23.88	36.65	35.87	8819	2200
长安区	Chang'an	38.05	122.09	57.98	60.66	61.43	82379	7071
高陵区	Gaoling	11.27	35.77	23.65	17.71	18.06	18539	1158
鄠邑区	Huyi	18.52	62.55	21.30	32.10	30.45	17088	7592
蓝田县	Lantian	19.41	65.53	18.23	34.02	31.51	4158	7584
周至县	Zhouzhi	18.32	69.17	16.42	36.44	32.73	4366	7379

注：本表均为公安年报数据，为西安原口径数据。总户数未机械配平。

4-5 全市及各区县常住人口数和人口变动情况（2018年）

Permanent Population and Population Changes by Region（2018）

区 县	Region	常住人口（万人） Permanent Population (10 000 persons)	城镇 Urban	出生率（‰） Birth Rate（‰）	死亡率（‰） Death Rate（‰）	自然增长率（‰） Natural Growth Rate（‰）
全 市	**Total**	**1000.37**	**740.37**	**12.47**	**5.48**	**6.99**
新城区	Xincheng	64.13	64.13	9.92	3.59	6.33
碑林区	Beilin	67.97	67.97	11.45	4.13	7.32
莲湖区	Lianhu	76.86	76.86	11.01	3.91	7.10
灞桥区	Baqiao	67.73	64.35	12.95	5.57	7.38
未央区	Weiyang	77.74	75.58	12.81	5.45	7.36
雁塔区	Yanta	134.32	134.32	11.98	4.55	7.43
阎良区	Yanliang	30.12	17.29	11.41	5.61	5.80
临潼区	Lintong	69.69	24.42	12.09	5.75	6.34
长安区	Chang'an	104.28	63.26	13.72	7.03	6.69
高陵区	Gaoling	36.26	23.42	13.25	5.95	7.30
鄠邑区	Huyi	55.86	23.60	13.35	6.28	7.07
蓝田县	Lantian	53.68	17.92	14.19	7.18	7.01
周至县	Zhouzhi	59.41	20.17	14.10	7.31	6.79
西咸新区	Xixian	102.32	67.08	12.54	5.53	7.01

注：本表数据均为人口变动抽样调查推算数据。自2017年起常住口径数据为大西安范围，含西咸新区。

4-6 主要年份常住人口数

Permanent Population in Representative Years

单位：万人 （10 000 persons）

年 份 Year	年末常住人口 Permanent Population（year-end）	城镇 Urban	乡村 Rural
2000	741.14	450.36	290.78
2005	806.81	510.55	296.26
2006	822.52	530.94	291.58
2007	830.54	548.99	281.55
2008	837.52	565.16	272.36
2009	843.46	581.40	262.06
2010	847.41	584.71	262.70
2011	851.34	596.79	254.55
2012	855.29	611.62	243.67
2013	858.81	618.77	240.04
2014	862.75	626.44	236.31
2015	870.56	635.68	234.88
2016	883.21	648.54	234.67
2017	961.67	706.06	255.61
2018	1000.37	740.37	260.00

注：2000年常住人口为普查数据。2010年常住人口为年末常住人口数，根据第六次人口普查数据推算得出。2005-2009、2011-2018年常住人口为人口变动抽样调查推算数据。自 201?年起常住口径数据为大西安范围，含西咸新区。

4-7 主要年份社会从业人数

Number of Social Laborers in Representative Years

单位：万人 (10 000 persons)

年份 Year	合计 Total	一、按城乡分 Grouped by Urban Area and Rural Area					二、按三次产业分 Grouped by Industry		
		1.城镇 Urban	国有经济 State-owned Enterprises	集体经济 Collective Enterprises	其他经济 Others	2.乡村 Village	第一产业 Primary Industry	第二产业 Secondary Industry	第三产业 Tertiary Industry
1985	**296.80**	129.07	96.80	29.07	3.20	167.73	135.89	98.61	62.30
1986	**299.45**	132.82	101.28	28.43	3.11	166.63	127.46	100.61	71.38
1987	**312.16**	138.56	104.58	30.72	3.26	173.60	130.36	107.75	74.05
1988	**327.76**	142.24	106.46	30.73	5.05	185.52	138.87	108.12	80.77
1989	**332.65**	145.65	108.80	30.44	6.41	187.00	142.21	106.40	84.04
1990	**343.06**	147.93	110.95	29.78	7.20	195.13	149.64	106.74	86.68
1991	**347.65**	149.48	111.87	29.80	7.81	198.17	152.24	108.19	87.22
1992	**357.51**	151.67	113.19	29.97	8.51	205.84	154.75	110.22	92.54
1993	**363.70**	155.72	112.98	29.77	12.97	207.98	154.02	114.02	95.66
1994	**364.56**	154.88	113.39	27.97	13.52	209.68	153.51	108.53	102.52
1995	**372.60**	158.80	113.79	25.58	19.43	213.80	153.39	109.67	109.54
1996	**379.29**	164.54	113.29	24.82	26.43	214.75	153.43	109.17	116.69
1997	**385.14**	169.52	112.44	23.52	33.56	215.62	153.23	109.46	122.45
1998	**393.95**	177.20	106.06	21.50	49.64	216.75	153.00	110.45	130.50
1999	**400.43**	180.27	105.08	20.50	54.69	220.16	154.64	110.58	135.21
2000	**389.10**	176.45	103.46	18.40	54.59	212.65	147.03	107.26	134.81
2001	**389.30**	177.94	100.47	17.10	60.37	211.36	145.09	108.96	135.25
2002	**397.16**	181.85	100.54	16.90	64.41	215.31	143.04	111.62	142.50
2003	**404.92**	183.23	94.51	16.78	71.94	221.69	146.67	109.09	149.16
2004	**409.57**	187.53	93.43	15.41	78.69	222.04	141.81	111.70	156.06
2005	**415.83**	192.53	93.27	14.47	84.79	223.30	136.31	114.20	165.32
2006	**422.15**	196.16	84.46	14.41	97.29	225.99	135.10	116.09	170.96
2007	**436.36**	214.27	90.58	11.38	111.81	222.09	133.33	125.06	177.97
2008	**448.05**	224.20	90.17	10.60	123.43	223.85	127.87	130.23	189.95
2009	**462.52**	239.39	90.83	7.63	140.93	223.13	122.13	131.57	208.82
2010	**477.58**	252.54	94.01	5.48	153.05	225.04	117.27	145.40	214.91
2011	**495.99**	265.43	91.62	5.33	168.48	230.56	121.05	151.33	223.61
2012	**514.57**	287.65	95.33	5.10	187.22	226.92	114.92	162.35	237.30
2013	**530.71**	308.04	86.06	7.29	214.69	222.67	110.45	151.50	268.76
2014	**532.92**	316.59	84.83	6.67	225.09	216.33	105.02	151.85	276.05
2015	**528.06**	327.68	84.52	5.29	237.87	200.38	107.68	129.51	290.87
2016	**539.18**	335.07	87.15	4.85	243.07	204.11	105.12	127.88	306.18
2017	**596.21**	370.33	86.06	4.46	279.81	225.88	113.17	135.52	347.52
2018	**621.22**	398.23	80.83	3.53	313.87	222.99	101.25	154.02	365.95

注：第一产业从业人员中包括城镇农林牧渔及服务业企业人员。

4-8 按国民经济行业分从业人数（2018年）

单位：万人

行 业	Sector	合计 Total
总计	**Total**	**621.22**
（一）农、林、牧、渔业	Agriculture ,Forestry,Animal Husbandry and Fishery	101.25
（二）采矿业	Mining	2.10
（三）制造业	Manufacturing	83.41
（四）电力、燃气及水的生产供应业	Production and Distribution of Electricity,Gas and Water	5.49
（五）建筑业	Construction	63.02
（六）批发和零售业	Wholesale and Retail Trades	99.95
（七）交通运输、仓储和邮政业	Traffic,Transport,Storage and Post	37.29
（八）住宿和餐饮业	Hotels and Catering Services	49.56
（九）信息传输、软件和信息技术服务业	Information Transmission,Software and Information Technology Services	15.21
（十）金融业	Financial Intermediation	11.24
（十一）房地产业	Real Estate	13.71
（十二）租赁和商务服务业	Leasing and Business Services	22.54
（十三）科学研究和技术服务业	Scientific Research and Technical Services	16.74
（十四）水利、环境和公共设施管理业	Management of Water Conservancy, Environment and Public Facilities	3.64
（十五）居民服务、修理和其他服务业	Services to Households, Repairs and Other Services	30.77
（十六）教育	Education	26.20
（十七）卫生和社会工作	Health and Social Work	19.51
（十八）文化、体育和娱乐业	Culture, Sports and Entertainment	4.98
（十九）公共管理、社会保障和社会组织	Public Administration, Social Security and Social Organizations	14.61
（二十）国际组织	International Organizations	

Number of Employed Persons Grouped by Industry of the National Economy (2018)

(10 000 persons)

国有经济 State-owned Enterprises	集体经济 Collective Enterprises	城镇其他经济 Urban Other Enterprises	城镇私营经济及个体劳动者 Urban Private Enterprises and Individual Labors	乡村从业人员 Rural Employed Persons
80.83	**3.53**	**111.87**	**202.00**	**222.99**
0.15			3.44	97.65
		1.23	0.82	
15.09	0.14	28.77	23.28	16.14
3.05		1.85	0.58	
1.43	2.13	19.09	22.42	17.95
1.05	0.13	9.96	66.96	21.85
11.23	0.03	4.99	9.05	11.99
0.26	0.02	5.04	31.51	12.75
0.07	0.01	10.09	4.06	0.98
1.67	0.18	8.19	0.37	0.82
0.48	0.03	7.30	5.90	
0.68	0.58	4.06	7.54	9.68
8.18	0.08	4.51	3.18	0.78
1.35	0.02	1.50	0.77	
0.78	0.04	0.47	15.89	13.59
14.44	0.02	2.10	1.97	7.68
7.02	0.12	0.85	1.84	9.68
1.02		1.54	2.42	
12.89		0.27		1.45

4-9 城镇非私营单位从业人员情况（2018年）

单位：人

分 组	Classify	单位从业人员 Employed Persons	女性 Female
总计	**Total**	**1962340**	**742577**
一、按机构类型分组	**Grouped by Organization Type**		
#企业	Enterprises	1559443	547427
事业	Public Institutions	281823	152640
机关	Government Units	111507	36563
二、按国民经济行业分组	**Grouped by Economic Sector**		
（一）农业	Agriculture ,Forestry,Animal Husbandry and Fishery	1582	453
（二）采矿业	Mining	12837	3247
（三）制造业	Manufacturing	439950	140602
（四）电力、燃气及水的生产供应业	Production and Distribution of Electricity,Gas and Water	49077	19541
（五）建筑业	Construction	226439	36449
（六）批发和零售业	Wholesale and Retail Trades	111344	59907
（七）交通运输、仓储和邮政业	Traffic,Transport,Storage and Post	162481	41952
（八）住宿和餐饮业	Hotels and Catering Services	53231	30782
（九）信息传输、软件和信息技术服务业	Information Transmission,Software and Information Technology Services	101678	38491
（十）金融业	Financial Intermediation	100430	51571
（十一）房地产业	Real Estate	78113	32799
（十二）租赁和商务服务业	Leasing and Business Services	53205	22728
（十三）科学研究和技术服务业	Scientific Research and Technical Services	127739	40159
（十四）水利、环境和公共设施管理业	Management of Water Conservancy, Environment and Public Facilities	28745	12899
（十五）居民服务、修理和其他服务业	Services to Households, Repairs and Other Services	12883	6153
（十六）教育	Education	165520	92137
（十七）卫生和社会工作	Health and Social Work	79874	56079
（十八）文化、体育和娱乐业	Culture, Sports and Entertainment	25606	12213
（十九）公共管理、社会保障和社会组织	Public Administration, Social Security and Social Organizations	131606	44415
（二十）国际组织	International Organizations		

注：2018年表名中“全部单位”改为“城镇非私营单位”。下同。

Basic Facts on Employees in Urban Non-Private Units （2018）

(person)

在岗职工合计 Total Fully Employed Staff and Workers	其他从业人员 Other Employed Persons	单位从业人员平均人数 Average Employment	在岗职工合计 Staff and Workers	其他从业人员 Other Employed Persons
1817568	**144772**	**2001383**	**1862515**	**138868**
1443809	115634	1587613	1477162	110451
266834	14989	292270	278026	14244
98077	13430	112127	98598	13529
1572	10	1575	1565	10
12067	770	16017	15311	706
432493	7457	458186	450529	7657
47762	1315	64047	62701	1346
204434	22005	215383	194018	21365
107325	4019	112473	108214	4259
157285	5196	165803	160789	5014
47153	6078	51773	45899	5874
100452	1226	97787	96523	1264
59950	40480	101580	62062	39518
75822	2291	78134	75726	2408
35853	17352	50622	36973	13649
123961	3778	132873	128909	3964
26237	2508	28775	26376	2399
12839	44	14277	14242	35
153738	11782	172603	161262	11341
77171	2703	82074	79758	2316
24152	1454	25204	23876	1328
117302	14304	132197	117782	14415

4-10 城镇国有单位从业人员情况（2018年）

单位：人

分 组	Classify	单位从业人员 Employed Persons	女性 Female
总计	**Total**	**808251**	**326392**
一、按机构类型分组	**Grouped by Organization Type**		
#企业	Enterprises	422188	140862
事业	Public Institutions	273998	148829
机关	Government Units	111099	36372
二、按国民经济行业分组	**Grouped by Economic Sector**		
（一）农业	Agriculture ,Forestry,Animal Husbandry and Fishery	1545	437
（二）采矿业	Mining		
（三）制造业	Manufacturing	150890	50987
（四）电力、燃气及水的生产供应业	Production and Distribution of Electricity,Gas and Water	30517	13693
（五）建筑业	Construction	14270	2109
（六）批发和零售业	Wholesale and Retail Trades	10457	5568
（七）交通运输、仓储和邮政业	Traffic,Transport,Storage and Post	112275	25126
（八）住宿和餐饮业	Hotels and Catering Services	2576	1498
（九）信息传输、软件和信息技术服务业	Information Transmission,Software and Information Technology Services	747	178
（十）金融业	Financial Intermediation	16717	8178
（十一）房地产业	Real Estate	4780	1792
（十二）租赁和商务服务业	Leasing and Business Services	6767	3152
（十三）科学研究和技术服务业	Scientific Research and Technical Services	81833	27277
（十四）水利、环境和公共设施管理业	Management of Water Conservancy, Environment and Public Facilities	13532	6560
（十五）居民服务、修理和其他服务业	Services to Households, Repairs and Other Services	7755	3266
（十六）教育	Education	144352	79364
（十七）卫生和社会工作	Health and Social Work	70203	49305
（十八）文化、体育和娱乐业	Culture, Sports and Entertainment	10175	4679
（十九）公共管理、社会保障和社会组织	Public Administration, Social Security and Social Organizations	128860	43223
（二十）国际组织	International Organizations		

Basic Facts on Employees in State-owned Units（2018）

(person)

		单位从业人员 平均人数 Average Employment		
在岗职工合计 Total Fully Employed Staff and Workers	其他从业人员 Other Employed Persons		在岗职工合计 Staff and Workers	其他从业人员 Other Employed Persons
767479	**40772**	**852564**	**812943**	**39621**
409458	12730	455427	443149	12278
259617	14381	284458	270825	13633
97700	13399	111719	98221	13498
1535	10	1538	1528	10
149116	1774	164970	163419	1551
30430	87	45704	45617	87
13511	759	12889	12043	846
9909	548	10059	9670	389
109529	2746	115069	112323	2746
2143	433	2584	2145	439
554	193	770	598	172
13403	3314	17327	14417	2910
4741	39	4774	4726	48
6378	389	6876	6428	448
79973	1860	83768	81723	2045
11546	1986	13635	11671	1964
7724	31	8819	8798	21
134901	9451	151506	142426	9080
67667	2536	72671	70521	2150
9829	346	10162	9828	334
114590	14270	129443	115062	14381

4-11 城镇集体单位从业人员情况（2018年）

单位：人

分 组	Classify	单位从业人员 Employed Persons	女性 Female
总计	**Total**	**35341**	**7266**
一、按机构类型分组	**Grouped by Organization Type**		
#企业	Enterprises	34212	6618
事业	Public Institutions	1047	584
机关	Government Units	26	16
二、按国民经济行业分组	**Grouped by Economic Sector**		
（一）农业	Agriculture ,Forestry,Animal Husbandry and Fishery		
（二）采矿业	Mining		
（三）制造业	Manufacturing	1378	470
（四）电力、燃气及水的生产供应业	Production and Distribution of Electricity,Gas and Water	15	3
（五）建筑业	Construction	21314	2648
（六）批发和零售业	Wholesale and Retail Trades	1334	454
（七）交通运输、仓储和邮政业	Traffic,Transport,Storage and Post	308	114
（八）住宿和餐饮业	Hotels and Catering Services	208	111
（九）信息传输、软件和信息技术服务业	Information Transmission,Software and Information Technology Services	62	25
（十）金融业	Financial Intermediation	1824	878
（十一）房地产业	Real Estate	310	114
（十二）租赁和商务服务业	Leasing and Business Services	5813	903
（十三）科学研究和技术服务业	Scientific Research and Technical Services	821	436
（十四）水利、环境和公共设施管理业	Management of Water Conservancy, Environment and Public Facilities	172	107
（十五）居民服务、修理和其他服务业	Services to Households, Repairs and Other Services	396	180
（十六）教育	Education	183	140
（十七）卫生和社会工作	Health and Social Work	1150	661
（十八）文化、体育和娱乐业	Culture, Sports and Entertainment	14	2
（十九）公共管理、社会保障和社会组织	Public Administration, Social Security and Social Organizations	39	20
（二十）国际组织	International Organizations		

Basic Facts on Employees in Urban Collective-owned Units（2018）

(person)

		单位从业人员		
在岗职工合计 Total Fully Employed Staff and Workers	其他从业人员 Other Employed Persons	平均人数 Average Employment	在岗职工合计 Staff and Workers	其他从业人员 Other Employed Persons
33832	**1509**	**33409**	**32014**	**1395**
32756	1456	32286	30944	1342
994	53	1049	996	53
26		26	26	
1269	109	1427	1324	103
15		15	15	
20293	1021	19601	18700	901
1128	206	1321	1116	205
308		323	323	
208		191	191	
62		68	68	
1773	51	1874	1808	66
279	31	311	280	31
5813		5534	5534	
744	77	817	742	75
172		172	172	
396		434	434	
183		183	183	
1136	14	1085	1071	14
14		14	14	
39		39	39	

4-12　城镇非私营其他经济类型单位从业人员情况（2018年）

单位：人

分　组	Classify	单位从业人员 Employed Persons	女性 Female
总计	**Total**	**1118748**	**408919**
一、按机构类型分组	**Grouped by Organization Type**		
#企业	Enterprises	1103043	399947
事业	Public Institutions	6778	3227
机关	Government Units	382	175
二、按国民经济行业分组	**Grouped by Economic Sector**		
（一）农业	Agriculture ,Forestry,Animal Husbandry and Fishery	37	16
（二）采矿业	Mining	12837	3247
（三）制造业	Manufacturing	287682	89145
（四）电力、燃气及水的生产供应业	Production and Distribution of Electricity,Gas and Water	18545	5845
（五）建筑业	Construction	190855	31692
（六）批发和零售业	Wholesale and Retail Trades	99553	53885
（七）交通运输、仓储和邮政业	Traffic,Transport,Storage and Post	49898	16712
（八）住宿和餐饮业	Hotels and Catering Services	50447	29173
（九）信息传输、软件和信息技术服务业	Information Transmission,Software and Information Technology Services	100869	38288
（十）金融业	Financial Intermediation	81889	42515
（十一）房地产业	Real Estate	73023	30893
（十二）租赁和商务服务业	Leasing and Business Services	40625	18673
（十三）科学研究和技术服务业	Scientific Research and Technical Services	45085	12446
（十四）水利、环境和公共设施管理业	Management of Water Conservancy, Environment and Public Facilities	15041	6232
（十五）居民服务、修理和其他服务业	Services to Households, Repairs and Other Services	4732	2707
（十六）教育	Education	20985	12633
（十七）卫生和社会工作	Health and Social Work	8521	6113
（十八）文化、体育和娱乐业	Culture, Sports and Entertainment	15417	7532
（十九）公共管理、社会保障和社会组织	Public Administration, Social Security and Social Organizations	2707	1172
（二十）国际组织	International Organizations		

Basic Facts on Employees in Urban Non-Private Other Units（2018）

(person)

		单位从业人员 平均人数 Average Employment		
在岗职工合计 Total Fully Employed Staff and Workers	其他从业人员 Other Employed Persons		在岗职工合计 Staff and Workers	其他从业人员 Other Employed Persons
1016257	**102491**	**1115410**	**1017558**	**97852**
1001595	101448	1099900	1003069	96831
6223	555	6763	6205	558
351	31	382	351	31
37		37	37	
12067	770	16017	15311	706
282108	5574	291789	285786	6003
17317	1228	18328	17069	1259
170630	20225	182893	163275	19618
96288	3265	101093	97428	3665
47448	2450	50411	48143	2268
44802	5645	48998	43563	5435
99836	1033	96949	95857	1092
44774	37115	82379	45837	36542
70802	2221	73049	70720	2329
23662	16963	38212	25011	13201
43244	1841	48288	46444	1844
14519	522	14968	14533	435
4719	13	5024	5010	14
18654	2331	20914	18653	2261
8368	153	8318	8166	152
14309	1108	15028	14034	994
2673	34	2715	2681	34

4-13 城镇非私营单位分行业从业人员年平均工资

单位：元

分 组	Classify	2010
总计	**Grouped by Economic Sector**	**37870**
（一）农、林、牧、渔业	Agriculture ,Forestry,Animal Husbandry and Fishery	21436
（二）采矿业	Mining	32154
（三）制造业	Manufacturing	26663
（四）电力、燃气及水的生产供应业	Production and Distribution of Electricity,Gas and Water	39508
（五）建筑业	Construction	26875
（六）批发和零售业	Wholesale and Retail Trades	25103
（七）交通运输、仓储和邮政业	Traffic,Transport,Storage and Post	41737
（八）住宿和餐饮业	Hotels and Catering Services	19647
（九）信息传输、软件和信息技术服务业	Information Transmission,Software and Information Technology Services	45904
（十）金融业	Financial Intermediation	63952
（十一）房地产业	Real Estate	45273
（十二）租赁和商务服务业	Leasing and Business Services	30267
（十三）科学研究和技术服务业	Scientific Research and Technical Services	55456
（十四）水利、环境和公共设施管理业	Management of Water Conservancy, Environment and Public Facilities	25322
（十五）居民服务、修理和其他服务业	Services to Households, Repairs and Other Services	26443
（十六）教育	Education	53084
（十七）卫生和社会工作	Health and Social Work	44035
（十八）文化、体育和娱乐业	Culture, Sports and Entertainment	31925
（十九）公共管理、社会保障和社会组织	Public Administration, Social Security and Social Organizations	39964
（二十）国际组织	International Organizations	

Average Wages of Urban Non-private Employees by Industry

(yuan)

2011	2012	2013	2014	2015	2016	2017	2018
41679	**44533**	**49350**	**54573**	**60557**	**67205**	**75262**	**83821**
23567	31846	36658	42881	43426	48626	52020	72890
38551	33489	40605	42116	46645	108827	118026	99400
34698	38957	44321	49482	56686	61434	66067	73733
47705	55409	59955	61252	65887	69092	77674	70021
29773	35828	39507	48275	52783	60475	68025	73963
27996	34382	37362	40915	46203	48210	55793	62362
48231	48760	54147	59189	62816	63583	69469	88547
22925	26637	29497	30914	33746	37507	41147	42970
51135	63328	67495	100550	109448	137210	142407	150081
72195	75652	97140	104433	106807	108569	114884	108643
34626	37567	44832	48120	52423	56979	57970	65726
31549	34291	42109	46828	52637	54395	53474	54940
64448	68274	69951	69958	72731	79539	86199	103604
26009	29938	38429	43033	45356	44062	48277	54127
23993	25103	32066	32478	37019	35721	35979	56707
54442	54581	59143	58451	63761	71635	86672	98158
48836	56764	61602	59892	61623	74797	86521	99523
34717	40833	50201	57239	61561	65974	70202	74588
42163	47691	49893	47000	51681	59437	77660	84567

4-14 主要年份城镇非私营单位从业人数及工资总额

Number of Urban Non-Private Employees and Remuneration in Representative Years

年份 year	单位从业人员（万人） Number of Employed Persons (10 000 persons)	从业人员工资总额（亿元） Remuneration of Employed Persons (100mil. yuan)	城镇非私营单位从业人员年平均工资（元） Annual Average Wage of Employees in Urban Non-private Units(yuan)	城镇国有单位从业人员年平均工资（元） Annual Average Wage of Employees in State-owned Units(yuan)	城镇集体单位从业人员年平均工资（元） Annual Average Wage of Employees in Urban Collective Units(yuan)	城镇非私营其它经济类型单位从业人员年平均工资（元） Average Wages of Urban Non-private Basic Facts on Employees in other Units(yuan)
1978	93.56	6.28	688	705	609	
1980	103.09	8.17	818	849	699	
1985	127.04	14.17	1148	1215	923	1409
1986	132.78	16.87	1311	1388	1048	1659
1987	135.48	19.13	1446	1544	1107	1583
1988	137.56	22.81	1702	1842	1216	2065
1989	139.86	25.64	1873	2010	1385	2188
1990	141.55	29.48	2133	2290	1545	2044
1991	142.86	26.88	2276	2435	1657	2966
1992	144.51	30.80	2545	2758	1709	3504
1993	146.03	43.25	2999	3274	1910	3551
1994	142.37	58.87	4172	4588	2337	5243
1995	141.17	67.23	4763	5168	2837	5863
1996	140.60	75.64	5407	5858	3216	6225
1997	138.89	80.83	5785	6204	3437	7487
1998	138.78	82.85	6900	7445	3964	6942
1999	115.88	90.13	7764	8238	4374	8217
2000	112.45	103.80	9179	9742	5178	9451
2001	113.93	123.12	10786	11570	5431	10781
2002	115.77	138.88	12138	12877	6230	12543
2003	116.68	155.95	13504	14217	6892	14215
2004	118.15	184.63	15473	15994	7428	17030
2005	123.66	215.67	17728	18420	7612	19066
2006	125.10	250.87	20475	21392	8494	21859
2007	129.40	319.23	25012	25696	9768	27400
2008	130.85	379.29	29749	30246	10834	33344
2009	135.64	450.48	34032	34611	11940	37307
2010	140.38	520.88	37870	38122	12505	40721
2011	154.33	658.73	41679	45217	23241	37643
2012	165.59	770.86	44533	47493	29988	41218
2013	198.42	1031.46	49350	52782	34591	47462
2014	199.41	1151.53	54573	54138	41006	55766
2015	198.46	1255.75	60557	60301	43291	61590
2016	199.19	1358.95	67205	66295	48098	68847
2017	202.29	1542.35	75262	76682	54755	74999
2018	196.23	1677.57	83821	87096	53048	82239

注：因1989年以前，西安市行政区划有几次调整，本表按1989年西安行政区划对1989年前的历史数据进行了调整。

4-15 城镇非私营单位从业人员工资总额（2018年）

Total Wages of Urban Non-Private Units Employees（2018）

单位：万元　　　　(10 000yuan)

分　组	Classify	单位从业人员工资总额 Total Wages of Employment	在岗职工工资总额 Total Wages of Employed Staff and Workers
总计	**Total**	**16775748**	**16227249**
一、按机构类型分组	**Grouped by Organization Type**		
#企业	Enterprises	12936106	12480964
事业	Public Institutions	2841496	2785015
机关	Government Units	949778	914975
二、按国民经济行业分组	**Grouped by Economic Sector**		
（一）农业	Agriculture ,Forestry,Animal Husbandry and Fishery	11480	11458
（二）采矿业	Mining	159209	153075
（三）制造业	Manufacturing	3378358	3341844
（四）电力、燃气及水的生产供应业	Production and Distribution of Electricity, Gas and Water	448466	444620
（五）建筑业	Construction	1593046	1467535
（六）批发和零售业	Wholesale and Retail Trades	701399	685337
（七）交通运输、仓储和邮政业	Traffic,Transport,Storage and Post	1468137	1439250
（八）住宿和餐饮业	Hotels and Catering Services	222471	209656
（九）信息传输、软件和信息技术服务业	Information Transmission,Software and Information Technology Services	1467594	1460069
（十）金融业	Financial Intermediation	1103592	985750
（十一）房地产业	Real Estate	513543	503681
（十二）租赁和商务服务业	Leasing and Business Services	278118	231555
（十三）科学研究和技术服务业	Scientific Research and Technical Services	1376615	1353945
（十四）水利、环境和公共设施管理业	Management of Water Conservancy, Environment and Public Facilities	155750	147912
（十五）居民服务、修理和其他服务业	Services to Households, Repairs and Other Services	80961	80820
（十六）教育	Education	1694241	1647460
（十七）卫生和社会工作	Health and Social Work	816824	802703
（十八）文化、体育和娱乐业	Culture, Sports and Entertainment	187992	180061
（十九）公共管理、社会保障和社会组织	Public Administration, Social Security and Social Organizations	1117952	1080517
（二十）国际组织	International Organizations		

4-15 续表 continued

单位：万元 (10 000 yuan)

分　组	Classify	其他从业人员工资总额 Remuneration of Other Employed Persons	从业人员年平均工资（元） Average Wages of Employees (yuan)
总计	**Total**	**548499**	**83821**
一、按机构类型分组	**Grouped by Organization Type**		
#企业	Enterprises	455142	81481
事业	Public Institutions	56481	97222
机关	Government Units	34803	84706
二、按国民经济行业分组	**Grouped by Economic Sector**		
（一）农业	Agriculture ,Forestry,Animal Husbandry and Fishery	22	72890
（二）采矿业	Mining	6134	99400
（三）制造业	Manufacturing	36513	73733
（四）电力、燃气及水的生产供应业	Production and Distribution of Electricity, Gas and Water	3845	70021
（五）建筑业	Construction	125513	73963
（六）批发和零售业	Wholesale and Retail Trades	16062	62362
（七）交通运输、仓储和邮政业	Traffic,Transport,Storage and Post	28887	88547
（八）住宿和餐饮业	Hotels and Catering Services	12815	42970
（九）信息传输、软件和信息技术服务业	Information Transmission,Software and Information Technology Services	7525	150081
（十）金融业	Financial Intermediation	117842	108643
（十一）房地产业	Real Estate	9862	65726
（十二）租赁和商务服务业	Leasing and Business Services	46563	54940
（十三）科学研究和技术服务业	Scientific Research and Technical Services	22670	103604
（十四）水利、环境和公共设施管理业	Management of Water Conservancy, Environment and Public Facilities	7837	54127
（十五）居民服务、修理和其他服务业	Services to Households, Repairs and Other Services	140	56707
（十六）教育	Education	46782	98158
（十七）卫生和社会工作	Health and Social Work	14121	99523
（十八）文化、体育和娱乐业	Culture, Sports and Entertainment	7932	74588
（十九）公共管理、社会保障和社会组织	Public Administration, Social Security and Social Organizations	37435	84567
（二十）国际组织	International Organizations		

4-16 城镇国有单位从业人员工资总额（2018年）

Total Average of Urban State-owned Units Employees（2018）

单位：万元 （10 000yuan）

分 组	Classify	单位从业人员工资总额 Total Wages of Employment	在岗职工工资总额 Total Wages of Employed Staff and Workers
总计	**Total**	**7425512**	**7276514**
一、按机构类型分组	**Grouped by Organization Type**		
#企业	Enterprises	3697731	3638532
事业	Public Institutions	2775857	2721248
机关	Government Units	946300	911603
二、按国民经济行业分组	**Grouped by Economic Sector**		
（一）农业	Agriculture ,Forestry,Animal Husbandry and Fishery	11357	11334
（二）采矿业	Mining		
（三）制造业	Manufacturing	1082093	1076380
（四）电力、燃气及水的生产供应业	Production and Distribution of Electricity, Gas and Water	284693	284510
（五）建筑业	Construction	83089	79042
（六）批发和零售业	Wholesale and Retail Trades	64565	63155
（七）交通运输、仓储和邮政业	Traffic,Transport,Storage and Post	1089801	1075114
（八）住宿和餐饮业	Hotels and Catering Services	10436	9305
（九）信息传输、软件和信息技术服务业	Information Transmission,Software and Information Technology Services	4235	3470
（十）金融业	Financial Intermediation	268236	260673
（十一）房地产业	Real Estate	28968	28724
（十二）租赁和商务服务业	Leasing and Business Services	46885	45323
（十三）科学研究和技术服务业	Scientific Research and Technical Services	821970	807761
（十四）水利、环境和公共设施管理业	Management of Water Conservancy, Environment and Public Facilities	72820	66749
（十五）居民服务、修理和其他服务业	Services to Households, Repairs and Other Services	54684	54588
（十六）教育	Education	1558140	1519420
（十七）卫生和社会工作	Health and Social Work	756341	743227
（十八）文化、体育和娱乐业	Culture, Sports and Entertainment	92628	90492
（十九）公共管理、社会保障和社会组织	Public Administration, Social Security and Social Organizations	1094571	1057247
（二十）国际组织	International Organizations		

4-16 续表 continued

单位：万元 (10 000yuan)

分 组	Classify	其他从业人员工资总额 Remuneration of Other Employed Persons	从业人员年平均工资（元） Average Wages of Employees (yuan)
总计	**Total**	**148998**	**87096**
一、按机构类型分组	**Grouped by Organization Type**		
#企业	Enterprises	59198	81193
事业	Public Institutions	54609	97584
机关	Government Units	34697	84704
二、按国民经济行业分组	**Grouped by Economic Sector**		
（一）农业	Agriculture ,Forestry,Animal Husbandry and Fishery	22	73841
（二）采矿业	Mining		
（三）制造业	Manufacturing	5713	65593
（四）电力、燃气及水的生产供应业	Production and Distribution of Electricity, Gas and Water	183	62291
（五）建筑业	Construction	4046	64464
（六）批发和零售业	Wholesale and Retail Trades	1410	64186
（七）交通运输、仓储和邮政业	Traffic,Transport,Storage and Post	14688	94708
（八）住宿和餐饮业	Hotels and Catering Services	1131	40386
（九）信息传输、软件和信息技术服务业	Information Transmission,Software and Information Technology Services	765	55003
（十）金融业	Financial Intermediation	7563	154808
（十一）房地产业	Real Estate	244	60678
（十二）租赁和商务服务业	Leasing and Business Services	1562	68187
（十三）科学研究和技术服务业	Scientific Research and Technical Services	14209	98125
（十四）水利、环境和公共设施管理业	Management of Water Conservancy, Environment and Public Facilities	6071	53407
（十五）居民服务、修理和其他服务业	Services to Households, Repairs and Other Services	96	62007
（十六）教育	Education	38720	102843
（十七）卫生和社会工作	Health and Social Work	13115	104077
（十八）文化、体育和娱乐业	Culture, Sports and Entertainment	2136	91151
（十九）公共管理、社会保障和社会组织	Public Administration, Social Security and Social Organizations	37324	84560
（二十）国际组织	International Organizations		

4-17 城镇集体单位从业人员工资总额（2018年）

Total Average of Basic Facts on Employees in Urban Collective-owned Units（2018）

单位：万元 （10 000yuan）

分组	Classify	单位从业人员工资总额 Total Wages of Employment	在岗职工工资总额 Total Wages of Employed Staff and Workers
总计	**Total**	**177229**	**169671**
一、按机构类型分组	**Grouped by Organization Type**		
#企业	Enterprises	169987	162510
事业	Public Institutions	6836	6756
机关	Government Units	231	231
二、按国民经济行业分组	**Grouped by Economic Sector**		
（一）农业	Agriculture ,Forestry,Animal Husbandry and Fishery		
（二）采矿业	Mining		
（三）制造业	Manufacturing	5782	5353
（四）电力、燃气及水的生产供应业	Production and Distribution of Electricity, Gas and Water	48	48
（五）建筑业	Construction	98832	93310
（六）批发和零售业	Wholesale and Retail Trades	5075	4402
（七）交通运输、仓储和邮政业	Traffic,Transport,Storage and Post	3102	3102
（八）住宿和餐饮业	Hotels and Catering Services	792	792
（九）信息传输、软件和信息技术服务业	Information Transmission,Software and Information Technology Services	427	427
（十）金融业	Financial Intermediation	23533	23051
（十一）房地产业	Real Estate	1642	1575
（十二）租赁和商务服务业	Leasing and Business Services	22350	22350
（十三）科学研究和技术服务业	Scientific Research and Technical Services	6263	5944
（十四）水利、环境和公共设施管理业	Management of Water Conservancy, Environment and Public Facilities	623	623
（十五）居民服务、修理和其他服务业	Services to Households, Repairs and Other Services	2512	2512
（十六）教育	Education	1233	1233
（十七）卫生和社会工作	Health and Social Work	4673	4608
（十八）文化、体育和娱乐业	Culture, Sports and Entertainment	41	41
（十九）公共管理、社会保障和社会组织	Public Administration, Social Security and Social Organizations	301	301
（二十）国际组织	International Organizations		

4-17 续表 continued

单位：万元 (10 000 yuan)

分 组	Classify	其他从业人员工资总额 Remuneration of Other Employed Persons	从业人员年平均工资（元） Average Wages of Employees (yuan)
总计	**Total**	**7558**	**53048**
一、按机构类型分组	**Grouped by Organization Type**		
#企业	Enterprises	7478	52650
事业	Public Institutions	80	65169
机关	Government Units		88654
二、按国民经济行业分组	**Grouped by Economic Sector**		
（一）农业	Agriculture ,Forestry,Animal Husbandry and Fishery		
（二）采矿业	Mining		
（三）制造业	Manufacturing	429	40516
（四）电力、燃气及水的生产供应业	Production and Distribution of Electricity, Gas and Water		32067
（五）建筑业	Construction	5522	50422
（六）批发和零售业	Wholesale and Retail Trades	673	38421
（七）交通运输、仓储和邮政业	Traffic,Transport,Storage and Post		96037
（八）住宿和餐饮业	Hotels and Catering Services		41455
（九）信息传输、软件和信息技术服务业	Information Transmission,Software and Information Technology Services		62750
（十）金融业	Financial Intermediation	483	125580
（十一）房地产业	Real Estate	68	52807
（十二）租赁和商务服务业	Leasing and Business Services		40387
（十三）科学研究和技术服务业	Scientific Research and Technical Services	319	76660
（十四）水利、环境和公共设施管理业	Management of Water Conservancy, Environment and Public Facilities		36192
（十五）居民服务、修理和其他服务业	Services to Households, Repairs and Other Services		57889
（十六）教育	Education		67366
（十七）卫生和社会工作	Health and Social Work	64	43065
（十八）文化、体育和娱乐业	Culture, Sports and Entertainment		29214
（十九）公共管理、社会保障和社会组织	Public Administration, Social Security and Social Organizations		77179
（二十）国际组织	International Organizations		

4-18 城镇非私营其他经济类型单位从业人员工资总额（2018年）

Average Wages of Urban Non-private Basic Facts on Employees in other Units (2018)

单位：万元 (10 000yuan)

分 组	Classify	单位从业人员工资总额 Total Wages of Employment	在岗职工工资总额 Total Wages of Employed Staff and Workers
总计	**Total**	**9173007**	**8781064**
一、按机构类型分组	**Grouped by Organization Type**		
#企业	Enterprises	9068388	8679923
事业	Public Institutions	58803	57011
机关	Government Units	3247	3142
二、按国民经济行业分组	**Grouped by Economic Sector**		
（一）农业	Agriculture ,Forestry,Animal Husbandry and Fishery	123	123
（二）采矿业	Mining	159209	153075
（三）制造业	Manufacturing	2290483	2260112
（四）电力、燃气及水的生产供应业	Production and Distribution of Electricity, Gas and Water	163723	160062
（五）建筑业	Construction	1411128	1295183
（六）批发和零售业	Wholesale and Retail Trades	631759	617780
（七）交通运输、仓储和邮政业	Traffic,Transport,Storage and Post	375234	361034
（八）住宿和餐饮业	Hotels and Catering Services	211243	199560
（九）信息传输、软件和信息技术服务业	Information Transmission,Software and Information Technology Services	1462932	1456172
（十）金融业	Financial Intermediation	811822	702026
（十一）房地产业	Real Estate	482933	473383
（十二）租赁和商务服务业	Leasing and Business Services	208882	163882
（十三）科学研究和技术服务业	Scientific Research and Technical Services	548382	540240
（十四）水利、环境和公共设施管理业	Management of Water Conservancy, Environment and Public Facilities	82307	80541
（十五）居民服务、修理和其他服务业	Services to Households, Repairs and Other Services	23765	23720
（十六）教育	Education	134868	126807
（十七）卫生和社会工作	Health and Social Work	55810	54868
（十八）文化、体育和娱乐业	Culture, Sports and Entertainment	95324	89528
（十九）公共管理、社会保障和社会组织	Public Administration, Social Security and Social Organizations	23080	22969
（二十）国际组织	International Organizations		

4-18 续表 continued

单位：万元 (10 000 yuan)

分 组	Classify	其他从业人员工资总额 Remuneration of Other Employed Persons	从业人员年平均工资（元） Average Wages of Employees (yuan)
总计	**Total**	**391943**	**82239**
一、按机构类型分组	**Grouped by Organization Type**		
#企业	Enterprises	388465	82447
事业	Public Institutions	1792	86949
机关	Government Units	106	85003
二、按国民经济行业分组	**Grouped by Economic Sector**		
（一）农业	Agriculture ,Forestry,Animal Husbandry and Fishery		33351
（二）采矿业	Mining	6134	99400
（三）制造业	Manufacturing	30372	78498
（四）电力、燃气及水的生产供应业	Production and Distribution of Electricity, Gas and Water	3662	89330
（五）建筑业	Construction	115945	77156
（六）批发和零售业	Wholesale and Retail Trades	13979	62493
（七）交通运输、仓储和邮政业	Traffic,Transport,Storage and Post	14200	74435
（八）住宿和餐饮业	Hotels and Catering Services	11683	43113
（九）信息传输、软件和信息技术服务业	Information Transmission,Software and Information Technology Services	6760	150897
（十）金融业	Financial Intermediation	109795	98547
（十一）房地产业	Real Estate	9550	66111
（十二）租赁和商务服务业	Leasing and Business Services	45000	54664
（十三）科学研究和技术服务业	Scientific Research and Technical Services	8142	113565
（十四）水利、环境和公共设施管理业	Management of Water Conservancy, Environment and Public Facilities	1766	54989
（十五）居民服务、修理和其他服务业	Services to Households, Repairs and Other Services	44	47302
（十六）教育	Education	8062	64487
（十七）卫生和社会工作	Health and Social Work	943	67096
（十八）文化、体育和娱乐业	Culture, Sports and Entertainment	5796	63431
（十九）公共管理、社会保障和社会组织	Public Administration, Social Security and Social Organizations	111	85007
（二十）国际组织	International Organizations		

4-19 主要年份城镇登记失业人数及失业率

Registered Unemployed Persons and Unemployment Rate in Urban Area in Representative Years

年份 year	城镇登记失业人员数（万人） Real Number of Registered Unemployed Persons (10 000 persons)	城镇登记失业率（%） Registered Unemployment in Urban Area (%)
2002		3.7
2003		4.5
2004	8.29	4.3
2005	8.45	4.3
2006	8.74	4.3
2007	8.77	4.3
2008	9.40	4.2
2009	10.02	4.3
2010	10.46	4.2
2011	10.37	3.9
2012	9.60	3.5
2013	10.13	3.4
2014	10.84	3.4
2015	10.74	3.4
2016	11.29	3.3
2017	11.51	3.3
2018	12.48	3.3

注：本表数据由西安市人力资源与社会保障局提供。

主要统计指标解释

人口数 指一定时点、一定地区范围内的有生命的个人的总和。年度统计的年末人口数，指每年12月31日24时的人口数。

常住人口 指实际经常居住在某地区一定时间（半年以上，含半年）的人口。常住人口包括户口在本辖区人也在本辖区居住的人，户口在本辖区之外但在户口登记地半年以上的人，户口待定（无户口和口袋户口）的人，户口在本辖区但离开本辖区半年以下的人。

城镇人口和乡村人口 城镇人口是指居住在城镇范围内的全部常住人口；乡村人口是除上述人口以外的全部人口。

出生率（又称粗出生率） 指在一定时期内（通常为一年）平均每千人所出生的人数的比率，一般用千分率表示。其计算公式为：

出生率＝年出生人数／年平均人数×1000‰

式中：出生人数指活产婴儿，即胎儿脱离母体时（不管怀孕月数），有过呼吸或其他生命现象。年平均人数指年初、年底人口数的平均数，也可用年中人口数代替。

死亡率（又称粗死亡率） 指在一定时期内（通常为一年）一定地区的死亡人数与同期内平均人数（或期中人数）之比，一般用千分率表示。本资料中的死亡率指年死亡率，其计算公式为：

死亡率＝年死亡人数／年平均人数×1000‰

人口自然增长率 指在一定时期内（通常为一年）人口自然增加数（出生人数减死亡人数）与该时期内平均人数（或期中人数）之比，一般用千分率表示。计算公式为：

人口自然增长率＝（本年出生人数—本年死亡人数）／年平均人数×1000‰。

从业人员 指在16周岁及以上，从事一定社会劳动并取得劳动报酬或经营收入的人员。这一指标反映了一定时期内全部劳动力资源的实际利用情况，是研究我国基本国情国力的重要指标。

单位从业人员 指在各级国家机关、政党机关、社会团体及企业、事业单位中工作，取得工资或其他形式的劳动报酬的全部人员。包括在岗职工、再就业的离退休人员、民办教师以及在各单位中工作的外方人员和港澳台方人员、兼职人员、借用的外单位人员和第二职业者。不包括离开本单位仍保留劳动关系的职工。各单位的就业人员反映了各单位实际参加生产或工作的全部劳动力。

城镇私营和个体就业人员 城镇私营就业人员指在工商管理部门注册登记，其经营地址设在县城关镇（含城关镇）以上的私营企业就业人员；包括私营企业投资者和雇工。城镇个体就业人员指在工商管理部门注册登记，并持有城镇户口或在城镇长期居住，经批准从事个体工商经营的就业人员；包括个体经营者和在个体工商户劳动的家庭帮工和雇工。

国有单位 指资产归国家所有的经济组织。包括按《中华人民共和国企业法人登记管理条例》规定登记注册的非公司制的经济组织，以及中央、地方各级国家机关、事业单位和社会团体。

集体单位 指生产资料归集体所有，并按《中华人民共和国企业法人登记管理条例》规定登记注册的经济组织。

其他单位 包括股份合作单位、联营单位、有限责任公司、股份有限公司、港澳台商投资单位以及外商投资单位等其他登记注册类型单位。

在岗职工 指在本单位工作并由单位支付工资的人员，以及有工作岗位，但由于学习、病伤产假等原因暂未工作，仍由单位支付工资的人员。

职工工资总额 指各单位在一定时期内直接支付给本单位全部职工的劳动报酬总额。工资总额的计算原则应以直接支付给职工的全部劳动报酬为根据。各单位支付给职工的劳动报酬以及其他根据有关规定支付的工资，不论是计入成本的还是不计入成本的，不论是按国家规定列入计征奖金税项目的，还是未列入计征奖金税项目的，不论是以货币形式支付的还是以实物形式支付的，均包括在工资总额内。

职工平均工资 指企业、事业、机关单位的职工在一定时期内平均每人所得的货币工资额。它表明一定时期职工工资收入的高低程度，是反映职工工资水平的主要指标。计算公式为：

职工平均工资＝报告期实际支付的全部职工工资总额/报告期全部职工平均人数

城镇登记失业人员 指有非农业户口，在一定的劳动年龄内，有劳动能力，无业而要求就业，并在当地就业服务机构进行求职登记的人员。

城镇登记失业率 指城镇登记失业人数同城镇从业人数与城镇从业人数与城镇登记失业人数之和的比。计算公式为：

$$\text{城镇登记失业率}=\frac{\text{城镇登记失业人数}}{\text{（城镇单位就业人员－使用的农村劳动力－聘用的离退休人员－聘用的港澳台及外方人员）＋不在岗职工＋城镇私营业主＋城镇个体户主＋城镇私营企业及个体就业人员＋城镇登记失业人数}}\times 100\%$$

Explanatory Notes on Main Statistical Indicators

The annual statistics on total population is taken at midnight, the 31st of December, not including residents in Taiwan province, Hong Kong SAR and Macao SAR and Chinese national residing abroad.

Permanent population refers to the population of actual habitual residence in a certain area six months or over six months. Permanent popul ation include the accounts in this area which are also living in this area, accounts outside this area but with more than half a year of household registration, accounts to be determined including people without accounts or pockets of accounts, and accounts in the area but leaving this area less than six months.

Urban Population and Rural Population Urban population refers to all people residing in cities and towns, while rural population refers to population other than urban population.

Birth Rate (or Crude Birth Rate) refers to the ratio of the number of births to the average population (or mid-period population) during a certain period of time (usually one year), expressed in ‰. Birth rate in the chapter refers to annual birth rate. The following formula is used:

$$\text{Birth Rate}=\frac{\text{Number of Births}}{\text{Annual Average Population}}\times 1000‰$$

Number of births in the formula refers to live births, i.e. when a baby has breathed or showed any vital phenomena regardless of the length of pregnancy.

Annual average population is the average of the number of population at the beginning of the year and that at the end of the year. Sometimes it is substituted by the mid-year population.

Death Rate (or Crude Death Rate) refers to the ratio of the number of deaths to the average population (or mid-period population) during a certain period of time (usually one year), expressed in ‰. Death rate in the chapter refers to annual death rate. The following formula is used:

$$\text{DeathRate}=\frac{\text{Number of Deaths}}{\text{Annual Average Population}}\times 1000‰$$

Natural Growth Rate of Population refers to the ratio of natural increase in population (number of births minus number of deaths) in a certain period of time (usually one year) to the average population (or mid-period population) of the same period, expressed in ‰ . The following formula is applied:

Natural Growth Rate of Population =(Number of Births-Number of Deaths)/Annual Average Population× 1000‰

Employed Persons refer to the ones aged 16 and over who are engaged in gainful employment and thus receive remuneration payment or earn business income. This indicator reflects the actual utilization of total labour force during a certain period of time and is often used for the research on China's economic situation and national power.

Persons Employed in Various Units refer to all the persons working in government agencies of various levels, political and party organizations, social organizations, enterprises and institutions, and receiving wages or other forms of payment. They include fully-employed staff and workers, re-employed retirees, teachers in the schools run by the local people, foreigners and Chinese compatriots from Hong Kong, Macao, and Taiwan working in various units, part-time employees, employees of other units working temporarily at current posts, and employees holding the second job, but do not include persons who have left their working units while keeping their labour contract (employment relation) unchanged. This indicator reflects the total number of laborers actually engaged in production or other operations in various units.

Persons Employed in Private Enterprises and Self- Employed Individuals in Urban Areas Persons employed in private enterprises refer to the persons employed in the private enterprises which have been registered at the departments of industrial and commercial administration for which the business operation are situated at a county town (i.e. a town where the county government is located), or at urban areas with administrative hierarchy higher than a county town. The self-employed individuals in urban areas refer to persons who hold the certificates of residence in urban areas or have resided in the urban areas for a long time and have been registered at the departments of industrial and commercial administration and approved to be engaged in individual industrial or commercial business, including self-employed persons as well as helpers and hired labourers who work in individual households.

State–owned Units refer to economic units whose assets are owned by the state, including non-corporation units registered according to Regulation of the People's Republic of China on the Registration of Enterprises and

Corporations, state organs, institutions and social organizations at the central-level and local levels.

Collective–owned Units refer to economic units registered according to Regulation of the People's Republic of China on the Registration of Enterprises and Corporations where the means of production are collectively owned.

Units of Other Types of Ownership refer to units registered with other types of ownership, including cooperative units, joint ownership units, limited liability corporations, share holding corporations, units funded by entrepreneurs from Hong Kong, Macao, and Taiwan, and foreign- funded units.

Employed Staff and Workers refer to persons who work in, and receive wages from their working units, including persons who have their work posts but are temporarily absent from work for reasons of study or on sick, injury or maternal leave and still receive wages from their working units.

Total Wage Bill refers to the total remuneration payment to employed persons in various units during a certain period of time. The calculation of total wage bill is based on the total remuneration payment to employed persons . Therefore, all the wages and salaries and other payments to employed persons are included in the total wage bill regardless of sources, reckoning the cost of production or not, category, listing as items of premium taxation or not, and forms, paying in cash or in kind.

Average Wage refers to the average wage in money terms per person during a certain period of time for employed persons in enterprises, institutions, and government agencies, which reflects the general level of wage income during a certain period of time and is calculated as follows:

$$\text{AverageWage} = \frac{\text{TotalWage Billof Employed Personsat Reference Time}}{\text{Average Number of Persons Employedat Reference Time}}$$

Registered Unemployed Persons in Urban Areas refer to the persons with non-agricultural household registration at certain working ages (16 years old to retirement age), who are capable of working, unemployed and willing to work, and have been registered at the local employment service agencies to apply for a job.

Registered Unemployment Rate in Urban Areas refers to the ratio of the number of the registered unemployed persons to the sum of the number of persons employed in various units (minus the employed rural labour force, re-employed retirees, and Hong Kong, Macao, Taiwan or foreign employees), laid-off staff and workers in urban units, owners of private enterprises in urban areas, owners of self-employed individuals in urban areas, employees of private enterprises in urban areas, employee of self-employed individuals in urban areas, and the registered unemployed persons in urban areas. The formula is as follows:

$$\text{Registered Unemployment rate in urban areas} = \frac{\text{numberof registered urban unemployed persons}}{\begin{array}{c}\text{number of persons employed in}\\ \text{urbanunits-employed rurallabour force}\\ \text{re-employed retirees - HongKong,}\\ \text{Macao,Taiwan or foreign employees}\\ \text{+ laid-off staff and workers+owners of}\\ \text{urban private Enterprises+ owners of}\\ \text{urbanself-employed Individuals + employees}\\ \text{ofurbanprivate Enterprises+employees of}\\ \text{urbanself- employed Individuals+ registered}\\ \text{unemployed persons in urbanareas}\end{array}} \times 100\%$$

5 固定资产投资

INVESTMENT IN FIXED ASSETS

资料整理：康 敏 王 峰
Data management： Kang Min Wang Feng
数据审核：陈 英
Data audit：Chen Ying

第五部分　固定资产投资

一、简要说明

1.本章资料通过对一定时期全社会建造和购置固定资产活动的数量方面的描述，反映报告期内西安固定资产投资的规模和速度、固定资产投资的结构和比例关系、固定资产投资的资金来源及固定资产投资的效果等。主要包括全社会固定资产投资、项目投资、房地产开发投资和农户投资以及分区县、开发区投资情况等。

2.固定资产投资统计的范围包括：城乡建设项目投资、房地产开发投资及农户投资。

3.固定资产投资统计的资料来源主要为国家统计局的全面统计报表。除农户固定资产投资统计采用抽样调查方法外，其他均为全面统计报表。

4.统计口径的变化。

自1997年起，除房地产开发投资、非农户投资、农户投资及城镇和工矿区私人建房投资外，固定资产投资的统计起点由5万元提高到50万元。

自2006年起，非农户固定资产投资统计改为按项目统计，调查方法由抽样调查改为全面统计报表，起点提高到50万元。城镇和工矿区私人建房投资改为按项目统计，起点为50万元。

自2011年起，除房地产开发投资、农户投资外，固定资产投资项目统计起点，由计划总投资50万元提高到500万元；统计范围从城镇扩大到农村企事业组织，并将这一统计范围定义为“固定资产投资（不含农户）”。

5.2018年数据口径与往年相同。

二、主要指标

全社会固定资产投资	比上年增长	8.4 %
#国有经济单位	比上年增长	−2.9 %
集体经济单位	比上年增长	−54.5 %
#固定资产投资	比上年增长	8.5 %
#房地产开发投资	比上年增长	7.9 %
商品房销售面积	比上年增长	8.1 %
全市新增固定资产	比上年增长	−12.2 %
全市竣工住宅面积	比上年增长	−53.0 %

5 INVESTMENT IN FIXED ASSETS

Ⅰ.Brief Introduction

1.This chapter reflects the scale and speed of investment in fixed assets in Xi'an, the structure and proportional relationship of investment in fixed assets, the source of funds for investment in fixed assets and the effects of them during a certain period of time by describing the quantity of fixed asset activities built and purchased in the whole society during a certain period of time, mainly including total investment in fixed assets in the whole province, project investment, real estate development, farmer investment by Region and Development Zone.

2.Statistics on the investment in fixed assets cover investments in capital construction projects in urban and rural areas, investments in real estate development and rural household investment.

3.The data sources for the statistics of investment in fixed assets mainly come from complete statistical report forms, Investment in fixed assets by farm households are calculated with sample survey, and the others come from complete statistical report forms.

4.Changes in Statistical Scope

Since 1997, the cut-off point of projects covered by statistics of investment in fixed assets are raised from an investment of 50,000 yuan to 500,000 yuan, except investment in real estate development, non-farm household investment, farm household investment and private investment in housing construction in urban areas and industrial and mining areas.

Since 2006, statistics on investments in fixed assets of rural non-farm households are changed to project-based. Survey method is changed from sample survey to the system of reporting form with complete enumeration. The cut-off point has been raised to 500,00 yuan. Statistics on private investment in housing construction in urban areas and industrial and mining areas have become project-based. The cut-off point has been raised to 500,000 yuan.

Since 2011, except investment in real estate development and rural household investment , the cut-off point of statistics on investments in fixed assets are raised, amount of intended investment are raised from 500,000 yuan to 5000,000. The scope of investment statistics expends from urban to rural enterprises, and this scope of statistics is defined "investments in fixed assets(non-farm)" .

5.The data caliber of 2018 is same as the previous years.

Ⅱ.Major Indicators

	Increase over Preceding Year
Total Investment In Fixed Assets	8.4 %
State-owned Enterprises	-2.9 %
Collective-owned Enterprises	-54.5 %
Project Investment	8.5 %
Real Estate Development	7.9 %
Floor Space of Commercialized Buildings Sold	8.1 %
Investment Newly Increased Fixed Assets	-12.2 %
Total Floor Space of Building Completed	-53.0 %

5-1 主要年份按类别分全社会固定资产投资增长速度

The Growth Rate of Total Investment in Fixed Assets in the Whole Country by Classifications in Representative Years

单位：%　　(%)

年 份 Year	全社会固定资产投资 Total Investment in Fixed Assets in the Whole Country	固定资产投资 Investment in Fixed Assets	房地产开发投资 Real Estate Investment	农户投资 Farmer Investment
1979	22.9			
1980	50.0	48.8		53.3
1981	-8.7	1.8		-37.2
1982	69.8	75.9		42.7
1983	10.2	14.3		-12.2
1984	23.2	16.6		70.5
1985	43.1	35.1		81.8
1986	20.1	28.4		-9.8
1987	22.1	24.9		8.0
1988	7.7	5.5		20.8
1989	-2.9	-2.4		-5.5
1990	-6.7	-3.1		-26.1
1991	16.6	10.6	120.9	58.4
1992	25.1	28.6	65.2	8.1
1993	95.1	102.9	122.6	49.4
1994	14.0	10.2	62.7	43.9
1995	20.9	20.5	80.1	23.3
1996	10.6	9.6	13.9	16.6
1997	2.2	-1.9	0.1	24.9
1998	32.4	45.7	54.8	-25.8
1999	27.5	24.5	15.9	53.0
2000	17.8	17.6	17.0	19.0
2001	23.8	26.6	30.0	4.8
2002	17.5	19.6	17.7	0.5
2003	41.4	45.1	57.3	4.7
2004	35.3	37.3	35.9	7.1
2005	29.1	26.8	32.7	69.6
2006	27.7	25.2	26.9	61.3
2007	34.6	37.9	35.5	
2008	32.8	33.3	39.5	26.4
2009	31.1	32.5	28.9	10.7
2010	30.0	31.1	21.0	9.9
2011	30.0	33.2	18.3	-5.0
2012	26.8	28.0	28.6	-1.7
2013	21.0	21.3	24.5	12.1
2014	15.0	14.1	10.4	45.5
2015	-12.5	-10.5	4.0	-64.3
2016	2.0	3.4	6.8	-0.5
2017	12.9	13.0	15.0	持平
2018	8.4	8.5	7.9	2.1

注：2015年国家取消了城乡投资分组，表中"农户投资"2014年以前为原先的农村投资。
　　2016年全社会固定资产投资不含跨省项目，固定资产投资不含跨省和跨市项目。

5-2 主要年份按经济类型分全社会固定资产投资增长速度

The Growth Rate of Total Investment in Fixed Assets in the Whole Country by Economic Type in Representative Years

单位：%　　　　(%)

年份 Year	合计 Total	国有经济 State-owned	集体经济 Collective-owned	个体经济 Self-employed Individual	其他经济 Others
1985	43.1	34.8	72.0	79.0	
1986	20.1	29.3	-28.7	0.3	
1987	22.1	22.9	54.6	7.7	
1988	7.7	6.9	24.0	5.6	
1989	-2.9	-2.1	-21.5	1.7	
1990	-6.7	-4.3	-1.4	-24.3	
1991	16.6	10.0	56.9	48.9	
1992	25.1	31.2	-35.8	22.3	
1993	95.1	86.2	109.0	31.3	
1994	14.0	8.5	36.6	54.0	13.9
1995	20.9	6.8	136.2	10.3	102.6
1996	10.6	16.8	-10.7	12.3	-7.0
1997	2.2	-4.0	17.0	20.9	13.1
1998	32.4	46.0	-22.7	-29.9	64.7
1999	27.5	20.7	72.6	53.2	33.2
2000	17.8	16.9	7.6	50.4	8.9
2001	23.8	10.0	0.1	58.1	74.7
2002	17.5	13.9	-6.6	15.8	35.3
2003	41.4	32.4	63.0	64.3	47.4
2004	35.3	24.3	79.4	-33.3	94.5
2005	29.1	13.5	47.9	61.5	41.4
2006	27.7	7.3	86.9	35.8	38.5
2007	34.6	18.9	87.1	70.6	27.0
2008	32.8	45.7	19.2	-72.5	60.8
2009	31.1	34.3	17.4	94.1	29.0
2010	30.0	44.6	12.6	-44.1	28.9
2011	30.0	24.8	10.4	36.4	18.9
2012	26.8	37.9	-24.6	10.8	27.4
2013	21.0	6.6	12.9	2.1	32.7
2014	15.0	8.2	-7.5	-1.4	21.0
2015	-12.5	-4.7	-22.2	-3.4	-16.2
2016	2.0	15.9	-17.5	1.5	-15.3
2017	12.9	19.4	-9.9	15.0	21.2
2018	8.4	-2.9	-54.5		8.6

注：集体经济：包括城镇集体和农村集体。
　　个体经济：包括私营个体投资及城镇工矿区私人建房和农村私人建房。
　　2017年后数据为含西咸数据

5-3 主要年份按产业分全市固定资产投资增长速度

The Growth Rate of Total Investment in Fixed Assets in the Whole City by Three Strata of Industry in Representative Years

单位：%　　　　　　　　　　　　　　　　　　　　　　　　　　　　　　　　　　　　　　　（%）

年　份 Year	全市固定资产投资 Total Investment in Fixed Assets in The Whole City	第一产业 Primary Industry	第二产业 Secondary Industry	工业 Industry	第三产业 Tertisry Industry
1979					
1980	48.8	3.2	68.5	65.0	36.1
1981	1.8	83.3	0.5	-8.0	0.9
1982	75.9	-63.6	93.8	98.4	66.4
1983	14.3	175.0	22.1	21.5	4.6
1984	16.6	72.7	-8.2	-9.5	45.2
1985	35.1	-5.3	58.3	61.7	18.5
1986	28.4	-11.1	24.4	29.8	33.5
1987	24.9	18.8	31.5	34.5	18.6
1988	5.5	-21.1	1.2	-0.5	10.6
1989	-2.4	-13.3	-0.1	2.7	-4.5
1990	-3.1	92.3	-7.6	-7.9	0.3
1991	10.6	8.0	13.1	12.8	8.3
1992	28.6	-63.0	25.0	23.3	34.0
1993	102.9	-30.0	57.1	52.3	145.4
1994	10.2	-57.1	10.4	15.2	10.3
1995	20.5	365.7	6.5	7.2	28.4
1996	9.6	-7.1	-9.9	-12.5	19.0
1997	-1.9	84.6	-8.9	-10.6	0.6
1998	45.7	100.0	49.4	37.9	44.3
1999	24.5	95.8	12.9	21.9	28.1
2000	17.6	-19.1	43.5	49.4	10.0
2001	26.6	13.2	10.7	12.7	32.9
2002	19.6	393.8	17.4	11.7	18.6
2003	45.1	-22.1	12.0	14.6	57.1
2004	37.3	1.2	17.3	22.0	42.3
2005	26.8	55.6	47.7	46.8	22.7
2006	25.2	90.9	48.0	47.0	19.4
2007	37.9	1.6	39.4	38.8	38.0
2008	33.3	132.8	24.3	24.3	34.9
2009	32.5	3.0	24.0	24.3	35.3
2010	31.1	62.8	21.3	12.6	33.1
2011	30.0	22.2	21.3	18.5	31.8
2012	29.9	130.5	41.5	48.1	26.2
2013	21.3	-26.4	46.3	50.2	17.8
2014	15.2	2.7	28.3	38.8	12.2
2015	-12.7	32.8	-8.2	-5.8	-14.7
2016	3.4	-10.1	-12.3	-12.0	8.3
2017	13.0	2.3	-10.2	-10.6	18.6
2018	8.5	20.8	28.6	28.7	5.4

5-4 按资金来源及建设性质分全市固定资产投资增长速度（2018年）

The Growth Rate of Total Investment in Fixed Assets in the Whole City by Sources of Funds and Type of Construction （2018）

单位：%　　　　(%)

指　标	Item	增长速度 Growth
一. 投资总额	**Total Investment**	**8.5**
（一）按资金来源分	Grouped by Funds Source	
1. 国家预算内投资	State Budgetary Funds	84.1
2. 国内贷款	Domestic Loans	-22.3
3. 债券	Bonds	
4. 利用外资	Utilization of Foreign Funds	3.3
5. 自筹资金	Self-raising Funds	16.5
6. 其他资金	Others	-80.2
（二）按构成分	Grouped by Composition of Funds	
1. 建筑安装工程	Construction and Installation Projects	4.2
2. 设备、工器具购置	Purchasing of Equipment and Instruments	-14.1
3. 其它费用	Others	25.9
（三）按建设性质分	Grouped by Type of Construction	
#新建	New Construction	8.2
扩建	Expansion	-21.9
改建和技术改造	Reconstruction and Technical Transformation	39.8
二. 房屋施工面积	**Floor Space Under Construction**	**-0.9**

5-5 主要年份全市新增固定资产投资及房屋竣工面积增长速度

The Growth Rate of Newly Added Fixed Assets and Floor Spaces Completed of Municipal Units in Representative Years

单位：%　　　　(%)

年份 Year	新增固定资产 Newly Increased Fixed Assets	房屋竣工面积 Floor Space of Buildings Completed	住宅 Residential Buildings
1980	44.2	38.3	41.7
1985	1.1	-4.6	-5.9
1986	55.5	22.7	20.8
1987	24.8	-11.5	-23.5
1988	0.6	-12.3	-14.1
1989	-1.4	-15.8	-14.3
1990	22.4	18.7	26.5
1991	-12.0	-12.5	-13.7
1992	25.0	10.5	17.6
1993	86.7	26.0	28.6
1994	32.8	9.7	27.3
1995	13.0	26.4	37.0
1996	-4.1	-7.1	-1.3
1997	4.7	12.7	14.8
1998	27.6	2.2	-3.8
1999	48.2	77.9	99.8
2000	26.3	5.0	-1.1
2001	11.7	-3.1	-7.8
2002	18.6	11.7	-3.2
2003	40.4	18.7	18.9
2005	-6.3	-15.4	-13.8
2004	56.4	45.7	20.1
2006	10.6	6.0	-2.6
2007	47.5	39.4	59.4
2008	8.6	-33.4	-25.4
2009	39.8	37.3	18.6
2010	17.7	-49.3	-36.7
2011	86.7	58.9	65.3
2012	36.1	32.0	38.0
2013	6.2	-31.2	-29.4
2014	32.1	66.0	74.1
2015	-17.2	-40.3	-43.5
2016	-4.7	69.9	61.2
2017	24.6	5.5	0.6
2018	-12.2	-44.5	-53.0

5-6 全市固定资产投资增长速度（2018年）

The Growth Rate of Total Investment in Fixed Assets in the Whole City（2018）

单位：%

指　标	Item	固定资产投资 Investment in Fixed Assets	房地产开发投资 Real Estate Investment
一、本年完成投资（万元）	**Investment Completed This Year(10 000 yuan)**	**8.5**	**7.9**
#住宅	Residential Buildings	4.4	5.7
（一）按登记注册类型分	**Grouped by Registion Status**		
内资	Domestic Funded Enterprises	8.0	7.5
国有	State-owned Enterprises	-2.9	1.8
集体	Collective-owned Enterprises	-54.5	
股份合作	Cooperative Enterprises		
联营	Joint Ownership Enterprises		
国有联营	State Joint Ownership Enterprises		
集体联营	Collective Joint Ownership Enterprises		
国有与集体联营	Joint State-collective Ownership Enterprises		
其他联营	Other Joint Ownership Enterprises		
有限责任公司	Limited Liability Corporations	-11.9	-19.3
国有独资公司	State-funded Corporations	7.6	-50.7
其他有限责任公司	Other Limited Liability Corporations	-16.0	-16.4
股份有限公司	Stock Limited Corporation	17.0	1.1
私营	Private Enterprises	28.4	84.5
私营独资	Private -funded Enterprises	-21.6	
私营合伙	Private Limited Liability Corporations	-100.0	
私营有限责任公司	Private Limited Liability Corporations	34.7	88.4
私营股份有限公司	Private Share Holding Corporations	-13.8	23.6
其他	Others	-74.4	
港澳台商投资	Enterprises Funded by Hong Kong, Macao and Taiwan	-41.5	-22.1
与港澳台合资经营	Joint-venture Enterprises	-53.8	84.6
与港澳台合作经营	Cooperative Enterprises	-23.3	-23.3
港澳台独资	Wholly Funded from Hong Kong,Macao and Taiwan	-49.3	-37.5

5-6 续表 continued

(%)

指 标	Item	固定资产投资 Investment in Fixed Assets	房地产开发投资 Real Estate Investment
港澳台投资股份有限公司	Share-holding Corporations Ltd.		
其他港澳台投资	Investment From Hongkong,Macao,Taiwan		
外商投资	Foreign Owned Enterprises	59.9	78.2
中外合资经营	Joint-venture Enterprises	-49.5	-8.2
中外合作经营	Cooperation Enterprises		
外资企业	Foreign Funded Enterprises	91.8	15.4
外商投资股份有限公司	Share-holding Corporations Ltd. With Foreign Funds	392.3	392.3
其他外商投资	Foreign Investment		
（二）按建设性质分	**Grouped by Type of Construction**		
#新建	New Construction	8.2	
扩建	Expansion	-21.9	
改建和技术改造	Reconstruction	39.8	
（三）按构成分	**Grouped by Composition**		
1. 建筑工程	Construction Projects	4.2	-2.5
2. 安装工程	Installment Projects	8.9	-15.0
3. 设备、工器具购置	Purchasing of Equipment and Instruments	14.1	-53.6
4. 其他费用	Others	25.9	63.9
二、本年新增固定资产	**Newly Increase in Fixed Assets This Year**	-12.2	-49.3
三、房屋面积	**Floor Space**		
房屋施工面积	Floor Space of Buildings Under Construction	-0.9	1.3
#住宅	Residential Buildings	-1.0	0.7
房屋竣工面积	Floor Space of Buildings Completed	-44.5	-40.2
#住宅	Residential Buildings	-53.0	-51.4
四、本年房屋竣工价值	**Value of the Building Completed This Year**	-39.2	-42.2
#住宅	Residential Buildings	-54.0	-53.4

5-7 按国民经济行业分全市固定资产投资增长速度（2018年）

The Growth Rate of Investment in Fixed Assets in the Whole Country by Industry（2018）

单位：%　　　　(%)

行业	Sector	固定资产投资 Investment in Fixed Assets	工业企业技术改造 Technological Transformation of Industrial Enterprises
本年完成固定资产投资（%）	**Grouped by Sector (%)**	**8.5**	**25.5**
（一）农、林、牧、渔业	Agriculture,Forestry,Animal Husbandry and Fishery	18.1	
（二）采矿业	Mining	21.0	130.4
（三）制造业	Manufacturing	31.8	-12.4
农副食品加工业	Processing of Food from Agricultural Products	28.0	204.2
食品制造业	Manufacture of Foods	-32.6	-68.8
酒、饮料和精制茶制造业	Wine, Soft Drinks and Refined Tea Industry	-44.2	-74.4
烟草制品业	Tobacco Processing	-84.5	
纺织业	Textile Industry	-73.1	110.0
纺织服装、服饰业	Textile, Apparel Industry	-100.0	
皮革、毛皮、羽毛及其制品和制鞋业	Leather, Fur, Feather (eiderdown) and Their Products Industry	-100.0	
木材加工和木、竹、藤、棕、草制品业	Timber Processing,Bamboo,Cane, Palm Fiber and Straw Products	-40.5	
家具制造业	Furniture Manufacturing	-49.4	-39.0
造纸及纸制品业	Papermaking and Paper products	113.1	152.7
印刷和记录媒介复制业	Printing,Record Medium Reproduction	-2.8	21.4
文教、工美、体育和娱乐用品制造业	Culture, Education, Craft Art, Sports and Entertainment Goods Manufacturing Industry	-91.8	-88.5
石油、煤炭及其他燃料加工业	Oil, Coal and Other Fuel Processing Industries	2312.4	-30.3
化学原料和化学制品制造业	Raw Chemical Materials and Chemical Products	71.8	95.3
医药制造业	Medical and Pharmaceutical Products	3.1	-45.0
化学纤维制造业	Chemical Fiber		
橡胶和塑料制品业	Rubber and Plastic Products Industry	-78.8	-16.6
非金属矿物制品业	Nonmetal Mineral Products	-10.8	-48.9
黑色金属冶炼和压延加工业	Smelting and Pressing of Ferrous Metals	-31.0	119.5
有色金属冶炼和压延加工业	Smelting and Pressing of Nonferrou Metals	151.3	-9.0
金属制品业	Metal Products	17.5	95.5

5-7 续表 continued

单位：% (%)

行 业	Sector	固定资产投资 Investment in Fixed Assets	工业企业技术改造 Technological Transformation of Industrial Enterprises
通用设备制造业	General Equipment Manufacturing Industry	46.4	-59.7
专用设备制造业	Special Purpose Equipment	-13.0	-42.3
汽车制造业	Automotive Manufacturing	60.4	77.4
铁路、船舶、航空航天和其他运输设备制造业	Railroad, Marine, Aerospace and other Transportation Equipment Manufacturing	5.7	8.5
电气机械和器材制造业	Electric Equipment and Machinery	-12.9	-39.2
计算机、通信和其他电子设备制造业	Communication Equipment, Computer and Other Electronic Equipment Manufacturing Industry	149.0	14.9
仪器仪表制造业	Instrument Manufacturing Industry	2.8	-69.9
其他制造业	Other Manufacturing	725.2	
废弃资源综合利用	Comprehensive Utilization of waste Resources	404.3	-89.8
金属制品、机械和设备修理业	Metal Products, Machinery and Equipment Repair Industry	-94.8	
（四）电力、燃气及水的生产供应业	Production & Supply of Electricity,Gas & Water	17.0	-45.3
（五）建筑业	Construction	-62.7	
（六）批发和零售业	Wholesale and Retail Trades	-16.6	
（七）交通运输、仓储和邮政业	Transport, Storage and Post	17.6	
（八）住宿和餐饮业	Hotels and Catering Services	133.3	
（九）信息传输、软件和信息技术服务业	Information Transmission,Computer Service and Software	15.4	
（十）金融业	Financial Intermediation	-50.3	
（十一）房地产业	Real Estate	5.7	
（十二） 租赁和商务服务业	Leasing and Business Services	-6.6	
（十三）科学研究和技术服务业	Scientific Research,Technical Service and Geologic Prospecting	-12.1	
（十四）水利、环境和公共设施管理业	Management of Water Conservancy, Environment and Public Facilities	7.1	
（十五）居民服务、修理和其他服务业	Services to Households, Repairs and Other Services	-15.7	
（十六）教育	Education	-38.6	
（十七）卫生和社会工作	Health and Social Work	22.4	
（十八）文化、体育和娱乐业	Culture, Sports and Entertainment	19.4	
（十九）公共管理、社会保障和社会组织	Public Administration, Social Security and Social Organizations	10.7	
（二十）国际组织	International Organizations		

5-8 按国民经济行业分民间投资增长速度（2018年）

The Growth Rate of Private Investment of Municipal Units by Industry（2018）

单位：%　　　　(%)

行　业	Sector	民间投资 Private Investment	占民间投资比重 Rate
民间投资总计	**Total**	**20.3**	**100.0**
（一）农、林、牧、渔业	Agriculture, Forestry, Animal Husbandry and Fishery	35.3	1.5
（二）采矿业	Mining	-75.9	
（三）制造业	Manufacturing	21.5	14.0
（四）电力、燃气及水的生产供应业	Generation and Supply of Electricity, Production and Supply of Gas and Water	77.5	1.2
（五）建筑业	Construction	75.1	
（六）批发和零售业	Wholesale and Retail Trades	-23.8	1.3
（七）交通运输、仓储和邮政业	Transportation, Storage and Post	58.1	2.3
（八）住宿和餐饮业	Hotels and Catering Services	205.4	1.0
（九）信息传输、软件和信息技术服务业	Information Transmission, Computer Service and Software	115.6	1.0
（十）金融业	Financial Intermediation	46.4	
（十一）房地产业	Real Estate	19.3	67.4
（十二） 租赁和商务服务业	Leasing and Business Services	-59.4	0.9
（十三）科学研究和技术服务业	Scientific Research and Technical Service	7.5	0.7
（十四）水利、环境和公共设施管理业	Management of Water Conservancy, Environment and Public Facilities	26.4	3.9
（十五）居民服务、修理和其他服务业	Services to Households, Repairs and Other Services	697.4	0.1
（十六）教育	Education	32.3	1.0
（十七）卫生和社会工作	Health and Social Work	65.4	1.7
（十八）文化、体育和娱乐业	Culture, Sports and Entertainment	35.2	2.0
（十九）公共管理、社会保障和社会组织	Public Administration, Social Security and Social Organizations	-96.1	
（二十）国际组织	International Organizations		

5-9 按国民经济行业分基础设施投资增长速度（2018年）

The Growth Rate of Investment for Basic Infrastructure of Municipal Units by Industry（2018）

单位：%　　　　(%)

指　标	Item	基础设施投资 Infrastructure Investment	占基础设施投资比重 Rate
基础设施投资总计	**Total Investment of Infrastructure**	**8.3**	**100.0**
一、交通运输、仓储和邮政业	**Traffic, Transport, Storage and Post**	**17.6**	**17.4**
铁路运输业	Railway Transport Industry	-0.5	2.6
道路运输业	The Road Transport Industry	41.1	13.8
水上运输业	Water Transportation		
航空运输业	The Air Transport Industry	-23.8	0.7
管道运输业	Pipeline Transportation	457.8	0.1
装卸搬运和运输代理服务业	Handling and Transport Industry	141.7	0.1
仓储业	Warehousing Industry		5.5
邮政业	The Postal Service	-57.5	0.1
二、信息传输、软件和信息技术服务业	**Information Transmission,Software and Information Technology Services**	**15.4**	**3.0**
三、水利、环境和公共设施管理业	**Management of Water Conservancy, Environment and Public Facilities**	**7.1**	**73.7**
水利管理业	Water Resources Management Industry	-29.2	3.2
生态保护和环境治理业	Ecological Protection and Environmental Control Industries	-22.1	1.4
公共设施管理业	Public Facilities Management Industry	10.6	69.1

5-10 全市固定资产投资资金来源增长速度（2018年）

The Growth Rate of Source of Funds for Total Fixed Assets Investment of Whole City（2018）

单位：%　　　　(%)

指　标	Item	固定资产投资 Investment in Fixed Assets	房地产开发 Real Estate
一、本年资金来源合计	**Total of Sources of Funds This Year**	**-17.3**	**-10.8**
1. 上年末结余资金	Balance of Last Year	12.1	12.3
2. 本年实际到位资金	Fully Funded Capital this Year	9.4	
(1) 国家预算资金	State Budgetary Funds	10.3	
(2) 国内贷款	Domestic Loans	-13.5	-10.4
(3) 债券	Bonds		
(4) 利用外资	Utilization of Foreign Funds	-57.2	
(5) 自筹资金	Self-raising Funds	10.7	22.0
(6) 其他资金来源	Others	17.3	-90.0
二、各项应付款合计	**Total Sums of Money to be Paid This Year**	**8.0**	**16.8**

5-11 全市按行业分施工项目（2018年）

Construction Project Grouped by Industry in the Whole City（2018）

行 业	Sector	本年新增固定资产增长速度（%） The Growth Rate of Newly Increased Fixed Assets This Year(%)	施工项目个数（个） Number of Constructing Projects(unit)
总计	**Total**	**-12.2**	**3270**
（一）农、林、牧、渔业	Agriculture, Forestry, Animal Husbandry and Fishery	-79.1	156
（二）采矿业	Mining	-32.5	6
（三）制造业	Manufacturing	-12.4	756
（四）电力、燃气及水的生产供应业	Generation and Supply of Electricity,Production and Supply of Gas and Water	-21.1	172
（五）建筑业	Construction	-93.7	4
（六）批发和零售业	Wholesale and Retail Trades	-13.6	87
（七）交通运输、仓储和邮政业	Transportation, Storage and Post	50.4	143
（八）住宿和餐饮业	Hotels and Catering Services	-37.9	67
（九）信息传输、软件和信息技术服务业	Information Transmission, Computer Service and Software	11.2	87
（十）金融业	Financial Intermediation	-31.2	5
（十一）房地产业	Real Estate	12.9	167
（十二） 租赁和商务服务业	Leasing and Business Services	-51.3	63
（十三）科学研究和技术服务业	Scientific Research and Technical Service	-64.6	60
（十四）水利、环境和公共设施管理业	Management of Water Conservancy, Environment and Public Facilities	-44.6	1141
（十五）居民服务、修理和其他服务业	Services to Households, Repairs and Other Services	2.7	12
（十六）教育	Education	-69.3	184
（十七）卫生和社会工作	Health and Social Work	-52.7	57
（十八）文化、体育和娱乐业	Culture, Sports and Entertainment	9.8	70
（十九）公共管理、社会保障和社会组织	Public Administration, Social Security and Social Organizations	3.5	33
（二十）国际组织	International Organizations		

5-11 续表 continued

行 业	Sector	本年新开工 Newly Started This Year	本年投产项目个数（个） Projects put into Use (unit)
总计	**Total**	**1486**	**1186**
（一）农、林、牧、渔业	Agriculture, Forestry, Animal Husbandry and Fishery	113	66
（二）采矿业	Mining	3	3
（三）制造业	Manufacturing	363	287
（四）电力、燃气及水的生产供应业	Generation and Supply of Electricity,Production and Supply of Gas and Water	71	44
（五）建筑业	Construction	4	2
（六）批发和零售业	Wholesale and Retail Trades	27	46
（七）交通运输、仓储和邮政业	Transportation, Storage and Post	55	66
（八）住宿和餐饮业	Hotels and Catering Services	46	29
（九）信息传输、软件和信息技术服务业	Information Transmission, Computer Service and Software	57	14
（十）金融业	Financial Intermediation		1
（十一）房地产业	Real Estate	44	52
（十二） 租赁和商务服务业	Leasing and Business Services	29	49
（十三）科学研究和技术服务业	Scientific Research and Technical Service	21	24
（十四）水利、环境和公共设施管理业	Management of Water Conservancy, Environment and Public Facilities	502	358
（十五）居民服务、修理和其他服务业	Services to Households, Repairs and Other Services	5	7
（十六）教育	Education	80	64
（十七）卫生和社会工作	Health and Social Work	24	36
（十八）文化、体育和娱乐业	Culture, Sports and Entertainment	29	22
（十九）公共管理、社会保障和社会组织	Public Administration, Social Security and Social Organizations	13	16
（二十）国际组织	International Organizations		

5-12 全市固定资产投资效果（2018年）

Achievements of Total Assets Investment of Whole City（2018）

指　标	Item	固定资产投资 Investment in Fixed Assets	房地产开发投资 Real Estate Investment
一、建设项目投产率（%）	**Rate of Projects Put Into Use(%)**	**36.3**	
施工项目个数（个）	Number of Constructing Projects (unit)	3270	
本年投产项目个数（个）	Number of Projects Put into Use (unit)	1186	
二、固定资产交付使用率（%）	**Rate of Fixed Assets Put into Use(%)**	**26.9**	**16.2**
本年新增固定资产增长速度（%）	The Growth Rate of Newly Increased Fixed Assets This Year(%)	-12.2	-49.3
本年完成投资增长速度（%）	The Growth Rate of Investment Completed This Year(%)	8.5	7.9
三、建设周期（年）	**Construction Period (year)**	**4.9**	**6.6**
计划总投资增长速度（%）	The Growth Rate of Total Planned Investment(%)	3.6	11.8
本年完成投资额增长速度（%）	The Growth Rate of Investment Completed This Year(%)	8.5	7.9
四、房屋建筑面积竣工率（%）	**Completion Rate of Buildings (%)**	**6.4**	**6.1**
本年房屋施工面积增长速度（%）	The Growth Rate of Floor Space of the Constructing Buildings This Year(%)	-0.9	1.3
本年房屋竣工面积增长速度（%）	The Growth Rate of Floor Space of the Buildings Completed This Year(%)	-44.5	-40.2

5-13 固定资产投资新增生产能力或效益（2018年）

Newly Increased Production Capacity or Project Efficiency through Investment（2018）

能源名称	Name	累计新增生产能力或效益 Cumulative Newly Increased Production Capacity or Project Efficiency
石油加工：蒸馏设备能力（处理万吨/年）	Oil Processing : Distillation Equipment Capacity (10 000 tons/year)	21
石油加工：裂变设备能力（处理万吨/年）	Oil Processing : Fission Equipment Capacity (10 000 tons/year)	12
太阳能发电（万千瓦）	Solar Energy (10 000 kw)	0.03
其他发电（万千瓦）	Others (10 000 kw)	
输电线路长度（11万伏及以上）（公里）	Length of Transmission Lines (above 110 000 VA) (km)	13.6
载货汽车制造（辆/年）	Truck Manufacturing (car/year)	
客车制造（辆/年）	Bus Manufacturing (car/year)	
轿车制造（辆/年）	Car Manufacturing (car/year)	
其他汽车制造（辆/年）	Other cars Manufacturing (car/year)	770
啤酒（万吨/年）	Beer (10 000 tons/year)	
白酒（万吨/年）	White Spirit (10 000 tons/year)	0.26
其他酒（万吨/年）	Other Alcohols (10 000 tons/year)	
新建公路（公里）	Newly Highways (km)	12.9
#高速公路（公里）	Expressway (km)	
一级公路（公里）	First Class (km)	
二级公路（公里）	Second Class (km)	8.5
改建公路（公里）	Reconstructed Highways (km)	42.0
新（扩）建客、货运站（个）	New (expanded) Passenger and Freight Stations (unit)	1
新（扩）建公路客、货运站（平方米）	New (expanded) Road Passenger and Freight Station (square meter)	120
飞机购置（驾）	Airplane Purchasing (set)	
城市自来水供水能力（万吨/日）	Tap Water Supply Capacity in City(10 000 tons/day)	27.7
城市污水处理能力（万吨/日）	Waste Water Treated Capacity in City(10 000 tons/day)	1.5

5–14 全市按国民经济行业分房屋建筑面积增长速度（2018年）

单位：%

行　业	Sector	本年施工房屋面积 Floor Space of Buildings Under Construction This Year	住宅 Residential Residence
总　计	**Total**	**-0.9**	**-1.5**
（一）农、林、牧、渔业	Agriculture, Forestry, Animal Husbandry and Fishery	-92.3	71.2
（二）采矿业	Mining		
（三）制造业	Manufacturing	-40.7	-83.1
（四）电力、燃气及水的生产供应业	Generation and Supply of Electricity, Production and Supply of Gas and Water	-84.0	
（五）建筑业	Construction		
（六）批发和零售业	Wholesale and Retail Trades	-29.2	-53.1
（七）交通运输、仓储和邮政业	Transportation, Storage and Post	-27.0	
（八）住宿和餐饮业	Hotels and Catering Services	-9.3	
（九）信息传输、软件和信息技术服务业	Information Transmission, Computer Service and Software	-74.9	
（十）金融业	Financial Intermediation		
（十一）房地产业	Real Estate	-1.4	-0.9
（十二） 租赁和商务服务业	Leasing and Business Services	4.8	
（十三）科学研究和技术服务业	Scientific Research and Technical Service	-70.6	
（十四）水利、环境和公共设施管理业	Management of Water Conservancy, Environment and Public Facilities	-12.2	
（十五）居民服务、修理和其他服务业	Services to Households, Repairs and Other Services	-97.3	
（十六）教育	Education		
（十七）卫生和社会工作	Health and Social Work	100.2	323.7
（十八）文化、体育和娱乐业	Culture, Sports and Entertainment	56.5	
（十九）公共管理、社会保障和社会组织	Public Administration, Social Security and Social Organizations	-48.5	
（二十）国际组织	International Organizations		

The Growth Rate of Floors Space of Buildings Construction of Municipal Units by Industry（2018）

（%）

本年竣工房屋面积 Floor Space of Buildings Completed This Year	住宅 Residential Residence	本年竣工房屋价值 Value of Buildings Completed this Year	住宅 Residential Residence
-44.5	**-53.0**	**-42.2**	**-53.4**
-90.1	671.9		
-41.2	-87.6		
-62.5			
386.0			
-71.0			
-43.3	-52.6	-42.2	-53.4
78.1			
-21.5			
-64.9			
-95.8			
36.6			
-76.9			

5–15 分区县、开发区全社会固定资产投资增长速度（2018年）

The Growth Rate of Total Investment in Fixed Assets by Region and Development Zone（2018）

单位：% (%)

区县、开发区	Region	全社会固定资产投资 Fixed Assets Investment	固定资产投资 Investment in Fixed Assets	房地产开发投资 Real Estate Investment	农户投资 Farmer Investment
全市	**Total**	**8.4**	**8.5**	**7.9**	**2.1**
新城区	Xincheng	-49.1	-49.1	-75.1	
碑林区	Beilin	0.3	0.3	-52.1	
莲湖区	Lianhu	3.8	3.8	-1.8	
灞桥区	Baqiao	20.3	20.4	32.0	6.2
未央区	Weiyang	-11.8	-11.7	-14.1	-64.7
雁塔区	Yanta	4.0	4.0	2.4	
阎良区	Yanliang	13.8	13.9	7.2	7.2
临潼区	Lintong	34.9	37.7	70.1	5.9
长安区	Chang'an	38.3	39.9	9.5	-18.3
高陵区	Gaoling	7.9	7.9	-15.3	5.6
鄠邑区	Huyi	0.8	2.2	-31.5	-0.8
蓝田县	Lantian	21.5	23.7	183.6	2.8
周至县	Zhouzhi	4.6	0.3	-47.1	5.8
西咸新区	Xixian	12.6	12.5	104.4	22.6
#开发区	**Development Zones**				
高新区	GaoXin		14.1	-17.6	
经开区	JingKai		0.1	-36.2	
曲江新区	Qujiang		10.8	19.6	
浐灞生态区	Chanba Eco-District		10.2	15.1	
航空基地	Aviation Industry Base		17.3	1.4	
航天基地	Aerospace Base		9.2	3.7	
国际港务区	International Trade&Logistic Park		17.7	164.4	

5-16 分区县工业投资增长速度（2018年）

The Growth Rate of Industrial Investment by Region（2018）

单位：% (%)

区县	Region	工业投资 Industrial Investment	工业企业技术改造 Technological Transformation of Industrial Enterprises
全　市	**Total**	**28.7**	**25.5**
新城区	Xincheng	-21.7	-46.4
碑林区	Beilin	3.5	-57.8
莲湖区	Lianhu	-51.9	-25.3
灞桥区	Baqiao	70.9	-51.7
未央区	Weiyang	30.8	51.6
雁塔区	Yanta	6.9	-7.8
阎良区	Yanliang	32.9	151.4
临潼区	Lintong	6.0	125.1
长安区	Chang'an	106.4	39.7
高陵区	Gaoling	48.4	94.7
鄠邑区	Huyi	-38.1	1.5
蓝田县	Lantian	13.3	-56.9
周至县	Zhouzhi	2.3	-56.8
西咸新区	Xixian	-6.4	14.8

5-17 分区县、开发区新增固定资产及房屋施工、竣工面积增长速度（2018年）

单位：%

区县、开发区	Region	本年新增固定资产 Increased Fixed Assets this Year	房屋施工面积 Floor Space of Buildings Under Construction	住宅 Residential Buildings
区县	**Region**	**-27.3**	**5.1**	**6.3**
新城区	Xincheng	-64.7	-38.8	-37.3
碑林区	Beilin	-74.7	-33.8	-33.3
莲湖区	Lianhu	-82.5	-10.8	-11.6
灞桥区	Baqiao	-72.9	4.5	4.3
未央区	Weiyang	-23.4	-3.8	-1.1
雁塔区	Yanta	-39.8	-0.8	-3.1
阎良区	Yanliang	-73.3	2.2	-3.3
临潼区	Lintong	-71.8	10.8	20.6
长安区	Chang'an	-46.9	8.0	9.8
高陵区	Gaoling	-47.9	-7.3	13.2
鄠邑区	Huyi	-9.0	3.8	11.5
蓝田县	Lantian	-72.0	10.1	-1.1
周至县	Zhouzhi	-76.7	0.8	-42.3
西咸新区	Xixian	-37.5	23.2	31.8
开发区	**Development Zones**	**28.7**	**28.1**	**35.2**
高新区	GaoXin	-0.1	29.2	57.7
经开区	JingKai	-7.6	-2.1	-2.0
曲江新区	Qujiang	-73.6	-5.5	3.8
浐灞生态区	Chanba Eco-District	-44.6	5.9	5.1
航空基地	Aviation Industry Base	-64.0	-2.0	-10.1
航天基地	Aerospace Base	-71.5	-0.2	-2.7
国际港务区	International Trade&Logistic Park	-87.8	71.9	130.7

The Growth Rate of Newly Added Fixed Assets and Floor Space of Constructing and Completed Buildings by Region and Development Zone（2018）

(%)

本年房屋竣工面积 Floor Space of Buildings this Year Completed	住宅 Residential Buildings	本年房屋竣工价值 Value of Buildings Completed this Year	住宅 Residential Buildings	本年商品房销售面积 Floor Space of Houses Sales this year	本年商品房销售额 Sales Income of Commercial Houses this year
-39.7	**-50.0**	**-39.2**	**-50.8**	**13.1**	**34.9**
-72.1	-67.9	-76.6	-61.8	-17.6	30.6
-68.5	-65.6	-63.2	-55.1	-32.5	-12.4
-93.9	-94.9	-95.1	-94.9	-4.5	9.3
-53.9	-65.3	-44.8	-65.3	23.5	63.0
-10.6	-26.6	-23.7	-38.4	-6.1	16.8
-19.4	-46.7	-23.9	-49.8	10.2	18.3
-71.8	-80.3	-85.4	-81.8	10.1	23.1
-90.2	-89.0	-61.6	-62.3	62.0	127.7
-41.7	-49.1	-53.9	-53.4	2.6	24.8
-9.9	11.9	7.9	9.6	-1.4	24.6
41.0	-59.7	-63.9	-65.9	-20.4	-3.2
-87.6	-81.0	-77.3	-79.5	40.5	99.3
-35.1	80.0	-42.2	-32.6	-12.8	-2.9
-94.9	-98.7	-87.8	-95.9	115.6	185.0
32.4	**-13.6**	**12.2**	**-25.3**	**22.1**	**39.2**
321.8	159.5	328.6	176.0	26.5	18.0
59.5	13.5	51.5	-1.5	-3.3	23.6
-86.5	-85.2	-90.4	-88.8	-7.9	13.1
-39.4	-61.1	-37.2	-54.7	1.9	23.6
-80.8	-83.6	-88.2	-90.0	39.0	26.5
-76.8	-79.9	-73.8	-76.4	7.7	14.5
				62.4	148.9

5-18 主要年份房地产开发投资主要指标

单位：万平方米

指 标	Item	1998	1999	2000	2001	2002	2003
本年完成投资额（亿元）	Investment Completed This Year(100 million yuan)	38.21	44.30	51.85	67.42	79.37	124.82
本年房屋施工面积	Floor Space of Buildings Under Construction This Year	678.87	793.46	763.18	743.78	1172.58	1343.12
#住宅	Residential Buildings	552.37	649.53	619.85	580.43	964.68	943.61
本年房屋竣工面积	Floor Space of Buildings Completed This Year	156.17	377.79	321.10	316.24	329.71	339.67
#住宅	Residential Buildings	133.33	352.28	295.55	269.61	290.30	289.56
本年房屋竣工价值（亿元）	Value of Floor Space of Buildings Completed this Year(100million yuan)	14.36	38.22	26.94	37.20	36.93	54.73
#住宅	Residential Buildings	11.00	33.02	22.97	28.62	30.46	44.01
本年商品房销售面积	Floor Space of Commercialized Buildings Sold	117.11	296.97	212.92	225.35	252.90	252.74
#住宅	Residential Buildings	108.61	284.95	200.77	192.20	237.04	230.28
本年商品房销售额（亿元）	Total Sales of Commercialized Buildings(100 million yuan)	17.74	35.19	32.52	47.22	51.35	54.29
#住宅	Residential Buildings	15.46	32.35	29.46	35.53	45.46	44.25
本年批准预售面积	Approved Pre-sale Area of This Year	252.02	30.25	253.03	67.44	61.02	52.35
#住宅	Residential Buildings	246.77	27.34	253.03	65.20	55.73	49.12
待售面积	Area for Sale	32.52	62.38	36.41	50.82	57.14	63.85
#住宅	Residential Buildings	22.81	52.32	24.02	34.18	44.70	52.34
房屋出租面积	Rental Housing Area	1.04	1.88	1.17	9.19	15.75	10.56
#住宅	Residential Buildings	0.01	0.15	0.02	0.10	1.13	5.43
本年新增固定资产（亿元）	Newly Increased Fixed Assets This Year(100 million yuan)	19.93	43.10	38.38	50.77	48.43	62.13

Main Indicators of Investment in Real Estate Development in Representative Years

2004	2005	2006	2007	2008	2009	2010	2011	2012	2013	2014	2015	2016	2017	2018
169.67	225.23	285.76	387.33	540.26	696.34	842.34	996.81	1281.90	1595.64	1761.88	1831.67	1955.82	2333.34	2518.01
1633.68	2174.29	2383.56	2915.95	3632.87	5708.63	6697.39	8247.69	9947.89	10454.27	12422.10	13392.94	14727.10	15843.92	16044.57
1204.01	1783.36	1890.27	2376.82	3079.13	4901.59	5777.71	7108.27	8294.92	8461.71	9727.60	9777.23	10468.80	11134.28	11208.59
380.84	361.62	399.64	483.30	443.96	542.81	463.65	631.03	1063.70	795.35	1533.70	976.64	1560.18	1634.63	977.28
308.06	316.52	342.15	422.47	412.46	453.49	412.44	564.59	903.82	663.20	1307.64	766.58	1259.24	1281.71	623.40
73.75	80.58	82.02	101.13	106.50	168.08	145.62	213.29	310.57	279.63	442.74	301.86	456.48	571.96	330.61
55.58	68.11	65.80	77.13	96.02	137.42	128.69	185.31	260.04	222.64	368.25	236.66	351.46	448.02	208.68
305.47	497.34	621.50	833.92	760.72	1256.02	1587.81	1778.02	1538.91	1662.75	1707.71	1763.68	2047.67	2509.78	2713.46
279.90	476.39	584.06	782.91	715.76	1202.12	1523.24	1674.85	1383.84	1522.50	1525.95	1584.08	1877.78	2147.67	2221.27
81.35	171.29	206.15	281.79	296.44	488.55	707.00	1091.31	1017.74	1112.87	1100.71	1146.79	1347.08	2123.34	2753.13
71.27	158.03	179.47	251.74	268.92	450.71	661.27	973.71	858.53	976.19	928.74	985.35	1194.41	1743.43	2214.18
176.40	300.07	428.20	491.07	569.22	1125.44	1510.20	3105.76	2627.73	1787.89	842.98	751.15	717.54	634.50	1047.65
159.10	287.13	408.11	457.54	541.20	1095.17	1452.20	2826.79	2340.69	1597.82	727.31	583.55	508.17	515.34	865.40
108.52	123.59	112.49	45.42	55.40	40.68	34.32	59.76	102.58	74.59	187.13	296.50	378.24	379.66	240.04
72.76	99.17	85.89	38.62	35.40	28.73	26.23	45.41	83.78	61.24	143.21	185.96	215.40	176.90	59.98
11.18	17.32	8.53	10.84	34.94	38.23	28.60	8.01	15.16	15.57	7.15	19.64	48.67	57.12	51.95
5.78	4.09	3.74	5.36	4.53	6.55	0.70	3.25	4.03	0.73	0.07	1.47	1.47		2.37
83.36	92.78	100.22	143.17	124.02	195.71	168.20	25.53	358.03	334.41	531.44	335.91	574.54	807.26	409.04

5-19 分区县、开发区房地产开发主要指标（2018年）

单位：万元

区县、开发区	Region	企业（单位）个数（个） Number of Enterprises (unit)	本年完成投资 Investment Completed This Year	本年新增固定资产 Increased Fixed Assets This Year
全　市	**Total**	**1129**	**25180087**	**4090439**
新城区	Xincheng	39	307610	194982
碑林区	Beilin	75	370161	283611
莲湖区	Lianhu	86	1611249	14545
灞桥区	Baqiao	113	3005736	185359
未央区	Weiyang	183	4008101	1477626
雁塔区	Yanta	227	6660305	1540057
阎良区	Yanliang	39	375231	13558
临潼区	Lintong	28	612772	6063
长安区	Chang'an	98	2176064	121938
高陵区	Gaoling	41	526893	161463
鄠邑区	Huyi	41	181735	8370
蓝田县	Lantian	19	110137	3650
周至县	Zhouzhi	20	40238	4770
西咸新区	Xixian	120	5193855	74447
#开发区	**Development Zones**	450	12118084	2492842
高新区	GaoXin	111	2836209	1188905
经开区	JingKai	88	1727041	761792
曲江新区	Qujiang	84	3196756	144142
浐灞生态区	Chanba Eco-District	87	2386229	321664
航空基地	Aviation Industry Base	12	253008	2000
航天基地	Aerospace Base	49	973262	74339
国际港务区	International Trade&Logistic Park	19	745579	

Main Indicators of Real Estate Development by Region and Development Zone（2018）

(10 000 yuan)

房屋施工面积（平方米）Floor Space of Buildings Under Constmction(sq.m)	住宅 Residential Buildings	本年房屋竣工面积（平方米）Floor Space of Buildings Completed this Year(sq.m)	住宅 Residential Buildings	本年房屋竣工价值 Value of Buildings Completed this Year	住宅 Residential Buildings
160445715	**112085903**	**9772813**	**6234005**	**3306138**	**2086791**
4771532	3599011	330726	256893	90602	75713
6129650	4447354	741744	728545	266904	263082
13672998	10869183	45606	44035	14494	13801
17225235	13002996	468036	285936	181861	88650
35835164	23350027	3930303	2289593	1228851	702677
37160090	22319181	3029948	1645031	1193666	689453
1971258	1308468	42560	41839	12654	12459
2495334	2091230	28886	27310	6063	5827
17956766	13072002	387363	284398	100053	79535
5222028	4442078	660001	567469	159283	132475
1776620	1194789	28893	24693	8370	7170
1127740	887880	21225	17658	3650	3043
536972	367153	13874	9557	4770	3060
14564328	11134551	43648	11048	34917	9846
74112266	47797766	5381790	2875012	1999091	1079364
15296234	7441543	2466406	1272600	994764	538699
15441195	8473432	2097994	1087134	627564	289735
14769214	11044054	67514	66414	50000	49000
17059378	13305207	562337	331303	273013	161852
787095	379735	4800	4079	1296	1101
8164365	5570065	182739	113482	52454	38977
2594785	1583730				

5-20 房地产开发投资主要指标（2018年）

Main Indicators of Investment in Real Estate Development（2018）

单位：万元 (10 000 yuan)

指标	Item	全市合计 Total	国有 State-owned	市区 Urban	市属 Municipal
一、企业（单位）个数（个）	**Number of Enterprises(unit)**	**1129**	**27**	**1014**	**1059**
二、本年完成投资	**Investment Completed This Year**	**25180087**	**1163265**	**22073356**	**23931741**
按工程用途分	Grouped by Function				
住宅	Residential Buildings	16553911	954840	14457850	15733619
#别墅、高档公寓	Villas and Top-Grade Apartments	772426		493270	717649
办公楼	Office Buildings	2082622	69563	1864156	2001162
商业营业用房	Houses for Business Use	3267080	77412	2669278	3092558
其他	Others	3276474	61450	3082072	3104402
三、本年新增固定资产	**Increased Fixed Assets This Year**	**4090439**	**493303**	**4052606**	**3910065**
四、房屋施工面积（平方米）	**Floor Space of Buildings Under Construction (sq.m)**	**160445715**	**7581863**	**151157035**	**150288334**
#住宅	Residential Buildings	112085903	5987882	105159899	104892618
五、本年房屋竣工面积（平方米）	**Floor Space of Buildings this Year Completed (sq.m)**	**9772813**	**1121564**	**9718241**	**9451437**
#住宅	Residential Buildings	6234005	982238	6195742	6058524
六、本年房屋竣工价值	**Value of Buildings Completed this Year**	**3306138**	**375162**	**3286976**	**3156977**
#住宅	Residential Buildings	2086791	314920	2070842	1997415
七、本年商品房屋销售面积（平方米）	**Floor Space of Commercialized Buildings Sold this Year(sq.m)**	**27134577**	**699386**	**26029260**	**25606007**
本年商品房销售额	Sales Income of Commercialized Buildings	27531301	456645	26602440	26099899

5-21 商品房销售情况（2018年）

Sales of Commercial Houses（2018）

指 标	Item	全市合计 Total	国有 State-owned	市区 Urban	市属 Municipal
本年商品房销售面积（平方米）	**Floor Space of Commercialized Buildings Sold(sq.m)**	**27134577**	**699386**	**26029260**	**25606007**
现房销售面积（平方米）	**Floor Space of Completed Apartment Sales(sq.m)**	**3636196**	**122843**	**3320788**	**3428254**
期房销售面积（平方米）	**Floor Space of Forward Delivery Housing Sales(sq.m)**	**23498381**	**576543**	**22708472**	**22177753**
住宅	Residential Buildings	22212699	640735	21214543	20935363
#别墅、高档公寓	Villas and High-grade Apartments	353713		319960	343129
办公楼	Office Buildings	2104051	33171	2096129	2052619
商业营业用房	Houses for Business Use	1689091	18953	1599061	1593744
其他	Others	1128736	6527	1119527	1024281
本年商品房销售额（万元）	**Real estate sales this year(10 000Yuan)**	**27531301**	**456645**	**26602440**	**26099899**
现房销售额（万元）	**Floor Space of Completed Apartment Sales**	**2727443**	**72471**	**2503895**	**2596111**
期房销售额（万元）	**Floor Space of Forward Delivery Housing Sales**	**24803858**	**384174**	**24098545**	**23503788**
住宅	Residential Buildings	22141762	373818	21303352	20940626
#别墅高档公寓	Villas and High-grade Apartments	529396		480517	495196
办公楼	Office Buildings	2492080	51308	2482420	2415792
商业营业用房	Houses for Business Use	2204552	27688	2128943	2099287
其他	Others	692907	3831	687725	644194
待售面积（平方米）	**Area for Sale(sq.m)**	**2400434**	**48362**	**2235444**	**2277015**
#待售一年以上（一到三年）	Being Idle for One Year	489963	13749	452770	432898
待售三年以上（含三年）	Being Idle for Three Years	145295	34449	115276	140814
住宅	Residence	599810	28578	536354	566289
#别墅高档公寓	Villas and High-grade Apartments	30781		30355	30781
办公楼	Office Buildings	299642		299642	299642
商业营业用房	Houses for Business Use	869824	19536	780870	837518
其他	Others	631158	248	618578	573566
房屋出租面积（平方米）	**Rental area(sq.m)**	**519505**		**519505**	**519505**
住宅	Residential Buildings	23728		23728	23728
办公楼	Office Buildings	99905		99905	99905
商业营业用房	Houses for Business Use	374974		374974	374974
其他	Others	20898		20898	20898

5-22 房地产开发投资资金来源（2018年）

Source of Funds for Investment in Real Estate Development（2018）

单位：万元 (10 000 yuan)

指 标	Item	全市合计 Total	国有 State-owned	市区 Urban	市属 Municipal
一、本年资金来源合计	**Total**	**43727553**	**1428462**	**39944435**	**41490004**
1. 上年末结余资金	Balance of Last Year	9463575	376646	8983142	9072885
2. 本年实际到位资金	Fully Funded Capital this Year	34263978	1051816	30961293	32417119
(1) 国内贷款	Domestic Loans	2777727	232579	2492473	2632153
#银行贷款	Bank Loan	2092782	80000	1865888	1970261
非银行金融机构贷款	Loans from financial Institutions except Bank	684945	152579	626585	661892
(2) 自筹资金	Self-raising Funds	15063469	567125	12705241	14360278
(3) 定金及预收款	Earnest Money and Advance payment	11186721	175091	10771234	10532632
(4) 个人按揭贷款	Personal Mortgage Loan	3870629	11511	3749953	3583355
(5) 其他资金	Others	1365432	65510	1242392	1308701
二、本年各项应付款合计	**Total Sums of Money to be Paid This Year**	7018937	399420	6254780	6241373
#工程款	Project Fund	3838141	120293	3500936	3514645

5-23 房地产开发经营情况（2018年）

Running of Real Estate Development（2018）

单位：万元 (10 000 yuan)

指　标	Item	全市合计 Total	国有 State-owned	市区 Urban	市属 Municipal
一、资产负债情况	**Assets and Liabilities**				
1. 资产总计	Total Assets	116912727	9852095	111572243	108269257
2. 负债合计	Total Liabilities	101802708	7936241	97127657	94196301
3. 所有者权益合计	Total Creditor's Equity	15110019	1915853	14444585	14072957
#实收资本	Held Capital	11063361	901475	10563343	10223676
二、损益及分配情况	**Profit or Loss and the Distribution**				
1. 主营业务收入	Revenue from Principal Business	12603487	1167048	12076350	11772637
土地转让收入	Revenue of Land Transferred	55525	1000	55063	55525
商品房屋销售收入	Revenue of Commercial Houses Sold	12015148	980395	11500876	11207069
自持物业收入	Self-owned Property Income	184278	29958	182994	184184
房屋出租收入	Revenue of Houses Leased	122628	17474	121444	122534
其他收入	Other Revenue	348535	155695	337416	325859
2. 主营业务成本	Cost of Principal Business	9815010	934887	9399628	9146040
3. 主营业务税金及附加	Taxes and Other Charges on Principal Business	507300	40797	484868	464162
4. 其他业务利润	Other Business Profit	18812	1306	18833	18706
5. 销售费用	Sales Expenditures	666380	26817	628113	634043
6. 管理费用	Management Cost	568162	67609	537845	545142
7. 财务费用	Fiscal Expenditure	306804	38810	297553	299724
#利息支出	Interest Exchange	254009	58449	253312	248221
8. 营业利润	Operating Profit	934333	111100	886097	866537
投资收益	Investment Revenue	44086	9440	36499	36094
营业外收入	Non-business Revenue	49639	7765	47675	49064
营业外支出	Non-business Expenditures	115890	2982	103459	100013
9. 利润总额	Total Profit	931181	261194	917216	878699
10. 应付职工薪酬	Salary Payable	491168	56012	457960	466388
11. 应交增值税	Value-added Tax Payable	678332	48737	656322	624608
三、全部从业人员年平均人数	**Average Number of Employed Persons**	**78134**	**4774**	**77833**	**77833**
四、本年应付工资总额	**Total Wages This Year**	**513543**	**28968**	**512181**	**512181**

主要统计指标解释

全社会固定资产投资 是以货币形式表现的在一定时期内全社会建造和购置固定资产的工作量以及与此有关的费用的总称。该指标是反映固定资产投资规模、结构和发展速度的综合性指标，又是观察工程进度和考核投资效果的重要依据。全社会固定资产投资按登记注册类型可分为国有、集体、联营、股份制、私营和个体、港澳台商、外商、其他等。

固定资产投资(不含农户) 指城镇和农村各种登记注册类型的企业、事业、行政单位及城镇个体户进行的计划总投资500万元及500万元以上的建设项目投资和房地产开发投资，包含原口径城镇固定资产投资加上农村企事业组织项目投资，该口径自2011年起开始使用。

房地产开发投资 指各种登记注册类型的房地产开发公司、商品房建设公司及其他房地产开发法人单位和附属于其他法人单位实际从事房地产开发或经营活动的单位统一开发的包括统代建、拆迁还建的住宅、厂房、仓库、饭店、宾馆、度假村、写字楼、办公楼等房屋建筑物和配套的服务设施，土地开发工程（如道路、给水、排水、供电、供热、通讯、平整场地等基础设施工程)的投资；不包括单纯的土地交易活动。

农产投资 是指以农户为单位进行的房屋建设(主要指住宅建设)投资、农村对农、林、牧、渔及服务行业进行的投资(如农户近年广泛进行的设施农业投资)、以及农户购买生产性固定资产的投资。

固定资产投资的资金来源 根据固定资产投资的资金来源不同，分为国家预算资金、国内贷款、利用外资、自筹资金和其他资金。

（1）国家预算资金：包括一般预算、政府性基金预算、国有资本经营预算和社保基金预算等资金。

（2）国内贷款：指报告期固定资产投资单位向银行及非银行金融机构借入的用于固定资产投资的各种国内借款，包括银行利用自有资金及吸收的存款发放的贷款、上级主管部门拨入的国内贷款、国家专项贷款、地方财政专项资金安排的贷款、国内储备贷款、周转贷款等。

（3）利用外资：指报告期收到的用于固定资产建造和购置的境外资金（包括设备、材料、技术在内）。包括对外借款（外国政府、国际金融组织贷款、出口信贷、外国银行商业贷款、对外发行债券和股票）、外商直接投资及外商其他投资。不包括我国自有外汇资金（国家外汇、地方外汇、留成外汇、调剂外汇和中国银行自有资金发行的外汇贷款等）。计算利用外资时，需要折算成人民币，折算中所使用的外汇汇率按现汇计算，即按使用外汇时的汇率计算。

（4）自筹资金：指固定资产投资单位报告期收到的，由各地区、各部门及企、事业单位筹集用于固定资产投资的预算外资金，包括中央各部门、各级地方和企、事业单位的自筹资金。

（5）其他资金：指在报告期收到的除以上各种资金之外其他用于固定资产投资的资金，包括企业或金融机构通过发行各种债券筹集到的资金、社会集资、个人资金、无偿捐赠的资金及其他单位拨人的资金等。

固定资产投资按国民经济行业分 根据现有企业、事业、行政单位和建设项目建成投产后的主要产品种类或主要用途及社会经济活动性质来确定国民经济行业。一般情况下，一个建设项目或一个企业、事业单位只能属于一种国民经济行业。

固定资产投资按隶属关系分 是按建设单位或企业、事业、行政单位的主管上级机关确定的。

（1）中央：是指中共中央、人大常委会和国务院各部、委、局、总公司以及直属机构直接领导的建设项目和企业、事业、行政单位。这些单位的固定资产投资计划由国务院各部门直接编制和下达，建设中所需物资、主要设备以及建设中的问题都由中央有关部门安排和解决。

（2）地方：是由省（自治区、直辖市）、地区（州、盟、省辖市）、县（旗、县级市）三级政府及业务主管部门直接领导和管理的建设项目、企业、事业、行政单位。地方项目还包括不隶属以上各级政府及主管部门的建设项目和企业、事业单位，如外商投资企业和无主管部门的企业等。

固定资产投资按建设性质分 根据整个建设项目情况来确定。建设项目的性质一般分为新建、扩建、改建和技术改造、单纯建造生活设施、迁建、恢复、单纯购置。房地产开发单位、农户投资不划分建设性质。

（1）新建：一般指从无到有开始建设的企业、事业和行政单位或建设项目。有的单位原有基础很小，经过建设后新增的固定资产价值超过该企、事业、行政单位原有固定资产价值（原值）三倍以上的也应作为新建。

（2）扩建：指在厂内或其他地点，为扩大原有产品的生产能力（或效益）或增加新的产品生产能力，而增建主要的生产车间（或主要工程）、分厂、独立的生产线。行政、事业单位在原单位增建业务用房（如学校增建教学用房、医院增建门诊部、病房等）也作为扩建。

现有企、事业单位为扩大原有主要产品生产能力或增加新的产品生产能力，增建一个或几个主要生产车间（或主要工程）、分厂，同时进行一些更新改造工程的，也应作为扩建。

（3）改建和技术改造：指现有企业、事业单位，对原有设施进行技术改造或更新（包括相应配套的辅助性生产、生活福利设施）的建设项目。现有企业、事业单位为适应市场变化的需要，而改变企业的主要产品种类（如军工企业转产民用品等）的建设项目，应作为改建。原有产品生产作业线由于各工序（车间）之间能力不平衡，为填平补齐充分发挥原有生产能力而增建不增加本企业主要产品设计能力的车间，也应作为改建。技术改造是指企业、事业单位在现有基础上，用先进的技术代替落后的技术，用先进的工艺和装备代替落后的工艺和装备，以改变企业落后的技术经济面貌，实现以内涵为主的扩大再生产，达到提高产品质量、促进产品更新换代、节约能源、降低消耗、扩大生产规模、全面提高社会经济效益的目的。技术改造具体包括以下内容：机器设备和工具的更新改造；生产工艺改革、节约能源和原材料的改造；厂房建筑和公共设施的改造；劳动条件和生产环境的改造等。

固定资产投资按构成分 固定资产投资活动按其工作内容和实现方式分为建筑安装工程，设备工具器具购置和其他费用三个部分。

（1）建筑安装工程（建筑安装工作量）：指各种房屋、建筑物的建造工程和各种设备、装置的安装工程。包括各种房屋建造工程；各种用途设备基础和各种工业窑炉的砌筑工程及金属结构工程；为施工而进行的各种准备工作和临时工程以及完工后的清理工作等；铁路、道路的铺设，矿井的开凿及石油管道的架设等；水利工程；防空地下建筑等特殊工程；列入房屋工程预算内的暖气、卫生、通风、照明、煤气等设备的价值及装设油饰工程；列入建筑工程预算内的各种管道（蒸汽、压缩空气、石油、给排水等管道）、电力、电讯电缆导线等的敷设工程；以及各种机械设备的安装下程；为测定安装工程质量，对设备进行的试运工作；房地产开发单位进行的商品房屋开发建设工程、土地开发工程。

在建筑安装工程中，不包括被安装设备本身的价值。

（2）设备工具器具购置：指建设单位或企、事业单位购置或自制的，达到固定资产标准的设备、工具、器具的价值。新建单位及扩建单位的新建车间，按照设计或计划要求购置或自制的全部设备、工具、器具，不论是否达到固定资产标准均计入“设备工具器具购置”中。

（3）其他费用：指在固定资产建造和购置过程中发生的，除上述几项内容以外的各种应分摊计入固定资产的费用。

施工项目 指报告期内所有施工的建设项目个数，包括本年新开工的项目和以前年度开工在本年继续施工的建设项目。凡是报告期内施过工的建设项目，不论施工时间长短，均作为施工项目统计。施工项目个数可以反映一定时期固定资产投资的实际规模，与同期全部建成投产项目个数相比，可以从建设速度的角度反映固定资产投资的效果。

全部建成投产项目 指报告期内按设计文件规定的全部生产能力（或效益）建成投产，经验收合格交付使用的建设项目。

新增生产能力（或工程效益） 指通过固定资产投资活动而增加的设计能力（或工程效益）。主要指标包括建设规模、本年施工规模、自开始建设累计新增生产能力（或工程效益）、本年新增生产能力（或工程效益）等。

建设规模 指建设项目或工程设计文件中规定的全部设计能力（或工程效益）。包括已经建成投产和尚未建成投产的工程的生产能力（或工程效益）。

本年施工规模 指报告期内施工的单项工程的设计能力（或工程效益），即全部建设规模中在本年正式施工的部分。

自开始建设累计新增生产能力（或工程效益） 指自开始建设至本年底止建成投产的全部单项工程累计的新增生产能力（或工程效益）。

本年新增生产能力（或工程效益） 指在本年度内按照新增生产能力（或工程效益）的计算条件和标准，实际建成投入生产或交付使用的生产能力（或工程效益）。

施工房屋面积 指报告期内施工的全部房屋（包括地下室、半地下室以及配套房屋）建筑面积。包括本期新开工的面积和上期开工跨入本期继续施工的房屋面积，以及上期已停建在本期恢复施工的房屋面积。本期竣工和本期施工后又停缓建的房屋，其建筑面积仍计入本期房屋施工面积中。

竣工房屋面积 指在报告期内房屋建筑按照设计要求已经全部完工，达到住人和使用条件，经验收鉴定合格（或达到竣工验收标准），可正式移交使用单位的各栋房屋建筑面积的总和。

新增固定资产 指报告期内交付使用的固定资产价值。包括本年内建成投入生产或交付使用的工程投资和达到固定资产标准的设备、工具、器具的投资及有关应摊入的费用。该指标是表示固定资产投资成果的价值指标，也是反映建设进度，计算固定资产投资效果的重要指标。

项目建成投产率 指一定时期内全部建成投产项目个数与同期施工项目个数的比率。该指标是从建设单位建设速度的角度反映投资效果的指标。

固定资产交付使用率 指一定时期新增固定资产与同期完成投资额的比率。该指标是反映固定资产动用速度，衡量建设过程中宏观投资效果的综合指标。由于新增固定资产是较长时期内形成的结果，而投资额则是当年完成的，因此，该指标一般适宜于反映较长时期内固定资产的动用情况。

商品房销售面积 指报告期内出售商品房屋的合同总面积（即双方签署的正式买卖合同中所确定的建筑面积）。由现房销售建筑面积和期房销售建筑面积两部分组成。

商品房销售额 指报告期内出售商品房屋的合同总价款（即双方签署的正式买卖合同中所确定的合同总价）。该指标与商品房销售面积同口径，由现房销售额和期房销售额两部分组成。

经济适用房 指根据经济适用房计划安排建设的政策性住宅。经济是指房屋建筑造价和销售价格低于一般商品住宅；适用是指适合中低收入家庭购买使用。经济适用房主要是由地方政府统一下达投资计划，房地产公司开发，对外销售；用地一般采用行政划拨或招标投标方式，免收土地出让金；对各种经批准的收费减半征收，开发利润不超过3%；销售价格实行政府指导价。该指标可以分析房地产投资结构，反映中低收入家庭商品住宅的供求平衡情况。

Explanatory Notes on Main Statistical Indicators

Total Investment in Fixed Assets in the Whole Country refers to the volume of activities in construction and purchases of fixed assets of the whole country and related fees, expressed in monetary terms during the reference period. It is a comprehensive indicator which shows the size, structure and growth of the investment in fixed assets, providing a basis for observing the progress of construction projects and evaluating results of investment. Total investment in fixed assets in the whole country includes, by type of ownership, the investment by State-owned units, collective-owned units, joint ownership units, share-holding units, private units individuals as well as investments by entrepreneurs from Hong Kong, Macao and Taiwan, foreign investors and others.

Investment in Fixed Assets (Excluding Rural Households) refers to the investment in construction projects with a total planned investment of 5 million yuan and above by enterprises of various ownerships, public institutions, administrative units and urban self-employed individuals, and the investment in real estate development in both urban and rural areas. Since 2011, it covers the urban investment in fixed assets of original statistical ranges and project investments by rural enterprises and public institutions.

Investment in Real Estate Development refers to investment by real estate development companies, commercialized buildings construction companies and other real estate development units of various types of ownership in the construction of buildings, such as residential buildings, factory buildings, warehouses, hotels, guesthouses, holiday villages, office buildings, and the complementary service facilities and land development projects, such as roads, water supply, water drainage,power supply,heating sup ply, telecommunications, land leveling and other infrastructural projects. It does not include activities in pure land transactions.

Investmentof Rural Households refers to the Housing construction investment (mainly residential construction) taken by the Rural Households as one unit, rural investment in agriculture, forestry, animal husbandry, fishery and service industries (such as the extensive facility agriculture investment of farmers in recent years) and investment in productive fixed assets purchased by farmers.

Sources of Funds for Investment in Fixed Assets are categorized as funds from the State budget, domestic loans, foreign investment, self-raised funds, and others, depending on the sources of investment.

(1) Fund from the State budget consists of budgetary appropriation and loans from the State budget. More specifically, it includes, from the budget of the central government, capital construction fund (operation fund and non-operational fund), special expenses, loans from repayment, discount fund, expenses on innovation and trial production of new products, expenses on urban construction, expenses on temporary construction from business departments, development fund for less developed areas, as well as local budgetary fund transferred from the central budget.

(2) Domestic loans refer to loans of various forms borrowed by investing units from banks and non-bank financial institutions during the reference period for the purpose of investment in fixed assets, including loans issued by banks from their self-owned funds and deposit, loans appropriated by higher authorities, special loans by government, loans arranged by local government from special funds, domestic reserve loan, and working loan.

(3) Foreign investment refers to overseas funds received during the reference period for the construction and purchase of investment in fixed assets (covering equipment, materials and technology), including foreign borrowings (loans from foreign governments and international financial institutions, export credit, commercial loans from foreign banks, issue of bonds and stocks overseas), foreign direct investment and other foreign investments. Excluded from this category is capital in foreign exchanges owned by China (foreign exchanges owned by the central and local governments, foreign exchanges retained by enterprises, foreign exchanges by enterprises through the regulating mechanism, loans in foreign exchanges issued by the Bank of China with its own fund, etc). In calculating the utilization of foreign capital, foreign currencies are converted into Chinese Renminbi applying the current exchange rate when the foreign capitals are actually used.

(4) Self-raised funds refer to extra-budgetary funds for investment in fixed assets received during the reference period by investing units from central government ministries, local governments, enterprises and institutions, including their self-raised funds.

(5) Others refer to funds for investment in fixed assets received from sources other than those listed above, including capital raised through issuing bonds by

enterprises or financial institutions, funds raised from individuals and through donations, and funds transferred from other units.

Investment in Fixed Assets by Sector The classification of construction projects by sector is determined by enterprises, institutions, administrative units and the major products or the purpose of the projects of existing enterprises, institutional and administrative units when they are put into production or use, and by the nature of their social economic activities. In general, one project or one enterprise or institution can only be classified into one sector.

Investment in Fixed Assets by Jurisdiction of Management refers to the classification of investment by the competent authorities under which investment is made by construction units, enterprises, institutions or administrative units.

(1) Central investment refers to the investment in projects or by enterprises, institutions or administrative units which are under the direct leadership and management of the State Council and of the national commissions, ministries, agencies and State-owned large corporations. Various ministries and departments of the State Council prepare and implement plans for investment in fixed assets by those departments, and arrange and ensure the supply of materials and key equipment required for the projects.

(2) Local investment refers to the investment in projects or by enterprises, institutions or administrative units which are under the direct leadership and management of departments under the provincial, prefecture and county governments. Also included are projects by foreign-invested enterprises and enterprises without competent managing authorities.

Investment in Fixed Assets by Type of Construction Construction projects in general can be classified, by the type of construction, into new construction, expansion, reconstruction and technical transformation, purely construction of living facilities, moving, restoration and purely purchasing. However, investment by type of construction is not applied to investment by real-estate development units and investment by rural households.

(1) New construction in general refers to construction projects, which start from scratch, of enterprises, institutions, administrative agencies. In case the size of the existing unit is quite small, and the value of newly added fixed assets is more than three times of the original value, the expansion will be considered as new construction.

(2) Expansion refers to construction of new major production workshop, branch factory or independent production line within a factory or in other locations, for the purpose of increasing the production capacity (or improving efficiency) or adding new production capacity. Newly constructed accommodation for the operation of institutions and administrative organizations (such as newly constructed buildings for teaching in schools, buildings for clinics or wards in hospitals, etc.) are also classified as expansion.

Also included in expansion are investments by existing enterprises or institutions in building major production line(s) or branch factory(ies) along with some work on innovation, for the purpose of expanding the production capacity of original products or producing new products.

(3) Reconstruction and technical transformation refers to construction projects by existing enterprises or institutions in innovation or technical transformation of the old facilities (including auxiliary production equipment and welfare facilities). Also considered as reconstruction is the construction of new workshops by the existing enterprises or institutions to change the variety of products to meet the market demand (such as the production of civil products by defence industries), or to bring the designed production capacity into full play through a more balanced production process on production lines. Technical transformation refers to replacement of old technology or equipment by new technology or equipment, in order to expand the reproduction through improvement of technology contents in production, to improve product quality, to promote new products to save energy,to reduce consumption, to expand the production scale and to improve overall social-economic efficiency. Contents of technical transformation include: updating of machinery, equipment and tools; reforming production process by using energy or materials saving technology; construction of factory workshops and transformation of public facilities; improvement of working conditions and environment, etc.

Investment in Fixed Assets by Structure By their

contents and the mode of implementation, investment activities are classified into 3 categories, i.e. construction and installation, purchase of equipment and instrument, and other expenses.

(1) Construction and installation (work volume of construction and installation) refers to the construction of houses and buildings and the installation of various kinds of equipment and instruments. They include construction of houses; equipment foundations, industrial kilns and stoves, and metal structure work; preparation works and temporary works for project construction, and clearing up works post project construction; pavement of railways and roads, drilling of mines and putting up of oil pipes; construction of water conservancy; construction of underground air-raid shelters and construction of other special projects; value of equipment for heating, sanitation, ventilation, lighting, gas, painting, etc. that are covered by the budget of housing projects; laying out of various pipelines (for steam, compressed air, petroleum, tap water and sewage) and wiring and cabling for electric power and for communications; installation of various machinery and equipment; testing operation for pre- testing the quality of installation projects, and land and other development work conducted by real estate developers for commercialized housing.

The value of equipment installed is itself not included in the value of construction and installation projects.

(2) Purchase of equipment and instruments refers to the total value of equipment, tools, and instruments purchased or self-produced which come up to the cut-off point for fixed assets by the construction units or investing enterprises or institutions. Equipment, tools and instruments purchased or self-produced for new workshops by newly established or expanded units are categorized as "purchase of equipment and instruments" no matter whether they come up to the cut-off point for fixed assets.

(3) Other expenses refer to expenses arising during the construction or purchase of fixed assets other than those mentioned above.

Projects under Construction refer to number of all projects with construction activities newly started in current year or left-over from the previous year in the reference period. All projects that have construction activities undertaken during the reference period are reported as projects under construction irrespective of the length of construction work. The number of projects under construction can reflect the actual size of investment in fixed assets during a given period, and when compared with the number of projects completed and put into use during the same period, it demonstrates the results of investment in fixed assets from the angle of the speed of the construction.

Projects Completed and Put into Use refer to projects have been completed in accordance with the design documents, resulting in forming production capacity (efficiency) and have been checked and accepted after relevant tests, and have been formally delivered for use.

Newly Increased Production Capacity (or Project Efficiency) refers to the increase in design capacity (or project efficiency) through investment in fixed assets. The main indicators include: construction scale, scale of projects under construction in current year, the accumulated newly increased production capacity (project efficiency) since the start of the projects and the newly increased production capacity (project efficiency) of current year.

Construction Scale refers to the total designed production capacity (project efficiency) of the construction projects in accordance with the design document, including those have been put into operation and those that have not been completed.

Scale of Projects under Construction in Current Year refers to the designed production capacity (project efficiency) of a single project under construction in the reference period, i.e. the part of the total scale of project which is officially under construction in current year.

The Accumulated Newly Increased Production Capacity (project efficiency) since the Start of the Projects refers to the accumulated newly increased production capacity of all the single projects which have been put into use from the beginning of the projects till the end of current year.

The Newly Increased Production Capacity (project efficiency) of Current Year refers to the production capacity (project efficiency) that has been completed and put into operation in current year according to the calculation conditions and standards on newly increased production capacity (project efficiency).

Floor Space of Buildings under Construction refers to the total floor space of all the buildings (including basement, semi-basement and auxiliary buildings), including the effective area and the area occupied by the structure. This indicator is one of the important indicators in physical terms to reflect the scale and accomplishment of the construction industry and also an important basis for monitoring the progress, Calculating the cost, analyzing the efficiency and studying the supply of building materials in relation to the construction projects.

Floor Space Completed refers to the floor space of all buildings completed in the reference period, which have been appraised and accepted (or come up to the designed standards) and have been transferred to owner units.

Newly Increased Fixed Assets refer to the value of fixed that has been put into use, including investment in projects that have been completed and put into operation in current year and the investment in equipment, tools and appliance that meet the standard of fixed assets and fees that should be apportioned. This is an indicator that demonstrates the results of investment in fixed assets in monetary terms, and an important indicator to reflect the speed of construction and to calculate the efficiency of investment.

Rate of Construction Projects Completed and Put into Use refers to the ratio of the number of construction projects completed and put into use in a certain period of time to the number of projects under construction in the same period. This reflects the investment efficiency from the perspective of the speed of projects construction.

Rate of Projects of Fixed Assets Completed and Put into Operation refers to the ratio of the newly increased fixed assets to the total investment made in the same period. This is a comprehensive indicator reflecting the speed of the employment of fixed assets and the investment efficiency at the macro-level. As the newly increase fixed assets is the result of a long period while the investment is completed in the current year, this indicator is expected to be used to reflect the employment of fixed assets over a long period of time.

6 财 政

GOVERNMENT FINANCE

资料整理：罗延庆
Data management:Luo Yanqing
数据审核：刘　婷
Data audit:Liu Ting

第六部分　财政

一、简要说明

本章资料主要包括地方财政收入、支出总额构成及分区县情况，由西安市统计局综合处根据西安市财政局提供资料整理。

二、主要指标

财政总收入（亿元）	1460.39	比上年增长	13.6%
一般公共预算收入（亿元）	684.70	比上年增长	10.8%
一般公共预算支出（亿元）	1151.87	比上年增长	10.2%

6 GOVERNMENT FINANCE

Ⅰ.Brief Introduction

This chapter consists of primarily data on regional revenue, expenditure of the municipal government, regional revenue and expenditure of the districts and the counties. The data are provided by the Xi'an Bureau of Finance and are compiled by Integration division of the Xi'an Bureau of Statistics.

Ⅱ.Major Indicators

		Increase over Preceding Year
Total Government Revenue(100 mil. yuan)	1460.39	13.6%
General Pubilc Budgetary Revenue(100 mil. yuan)	684.70	10.8%
General Pubilc Budgetary Expenditures(100 mil. yuan)	1151.87	10.2%

6-1 主要年份地方财政一般预算收入及支出

General Public Budgetary Revenue and Expenditure of Local Finance in Representative Years

单位：亿元 (100 million yuan)

年 份 Year	财政总收入 Fiscal Revenue	一般公共预算收入 General Public Budgetary Revenue	一般公共预算支出 General Public Budgetary Expenditure	收支差额 Balance of Payments	财政总收入比上年增长（%） Fiscal Revenue Increased over the Previous Year（%）	一般公共预算收入比上年增长（%） General Public Budget Revenue Growth over the Previous Year（%）	一般公共预算支出比上年增长（%） General Public Budget Expenditures Growth over the Previous Year（%）
2000	61.57	41.39	46.50	-5.11		14.4	
2001	75.79	51.45	54.21	-2.76	23.1	9.9	10.2
2002	99.84	54.49	63.80	-9.32	31.7	16.9	11.3
2003	120.64	64.80	72.37	-7.57	20.8	21.6	22.6
2004	133.52	75.31	84.20	-8.88	10.7	20.0	16.3
2005	163.87	73.05	97.82	-24.76	22.7	18.2	16.2
2006	195.96	85.89	119.22	-33.33	19.6	18.6	21.9
2007	260.70	112.92	161.25	-48.33	33.0	31.5	35.3
2008	324.49	145.61	226.99	-81.38	24.5	28.9	40.8
2009	399.53	181.40	276.85	-95.45	23.4	24.6	22.0
2010	510.69	241.86	371.62	-129.76	27.6	33.3	34.2
2011	649.88	318.55	494.58	-176.03	27.3	31.7	33.1
2012	753.08	396.96	597.49	-200.53	15.9	24.6	20.8
2013	902.76	501.98	729.81	-227.84	19.9	26.5	22.1
2014	1019.69	583.79	819.54	-235.75	13.0	16.3	12.3
2015	1114.98	650.99	917.24	-266.25	9.3	16.3	12.9
2016	1135.68	641.07	942.52	-301.46	8.5	11.1	2.8
2017	1364.71	654.50	1045.09	-390.59	12.6	9.8	7.1
2018	1460.39	684.70	1151.87	-467.17	13.6	10.8	10.2

注：本表数据来源于市财政局，对部分历史年份数据进行了修订。

6-2 财政收入（2018年）

Government Revenue（2018）

单位：万元 （10 000 yuan）

指 标	Item	2018
财政总收入	**Total Government Revenue**	**14603854**
#一般公共预算收入	**General Public Budgetary Revenue**	**6847035**
一、税收收入	**Total Tax Revenue**	**5565811**
1. 国内增值税	Value-added Tax	813593
2. 改征增值税	Levying VAT	1319441
3. 营业税	Business Tax	3701
4. 企业所得税	Corporate Income Tax	539562
5. 个人所得税	Individual Income Tax	312332
6. 城建税	City Maintenance and Construction Tax	453433
7. 房产税	House Property Tax	262192
8. 城镇土地使用税	Urban Land Use Tax	110558
9. 印花税	Stamp Tax	153164
10. 车船税	Tax on the Use of Vehicles and Ships	98257
11. 土地增值税	Land Appreciation Tax	736785
12. 资源税	Resource Tax	18041
13. 环境保护税	Environmental Protection Tax	548
14. 耕地占用税	Farm Land Occupatian Tax	107508
15. 契税	Deed Tax	636696
二、非税收入	**Total Non-tax Revenue**	**1281224**
1. 行政性收费收入	Charge of Adminnistrative and Institutional Units	151928
2. 罚没收入	Penalty Receipts	185509
3. 专项收入	Special Program Receipts	474231
4. 国有资源（资产）有偿使用收入	Revenue for the Use of State-owned Assets (Resources)	356158
5. 捐赠收入	Donation Income	158
6. 政府住房基金收入	Governmental Housing Fund Income	92376
7. 其他收入	Other Revenue	20864
政府性基金预算收入	**Governmental Fund Budgetary Revenue**	**7683433**

注：本表数据来源于市财政局。

6-3 财政支出（2018年）

Government Expenditures (2018)

单位：万元 (10 000 yuan)

指 标	Item	2018
一般公共预算支出	**General Public Budgetary Expenditure**	**11518741**
1. 一般公共服务支出	Expenditure for General Public Services	1050070
2. 国防支出	Expenditure for National Defense	15976
3. 公共安全支出	Expenditure for Public Security	693634
4. 教育支出	Expenditure for Education	1571932
5. 科学技术支出	Expenditure for Science and Technology	482295
6. 文化体育与传媒支出	Expenditure for Cultural, Sports and Media	280503
7. 社会保障和就业支出	Expenditure for Social Safety Net and Employment Effort	1307951
8. 医疗卫生与计划生育支出	Expenditure for Medical 、 Health Care and Brith Control Planning	929633
9. 节能环保支出	Expenditure for Energy Saving	534790
10. 城乡社区事务支出	Expenditure for Urban and Rural Community Affairs	2474744
11. 农林水事务支出	Expenditure for Agriculture, Forestry and Water Conservancy	629817
12. 交通运输支出	Expenditure for Transportation	147637
13. 资源勘探电力信息等事务支出	Expenditure for Exploration of the Power of Information	227078
14. 商业服务业等事务支出	Expenditure for Business Services	249238
15. 金融支出	Expenditure for Finance	16856
16. 国土海洋气象等支出	Expenditure for Land and Marine Meteorology	54974
17. 住房保障支出	Expenditure for Housing Security	439600
18. 粮油物资储备支出	Expenditure for Grain and Oil Stockpiles	18685
19. 债务付息支出	Debt Service Expenditure	264063
20. 其它支出	Other Expenditure	128101
21. 债务发行费用支出	Debt Issuance Expenditure	1164
政府性基金支出	**Governmental Fund Budgetary Expenditure**	**7360299**

注：本表数据来源于市财政局。

6-4 各区县、开发区财政收入（2018年）

单位：万元

区县、开发区	Region	一般公共预算收入 General Public Budgetary Revenue	税收收入 Tax Revenue	增值税 Value Added Tax	营业税 Business Revenue	企业所得税 Corporate Income Tax
合计	**Total**	**6847035**	**5565811**	**2133034**	**3701**	**539562**
市本级合计	Sum of City Level	1137239	612409	310872	-156	52458
新城区	Xincheng	218916	199683	75870	66	40982
碑林区	Beilin	438308	398982	177698	681	73321
莲湖区	Lianhu	488104	363252	173808	72	33943
雁塔区	Yanta	484137	443921	186442	579	45027
灞桥区	Baqiao	196462	168549	61204	93	12697
未央区	Weiyang	354078	309345	115823	751	29597
阎良区	Yanliang	96672	84935	16384	44	4029
临潼区	Lintong	134213	113628	33647	678	4985
长安区	Chang'an	243684	196123	78687	100	19486
高陵区	Gaoling	124008	109692	44618	331	5907
鄠邑区	Huyi	117810	67306	31333	81	3743
蓝田县	Lantian	30470	20216	9584	3	1403
周至县	Zhouzhi	26801	19622	9492		527
西咸新区	Xixian	519693	443213	165578	36	28385
全市中：高新区	Total City: Gao Xin	1053726	934615	337206	942	112237
经开区	JingKai	417628	386854	154882	246	29396
曲江新区	Qujiang	419665	382201	77899	-836	22082
浐灞生态区	Chanba Eco-District	185087	161038	28906	-127	9180
航天基地	Aerospace Base	63344	57771	11810	63	4282
航空基地	Aviation Industry Base	14030	13062	4633	53	1009
国际港务区	International Trade&Logistic Park	82960	79394	26658	1	4886

注：本表数据来源于市财政局。

Government Revenue by Region and Development Zone（2018）

（10 000 yuan）

一般公共预算收入 General Public Budgetary Revenue					
税收收入 Tax Revenue					
个人所得税 Individual Income Tax	资源税 Resource Tax	城市维护建设税 City Maintenance and Construction Tax	耕地占用税 Farm Land Occupation Tax	契税 Deed Tax	其他各项税收收入 Other Tax Revenue
312332	**18041**	**453433**	**107508**	**636696**	**1361504**
52893	16558	62836			116948
11473		16888		11890	42514
37321		35110		28325	46526
22490	4	35745		33454	63736
28439	3	37508	597	48993	96333
4250		12943	2015	15914	59433
12042	1	28418	6064	29978	86671
4805		3137	10754	32779	13003
3063	104	7044	38136	10609	15362
8184	44	13767	4178	30608	41069
4814		9703	3231	15469	25619
2024	363	4920	5370	4194	15278
581	34	1537	751	2409	3914
991	13	1360	2288	661	4290
9966	917	35292	23901	82371	96767
80650		82432	2267	78092	240789
13419		31195		42021	115695
7981		15894		82777	176404
1957		6437		61891	52794
2731		4079		10008	24798
646		1511		1435	3775
1612		5677	7956	12818	19786

6-4 续表1

单位：万元

区县、开发区	Region	一般公共预算收入 General Public Budgetary Revenue		
		非税收入 Non-tax Revenue	专项收入 Special Program Receipts	行政事业性收费收入 Charge of Adiministrative and Institutional Units
合计	**Total**	**1281224**	**474231**	**151928**
市本级合计	Sum of City Level	524830	187044	79382
新城区	Xincheng	19233	9408	2803
碑林区	Beilin	39326	19714	2527
莲湖区	Lianhu	124852	20665	6084
雁塔区	Yanta	40216	20259	9474
灞桥区	Baqiao	27913	6840	1508
未央区	Weiyang	44733	20725	4114
阎良区	Yanliang	11737	1766	2733
临潼区	Lintong	20585	4012	3457
长安区	Chang'an	47561	18446	7580
高陵区	Gaoling	14316	5222	2475
鄠邑区	Huyi	50504	6562	4995
蓝田县	Lantian	10254	2820	661
周至县	Zhouzhi	7179	1667	1536
西咸新区	Xixian	76480	46046	15981
全市中：高新区	Total City: Gao Xin	119111	47006	3795
经开区	JingKai	30774	18755	678
曲江新区	Qujiang	37464	9295	977
浐灞生态区	Chanba Eco-District	24049	18587	1101
航天基地	Aerospace Base	5573	5095	15
航空基地	Aviation Industry Base	968	842	52
国际港务区	International Trade&Logistic Park	3566	3455	

continued 1

(10 000 yuan)

一般公共预算收入 General Public Budgetary Revenue			政府性基金预算收入 Governmental Funds Budgetary Revenue
非税收入 Non-tax Revenue			
罚没收入 Penalty Receipts	国有资源(资产)有偿使用收入 The Revenues of the Compensation for the Use of State-owned Resoures(Assants)	其他收入 Other Income	
185509	**356158**	**113398**	**7683433**
100352	75232	82820	761156
4378	2644		280
2674	14411		
3302	94801		103847
2617	7861	5	
2093	17419	53	193909
2583	7033	10278	55318
1328	5910		17554
3394	9609	113	168214
13462	6475	1598	303080
1759	4860		239792
31555	6818	574	50812
2337	4389	47	13095
2909	881	186	37194
4076	7324	3053	2328719
3073	52411	12826	422060
1459	8332	1550	263992
1123	26069		803009
702	3496	163	1192197
258	73	132	312615
65	9		38636
10	101		377954

6-5 各区县、开发区财政支出（2018年）

单位：万元

区县、开发区	Region	一般公共预算支出 General Public Budgetary Expenditures	一般公共服务支出 General Public Services Expenditure	国防支出 Expenditure for National Defense	公共安全支出 Expenditure for Public Safety
合计	**Total**	**11518741**	**1050070**	**15976**	**693634**
市本级合计	Sum of City Level	3421794	233440	11542	377677
新城区	Xincheng	220282	13205	208	19716
碑林区	Beilin	320013	36722		26361
莲湖区	Lianhu	401303	36026	340	21706
雁塔区	Yanta	347208	30347	442	33881
灞桥区	Baqiao	330784	26331	519	20216
未央区	Weiyang	340916	25275	410	23923
阎良区	Yanliang	217355	17304	44	11549
临潼区	Lintong	436318	26526	168	14692
长安区	Chang'an	569454	53823	496	28055
高陵区	Gaoling	340275	40001	322	16845
鄠邑区	Huyi	430238	27991	228	13109
蓝田县	Lantian	387317	35604	233	11832
周至县	Zhouzhi	458309	24577	116	10138
西咸新区	Xixian	872338	181561	37	26238
全市中：高新区	Total City: Gao Xin	885292	68351	871	15796
经开区	JingKai	274239	32466		8025
曲江新区	Qujiang	462313	52728		2564
浐灞生态区	Chanba Eco-District	292270	45639		6859
航天基地	Aerospace Base	74786	6205		663
航空基地	Aviation Industry Base	28786	1837		
国际港务区	International Trade&Logistic Park	407151	34111		3789

注：本表数据来源于市财政局。

Government Expenditure by Region and Development Zone（2018）

（10 000 yuan）

一般公共预算支出 General Public Budgetary Expenditures					
教育支出 Expenditure for Education	科学技术支出 Expenditure for Science and Technology	文化体育与传媒支出 Expenditure for Culture,Sport and Media	社会保障和就业支出 Expenditure for Social Safety Net and Employment Effort	医疗卫生与计划生育支出 Medical 、 Health and Family Planning Expenditure	节能环保支出 Expenditure for Energy Saving and Environment Protection
1571932	**482295**	**280503**	**1307951**	**929633**	**534790**
124290	97208	67750	383490	296088	234138
56115	1920	1282	60394	18881	871
67085	10258	2052	88411	23360	4840
101521	4724	1985	78961	24858	1710
90943	3037	2444	55989	38105	5648
67023	421	2588	41481	26219	9380
93920	2915	3102	37028	27167	4861
48072	2146	1943	30784	25387	4468
101002	1135	5231	92642	57294	12108
140975	803	9105	87486	90268	12780
73632	1388	4207	31159	47219	5671
95226	431	4373	54215	53443	27494
88537	451	4243	73251	53501	5823
110865	1145	5247	51487	65252	17430
136941	500	6599	116140	70593	37622
38571	317415	5515	12334	2928	82770
20301	23276	80	959		56405
46374		147885	121	30	3094
15194	608	183	120		1404
16387	10714	310	500		3541
1200	1300				840
37758	500	4379	10999	9040	1892

6-5 续表1

单位：万元

区县、开发区	Region	一般公共预算支出 General Public Budgetary Expenditures			
		城乡社区支出 Expenditure for Urban and Rural Community Affairs	农林水支出 Expenditure for Agriculture, Foresty and Water Conservancy	交通运输支出 Expenditure for Transportation	资源勘探信息等支出 Expenditure for Exploration of the Power of Information
合计	**Total**	**2474744**	**629817**	**147637**	**227078**
市本级合计	Sum of City Level	898932	89051	72808	69635
新城区	Xincheng	29520	691	1767	1766
碑林区	Beilin	55686	70	646	804
莲湖区	Lianhu	110881	2457	675	1789
雁塔区	Yanta	69366	6214	1380	2519
灞桥区	Baqiao	63334	23387	2163	1979
未央区	Weiyang	91499	8150	1707	1085
阎良区	Yanliang	29252	34112	2277	3967
临潼区	Lintong	27469	54624	4476	3107
长安区	Chang'an	48953	66971	9205	1557
高陵区	Gaoling	41865	39777	10833	1871
鄠邑区	Huyi	68756	62207	6594	5505
蓝田县	Lantian	33274	50625	7922	1778
周至县	Zhouzhi	12922	131718	15245	1809
西咸新区	Xixian	66580	38906	5085	10793
全市中：高新区	Total City: Gao Xin	180311	7808		80350
经开区	JingKai	107144	149	674	19524
曲江新区	Qujiang	174802	5111		321
浐灞生态区	Chanba Eco-District	197348	990		2152
航天基地	Aerospace Base	22717			9856
航空基地	Aviation Industry Base	11005			4682
国际港务区	International Trade&Logistic Park	133128	6799	4180	229

continued 1

(10 000 yuan)

一般公共预算支出 General Public Budgetary Expenditures				
商业服务业等支出 Expenditure for Business Services	金融支出 Expenditure for Finance	国土海洋气象等支出 Land and Marine Meteorological and Other Expenses	住房保障支出 Expenditure for Housing Support	粮油物资储备支出 Expenditure for Grain and Oil Stockpiles
249238	**16856**	**54974**	**439600**	**18685**
70759	7212	12341	192025	13538
2726	1770	632	7422	178
1566		900	229	38
2566	347	800	5881	39
3677	88	2439	55	
1657		1719	32345	1546
2466	208	2180	6259	50
920	471	973	179	387
3975	900	2611	25249	263
4316		6801	5901	961
1364		3715	16552	512
1140	78	2449	4980	416
1368	23	7327	7643	483
1850	50	2419	2945	274
8172	658	2460	47833	
3837	2826	3692	6149	
2348	170	53	1550	
1347	1607		24396	
7221	40	1139	9805	
296	188	160	3089	
618	120		5980	
125049	100	164	33133	

6-5 续表2 continued 2

单位：万元 （10 000 yuan）

区县、开发区	Region	一般公共预算支出 General Public Budgetary Expenditures			政府性基金预算支出 Governmental Fund Budgetary Expenditure
		债务付息支出 Debt Service Expenditure	债务发行费用支出 Debt Issuance Expenditure	其他支出 Other Expenditure	
合计	**Total**	**264063**	**1164**	**128101**	**7360299**
市本级合计	Sum of City Level	145494	1060	23316	1273216
新城区	Xincheng	1218			35745
碑林区	Beilin	985			7960
莲湖区	Lianhu	3787		250	85149
雁塔区	Yanta	563		71	10005
灞桥区	Baqiao	5598		2878	115779
未央区	Weiyang	8711			66503
阎良区	Yanliang	3020		100	62089
临潼区	Lintong	2842		4	185305
长安区	Chang'an	826		172	232177
高陵区	Gaoling	3082		260	125804
鄠邑区	Huyi	1383		220	36532
蓝田县	Lantian	3065		334	10164
周至县	Zhouzhi	1314		1506	28618
西咸新区	Xixian	37716	104	77800	2081767
全市中：高新区	Total City: Gao Xin	35028		20740	412714
经开区	JingKai	1085		30	272658
曲江新区	Qujiang	1883		50	773076
浐灞生态区	Chanba Eco-District	3508		60	1001436
航天基地	Aerospace Base	60		100	267659
航空基地	Aviation Industry Base	1124		80	38900
国际港务区	International Trade&Logistic Park	1771		130	237043

主要统计指标解释

财政收入 指国家财政参与社会产品分配所取得的收入，是实现国家职能的财力保证。主要包括：

(1)税收收入：包括增值税、消费税、营业税、企业所得税、企业所得税退税、个人所得税、资源税、城市维护建设税、房产税、印花税、城镇土地使用税、土地增值税、车船税、船舶吨税、车辆购置税、关税、耕地占用税、契税、烟叶税等。

(2)非税收入：包括专项收入、行政事业性收费、罚没收入、国有资本经营收入、国有资源(资产)有偿使用收入、捐赠收入、政府住房基金收入和其他收入。

财政支出 指国家财政将筹集起来的资金进行分配使用，以满足经济建设和各项事业的需要。主要包括：

(1)一般公共服务支出：指政府提供基本公共管理与服务的支出，包括人大事务、政协事务、政府办公厅(室)及相关机构事务、发展与改革事务、统计信息事务、财政事务、税收事务、审计事务、海关事务、人力资源事务、纪检监察事务、商贸事务、知识产权事务、工商行政管理事务、质量技术监督与检验检疫事务、民族事务、宗教事务、港澳台侨事务、档案事务、民主党派及工商联事务、群众团体事务、党委办公厅（室）及相关机构事务、组织事务、宣传事务、统战事务、对外联络事务、其他共产党事务支出等。

(2)外交支出：指政府外交事务支出，包括外交管理事务、驻外机构、对外援助、国际组织、对外合作与交流、对外宣传、边界勘界联检等方面的支出。

(3)国防支出：指政府用于国防方面的支出，包括用于现役部队、国防科研事业、专项工程、国防动员等方面的支出。

(4)公共安全支出：指政府维护社会公共安全方面的支出，包括武装警察部队、公安、国家安全、检察、法院、司法、监狱、强制隔离戒毒、国家保密、缉私警察、海警等。

(5)教育支出：指政府教育事务支出，包括教育管理事务、普通教育、职业教育、成人教育、广播电视教育、留学教育、特殊教育、进修及培训、教育费附加安排的支出等。

(6)科学技术支出：指用于科学技术方面的支出，包括科学技术管理事务、基础研究、应用研究、技术研究与开发、科技条件与服务、社会科学、科学技术普及、科技交流与合作、科技重大项目等。

(7)文化体育与传媒支出：指政府在文化、文物、体育、新闻出版、广播影视等方面的支出。

(8)社会保障和就业支出：指政府在社会保障与就业方面的支出，包括人力资源和社会保障管理事务、民政管理事务、补充全国社会保障基金、行政事业单位离退休、企业改革补助、就业补助、抚恤、退役安置、社会福利、残疾人事业、自然灾害生活救助、红十字事业、最低生活保障、临时救助、特困人员救助供养、补充道路交通事故社会救助基金、其他生活救助、财政对基本养老保险基金的补助、财政对其他社会保险基金的补助等。

(9)医疗卫生和计划生育支出：指政府医疗卫生方面的支出，包括医疗卫生与计划生育管理事务、公立医院、基层医疗卫生机构、公共卫生、中医药、计划生育事务、食品和药品监督管理事务、行政事业单位医疗、财政对基本医疗保险基金的补助、医疗救助、优抚对象医疗等 。

(10)节能环保支出：指政府节能环保支出，包括环境保护管理事务、环境监测与监察、污染防治、自然生态保护、天然林保护、退耕还林、风沙荒漠治理、退牧还草、已垦草原退耕还草、能源节约利用、污染减排、可再生能源和循环经济、能源管理事务等支出。

(11)城乡社区支出：指政府城乡社区事务支出，包括城乡社区管理事务、城乡社区规划与管理、城乡社区公共设施、城乡社区环境卫生、建设市场管理与监督等。

(12)农林水支出：指政府用于农林水事务支出，包括农业、林业和草原、水利、南水北调、扶贫、农业综合开发、农村综合改革、普惠金融支农发展支出、目标价格补贴等。

(13)交通运输支出：指政府交通运输和邮政业方面的支出，包括公路水路运输、铁路运输、民用航空运输、成品油价格改革对交通运输的补贴、邮政业、车辆购置税等。

(14)资源勘探信息等支出：指政府用于资源勘探、制造业、建筑业、工业信息等方面的支出，包括资源勘探开发、制造业、建筑业、工业和信息产业监管、安全生产监管、国有资产监管、支持中小企业发展和管理等。

(15)商业服务业支出：指政府用于商业服务业方面的支出，包括商业流通事务、旅游业管理与服务、涉外发展服务等。

(16)金融支出：指政府用于金融方面的支出，包括金融部门行政、金融部门监管、金融发展、金融调控等。

(17)援助其他地区支出：指用于援助方政府安排并管理的对其他地区各类援助、捐赠等资金支出。

(18)国土海洋气象等支出：指政府用于国土资源、海洋管理、测绘、地震、气象等公益服务事业方面的支出。

(19)住房保障支出：指政府用于住房方面的支出，包括保障性安居工程、住房改革、城乡社区住宅等。

(20)粮油物资储备支出：指政府用于粮油物资储备方面的支出，包括粮油事务、物资事务、能源储备、粮油储备、重要商品储备等。

（21）债务付息支出：指政府用于归还债务利息等所发生的支出。

（22）债务发行费用支出：指政府用于债务发行兑付费用的支出。

（23）其他支出：指不能划分到上述功能科目的其他政府支出。

中央财政收入和地方财政收入 指按现行分税制财政体制划分的中央本级收入和地方本级收入。属于中央财政的收入包括关税，进口货物增值税和消费税，出口货物退增值税和消费税，消费税，铁道部门、各银行总行、各保险公司总公司等集中缴纳的城市维护建设税，增值税50%部分，纳入共享范围的企业所得税60%部分，未纳入共享范围的中央企业所得税、中央企业上交的利润，个人所得税60%部分，车辆购置税，船舶吨税，证券交易印花税，海洋石油资源税，中央非税收入等。属于地方财政的收入包括地方企业上交利润，城市维护建设税（不含铁道部门、各银行总行、各保险公司总公司集中缴纳的部分），房产税，城镇土地使用税，土地增值税，车船税，耕地占用税，契税，烟叶税，印花税（不含证券交易印花税），增值税50%部分，纳入共享范围的企业所得税40%部分，个人所得税40%部分，海洋石油资源税以外的其他资源税，地方非税收入等。

中央财政支出和地方财政支出 指根据政府在经济和社会活动中的不同职责，划分中央和地方政府的责权，按照政府的责权划分确定的支出。中央财政支出包括一般公共服务，外交支出，国防支出，公共安全支出，以及中央政府调整国民经济结构、协调地区发展、实施宏观调控的支出等。地方财政支出包括一般公共服务，公共安全支出，地方统筹的各项社会事业支出等。

Explanatory Notes on Main Statistical Indicators

Government Revenue refers to income for the government finance through participating in the distribution of social products. It is the financial guarantee to ensure government functioning. The contents of government revenue include the following main items:

(1) Tax revenue, including value added tax(VAT), consumption tax, business tax, corporate income tax, corporate income tax refund ,individual income tax, resource tax, city maintenance and construct tax, house property tax, stamp tax, urban land use tax, land appreciation tax, tax on vehicles and boat operation, ship tonnage tax, vehicle purchase tax, tariffs, farm land occupation tax, deed tax, and tobacco leaf tax, etc.

(2) Non-tax revenue, including special program receipts, charge of administrative and institutional units, penalty receipts, state-owned capital operating income, state-owned resources (assets) compensation for the use of income, donation income, government housing fund income and others non-tax receipts.

Government Expenditure refers to the distribution and use of the funds which the government finance has raised, so as to meet the needs of economic construction and various causes. It includes the following main items:

(1) Expenditure for general public services: It refers to the spending on the basic public management and services which provided by governments, including the expense on affairs of People's Congress, affairs of People's Political Consultative Conference, affairs of government general office and relative institutions, affairs of development and reform, affairs of statistics, affairs of finance, affairs of taxation, affairs of audit, affairs of customs, affairs of human resources and social security, affairs of discipline inspection and supervision, affairs of population and family planning, affairs of commerce and trade, affairs of intellectual property, affairs of administration for industry and commerce, affairs of land and resources, affairs of oceanic administration, affairs of surveying and mapping, affairs of earthquake, ethnic affairs, religious affairs, affairs of Hong Kong, Macao, Taiwan, and Overseas Chinese, affairs of archives administration, affairs of democratic parties and federation of industry and commerce, affairs of mass organization, and affairs of lottery, affairs of the general office of the Party Committee and related institutions, affairs of propaganda, affairs of united front, affairs of external liaison, affairs of expenditure on other Communist Party, other affairs of Chinese Communist Party, etc.

(2) Expenditure for foreign affairs: It refers to the spending of government on foreign affairs, including the expense on administration of foreign affairs, missions overseas, external assistance, international organizations, foreign cooperation and communication, surveying and joint inspection on borderline, etc.

(3) Expenditure for national defense: It refers to the spending of government on national defense, including the expense on active force, scientific research on national defense, special projects, mobilization of national defense, etc.

(4) Expenditure for public security: It refers to the spending of government on maintaining social and public security, including the expense on armed police force, public security, state security, prosecution, courts, justice, prison, compulsory isolation and drug treatment, state secrecy, anti-smuggling police, maritime police, etc.

(5) Expenditure for education: It refers to the spending of government on education, including the expense on the administration of education, general education, regular vocational school education, adult education, radio and television education, student abroad education, special education, education and training, education surtax arrangements spending, etc.

(6) Expenditure for science and technology: It refers to the spending of government on science and technology (S&T), including the expense on the administration of S&T, basic research, applied research, research and development, conditions and services of S&T, social science, popularization of science and technology, exchanges and cooperation of S&T, major project of S&T, etc.

(7) Expenditure for culture, sport and media: It refers to the spending of government on culture, cultural

heritage, sports, radio, film, television, press and publication, etc.

(8) Expenditure for social safety net and employment effort: It refers to the spending of government on social safety net and employment, including the expense on administration of social safety net and employment, civil affairs, subsidy on National Social Security Fund, retirees of administrative units and institutions, subsidy on enterprise reform, subsidy on employment effort, pension, placement of ex-serviceman, social welfare, the handicapped undertakings, living relief of natural disasters, affairs of Red Cross Society, minimum subsistence security, temporary assistance, relief and assistance for the residents living in extreme poverty, supplementary social assistance fund for road traffic accidents, other life assistance, financial subsidy for basic old-age insurance fund, financial subsidy for other social insurance funds, etc.

(9) Expenditure for medical health care and birth control planning: It refers to government spending on health care, including health management services, public hospitals, primary health care institutions, public health, the pharmaceutical, family planning affairs, food and drug supervision and administration affairs, medical treatment of administrative institutions, financial subsidies to basic medical insurance funds, medical assistance, preferential care for the target medical treatment, etc.

(10) Expenditure for energy saving: It refers to the government energy-saving and environmental protection expenditures, including environmental management services, environmental monitoring and surveillance, pollution control, ecological protection, natural forest protection project, forest, desert sand control, pasture, grassland of cultivated farmland, energy conservation and utilization expenditure pollution reduction, renewable energy and comprehensive utilization of resources, etc.

(11) Expenditure for urban and rural community affairs: It refers to the spending of government on urban and rural community affairs, including the expense on administration of urban and rural community, planning and management of urban and rural community, public facilities of urban and rural community, housing of urban and rural community, sanitation of urban and rural community, management and supervision on the construction market, etc.

(12) Expenditure for agriculture, forestry and water conservancy: It refers to the spending of government on agriculture, forestry and water conservancy, including the expense on agriculture, forestry, water conservancy, South-to-North Water Diversion Project, poverty alleviation, agricultural comprehensive development, comprehensive agricultural reform, inclusive financial development expenditure and target price subsidies, etc.

(13) Expenditure for transportation: It refers to the spending of government on transportation and postal services, including the expense on road transport, sea transport, rail transport, civil aviation transportation, oil price reform subsidies for transportation, postal services, vehicle purchase tax, etc.

(14) Expenditure for exploration of the power of information: It refers to the spending on exploration, manufacturing, construction, industry information and other aspects of information, including resource exploration and development, manufacturing, construction, industry and information industry regulation, safety supervision, the state-owned assets supervision and support of small and medium enterprise development and management, etc.

(15) Expenditure for business services: It refers to government spending on commercial aspects of services, including commercial distribution business, tourism management and services, foreign development services, etc.

(16) Expenditure for financial: It refers to government spending on financial aspects, including administrative of financial sector, financial sector supervision, financial development, financial control, etc.

(17) Expenditure for assistance to other parts: It refers to the various types of assistance to other regions, financial donations, donors, government expenditure and management arrangements, etc.

(18) Expenditure for Land and Marine Meteorology:

It refers to government spending on land resources, marine, mapping, seismic, weather and other aspects of public service undertakings, etc.

(19) Expenditure for housing security: It refers to government spending on housing, including affordable housing projects, housing reform, urban and rural communities housing, etc.

(20) Expenditure for Grain and Oil stockpiles: It refers to government spending on supplies of grain and oil reserves, including grain and oil services, supplies services, energy reserves, grain and oil reserves, reserves of other important commodities, etc.

(21) Expenditure for debt interest payment: It refers to the government expenditure for repayment of interest on debts, etc.

(22) Expenditure for debt issuance: It refers to the Government expenditure on debt issuance and payment fees.

(23) Other expenditure: It refers to other government spending cannot be divided into the above functions subjects.

Revenue of the Central Government and Revenue of the Local Governments refers to the revenue collected by the Central Government and that by the local governments as defined by the decentralized taxation system. In accordance with this system, the revenue of the Central Government includes tariff, VAT and consumption tax from imports, VAT and consumption tax rebate for exports, consumption tax, city maintenance and construct tax from the Ministry of Railways, head offices of banks, head offices of insurance company, which are handed over to the government in a centralized way, 50% of the value added tax, 60% the share part of the corporate income tax, unshared part of corporate income tax of the central enterprises, profit handed in by the central enterprises, 60% of individual income tax, vehicle purchase tax, ship tonnage tax, stamp tax on securities transactions, resource tax on the offshore petroleum resources, Central Government non-tax revenue, etc. The revenue of the local governments includes profit handed in by the local enterprises, city maintenance and construct tax (excluding the part of the Ministry of Railways, head offices of banks, head offices of insurance company, which are handed over to the government in a centralized way), house property tax, urban land use tax, land appreciation tax, tax on vehicles and boat operation, farm land occupation tax, deed tax, and tobacco leaf tax, stamp tax, 50% of the value added tax, 40% the share part of the corporate income tax, 40% of individual income tax, resource tax other than the tax on offshore petroleum resources, local non-tax revenue, etc.

Expenditure of the Central Government and Expenditure of the Local Governments according to the different functions of the Central Government and local governments in economic and social activities, the rights of affairs administration are demarcated between those of the Central Government and those of local governments; and the classification of the expenditure between the Central Government and local governments are made on the basis of the classification of the rights of affairs administration between them. The expenditure of the Central Government includes the expenditure for general public services, expenditure for foreign affairs, expenditure for defense, expenditure for public security, and the expenditure of the Central Government for adjusting the national economic structure; coordinating the development among different regions; and exercising macroeconomic regulation. The expenditure of the local governments includes mainly the expenditure for general public services, expenditure for public security, and expenditures for social development which are planned by local governments, etc.

7 物价指数

PRICE INDICES

资料整理：冯诗玮　乔兴录
Data management: Feng Shiwei Qiao Xinglu
数据审核：李　航　高小琴　赵　剑
Data audit: Li Hang Gao Xiaoqin Zhao Jian

第七部分　物价指数

一、简要说明

1.本章资料主要反映生产、流通、消费、投资与房地产等环节价格变动趋势和变动幅度。主要包括居民消费价格指数、商品零售价格指数、工业生产者出厂价格指数、工业生产者购进价格指数、固定资产投资价格指数和住宅销售价格指数。

2.本章资料由国家统计局西安调查队提供。

3.居民消费价格指数、商品零售价格指数资料的获取，是通过抽样调查和重点调查相结合的方式。在西安市区域内选定经营规模大、商品种类多的大型商场、超市、农贸市场和服务网点作为调查点，选择具有代表性的商品和服务项目作为样本，对其市场价格进行定期调查，以样本推断总体。

4.工业生产者出厂价格指数、工业生产者购进价格指数、固定资产投资价格指数，采取抽样调查和重点调查的方法。工业生产者出厂、工业生产者购进价格指数通过西安工业企业网上直报获取。固定资产投资价格指数通过西安建筑安装企业季报获取。住宅销售价格指数通过西安市月度住宅销售网签数据获取。

二、主要指标

商品零售价格总指数（上年=100）	102.2	比上年上升0.5
居民消费价格总指数（上年=100）	101.9	比上年下降0.1

7 PRICE INDICES

Ⅰ.Brief Introduction

1.The data on price indices in this chapter show the changing trends and change rates in the price of production, circulation, consumption, investment and real estate, including mainly consumer price indices, retail price indices, producer price indices for industrial producers, purchasing price indices for industrial producers, price indices for investment in fixed assets, and selling price indices of residential buildings.

2.The data are provided by NBS Survey Office in Xi' an.

3.The data for the calculation of consumer price indices and retail prices and retail price indices in the province are collected through stratified random sampling. Large-scale shops, supermarkets, fairs and service outlets with wide variety of commodities in Xi' an are selected as survey points. Representative commodities and services are selected as sample commodities and services. Regular surveys are conducted to collect data on market prices. The data on the population are estimated on the basis of the sample.

4.The producer price indices for industrial producers, purchasing price indices for industrial producers and price indices for investment in fixed assetsare collected through stratified random sampling. The producer price indices for industrial producers and purchasing price indices for industrial producers are collected by online direct report of Xi'an industrial enterprises. Price indices for investment in fixed assetsare collected by quarterly report of Xi'an construction and installation enterprises. Selling price indices of residential buildings are collected by monthly data of online residential sales record.

Ⅱ.Major Indicators

		Increase over Preceding Year
Retail Price Index(the price of preceding year=100)	102.2	0.5 percentage points
Consumer Price Index(the price of preceding year=100)	101.9	−0.1 percentage points

7-1 主要年份各种价格指数

Price Indices in Representative Years

(以上年价格为100) (the price of preceding year= 100)

年 份 Year	居民消费价格指数 Consumer Price Index	商品零售价格指数 Retail Price Index	工业生产者出厂价格指数 Producer Price Indices (PPI) for Industrial Producers	工业生产者购进价格指数 Industrial Purchasing Indices (IPI) for Industrial Producers	固定资产投资价格指数 Price Index for Investment in Fixed Assets
1980	108.7	109.3			
1981	102.4	102.7			
1982	100.9	101.0			
1983	102.6	102.0			
1984	104.7	104.8			
1985	109.7	109.3			
1986	108.5	107.4			
1987	110.6	111.4			
1988	122.8	123.2			
1989	118.3	117.8			
1990	102.5	100.9			
1991	109.4	108.3			
1992	112.2	112.4			
1993	117.2	112.8	102.5	104.3	
1994	128.5	126.2	132.2	115.0	
1995	117.0	114.6	110.8	113.1	
1996	110.9	107.9	100.7	103.8	
1997	106.0	101.5	98.6	102.5	
1998	97.9	95.5	94.4	97.5	
1999	96.8	97.4	97.5	96.9	100.8
2000	100.2	98.7	99.4	102.4	102.1
2001	99.9	98.9	99.3	101.0	101.3
2002	98.6	98.5	98.2	98.4	101.2
2003	100.5	100.0	101.5	105.3	102.4
2004	102.3	101.9	102.7	110.4	103.3
2005	100.3	99.7	103.9	109.6	102.4
2006	101.6	101.5	103.2	106.1	102.0
2007	104.7	103.7	101.9	106.2	103.5
2008	106.0	105.4	103.7	108.5	110.5
2009	99.7	99.5	99.9	100.7	97.9
2010	103.5	102.7	102.3	106.3	103.8
2011	105.6	104.4	102.5	108.8	105.4
2012	102.8	102.3	100.5	97.2	101.9
2013	102.7	101.7	99.5	97.2	100.8
2014	101.4	100.7	99.5	99.5	100.8
2015	100.7	99.7	98.5	94.5	97.9
2016	100.9	100.1	97.8	97.6	100.0
2017	102.0	101.7	100.3	104.7	105.4
2018	101.9	102.2	101.1	102.7	104.7

注：本表数据来源国家统计局西安调查队。

本表2017年数据为西安原口径数据。下同。

本表2018年PPI、IPI、住宅销售价格指数和固定资产投资价格指数包含西咸地区，其他指标为西安原口径数据。下同。

7-2 居民消费价格指数（2018年）

Residents Consumer Price Indices（2018）

（以上年价格为100） (the price of preceding year=100)

指 标	Item	2018
居民价格消费指数	**Consumer Price Index**	**101.9**
非食品烟酒价格指数	Non-Food，Tobaccol and Liquor Price Index	101.8
服务价格指数	Price Index of Service	102.2
工业品价格指数	Industrial Price Index	101.5
鲜活食品价格指数	Price Index of Fresh Food	102.1
消费品价格指数	Price Index of Consumer Goods	101.8
能源价格指数	Energy Price Index	103.8
非食品价格指数	Non-foodstuff Price Index	102.0
扣除食品和能源价格指数	Price Index with Food And Energy Excluded	101.8
扣除鲜菜鲜果价格指数	Price Index with Fresh Vegetables Fruits Excluded	101.8
扣除自有住房价格指数	Price Index with Self-owned Housing Excluded	102.0
居住（扣自有住房）价格指数	Housing (Self-owned Housing Excluded) Price Index	101.8
一、食品和烟酒	**Food，To bacco and Liquor**	**102.2**
1. 食品	Food	101.8
（1）粮食	Grain	101.6
（2）薯类	Potato	103.4
（3）豆类	Beans	99.2
（4）食用油	Cooking Oil	101.6
（5）菜	Vegetables	103.5
（6）畜肉类	Livestock Meat	97.3
（7）禽肉类	Poultry Meat	101.7
（8）水产品	Aquatic Products	98.4
（9）蛋类	Eggs	115.6
（10）奶类	Milk	103.1
（11）干鲜瓜果类	Dried Fresh Melons and Fruits	102.7
（12）糖果糕点类	Sweets and Cakes	104.7
（13）调味品	Flavouring	99.0
（14）其他食品类	Other Food	100.0
2. 茶及饮料	Tea and Drinks	100.7
3. 烟酒	Tobacco and Liquor	100.3
（1）烟草	Tobacco	99.8
（2）酒类	Liquor	101.2
4. 在外用餐	Dining Out	103.6
二、衣着	**Clothing**	**100.9**
1. 服装	Garments	100.7
2. 服装材料	Clothing Material	100.0
3. 其他衣着及配件	Other Clothing And Accessories	96.8
4. 衣着加工服务费	Clothing Manufacturing Services	106.9
5. 鞋类	Footwear	101.8
三、居住	**Residence**	**101.7**
1. 租赁房房租	Rental Housing	102.5
2. 住房保养维修及管理	Housing Maintenance And Management	102.5
3. 水电燃料	Water,Electricity, Fuels	101.1
4. 自有住房	Private Housing	101.6

注：本表数据来源国家统计局西安调查队。

7-2 续表 continued

(以上年价格为100) (the price of preceding year= 100)

指 标	Item	2018
四、生活用品及服务	**Daily Necessities and Services**	**102.8**
1. 家具及室内装饰品	Furniture and Interior Decorations	103.4
2. 家用器具	Household Appliances	99.2
3. 家用纺织品	Home Textiles	101.6
4. 家庭日用杂品	Daily Use Household Articles	102.8
5. 个人护理用品	Personal Care Articles	101.1
6. 家庭服务	Home Services	113.4
五、交通和通信	**Transportation And Communication**	**100.7**
1. 交通	Transportation	100.9
（1）交通工具	Transportation Facility	98.5
（2）交通工具用燃料	Fuels For Vehicles	112.8
（3）交通工具使用和维修	Vehicles Use And Maintenance	99.7
（4）交通费	Traffic Fare	101.9
2. 通信	Communications	100.3
（1）通信工具	Telecommunication facility	101.1
（2）通信服务	Telecommunication Service	100.0
（3）邮递服务	Postal Service	99.9
六、教育文化和娱乐	**Education, Culture And Recreation**	**101.6**
1. 教育	Education	102.2
（1）教育用品	Educational Articles	102.7
（2）教育服务	Education Service	102.2
2. 文化娱乐	Culture And Recreation	100.9
（1）文娱耐用消费品	Durable Consumer Goods for Cultural and Recreational Use and Service	99.3
（2）其他文娱用品	Other Recreational Articles	105.0
（3）文化娱乐服务	Cultural And Recreational Services	98.7
（4）旅游	Touring	101.2
七、医疗保健	**Health Care**	**104.3**
1. 药品及医疗器具	Medical Instrument Articles	104.3
（1）中药	Traditional Chinese Medicine	110.4
（2）西药	Western Medicine	102.7
（3）滋补保健品	Health Care Articles	100.8
（4）医疗卫生器具	Medical Apparatus	100.0
（5）保健器具	Health Care Appliances	100.0
2. 医疗服务	Medical Service	104.3
八、其他用品和服务	**Other Supplies And Services**	**100.1**
1. 其他用品类	Other Supplies	98.3
（1）首饰手表	Jewelry and Watches	96.6
（2）其他杂项用品	Other Miscellaneous Articles	100.5
2. 其他服务类	Other Service	102.4

7-3 商品零售价格指数（2018年）

Retail Price Indices（2018）

(以上年价格为100) (the price of preceding year= 100)

指　标	Item	2018
商品零售价格指数	**Retail Price Indices**	**102.2**
一、食品	**Food**	**102.2**
1. 粮食	Grain	101.6
2. 薯类	Potato	103.4
3. 豆类	Beans	99.2
4. 食用油	Cooking Oil	101.5
5. 菜	Vegetables	103.5
6. 畜肉类	Livestock Meat	96.2
7. 禽肉类	Poultry Meat	101.7
8. 水产品	Aquatic Products	98.9
9. 蛋类	Eggs	115.6
10. 奶类	Milk	103.1
11. 干鲜瓜果类	Dried Fresh Melons and Fruits	102.7
12. 糖果糕点类	Sweets and Cakes	104.7
13. 调味品	Flavouring	99.0
14. 其他食品类	Other Food	100.0
15. 在外餐饮	Dining Out	103.6
二、饮料、烟酒	**Drinks, Tobacco and Liquor**	**100.5**
1. 茶及饮料	Tea and Drinks	100.7
2. 烟草	Tobacco	99.8
3. 酒类	Liquor	101.2
三、服装、鞋帽	**Garments, Shoes And Hats**	**100.8**
1. 服装	Garments	100.7
2. 鞋帽袜	Footwear and Hats	101.3
3. 其他衣着配件	Other Clothing Accessories	98.8
四、纺织品	**Textiles**	**102.5**
1. 服装材料	Cotton Cloth	100.0
2. 床上用品	Blend Cloth	102.8
五、家用电器及音像器材	**Household Appliances，Music and Video Equipment**	**98.8**
1. 家庭设备	Household Facility	99.1
2. 文娱用耐用消费品	Durable Consumer Goods for Cultural and Recreational Use	98.0
3. 专业音响器材	Music and Video Equipment	99.8

注：本表数据来源国家统计局西安调查队。

7-3 续表 continued

(以上年价格为100) (the price of preceding year= 100)

指 标	Item	2018
六、文化办公用品	**Cultural and Office Appliances**	**102.3**
七、日用品	**Articles for Daily Use**	**103.2**
1. 日用百货	General Merchandise for Daily Use	100.5
2. 厨具餐具茶具	Kitchenware, Tableware, Tea Set	103.0
3. 清洗用品	Daily Use Articles For Washing	107.7
4. 其他日用品	Other Daily Articles	100.8
八、体育娱乐用品	**Sports And Recreation Articles**	**100.8**
1. 体育户外用品	Sports Outdoor Articles	100.4
2. 娱乐用品	Recreation Articles	101.0
九、交通、通信用品	**Transportation And Communication Goods**	**99.6**
1. 交通运输机械	Transportation Machinery	99.2
2. 通信器材	Communication Equipment	102.0
十、家具	**Furniture**	**104.6**
十一、化妆品	**Cosmetics**	**101.6**
十二、金银饰品	**Gold , Silver and Jewelry**	**95.8**
十三、中西药品及医疗保健用品	**Traditional Chinese And Western Medicines And Health Care Articles**	**104.3**
1. 医疗卫生器具	Medical Apparatus	100.0
2. 中药	Traditional Chinese Medicine	110.4
3. 西药	Western Medicine	102.7
4. 保健器具及用品	Health Care Apparatus and Article	100.4
十四、书报杂志及电子出版物	**Books, Newspapers,Magazines And Electronic Publications**	**105.9**
1. 教材及参考书	Teaching Materials and Reference Books	102.7
2. 书报杂志	Books, Newspapers,Magazines	114.2
3. 计算机办公软件	Computer Office Software	100.8
十五、燃料	**Fuel**	**109.5**
1. 煤炭及制品	Coal and Its Products	117.5
2. 石油及制品	Oil and Its Products	107.6
十六、建筑材料及五金电料	**Building Materials And Hardware**	**101.8**
1. 建筑装潢材料	Building Decoration Materials	101.9
2. 五金水暖	Hardware Plumbing	101.4

7–4 主要年份工业生产者出厂价格指数

（上年价格=100）

类 别	Classify	1997	1998	1999	2000	2001	2002
工业生产者出厂价格指数	**Producer Price Index**	**98.6**	**94.4**	**97.5**	**99.4**	**99.3**	**98.2**
按轻重工业分	Grouped by Light Industry and Heavy Industry						
轻工业	Light Industry	98.2	91.1	95.9	97.8	99.6	98.4
以农产品为原料	Using Farm Products as Raw Materials	99.2	89.5	95.2	99.2	99.0	98.4
以非农产品为原料	Using Non-farm Products as Raw Materials	96.8	93.4	97.0	95.5	100.6	98.6
重工业	Heavy Industry	99.0	97.3	98.9	100.8	99.2	98.2
采掘	Mining & Quarrying		104.1	101.5	97.5	94.8	101.3
原料	Raw Materials	101.0	100.7	102.3	107.7	101.1	101.3
加工	Processing	97.9	95.6	98.0	98.4	98.5	97.7
按生产生活资料分	by means of production and livelihood						
生产资料	Means of Production	99.6	96.6	98.3	100.5	99.1	98.0
采掘	Mining & Quarrying		104.1	101.5	97.5	94.8	101.3
原料	Raw Materials	100.9	100.6	100.2	106.4	101.1	101.0
加工	Processing	98.9	94.7	97.6	98.7	98.5	97.4
生活资料	Consumer Goods	97.0	91.4	96.5	97.3	99.9	99.1
（1）食品	Food	108.2	97.8	95.8	94.4	99.6	101.2
（2）衣着	Clothing	93.0	83.9	95.2	101.6	99.4	100.8
（3）一般日用品	Articles for Daily Use	91.6	95.1	97.6	96.9	101.9	97.9
（4）耐用消费品	Durable Consumer Goods	99.7	95.4	98.0	95.9	97.0	98.1
按工业部门分	Grouped by Industrial Sector						
1. 冶金工业	Metallurgical Industry	99.2	97.5	91.2	98.2	97.2	98.7
2. 电力工业	Power Industry	111.3	111.2	109.3	109.6	102.4	100.0
3. 煤炭及炼焦工业	Coal and Coking Industry	98.9	98.5	96.3	100.5	110.3	106.7
4. 石油工业	Petroleum Industry			107.1	134.2	96.6	100.7
5. 化学工业	Chemical Industry	91.8	92.9	96.6	96.7	100.5	99.2
6. 机械工业	Machine Manufacturing Industry	98.8	94.6	98.1	98.0	98.3	97.6
7. 建筑材料工业	Building Materials Industry	98.2	99.3	96.7	98.5	100.6	99.6
8. 森林工业	Timber Industry	107.6	104.5	97.9	98.9	98.1	98.9
9. 食品工业	Food Industry	106.8	95.3	95.5	94.3	99.8	101.1
10. 纺织工业	Textiles Industry	94.3	82.6	93.7	103.4	97.5	94.9
11. 缝纫工业	Tailoring Industry	100.1	97.3	99.1	103.5	100.0	101.1
12. 皮革工业	Leather Industry	91.2	96.8	98.0	99.2	101.0	101.8
13. 造纸工业	Paper Industry			95.3	96.7	102.3	95.0
14. 文教艺术用品工业	Cultural,Educational & Handicrafts Articles			96.7	96.4	101.1	103.4
15. 其它工业	Other Industry	109.5	109.2	98.9	104.8	107.1	99.4

注：本表数据来源国家统计局西安调查队。

Producer Price Indices (PPI) for Industrial Producers in Representative Years

(the price of preceding year= 100)

2003	2004	2005	2006	2007	2008	2009	2010	2011	2012	2013	2014	2015	2016	2017	2018
101.5	**102.7**	**103.9**	**103.2**	**101.9**	**103.7**	**99.9**	**102.3**	**102.5**	**100.5**	**99.5**	**99.5**	**98.5**	**97.8**	**100.3**	**101.1**
101.3	103.4	99.9	100.2	101.8	103.7	100.6	102.5	107.0	100.4	100.7	100.9	100.3	98.5	100.5	102.5
104.5	108.7	97.3	100.1	103.3	106.0	98.9	104.0	109.3	100.3	101.0	100.8	99.1	97.8	100.9	103.0
99.9	100.8	101.2	100.2	100.8	102.1	101.8	101.4	100.9	100.5	99.9	101.3	103.3	100.1	99.7	101.3
101.6	101.9	107.9	105.5	101.9	103.8	99.3	102.2	101.6	100.5	99.2	99.2	98.2	97.6	100.3	100.7
103.4	140.5	107.9	100.6	111.6	122.3	90.0	150.2	102.6	101.8	100.6	100.6	99.8	99.8	106.0	107.1
111.2	109.0	114.2	111.8	104.9	110.8	99.5	108.9	111.2	108.6	95.1	97.6	90.4	91.4	103.4	106.1
100.1	100.6	106.7	104.2	101.2	101.9	99.4	100.8	100.1	99.2	99.9	99.5	99.3	98.3	99.8	100.0
101.8	102.7	105.3	104.2	101.3	103.4	99.3	102.2	101.9	100.3	99.2	99.5	98.3	97.4	100.7	101.7
103.4	140.5	107.9	100.6	111.6	122.3	90.0	150.2	102.6	101.8	100.6	100.6	99.8	99.8	106.0	107.1
108.1	106.6	111.3	111.6	104.8	110.2	99.7	109.0	111.3	108.7	95.2	97.7	90.5	91.2	102.7	106.0
100.9	102.0	104.3	103.0	100.6	102.0	99.3	101.0	100.3	98.9	99.9	99.7	99.6	98.3	100.3	101.0
100.5	102.5	100.4	100.4	103.5	104.7	101.4	102.5	104.5	100.8	100.4	99.7	99.4	98.6	99.7	100.1
101.0	103.6	100.3	100.4	105.3	106.6	100.3	103.3	109.5	101.6	100.9	101.2	100.1	97.7	100.3	102.5
99.4	102.7	102.0	103.3	104.6	105.1	102.7	101.2	111.9	99.4	100.4	99.1	96.0	100.2	101.3	100.4
101.2	101.2	101.3	100.8	100.1	102.7	102.6	101.2	101.5	101.5	99.1	101.3	102.1	98.9	99.6	96.8
97.2	98.3	99.1	99.4	100.7	100.7	103.9	101.9	99.5	99.0	100.9	95.9	95.6	99.5	98.5	101.3
103.8	107.1	103.9	106.5	103.2	104.8	92.0	105.8	116.3	100.7	97.5	97.5	96.5	95.2	104.9	107.3
103.2	104.1	110.6	107.9	105.5	110.0	109.0	101.2	104.7	111.2	100.6	99.4	98.9	92.3	99.4	102.3
136.8	131.4	97.1	95.4	106.8	104.8	101.7	110.6	109.3	101.5	100.0	100.0	100.0			
118.6	110.5	121.7	117.6	104.8	115.6	96.7	114.2	108.4	108.2	89.7	97.2	81.0	95.4	102.5	107.3
100.2	100.8	103.2	100.8	101.1	104.1	102.6	100.8	104.2	100.3	99.6	100.9	100.6	96.8	100.6	97.9
99.8	100.6	104.9	103.4	101.0	101.7	99.9	100.9	99.5	99.0	100.0	99.4	99.5	98.6	99.5	100.1
99.7	100.0	98.6	98.9	98.9	101.8	101.9	99.9	100.6	99.6	99.3	99.1	99.5	98.0	106.1	118.8
100.1	100.2	101.6	101.6	101.1	101.1	101.1	101.7	105.2	103.2	103.4	101.6	91.7	99.9	100.0	102.0
102.8	107.5	98.3	99.0	106.1	109.3	98.3	104.3	110.1	101.7	101.0	101.3	99.8	97.0	99.9	102.6
117.3	119.1	89.9	102.4	98.4	99.7	97.5	108.9	107.2	88.7	103.9	99.3	96.0	93.7	103.5	102.8
100.2	103.6	100.8	103.5	104.6	105.1	102.6	101.3	113.4	99.4	100.4	99.0	93.4	100.5	102.7	100.7
98.7	99.6	101.2	100.0	99.0	99.6	99.7	99.6	98.0	99.9	99.9	100.0	118.9	99.8	99.6	100.0
96.9	100.2	101.2	100.0	100.1	104.5	98.4	100.4	103.4	99.2	98.4	98.1	98.1	100.9	109.7	106.3
97.5	96.5	98.1	100.1	99.1	99.2	102.2	99.9	100.7	106.0	97.5	100.0	102.6	98.0	99.0	100.9
103.3	105.0	103.4	105.7	111.4	104.3	99.7	100.5	104.3	101.2	99.6	100.0	100.0	99.7	96.2	93.6

7-5 主要年份工业生产者购进价格指数

Industrial Purchasing Indices (IPI) for Industrial Producers in Representative Years

(上年价格=100) (the price of preceding year= 100)

指　标	Item	2000	2001	2002	2003	2004	2005	2006	2007	2008
工业生产者购进价格指数	**Industrial Producer Price Index**	**102.4**	**101.0**	**98.4**	**105.3**	**110.4**	**109.6**	**106.1**	**106.2**	**108.5**
(一)燃料、动力类	Fuel and Power	105.0	101.8	100.9	105.7	109.4	123.5	112.6	107.0	109.8
(二)黑色金属材料类	Ferrous Metals	102.7	102.1	98.5	107.4	117.4	107.6	99.2	104.8	111.3
#钢材	Steel	103.4	102.4	97.9	106.0	114.8	107.5	98.5	104.9	111.7
(三)有色金属材料和电线类	Non-ferrous Metals and Electric Wires	105.2	95.5	96.8	105.8	114.1	107.8	116.5	110.7	99.1
(四)化工原料类	Raw Chemical Materials	104.6	102.5	97.9	102.4	106.3	106.1	101.6	105.6	111.4
(五)木材及纸浆类	Timber and Paper Pulp	101.2	102.8	99.4	101.2	100.3	108.2	111.7	105.9	106.5
(六)建筑材料及非金属矿类	Building Materials and Non-metal ores	100.3	99.7	98.6	99.6	110.4	99.3	100.7	104.0	104.8
(七)其它工业原材料及半成品类	Other Industrial Raw Materials and Semi-Products	98.8	100.8	98.9	102.5	111.2	106.1	104.3	108.8	110.6
(八)农副产品类	Agricultural Products	100.4	102.8	98.2	113.7	112.7	100.9	107.2	107.2	108.9
(九)纺织原料类	Textile Materials	98.0	96.8	90.6	103.4	103.9	97.6	101.5	100.5	99.8

注：本表数据来源国家统计局西安调查队。

7-5 续表 continued

(上年价格=100) (the price of preceding year= 100)

指　标	Item	2009	2010	2011	2012	2013	2014	2015	2016	2017	2018
工业生产者购进价格指数	**Industrial Producer Price Index**	**100.7**	**106.3**	**108.8**	**97.2**	**97.2**	**99.5**	**94.5**	**97.6**	**104.7**	**102.7**
(一)燃料、动力类	Fuel and Power	105.1	108.6	113.5	102.3	96.8	98.2	95.3	98.3	101.6	99.8
(二)黑色金属材料类	Ferrous Metals	99.2	103.1	102.9	93.4	98.0	97.9	91.6	96.0	109.0	104.1
#钢材	Steel	98.7	103.5	102.9	93.3	98.0	97.9	91.5	96.0	109.0	104.0
(三)有色金属材料和电线类	Non-ferrous Metals and Electric Wires	93.9	113.6	118.9	93.0	94.5	96.6	96.3	99.3	117.7	115.1
(四)化工原料类	Raw Chemical Materials	95.0	103.9	108.1	87.7	90.8	104.6	91.3	94.1	104.2	99.2
(五)木材及纸浆类	Timber and Paper Pulp	102.6	101.1	105.4	100.9	99.2	100.7	101.0	98.7	107.3	103.9
(六)建筑材料及非金属矿类	Building Materials and Non-metal ores	106.8	102.1	102.9	97.4	102.2	101.1	98.1	97.1	101.0	111.1
(七)其它工业原材料及半成品类	Other Industrial Raw Materials and Semi-Products	101.4	108.1	109.4	100.3	98.9	100.9	99.1	98.9	100.8	100.4
(八)农副产品类	Agricultural Products	99.6	106.5	107.4	103.4	100.5	98.8	92.8	100.4	101.0	102.3
(九)纺织原料类	Textile Materials	97.6	104.6	107.0	89.1	97.6	99.3	89.7	94.1	102.7	99.4

7-6 住宅销售价格指数（2018年）

Selling Price Indices of Residential Buildings（2018）

(上年价格=100) (the price of preceding year= 100)

指　标	Item	2018
新建住宅	**Newly built residential buildings**	
一、保障性住房	guaranteed house	
二、新建商品住宅	New commodity residential house	114.6
（一）90平方米及以下	90 square meters and less	114.1
（二）90-144平方米	90-144 square meters	114.8
（三）144平方米以上	144 square meters and more	114.8
二手住宅	**used/second hand residential buildings**	**111.3**
一、90平方米及以下	90 square meters and the following	113.3
二、90-144平方米	90-144 square meters	110.3
三、144平方米以上	144 square meters and more	110.4

注：本表数据来源国家统计局西安调查队。

7-7 主要年份固定资产投资价格指数

Price Indices for Investment in Fixed Assets in Representative Years

(上年价格=100) (the price of preceding year= 100)

指　标	Item	2000	2004	2005	2006	2007	2008	2009	2010	2011	2012	2013	2014	2015	2016	2017	2018
固定资产投资价格指数	**Price Indices for Investment in Fixed Assets**	**102.1**	**103.3**	**102.4**	**102.0**	**103.5**	**110.5**	**97.9**	**103.8**	**105.4**	**101.9**	**100.8**	**100.8**	**97.9**	**100.0**	**105.4**	**104.7**
一、建筑安装工程	**Construction and Installation Engineering**	**103.9**	**104.6**	**102.3**	**102.6**	**104.9**	**114.9**	**97.1**	**105.5**	**107.2**	**102.6**	**101.0**	**100.8**	**97.0**	**100.5**	**107.8**	**106.7**
1. 材料费	Material Costs	104.4	105.1	101.4	101.1	104.3	117.6	94.1	105.2	106.3	99.0	97.5	98.1	93.3	99.8	111.9	109.6
钢材	Steel	109.0	108.6	101.4	97.0	104.5	127.2	86.7	106.4	107.9	94.7	92.9	93.7	84.6	100.0	120.3	107.6
木材	Wood	103.6	102.2	101.9	101.9	102.5	106.9	101.8	105.0	104.5	104.9	104.5	105.2	107.6	101.4	102.0	101.8
水泥	Cement	101.5	101.8	100.1	101.1	102.7	107.8	109.4	103.8	100.9	100.3	101.4	100.4	97.3	98.1	104.4	110.1
地方材料	Local Materials	101.6	102.4	101.4	102.6	103.5	108.5	103.8	104.7	105.8	102.0	102.4	102.0	100.4	100.0	105.3	114.9
化工材料	Chemical Materials	107.1	104.8	104.6	113.6	113.0	110.0	95.5	104.5	105.4	104.2	102.5	100.9	95.6	95.3	102.7	103.3
电料	Electrical Materials and Sppliances	100.6	101.3	100.9	107.5	110.4	110.1	102.6	104.1	104.1	101.5	100.9	99.9	97.8	99.1	104.2	102.7
其他材料	Other Materials	103.4	101.9	101.7	103.2	107.4	108.5	101.6	102.7	104.5	102.7	101.6	100.7	100.4	100.7	101.4	102.0
2. 人工费	Labor Costs	103.6	105.2	106.9	108.3	109.1	114.5	110.6	111.9	114.0	112.9	109.7	108.8	105.7	102.9	103.2	104.4
3. 机械使用费	Mechanical Service Costs	103.9	102.8	102.5	104.5	104.5	106.5	99.3	103.3	106.7	104.8	104.0	102.2	100.8	100.7	100.8	101.2
二、设备、工器具购置	**Purchase of Equipment and Instruments**	**97.9**	**100.5**	**104.5**	**100.8**	**100.7**	**101.0**	**98.6**	**100.0**	**100.6**	**99.1**	**99.5**	**99.9**	**99.1**	**99.1**	**99.7**	**100.2**
三、其他费用	**Others**	**100.0**	**100.6**	**100.5**	**100.5**	**100.6**	**101.9**	**100.9**	**100.8**	**102.8**	**102.7**	**101.9**	**101.8**	**100.4**	**99.0**	**100.9**	**101.1**

注：本表数据来源国家统计局西安调查队。

主要统计指标解释

居民消费价格指数 是反映一定时期内城乡居民所购买的生活消费品和服务项目价格变动趋势和程度的相对数，是对城市居民消费价格指数和农村居民消费价格指数进行综合汇总计算的结果。通过该指数可以观察和分析消费品的零售价格和服务项目价格变动对城乡居民实际生活费支出的影响程度。

商品零售价格指数 是反映一定时期内城乡商品零售价格变动趋势和程度的相对数。商品零售价格的变动与国家的财政收入、市场供需的平衡、消费与积累的比例关系有关。因此，该指数可以从一个侧面对上述经济活动进行观察和分析。

工业生产者价格指数 是反映工业产品价格变化趋势和变动幅度的统计指标，是工业企业的产品价格在不同的时间和空间条件下平均变动的相对数。工业生产者价格包括工业品第一次出售时的出厂价格和企业作为中间投入的原材料、燃料、动力购进价格，简称工业生产者出厂价格和工业生产者购进价格。工业生产者价格指数是进行国民经济核算和经济管理的主要依据。

住宅销售价格指数 是综合反映住宅商品价格水平总体变化趋势和变化辐度的相对数。

固定资产投资价格指数 是反映一定时期内固定资产投资品和取费项目价格的变动趋势和变动幅度的相对数。固定资产投资额是由建筑安装工程投资完成额、设备工器具购置投资完成额和其他费用投资完成额三部分组成的。编制固定资产投资价格指数应首先分别编制上述三部分投资的价格指数，然后采用加权算术平均法求出固定资产投资价格总指数。

该指数可以准确地反映固定资产投资中涉及的各类投资品和取费项目价格变动趋势和变动幅度，消除按现价计算的固定资产投资指标中的价格变动因素，真实地反映固定资产投资的规模、速度、结构和效益，为国家科学地制定、检查固定资产投资计划和进行国民经济核算提供科学的、可靠的依据。

Explanatory Notes on Main Statistical Indicators

Consumer Price Indices reflect the trend and degree of changes in prices of consumer goods and services purchased by urban and rural households during a given period. They are obtained by combining Consumer Price Indices of Urban Household and Consumer Price Indices of Rural Household. The Indices enable the observation and analysis of the degree of impact of the changes in the prices of retailed goods and services on the actual living expenses of urban and rural residents.

Retail Price Indices reflect the trend and degree of change in retail prices of commodities during a given period. The change in retail prices of commodities is related to government revenue, the equilibrium of market supply and demand, and the ratio of consumption to accumulation. Therefore, the retail price indices are useful from an oblique perspective for observing and analyzing the changes of the above economic activities.

Industrial Producer Price Index refelct the trend and degree of changes of industrial product price, which is the relative number of average change prices of industrial enterprises products under different condition of time and space. Including the first time of sale prices of industrial products and the price of raw materials, fuel and power as intermediate inputs, be called for short of PPI and IPI.

Industrial producer price Index is an important basis for national accounts and economic manegement.

Price Indices for Investment in Fixed Assets reflect the trend and degree of changes in prices of investment goods and projects in fixed assets during a given period. The investment in fixed assets consists of three components, namely the investment in construction and installation, the investment in purchases of equipment and instrument, and the investment in other items. Price indices for investment in fixed assets are calculated as the weighted arithmetic mean of the price indices for the three components of investment in fixed assets.

Removing the factor of price change in the aggregates of investment at current prices, this indicator shows the changes in the prices of commodities and fees involved in the investment of fixed assets, and can be used to observe the actual size, growth, structure, and efficiency of investment in fixed assets and provides reliable and scientific data for government planning and further improving the current national accounting .

8 人民生活

PEOPLE´S LIVELIHOOD

资料整理：张　磊　宋　洁

Data management：Zhang Lei Song Jie

数据审核：罗朝晖

Data audit：Luo Zhaohui

第八部分　人民生活

一、简要说明

1.本章资料反映我市城乡居民生活现状和变化情况，主要包括居民家庭基本情况及生活状况、收入及支出、住房等。

2.本章资料来源于国家统计局西安调查队城乡一体化住户收支与生活状况抽样调查。

3.统计资料范围及口径变化：①2014年西安开始实施城乡住户一体化改革，新老口径存在差距，本年起调查资料为新口径数据。②因2018年是分市、分省数据衔接年的基数年，衔接后西安各区县新口径与老口径数据相比，绝对额有所下降，除8-1、8-3表外，其余表格不再公布2017年相关数据。③自2018年起本章调查资料包含13区、县及西咸新区城乡住户调查数据。

4.统计调查方法：住户收支与生活状况以各市（区）为总体，采用分层、多阶段、与人口规模大小成比例的概率抽样方法，随机抽选调查住宅，确定调查户。在全市抽选出调查小区，对抽中小区中的住户进行全面摸底调查，在此基础上随机等距选出调查户参与记账调查。定期对调查小区和调查住宅进行轮换。

二、主要指标

全体居民人均可支配收入（元）	31406.7	比上年增长	8.7%
城镇常住居民人均可支配收入（元）	38729.1	比上年增长	8.1%
城镇常住居民人均消费支出（元）	25961.5		
农村常住居民人均可支配收入（元）	13286.3	比上年增长	9.0%
农村常住居民人均消费支出（元）	11231.1		

8 PEOPLE'S LIVELIHOOD

Ⅰ.Brief Introduction

1.The data in this chapter reflects the people's living conditions and their changes in Xi'an, consisting of the basic conditions of all households, income, expenditure, the inhabit situation and etc.

2.The data are provided by NBS Survey Office in Xi'an, collected though sample survey.

3.The field of investigation and statistics range have been changed. ①In 2014, reformed household survey programme was used in Xi'an in order to produce aggregates with the same concepts and definitions for the urban and rural population. Since 2014, the data of this yearbook are new range data. They are different from the old range data. ② Since 2018 is the base year for the data convergence of cities and provinces, the absolute amount of new caliber data of Xi'an districts and counties has declined compared with the old caliber data. Except for the tables 8-1 and 8-3, the remaining sheets in chapter VIII are not publishing the relevant data in 2017.③Since 2018, the data in this chapter consists of 13 Districts (Counties) and Xi Xian new area.

4. Methodology on household survey. The household survey is conducted by selecting sampled houses randomly, deciding surveyed households, with all households in the city (district) as the population, with stratified sampling, multi-stage sampling, probability sampling in proportion scale. The households in selected communities are surveyed comprehensively, and then on the basis, randomly select some households for keeping diaries. Communities and households surveyed rotate regularly.

Ⅱ.Major Indicators

		Increase over Preceding Year
Per capita disposable income of all residents(yuan)	31406.7	8.7%
Per capita disposable income of Urban residents (yuan)	38729.1	8.1%
Per capita consumption expenditure of Urban residents (yuan)	25961.5	
Per capita disposable income of Rural residents (yuan)	13286.3	9.0%
Per capita consumption expenditure of Rural residents(yuan)	11231.1	

8-1 主要年份城乡居民人均收入及恩格尔系数

Per Capita Annual Income and Engel's Coefficient of Urban and Rural Households in Representative Years

年　份 Year	城镇居民人均可支配收入 Per Capita Annual Disposable Income of Urban		农村居民人均纯收入（可支配收入） Per Capita Annual Net Income of Rural （Disposable Income）		城镇居民家庭恩格尔系数（%） Engel's Coefficient of Urban Households（%）	农村居民家庭恩格尔系数（%） Engel's Coefficient of Rural Households（%）
	绝对数(元) Absolute number (yuan)	指数 1980年=100 Index year of 1980=100	绝对数(元) Absolute number (yuan)	指数 1978年=100 Index year of 1978=100		
1978			140	100.0		
1979						
1980	414	100.0	190	135.7	53.3	53.3
1981	446	107.7	207	147.9	52.9	53.7
1982	479	115.6	254	181.4	55.1	56.7
1983	509	122.9	245	175.0	55.1	58.4
1984	540	130.3	299	213.6	54.9	51.7
1985	719	173.5	351	250.7	49.5	48.5
1986	911	219.8	390	278.6	49.9	47.9
1987	1034	249.7	434	310.0	50.6	50.3
1988	1142	275.6	482	344.3	44.9	47.5
1989	1344	324.3	530	378.6	51.7	48.2
1990	1518	366.5	610	435.7	53.1	49.5
1991	1619	390.9	707	505.0	51.6	46.7
1992	1992	481.0	783	559.3	52.5	50.9
1993	2661	642.5	870	621.4	46.4	46.0
1994	3517	849.1	1078	770.0	45.2	50.1
1995	4153	1002.5	1353	966.4	44.7	50.3
1996	5023	1212.6	1586	1132.9	42.6	49.9
1997	5344	1290.1	1846	1318.6	40.7	49.2
1998	5670	1368.7	2052	1465.7	39.8	42.4
1999	5999	1448.3	2203	1573.6	36.3	39.1
2000	6364	1536.5	2344	1674.3	36.5	36.6
2001	6705	1618.8	2490	1778.6	34.8	33.9
2002	7184	1734.3	2641	1886.4	34.4	31.1
2003	7748	1870.7	2838	2027.1	34.8	37.6
2004	8544	2062.8	3143	2245.0	36.1	35.7
2005	9628	2324.5	3460	2471.4	37.0	36.3
2006	10905	2632.9	3808	2720.0	34.4	36.8
2007	12662	3057.0	4399	3142.1	36.6	38.2
2008	15207	3671.4	5212	3722.9	36.4	37.0
2009	18963	4578.2	6275	4482.3	32.4	35.8
2010	22244	5370.4	7750	5535.7	31.3	32.5
2011	25981	6272.6	9788	6991.4	31.3	31.9
2012	29982	7238.5	11442	8172.9	32.5	33.8
2013	33100	7991.3	12930	9235.7	32.5	33.0
2014	30715	8718.5	12898	10334.7	32.3	34.2
2015	33188	9422.0	14072	11270.0	32.7	32.2
2016	35630	10119.2	15191	12171.6	29.3	26.9
2017	35837	10948.9	12190	13267.0	29.4	27.3
2018	38729	11835.8	13286	14461.0	27.1	24.4

注：2014年实施城乡住户一体化调查后，统计口径发生变化，新老口径存在差异。本表2014年开始为新口径数据，“农村居民人均纯收入”改为“农村居民人均可支配收入”。2014-2015年恩格尔系数按新口径进行了修订。

本表2018年数据包含西咸新区数据。下同。

8-1表、8-3表中2017年城镇、农村居民人均可支配收入已依据2018年口径进行衔接，其他年份不可比。

8-2 主要年份城乡居民人民币储蓄存款

Savings Deposit of Urban and Rural Households in Representative Years

单位：亿元 (100 million yuan)

年 份 Year	年末余额 Balance at Year-end	指数（上年=100） Index(preceding year=100)
1978	2.57	
1979	3.30	128.4
1980	4.22	127.8
1981	4.90	116.0
1982	5.97	121.9
1983	7.35	123.1
1984	10.73	146.0
1985	14.26	132.9
1986	19.45	136.4
1987	33.95	174.6
1988	40.77	120.1
1989	56.65	138.9
1990	77.09	136.1
1991	97.42	126.4
1992	120.27	123.5
1993	158.28	131.6
1994	218.74	138.2
1995	291.46	133.2
1996	394.02	135.2
1997	433.56	110.0
1998	499.68	115.3
1999	586.40	117.4
2000	675.83	115.3
2001	800.86	118.5
2002	988.04	123.4
2003	1210.56	122.5
2004	1432.86	118.4
2005	1716.76	119.8
2006	1950.53	113.6
2007	2002.38	102.7
2008	2513.70	125.5
2009	3084.20	122.7
2010	3641.09	118.1
2011	4155.65	114.1
2012	4787.03	115.2
2013	5357.05	111.9
2014	5698.15	106.4
2015	6571.18	115.3
2016	7035.81	107.1
2017	7497.30	106.6
2018	8360.33	111.5

注：1.本表数据来源于人民银行西安分行营管部,对部分历史年份数据进行了修订。
2.2015年以后“储蓄存款”为“住户存款”。

8-3 各区县城乡居民人均可支配收入

Per Capita Income of Urban and Rural Households by Region

区　县	Region	城镇居民人均可支配收入 Per Capita Disposable Income of Urban Households			农村居民人均可支配收入 Per Capita Disposable Income of Rural Households		
		绝对数（元） Absolute number(yuan)		2018年比2017年增长% Growth of 2018 than 2017 (%)	绝对数（元） Absolute number(yuan)		2018 年比2017年增长% Growth of 2018 than 2017 (%)
		2017	2018		2017	2018	
全　市	**Total**	**35837**	**38729**	**8.1**	**12190**	**13286**	**9.0**
新城区	Xincheng	41285	44637	8.1			
碑林区	Beilin	41087	44382	8.0			
莲湖区	Lianhu	41221	44440	7.8			
灞桥区	Baqiao	34440	37306	8.3	15041	16395	9.0
未央区	Weiyang	38043	41056	7.9			
雁塔区	Yanta	41655	44995	8.0			
阎良区	Yanliang	34603	37448	8.2	13256	14423	8.8
临潼区	Lintong	26311	28449	8.1	12260	13363	9.0
长安区	Chang'an	35878	38900	8.4	13309	14520	9.1
高陵区	Gaoling	33069	35788	8.2	13665	14936	9.3
鄠邑区	Huyi	21147	22909	8.3	11390	12415	9.0
蓝田县	Lantian	20440	22082	8.0	12309	13404	8.9
周至县	Zhouzhi	19116	20633	7.9	10927	11954	9.4
西咸新区	Xixian	21654	23333	7.8	11768	12775	8.6

注：8-1表、8-3表中2017年城镇、农村居民人均可支配收入已依据2018年口径进行衔接。

8-4　全市居民家庭基本情况

Basic Conditions of All Households

指标名称	Item	2018
调查户数（户）	**Number of Households Surveyed (household)**	**2460**
调查户人口（人）	**Residents Surveyed(person)**	
平均每户常住人口	Average Household Size	3.0
平均每户劳动力人数	Average Number of Employed Persons	2.2
平均每劳动力负担人口	Average Number of Persons Supported by a Laborer	1.4
人均可支配收入（元）	**Annual Per Capita Disposable Income(yuan)**	**31406.7**
工资性收入	Wages Income	19251.7
经营净收入	Net Income from Business	2444.7
财产净收入	Net Income from Property	2847.8
转移净收入	Net Income from Transfer	6862.5
人均消费支出（元）	**Annual Per Capita Consumption Expenditure (yuan)**	**21722.6**
食品烟酒	Food,Tobacco and Alcohol	5797.1
衣着	Clothing	1653.9
居住	Residence	4463.4
生活用品及服务	Living Articles and Services	1701.2
交通通信	Transport and Communication Services	2548.7
教育文化娱乐	Recreation, Education and Culture Services	3003.9
医疗保健	Medical and Health Care Services	2048.8
其他用品和服务	Other Commodities and Services	505.6

8-5 全市居民人均可支配收入

Per Capita Annual Disposable Income of All Households

单位：元 (yuan)

指标名称	Item	2018
可支配收入	**Disposable income**	**31406.7**
一、工资性收入	**Wage income**	**19251.7**
（一）工资	Wage	18355.1
（二）实物福利	Benefits in kind	65.3
（三）其他	Others	831.3
二、经营净收入	**Net Income from Business**	**2444.7**
（一）第一产业经营净收入	Net Income from Primary Industry Business	401.4
（二）第二产业经营净收入	Net Income from Secondary Industry Business	205.6
（三）第三产业经营净收入	Net Income from Tertiary Industry Business	1837.7
三、财产净收入	**Net Income from Properties**	**2847.8**
#利息净收入	Net interest	81.3
红利收入	Bonus	497.1
转让承包土地经营权租金净收入	Net Rental from Transfer of Contracted Land Management Rights	36.6
出租房屋财产性收入	The Property Income by Renting House	1009.7
出租机械、专利、版权等资产的收入	The Income by Renting Assets like Mechanical, Patents, Copyright ect.	15.0
四、转移净收入	**Net Income from Transfer**	**6862.5**
（一）转移性收入	Net Income from Transfer	8297.6
（二）转移性支出	Transfer Expenditure	1435.1

8-6 全市居民年人均消费支出

Per Capita Living Expenditure of All Households

单位：元 （yuan）

指标名称	Item	2018
消费支出	**Total Living Expenditure**	**21722.6**
一、食品烟酒	**Food,Tobacco and Alcohol**	**5797.1**
1.食品	food	3433.2
2.烟酒	Alcohol and tobacco	513.5
3.饮料	Drink	160.2
4.饮食服务	Catering Services	1690.2
二、衣着	**Clothing**	**1653.9**
衣类	Garments	1297.6
鞋类	Footwear	356.3
三、居住	**Residence**	**4463.4**
#租赁房房租	Rental Housing Rent	287.7
住房维修及管理	Housing Repair and Management	445.6
水电燃料及其他	Water,Electric Power Fuel and Others	1101.2
四、生活用品及服务	**Living Articles and Services**	**1701.2**
家具及室内装饰品	Furniture and Interior Decorations	266.6
家用器具	Household Appliances	487.7
家用纺织品	Household textile	133.8
家庭日用杂品	Household Articles of Daily Use	375.9
个人用品	Personal Items	370.6
家庭服务	Household Services	66.6
五、交通通信	**Transportation and Communications**	**2548.7**
交通	Transportation	1758.3
通信	Communications	790.4
六、教育文化娱乐	**Recreation, Education and Culture Services**	**3003.9**
教育	Education	1760.5
文化娱乐	Recreation	1243.4
七、医疗保健	**Medicine and Medical Services**	**2048.8**
医疗器具及药品	Medical Instruments and Medicines	754.8
医疗服务	Medical Services	1294.0
八、其他用品和服务	**Others**	**505.6**

8-7 全市居民家庭人均购买主要商品数量

Per Capita Annual Purchases of Major Commodities of All Households

单位：千克 (kg)

指标名称	Item	2018
面粉	Flour	20.6
大米	Rice	16.0
薯类	Potato	13.8
豆类	Beans	10.6
食用植物油	Edible vegetable oil	10.7
鲜菜	Fresh vegetables	90.5
猪肉	Pork	10.8
牛肉	Beef	1.9
羊肉	Lamb	0.7
鸡	Chicken	2.5
鱼类	Fish	3.1
虾类	Shrimp	0.8
鲜蛋	Eggs	10.1
鲜奶	Milk	13.3
酸奶	Yogurt	6.8
奶粉	Milk	0.9
鲜瓜果	Fresh fruit	59.4
糕点	Cake	5.5
茶叶	Tea	0.5
卷烟（盒）	Cigarettes (box)	27.4
啤酒	Beer	3.3
白酒	Liquor	1.2
果酒	Wine	0.3
鞋（双）	Footwear (pair)	2.9
水（吨）	Water (tons)	28.8
电（度）	Electricity （kwh）	786.3
煤炭	Coal	23.7
管道天燃气（立方米）	Gas pipeline (cu.m)	98.0
罐装液化石油气	Bottled liquefied petroleum gas	4.0

8-8 全市居民家庭每百户年末耐用品拥有情况

Ownership of Major Durable Consumer Goods Every 100 Households

指标名称	Item	2018
家用汽车（辆）	Automobile (unit)	38.6
摩托车（辆）	Motorcycles (unit)	14.4
助力车（台）	Strength-aid Cycle (unit)	43.9
洗衣机（台）	washing machine (unit)	99.0
电冰箱（柜）	Refrigerator (unit)	96.4
微波炉（台）	Microwave Oven (unit)	45.5
彩色电视机（台）	Color TV Set (unit)	107.9
#接入有线电视（台）	Cable TV Set(unit)	43.2
空调（台）	Air conditioning(unit)	156.3
热水器（台）	Water heaters(unit)	89.5
#太阳能热水器（台）	Solar water heaters (unit)	30.1
洗碗机（台）	Dishwasher (unit)	1.7
排油烟机（台）	Exhauster (unit)	73.7
固定电话（部）	Ordinary Telephone (unit)	21.5
移动电话（部）	Mobile phones (unit)	251.9
#接入互联网（部）	Access to the Internet(unit)	171.8
计算机（台）	Computer (a)	58.7
#接入互联网（台）	Access to the Internet(unit)	42.6
照相机（台）	Camera (unit)	19.6
中高档乐器（架）	High-end Instruments (unit)	6.3
健身器材（台）	Setting-up Apparatus (unit)	5.5

8-9 城镇常住居民家庭基本情况

Basic Conditions of Urban Households

指标名称	Item	2018
调查户数（户）	**Number of Households Surveyed (household)**	**1800**
调查户人口（人）	**Residents Surveyed(person)**	
平均每户常住人口	Average Household Size	2.8
平均每户劳动力人数	Average Number of Employed Persons	2.1
平均每劳动力负担人口	Average Number of Persons Supported by a Laborer	1.3
人均可支配收入（元）	**Annual Per Capita Disposable Income(yuan)**	**38729.1**
工资性收入	Wages Income	23797.3
经营净收入	Household Business Income	2513.1
财产净收入	Property Income	3879.4
转移净收入	Transfer Income	8539.3
人均消费支出（元）	**Annual Per Capita Consumption Expenditure (yuan)**	**25961.5**
食品烟酒	Food,Tobacco and Alcohol	7030.5
衣着	Clothing	2052.6
居住	Residence	5195.7
生活用品及服务	Living Articles and Services	2040.8
交通通信	Transport and Communication Services	3047.2
教育文化娱乐	Recreation, Education and Culture Services	3616.2
医疗保健	Medical and Health Care Services	2329.8
其他用品和服务	Other Commodities and Services	648.7

8-10 城镇常住居民人均消费支出

Per Capita Living Expenditure of Urban Households

单位：元 (yuan)

指标名称	Item	2018
消费支出	**Total Living Expenditure**	**25961.5**
一、食品烟酒	**Food,Tobacco and Alcohol**	**7030.5**
1.食品	food	4054.8
2.烟酒	Alcohol and tobacco	566.4
3.饮料	Drink	200.4
4.饮食服务	Catering Services	2208.9
二、衣着	**Clothing**	**2052.6**
衣类	Garments	1611.6
鞋类	Footwear	441.0
三、居住	**Residence**	**5195.7**
#租赁房房租	Rental Housing Rent	359.8
住房维修及管理	Housing Repair and Management	474.4
水电燃料及其他	Water,Electric Power Fuel and Others	1330.1
四、生活用品及服务	**Living Articles and Services**	**2040.8**
家具及室内装饰品	Furniture and Interior Decorations	326.0
家用器具	Household Appliances	548.1
家用纺织品	Household textile	163.3
家庭日用杂品	Household Articles of Daily Use	443.1
个人用品	Personal Items	474.5
家庭服务	Household Services	85.8
五、交通通信	**Transportation and Communications**	**3047.2**
交通	Transportation	2109.4
通信	Communications	937.8
六、教育文化娱乐	**Recreation, Education and Culture Services**	**3616.2**
教育	Education	1979.1
文化娱乐	Recreation	1637.1
#健身器材	Fitness Equipment	2.4
体育及户外用品	Sports and outdoor products	30.1
体育健身活动	Sports fitness activity	56.3
七、医疗保健	**Medicine and Medical Services**	**2329.8**
医疗器具及药品	Medical Instruments and Medicines	917.7
医疗服务	Medical Services	1412.1
八、其他用品和服务	**Others**	**648.7**

8-11 城镇常住居民家庭人均购买主要商品数量

Per Capita Annual Purchases of Major Commodities of Urban Households

单位：千克 (kg)

指标名称	Item	2018
面粉	Flour	19.0
大米	Rice	17.7
薯类	Potato	14.9
豆类	Beans	11.3
食用植物油	Edible vegetable oil	10.1
鲜菜	Fresh vegetables	100.5
猪肉	Pork	11.9
牛肉	Beef	2.5
羊肉	Lamb	0.9
鸡	Chicken	3.2
鱼类	Fish	4.0
虾类	Shrimp	1.0
鲜蛋	Eggs	11.5
鲜奶	Milk	15.9
酸奶	Yogurt	8.7
奶粉	Milk	0.9
鲜瓜果	Fresh fruit	69.3
糕点	Cake	6.5
茶叶	Tea	0.6
卷烟（盒）	Cigarettes (box)	25.5
啤酒	Beer	3.3
白酒	Liquor	1.4
果酒	Wine	0.3
鞋（双）	Footwear (pair)	3.1
水（吨）	Water (tons)	34.8
电（度）	Electricity （kwh）	867.9
煤炭	Coal	9.6
管道天然气（立方米）	Gas pipeline (cu.m)	136.0
罐装液化石油气	Bottled liquefied petroleum gas	2.5

8-12 城镇常住居民家庭每百户耐用品拥有情况

Ownership of Major Durable Consumer Goods Every 100 Urban Households

指标名称	Item	2018
家用汽车（辆）	Automobile (unit)	40.2
摩托车（辆）	Motorcycles (unit)	5.4
助力车（台）	Strength-aid Cycle (unit)	33.1
洗衣机（台）	washing machine (unit)	99.3
电冰箱（柜）	Refrigerator (unit)	96.9
微波炉（台）	Microwave Oven (unit)	55.2
彩色电视机（台）	Color TV Set (unit)	104.2
#接入有线电视（台）	The Number of Cable Television Accessed to Network	48.6
空调（台）	Air conditioning(unit)	168.8
热水器（台）	Water heaters(unit)	93.2
#太阳能热水器（台）	Solar water heaters (unit)	22.6
洗碗机（台）	Dishwasher (unit)	2.0
排油烟机（台）	Exhauster (unit)	87.1
固定电话（部）	Ordinary Telephone (unit)	24.3
移动电话（部）	Mobile phones (unit)	234.5
#接入互联网（部）	Access to the Internet(unit)	163.8
计算机（台）	Computer (a)	67.4
#接入互联网（台）	Access to the Internet(unit)	49.9
照相机（台）	Camera (unit)	24.8
中高档乐器（架）	High-end Instruments (unit)	7.6
健身器材（台）	Setting-up Apparatus (unit)	6.5

8-13 城镇常住居民家庭居住情况

Housing Conditions of Urban Households

指标名称	Item	2018
调查户数（户）	**Number of Households Surveyed (household)**	**1800**
平均每户居住人口（人）	**Average Number of Resident Population (person)**	**2.8**
人均现住房建筑面积（平方米/人）	**The Average Floor Area Per Person (sq.m / person)**	**34.4**
一、按居住空间样式分（%）	**by Living space style（%）**	**100.0**
单栋楼房	Single building Room	10.9
单栋平房	Single-storey House	3.9
单元房	Apartment	80.2
筒子楼或连片平房	Tube-shaped Apartment or Lace Single-storey Houses	5.0
其他	Other	
二、按主要建筑材料分（%）	**by main construction materials（%）**	**100.0**
钢筋混凝土	Reinforced concrete soil	59.9
砖混材料	Brick and concrete material	39.5
砖瓦砖土	Tile and brick earth	0.5
其他	Others	0.1
三、按房屋来源分（%）	**by Source of Housing（%）**	**100.0**
租赁住房	Rental housing	10.9
自建住房	Self-establish Housing	14.6
购买商品房	Commercial Residential Housing	37.2
购买房改住房	Private Housing through Housing Reform	18.0
购买保障性住房	Indemnificatory Housing	4.7
拆迁安置房	Resettlement Housing	8.4
继承或获赠住房	Inheriting and Donation Housing	2.5
其他	Others	3.7
四、住房外道路为硬化路面的户比重（%）	**proportion of households which outer road is Hardened road（%）**	**99.7**
五、按住宅有管道供水情况分（%）	**By Piped Water Supply Condition（%）**	**100.0**
管道供水入户	Pipe water into People's Homes	98.3
管道供水至公共取水点	Pipe water to Public Watering Points	1.0
没有管道设施	No Pipeline Facilities	0.7
六、按住户主要饮水来源情况分（%）	**By Source of main Drinking Water（%）**	**100.0**
经过净化处理的自来水	Purified Tap Water	90.6
受保护的井水和泉水	Protected Wells and Springs	6.6
不受保护的井水和泉水	Unprotected Wells and Springs	1.3
江河湖泊水	Rivers and Lakes Water	0.8
其他饮用水来源	Others	0.7
七、按住宅内厕所类型分（%）	**By Household Lavatory Type (%)**	**100.0**
水冲式卫生厕所	Sanitary Water Closet	95.9
水冲式非卫生厕所	Insanitary Water Closet	1.2
卫生旱厕	Sanitary Latrine	1.2
普通旱厕	Latrine	1.4
无厕所	No Lavatory	0.3
八、按主要炊用能源状况分（%）	**By Cooking Fuel Condition（%）**	**100.0**
天然气、煤气、液化石油气	Pipeline Natural Gas，Pipeline Gas，Pipeline Liquified Petroleum Gas	80.9
煤炭	Coal	
电	Electricity	17.3
沼气	Methane	
其他	Others	1.8

8-14 农村常住居民家庭基本情况

Basic Conditions of Rural Households

指标名称	Item	2018
调查户数（户）	**Number of Households Surveyed (household)**	**660**
调查户人口（人）	**Residents Surveyed(person)**	
平均每户常住人口	Average Household Size	3.7
平均每户劳动力人数	Average Number of Employed Persons	2.4
平均每劳动力负担人口	Average Number of Persons Supported by a Laborer	1.5
人均可支配收入（元）	**Annual Per Capita Disposable Income(yuan）**	**13286.3**
工资性收入	Wages Income	8000.8
经营净收入	Household Business Income	2275.4
财产净收入	Property Income	294.6
转移净收入	Transfer Income	2715.5
人均消费支出（元）	**Annual Per Capita Consumption Expenditure (yuan)**	**11231.1**
食品烟酒	Food,Tobacco and Alcohol	2744.5
衣着	Clothing	667.1
居住	Residence	2650.9
生活用品及服务	Living Articles and Services	860.6
交通通信	Transport and Communication Services	1314.8
教育文化娱乐	Recreation, Education and Culture Services	1488.5
医疗保健	Medical and Health Care Services	1353.3
其他用品和服务	Other Commodities and Services	151.4

8-15 农村常住居民人均消费支出

Per Capita Living Expenditure of Rural Households

单位：元 (yuan)

指标名称	Item	2018
消费支出	**Total Living Expenditure**	**11231.1**
一、食品烟酒	**Food,Tobacco and Alcohol**	**2744.5**
1.食品	food	1894.9
2.烟酒	Alcohol and tobacco	382.6
3.饮料	Drink	60.6
4.饮食服务	Catering Services	406.4
二、衣着	**Clothing**	**667.1**
衣类	Garments	520.5
鞋类	Footwear	146.6
三、居住	**Residence**	**2650.9**
#租赁房房租	Rental Housing Rent	109.2
住房维修及管理	Housing Repair and Management	374.5
水电燃料及其他	Water,Electric Power Fuel and Others	534.7
四、生活用品及服务	**Living Articles and Services**	**860.6**
家具及室内装饰品	Furniture and External Decorations	119.8
家用器具	Household Appliances	338.2
家用纺织品	Household textile	60.8
家庭日用杂品	Household Articles of Daily Use	209.5
个人用品	Personal Items	113.4
家庭服务	Household Services	18.9
五、交通通信	**Transportation and Communications**	**1314.8**
交通	Transportation	889.3
通信	Communications	425.5
六、教育文化娱乐	**Recreation, Education and Culture Services**	**1488.5**
教育	Education	1219.5
文化娱乐	Recreation	269.0
七、医疗保健	**Medicine and Medical Services**	**1353.3**
医疗器具及药品	Medical Instruments and Medicines	351.7
医疗服务	Medical Services	1001.6
八、其他用品和服务	**Others**	**151.4**

8-16 农村常住居民家庭人均购买主要商品数量

Per Capita Annual Purchases of Major Commodities of Rural Households

单位：千克 (kg)

指标名称	Item	2018
面粉	Flour	24.5
大米	Rice	11.6
薯类	Potato	10.9
豆类	Beans	8.9
食用植物油	Edible vegetable oil	12.1
鲜菜	Fresh vegetables	65.7
猪肉	Pork	8.3
牛肉	Beef	0.4
羊肉	Lamb	0.1
鸡	Chicken	1.0
鱼类	Fish	0.8
虾类	Shrimp	0.1
鲜蛋	Eggs	6.8
鲜奶	Milk	6.7
酸奶	Yogurt	2.1
奶粉	Milk	0.8
鲜瓜果	Fresh fruit	34.8
糕点	Cake	3.1
茶叶	Tea	0.3
卷烟（盒）	Cigarettes (box)	32.3
啤酒	Beer	3.4
白酒	Liquor	0.7
果酒	Wine	0.3
鞋（双）	Footwear (pair)	2.3
水（吨）	Water (tons)	14.1
电（度）	Electricity （kwh）	584.4
煤炭	Coal	58.8
管道天燃气（立方米）	Gas pipeline (cu.m)	3.9
罐装液化石油气	Bottled liquefied petroleum gas	7.8

8-17 农村常住居民家庭平均每百户耐用品拥有情况

Ownership of Major Durable Consumer Goods Every 100 Rural Households

指标名称	Item	2018
家用汽车（辆）	Automobile (unit)	33.2
摩托车（辆）	Motorcycles (unit)	43.5
助力车（台）	Strength-aid Cycle (unit)	78.9
洗衣机（台）	washing machine (unit)	98.1
电冰箱（柜）	Refrigerator (unit)	94.7
微波炉（台）	Microwave Oven (unit)	14.3
彩色电视机（台）	Color TV Set (unit)	119.9
#接入有线电视（台）	The Number of Cable Television Accessed to Network	25.7
空调（台）	Air conditioning(unit)	116.0
热水器（台）	Water heaters(unit)	77.8
#太阳能热水器（台）	Solar water heaters (unit)	54.4
洗碗机（台）	Dishwasher (unit)	0.7
排油烟机（台）	Exhauster (unit)	30.4
固定电话（部）	Ordinary Telephone (unit)	12.4
移动电话（部）	Mobile phones (unit)	308.0
#接入互联网（部）	Access to the Internet(unit)	197.8
计算机（台）	Computer (a)	30.6
#接入互联网（台）	Access to the Internet(unit)	19.1
照相机（台）	Camera (unit)	3.0
中高档乐器（架）	High-end Instruments (unit)	1.9
健身器材（台）	Setting-up Apparatus (unit)	2.3

8-18 农村常住居民家庭居住情况

Housing Conditions of Rural Households

指标名称	Item	2018
调查户数（户）	**Number of Households Surveyed (household)**	**660.0**
平均每户居住人口（人）	**Average Number of Resident Population (person)**	**3.7**
人均现住房建筑面积（平方米/人）	**The Average Floor Area Per Person (sq.m / person)**	**51.4**
一、按居住空间样式分（%）	**by Living space style（%）**	**100.0**
单栋楼房	Single building Room	49.4
单栋平房	Single-storey House	47.2
单元房	Apartment	1.6
筒子楼或连片平房	Tube-shaped Apartment or Lace Single-storey Houses	0.3
其他	Other	1.5
二、按主要建筑材料分（%）	**by main construction materials（%）**	**100.0**
钢筋混凝土	Reinforced concrete soil	16.5
砖混材料	Brick and concrete material	76.5
砖瓦砖土	Tile and brick earth	5.9
竹草土坯	Bamboo grass mud	0.6
其他	Others	0.5
三、按房屋来源分（%）	**by Source of Housing（%）**	**100.0**
租赁住房	Rental housing	0.6
自建住房	Self-establish Housing	97.7
购买商品房	Commercial Residential Housing	0.3
购买房改住房	Private Housing through Housing Reform	
购买保障性住房	Indemnificatory Housing	
拆迁安置房	Resettlement Housing	1.3
继承或获赠住房	Inheriting and Donation Housing	
其他	Others	0.1
四、住房外道路为硬化路面的户比重（%）	**proportion of households which outer road is Hardened road（%）**	**99.9**
五、按住宅有管道供水情况分（%）	**By Piped Water Supply Condition（%）**	**100.0**
管道供水入户	Pipe water into People's Homes	93.1
管道供水至公共取水点	Pipe water to Public Watering Points	1.1
没有管道设施	No Pipeline Facilities	5.8
六、按住户主要饮水来源情况分（%）	**By Source of main Drinking Water（%）**	**100.0**
经过净化处理的自来水	Purified Tap Water	51.7
受保护的井水和泉水	Protected Wells and Springs	40.7
不受保护的井水和泉水	Unprotected Wells and Springs	4.6
江河湖泊水	Rivers and Lakes Water	0.7
其他饮用水来源	Others	2.3
七、按住宅内厕所类型分（%）	**By Household Lavatory Type (%)**	**100.0**
水冲式卫生厕所	Sanitary Water Closet	33.1
水冲式非卫生厕所	Insanitary Water Closet	8.3
卫生旱厕	Sanitary Latrine	29.3
普通旱厕	Latrine	29.0
无厕所	No Lavatory	0.3
八、按主要炊用能源状况分（%）	**By Cooking Fuel Condition（%）**	**100.0**
天然气、煤气、液化石油气	Pipeline Natural Gas，Pipeline Gas，Pipeline Liquified Petroleum Gas	17.9
煤炭	Coal	2.1
电	Electricity	61.0
沼气	Methane	0.2
其他	Others	18.8

主要统计指标解释

住户 指居住在一个住宅内，共同分享生活开支或收入的一群人。居住在同一房间内、不共同分享生活开支的人群，每个人都视为一个住户。住家保姆、住家家庭帮工视为单独的住户。

常住成员指住户成员中，经常在家居住、或者调查期内居住时间超过一半的人员，以及本住户供养的学生。

可支配收入 指调查户在调查期内获得的、可用于最终消费支出和储蓄的总和，即调查户可以用来自由支配的收入。可支配收入既包括现金，也包括实物收入。按照收入的来源，可支配收入包含四项，分别为：工资性收入、经营净收入、财产净收入和转移净收入。计算公式为：

可支配收入 = 工资性收入 + 经营净收入 + 财产净收入 + 转移净收入

工资性收入 指就业人员通过各种途径得到的全部劳动报酬和各种福利，包括受雇于单位或个人、从事各种自由职业、兼职和零星劳动得到的全部劳动报酬和福利。

经营净收入 指住户或住户成员从事生产经营活动所获得的净收入，是全部经营收入中扣除经营费用、生产性固定资产折旧和生产税之后得到的净收入。计算公式具体为：

经营净收入 = 经营收入 – 经营费用 –生产性固定资产折旧–生产税

财产净收入 指住户或住户成员将其所拥有的金融资产、住房等非金融资产和自然资源交由其他机构单位、住户或个人支配而获得的回报并扣除相关的费用之后得到的净收入。

财产性净收入=财产性收入– 财产性支出

转移性收入 指国家、单位、社会团体对住户的各种经常性转移支付和住户之间的经常性收入转移。包括养老金或退休金、社会救济和补助、政策性生产补贴、政策性生活补贴、经常性捐赠和赔偿、报销医疗费、住户之间的赡养收入，以及本住户非常住成员寄回带回的收入等。计算公式为：

转移净收入 = 转移性收入 –转移性支出

消费支出 指住户用于满足家庭日常生活消费需要的全部支出，包括用于消费品的支出和用于服务性消费的支出。根据用途不同，消费支出可划分为食品烟酒、衣着、居住、生活用品及服务、交通通信、教育文化娱乐、医疗保健、其他用品及服务八大类。

农村居民人均纯收入（老口径） 指农村住户当年从各个来源得到的家庭总收入扣除相关费用性支出后，最终归农村居民所有的收入总和，按照农村住户人口平均的纯收入水平。计算公式为：

纯收入=总收入 –家庭经营费用支出–税费支出–生产性固定资产折旧–赠送农村内部亲友

Explanatory Notes on Main Statistical Indicators

Households refer to persons living and sharing economically together in one house. When people don`t share living expenses, every single person are deemed to be one household. Live-in Nanny and family helpers are deemed to be one household.

Usual Resident Population refers to persons staying at home regularly or for over half of time in survey period and students provided by the by the household.

Disposable Income of Households refers to the actual income of households for purpose of final expenditure and savings in survey period, households can use that at their disposable. It includes income both in cash and in kind. By sources of income, disposable income includes four categories: income from wages and salaries, net business income, net income from properties and net income from transfer. The formula is:

Disposable Income of Households = Income from Wages and Salaries + Net Business Income + Net Income from Properties + Net Income from Transfer

Income from Wages and Salaries refers to remuneration of labour and salaries from all kinds of sources, including those employed by other units or individuals, freelance work, part-time jobs, and sporadic labour.

Net Business Income refers to net income earned by households and their members engaged in production and business activities. It refers to the operating revenue minus operating costs, depreciation of productive fixed assets, and production tax. The formula is:

Net Business Income = Operating Revenue - Operating Costs - Depreciation of Productive Fixed Assets - Production Tax

Net Income from Properties refers to net income received as returns by households or members of financial assets, non-financial assets such as housing, to other institutions, households and individuals, and minus relevant costs. The formula is:

Net Income from Properties = Property Income – Property Expenditure

Income from Transfer refersto the regular transfer from country, institutions, social communities to households and between households. It includes old-age and retirement pension, regular donation and compensation, applying for medical fees, supporting income between households, income from non-usual-residing members of households, etc.

Net Income from Transfer The formula is:

Net Income from Transfer = Income from Transfer – Expenditure from Transfer

Consumption Expenditure of Households refers to all expenditure of households for living expenditure to satisfy family daily living. It includesexpenditure on eight categories: food tobacco and liquor; clothing; residence; household facilities, articles and services; transport and communications; education, cultural and recreational activities; health care and medical services, and miscellaneous goods and services.

The Average Per Capita Net Income of Rural Residents (the old range) refers to the total income of rural households from all sources minus all corresponding expenses. The formula is:

Net Income = Total Income –Household Operation Expenses – Taxes and Fees Paid – Taxes and Fees Depreciation of Fixed Assets for Production – Gifts to Non-rural Relatives

9 城市公用事业

URBAN PUBLIC UTILITIES

资料整理：郝　静
Data management：Hao Jing
数据审核：王金桂
Data audit：Wang Jingui

第九部分　城市公用事业

一、简要说明

本章资料主要包括城市供水、供燃气、供热、公共交通、市政设施、市政设施水平、城市规模及用地状况、园林绿地、环境卫生等情况，由西安市统计局服务业和社会科技处根据西安市建委、市交通局、市地铁办及市水务局提供的数据整理。建委提供的数据为初步数据。

二、主要指标

人均公园绿地面积（平方米）	9.97	比上年减少	2.07
人均城市道路面积（平方米）	17.97	比上年减少	1.76
供水普及率（%）	97.85	比上年降低	1.40个百分点
燃气普及率（%）	99.90	比上年提高	3.83个百分点

9　URBAN PUBLIC UTILITIES

Ⅰ.Brief Introduction

Data in this chapter reflects basic condition of urban public utilities of Xi'an City. Data on public utilities primarily consists of urban water supply, gas sales, urban heating, public transportation, municipal facilities, level of municipal construction, scale of the city, condition of land utilization, parks, greenbelt and environmental sanitation. Data in this chapter is compiled by Tertiary Industry and Social Science & Technology Division of Xi'an Bureau of Statistics according to the data provided by Committee of Urban Construction of Xi'an, Xi'an Burean of Transportation and Xi'an Metro Office.

Ⅱ.Major Indicators

		Increase over Preceding Year
Per Capita Public Green Areas (sq.m)	9.97	-2.07
Per Captia Area of Roads (sq.m)	17.97	-1.76
Water-Consuming Popularization (%)	97.85	-1.40 percenage points
Gas-Consuming Popularization (%)	99.90	3.83 percenage points

9-1 城市（县城）供水

Urban（County）Water Supply

指　标	Item	2010	2014	2015	2016	2017	2018
年末水厂个数（个）	Number of Water Factory at Year-end (units)	9	16	22	22	24	22
供水综合生产能力（万立方米/日）	Total Volume of Water Supply (10 000 cu.m/day)	197.40	196.50	211.50	219.38	206.47	215.10
# 地下水	Undergronnd Water	55.80	51.33	62.86	64.61	65.11	89.86
年末供水管道总长度（公里）	Length of Water Supply Pipelines at Year-end (kms)	2416.00	3499.97	4371.05	4522.46	4899.56	4959.94
全年供水总量（万立方米）	Total Annual Volume of Water Supply (10 000 cu.m)	41089.00	53798.99	56055.25	59953.03	89215.62	90394.45
#生产运营用水	For Productive Use	6267.00	15680.53	16146.29	16567.21	43095.31	39453.60
居民家庭用水	For Residential Use	20944.00	28497.40	30742.79	32182.87	34896.60	39078.56
用水人口（万人）	Population with Access to Tap Water (10 000 persons)	410.90	452.57	463.05	475.00	506.26	589.90

注：本表数据来源于市建委和市水务局。
本表2017年及以后年份数据含西咸新区。

9-2 城市（县城）供燃气

Gas Supply in Urban Area（County）

指　标	Item	2010	2014	2015	2016	2017	2018
一、天然气	**Natural Gas**						
供气管道长度（公里）	Total Length of Gas Pipelines (km)	4488	6892.25	7465.73	8199.80	9174.87	10659.68
供气总量（万立方米）	Total Gas Supply(10 000 cu.m)	109052	186259.15	196826.38	206068.05	231168.38	285215.47
#销售气量	Volume of Gas Sales	104055	179536.78	189066.21	201078.36	224419.93	279030.23
#家庭用量	Residential Households	20989	59057.38	65952.81	67024.75	105249.81	100959.64
用气人口（万人）	Population with Access to Gas (10 000 persons)	333	425.72	437.96	452.11	477.01	588.40
二、液化石油气	**Liquefied Petroleum Gas**						
供气总量（吨）	Total Gas Supply (tons)	11469	5299.70	5030.30	4955.50	7607.20	31023.54
#销售气量	Volume of Gas Sales	11441	5244.00	4950.00	4875.20	7478.90	30397.32
#家庭用量	Residential Households	7376	4281.00	4064.00	4056.00	6081.47	8881.82
用气人口（万人）	Population with Access to Gas (10 000 persons)	31.20	21.00	19.50	17.60	13.02	13.65

注：本表数据来源于市建委。
本表2017年及以后年份数据含西咸新区。

9-3 城市（县城）集中供热

Heating in Urban Area（County）

指　标	Item	2010	2014	2015	2016	2017	2018
供热能力	Heating Capacity						
蒸气（吨/小时）	Steam (tons/hour)	2235	2893	3013	3013	6200	4325
热水（兆瓦）	Hot Water (megawatts)	3531	13967.00	17191.90	17765.90	14477.00	14465.47
供热总量(万吉焦)	Volume Supplied (10 000 gigajoules)						
蒸气	Steam	1674	1743.87	1671.14	1789.13	2813.00	1972.08
热水	Hot Water	2570	3726.89	4241.30	5032.84	6338.00	6532.89
集中供热管道长度（公里）	Length of Centralized Heating Pipelines(km)	541	894.24	1054.41	1141.24	1842.00	1516.83
集中供热面积（万平方米）	Heated Area (10 000sq.m)	6094	13492.55	16690.65	19566.81	29118.90	24922.93
#住宅	Residential Buildings	5009	11828.59	14730.49	17282.39	17541.10	20751.73

注：本表数据来源于市建委。
　　本表2017年及以后年份数据包含西咸新区。

9-4 城市公共交通

Urban Public Traffic

指　标	Item	2010	2014	2015	2016	2017	2018
运营车辆（辆）	Operating Vehicles (units)	7107	7769	7781	7829	7780	8743
标准运营车辆（标台）	Standard Vehicles (units)	8139	9050	9061	9140	9243	10712
公交客运总量（万人次）	Total of Bus Passenger(10 000 person-times)	162400	170960	161032	147089	133465	135919
公交客运收入（万元）	Bus Passenger Transport Income (10 000 yuan)	129397	140914	137492	129132	165072	126590
出租汽车数（辆）	Number of Taxis (units)	12786	14159	14459	14459	14509	14609
地铁运营线路长度（公里）	Length of Subway Lines in Operation(km)		50.94	50.94	88.97	88.97	126.70
地铁客运量（万人次）	Total of Subway Passenger(10 000 person-times)		29953.07	34209.35	40815.75	60534.01	74624.64

注：本表数据来源于市交通局和地铁办。
　　本表数据为西安原口径。

9-5 市政设施

Municipal Facilities

指 标	Item	2010	2014	2015	2016	2017	2018
一、道路长度（公里）	Length of Roads (km)	2662	3461.18	3570.58	3683.14	4398.83	4712.47
二、道路面积（万平方米）	Area of Roads (10 000 sq.m)	5965	8144.22	8457.14	8618.93	10063.55	10834.70
三、人行道面积（万平方米）	Area of Sidewalks (10 000 sq.m)	1834	2310.46	2381.20	2423.70	2814.31	2886.16
四、桥梁数（座）	Number of Bridges (units)	347	437	448	449	491	502
#立交桥	Overpasses	71	105	106	107	127	126
五、路灯盏数（盏）	Number of Street Lights (units)	291754	337991	343465	349808	382979	383174
六、排水管道长度（公里）	Length of Drainage Pipelines (km)	3765	4839.49	4984.94	5161.83	5802.36	6126.11
七、污水年排放量（万立方米）	Annual Discharge Volume of Sewage (10 000 cu.m)	34706	51673	62092	56578	58303	70374
八、污水处理厂处理能力（万立方米/日）	Daily Disposal Capacity of Sewage (10 000 cu.m/day)	106.5	153.1	200.6	212.1	147.6	225.1
九、污水年处理量（万立方米）	Yearly Disposal Capacity of Sewage Disposal Plant (10 000 cu.m)	25088	47907	57034	52011	54279	66048

注：本表数据来源于市建委。

本表2017年及以后年份数据包含西咸新区。

9-6 城市（县城）设施水平

Urban (County) Municipal Facilities

指 标	Item	2010	2014	2015	2016	2017	2018
一、人均日生活用水量（升）	Per Capita Daily Consumption of Tap Water For Residential Use (liters)	186.20	178.45	187.79	191.35	199.09	189.56
二、供水普及率(%)	Water-Consuming Popularization (%)	98.8	100	100	100	99.25	97.85
三、每万人拥有公共交通车辆（标台）	Number of Public Transport Vehicles Per 10 000 Population (units)	13.9	14.4	14.3	13.9	14.4	16.1
四、燃气普及率(%)	Gas-Consuming Popularization (%)	97.0	98.71	98.79	98.89	96.07	99.90
五、人均城市道路面积（平方米）	Per Captia Area of Roads (sq.m)	15.4	18.00	18.26	18.15	19.73	17.97
六、建成区排水管道密度（公里/平方公里）	Density of Drainage Pipelines in Developed Areas (km/sq.km)	9.5	9.27	9.09	9.12	1.46	7.88
七、污水处理率(%)	Rate of Sewerage Disposal (%)	84.0	92.71	91.85	91.93	93.10	93.85
八、园林绿化	Afforestation and Parks and Gardens						
人均公园绿地面积（平方米）	Per Capita Public Green Areas (sq.m)	9.1	11.22	11.47	11.61	12.04	9.97
建城区绿地率（%）	Rate of Green Areas in Developed Areas (%)	29.2	32.60	34.03	34.95	36.78	35.23
九、生活垃圾无害化处理率(%)	Rate of No Harm Disposal of Garbage (%)	93.9	93.48	98.09	96.70	98.11	98.97

注：本表数据来源于市建委。

本表2017年及以后年份数据包含西咸新区。其中，“每万人拥有公共交通车辆”指标数据仍为西安原口径。

本表供水普及率指标2016年及以前数据为用水普及率。

9–7 城市（县城）规模及用地情况

City（County） Scale and Land Use

单位：平方公里 (sq.km)

指　标	Item	2010	2014	2015	2016	2017	2018
建成区面积	Area of the Constructed Regions	395	521.91	548.60	565.75	683.09	723.68
城市建设用地	Land use for Construction	336	507.66	536.10	553.29	646.54	679.35

注：本表数据来源于市建委。
本表2017年及以后年份数据包含西咸新区。

9–8 城市（县城）园林绿化

Urban（County） Parks,Gardens and Green Areas in Cities

指　标	Item	2010	2014	2015	2016	2017	2018
一、公园个数（个）	**Number of Parks (units)**	**68**	**85**	**91**	**95**	**103**	**104**
二、公园面积（公顷）	**Area of Parks (hectares)**	**1335**	**2483.83**	**2599.83**	**2647.40**	**3259.70**	**3272.70**
三、绿地面积（公顷）	**Total Area of Parks,Gardens and Green Areas (hectares)**	**12140**	**18914.05**	**20582.44**	**22502.87**	**30703.66**	**31680.89**
#公园绿地面积	Public Green Areas	3526	5075.85	5310.58	5517.08	6142.98	6010.08
四、年末绿化覆盖面积（公顷）	**Coverage Space of Green Areas at year-end (hectares)**	**15646**	**23216.65**	**25639.88**	**27617.83**	**35936.49**	**35939.67**
五、建成区绿化覆盖率（%）	**Coverage of Green Areas in Developed Areas (%)**	**37.50**	**40.76**	**42.04**	**42.57**	**40.79**	**38.53**

注：本表数据来源于市建委。
建成区绿化覆盖率2018年数据不含蓝田和周至。
本表2017年及以后年份数据包含西咸新区。

9-9 城市（县城）环境卫生

Urban（County）Environment Sanitation

指 标	Item	2010	2014	2015	2016	2017	2018
清扫面积（万平方米）	Area Under Cleaning Program (10 000 sq.m)	6290	10110	9842	9137	12241	7790
生活垃圾清运量（万吨）	Volume of Residential Garbage Disposal (10 000 tons)	237	359.37	359.16	371.51	189.93	430.68
公共厕所（座）	Number of Public Lavatories (units)	1257	2151	2239	2314	3274	4030
市容环卫专用车辆设备总数（辆）	Special Vehicles of Environmental Sanitation (units)	1042	1990	2050	2000	2571	3305

注：本表数据来源于市建委。
本表2017年及以后年份数据包含西咸新区。
2017年及以后年份生活垃圾清运量统计口径与以前不同。

9-10 市区及县供水（2018年）

Urban and County Water Supply（2018）

指 标	Item	西安 Xi'an	市区 City	蓝田 Lantian	周至 ZhouZhi
年末水厂个数（个）	Number of Water Factory at Year-end (units)	22	20	1	1
供水综合生产能力（万立方米/日）	Total Volume of Water Supply (10 000 cu.m/day)	215.10	210.06	2.54	2.50
#地下水	Groundwater	89.86	86.30	1.74	1.82
年末供水管道总长度（公里）	Length of Water Supply Pipelines at Year-end (km)	4959.94	4762.42	124.92	72.60
全年供水总量（万立方米）	Total Annual Volume of Water Supply (10 000 cu.m)	90394.45	89259.52	617.03	517.90
#生产运营用水	For Productive Use	39453.60	39174.03	266.57	13.00
居民家庭用水	For Residential Use	39078.56	38435.84	267.72	375.00
用水人口（万人）	Population with Access to Tap Water (10 000 persons)	589.90	574.47	8.13	7.30

注：本表数据来源于市建委及市水务局。
本表数据含西咸新区。

9-11 市区及县供燃气（2018年）

Urban and County Gas Supply (2018)

指 标	Item	西安 Xi'an	市区 Urban	蓝田 Lantian	周至 ZhouZhi
一、天然气	**Natural Gas**				
管道长度（公里）	Total Length of Gas Pipelines (km)	10659.68	10484.54	109.14	66.00
供气总量（万立方米）	Total Gas Supply(10 000 cu.m)	285215.47	280611.35	1949.12	2655.00
#销售气量	Volume of Gas Sales	279030.23	274458.01	1919.12	2653.10
#家庭用量	Residential Households	100959.64	99005.96	1197.12	756.56
用气人口（万人）	Population with Access to Gas (10 000 persons)	588.40	574.75	7.15	6.50
二、液化石油气	**Liquefied Petroleum Gas**				
供气总量（吨）	Total Gas Supply (tons)	31023.54	28725.84	1087.50	1210.20
#销售气量	Volume of Gas Sales	30397.32	28132.32	1055.00	1210.00
#家庭用量	Residential Households	8881.82	6696.82	975.00	1210.00
用气人口（万人）	Population with Access to Gas (10 000 persons)	13.65	11.46	0.98	1.21

注：本表数据来源于市建委。
本表数据含西咸新区。

9-12 市区及县集中供热（2018年）

Urban and County Heating (2018)

指 标	Item	西安 Xi'an	市区 Urban	蓝田 Lantian	周至 ZhouZhi
供热能力	Heating Capacity				
蒸气（吨/小时）	Steam (tons/hour)	4325	4325		
热水（兆瓦）	Hot Water (megawatts)	14465	14459		6
供热总量(万吉焦)	Volume Supplied(10 000 gigajoules)				
蒸气	Steam	1972	1972		
热水	Hot Water	6533	6527		5
集中供热管道长度（公里）	Length of Centralized Heating Pipelines(km)	1517	1514		3
供热面积（万平方米）	Heated Area (10 000sq.m)	24922.9	24912.0		11.0
#住宅	Residential Buildings	20751.7	20742.3		9.4

注：本表数据来源于市建委。
本表数据含西咸新区。

9-13 市区及县市政设施（2018年）

Urban and County Municipal Facilities (2018)

指 标	Item	西安 Xi'an	市区 Urban	蓝田 Lantian	周至 ZhouZhi
一、道路长度（公里）	**Length of Roads (km)**	**4712.47**	**4590.31**	**75.60**	**46.56**
二、道路面积（万平方米）	**Area of Roads (10 000 sq.m)**	**10834.70**	**10600.54**	**136.18**	**97.98**
三、人行道面积（万平方米）	**Area of Sidewalks (10 000 sq.m)**	**2886.16**	**2792.36**	**58.96**	**34.84**
四、桥梁数（座）	**Number of Bridges (units)**	**502**	**486**	**11**	**5**
#立交桥	Crossroads	126	126		
五、路灯盏数（盏）	**Number of Street Lights (units)**	**383174**	**375731**	**2232**	**5211**
六、排水管道长度（公里）	**Length of Drainage Pipelines (km)**	**6126.11**	**5972.90**	**92.81**	**60.40**
七、污水年排放量（万立方米）	**Annual Discharge Volume of Sewage (10 000 cu.m)**	**70374**	**69425**	**534**	**415**
八、污水处理厂处理能力（万立方米/日）	**Daily Disposal Capacity of Sewage (10 000 cu.m/day)**	**225.1**	**222.5**	**1.5**	**1.1**
九、污水年处理量（万立方米）	**Yearly Disposal Capacity of Sewage Disposal Plant (10 000 cu.m)**	**66048**	**65275**	**435**	**337**

注：本表数据来源于市建委。
本表数据含西咸新区。

9-14 市区及县市政设施水平（2018年）

Urban and County Municipal Facilities Level (2018)

指 标	Item	西安 Xi'an	市区 Urban	蓝田 Lantian	周至 ZhouZhi
一、人均日生活用水量（升）	**Per Capita Daily Consumption of Tap Water For Residential Use (liters)**	**189.56**	**191.02**	**107.59**	**165.51**
二、供水普及率(%)	**Water-Consuming Popularization (%)**	**97.85**	**97.93**	**98.78**	**91.02**
三、燃气普及率（%）	**Gas-Consuming Popularization (%)**	**99.90**	**99.97**	**98.78**	**96.13**
四、人均城市道路面积（平方米）	**Per Captia Area of Roads (sq.m)**	**17.97**	**18.07**	**16.55**	**12.22**
五、建成区排水管道密度（公里/平方公里）	**Density of Drainage Pipelines (km/sq.km)**	**7.88**	**8.00**	**4.19**	**3.63**
六、污水处理率(%)	**Rate of Sewerage Disposal (%)**	**93.85**	**94.02**	**81.52**	**81.20**
七、园林绿化	**Afforestation and Parks and Gardens**				
人均公园绿地面积（平方米）	Per Capita Public Green Areas (sq.m)	9.97	9.98	8.86	10.22
建城区绿地率（%）	Rate of Green Areas in Developed Areas(%)	35.23	35.55	31.33	17.00
八、生活垃圾无害化处理率(%)	**Rate of No Harm Disposal of Garbage (%)**	**98.97**	**99.80**		**94.13**

注：本表数据来源于市建委。
本表数据含西咸新区。

主要统计指标解释

建成区面积 城市行政区内实际已成片开发建设、市政公用设施和公共设施基本具备的区域。对核心城市，它包括集中连片的部分以及分散的若干个已经成片建设起来，市政公用设施和公共设施基本具备的地区；对一城多镇来说，它包括由几个连片开发建设起来的，市政公用设施和公共设施基本具备的地区组成。因此建成区范围，一般是指建成区外轮廓线所能包括的地区，也就是这个城市实际建设用地所达到的范围。

供水综合生产能力 指按供水设施取水、净化、送水、出厂输水干管等环节设计能力计算的综合生产能力。包括在原设计能力的基础上，经挖、革、改增加的生产能力。计算时，以四个环节中最薄弱的环节为主确定能力。

供水管道长度 指从送水泵至用户水表之间所有管道的长度。不包括新安装尚未使用、水厂内以及用户建筑物内的管道。在同一条街道埋设两条或两条以上管道时，应按每条管道的长度计算。

供水总量 指报告期供水企业（单位）供出的全部水量。包括有效供水量和漏损水量。

用水普及率 指报告期末城区内用水人口与总人口的比率。计算公式:

$$用水普及率=\frac{用水人口（含暂住人口）}{人口+暂住人口}\times 100\%$$

供气管道长度 指报告期末从气源厂压缩机的出口或门站出口至各类用户引入管之间的全部已经通气投入使用的管道长度。不包括煤气生产厂、输配站、液化气储存站、灌瓶站、储配站、气化站、混气站、供应站等厂（站）内的管道。

供气总量 指报告期燃气企业（单位）向用户供应的燃气数量。包括销售量和损失量。

燃气普及率 指报告期末城区内使用燃气的人口与总人口的比率。计算公式：

$$燃气普及率=\frac{用气人口（含暂住人口）}{人口+暂住人口}\times 100\%$$

供热能力 指供热企业（单位）向城市热用户输送热能的设计能力。不是热电厂的生产能力。

供热总量 指在报告期供热企业（单位）向城市热用户输送全部蒸汽和热水的总热量。

供热管道长度 指从各类热源到热用户建筑物接入口之间的全部蒸汽和热水的管道长度。不包括各类热源厂内部的管道长度。

供热面积 指供热企业（单位）向城市各类房屋建筑物、构筑物及其附属设施供热的全部建筑面积。

道路长度 指道路长度和与道路相通的桥梁、隧道的长度，按车行道中心线计算。

道路面积 指道路实际铺装面积和与道路相通的广场、桥梁、隧道的铺装面积（统计时，将人行道面积单独统计）。

人行道面积按道路两侧面积相加计算，包括步行街和广场，不含人车混行的道路。

排水管道长度 指所有排水总管、干管、支管、检查井及连接井进出口等长度之和。计算时按单管计算，即在同一条街道上如有两条或两条以上并排的排水管道时，应按每条排水管道的长度相加计算。

绿化覆盖面积 指城市中的乔木、灌木、草坪等所有植被的垂直投影面积。包括公园绿地、防护绿地、生产绿地、附属绿地、其他绿地的绿化种植覆盖面积、屋顶绿化覆盖面积以及零散树木的覆盖面积，不含各类绿地中的水域面积以及没有被植被覆盖的面积（硬化道路、无屋顶绿化的建筑物等）。乔木树冠下重迭的灌木和草本植物不重复计算。

人均城市道路面积 指报告期末城区内平均每人拥有的城市道路面积。计算公式：

$$人均城市道路面积=\frac{城区道路面积}{城区人口+城区暂住人口}$$

建成区排水管道密度 指报告期末建成区排水管道分布的疏密程度，计算公式：

$$排水管道密度=\frac{排水管道长度}{建成区面积}$$

污水处理率 指报告期内污水处理总量与污水排放总量的比率。计算公式：

$$污水处理率=\frac{污水处理总量}{污水排放总量}\times 100\%$$

人均公园绿地面积 指报告期末城区内平均每人拥有的公园绿地面积。计算公式：

$$人均公园绿地面积=\frac{城区公园绿地面积}{城区人口+城区暂住人口}$$

建成区绿地率 指报告期末建成区内绿地面积与建成区面积的比率。计算公式：

$$建成区绿地率\frac{建成区绿地面积}{建成区面积}\times 100\%$$

Explanatory Notes on Main Statistical Indicators

Area of the Constructed Regions refers to developed and built city administrative area where basic municipal utilities and public facilities complete constructed. To core city, it includes part of contiguous centralized and a number of decentralized part where basic municipal utilities and public facilities complete constructed. To a multi-city town, it consists of several contiguous developed and build area where municipal utilities and public facilities with basic composition. Therefore, the range of built-up area, generally refers to the built-up areas in the contour line, which is the actual construction site of the city achieved range.

Production Capacity of Water Supply refers to the designed overall production capacity of water facilities, covering the four segments of water collection, purification, conveyance, and out flow through trunk pipelines. Increased capacity through transformation and innovation projects is included as well. The capacity is determined mainly on the weakest of the above-mentioned four segments.

Length of Water Supply Pipelines at Year-end refers to the total length of all the pipelines between the water pumps and the user water meters, excluding pipelines newly installed but not used yet, pipeline in the water factory, and pipeline in the user's buildings.

Volume of Water Supply refers to the total volume of water supplied by water-works(units) during the reference period, including both the effective water supply and loss during the water supply.

Coverage Rate of Urban Population with Access to Tap Water refers to the ratio of the urban population with access to tap water to the total urban population . The formula is :

$$\text{Coverage of urban population with access to tap water} = \frac{\text{population with access to tap water}}{\text{population}} \times 100\%$$

Length of Gas Pipeline refers to the total length of pipelines in use between the outlet of the compressor of gas-work of outlet gas stations and the leading pipe of users , excluding pipelines within gasworks , delivery stations ,LPG storage stations ,refilling stations, gas-mixing stations and supply stations.

Volume of Gas Supply refers to the total volume of gas provided to users by gas-producing enterprises (units) in a year ,including the volume sold and the volume lost .

Coverage Rate of Urban Population with Access to Gas refers to the ratio of the urban population with access to gas to the total urban population at the end of the reference period. The formula is :

$$\text{Coverage rate of urban population with access to gas} = \frac{\text{population with access to gas}}{\text{population}} \times 100\%$$

City Heating capacity in Urban Areas refers to the designed capacity of heating enterprises (units) in supplying heating energy to urban users during the reference period .

City Quantity of Heat Supplied in Urban Areas refers to the total quantity of heat from steam and hot water urban users by heating enterprises (units) during the reference period .

City Length of Urban Heating Pipelines refers to the total length of steam or hot water pipelines for sources of heat to the leading pipelines of the building of the users ,excluding internal pipelines in heat generating enterprises

Heated Area refers to the total structure area of heat supplied to urban constructions, structures and ancillary facilities by heating enterprises (units) during the reference period .

Length of Paved Roads refers to the length of roads with paved surface including bridges and tunnels connected with roads. Length of the roads is measured by the central lines .

Area of Paved Roads refers to the actual pavement area of roads and the actual pavement area of squares, bridges and tunnels connecting to the roads (the area of sidewalk pavements is calculated separately).

The area of sidewalk pavements is the sum of area of roads on sides of road, including pedestrian streets and squares, excluding roads for both pedestrians and vehicles .

Length of exhaust pipelines refers to the total length of all main drain piles ,trunk pipes ,branch pipes

,access manholes ,and connector well entrances and exits ,and so on . The whole length is calculated as of single pipes. Namely ,if there are two or more drain pipes parallel on a street ,the length of every pipe shall be summed .

Total area of green land refers to vertical projection area of all vegetation including trees, shrubs, lawns. Including parks, protective green space, production green space, green subsidiaries, green plants covering area, covering an area other green spaces, green roofs and covering area of scattered trees, excluding kinds of water area in kinds of green area and the area not covered by vegetation(hardened road, building of no green roof). shrubs and herbaceous plants overlap under the canopy of trees do not double counting.

Per Capita Area of Paved Roads refers to the area of urban roads per capita at the end of the reporting period. The formula is :

$$\text{Per capita area of paved roads} = \frac{\text{Area of urban roads}}{\text{Urban population+temporary resident population}}$$

Density of Drainage Pipelines refers to density of drainage pipelines in developed areas at the end of the reporting period .The formula is :

$$\text{Density of drainage pipelines} = \frac{\text{Length of drainage pipelines}}{\text{Ares of developed areas}}$$

Rate of Sewerage Disposal refers to the ratio of waste water disposed with the total discharge of waste water in the reporting period .The formula is:

$$\text{Rate of Sewerage Disposal} = \frac{\text{Waste Water Disposed}}{\text{Total Discharge of Waste Water}} \times 100\%$$

Per Capita Area of Public Green refers to the area of public green areas per capita at end of the reporting period .The formula is :

$$\text{Per capita area of public green} = \frac{\text{Area of public green areas}}{\text{Urban population+temporary resident population}}$$

Coverage of Green Areas in Developed Areas refers to the ratio of green areas in built-up areas with the area of developed areas at the end of reporting period . The formula is:

$$\text{Coverage of green land in developed areas} = \frac{\text{Area of green land in developed aresa}}{\text{Area of developed areas}} \times 100\%$$

10 环境保护

ENVIRONMENT PROTECTION

资料整理：张　育
Data management：Zhang Yu
数据审核：马建华
Data audit：Ma Jianhua

第十部分　环境保护

一、简要说明

本章资料反映环境保护、工业污染排放及处理利用情况、危险废物集中处置情况、生活及其他污染情况和工业污染治理项目建设情况，由西安市统计局能源与环境处根据西安市环保局提供的数据资料整理。本部分2017年及以后数据不包含西咸新区。

二、主要指标

全年环境空气质量达标天数（天）	188	比上年增加	8天
工业固体废物综合利用率（%）	59.5	比上年下降	24.5个百分点

10 ENVIRONMENT PROTECTION

Ⅰ.Brief Introduction

This chapter contains information that reflect environment protection, discharge and treatment of industrial pollutant, centralized treatment of dangerous wastes, domestic pollution and other pollution, construction of projects of industrial pollution treatment. Data in this chapter is compiled by General Division of the Xi'an Bureau of Statistics according to the reported data from Xi'an Environment Protection Bureau. Data from Xixian is not contained in this chapter from 2017.

Ⅱ.Major Indicators

		Increase over Preceding Year
Days of Air Quality up to the Standards（days）	188	8 days
Percentage of InduStrial Solid Waste Utilized（%）	59.5	-24.5 percentage points

10-1 城市环境保护（2018年）

Urban Environmental Protection（2018）

指 标	Item	2018
一、饮用水环境	**Potable Water Environment**	
全市饮用水水质达标率(%)	Compliance Rate of the City's Potable Water Quality (%)	99.7
二、大气环境	**Atmospheric Environment**	
颗粒物（PM10）年平均浓度（微克/立方米）	Particulate matter (PM10) Annual average concentration (μg / m^3)	122
颗粒物（PM2.5）年平均浓度（微克/立方米）	Particulate matter (PM2.5) Annual average concentration (μg / m^3)	63
二氧化硫浓度年平均值（微克/立方米）	Annual Average Concentration of Sulphur Dioxide (μg / m^3)	15
二氧化氮浓度年平均值（微克/立方米）	Annual Average Concentration of Nitrogen Dioxide (μg / m^3)	55
一氧化碳第95百分位数（微克/立方米）	The 95th percentile of carbon monoxide (μg / m^3)	2.2
臭氧八小时第90百分位数（微克/立方米）	Ozone eight hours 90th percentile (μg / m^3)	180
全年环境空气质量达标天数(天)	Days of Air Quality up to the Standards(days)	188
全年环境空气质量达标率(%)	Annual compliance rate of Ambient Air Quality(%)	51.5
三、声环境	**Voice**	
1、功能区噪声平均值(dB(A))	Average Noise Value of Functional Districts(dB(A))	
0类区	Class 0	54
1类区	Class 1	58
2类区	Class 2	59
3类区	Class 3	62
4类区	Class 4	71
2、道路交通噪声平均值(dB(A))	Average Noise Value of Road Traffic(dB(A))	69.8
3、区域噪声平均值(dB(A))	Average Noise Value of Region(dB(A))	56.1
四、环境污染治理	**Environmental pollution treatment**	
当年完成环保验收项目环境保护投资（亿元）	Year Completed Investment in Environmental Protection Projects of Environmental acceptance(100 million yuan)	14.21

注：本表数据来源于市环保局。
2017年起数据为不含西咸新区口径。下同

10-2 主要年份工业“三废”排放及处理利用情况

指　标	Item	2000	2010
一、工业废水排放量（万吨）	**Volume of Waste Water Discharge (10 000 tons)**	**9145**	**13840**
工业废水处理量（万吨）	Volume of Industrial Wastewater Disposal (10 000 tons)		10673.52
废水治理设施数（套）	Number of Facilities for Treatment of Waste Water (sets)		267
二、工业废气排放量（亿立方米）	**Total Volume of Industrial Waste Gas Emission (100 million cu.m)**	**275.97**	**791.56**
废气治理设施数（套）	Number of Facilities for Treatment of Waste Gas(sets)		816
三、工业固体废物产生量（万吨）	**Volume of Industrial Solid Wastes Produced (10 000 tons)**	**107**	**267.29**
工业固体废物处置量（万吨）	Volume of Industrial Solid Wastes Treated (10 000 tons)	20	3.56
工业固体废物综合利用量（万吨）	Volume of Industrial Solid Waste Utilized (10 000 tons) in a Comprehensive Way	63	262
工业固体废物综合利用率（%）	Percentage of Volume of Industrial Solid Waste Utilized in a Comprehensive Way(%)	58.88	98.05
四、工业锅炉（台/蒸吨）	**Industrial Boilers (units/tons)**		

注：1.本表数据来源于市环保局。
2.2010年全国统一进行了污染源普查动态更新调查工作，“十二五”的环境统计体系与污染源普查体系相衔接，与“十一五”环境统计口径不同。
3.工业固体废物综合利用率依据环境统计口径计算。

Discharge and Treatment of Waste Gas, Water & Solid Wastes in Repersentative Years

2011	2012	2013	2014	2015	2016	2017	2018
13148	**10223.73**	**8972.97**	**6339.85**	**5203.56**	**4029.83**	**4247.57**	**4163.40**
12632.38	9089.04	6798.71	5818.27	4783.60	4264.99	4448.08	4091.10
314	312	295	305	315	266	275	299
1018.46	**1043.31**	**844.11**	**901.23**	**1108.48**	**1034.46**	**1444.60**	**1040.40**
745	649	661	740	801	834	1048	1225
279	**259.14**	**255.78**	**252.66**	**238.53**	**195.99**	**190.30**	**198.70**
6	9.24	9.68	17.54	20.95	28.66	28.00	78.10
271	248.58	244.08	233.52	216.64	167.20	159.80	118.30
97.30	95.92	95.43	92.43	90.82	85.31	83.97	59.50
	503/8785	**576/13466**	**520/14177**	**501/18278**	**480/12791.8**	**457/14682.3**	**466/17078.21**

10-3 工业污染排放及处理利用情况（2018年）

Discharge and Treatment of Industrial Pollution （2018）

指　标	Item	2018
一、被调查企业基本情况	**Basic condition of Enterprises investigated**	
1. 企业数（个）	Number of Enterprises (units)	524
2. 工业总产值（亿元）	Gross Industry Output Value (100 millian yuan)	3314.8
3. 工业锅炉数（台/蒸吨）	Industrial Boilers (units/tons)	466/17078.21
4. 工业炉窑数（座）	Number of Industrial Grates (items)	247
二、工业废水	**Industrial Waste Water**	
1. 工业取水量（万吨）	Industrial water intake (10000 tons)	8843.6
#新鲜水量	Volume of Fresh Water	
重复用水量	Volume of Water Recycled	
2. 工业用水重复利用率（%）	Percentage of Industrial Water Recycled (%)	
3. 废水治理设施数（套）	Number of Facilities for Treatment of Waste Water (sets)	299
4. 废水治理设施处理能力（万吨/日）	Disposal Capacity of Facilities for Treatment of Waste Water (10 000 tons/day)	25.5
5. 废水治理设施运行费用（万元）	Operating Expense of Facilities for Treatment of Waste Water (10 000 yuan)	30084.4
6. 工业废水排放量（万吨）	Volume of Industrial Waste Water Discharged (10 000 tons)	4163.4
三、工业废气	**Industrial Waste Gas**	
1. 煤炭消费量（万吨）	Total Coal Consumption (10 000 tons)	631.4
2. 燃料油消费量（不含车船用）（万吨）	Fuel Oil Consumption (10 000 tons)	0.3
3. 天然气消费量（亿立方米）	Natural Gas Consumption (100 millian cu.m)	4.5
4. 工业废气排放总量（亿立方米）	Total Volume of Industrial Waste Gas Emission (100 millian cu.m)	1040.4
5. 废气治理设施数（套）	Number of Facilities for Treatment of Waste Gas (sets)	1225
6. 废气治理设施处理能力（万立方米/时）	Disposal Capacity of Facilities for Treatment of Waste Gas (10 000 cu.m./h)	8034.1
7. 废气治理设施设备运行费用（万元）	Operating Expense of Facilities for Treatment of Waste gas(10 000 yuan)	31218.8
8. 二氧化硫产生量（吨）	Sulfur dioxide production (tons)	82011.6
9. 二氧化硫排放量（吨）	Volume of Sulphur Dioxide Emission (tons)	3064.4
10. 氮氧化物产生量（吨）	Production of nitrogen oxides(tons)	23578.96
11. 氮氧化物排放量（吨）	Nitrogen oxide emissions(tons)	5574.8
12. 烟（粉）尘产生量（吨）	Tobacco (powder) dust production(tons)	672281.4
13. 烟（粉）尘排放量（吨）	The smoke (powder) dust emissions(tons)	2322.5
四、工业固体废物	**Industrial Solid Waste**	
1. 工业固体废物产生量（万吨）	Volume of Industrial Solid Waste Produced (10 000tons)	198.7
2. 工业固体废物综合利用量（万吨）	Volume of Industrial Solid Waste Utilized (10 000tons)	118.3
3. 工业固体废物综合利用率（%）	Percentage of Industrial Solid Waste Utilized (%)	59.5
4. 工业固体废物贮存量（万吨）	Volume of Industrial Solid Waste Accumulated (10 000tons)	2.3
5. 工业固体废物处置量（万吨）	Volume of Industrial Solid Waste Treated (10 000tons)	78.1
6. 工业固体废物倾倒丢弃量（吨）	Volume of Industrial Solid Waste Discharged (tons)	

注：本表数据来源于市环保局。

10-4 城市污水处理情况（2018年）

Urban Sewage Treatment（2018）

指　标	Item	2018
一、污水处理厂数（座）	**Number of Sewage Treatment Works(units)**	**41**
污水处理厂处理能力（万吨/日）	Daily Disposal Capacity of Sewage(10 000 tons/day)	274
二、污水处理	**Sewgae Disposal**	
污水实际处理量（万吨）	Volume of Sewgae Disposal(10 000 tons)	85606.6
生活污水处理量	Volume of Domestic Sewgae Disposal	81731.4
工业污水处理量	Volume of Industrial Sewage Disposal	3875.3
三、再生水（万吨）	**Recycled water (10 000 tons)**	
生产量	Production	6693.8
利用量	Utilization	5586
四、化学需氧量去除量（吨）	**Volume of COD Removed (tons)**	**319521.4**
五、氨氮去除量（吨）	**Volume of Ammonia and Nitrogen Removed(tons)**	**28788.3**
六、总磷去除量（吨）	**Volume of Total Phosphorus Removed(tons)**	**4266.3**
七、污泥产生量（吨）	**Volume of Sludge Produced(tons)**	**13.1**
八、污泥处置量（吨）	**Volume of Sludge Disposal(tons)**	**13.1**
九、污泥倾倒丢弃量（吨）	**Dumping sludge discards (tons)**	
十、本年运行费用（万元）	**Operating Expense(10 000 yuan)**	**80339.53**

注：本表数据来源于市环保局。

10-5 危险废物（医疗废物）集中处理情况（2018年）

Condition of Concentrated Disposal of Dangerous Wastes（Medical Wastes）（2018）

指　标	Item	2018
一、危险废物集中处理（置）厂数（个）	**Number of Colleted Dangerous Wastes Treated Plants(items)**	**1**
二、医疗废物集中处理（置）厂数（个）	**The number of Manufacturing Plants of Medical waste treatment (units)**	**1**
三、危险废物设计处置能力（吨/日）	**Design hazardous waste disposal capacity (tons / day)**	**52**
四、实际处置危险废物量（吨）	**The actual amount of hazardous waste disposal (tons)**	**14100.8**
五、危险废物综合利用量（吨）	**Volume of Dangerous Wastes Utilized in a Comprehensive Way (tons)**	
六、焚烧残渣流向（千克）	**Flow Direction of Residuum after Burning (kg)**	
1. 焚烧残渣量	Volume of Residuum after Burning	642119.5
2. 焚烧残渣安全填埋处置量	Secure landfill disposal incineration residues	633119.5
3. 焚烧飞灰产生量	Fly ash production	70345.9
4. 焚烧飞灰安全填埋处置量	Fly ash landfill disposal safety	70345.9
七、当年运行费用（万元）	**Operating Expenses in Current year(10 000 yuan)**	**4330**

注：本表数据来源于市环保局。

10-6 生活及其他污染情况（2018年）

Domestic Pollution and Other Conditions（2018）

指　标	Item	2018
一、基本情况	**Basic Condition**	
1. 生活天然气消费量（万立方米）	Volume of Living natural gas consumption (10 000 cu.m)	104990
2. 生活用水总量（万吨）	Volume of Living water (10 000 tons)	100803
二、污染排放情况	**Discharge of Pollutant**	
1. 城镇生活污水排放量（万吨）	Volume of Urban Domestic Sewage Discharged(10 000 tons)	85137
2. 生活污水处理量（万吨）	Volume of Domestic Sewgae Disposal(10 000 tons)	81731
3. 生活CDD产生量（吨）	Volume of Life CDD production (tons)	330531
4. 生活CDD排放量（吨）	Volume of Life CDD emissions (tons)	24215
5. 生活氨氮产生量（吨）	Volume of Ammonia and Nitrogen in Urban Domestic Sewage Produced (tons)	29981
6. 生活氨氮排放量（吨）	Volume of Ammonia and Nitrogen in Urban Domestic Sewage Discharged (tons)	2382
7. 二氧化硫排放量（吨）	Volume of Domestic and Other Sulphur Dioxide Emission (tons)	32232
8. 氨氮化物排放量（吨）	Volume of Ammonia and Nitrogen in Urban Domestic Sewage Discharged (tons)	5580
9. 烟尘排放量（吨）	Volume of Soot Emission (tons)	23463

注：本表数据来源于市环保局。

10-7 工业污染治理项目建设情况（2018年）

Condition of Anti-Industrial-Pollution Projects（2018）

指　标	Item	2018
一、工业企业数（个）	**Number of Industrial Enterprises (units)**	**18**
二、老工业污染源项目治理本年施工总数（个）	**The total number of construction projects of Old industrial pollution sources control this year(units)**	**14**
#工业废水治理项目	Treatment of Waste Water	1
工业废气治理项目	Treatment of Waste Gas	9
工业固体废物治理项目	Treatmen of Solid Wastes	1
三、老工业污染源项目治理本年竣工总数（个）	**The Total Number of Old Industrial Pollution Control Projects Completed this year(units)**	**10**
#工业废水治理项目	Treatment of Waste Water	
工业废气治理项目	Treatment of Waste Gas	8
工业固体废物治理项目	Treatmen of Solid Wastes	
四、老工业污染源治理项目本年完成投资（万元）	**Investment completed in Old industrial pollution control projects this Year(10 000 yuan)**	**6638**
#废水治理项目	Treatment of Waste Water	60
废气治理项目	Treatment of Waste Gas	1243
固体废物治理项目	Treatmen of Solid Wastes	120
五、老工业污染源治理项目本年投资来源（万元）	**Source of Investment in Old industrial pollution control projects this Year(10 000 yuan)**	
#排污费补助	Pollution Charges Subsidies	5
政府其他补助	Other Government Subsidies	
企业自筹	Self-raising Funds	6628
#银行贷款	Lonans	36
六、“三同时”项目竣工验收数（个）	**Number of "Three simultaneous 'project completion and acceptance (a)**	**7**
七、“三同时”竣工验收项目实际环保投资（万元）	**"Three simultaneous" actual environmental investment completed and accepted (10 000 yuan)**	**933**
八、“三同时”项目废水治理新增处理能力（万吨/日）	**"Three simultaneous"Add processing capacity of wastewater treatment (10 000 tons / day)**	**0.08**
九、“三同时”项目废气治理新增处理能力（万立方米/时）	**"Three simultaneous"Add processing capacity of Exhaust treatment (10 000 cu.m/h)**	**0.01**

注：本表数据来源于市环保局。
“三同时”指建设项目中防治污染的措施，必须与主体工程同时设计，同时施工，同时投产使用。

10-8 各区县、开发区环境保护基本情况（2018年）

区县、开发区	Region	本年完成环保验收项目环保投资额（万元）Investment Completed in accepted Environmental projects this year (10 000 yuan)	工业二氧化硫排放量（吨）Volume of Industrial Sulphur Dioxide Discharged (tons)
全　市	**Total**	**142123.0**	**3064.4**
新城区	Xincheng	2516.1	1.3
碑林区	Beilin	225.0	73.3
莲湖区	Lianhu	1493.8	102.5
灞桥区	Baqiao	8021.0	424.2
未央区	Weiyang	5536.9	89.2
雁塔区	Yanta	4463.1	301.8
阎良区	Yanliang	1267.5	181.7
临潼区	Lintong	7137.8	23.7
长安区	Chang'an	215.1	300.8
高陵区	Gaoling		116.0
鄠邑区	Huyi	3185.0	268.6
蓝田县	Lantian	2534.5	198.6
周至县	Zhouzhi	1113.3	1.1
高新开发区	Gaoxinkaifaqu	20196.6	492.7
经济开发区	Jingjikaifaqu	5513.8	266.9
航天基地	Hangtianjidi	5314.0	222.0

注：本表数据来源于市环保局。
环境统计中污水处理厂个数包含部分大学园区及部分大型小区的污水处理厂。
区县、开发区环保验收项目环保投资额未包括市本级完成数。

Condition of Environment Protection by Regions（2018）

工业化学需氧量排放量（吨） Volume of COD Removed (tons)	垃圾处理站数（座） Number of Rubbish Disposal Works (units)	污水处理厂数（个） Number of Sewage Treatment Works (units)
1278.5	**2**	**41**
49.1		
70.7		2
50.9	1	4
62.3		6
34.7		2
39.9		2
43.2		2
38.2		5
75.1	1	1
394.9		3
5.7		3
8.7		2
243.7		7
111.9		2
49.7		

主要统计指标解释

工业用水 指工矿企业在生产过程中用于制造、加工、冷却、空调、净化、洗涤等方面的用水，按新水取用量计，不包括企业内部的重复利用水量。

工业废水排放量 指经过企业厂区所有排放口排到企业外部的工业废水量。包括生产废水、外排的直接冷却水、超标排放的矿井地下水和与工业废水混排的厂区生活污水，不包括外排的间接冷却水（清污不分流的间接冷却水应计算在内）。

直接排入海的 指经企业位于海边的排放口，直接排入海的废水量。直接排放指废水经过工厂的排污口直接排入海，而未经过城市下水道或其他中间体，也不受其他水体的影响。

工业废水排放达标量 指报告期内废水中各项污染物指标都达到国家或地方排放标准的外排工业废水量，包括未经处理外排达标的，经废水处理设施处理后达标排放的，以及经污水处理厂处理后达标排放的。

生活污水排放量 指城镇居民每年排放的生活污水。用人均系数法测算。测算公式为：

$$\text{生活污水排放量} = \text{城镇生活污水排放系数} \times \text{市镇非农业人口} \times 365$$

生活污水中化学需氧量（COD）排放量 指城镇居民每年排放的生活污水中的COD的量。用人均系数法测算。测算公式为：

$$\text{城镇生活污水中COD产生系数} = \text{城镇牛活污水中COD排放量} \times \text{市镇非农业人口} \times 365$$

化学需氧量（COD） 指用化学氧化剂氧化水中有机污染物时所需的氧量。COD值越高，表示水中有机污染物污染越重。

工业废气排放量 指报告期内企业厂区内燃料燃烧和生产工艺过程中产生的各种排入大气的含有污染物的气体的总量，以标准状态（273K，101325Pa）计算。测算公式为：

$$\text{工业废气排放量} = \text{燃料燃烧过程中废气排放量} + \text{生产工艺过程中废气排放量}$$

生活及其他SO_2排放量 以生活及其他煤炭消费量和其含硫量为基础，根据以下公式计算：

$$\text{生活及其他}SO_2\text{排放量} = \text{生活及其他煤炭消费量} \times \text{含硫量} \times 0.8 \times 2$$

工业SO_2排放量 指报告期内企业在燃料燃烧和生产工艺过程中排入大气的SO_2总量，计算公式为：

$$\text{工业}SO_2\text{排放量} = \text{燃料燃烧过程中}SO_2\text{排放量} + \text{生产工艺过程中}SO_2\text{排放量}$$

工业烟尘排放量 指企业厂区内燃料燃烧过程中产生的烟气中夹带的颗粒物排放量。

生活及其他烟尘排放量 指除工业生产活动以外的所有社会、经济活动及公共设施的经营活动中燃烧所排放的烟尘纯重量。以生活及其他煤炭消费量为基础进行测算。

工业粉尘排放量 指企业在生产工艺过程中排放的能在空气中悬浮一定时间的固体颗粒物排放量。如钢铁企业的耐火材料粉尘、焦化企业的筛焦系统粉尘、烧结机的粉尘、石灰窑的粉尘、建材企业的水泥粉尘等。不包括电厂排入大气的烟尘。

工业固体废物产生量 指报告期内企业在生产过程中产生的固体状、半固体状和高浓度液体状废弃物的总量，包括危险废物、冶炼废渣、粉煤灰、炉渣、煤矸石、尾矿、放射性废物和其他废物等；不包括矿山开采的剥离废石和掘进废石（煤矸石和呈酸性或碱性的废石除外）。酸性或碱性废石指采掘的废石其流经水、雨淋水的pH值小于4或pH值大于10.5者。

危险废物 指列入国家危险废物名录或根据国家规定的危险废物鉴别标准和鉴别方法认定的，具有爆炸性、易燃性、易氧化性、毒性、腐蚀性、易传染疾病等危险特性之一的废物。

工业固体废物综合利用量 指报告期内企业通过回收、加工、循环、交换等方式，从固体废物中提取或者使其转化为可以利用的资源、能源和其他原材料的固体废物量（包括当年利用往年的工业固体废物贮存量），如用作农业肥料、生产建筑材料、筑路等。综合利用量由原产生固体废物的单位统计。

工业固体废物综合利用率 指工业固体废物综合利用量占丁业固体废物产生量（包括综合利用往年贮存量）的百分率。计算公式为：

$$\text{工业固体废物综合利用率}=\frac{\text{工业固体废物综合利用量}}{\text{工业固体废物产生量}+\text{综合利用往年贮存量}}\times 100\%$$

工业固体废物贮存量 指报告期内企业以综合利用或处置为目的，将固体废物暂时贮存或堆存在专设的贮存设施或专设的集中堆存场所内的数量。专设的固体废物贮存场所或贮存设施必须有防扩散、防流失、防渗漏、防止污染大气、水体的措施。

工业固体废物处置量 指报告期内企业将固体废物焚烧或者最终置于符合环境保护规定要求的场所，并不再回取的工业固体废物量（包括当年处置往年的工业固体废物贮存量）。处置方式有填埋（其中危险废物应安全填埋）、焚烧、专业贮存场（库）封场处理、深层灌注、回填矿井及海洋处置（经海洋管理部门同意投海处置）等。

工业固体废物排放量 指报告期内企业将所产生的固体废物排到固体废物污染防治设施、场所以外的数量，不包括矿山开采的剥离废石和掘进废石（煤矸石和呈酸性或碱性的废石除外）。

"三废"综合利用产品产值 指报告期内利用"三废"作为主要原料生产的产品价值（现行价）；已经销售或准备销售的应计算产品价值，留作生产自用的不应计算产品价值。

生活垃圾清运量 指报告期内收集和运送到各生活垃圾处理厂（场）和生活垃圾最终消纳点的生活垃圾数量。生活垃圾指城市日常生活或为城市日常生活提供服务的活动中产生的固体废物以及法律行政规定的视为城市生活垃圾的固体废物。包括：居民生活垃圾、商业垃圾、集市贸易市场垃圾、街道清扫垃圾、公共场所垃圾和机关、学校、厂矿等单位的生活垃圾。

生活垃圾无害化处理率 指报告期生活垃圾无害化处理量与生活垃圾产生量的比率。在统计上，由于生活垃圾产生量不易取得，可用清运量代替。计算公式为：

$$\text{生活垃圾无害化处理率}=\frac{\text{生活垃圾无害化处理量}}{\text{生活垃圾产生量}}\times 100\%$$

Explanatory Notes on Main Statistical Indicators

Water Used by Industry refers to new withdrawals of water, excluding reuse of water within enterprises.

Waste Water Discharged by Industry refers to the volume of waste water discharged by industrial enterprises through all their outlets, including waste water from production process, directly cooled water, groundwater from mining wells which does not meet discharge standards and sewage from households mixed with waste water produced by industrial activities, but excluding indirectly cooled water discharged (It should be included if the discharge is not separated from waste water).

Waste Water Directly Discharged into Sea refers to the volume of waste water directly discharged into sea through outlets of enterprises situated by sea without going through municipal sewerage networks or any other intermediates or being affected by any other water bodies.

Industrial Waste Water Meeting Discharge Standards refers to volume of industrial waste water discharge which, with or without treatment, reaches national or local standards with regard to all pollutants.

Urban Non-industrial Waste Water Discharge refers to annual discharge of non-industrial waste water by urban households. It is estimated by per capita coefficient using the formula:

$$\text{Urban non-industrial waste water discharge} = \text{urban non-industrial waste water discharge coefficient} \times \text{urban non-alagricultur population} \times 365$$

Volume of Chemical Oxygen Demand (COD) Generated by Urban Non-industrial Waster Water refers to chemical oxygen demand generated through the annual discharge of non-industrial waste water by urban households. It is estimated as:

$$\text{Volume of chemical oxygen demand (cod) generated by urban non-industrial waster water} = \text{Coefficient of COD generated through urban non-industrial waste water} \times \text{urban non-agricultura population} \times 365$$

Chemical Oxygen Demand (COD) refers to the amount of oxygen required when chemical oxidants are used to oxidize organic pollutants in water. A higher value of COD corresponds to more serious pollution by organic pollutants.

Industrial Waste Air Emission refers to the discharge into atmosphere of waste air containing pollutants generated from fuel burning and production processes in enterprises within a given period of time. It is calculated at standard status (273K, 101325Pa) as:

$$\text{Industrial waste air emission} = \text{tnoissimehrough fuel burning} + \text{tnoissimehrough production process}$$

SO_2 Emission through Non-industrial and Other Activities is calculated on the basis of consumption of coal by households and other activities and the sulphur content of coal with the following formula:

$$SO_2\ \text{emission through non-industrial and other activities} = \text{of coalby households andother activities} \times \text{sulphur content} \times 0.8 \times 2$$

SO_2 Emission through Industrial Activities refers to volume of sulphur dioxide emission from fuel burning and production process by enterprises during a given period of time. It is calculated as:

$$SO_2\ \text{emission through industrial activities} = SO_2\text{emIssIon from fuel burning} + SO_2\ \text{emission from production process}$$

Industrial Soot Emission refers to the volume of soot in smoke emitted in the process of fuel burning in the premises of enterprises.

Soot Emission by Consumption and Others refers to the net volume of soot emitted by fuel burning from all social and economic activities and operations of public facilities other than industrial activities. It is calculated on the basis of coal consumption by households and others.

Industrial Dust Emission refers to volume of dust emitted by production process of enterprises and suspended in the air for a given period of time, including dust from refractory material of iron and steel works, dust from coke-screening systems and sintering machines of coke plants, dust from lime kilns and dust from cement production in building material enterprises, but excluding soot and dust emitted from power plants.

Industrial Solid Wastes Produced refers to total volume of solid, semi-solid and high concentration liquid residues produced by industrial enterprises from production process in a given period of time, including hazardous wastes, slag, coal ash, gangue, tailings, radioactive residues and other wastes, but excluding stones stripped or dug out in mining - gangue and acid or alkaline stones not included (a stone is acid or alkaline according to the pH value of the water being below 4 or above 10.5 when the stone is in, or soaked by water).

Hazardous Wastes refers to those included in the national hazardous wastes catalogue or specified as any one of the following properties in the national hazardous wastes identification standards: explosive, ignitable, oxidizable, toxic, corrosive or liable to cause infectious diseases or lead to other dangers.

Industrial Solid Wastes Utilized refers to volume of solid wastes from which useful materials can be extracted or which can be converted into usable resources, energy or other materials by means of reclamation, processing, recycling and exchange (including utilizing in the year the stocks of industrial solid wastes of the previous year). Examples of such utilizations include fertilizers, building materials and road materials. The information shall be collected by the producing units of the wastes.

Rate of Utilization of Industrial Solid Wastes refers to the percentage of industrial solid wastes utilized over industrial solid wastes produced (including stocks of the previous years). It is calculated as:

$$\text{Rate of utilization of industrial solid wastes} = \frac{\text{volume of industrial solid wastes utilized}}{\text{industrial solid wastesproduced+ stock of previous years}} \times 100\%$$

Stock of Industrial Solid Wastes refers to the volume of solid wastes placed in special facilities or special sites for purposes of utilization or disposal. The sites or facilities should take measures against dispersion, loss, seepage, and air and water contamination.

Industrial Solid Wastes Disposed refers to the quantity of industrial solid wastes which are burnt or placed ultimately in the sites meeting the requirements for environmental protection and not salvaged or recycled (including disposition in the year of those wastes of previous years). The disposition includes landfill (Safe landfills should be conducted for hazardous wastes), incineration, containment spaces, deep underground disposal, backfill in mining pits and disposal at sea.

Industrial Solid Wastes Discharged refers to the volume of industrial solid wastes discharged by producing enterprises to disposal facilities or to other sites. The wastes exclude stones stripped or dug from mining (gangue and acid or alkaline waste stones not included).

Output Value of Products Made from Waste Gas, Waste Water and Solid Wastes refers to the current value of products with waste gas, waste water and solid wastes as main materials of production. Products sold and ready to sell shall be included while those produced for own use shall not be included.

Consumption Wastes Transported refers to volume of consumption wastes collected and transported to disposal factories or sites. Consumption wastes are solid wastes produced from urban households or from service activities for urban households, and solid wastes regarded by laws and regulations as urban consumption wastes, including those from households, commercial activities, markets, cleaning of streets, public sites, offices, schools, factories, mining units and other sources.

Ratio of Consumption Wastes Treated refers to consumption wastes treated over that produced. In practical statistics, as it is difficult to estimate, the volume of consumption wastes produced is replaced with that transported. It is calculated as:

$$\text{Ratio of consumption wastes treated} = \frac{\text{consumption wastes treated}}{\text{consumption wastes produced}} \times 100\%$$

11 农 业

AGRICULTURE

资料整理：张喜兰　马秋娟　薛　丰
Data management：Zhang Xilan　Ma Qiujuan　Xue Feng
数据审核：马　琰
Data audit：Ma yan

第十一部分　农业

一、简要说明

1.本章资料反映西安农业生产和农村经济的基本情况。内容主要包括耕地、农林牧渔业产值、主要农产品产量、造林、水利水保、农业机械拥有量、农村经济效益主要指标、区县农业生产情况等方面统计资料。

2.农业统计范围包括主要涉农区县的农业生产经营活动。

3.涉及主要年份数据资料，按照《陕西省根据第三次全国农业普查结果核定和修订常规年报相关数据方案》要求，对2007–2017年数据进行了修订。其中，畜牧业中猪牛羊禽修订了2013–2017年数据。11–1、11–3、11–5、11–7表不做修订。

二、主要指标

指标	数值	比较	幅度
年末常用耕地面积（万亩）	367.61	比上年下降	1.8%
农林牧渔业总产值（亿元）	461.21	比上年增长	3.5%
农作物播种面积（万亩）	547.46	比上年下降	0.2%
粮食产量（万吨）	142.14	比上年增长	1.6%

11 AGRICULTURE

Brief Introduction

1. Data in this chapter reflects basic condition of agriculture production of Xi'an city. The mainly including cultivated land, output of agriculture, forestry, animal husbandry and fishery, output of major products, forestation, water conservancy and protection, quantity of agricultural machinery and agricultural base county.

2. Rural social and economic statistics cover social and economic activities in all townships except county towns.

3. Data related to major years, revised the data from 2007 to 2017 by Shanxi Province in accordance with the results of the third national agricultural census approved and revised the regular annual report data programmed. Among them, animal husbandry such as hog, cattle, sheep are revised the data from 2013 to 2017.

		Increase over Preceding Year
Cultivated Area Year-end(10 000 mu)	367.61	-1.8%
Gross Output Value of Farming, Forestry, Animal Husbandry and Fishery (100 mil. Yuan)	461.21	3.5%
Sown Area of Crops(10 000 mu)	547.46	-0.2%
Grain Output(10 000 tons)	142.14	1.6%

11-1 主要年份乡村户数、劳动力及基础设施情况

Rural Households, Labor Force and Basic FaciLities in Representative Years

指 标	Item	2000	2005	2009	2010	2011	2012
一、乡村户数（万户）	**Rural Households(10000 households)**	**98.77**	**101.50**	**101.00**	**101.43**	**102.59**	**101.92**
二、农村劳动力和从业人员情况	**Condition of Rural Population and Employment**						
1.乡村劳动力资源总数（万人）	Total Rural Labor Force (10000 persons)	240.76	255.93	255.00	256.36	260.97	259.06
2.乡村从业人员数（万人）	Number of Rural Workers (10000 persons)	212.65	223.30	223.13	225.04	230.56	226.92
#女性	Female	99.07	103.22	102.76	103.25	109.61	107.63
#农林牧渔业	Forestry Animal Husbandry and Fishery	146.07	137.69	121.78	116.58	116.15	113.29
三、自来水受益村数（个）	**The Number of Tap Water Villages (unit)**	**1527**	**1756**	**2058**	**2184**	**2400**	**2545**
四、通汽车村数（个）	**The Number of Villages with Bus Service (unit)**	**2785**	**2952**	**2989**	**2989**	**2978**	**2936**
五、通电话村数（个）	**The Number of Villages with Telephone Service (unit)**	**2885**	**3101**	**3071**	**3052**	**3033**	**2974**

11-1 续表 continued

指 标	Item	2013	2014	2015	2016	2017	2018
一、乡村户数（万户）	**Rural Households(10000 households)**	**101.37**	**99.26**	**92.77**	**92.63**	**106.28**	**106.02**
二、农村劳动力和从业人员情况	**Condition of Rural Population and Employment**						
1.乡村劳动力资源总数（万人）	Total Rural Labor Force (10000 persons)	257.96	252.40	230.21	230.62	262.44	259.06
2.乡村从业人员数（万人）	Number of Rural Workers (10000 persons)	222.67	216.33	200.38	204.11	225.88	222.99
#女性	Female	106.70	104.03	96.46	98.10	107.16	105.88
#农林牧渔业	Forestry Animal Husbandry and Fishery	108.48	110.30	105.10	102.32	110.38	97.65
三、自来水受益村数（个）	**The Number of Tap Water Villages (unit)**	**2650**	**2765**	**2718**	**2507**	**2706**	**2027**
四、通汽车村数（个）	**The Number of Villages with Bus Service (unit)**	**2927**	**2186**	**2209**			
五、通电话村数（个）	**The Number of Villages with Telephone Service (unit)**	**2966**	**2536**	**2593**			

11-2 各区县乡村从业人员数（2018年）

Number of Rural Employees by Region (2018)

单位：万人　　(10 000 persons)

区 县	Region	乡村劳动力资源总数 Total rural labor force	乡村从业人员数合计 Total number of employees in rural areas	女性从业人员 Female employees	农林牧渔业 Forestry Animal Husbandry and Fishery
合 计	**Total**	**259.06**	**222.99**	**105.88**	**97.65**
新城区	Xingcheng				
碑林区	Beilin				
莲湖区	Lianhu				
灞桥区	Baqiao	18.78	14.86	6.15	4.37
未央区	Weiyang	1.65	0.10	0.02	0.02
雁塔区	Yanta				
阎良区	Yanliang	11.10	10.10	4.68	6.43
临潼区	Lintong	36.60	32.20	15.30	19.01
长安区	Chang'an	35.57	38.65	17.46	9.68
高陵区	Gaoling	9.77	8.24	3.70	2.58
鄠邑区	Huyi	31.45	26.68	12.45	11.97
蓝田县	Lantian	32.05	29.79	18.80	12.65
周至县	Zhouzhi	40.22	32.36	13.65	17.83
西咸新区	Xixian	41.88	30.00	13.66	13.12

11-3 主要年份耕地面积

Area of Cultivated Land in Representative Years

单位：万亩 (10 000 mu)

年 份 Year	年末常用耕地面积 Cultivated Area Year-end	水田 Paddy Field	水浇地 Irrigable Land
1970	554.09	18.20	297.05
1975	538.35	20.34	349.13
1978	530.96	16.70	370.46
1980	526.29	17.45	372.96
1985	508.88	17.63	328.10
1990	495.32	17.97	311.91
1991	492.09	17.03	309.17
1992	485.30	16.44	298.19
1993	479.04	14.36	304.49
1994	471.44	13.98	299.58
1995	463.97	17.04	278.01
1996	451.50	14.21	283.76
1997	456.62	11.90	290.49
1998	455.15	11.18	282.23
1999	450.74	11.31	281.96
2000	443.37	10.26	284.04
2001	431.69	9.00	274.73
2002	424.46	7.98	275.96
2003	413.84	6.65	263.75
2004	404.87	6.59	254.04
2005	400.17	5.55	254.04
2006	395.79	5.33	263.75
2007	391.77	4.80	255.95
2008	390.77	4.64	255.36
2009	387.89	4.39	260.71
2010	383.32	4.03	257.43
2011	377.10	3.80	253.46
2012	369.91	3.32	248.97
2013	366.23	5.33	263.75
2014	360.73	2.42	237.26
2015	356.89	2.37	228.14
2016	346.80	0.96	223.91
2017	374.45	0.62	242.13
2018	367.61	0.53	236.02

11-4 各区县耕地面积（2018年）

单位：万亩

区 县	Region	年末常用耕地面积 Cultivated Area Year-end	水田 Paddy Field	旱地 Dry Land	水浇地 Irrigable Land
合 计	**Total**	**367.61**	**0.53**	**367.08**	**236.02**
新城区	Xincheng				
碑林区	Beilin				
莲湖区	Lianhu				
灞桥区	Baqiao	6.66		6.66	4.82
未央区	Weiyang	0.18		0.18	0.18
雁塔区	Yanta				
阎良区	Yanliang	22.7		22.7	22.32
临潼区	Lintong	68.69		68.69	52.59
长安区	Chang'an	46.84	0.36	46.48	16.69
高陵区	Gaoling	22.21		22.21	20.36
鄠邑区	Huyi	50.53	0.06	50.47	43.73
蓝田县	Lantian	58.69	0.04	58.65	
周至县	Zhouzhi	49.09	0.07	49.02	36.21
西咸新区	Xixian	42.02		42.02	39.12

Area of Cultivated Land by Region（2018）

(10 000 mu)

当年增加的耕地面积 Area of Newly Increased Cultivated Land	新开荒地面积 Area of Newly Reclamation of Wasteland	当年减少的耕地面积 Decrease in Cultivated Area in the Year	国家基建占地 Capital Construction	退耕改果、茶、桑面积 Area for Change into Fruit, Tea and Mulberry	退耕造林面积 Area for Change into Woods
0.72	**0.29**	**11.16**	**5**	**1.4**	**2.3**
0.13		0.72		0.29	0.15
		0.15			
		0.11		0.07	
0.04	0.02	3.75	2	0.03	0.01
0.27	0.27	0.76			
		2.34			2.15
		0.18		0.05	
0.28		1.05		0.87	
		2.1	2	0.09	

11-5 主要年份农业机械拥有量（年末数）

指标	Item	2005	2009	2010
农用机械总动力（千瓦）	Total Power of Agricultural Machinery(kw)	2239001	2616053	2677334
大中型拖拉机（台）	Large and Medium Tractors(unit)	8415	11479	14675
小型拖拉机（台）	Mini-tractors(unit)	26326	18406	14194
拖拉机配套农具（台）	Number of Tactor Towing Farm Machinery(unit)	67217	55614	53608
农用排灌柴油机（台）	Agricultural Diesel Engines(unit)	2219	2691	3309
农用排灌电动机（台）	Agricultural Motors(unit)	79666	83243	79462
农用水泵（台）	Agricultural Water Pump(unit)	77567	80174	77367
节水灌溉类机械（套）	Equipment in Water-saving Irrigation(set)	1290	1799	1710
联合收割机（台）	Combine Harvesters(unit)	4802	6155	6718
自走式机动割晒机（台）	Self-propelled Motorized Swather(unit)	4226	1220	208
机动脱粒机（台）	Motorized Huller (unit)	13870	11960	13231
农用运输车（辆）	Agricultucal Transporter(unit)	47348	50671	51665

注：1.本表数据来源于市农业农村局，2017年、2018年数据不包含西咸新区。
2.2017年以前大中型拖拉机动力标准为14.7千瓦及以上，小型拖拉机动力标准为2.2-14.7千瓦，含2.2千瓦。2018年大中型拖拉机动力标准为22.1千瓦以上，小型拖拉机动力标准为22.1千瓦及以下。“农用排灌柴油机”、“农用排灌电动机”、“自走式机动割晒机”、“农用运输车”四项指标农业农村局报表调整取消。

Possession of Agricultural Machinery in Representative Years (Number of year-end)

2011	2012	2013	2014	2015	2016	2017	2018
2890247	2983979	3108354	3203302	3253733	2615435	2543023	2429137
12585	12987	12927	9946	9652	10177	9275	8580
13008	11471	8971	7538	8447	9175	8501	8226
65833	60035	58515	53257	54120	59805	50559	47582
2639	2891	2509	2409	2409	1772	1467	
87461	87056	86216	85244	84975	84734	80899	
75426	80982	80575	79849	79695	79681	76916	70533
1733	2106	2218	2562	2517	2476	2366	2135
7854	8502	9114	7815	8144	8458	7656	7390
187							
13407	14493	14700	14749	14504	14272	14169	14074
51838	51850	51710	51410	51365			

11-6 各区县农业机械拥有量（2018年）

指标	Item	西安市 Xi' an	新城区 Xincheng	碑林区 Peilin	莲湖区 Lianhu	灞桥区 Baqiao
农用机械总动力（千瓦）	Total Power of Agricultural Machinery(kw)	2429137				125500
大中型拖拉机（台）	Large and Medium Tractors(unit)	8580				82
小型拖拉机（台）	Mini-tractors(unit)	8226				22
拖拉机配套农具（台）	Number of Tactor Towing Farm Machinery(unit)	47582				297
农用排灌柴油机（台）	Agricultural Diesel Engines(unit)					
农用排灌电动机（台）	Agricultural Motors(unit)					
农用水泵（台）	Agricultural Water Pump(unit)	70533				1356
节水灌溉类机械（套）	Equipment in Water-saving Irrigation(set)	2135				43
联合收割机（台）	Combine Harvesters(unit)	7390				47
自走式机动割晒机（台）	Self-propelled Motorized Swather(unit)					
机动脱粒机（台）	Motorized Huller (unit)	14074				35

注：1.本表数据来源于市农业农村局，2017年、2018年数据不包含西咸新区。
2.2017年以前大中型拖拉机动力标准为14.7千瓦及以上，小型拖拉机动力标准为2.2−14.7千瓦，含2.2千瓦。2018年大中型拖拉机动力标准为22.1千瓦以上，小型拖拉机动力标准为22.1千瓦及以下。“农用排灌柴油机”、“农用排灌电动机”、“自走式机动割晒机”、“农用运输车”四项指标农业农村局报表调整取消。

Possession of Agricultural Machinery by Region（2018）

未央区 Weiyang	雁塔区 Yanta	阎良区 Yanliang	临潼区 Lintong	长安区 Chang'an	高陵区 Gaoling	鄠邑区 Huyi	蓝田县 Lantian	周至县 Zhouzhi	西咸新区 Xixian
41850	55320	125777	404008	354063	220900	500694	247042	353983	
13	17	456	1178	1492	1538	1782	898	1124	
	22	252		1132	137	1545	924	4192	
60	86	2081	9784	5597	6400	9943	6194	7140	
500	485	5796	16460	9718	3760	12735	2486	17237	
90		485	142	936		149	63	227	
6	14	467	1637	1220	730	2550	388	331	
6		1121	4948	792	545	2381	1815	2431	

11-7 主要年份农业机械化、化肥、水利情况

指标	Item	2000	2005	2008
一、农业机械化水平（万亩）	**Statistics on Agricultural Machinery (10 000 mu)**			
当年机械耕地面积（实际）	Area Ploughed by Tractors	366.81	360.68	404.42
当年机械播种面积（作业）	Seeded Area by Tractors	482.74	485.62	539.81
当年机械收获面积（作业）	Harvest Area by Tractors	272.83	271.77	313.11
二、农用化肥施用量（吨）	**Use of Agricultural Fertilizers and Insecticides(ton)**			
1. 按实物量计算合计	Practicality Consumption	697243	749802	767980
氮肥	Nitrogenous Fertilizer	392366	411161	413397
磷肥	Phosphate Fertilizer	155480	161444	157145
钾肥	Potash Fertilizer	31841	34114	34149
复合肥	Compound Fertilizer	78620	115458	132481
2. 按折纯法计算合计	Standard Consumption	196343	211790	225949
氮肥	Nitrogenous Fertilizer	102982	107645	112000
磷肥	Phosphate Fertilizer	18658	19368	18855
钾肥	Potash Fertilizer	15921	17055	17077
复合肥	Compound Fertilizer	39313	57009	66247
三、农用塑料薄膜使用量（公斤）	**Plastic Sheet for Agricultural Use(kg)**	**1622198**	**1855383**	**2122310**
四、农用柴油使用量（吨）	**Diesel Oil for Agricultural Use (ton)**	**52706**	**50832**	**51097**
五、农药使用量（公斤）	**Pesticide (kg)**	**1559333**	**1427879**	**1465819**
六、农村水利化情况（万亩）	**Irrigation and Water Conservancy (10 000 mu)**			
有效灌溉面积	Effective Irrigation Area	335.97	280.1	274.48
旱涝保收面积	Stable-Harvesting Arable Land	294.06	255.37	249.31
机电排灌面积	Electrical Irrigation Area	249.11	223.74	211.01

注：1.本表第一部分数据来源于市农业农村局，第六部分数据来源于市水务局，其中“机电排灌面积”2016年报表取消。
2.2017年起农业机械化水平数据不含西咸新区。

Agricultural Machinery,Chemical Fertilizers,Water Conservancy, in Representative Years

2009	2010	2011	2012	2013	2014	2015	2016	2017	2018
413.7	367.32	427.03	425.4	425.21	549.07	533.21	518.07	498.57	465.25
544.86	548.28	507.55	529.99	523.15	509.53	492.9	499.36	532.61	501.27
342.82	403.5	413.93	428.28	443.57	466.21	474.1	488.85	470.66	456.27
776319	781072	785885	807900	794361	820315	810849	771144	800468	783707
414481	397975	398395	414339	401140	412544	408396	374476	383467	374479
153825	152943	151005	151967	152565	156662	157601	152278	153808	146521
33069	37715	38195	43356	39630	42504	46284	46388	45866	45520
142137	158062	163797	198238	201026	208605	198568	198002	217327	217187
230299	235532	239497	243281	239701	251217	246284	242871	255267	252662
112275	108868	110412	113662	109497	116055	108833	111150	115631	113745
18457	18315	18026	18061	18023	18505	18584	18033	19072	18456
16534	17997	18095	21267	18973	20110	21986	21779	21486	21228
71042	78811	81764	90291	93208	96547	96881	91909	99078	99233
2141969	**2450496**	**2533372**	**2683201**	**2678745**	**2657870**	**2770750**	**2880480**	**3157710**	**3380130**
51346	**61917**	**61637**	**57451**	**62563**	**74935**	**59360**	**55982**	**67510**	**67091**
1325459	**1243105**	**1242773**	**1252490**	**1210060**	**1220638**	**1174883**	**1126305**	**1703736**	**1506859**
273.17	281.28	262.32	267.84	240.22	248.34	244.72	259.78	256.13	282.83
247.6	234.15	214.62	211.31	196.96	189.69	188.5	201.7	184.91	184.78
213.42	224.6	200.36	198.66	229.29	230.58	239.63			

11-8 各区县农业机械化、化肥、水利情况（2018年）

指标	Item	西安市 Xi'an	新城区 Xincheng	碑林区 Peilin	莲湖区 Lianhu
一、农业机械化水平（万亩）	**Statistics on Agricultural Machinery (10 000 mu)**				
当年机械耕地面积（实际）	Area Ploughed by Tractors	465.25			
当年机械播种面积（作业）	Seeded Area by Tractors	501.27			
当年机械收获面积（作业）	Harvest Area by Tractors	456.27			
二、农用化肥施用量（吨）	**Use of Agricultural Fertilizers and Insecticides(ton)**				
1. 按实物量计算合计	Practicality Consumption	783707			
氮肥	Nitrogenous Fertilizer	374479			
磷肥	Phosphate Fertilizer	146521			
钾肥	Potash Fertilizer	45520			
复合肥	Compound Fertilizer	217187			
2.按折纯法计算合计	Standard Consumption	252662			
氮肥	Nitrogenous Fertilizer	113745			
磷肥	Phosphate Fertilizer	18456			
钾肥	Potash Fertilizer	21228			
复合肥	Compound Fertilizer	99233			
三、农用塑料薄膜使用量（公斤）	**Plastic Sheet for Agricultural Use(kg)**	**3380130**			
四、农用柴油使用量（吨）	**Diesel Oil for Agricultural Use (ton)**	**67091**			
五、农药使用量（公斤）	**Pesticide (kg)**	**1506859**			
六、农村水利化情况（万亩）	**Irrigation and Water Conservancy (10 000 mu)**				
有效灌溉面积	Effective Irrigation Area	282.83			
旱涝保收面积	Stable-Harvesting Arable Land	184.78			
机电排灌面积	Electrical Irrigation Area				

注：1.本表第一部分数据来源于市农业农村局，第六部分数据来源于市水务局，其中“机电排灌面积”2016年报表取消。
2.农业机械化水平数据不含西咸新区。

Agricultural Machinery,Chemical Fertilizers, Water Conservancy by Region （2018）

灞桥区 Baqiao	未央区 Weiyang	雁塔区 Yanta	阎良区 Yanliang	临潼区 Lintong	长安区 Chang'an	高陵区 Gaoling	鄠邑区 Huyi	蓝田县 Lantian	周至县 Zhouzhi	西咸新区 Xixian
16.22			38.77	94.70	93.87	24.55	64.53	72.40	60.21	
10.97			24.26	98.36	88.72	35.50	81.76	92.60	69.10	
9.48			22.11	96.70	78.76	36.50	76.50	74.70	61.52	
17738	562		76787	152617	52780	55942	104196	122030	149488	51567
6224	125		33717	81053	24011	24475	57125	65583	62533	19633
1177	167		13099	44818	6928	14721	14496	25785	15950	9380
1686	101		5577	2905	6388	3461	5553	8545	9105	2199
8651	169		24394	23841	15453	13285	27022	22117	61900	20355
7121	204		28240	40674	16026	13297	31751	46737	52774	15838
2891	56		13149	21862	7027	4200	15075	28810	15358	5317
141	21		1686	5392	958	1829	1804	2950	1914	1761
844	49		2846	1468	2759	1698	2404	3777	4552	831
3245	78		10559	11952	5282	5570	12468	11200	30950	7929
11980	**19800**		**1480000**	**233680**	**160670**	**34450**	**573000**	**406000**	**98750**	**361800**
337	**395**		**3304**	**15516**	**7209**	**1929**	**10871**	**9750**	**3302**	**14478**
21491	**338**		**192895**	**288561**	**62668**	**155526**	**59979**	**74065**	**165011**	**486325**
10.38	0.86		22.58	53.94	39.63	25.89	51.41	17.43	60.71	
	0.38		22.56	46.58	19.71	21.20	43.10	0.00	31.25	

11-9 主要年份农林牧渔业总产值及指数

Gross Output Value of Farming,Forestry,Animal Husbandry,Fishery, Service and Related Indices in Representative Years

单位：万元　　　　(10 000 yuan)

年份 Year	农林牧渔业总产值（现价） Gross Output Value (At current prices)	农业 Farming	林业 Forestry	牧业 Animal Husbandry	渔业 Fishery	农林牧渔专业及辅助性活动 Farming, Forestry, Animal Husbandry, Fishery and AuxiliaryActivities	指数（上年=100）（可比价） Indices(preceding year= 100) (At cinstant prices)
1970	40617	35965	713	3896	43		111.2
1975	55322	47378	1509	6403	32		93.9
1978	65423	56519	1444	7427	33		104.7
1980	65322	54004	1177	10106	35		85
1985	134933	105888	2559	26186	300		106.4
1990	262073	191088	3134	65840	2011		102.5
1991	295620	208324	3362	81070	2864		108.6
1992	321155	219160	4225	94045	3725		108.6
1993	387068	261959	5031	115810	4268		112.8
1994	565056	359609	7819	192140	5488		102.4
1995	754597	513348	7185	228598	5466		106.8
1996	786003	552726	7573	219214	6490		102.1
1997	836201	585973	9226	233623	7379		110.3
1998	853279	625465	8146	212045	7623		107.5
1999	739905	530029	8883	194552	6441		100.7
2000	743712	514845	8482	212612	7773		104.3
2001	767511	527160	8427	223861	8063		102.8
2002	797444	539978	11378	238761	7327		103
2003	837857	551398	10550	269610	6299		101.5
2004	967946	580798	12773	314517	6728	53130	108.4
2005	1065437	657262	13086	329856	7340	57893	107.7
2006	1141484	686748	15188	346626	7017	85905	107.2
2007	1317442	790316	15845	395003	9147	107131	105.3
2008	1629892	943261	23365	521950	11348	129968	107.8
2009	1695468	1034208	22663	486142	11830	140625	106.5
2010	2124191	1389118	26787	538396	12830	157060	107.4
2011	2501236	1651250	34453	616943	14856	183734	106.6
2012	2785682	1827705	62291	643347	19877	232462	106
2013	3057732	2038346	80199	648800	22773	267614	104.9
2014	3232984	2196966	86889	633519	24030	291580	105.1
2015	3308141	2251512	97776	613417	19519	325917	105.1
2016	3467506	2357901	102222	621737	19640	366006	104.2
2017	4373298	3009278	135570	729219	22700	476531	104.8
2018	4612088	3230380	169157	679813	26268	506470	103.5

注：本表2007-2017年数根据第三次全国农业普查结果进行了修订。

11-10 主要年份农林牧渔业总产值指数

Related Indices of Gross Output Value of Farming,Forestry,Animal Husbandry and Fishery in Representative Years

年份 Year	农林牧渔业总产值指数（上年=100）（可比价） Gross Output Value Index of Farming, Forestry, Animal Husbandry and Fishery (preceding year = 100) (At constant prices)	农业 Farming	林业 Forestry	牧业 Animal Husbandry	渔业 Fishery	农林牧渔专业及辅助性活动 Farming, Forestry, Animal Husbandry, Fishery and Auxiliary Activities
2005	107.7	108.0	98.7	107.3	112.6	108.0
2006	107.2	106.0	102.5	109.3	104.5	109.0
2007	105.3	106.4	101.3	102.4	106.3	109.0
2008	107.8	107.9	112.2	106.0	100.5	114.0
2009	106.5	105.4	121.3	106.8	107.4	110.0
2010	107.4	108.7	115.2	104.3	92.7	109.0
2011	106.6	108.2	105.7	102.9	102.1	108.0
2012	106.0	105.6	143.0	104.8	113.4	109.0
2013	104.9	104.3	131.3	104.0	110.1	106.0
2014	105.1	105.8	105.7	103.2	106.0	106.0
2015	105.1	106.7	113.8	100.2	71.2	106.0
2016	104.2	104.8	114.7	100.6	100.1	107.0
2017	104.8	105.0	111.0	103.0	104.3	106.0
2018	103.5	102.8	131.0	100.1	111.4	105.0

11-11 主要年份农林牧渔业总产值构成

Gross Output Value and Its Composition of Farming, Forestry, Animal Husbandry and Fishery at Current Price in Representative Years

单位：% (%)

年份 Year	农林牧渔业总产值 Gross Output Value (At current prices)	农业 Farming	林业 Forestry	牧业 Animal Husbandry	渔业 Fishery	农林牧渔专业及辅助性活动 Farming, Forestry, Animal Husbandry, Fishery and Auxiliary Activities
2005	100	61.7	1.2	31.0	0.7	5.4
2006	100	60.9	1.3	31.5	0.6	5.7
2007	100	60.0	1.2	30.0	0.7	8.1
2008	100	57.9	1.4	32.0	0.7	8.0
2009	100	61.0	1.3	28.7	0.7	8.3
2010	100	65.4	1.3	25.3	0.6	7.4
2011	100	66.0	1.4	24.7	0.6	7.3
2012	100	65.6	2.2	23.1	0.7	8.4
2013	100	66.7	2.6	21.2	0.7	8.8
2014	100	68.0	2.7	19.6	0.7	9.0
2015	100	68.1	3.0	18.5	0.6	9.8
2016	100	68.0	2.9	17.9	0.6	10.6
2017	100	68.8	3.1	16.7	0.5	10.9
2018	100	70.0	3.7	14.7	0.6	11.0

11-12 各区县农林牧渔业总产值（2018年）

Gross Output Value of Farming, Forestry, Animal Husbandry and Fishery by Region（2018）

单位：万元 (10 000 yuan)

区县	Region	农林牧渔业总产值 Gross Output Value (At current prices)	农业 Farming	林业 Forestry	牧业 Animal Husbandry	渔业 Fishery	农林牧渔专业及辅助性活动 Farming, Forestry, Animal Husbandry, Fishery and Auxiliary Activities
合计	**Total**	**4612088**	**3230380**	**169157**	**679813**	**26268**	**506470**
新城区	Xincheng						
碑林区	Beilin						
莲湖区	Lianhu						
灞桥区	Baqiao	311278	246565	3853	20505	823	39532
未央区	Weiyang	8814	2680	1600	1758	1080	1696
雁塔区	Yanta						
阎良区	Yanliang	446310	348790	1993	51943	335	43249
临潼区	Lintong	601608	385467	4178	138318	5024	68621
长安区	Chang'an	455700	309130	7430	76256	5778	57106
高陵区	Gaoling	482906	316758	6098	82438	651	76961
鄠邑区	Huyi	447692	296872	20944	81945	2376	45555
蓝田县	Lantian	494077	298218	36663	105478	6403	47315
周至县	Zhouzhi	589596	391754	66902	70331	755	59854
西咸新区	Xixian	774107	634146	19496	50841	3043	66581

11-13 各区县农林牧渔业总产值指数和构成（2018年）

Gross Output Value and Its Composition of Farming, Forestry, Animal Husbandry and Fishery at Current Price by Region（2018）

单位：% (%)

区县	Region	农林牧渔业总产值 Gross Output Value (At current prices)	农业 Farming	林业 Forestry	牧业 Animal Husbandry	渔业 Fishery	农林牧渔专业及辅助性活动 Farming, Forestry, Animal Husbandry, Fishery and Auxiliary Activities
全市指数	**Total**	**103.5**	**102.8**	**131.0**	**100.1**	**111.4**	**105.1**
新城区	Xincheng						
碑林区	Beilin						
莲湖区	Lianhu						
灞桥区	Baqiao	103.4	102.3	107.7	104.8	72.3	110.0
未央区	Weiyang	55.7	46.5	109.3	29.9	153.5	90.2
雁塔区	Yanta						
阎良区	Yanliang	105.6	104.9	155.8	109.2	72.6	105.8
临潼区	Lintong	101.6	106.1	128.0	90.7	73.1	106.2
长安区	Chang'an	101.1	101.2	80.5	103.4	74.5	105.2
高陵区	Gaoling	105.2	105.0	131.6	102.5	181.6	106.9
鄠邑区	Huyi	104.6	102.1	133.0	107.5	82.5	105.9
蓝田县	Lantian	105.4	103.5	137.4	100.7	309.2	100.5
周至县	Zhouzhi	102.9	98.9	135.6	103.5	84.0	99.8
西咸新区	Xixian	104.0	102.7	139.7	100.6	676.3	107.0
全市构成	**Total**	**100.0**	**70.0**	**3.7**	**14.7**	**0.6**	**11.0**
新城区	Xincheng						
碑林区	Beilin						
莲湖区	Lianhu						
灞桥区	Baqiao	100.0	79.2	1.2	6.6	0.3	12.7
未央区	Weiyang	100.0	30.4	18.2	19.9	12.3	19.2
雁塔区	Yanta						
阎良区	Yanliang	100.0	78.1	0.4	11.6	0.1	9.8
临潼区	Lintong	100.0	64.1	0.7	23.0	0.8	11.4
长安区	Chang'an	100.0	67.8	1.6	16.7	1.3	12.6
高陵区	Gaoling	100.0	65.6	1.3	17.1	0.1	15.9
鄠邑区	Huyi	100.0	66.3	4.7	18.3	0.5	10.2
蓝田县	Lantian	100.0	60.4	7.4	21.3	1.3	9.6
周至县	Zhouzhi	100.0	66.4	11.3	11.9	0.1	10.3
西咸新区	Xixian	100.0	81.9	2.5	6.6	0.4	8.6

11-14 主要年份农林牧渔业增加值

Value-Added of Farming, Forestry, Animal Husbandry and Fishery in Representative Years

单位：万元 (10 000 yuan)

年份 Year	农林牧渔业增加值 Value-Added of Farming,Forestry,Animal Husbandry and Fishery	农业 Farming	林业 Forestry	牧业 Animal Husbandry	渔业 Fishery	农林牧渔专业及辅助性活动 Farming, Forestry, Animal Husbandry, Fishery and Auxiliary Activities
1995	413981	329662	4413	76746	3160	
2000	446481	336777	4323	101353	4028	
2001	458720	342427	4258	108096	3939	
2002	477691	351358	6419	116591	3323	
2003	458378	312849	5473	137236	2820	
2004	582009	393349	6811	164572	2919	14358
2005	660148	444320	6888	169701	3373	35866
2006	704427	465823	8556	177431	3227	49390
2007	810964	534266	8413	202542	4533	61210
2008	998801	630049	10551	277280	5735	75186
2009	1042178	679853	11866	265458	5937	79064
2010	1302739	902808	14215	291809	6532	87375
2011	1577644	1107767	18463	340097	7714	103603
2012	1752737	1225342	34155	352536	10156	130548
2013	1924233	1365967	44432	353361	11643	148830
2014	2036198	1471915	48367	343041	12294	160581
2015	2075195	1499915	54887	332210	10370	177813
2016	2163311	1560666	59309	335521	10062	197753
2017	2708351	1953733	78658	406750	11740	257470
2018	2861844	2097265	98148	379191	13586	273654

注：本表2007－2017年数根据第三次全国农业普查结果进行了修订。

11-15 主要年份农林牧渔业增加值指数

Indices of Value-Added of Farming, Forestry, Animal Husbandry and Fishery in Representative Years

年份 Year	农林牧渔业增加值指数（上年=100）（可比价） Value-Added Index of Farming, Forestry, Animal Husbandry and Fishery (preceding year = 100) (At constant prices)	农业 Farming	林业 Forestry	牧业 Animal Husbandry	渔业 Fishery	农林牧渔专业及辅助性活动 Farming, Forestry, Animal Husbandry, Fishery and Auxiliary Activities
2008	107.6	107.6	112.0	105.8	100.0	114.0
2009	106.3	103.6	114.6	111.2	106.3	108.8
2010	106.9	107.9	108.7	104.3	94.0	108.9
2011	106.7	108.1	106.1	102.8	102.7	108.1
2012	106.0	105.6	142.8	104.8	113.4	108.5
2013	104.8	104.3	131.3	104.0	110.1	105.9
2014	105.2	105.8	104.1	103.2	106.0	105.9
2015	105.1	106.5	114.0	100.5	71.3	106.2
2016	104.1	104.5	112.6	100.5	100.3	106.9
2017	104.8	105.1	111.0	102.3	104.3	106.2
2018	103.5	102.8	131.0	100.1	111.4	105.1

11-16 各区县农林牧渔业增加值（2018年）

Value-Added of Farming, Forestry, Animal Husbandry, Fishery and Service by Region（2018）

单位：万元 (10 000 yuan)

区县	Region	农林牧渔业增加值 Value-Added of Farming,Forestry,Animal Husbandry and Fishery	农业 Farming	林业 Forestry	牧业 Animal Husbandry	渔业 Fishery	农林牧渔专业及辅助性活动 Farming, Forestry, Animal Husbandry, Fishery and Auxiliary Activities
合计	**Total**	**2861844**	**2097265**	**98148**	**379191**	**13586**	**273654**
新城区	Xincheng						
碑林区	Beilin						
莲湖区	Lianhu						
灞桥区	Baqiao	203538	167291	2647	11675	340	21585
未央区	Weiyang	4974	1877	864	918	363	952
雁塔区	Yanta						
阎良区	Yanliang	239355	234089	1158	30012	175	23921
临潼区	Lintong	366504	250621	2547	72374	2188	38774
长安区	Chang'an	298893	225994	4792	34273	3832	30002
高陵区	Gaoling	297192	197578	3655	48371	279	47309
鄠邑区	Huyi	277530	191922	11916	51248	1469	20975
蓝田县	Lantian	296378	184011	22631	62115	2923	24698
周至县	Zhouzhi	359716	251978	35752	41270	404	30312
西咸新区	Xixian	467764	391904	12186	26935	1613	35126

11-17 各区县农林牧渔业增加值指数（2018年）

Indices of Value-Added of Farming, Forestry, Animal Husbandry and Fishery by Region（2018）

（上年 =100）（可比价） (preceding year = 100) (At constant prices)

区 县	Region	农林牧渔业增加值指数（上年=100）（可比价）Value-Added Index of Farming, Forestry, Animal Husbandry and Fishery (preceding year = 100) (At constant prices)	农业 Farming	林业 Forestry	牧业 Animal Husbandry	渔业 Fishery	农林牧渔专业及辅助性活动 Farming, Forestry, Animal Husbandry, Fishery and Auxiliary Activities
合 计	**Total**	**103.5**	**102.8**	**131.0**	**100.1**	**111.4**	**105.1**
新城区	Xincheng						
碑林区	Beilin						
莲湖区	Lianhu						
灞桥区	Baqiao	103.3	102.4	108.1	104.5	75.2	109.9
未央区	Weiyang	53.8	46.6	109.8	29.8	159.5	90.2
雁塔区	Yanta						
阎良区	Yanliang	105.6	104.9	156.4	108.9	75.5	105.7
临潼区	Lintong	102.2	106.2	128.5	90.5	76.0	106.1
长安区	Chang'an	101.0	101.2	80.8	103.1	77.5	105.1
高陵区	Gaoling	105.1	105.0	132.1	102.2	189.1	106.8
鄠邑区	Huyi	104.4	102.2	133.5	107.2	85.8	105.8
蓝田县	Lantian	105.3	103.5	137.9	100.5	321.4	100.4
周至县	Zhouzhi	102.4	98.9	136.1	103.2	87.4	99.7
西咸新区	Xixian	104.0	102.7	140.2	100.3	702.4	106.9

11-18 主要年份农作物播种面积

Sown Areas of Farm Crops In Representative Years

单位：万亩 （10 000mu）

年 份 Year	总播种面积 Total Sown Area	粮食 Grain Crops	小麦 Wheat	玉米 Corn	油料 Oil-bearing Crops	蔬菜 Vegetables
1980	835.43	706.35	324.17	273.14	10.01	24.02
1985	795.41	704.36	378.20	271.14	8.01	45.03
1990	816.41	731.42	387.20	282.14	12.00	51.03
1991	820.41	731.37	389.19	283.14	13.01	47.03
1992	820.65	715.50	384.60	273.60	16.20	54.60
1993	821.63	713.49	380.40	273.69	14.84	63.90
1994	821.10	719.00	375.90	272.40	13.80	59.90
1995	784.74	690.63	370.41	259.55	18.57	57.59
1996	797.40	709.00	366.30	286.80	18.80	55.50
1997	755.78	670.83	367.71	248.79	15.53	59.36
1998	789.99	705.03	370.17	285.45	14.69	60.95
1999	793.08	709.95	371.94	294.00	12.74	60.68
2000	784.94	697.55	369.89	283.70	13.46	64.35
2001	763.16	678.05	359.19	278.57	11.87	61.77
2002	751.10	655.59	350.64	271.95	11.40	67.71
2003	737.06	632.55	336.05	261.89	11.04	69.44
2004	753.83	630.63	311.52	286.50	9.74	77.55
2005	757.91	642.75	325.10	287.87	9.51	83.33
2006	769.49	648.00	313.23	307.89	8.58	87.03
2007	753.54	646.06	296.48	327.93	7.18	75.31
2008	710.48	605.57	294.42	292.34	8.04	75.86
2009	684.56	578.01	285.73	273.35	7.75	77.23
2010	665.89	559.09	277.34	264.07	7.77	78.06
2011	631.45	525.12	259.98	240.74	7.40	78.98
2012	612.90	508.16	256.22	233.84	6.25	79.54
2013	569.95	465.64	236.98	211.66	5.93	80.82
2014	543.19	437.10	224.27	200.39	5.21	81.72
2015	520.78	413.31	215.61	189.60	4.86	82.50
2016	502.63	401.95	209.78	180.80	4.13	81.43
2017	548.50	424.14	228.89	180.39	4.28	104.64
2018	547.46	419.56	227.84	177.58	4.61	107.74

注：本表2007-2017年数根据第三次全国农业普查结果进行了修订。

11–19 各区县主要农作物播种面积（2018年）

Sown Areas of Major Farm Crops by Region（2018）

单位：万亩 (10 000 mu)

区 县	Region	总播种面积 Total Sown Area	粮食 Grain Crops	小麦 Wheat	玉米 Corn	油料 Oil-bearing Crops	蔬菜 Vegetables	瓜果类 Fruits Class
合 计	**Total**	**547.46**	**419.56**	**227.84**	**177.58**	**4.61**	**107.74**	**14.92**
新城区	Xincheng							
碑林区	Beilin							
莲湖区	Lianhu							
灞桥区	Baqiao	13.29	8.14	5.29	2.77	0.20	4.59	0.31
未央区	Weiyang	0.05	0.02	0.02			0.03	
雁塔区	Yanta							
阎良区	Yanliang	50.07	27.77	14.45	13.32	0.08	15.11	7.11
临潼区	Lintong	118.15	100.30	53.08	42.42	0.40	15.60	1.78
长安区	Chang'an	58.87	46.39	28.02	18.13	0.64	10.01	1.82
高陵区	Gaoling	39.75	26.47	13.20	12.00	0.00	13.14	0.14
鄠邑区	Huyi	65.18	54.72	28.03	25.56	0.18	8.67	1.60
蓝田县	Lantian	69.98	60.45	35.34	20.80	2.45	5.80	1.09
周至县	Zhouzhi	47.84	38.32	18.95	17.81	0.48	8.64	0.11
西咸新区	Xixian	84.28	56.98	31.46	24.77	0.18	26.15	0.96

11-20 主要年份农作物产品产量

Yield of Major Farm Crops in Representative Years

单位：万吨 (10 000 ton)

年份 Year	粮食作物 Grain Crops	夏粮 Summer Grain	小麦 Wheat	秋粮 Autumn Grain	稻谷 Rice	玉米 Corn	油料 Oil-bearing Crops	油菜籽 Rapeseeds	蔬菜 Vegetables
1978	132.80	64.20	58.20	68.70	5.10	55.80	0.09	0.07	45.66
1979	145.70	81.80	74.20	63.90	4.50	53.40	0.33	0.29	49.11
1980	114.40	56.60	52.20	57.80	4.70	47.70	0.54	0.50	40.13
1981	116.10	78.70	74.30	37.40	3.40	31.50	0.76	0.75	34.06
1982	148.90	85.60	82.20	63.30	4.90	55.50	0.51	0.49	53.71
1983	148.10	81.80	79.60	66.30	4.80	58.50	0.36	0.34	46.99
1984	157.60	82.40	81.00	75.20	5.00	66.50	0.46	0.29	75.47
1985	150.10	76.10	74.80	74.00	5.10	65.10	0.75	0.39	86.44
1986	162.40	91.70	90.10	70.70	4.80	61.80	1.25	0.82	85.84
1987	171.20	87.00	85.20	84.20	5.00	74.30	1.57	1.22	95.16
1988	158.00	86.80	84.60	71.10	3.80	61.40	0.89	0.51	113.50
1989	173.60	93.50	91.20	80.20	4.70	70.40	1.33	0.94	129.32
1990	172.40	91.70	89.70	80.80	5.50	70.40	1.35	0.94	119.32
1991	178.80	91.10	89.20	87.70	5.00	77.50	1.20	0.74	117.41
1992	183.40	101.70	99.60	81.70	4.70	72.30	1.49	0.87	128.12
1993	190.00	101.10	99.00	88.90	4.90	78.60	1.40	1.00	145.80
1994	157.40	86.90	84.90	70.50	4.50	61.40	1.08	0.78	135.26
1995	175.30	99.80	97.40	75.50	3.40	67.80	2.17	1.90	133.60
1996	187.50	80.10	78.40	107.40	3.40	95.60	1.83	1.55	138.01
1997	190.50	114.30	112.30	76.30	3.50	69.40	1.86	1.65	142.11
1998	212.70	104.40	104.00	108.30	3.20	99.10	1.67	1.36	148.87
1999	204.40	95.50	94.40	108.90	2.90	99.70	1.30	1.00	153.24
2000	201.90	92.60	91.60	109.30	3.10	100.50	1.34	0.95	162.14
2001	197.10	98.10	97.20	98.90	2.70	91.30	1.23	0.90	152.80
2002	192.40	94.50	93.50	97.90	2.10	91.60	1.22	0.84	169.74
2003	176.30	98.20	96.70	78.20	1.60	72.30	1.13	0.70	169.67
2004	195.80	97.80	96.00	98.00	1.70	91.60	1.14	0.84	180.96
2005	205.50	100.00	99.10	105.50	1.60	99.30	1.16	0.89	195.70
2006	193.50	86.00	85.40	107.40	1.40	101.20	1.08	0.87	189.30
2007	192.52	73.97	71.97	118.55	1.51	113.83	0.93	0.74	168.98
2008	185.48	87.95	87.36	97.53	0.80	94.02	1.08	0.86	180.60
2009	177.91	81.90	81.03	96.01	0.73	92.49	1.04	0.84	195.07
2010	174.51	81.29	80.71	93.22	0.55	89.47	1.01	0.84	207.11
2011	167.05	78.35	76.66	88.70	0.54	84.37	1.00	0.84	214.13
2012	167.67	79.69	79.02	87.98	0.44	84.18	0.83	0.74	227.96
2013	151.68	67.73	67.05	83.95	0.29	80.04	0.77	0.71	243.92
2014	140.77	68.72	68.15	72.05	0.15	69.99	0.71	0.59	257.86
2015	141.42	72.34	71.95	69.08	0.00	67.71	0.68	0.57	267.91
2016	135.39	68.86	68.45	66.53	0.07	64.09	0.58	0.50	268.87
2017	139.89	75.26	74.90	64.63	0.05	60.96	0.62	0.55	354.74
2018	142.14	74.28	73.86	67.86	0.05	64.36	0.67	0.57	373.69

注：本表2007-2017年数根据第三次全国农业普查结果进行了修订。

11-21 各区县主要农作物产品产量（2018年）

Yield of Major Farm Crops by Region（2018）

单位：万吨 (10 000 tons)

区县	Region	粮食作物 Grain Crops	夏粮 Summer Grain	小麦 Wheat	秋粮 Autumn Grain	稻谷 Rice	玉米 Corn
合　计	**Total**	**142.14**	**74.28**	**73.86**	**67.86**	**0.06**	**64.36**
新城区	Xincheng						
碑林区	Beilin						
莲湖区	Lianhu						
灞桥区	Baqiao	2.77	1.88	1.88	0.89		0.87
未央区	Weiyang	0.01	0.01	0.01			
雁塔区	Yanta						
阎良区	Yanliang	12.03	6.13	6.13	5.90	0.00	5.90
临潼区	Lintong	32.91	16.51	16.51	16.40	0.00	14.76
长安区	Chang'an	15.62	8.84	8.84	6.78	0.05	6.72
高陵区	Gaoling	12.35	5.69	5.69	6.66	0.00	6.12
鄠邑区	Huyi	19.13	9.75	9.54	9.38	0.00	9.33
蓝田县	Lantian	17.04	9.71	9.56	7.33	0.01	6.67
周至县	Zhouzhi	11.91	5.83	5.77	6.08	0.00	5.79
西咸新区	Xixian	18.37	9.93	9.93	8.44	0.00	8.20

11-21 续表 continued

单位：万吨 (10 000 tons)

区县	Region	油料 Oil-bearing Crops	油菜籽 Rapeseeds	蔬菜 Vegetables	瓜果类 Fruits Class
合　计	**Total**	**0.67**	**0.57**	**373.69**	**51.14**
新城区	Xincheng				
碑林区	Beilin				
莲湖区	Lianhu				
灞桥区	Baqiao	0.03	0.02	17.93	0.65
未央区	Weiyang			0.11	0.00
雁塔区	Yanta				
阎良区	Yanliang	0.01	0.01	69.21	26.48
临潼区	Lintong	0.06	0.05	50.44	8.57
长安区	Chang'an	0.10	0.06	19.09	3.41
高陵区	Gaoling	0.00	0.00	58.62	1.06
鄠邑区	Huyi	0.03	0.02	28.51	4.90
蓝田县	Lantian	0.34	0.32	10.40	2.71
周至县	Zhouzhi	0.07	0.06	22.13	0.31
西咸新区	Xixian	0.03	0.03	97.26	3.04

11-22 主要年份农作物单位面积产量

Yield of Farm Crops Per Unit Area in Representative Years

单位：公斤/亩 (kg/mu)

年份 Year	粮食作物 Grain Crops	夏粮 Summer Grain	小麦 Wheat	秋粮 Autumn Grain	玉米 Corn	油料 Oil-bearing Crops	油菜籽 Rapeseeds	蔬菜 Vegetables
1990	236	232	232	241	249	103	101	2349
1991	245	229	229	264	274	94	89	2332
1992	256	259	259	253	264	92	101	2344
1993	266	260	260	274	287	94	107	2282
1994	219	226	226	211	225	79	84	2260
1995	254	263	263	243	261	117	128	2320
1996	265	214	214	321	333	86	100	2489
1997	284	305	306	257	279	76	129	2395
1998	302	278	279	328	347	114	121	2443
1999	288	253	254	327	339	102	106	2526
2000	289	247	248	338	354	102	112	2520
2001	291	270	271	314	328	104	113	2474
2002	293	266	267	326	337	107	115	2507
2003	279	287	288	269	276	102	110	2444
2004	310	308	308	313	320	117	129	2333
2005	320	304	305	336	345	121	132	2349
2006	299	273	273	323	329	125	135	2175
2007	298	247	246	342	347	130	131	2244
2008	306	297	297	315	322	134	137	2381
2009	308	284	284	331	338	134	130	2526
2010	312	292	291	333	339	130	130	2653
2011	318	297	295	340	350	135	133	2711
2012	330	309	308	352	360	133	129	2866
2013	326	284	283	370	378	129	122	3018
2014	322	304	304	342	349	136	129	3155
2015	342	333	334	352	357	139	132	3247
2016	337	326	326	349	354	141	132	3302
2017	330	325	327	333	338	144	138	3390
2018	339	324	324	357	362	146	137	3468

注：本表2007-2017年数根据第三次全国农业普查结果进行了修订。

11-23 各区县主要农作物单位面积产量（2018年）

The Output of Main Crops Per Unit Area by Region（2018）

单位：公斤/亩 (kg/mu)

区县	Region	粮食作物 Grain Crops	夏粮 Summer Grain	小麦 Wheat	秋粮 Autumn Grain	玉米 Corn
合计	**Total**	**339**	**324**	**324**	**357**	**362**
新城区	Xincheng					
碑林区	Beilin					
莲湖区	Lianhu					
灞桥区	Baqiao	340	356	356	310	314
未央区	Weiyang	351	349	349	360	360
雁塔区	Yanta					
阎良区	Yanliang	433	424	424	443	443
临潼区	Lintong	328	311	311	347	348
长安区	Chang'an	337	315	315	369	370
高陵区	Gaoling	467	431	431	502	510
鄠邑区	Huyi	350	338	340	363	365
蓝田县	Lantian	282	271	270	297	321
周至县	Zhouzhi	311	304	305	318	325
西咸新区	Xixian	322	316	316	331	331

11-23 续表 continued

单位：公斤/亩 (kg/mu)

区县	Region	油料 Oil-bearing Crops	油菜籽 Rapeseeds	蔬菜 Vegetables	瓜果类 Fruits Class
合计	**Total**	**146**	**137**	**3468**	**3427**
新城区	Xincheng				
碑林区	Beilin				
莲湖区	Lianhu				
灞桥区	Baqiao	148	137	3901	2100
未央区	Weiyang			3829	1700
雁塔区	Yanta				
阎良区	Yanliang	136	136	4580	3724
临潼区	Lintong	149	137	3234	4818
长安区	Chang'an	164	137	1908	1869
高陵区	Gaoling			4462	7467
鄠邑区	Huyi	156	136	3286	3067
蓝田县	Lantian	141	137	1792	2491
周至县	Zhouzhi	149	137	2562	2961
西咸新区	Xixian	137	137	3720	3162

11-24　设施农业生产情况（2018年）

Agricultural Production Facilities（2018）

指　标	Item	播种面积（亩） Seeded Area (mu)	产量（吨） output (ton)
一、蔬菜	**Vegetables**	**248156**	**1286247**
（一）芹菜	Celery	95068	355447
（二）油菜	Rape	9778	19933
（三）菠菜	Spinach	20873	51205
（四）生姜	Ginger	216	505
（五）黄瓜	Cucumber	24988	146136
（六）西葫芦	Squash	14410	87346
（七）四季豆	Green Beans	7683	45005
（八）茄子	Eggplant	17838	78095
（九）辣椒	Chilli	13094	58237
（十）西红柿	Tomato	28366	111827
（十一）其他蔬菜	Other Vegetables	15842	332511
二、瓜果类	**Fruits class**	**98242**	**343977**
其中：草莓	Strawberry	11014	22102
三、花卉苗木	**Flower seedling wood**	**18417**	
四、食用菌	**Edible Fungi**		**4732**
（一）干品	Dry Product		352
（二）鲜品	Fresh Product		4380
其中：蘑菇	Mushroom		4015
五、其他作物	**Other Crops**	**1001**	
补充资料：　设施数量数（个）	Number of Facilities (unit)		135583
设施占地面积（亩）	Area of Facilities(mu)	240673	

11-25　主要年份林业生产情况

Statistics on Forestry in Representative Years

指　标	Item	2000	2005	2010	2014	2015	2016	2017	2018
一、营林情况	**Afforestation**								
当年造林面积合计（万亩）	Build Forestry Areas(10 000 mu)	27.47	16.56	16.10	14.70	8.28	4.51	4.07	3.56
迹地更新面积（万亩）	Reforestation Area (10000 mu)	1.08	0.62						
封山育林面积（万亩）	Hill-closeure for Afforestation Areas (10 000 mu)	13.78	18.65	55.10	42.99	44.00	43.80	28.80	28.80
零星（四旁）植树（万株）	Planting(10 000 plants)	731.0	1064.0	509.2	621.0	516.0	462.0	686.7	656.2
育苗面积（万亩）	Raise Seedlings Areas(10 000 mu)	2.05	5.99	11.95	17.73	19.84	22.78	48.24	61.02
#本年新育	New Seedling of Current Year	1.69	2.54	1.75	2.70	1.00	1.72		
二、主要林产品产量（吨）	**Main Forestry Product(ton)**								
生漆	Lacquer	11	2	10					
核桃	Walnuts	997	3351	7875	16531	24344	19240	15010	13209
板栗	Chinese Chestnut	744	2076	7736	6922	8225	6694	6751	732
花椒	Pepper	140	525	1420	371	204	402	216	923
三、村及村以下采伐木材（万立方米）	**Timber Harvested at or below** Village Level (10 000 cu.m)	1.62	1.87	3.30		0.07	0.28		0.37

注：本表数据来源于市自然资源和规划局。

11-26 各区县林业生产情况（2018年）

Statistics On Forestry by Region （2018）

区 县 Region	当年造林面积（亩）Build Forestry Areasin in The Year(mu)	零星植树（万株）Planting (10 000 plants)	育苗面积（亩）Raise Seedlings Areas(mu)	核桃产量（吨）Output of Walnuts (ton)	板栗产量（吨）Output of Chinese Chestnut (ton)
合 计 Total	**35608**	**656.2**	**610200**	**13209**	**732**
新城区 Xincheng					
碑林区 Beilin					
莲湖区 Lianhu					
灞桥区 Baqiao	824	10	42540		4
未央区 Weiyang		41			
雁塔区 Yanta		1		360	
阎良区 Yanliang	1243		3900	12	
临潼区 Lintong	6596	72	12705	30	
长安区 Chang'an	3000		44325		
高陵区 Gaoling	1900	40	40500		
鄠邑区 Huyi	2143	267	66795		21
蓝田县 Lantian	11276	110	130140	8000	
周至县 Zhouzhi	6700	90	180540	4807	707
西咸新区 Xixian	1926	25.2	88755		

注：本表数据来源于市自然资源和规划局。

11-27 主要年份果业生产情况

Statistics on Fruits in Representative Years

指标	Item	2000	2005	2010	2014	2015	2016	2017	2018
果园面积合计（万亩）	**Areas of Orchards (10 000 mu)**	**47.86**	**55.55**	**63.26**	**63.44**	**61**	**62.73**	**72.72**	**74.28**
苹果园	Apple Orchards	12.15	5.96	3.07	0.91	1.04	0.99	6.03	6.08
梨园	Pears Orchards	5.79	3.01	1.64	0.84	0.74	1.06	0.95	0.97
葡萄园	Grapes Orchards	1.89	3.02	6.42	10.78	10.94	11.65	12.55	12.61
桃园	Peach Orchards	3.47	8.66	7.68	5.85	5.33	5.82	5.99	6.19
猕猴桃园	Chinese Goosebeery Orchards	16.83	4.33	20.36	27.88	27.69	27.97	28.19	29.32
杏园	Apricot Orchards	0.62	2.5	2.21	1.49	1.31	1.25	1.63	1.74
柿子园	Presimmons Orchards	1.96	2.69	2.08	0.35	0.21	0.22	0.19	0.27
石榴园	Pomegranate Orchards			3.31	3.3	2.93	2.93	3.33	3.24
水果产量（吨）	**Output of Fruits (ton)**	**343551**	**512869**	**661086**	**731144**	**733301**	**755316**	**898032**	**891522**
苹果	Apple	89416	53387	29612	14920	17117	17022	69335	69078
梨	Pears	65459	57059	36085	20897	21058	22018	22815	22673
葡萄	Grapes	16647	30951	62004	108081	114789	130650	164506	166175
桃	Peach	27010	89755	98523	75202	77610	86077	99241	105115
猕猴桃	Chinese Goosebeery	96640	137853	248681	350971	352995	354677	368411	358262
杏	Apricot			37124	30229	25672	25281	25687	24491
柿子	Persimmon			30081	11117	8130	2647	3349	3956
石榴	Pomegranate			29274	26643	25446	24419	31976	33180

注：本表2007-2017年数根据第三次全国农业普查结果进行了修订。

11-28 各区县果业生产情况（2018年）

Area and Output of Fruits by Region（2018）

区 县	Region	果园（万亩） Orchard (10 000 mu)	水果产量（吨） Output of Fruits(ton)
合 计	**Total**	**74.28**	**891522**
新城区	Xincheng		
碑林区	Beilin		
莲湖区	Lianhu		
灞桥区	Baqiao	7.88	94456
未央区	Weiyang	0.01	46
雁塔区	Yanta		
阎良区	Yanliang	1.8	31312
临潼区	Lintong	6.33	74242
长安区	Chang'an	3.34	43021
高陵区	Gaoling	1.94	26957
鄠邑区	Huyi	7.8	99932
蓝田县	Lantian	6.11	65075
周至县	Zhouzhi	29.78	345066
西咸新区	Xixian	9.29	111415

11-29 果品加工、销售及生产服务情况（2018年）

指标	Item	西安市 Xi' an	灞桥区 Baqiao	未央区 Weiyang
一、果品加工企业数（个）	**Number of Fruit Processing Enterprises(unit)**	**35**		
其中：苹果加工企业数量	Number of Apple Processing Enterprises			
猕猴桃加工企业数	Number of Kiwi Processing Enterprises	26		
二、果品加工企业果汁加工能力（吨）	**Processing Ability of Fruit Juice in Fruit Processing Enterprises**	**3910**		
其中：苹果汁加工能力	Processing Ability of Apple Juice			
三、当年果品加工企业鲜果消耗量(吨）	**Fresh Fruit Consumption of Fruit Processing Enterprise in the Year**	**45558**		
其中：加工消耗苹果数量	Number of Fresh Apple Consumption			
加工消耗猕猴桃数量	Number of Fresh Kiwi Consumption	40000		
四、仓储能力（吨）	**Storage Capacity(ton)**	**363622**	**200**	
其中：气调库	Gas Reservoir	129057	200	
机械库	Machine Shop	234565		
五、果业合作（个）	**Fruit Industry Cooperation(unit)**	**499**	**45**	
六、果苗木繁育中心（个）	**Fruit Seedling Breeding Center(unit)**	**5**		
七、果业服务投入（万元）	**Service Investment in Fruit Industry(10000 yuan)**	703	5	4
1. 技术培训投入	Technical Training Investment	150	5	
2. 科研投入	Scientific Research Investment	235		4
3. 生产技术指导投入	Production Technology Guidance Investment	318		
八、果品销售方式（吨）	**Fruit Sales Mode(ton)**	**1131885**	**63191**	
1. 产品批发市场	Product Wholesale Market	500617	24668	
2. 采供商	Supplier	324998	12334	
3. 专卖、直销店	Franchised and Direct Outlets	22588		
4. 超级市场	Supermarket	25882	6168	
5. 电子商务	Electronic Commerce	86491	1520	
6. 农产品加工厂	Agricultural Product Processing Plant	52863		
7. 其它	Others	118446	18501	
九、按销售区域分（吨）	**By the Sales Area(ton)**	**1131885**	**63191**	
1. 国内市场	Domestic market	1101885	63191	
2. 国际市场	International Market	30000		
附记：累计建成绿色果园面积（亩）	Cumulative Green Orchard Area(mu)	3550		
建成有机果园面积面积（亩）	Construction of Organic Orchard Area(mu)	600		

The Situation of Fruit Processing, Sales and Production Service (2018)

阎良区 Yanliang	临潼区 Lintong	长安区 Chang'an	高陵区 Gaoling	鄠邑区 Huyi	蓝田县 Lantian	周至县 Zhouzhi	西咸新区 Xixian
	4			**1**	**3**	**26**	**1**
						26	
	2600			**550**	**250**		**510**
	2600			**2000**	**650**	**40000**	**308**
						40000	
	3915	**700**	**5**	**7300**		**350000**	**1502**
	2650	700	5	4000		120000	1502
	1265			3300		230000	
19	**77**	**36**	**13**	**86**	**23**	**178**	**22**
				2		**2**	**1**
5	445		13	167	3	50	11
5	82		9	5		40	4
	74			156			1
	289		4	6	3	10	6
61808	**61550**	**54106**	**72546**	**147600**	**100650**	**390000**	**180434**
29760	12000	16232	20500	118000	60000	180000	39457
19040	11000		39906	15500	10000	90000	127218
568	300		4500	3050		10000	4170
304				6200		10000	3210
600	12000		700	1600	5000	60000	5071
5768	2000			3250	650	40000	1195
5768	24250	37874	6940		25000		113
61808	**61550**	**54106**	**72546**	**147600**	**100650**	**390000**	**180434**
61808	61550	54106	72546	147600	100650	360000	180434
						30000	
				2900	650		
					600		

11-30 主要年份畜牧业生产情况

Statistics on Livestock Husbandry in Representative Years

指标	Item	2013	2014	2015	2016	2017	2018
一、活牲畜年末存栏（头）	**Live Animals in Stock at Year-end (head)**	**55619**	**58737**	**56100**	**61179**	**51075**	**50705**
# 役畜	Draught Animals	7748	7235	6730	6203	578	555
1. 牛	Cattle	54900	58100	55900	61000	50900	50556
#肉牛	Farm Cattle	15673	17317	18465	23736	21509	21325
#奶牛	Dairy Cattle	31479	33887	30705	31061	28819	28681
2. 马（匹）	Horses	220	219	200	176	175	149
3. 驴	Donkeys	52	59				
4. 骡	Mules	447	359		3		
二、猪年末存栏（头）	**Pigs in Stock at Year-end**	**377300**	**377100**	**366800**	**363000**	**335700**	**312882**
# 能繁殖的母猪	Female Hogs of Reprductive Ability	60900	58700	56300	55600	51800	44304
三、羊年末存栏（只）	**Sheep and Goats in Stock at Year-end**	**84100**	**101700**	**107600**	**109800**	**75200**	**74200**
1. 山羊	Goats	82145	98974	104033	107260	73769	72942
# 奶山羊	Milch Goats	68370	69093	65180	66388	62120	60619
2. 绵羊	Sheeps	1955	2726	3567	2540	1431	1258
四、家禽年末存栏（万只）	**Poultry in Stock at Year-end (10 000 heads)**	**663.37**	**663.05**	**702.69**	**702.42**	**642.73**	**625.83**
五、年末养蜂箱数（箱）	**Honey (box)**	**23346**	**22485**	**19536**	**21420**	**20377**	**19129**

注：本表2013—2017年数根据第三次全国农业普查结果进行了修订。

11-31 各区县畜牧业生产情况（2018年）

Statistics On Livestock, Animal Husbandry by Region（2018）

区 县	Region	活牲畜年末存栏（头） Live Animals In Stock at Year-end (head)	能繁殖母畜 Female of Reproductive Ability	役畜 Draught Animals	牛（头） Cattle (head)	奶牛 Dairy Cattle	马（匹） Horses (head)	驴（头） Donkeys (head)
合 计	**Total**	**50705**		**555**	**50556**	**28681**	**149**	
新城区	Xincheng							
碑林区	Beilin							
莲湖区	Lianhu							
灞桥区	Baqiao	1397			1322	1300	75	
未央区	Weiyang	20			20	20		
雁塔区	Yanta							
阎良区	Yanliang	6254			6254	6003		
临潼区	Lintong	14091			14091	12105		
长安区	Chang'an	1824			1758	868	66	
高陵区	Gaoling	6190			6190	4510		
鄠邑区	Huyi	4042		10	4042	1063		
蓝田县	Lantian	10354		480	10351	1273	3	
周至县	Zhouzhi	5995		65	5990	1030	5	
西咸新区	Xixian	538			538	509		

11-31 续表 continued

区 县	Region	骡（头） Mutes (head)	猪（头） Swine (head)	能繁殖的母猪 breeding sows	羊（只） Sheep and Goats (head)	山羊 Goats	奶山羊 Milch Goats	家禽（万只） Poultry (10 000 head)	蜂（箱） Honey (box)
合 计	**Total**		**312882**	**44304**	**74200**	**72942**	**60619**	**625.83**	**19129**
新城区	Xincheng								
碑林区	Beilin								
莲湖区	Lianhu								
灞桥区	Baqiao		14661	976	1095	1095	1095	18.9	330
未央区	Weiyang								
雁塔区	Yanta								
阎良区	Yanliang		14700	2630	9180	9180	9180	38	700
临潼区	Lintong		81380	10821	21895	21895	21895	145.25	
长安区	Chang'an		19344	2961	3370	3370	2542	99.51	2393
高陵区	Gaoling		20220	2220	5200	5200	5200	91.8	
鄠邑区	Huyi		54077	7730	6772	6772	6772	73.13	6876
蓝田县	Lantian		35320	5098	23468	22368	12184	89.5	3760
周至县	Zhouzhi		60085	10010	1900	1870	650	51.32	5030
西咸新区	Xixian		13095	1858	1320	1192	1101	18.42	40

11-32 主要年份畜产品和水产品产量

单位：吨

年 份 Year	肉类总产量 Output of Meat	猪 肉 Pork	牛 肉 Beef	羊 肉 Mutton	禽 肉 Poultry
2013	66100	43900	4000	3300	13100
2014	70900	47400	4400	3700	13400
2015	72100	47100	4400	4100	14500
2016	68700	44200	3700	4400	14600
2017	58708	36900	4600	3300	12300
2018	54496	35932	3439	989	12473

注：1.2010年起，根据统计制度要求，水产品产量及养殖面积统计数据取自市水务局。
　　2.2013-2017年数根据第三次全国农业普查结果进行了修订。

Output of Livestock Products and Aquatic Products in Representative Years

(ton)

奶类产量 Output of Milk	牛　奶 Cow Milk	禽　蛋 Poultry Eggs	蜂蜜（公斤） Honey(kg)	水产品 Output of Aquatic Products	养殖面积（万亩） Water Raise Areas (10 000 mu)
73834	41700	48700	380000	14200	2.19
80961	42200	47900	376800	14218	2.31
76779	40800	51000	351582	14190	2.26
79281	43100	62900	371409	13449	1.96
116491	83300	52785	404337	13832	2.24
115200	80446	52610	308015	13528	2.23

11-33 各区县主要畜产品和水产品产量（2018年）

Output of Major Livestock Products and Aquatic Products by Region（2018）

单位：吨 (ton)

区 县	Region	肉类总产量 Output of Meat	猪 肉 Pork	牛 肉 Beef	羊 肉 Mutton	禽 肉 Poultry
合 计	**Total**	**54496**	**35932**	**3439**	**989**	**12473**
新城区	Xincheng					
碑林区	Beilin					
莲湖区	Lianhu					
灞桥区	Baqiao	1394	676	137	16	556
未央区	Weiyang	105	97		1	7
雁塔区	Yanta					
阎良区	Yanliang	2263	950	471	140	702
临潼区	Lintong	16537	13121	360	103	2362
长安区	Chang'an	5963	3133	171	97	2242
高陵区	Gaoling	3365	1717	165	100	1080
鄠邑区	Huyi	5895	3866	363	84	1406
蓝田县	Lantian	9371	4853	1175	402	2904
周至县	Zhouzhi	7294	5950	385	19	936
西咸新区	Xixian	2309	1569	212	27	278

11-33 续表 continued

区 县	Region	奶类产量 Output of Milk	牛 奶 Cow Milk	禽 蛋 Poultry Eggs	蜂蜜（公斤） Honey(kg)	水产品 Output of Aquatic Products	养殖面积（亩） Water Raise Areas (mu)
合 计	**Total**	**115200**	**80446**	**52610**	**308015**	**13528**	**22275**
新城区	Xincheng						
碑林区	Beilin						
莲湖区	Lianhu						
灞桥区	Baqiao	5141	4484	1579	8330	700	1245
未央区	Weiyang	38	38			750	585
雁塔区	Yanta						
阎良区	Yanliang	21398	15898	3100	19266	225	180
临潼区	Lintong	44289	32386	11758		3300	4965
长安区	Chang'an	4771	3292	10510	71773	5405	8655
高陵区	Gaoling	14726	11726	7705		235	180
鄠邑区	Huyi	6881	3271	5898	59956	1103	450
蓝田县	Lantian	12636	5092	7015	97253	1310	3705
周至县	Zhouzhi	3500	3100	4420	51110	500	2310
西咸新区	Xixian	1820	1159	625	327		

注：2010年起，根据统计制度要求，水产品产量及养殖面积统计数据取自市水务局。

11-34 农业科技、教育情况（2018年）

Agricultural Science and Technology Education（2018）

指标	Item	2018
农业研究开发机构（个）	Agricultural research and development institutions (unit)	225
农业科技人员（人）	Agricultural scientific and technical personnel(persons)	2735
农业科研成果（个）	Agricultural scientific research achievements (unit)	
农民技能培训人数（万人）	The number of peasants skills training(10000 persons)	158700
良种推广面积（万亩）	Thoroughbred promotion area (10000 mu)	587.7
农业信息站（个）	Information station of Agricultural (unit)	3104

注：本表数据来源于市农业农村局。

11-35 主要年份农产品人均占有量

Per Capita Output of Major Farm Products in Representative Years

单位：公斤/人 (kg/ person)

年份 Year	粮食 Grain	油料 Oil-bearing Crops	猪牛羊肉 Pork Beef and Mutton	禽蛋 Poultry Eggs	奶类 Milk	水果 Fruits	蔬菜 Vegetables
1978	266.7	0.2	5.4	0.9	3.3	6.8	91.7
1979	288.6	0.6	6.7	1.0	4.0	5.1	97.3
1980	223.5	1.1	5.9	1.2	4.1	6.9	78.4
1985	271.4	1.4	6.8	5.7	10.2	7.6	156.3
1990	298.7	2.1	9.4	9.2	14.2	11.5	196.0
1995	270.4	3.4	15.7	21.8	20.5	37.5	206.1
2000	293.5	1.9	17.9	20.1	35.7	49.9	235.7
2005	277.1	1.6	21.1	15.9	56.9	69.1	263.8
2010	206.4	1.2	13.8	14.6	74.8	78.2	245.0
2013	177.0	0.9	6.0	5.7	8.6	83.9	284.6
2014	163.5	0.8	6.4	5.6	9.4	84.9	299.6
2015	163.2	0.8	6.4	5.9	8.9	84.6	309.1
2016	154.4	0.7	6.0	7.2	9.0	86.1	306.6
2017	151.7	0.7	4.7	5.5	12.1	97.4	368.9
2018	144.9	0.7	4.1	5.4	11.6	90.9	380.9

11-36 主要年份农村经济效益指标

Main Indicators of Rural Economic Benefit in Representative Years

年份 Year	每一劳动力创造的 Average Labor Force Production 农林牧渔业总产值（元） Gross Output Value of Farming,Forestry, Animal Husbandry, Fishery (yuan)	粮食（公斤） Grain Crops(kg)	油料（公斤） Oil-bearing Crops(kg)	每亩耕地种植业总产值（元） Output of Each Unit of Area Planting(yuan)	每百元物耗生产的总产值（元） Output per 100-Yuan of Material Consumed(yuan)
1978	504.7	1024.6	0.7	104.3	
1979	549.0	1096.5	2.3	116.0	
1980	483.1	846.1	4.0	99.2	
1981	502.8	840.5	5.5	105.4	
1982	631.5	1058.9	3.6	139.3	
1983	606.5	1053.2	2.6	124.1	
1984	850.7	1154.2	3.4	163.6	
1985	1020.1	1134.6	5.6	183.1	
1986	1132.2	1236.4	9.5	204.6	
1987	1280.3	1277.2	11.7	231.5	
1988	1558.4	1148.0	6.5	273.2	
1989	1605.3	1231.9	9.5	295.0	
1990	1766.3	1279.1	10.0	343.4	233.3
1991	1958.8	1326.6	8.9	380.4	238.4
1992	2093.7	1360.7	11.1	451.6	241.8
1993	2528.9	1409.7	10.4	546.8	240.1
1994	3705.0	1167.8	8.0	762.8	227.6
1995	4953.0	1300.6	16.1	1106.5	225.9
1996	5154.8	1391.2	13.6	1224.2	234.5
1997	5493.0	1413.4	13.8	1283.3	239.2
1998	5615.9	1578.1	12.4	1374.3	247.0
1999	4826.5	1516.6	9.7	1175.9	251.7
2000	5091.5	1498.0	9.9	1161.1	250.2
2001	5328.5	1462.4	9.1	1221.1	248.6
2002	5617.4	1427.5	9.1	1272.0	265.9
2003	5761.2	1308.1	8.4	1332.4	254.3
2004	6885.4	1452.7	8.5	1434.6	261.7
2005	7737.9	1524.7	8.6	1642.3	262.9
2006	8415.5	1435.7	8.0	1756.9	263.1
2007	9983.6	1458.9	7.0	2017.3	259.6
2008	12888.6	1466.7	8.5	2413.9	257.7
2009	13922.4	1460.9	8.5	2666.2	259.7
2010	18220.9	1496.9	8.7	3623.9	258.7
2011	21534.5	1438.2	8.6	4378.8	271.0
2012	24588.9	1480.0	7.3	4940.9	269.8
2013	28187.1	1398.2	7.1	5565.8	269.9
2014	29310.8	1276.2	6.4	6090.3	270.3
2015	31476.1	1345.6	6.5	6308.7	268.3
2016	33888.8	1323.2	5.7	6799.0	265.9
2017	39620.4	1267.3	5.6	8036.5	262.7
2018	47231.8	1455.6	6.9	8787.5	263.5

主要统计指标解释

农林牧渔业总产值 指以货币表现的农、林、牧、渔业全部产品和对农林牧渔业生产活动进行的各种支持性服务活动的价值总量，它反映一定时期内农林牧渔业生产总规模和总成果。1957年以前的农林牧渔业总产值中包括了厩肥和农民自给性手工业（如农民自制衣服、鞋、袜，自己从事粮食初步加工等）。1958年及以后，林业中增加了村及村以下竹木采伐产值；牧业中取消了厩肥产值；副业中取消了农民自给性手工业产值，增加了村及村以下办的工业产值；渔业中增加了海洋捕捞水产品产值。1980年及以后，在副业中增加了农民家庭兼营工业商品部分的产值。从1984年起村及村以下工业产值划归工业。从1993年起取消副业，将野生动物的捕猎划入牧业，野生植物采集和农民家庭兼营商品性工业划归农业。从2003年起，执行新的国民经济行业分类标准，农林牧渔业总产值中包括了农林牧渔服务业产值。林业中增加了森林采运业产值。农业中取消了家庭兼营商品性工业产值，将野生林产品的采集划归林业。第一次农业普查以后，由于畜牧业产品年报数据与普查数据之间存在一定的差距，根据农业普查结果对畜牧业年报数据进行了修正，对畜牧业产值进行了相应修正。

农林牧渔业总产值的计算方法通常是按农、林、牧、渔业产品及其副产品的产量分别乘以各自单位产品价格求得；少数生产周期较长，当年没有产品或产品产量不易统计的，则采用间接方法匡算其产值；然后将四业产品产值及农林牧渔服务业产值相加即为农林牧渔业总产值。

粮食产量 指全社会的产量。包括国有经济经营的、集体统一经营的和农民家庭经营的粮食产量，还包括工矿企业办的农场和其他生产单位的产量。粮食除包括稻谷、小麦、玉米、高粱、谷子及其他杂粮外，还包括薯类和豆类。其产量计算方法，豆类按去豆荚后的干豆计算；薯类（包括甘薯和马铃薯，不包括芋头和木薯）1963年以前按每4公斤鲜薯折1公斤粮食计算，从1964年开始改为按5公斤鲜薯折1公斤粮食计算。城市郊区作为蔬菜的薯类（如马铃薯等）按鲜品计算，并且不作粮食统计。其他粮食一律按脱粒后的原粮计算。1989年以前全国粮食产量数据主要靠全面报表取得，1989年开始使用抽样调查数据。

棉花产量 指全社会的产量。包括春播棉和夏播棉。产量按皮棉计算。不包括木棉。

油料产量 指全部油料作物的生产量。包括花生、油菜籽、芝麻、向日葵籽、胡麻籽（亚麻籽）和其他油料。不包括大豆、木本油料和野生油料。花生以带壳干花生计算。

水产品产量 指人工养殖的水产品和天然生长的水产品的捕捞量。包括海水的鱼类、虾蟹类、贝类和藻类以及内陆水域的鱼类、虾蟹类和贝类，不包括淡水生植物。水产品产量是通过各级水产和统计部门逐级上报取得数据。1995年及以前，贝类中牡蛎按鲜肉计算；蚶、蛤、蛙按5斤鲜品折1斤计算。1996年以后则统一按鲜品计算。

猪、牛、羊肉产量 指当年出栏并已屠宰、除去头蹄下水后带骨肉（即胴体重）的重量。包括全社会范围内的产量。1996年前为各级逐级上报数据。1996年第一次农业普查以后，由于畜牧业产品年报数据与普查数据之间存在一定的差距，根据普查结果对畜牧业年报数据进行了修正。1999年以后，国家统计局在部分地区开展了猪、牛、羊、禽等主要畜禽品种的抽样调查，并用抽样数据作为国家定案数据使用。未开展抽样调查的地区和品种，仍使用各级统计部门逐级上报数据。2008年，根据第二次农业普查结果，对2006年2007年畜牧业年报数据进行了修正。

畜禽存栏头（只）数 指报告期末农村各种合作经济组织和国营农场、农民个人、机关、团体、学校、工矿企业、部队等单位以及城镇居民饲养的大牲畜、猪、羊、家禽等畜禽的存栏数。

常用耕地 是指耕地总资源中专门种植农作物并经常进行耕种、能够正常收获的土地。包括当年实际耕种的熟地；弃耕、休闲不满三年，随时可以复耕的地；开荒利用三年以上的地。不包括临时种植农作物的坡度在25度以上的陡坡地；在河套、湖畔、库区临时开发的成片或零星土地；也不包括已列为国家和省（区、市）退耕计划但临时耕种的土地。

农作物播种面积 指实际播种或移植有农作物的面积。凡是实际种植有农作物的面积，不论种植在耕地上还是种植在非耕地上，均包括在农作物播种面积中。在播种季节基本结束后，因遭灾而重新改种和补种的农作物面积，也包括在内。它是反映我国耕地面积利用情况的一个重要指标。目前，农作物播种面积主要包括粮食、棉花、油料、糖料、麻类、烟叶、蔬菜和瓜类、药材和其他农作物九大类。

有效灌溉面积 指具有一定的水源，地块比较平整，灌溉工程或设备已经配套，在一般年景下，当年能够进行正常灌溉的耕地面积。在一般情况下，有效灌溉面积应等于灌溉工程或设备已经配备，能够进行正常灌溉的水田和水浇地面积之和。它是反映我国耕地抗旱能力的一个重要指标。

农用化肥施用量 指本年内实际用于农业生产的化肥数量，包括氮肥、磷肥、钾肥和复合肥。化肥施用量要求按折纯量计算数量。折纯量是指把氮肥、磷肥、钾肥分别按含氮、含五氧化二磷、含氧化钾的百分之百成份进行折算后的数量。复合肥按其所含主要成分折算。公式为：

折纯量=实物量 × 某种化肥有效成份含量的百分比

农业机械总动力 指主要用于农、林、牧、渔业的各种动力机械的动力总和。包括耕作机械、排灌机械、收获机械、农用运输机械、植物保护机械、牧业机械、林业机械、渔业机械和其他农业机械【内燃机按引擎马力折成瓦（特）计算、电动机按功率折成瓦（特）计算】。不包括专门用于乡、镇、村、组办工业、基本建设、非农业运输、科学试验和教学等非农业生产方面用的动力机械与作业机械。这个指标的统计数据主要来源于农机部门。

Explanatory Notes on Main Statistical Indicators

Gross Output Value of Agriculture, Forestry, Animal Husbandry and Fishery refers to the total value of products of agriculture, forestry, animal husbandry and fishery, and total value of services in support of agriculture, forestry, animal husbandry and fishery activities. It reflects the total scale and results of agricultural production during a given period. Prior to 1957, China's gross agricultural output value included barnyard manure and handicraft products for self- consumption (clothes, shoes, stockings, and initial grain processing undertaken by peasants). Since 1958, cutting and felling of bamboo and trees by villages and other cooperative organizations under villages have been included in forestry; value of barnyard manure has been excluded from animal husbandry; self consumed handicrafts have not been included from sideline occupations, while the output value of industries run by villages and cooperative organizations under village has been included in sideline occupations; and the output value of fish catches by motor fishing boats has been added to fishery. Since 1980, the value of handicraft products made for sale by individuals in households has been added to sideline occupations. Since 1984, industries run by villages and under villages have been included in the sector of industry. Since 1993, the subdivision of sideline occupations has been cancelled, and the hunting of wild animals has been classified into animal husbandry, and the gathering of wild plants and commodity industry run by rural household have been included in farming. A new industrial classification of economic activities was introduced in 2003. Under the new classification, value of services to agriculture, forestry, animal husbandry and fishery is included in the gross output value of agriculture, value of wood felling and transport is included in forestry, value of industrial output by rural households is not included in agriculture, and the collection of wild forest products is taken from agriculture and included in forestry. The First Agriculture Census of China revealed some discrepancy between the production of animal products from the annual reports and that from the census. According to the result of the First Agriculture census, efforts were made to adjust the output value of animal husbandry to make the figures from the annual reports consistent with the census data.

Gross output value of agrieulture is obtained by multiplying the output of each product or by-product by its price, resulting in the output value of each single item. For a small number of products, annual output of which is not available or difficult to get due to the long production (growing) process involved, the output value is estimated through an indirect approach. The sum of output values of all products of agriculture, forestry, animal husbandry and fishery and services in support to those industries is then equal to the gross output value of agriculture.

Grain Output refers to the total output in the whole country including grains produced by State farms, collective units, rural households, as well as by farms affiliated to industrial and mining enterprises and other production units. Grain includes rice, wheat, corn, sorghum, millet and other miscellaneous grains as well as tubers and beans. Output of beans refers to dry beans without pods. The output of tubers (sweet potatoes and potatoes, not including taros and cassava) are converted into that of grain at the ratio 4:1, i.e. 4 kilograms of fresh tubers were equivalent to 1 kilogram of grain up to 1963. Since 1964 the ratio for conversion has been 5:1. Tubers supplied as vegetables (such as potatoes) in cities and suburbs are calculated as fresh vegetables and their output is not included in the output of grain. Output of all other grains refers to husked grain. Data on grain production before 1989 were obtained through the Comprehensive Statistical Reporting System. Since 1989, data from sample surveys are used.

Cotton Output refers to cotton production in the whole country including cotton planted in spring and in autumn. Output is measured as the weight of ginned cotton. Ceiba is not included.

Output of Oil–bearing Crops refers to the total production of oil-bearing crops of various kinds, including peanuts (dry, in shell), rapeseeds, sesame, sunflower seeds, flax seeds, and other oil-bearing crops. Soybeans, oil-bearing woody plants, and wild oil-bearing crops are not included.

Output of Aquatic Products refers to catches of both artificially cultured and naturally grown aquatic products, including fish, shrimps, crabs and shellfish in sea and inland water as well as seaweed. Freshwater plants are not included. Data on output of aquatic products are reported by aquatic product and statistical agencies level by level. Before 1995, among the shellfish, oyster was counted as fresh meat; 5 kilograms of ark shell, clams and frogs are equivalent to 1 kilogram of fresh aquatic products; they have all been counted as flesh aquatic products since 1996.

Output of Pork, Beef, and Mutton refers to the meat of slaughtered hogs, cattle, sheep and goats with head, feet, and offal taken away. Data refers to the production of the whole country. The First Agricultural Census of China in 1996 revealed some discrepancy between the production of animal products from the annual reports and that from the census. Efforts were made to adjust the output value of animal husbandry to make the figures from the annual reports consistent with the census data. Since 1999, the NBS conducted sample surveys for the major animal husbandry products, such as hogs, cattle, sheep and goats and fowls, and the data from sample surveys are used as national finalized data. Those products, which are not covered by the sample survey, are still reported by statistical agencies level by level. In 2007. the data on animal husbandry from 2000 to 2006 were revised according to the results of the Second Agriculture Census of China. In 2008, A Monitoring and Survey Program was set up on main livestock, the data on the main livestock such as hog, cattle, sheep and poultry became the official data based on the sampling survey.

Number of Livestock or Poultry in Stock at Beginning (or End) of Period refers to the total number of large animals, pigs, sheep, fowls, etc. raised by rural cooperative organizations, State farms, rural individuals, government agencies, schools, industrial and mining enterprises, army, and urban residents at the beginning (or end) of the reference period.

Regularly Cultivated Land refers to farmland among the total land resources which is exclusively used for farming and is under regular cultivation with harvest in normal years. Included are currently cultivated land, land that has been abandoned or put in idle for less than 3 years and could be re-used for cultivation at any time, and new-claimed land that has been put into cultivation for more than 3 years. Excluded under this category are steep slope land over 25 degrees under temporary cultivation, land (large or small plots) that is claimed along river bends, lake sides or banks of reservoirs, as well as land that has been designated under the "Green for Grain" programmes of the state and provincial governments but is still temporarily under cultivation.

Sown Area of Crops refers to area of transplanted with crops regardless of being land sown or in cultivated area or non-cultivated area. Area of land re-sown due to lso included. This is an important indicator that can reflect the utilization condition of the cultivated land in China. At present, the sown area of crops mainly include the following 9 categories of crops: grain, cotton, oil-bearing crops, sugar crops, flax crops, tobacco, vegetables and melons, medicinal materials and other farm crops.natural disasters is also included. This is an important indicator that can reflect the utilization condition of the cultivated land in China. At present, the sown area of crops mainly include the following 9 categories of crops: grain, cotton, oil-bearing crops, sugar crops, flax crops, tobacco, vegetables and melons, medicinal materials and other farm crops.

Irrigated Area refers to area of land that are effectively irrigated, i.e. relatively level land, where there are water sources or complete sets of irrigation facilities to lift and move adequate water for irrigation purpose under normal conditions. Under normal situations, irrigated area is the sum of watered fields and irrigated fields where irrigation systems or equipment have been installed for regular irrigation purpose. This important indicator reflects drought resistance capacity of the cultivated land in China.

Consumption of Chemical Fertilizers in Agriculture refers to the quantity of chemical fertilizers applied in agriculture in the year, including nitrogenous fertilizer, phosphate fertilizer, potash fertilizer, and compound fertilizer. The consumption of chemical fertilizers is calculated in terms of volume of effective components by means of converting the gross weight of the respective fertilizers into weight containing effective component (e.g. nitrogen content in nitrogenous fertilizer, phosphorous pentoxide contents in phosphate fertilizer, and potassium oxide contents in potash fertilizer). Compound fertilizer is converted in regard to its major components. The formula is:

Volume of effective component= physical quantity × effective component of certain chemical fertilizer (%)

Total Power of Agricultural Machinery refers to total mechanical power of machinery used in agriculture, forestry, animal husbandry and fishery, including machinery for ploughing, irrigation and drainage, harvesting, transport, plant protection, animal husbandry, forestry and fishery and other agricultural machineries. (For the power of internal combustion engines, it is converted from its horsepower into watts while for electric motors the output power is converted into watts.) Machinery employed for non-agricultural purposes, such as the machines used in township-run and village-run industry, construction, non-agricultural transport, scientific experiments and teaching, are not included. Data are mainly from agricultural machinery agencies.

12 工 业

INDUSTRY

资料整理：赵 晖 陈小兵 李 玫 沈佳慧 张思敏 王 玥

Data management：Zhao Hui Chen Xiaobing Li Mei Shen Jiahui Zhang Simin Wang Yue

数据审核：丁抗玲

Data audit：Ding Kangling

第十二部分　工业

一、简要说明

1.本章资料反映西安市工业经济方面的基本情况。

2.本章资料包括全部工业总产值、规模以上工业企业按企业登记类型、轻重工业、企业规模、工业行业大类分组的主要经济指标和经济效益指标，主要工业产品产量，主要产品生产能力。

3.规模以上工业企业统计范围。

1998年至2006年为全部国有及年主营业务收入在500万元以上非国有工业企业。

2007年至2010年为年主营业务收入在500万元以上工业企业。

2011年起提高到年主营业务收入在2000万元以上工业企业。

4.数据来源

根据国家统计局制定的《企业一套表统计调查制度》和《工业统计报表制度》，对规模以上工业法人单位采用全面调查的方法，从国家一套表平台采集。

5.数据说明

2018年规模以上工业数据为第四次经济普查上报数。

二、主要指标

规模以上工业企业单位数（个）	1474	比上年增长	5.1%
规模以上工业总产值（亿元）	6396.28	比上年增长	6.3%

12 INDUSTRY

Ⅰ.Brief Introduction

1. This chapter reflects the basic conditions of the industrial sector.

2. This chapter mainly including economic indicators of industrial enterprises above designated size; as well as their economic indicators, efficiency indicators, output and production capacity of key industrial products classified by type of registration by light and heavy industries, by size of enterprise, by branch of industry.

3. The Scopes of Industrial Statistics

The scopes of industrial statistics are all State-owned industrial enterprises and non-State-owned industrial enterprises with revenue from principal business over 5 million yuan from 1998 to 2006.

The scopes of industrial statistics are all industrial enterprises with revenue from principal business over 5 million yuan from 2007 to 2010.

The scopes of industrial statistics are raised to all industrial enterprises with revenue from principal business over 20 million yuan from 2011.

4.Sources of Data

According to the A set of table survey system for enterprises and System of industrial statistical report forms by the National Bureau of Statistics, the method of comprehensive investigation shall be adopted for industrial legal entities above the designated size, collected from a set of table platforms by the National Bureau of Statistics.

5. Data Collection

The industrial data in 2018 is the fourth economic census.

Ⅱ.Major Indicators

		Increase over Preceding Year
Number of industrial Enterprises Gross Output Above Designated Size(item)	1474	5.1%
Value Added of Industry Above Designated Size (100 million yuan)	6396.28	6.3%

12-1 主要年份全部工业总产值

Gross Output Value of Industry in Representative Years

单位：万元 (10 000 yuan)

年份 Year	全部工业总产值 Gross Industrial Output Value	工业总产值指数 （上年=100） Index of Gross Industry Output Value (Preceding Year=100)	国有经济 State-owned Enterprises	集体经济 Collective-owned Enterprises	其他经济类型 Enterprises of Other Ownership
1952	23512	139.6	9917	464	13131
1962	120833	86.8	102103	17599	1131
1965	200416	132.1	183164	17252	
1970	333386	143.5	305303	28083	
1975	385509	106.1	332982	52527	
1978	483262	116.9	405376	77886	
1979	517483	106.6	438850	78633	
1980	531755	101.8	440139	91577	39
1985	853196	120.4	632702	218893	1601
1986	976326	112.1	706380	267282	2664
1987	1142228	114.2	809186	328701	4341
1988	1429811	116.0	1012268	416217	1326
1989	1653472	106.1	1160877	486754	5814
1990	1771310	107.4	1196777	548605	25928
1991	2002727	110.0	1325242	604495	72990
1992	2300472	112.5	1488541	561369	250562
1993	3045988	121.7	1748145	1071122	226721
1994	3891584	120.6	1960533	1581321	349730
1995	4058952	108.7	2071755	1663536	323661
1996	5338510	133.4	2132140	2836176	370194
1997	5794532	121.8	1915536	2005610	1873386
1998	6738224	117.3	2593405	2077273	2067546
1999	7151528	117.1	2128243	2174220	2849065
2000	6394812	115.3	2749778	2094680	1550354
2001	7361510	116.4	3098431	2380910	1882169
2002	8379363	115.8	3472067	2312923	2594373
2003	9750800	115.1	4149015	1501372	4100413
2004	11853224	118.4	5414952	875412	5562860
2005	13085580	106.3	5916553	674900	6494127
2006	15573516	119.0	7527607	514810	7531099
2007	19798593	122.1	10179303	365329	9253961
2008	23881446	120.6	12479652	441987	10959807
2009	28270652	118.3	14440321	388777	13441554
2010	35628752	126.0	18353877	435206	16839669
2011	40933178	114.9	20654524	377199	19901455
2012	46560824	113.8	24303736	376427	21880661
2013	50426416	108.3	25358096	325004	24743316
2014	56606273	112.3	27352693	332712	28920867
2015	51599121	91.2	25008248	161009	26429864
2016	54624261	105.9	24498532	139018	29986711
2017	62853398	115.1	23750377	200886	33902135
2018	67594267	107.5	30615814	549287	36429166

注：2013年数据为全国第三次经济普查数据。

12-1 续表 continued

单位：万元 (10 000 yuan)

年份 Year	轻工业 Light Industry	重工业 Heavy Industry	大型工业 Large-size Industry Enterprises	中型工业 Medium-size Industry Enterprises	小型工业 Small-size Industry Enterprises
1952	20800	2712			
1962	68221	52618			
1965	98631	101785			
1970	124467	208919			
1975	167285	218224	145262	130592	109655
1978	220480	262782	168397	121813	193052
1979	243043	274440	189877	133759	193847
1980	283475	248280	193092	130053	208610
1985	401748	451448	333820	147488	371888
1986	458270	518056	401037	150644	424645
1987	516776	625452	472958	171698	497572
1988	699593	730210	615946	210089	603776
1989	712743	940729	696368	258414	698690
1990	787857	983453	716421	279098	775791
1991	897676	1105051	888052	303151	811524
1992	967104	1333368	988049	311628	1000795
1993	1121957	1924031	1258137	384255	1403596
1994	1578875	2312709	1479613	390233	2021738
1995	1636219	2422733	1575030	371156	2112766
1996	2347887	2990623	1693985	358913	3285612
1997	2700085	3094447	1675521	274888	3844123
1998	3232681	3505543	1821556	308424	4608244
1999	3488547	3662981	1744637	337795	5069096
2000	3121419	3273393	2320973	328494	3745345
2001	3518054	3843456	2656010	368497	4337003
2002	3935764	4443599	3038828	398834	4941701
2003	4028859	5721941	2911821	2217447	4621532
2004	4211592	7641632	3595150	3237701	5020373
2005	4078417	9007163	4640325	3228553	5216702
2006	4510970	11062546	5970535	3414468	6188513
2007	7331719	12466874	8351303	4171131	7276159
2008	6010865	17870581	10472686	5005676	8403084
2009	6636464	21634188	12309192	6186395	9775065
2010	7841869	27786884	15002737	8537140	12088876
2011	8992547	31940631	20882834	6261444	13788900
2012	10218288	36342536	23896868	6243799	16420157
2013	9297919	41128497	17390620	7271086	25764710
2014	10369659	46236614	24880136	8875553	22850583
2015	10089660	41509461	26485412	8432031	16681678
2016	9774967	44849294	28603440	8074967	17945853
2017	10986026	51867372	34454909	10051995	18346494
2018	12455919	55138348	35696720	11211514	20686033

12-2 主要年份各区县规模以上工业总产值

Gross Output Value of Industry above Designated Size in Representative Years

单位：亿元 (100 million yuan)

区 县	Region	1998	1999	2000	2001	2002	2003	2004	2005	2006	2007	2008
合 计	**Total**	**350.38**	**366.59**	**417.97**	**482.61**	**544.78**	**638.66**	**830.06**	**981.02**	**1187.74**	**1577.05**	**2007.85**
新城区	Xincheng	67.19	71.36	78.25	89.87	105.92	137.46	145.61	196.00	135.14	157.18	147.54
碑林区	Beilin	20.57	19.48	21.50	23.15	30.32	22.22	15.92	20.13	18.31	19.10	48.99
莲湖区	Lianhu	63.24	65.92	75.68	93.78	106.33	124.24	157.67	185.86	200.75	281.57	356.90
灞桥区	Baqiao	19.55	19.95	21.35	20.56	22.99	28.80	37.25	42.29	57.11	80.01	123.34
未央区	Weiyang	53.31	52.84	61.41	73.63	80.14	93.23	145.63	170.16	220.08	265.93	327.65
雁塔区	Yanta	65.00	75.88	94.38	102.58	107.75	113.99	151.61	144.51	167.58	204.70	262.32
阎良区	Yanliang	26.54	26.06	27.56	36.22	40.04	40.98	55.86	68.10	75.84	95.29	109.43
临潼区	Lintong	8.90	7.55	7.64	9.36	14.14	34.67	53.49	66.91	85.96	114.09	130.93
长安区	Chang'an	7.92	7.70	8.70	8.42	9.96	10.81	19.40	26.43	67.19	101.61	154.74
高陵区	Gaoling	1.60	1.83	2.58	3.28	3.97	7.09	14.89	16.50	97.94	177.65	256.55
鄠邑区	Huyi	12.75	13.24	13.07	15.27	16.58	18.74	24.48	35.28	49.55	61.28	65.09
蓝田县	Lantian	2.58	2.37	3.81	4.76	5.12	5.00	5.34	5.69	8.35	13.13	17.62
周至县	Zhouzhi	1.24	2.41	2.05	1.73	1.51	1.45	2.92	3.16	3.94	5.52	6.76
西咸新区	Xixian											

12-2 续表 continued

单位：亿元 (100 million yuan)

区 县	Region	2009	2010	2011	2012	2013	2014	2015	2016	2017	2018
合 计	**Total**	**2468.27**	**3130.15**	**3552.21**	**4066.31**	**4436.58**	**4961.12**	**4924.57**	**5266.25**	**6018.79**	**6396.28**
新城区	Xincheng	195.45	272.13	323.64	307.67	344.30	372.75	398.68	401.62	394.86	248.69
碑林区	Beilin	58.60	108.14	138.72	18.46	23.48	27.66	29.59	31.91	31.15	17.60
莲湖区	Lianhu	399.83	458.30	457.96	459.41	419.81	407.16	402.62	405.48	471.67	531.29
灞桥区	Baqiao	178.82	242.15	280.52	278.37	308.04	300.73	175.89	181.17	137.52	123.92
未央区	Weiyang	393.22	499.88	510.39	684.55	733.75	858.40	839.29	959.84	1014.93	1083.72
雁塔区	Yanta	249.69	286.19	367.97	587.65	624.55	694.34	677.00	648.80	721.42	663.32
阎良区	Yanliang	128.99	163.55	176.67	219.31	276.71	300.25	321.23	342.53	316.66	350.69
临潼区	Lintong	165.77	222.01	277.75	341.01	404.45	418.75	263.29	204.22	181.43	209.65
长安区	Chang'an	277.98	334.89	350.68	354.65	383.41	346.35	720.87	956.32	1001.19	1401.03
高陵区	Gaoling	305.94	402.98	516.33	662.99	741.34	854.73	869.60	835.74	939.03	1214.57
鄠邑区	Huyi	81.54	96.89	100.42	93.55	101.40	104.68	135.94	189.31	359.94	126.00
蓝田县	Lantian	23.40	31.93	35.87	41.60	49.33	46.22	49.32	55.47	74.43	73.47
周至县	Zhouzhi	9.03	11.11	15.29	17.08	26.01	29.10	41.25	53.84	65.64	44.26
西咸新区	Xixian										308.08

12-3 各区县规模以上工业企业工业总产值（2018年）

单位：亿元

区县	Regin	单位数（个） Number of Enterprises (unit)	工业总产值 Gross Industrial Output Value	国有经济 State-owned Enterprises	集体经济 Collective-owned Enterprises	其他经济类型 Enterprises of Other Ownership
新城区	Xincheng	13	248.69	131.45	1.01	116.23
碑林区	Beilin	9	17.60	6.18		11.42
莲湖区	Lianhu	26	531.29	514.13	1.39	15.77
灞桥区	Baqiao	84	123.92	71.97	2.90	49.05
未央区	Weiyang	188	1083.72	333.91	1.17	748.64
雁塔区	Yanta	267	663.32	340.92	26.54	295.86
阎良区	Yanliang	110	350.69	224.34	5.72	120.63
临潼区	Lintong	72	209.65	101.14	0.36	108.15
长安区	Chang'an	156	1401.03	158.87	4.01	1238.15
高陵区	Gaoling	161	1214.57	942.82	0.83	270.92
鄠邑区	Huyi	102	126.00	29.60	1.30	95.10
蓝田县	Lantian	52	73.47	6.29		67.18
周至县	Zhouzhi	53	44.26		0.91	43.35
西咸新区	Xixian	181	308.08	148.79	0.49	158.80

Gross Output Value of Industrial Enterprises above Designated Size by Region (2018)

(100 million yuan)

轻工业 Light Industry	重工业 Heavy Industry	大型工业 Large-size Industry Enterprises	中型工业 Medium-size Industry Enterprises	小型工业 Small-size Industry Enterprises
112.82	135.87	219.94	22.03	6.72
13.06	4.54	8.50	5.85	3.25
32.93	498.36	510.57	10.94	9.78
30.53	93.39	44.15	22.81	56.96
365.91	717.31	381.61	200.09	502.02
154.03	509.29	207.67	255.84	199.81
52.84	297.35	191.56	28.86	130.27
89.31	120.34	76.13	76.57	56.95
92.51	1308.52	1110.84	128.38	161.81
62.85	1151.72	724.30	220.20	270.07
57.03	68.97	18.96	37.17	69.87
38.47	35.00		3.93	69.54
32.29	11.97			44.26
45.25	262.83	75.44	108.48	124.16

12-4 主要年份规模以上工业企业主要经济指标

单位：亿元

年份 Year	企业单位数（个） Number of Enterprises (unit)	工业总产值（当年价格） Gross Industrial Output Value (At Current Prices)	平均用工人数（万人） Average Number of Employed Persons (10 000person)
1998	793	350.38	51.71
1999	770	366.59	45.64
2000	816	417.97	43.25
2001	785	482.61	40.12
2002	771	544.78	38.48
2003	735	638.66	36.55
2004	1066	830.06	38.08
2005	902	981.02	37.92
2006	904	1187.74	37.94
2007	937	1577.05	38.55
2008	1032	2007.85	40.17
2009	1131	2468.27	43.42
2010	1126	3130.15	47.11
2011	891	3552.21	50.42
2012	970	4066.31	49.23
2013	1056	4436.57	48.36
2014	1146	4961.12	49.65
2015	1150	4924.57	50.59
2016	1220	5266.25	49.54
2017	1403	6018.79	51.11
2018	1474	6396.28	51.40

注：2013年数据为全国第三次经济普查数据。

Major Economic Indicators of Industrial Enterprises above Designated Size in Representative Years

(100 million yuan)

资产总计 Total Assets	负债合计 Total Liabilites	所有者权益合计 Owners' Equities	主营业务收入 Revenue from Principal Business	利润总额 Total Profits	利税总额 Total Pre-tax Profits
810.56	548.68	261.88	346.84	-1.26	14.82
853.90	577.94	275.96	346.26	8.26	27.30
958.05	622.46	323.72	420.42	16.11	36.29
1054.36	657.88	384.65	451.62	17.97	40.84
1065.76	643.78	412.27	541.64	25.43	51.31
1195.69	733.04	460.97	645.53	33.82	64.99
1333.91	869.30	464.60	812.46	38.57	74.23
1503.85	977.42	508.82	980.97	28.72	67.25
1651.67	1062.11	578.33	1183.51	61.46	110.23
1940.52	1254.01	686.51	1561.25	106.22	168.54
2426.13	1518.86	907.27	1928.05	84.89	168.63
2913.56	1779.38	1130.76	2384.52	177.20	280.68
3592.13	2069.29	1515.65	3011.19	245.37	373.56
3975.38	2295.49	1678.19	3381.27	172.94	312.78
4775.92	2835.55	1926.72	3758.56	167.77	320.57
5127.69	3049.36	2071.72	4171.21	211.26	392.14
6048.34	3607.62	2436.06	4566.20	226.17	401.20
6740.26	3860.55	2926.55	4374.11	206.88	341.40
7473.07	4158.75	3302.36	5028.28	290.96	438.59
7862.59	4162.97	3595.73	5710.70	367.77	532.35
8294.08	4522.64	3771.44	6021.12	402.44	570.81

12-5 各区县规模以上工业企业主要经济指标（2018年）

单位：亿元

区县	Region	企业单位数（个）Number of Enterprises (unit)	平均用工人数（万人）Average Number of Employed Persons (10 000 persons)	资产合计 Total Assets
新城区	Xingcheng	13	2.69	348.14
碑林区	Beilin	9	0.33	72.06
莲湖区	Lianhu	26	5.49	931.77
灞桥区	Baqiao	84	1.98	216.57
未央区	Weiyang	188	6.88	977.09
雁塔区	Yanta	267	8.22	1297.05
阎良区	Yanliang	110	3.61	471.16
临潼区	Lintong	72	1.68	345.89
长安区	Chang'an	156	9.18	1983.58
高陵区	Gaoling	161	5.27	799.60
鄠邑区	Huyi	102	1.62	205.88
蓝田县	Lantian	52	0.60	57.58
周至县	Zhouzhi	53	0.37	31.45
西咸新区	Xixian	181	3.49	556.27

Major Economic Indicators of Industrial Enterprises above Designated Size by Region (2018)

(100 million yuan)

负债合计 Total Liabilites	所有者权益合计 Total Owners' Equities	营业收入 Revenue	利润总额 Total Profits	利税总额 Total Pre-tax Profits
203.59	144.55	239.87	12.73	29.07
46.70	25.36	28.74	3.69	5.20
421.74	510.03	488.31	35.43	56.08
143.83	72.74	128.53	2.82	6.36
516.27	460.82	1061.45	48.05	74.90
643.23	653.82	648.34	45.73	69.23
324.95	146.21	342.13	16.76	20.87
191.99	153.90	185.80	9.09	14.92
916.10	1067.48	1189.94	161.04	179.95
547.78	251.82	1161.43	39.23	60.01
139.12	66.76	119.96	6.06	11.68
35.76	21.82	66.68	7.87	9.79
12.22	19.23	32.25	2.64	3.51
379.37	176.90	327.69	11.30	29.25

12-6 规模以上工业企业主要工业产品产量（2018年）

Major Output of Industrial Enterprises above Designated Size（2018）

产品名称	Name of Products	2018	比上年增长(%) Increase over Preceding Year (%)
自来水生产量(亿立方米)	Tap Water Production (100 million cu.m)	5.52	9.1
大米(万吨)	Rice (10 000 ton)	1.76	-5.1
小麦粉(万吨)	Wheat Flour (10 000 ton)	55.57	8.2
精制食用植物油(万吨)	Edible Vegetable Oil (10 000 ton)	16.94	16.1
鲜、冷藏肉（万吨）	Fresh/Frozen Meat(10 000 ton)	10.09	7.7
饲料（万吨）	Mixed Feed(10 000 ton)	77.33	-10.8
#配合饲料	Compound feed	18.54	8.6
混合饲料	Mixed feed	58.65	-15.7
方便面(万吨)	instant Noodle(10 000 ton)	13.50	6.7
乳制品(万吨)	Dairy Products (10 000 ton)	74.86	13.1
液体乳	Milk	61.65	10.8
固体及半固体乳制品	Solid and semi-solid dairy products	13.21	25.1
饮料酒(万千升)	Beverage Wine (10 000 kiloliter)	51.08	2.5
#白酒（折65度，商品量）	Liquor (as 65 degree, amount of goods)	0.04	-24.8
啤酒	Beer	50.19	2.3
葡萄酒	Wine	0.72	24.2
软饮料(万吨)	Soft Beverage (10 000 ton)	174.23	-8.8
#碳酸饮料类（汽水）	Carbonated Beverage	38.20	12.6
果汁和蔬菜汁饮料	Juice and Fruit Beverage	30.64	-14.4
包装饮用水类	Canned Drinking Water	53.49	-7.7
纱(万吨)	Yarn (10 000 ton)	2.67	-1.3
1. 棉纱	Cotton Yarn	1.02	3.8
2. 棉混纺纱	Blend Fabric	0.63	12.9
3. 化学纤维纱	Pure Chemical-Fibre Yarn	1.02	-12.4
布(亿米)	Cloth (100 million m)	1.28	0.3

12-6 续表1 continued1

产品名称	Name of Products	2018	比上年增长(%) Increase over Preceding Year (%)
#1. 棉布	Cotton Cloth	0.55	19.6
2. 棉混纺布	Blend Fabric	0.30	2.0
3. 化学纤维布	Pure Chemical-Fibre Cloth	0.43	-17.7
人造板（万立方米）	Artificial Board (10 000 cu.m)	10.06	-49.7
纤维板	Fibre Board	10.06	-49.7
家具（万件）	Furniture (10 000unit)	38.52	8.6
#木质家具	Wooden Furniture	19.89	13.1
软体家具	Soft Furniture (inc.: Sofa ,Mattress etc.)	10.28	71.3
机制纸及纸板（外购原纸加工除外）（万吨）	Machine Made Paper(not including processing of procured base paper)(10 000 ton)	15.39	-15.4
纸制品（万吨）	Paper-Made Products (10 000 ton)	10.86	3.7
#瓦楞纸箱	Corrugated Paper	9.74	2.0
单色印刷（万令）	Monochrom Printed products(10 000 ream)	54.77	-5.8
多色印刷品（万对开色令）	Colored Printed products(10 000 ream)	985.05	17.0
化学农药原药(折有效成分100%)(万吨)	Chemical Pesticide(100% effective content)(10 000 ton)	0.13	-67.0
涂料（万吨）	Construction Paint(10 000 ton)	1.58	-7.1
合成洗涤剂（万吨）	Synthetic Detergents (10 000 ton)	4.66	-15.6
#合成洗衣粉	Washing Power	0.84	-26.4
液体洗涤剂	Liquid detergent	3.21	-8.7
化学原料药（万吨）	Chemical Medicine (10 000 ton)	0.02	-31.3
中成药（万吨）	Traditional Chinese Medicine (10 000 ton)	1.06	56.5
化学纤维（万吨）	Chemical Fiber	1.42	1.9
人造纤维（纤维素纤维）（万吨）	Man-made Fiber	1.42	1.9
塑料制品（万吨）	Plastic Product (10 000 ton)	18.17	29.1

12-6 续表2 continued2

产品名称	Name of Products	2018	比上年增长(%) Increase over Preceding Year (%)
水泥（万吨）	Cement (10 000 ton)	219.80	-4.5
硅酸盐水泥熟料（万吨）	Portland Cement Clinker (10 000 ton)	76.00	-5.7
水泥混凝土电杆（万根）	Cement Pole(10 000 unit)	1.88	-30.8
商品混凝土(万立方米)	Ready-mixed Concrete (10 000 cu.m)	2962.80	21.3
沥青和改性沥青防水卷材（万平方米）	Asphalt and Modified Bitumen Membrane(10 000 sq.m)	1667.50	-31.6
钢化玻璃(万平方米)	Toughened Glass(10 000 sq.m)	532.25	21.7
日用玻璃制品（万吨）	Glassware(10 000 ton)	2.15	-30.9
钢材（万吨）	Rolled-steel Final Products (10 000 ton)	33.40	15.3
线材（盘条）	Wire Rod	7.62	-12.0
其他钢材	Other steel	23.55	26.3
铝材(万吨)	Aluminum Material (10 000 ton)	2.41	-37.8
单晶硅（万千克）	Monocrystalline Silicon (10 000kg)	2038.32	25.1
工业锅炉（蒸发量吨）	industrial Boiler steam(ton)	2899.50	9.6
发动机（万千瓦）	Engine (10 000 kw)	383.33	12.8
#汽车发动机（万千瓦）	Motor Engine(10 000 kw)	383.33	12.8
金属切削机床(万台)	Metal-cutting Machines (10 000 unit)	0.43	-40.2
泵(万台)	Pump (Liquid pump)(10 000 unit)	0.28	-71.3
风机（万台）	Fan(10 000 unit)	0.61	-0.6
气体压缩机（万台）	Gas Compressor(10 000 unit)	27.55	-11.3
阀门（万吨）	Valves (10 000 ton)	0.16	-28.2
铸铁件（万吨）	iron Castings (10 000 ton)	1.76	-8.3
铸钢件（万吨）	Steel Castings (10 000 ton)	1.26	-6.8
锻件（万吨）	Forgings (10 000 ton)	0.06	-31.3
矿山专用设备（万吨）	Mining Equipment (10 000 ton)	1.00	-4.3

12-6 续表3 continued 3

产品名称	Name of Products	2018	比上年增长(%) Increase over Preceding Year (%)
炼油、化工生产专用设备（万吨）	Oil Refining and Chemical industry Machine(10 000 ton)	0.43	-28.0
金属冶炼设备（吨）	Metal Smelting Equipments(ton)	3563.40	-11.0
金属轧制设备（吨）	Metal-rolling Machine(ton)	3563.70	87.8
印刷专用设备（吨）	Printing Equipment(ton)	124.00	6.9
环境污染防治设备(台/套)	Special Equipment for Environment Protection	12833.00	42.8
大气污染防治设备	Equipment for Preventing Atmospheric Pollution	12257.00	36.4
汽车（万辆）	Motor Vehicle(10 000unit)	43.37	-2.6
其中：基本型乘用车（轿车）	Basic Type Passenger Vehicles(car)	18.08	-0.3
轿车（排量≤1升）	Car0L-1.0L Gas Displacement(1.0L included)	5.69	159.4
轿车（1升＜排量≤1.6升）	Car1.0L-1.6L Gas Displacement(1.6L included)	12.39	-22.3
运动型多用途乘用车（SUV）	Sports Utility Vehicle (SUV)	6.94	-5.7
客车	Passenger Vehicles	0.04	-66.5
#轻型客车（车长≤7米）	Light Buses（Length≤7m）	0.03	-64.3
载货汽车	Trucks	18.32	-3.1
其中：新能源汽车	New Energy Vehicles (10000 unit)	13.85	70.0
改装汽车（万辆）	Refit Trucks (10 000 unit)	0.10	9.5
铁路货车（万辆）	Freight(10 000 unit)	0.42	18.5
电动机（万千瓦）	Electric motor(Ten thousand kilowatts)	285.82	27.6
#直流电动机	DC motors	25.71	-1.0
交流电动机	Alternating Current Motor(10 000kw)	260.10	31.4
变压器（万千伏安）	Transformer(10 000KVA)	13192.59	-7.1
高压开关板（万面）	High-voltage Switch Panel(10 000 unit)	0.68	2.4
低压开关板（万面）	Low-voltage Switch Panel(10 000 unit)	1.18	23.8

12-6 续表4 continued 4

产品名称	Name of Products	2018	比上年增长(%) Increase over Preceding Year (%)
电力电缆(万千米)	Electric Power Cables(10 000 km)	13.28	11.8
通信及电子网络用电缆(万对千米)	Communication Cables(10 000 pair km)	3.39	-16.7
光缆（万芯千米）	Cable (10 000 Core.km)	716.10	22.1
绝缘制品(吨)	Insulating Products(ton)	15507.80	2.5
电子元件（亿只）	Electronic Components(100 million unit)	4.37	1.8
工业自动化调节仪表与控制系统（万台/套）	Automatization meter and system (10 000 unit)	3.84	17.4
分析仪器及装置（万台 / 套）	Analysis instruments and Apparatus(10 000 set)	2.78	17.7
化学试剂（万吨）	Chemicals Reagents(10000 ton)	53.03	22.8
起重机（吨）	Crane (ton)	686.00	130.2
减速机（台）	Reducer (a)	14161.00	42.8
模具（万套）	Molds (10 000set)	0.28	-38.4
电动自行车（万辆）	Electric bicycle (10 000car)	88.82	19.9
电力电容器（万千乏）	Power capacitors (10 000kW)	1754.79	-48.4
高压开关设备（11万伏以上）（万台）	High Voltage Switchgear (above 110,000 volt) (10 000a)	0.96	-53.5
灯具及照明装置（万套/台/个）	Lamps and lighting equipment (10 000set /a)	2.27	0.0
半导体分立器件（亿只）	Discrete semiconductor devices (100million unit)	55.27	18.9
光电子器件（万只/片）	Optoelectronic devices (100million unit)	152.20	328.7
工业仪表（万台/个）	Industrial Instrumentation (10 000a)	56.98	-18.4
环境监测专用仪器仪表（台）	Special equipment for prevention and control of environmental pollution(unit)	5811.00	-81.1
发电量（亿千瓦小时）	Power generation(One hundred million kilowatt-hours)	172.76	-4.1
火力发电量（亿千瓦小时）	Thermal power generation(One hundred million kilowatt-hours	167.11	-5.0
水力发电量（亿千瓦小时）	Hydropower(One hundred million kilowatt-hours)	0.83	-11.5
太阳能发电量(亿千瓦小时)	Solar energy generation(One hundred million kilowatt-hours)	4.82	44.5

12-7 主要年份规模以上工业企业经济效益指标

Indicators of Economic Performance of Industrial Enterprises above Designated Size in Representative Years

年 份 Year	总资产贡献率 (%) Ratio of Total Assets to Industrial Output Value (%)	资产负债率 (%) Assets-Liability Ratio (%)	流动资产周转次数 (次/年) Rate of Annual Turnover Working Capitals (times/year)	成本费用利润率 (%) Ratio of Profits to Cost (%)	全员劳动生产率 (元/人・年) Overall Labor Productivity (yuan/person year)	产品销售率 (%) Proportion of Industrial Products Sold (%)
1998		67.7	0.9	-266.1	19185	95.3
1999		67.7	0.9	2.5	22878	95.9
2000		65.0	1.0	4.2	29496	97.1
2001	5.8	62.4	0.9	4.1	38267	96.7
2002	6.2	60.4	1.1	5.1	46940	96.7
2003	7.0	61.3	1.1	5.7	58801	96.3
2004	6.9	65.2	1.2	5.0	66752	97.9
2005	8.4	65.0	1.3	3.1	82815	97.5
2006	7.8	64.3	1.4	5.5	97561	98.2
2007	10.2	64.6	1.6	7.3	129706	96.8
2008	8.6	62.6	1.5	4.6	150641	96.1
2009	11.3	61.1	1.7	8.1	161289	97.6
2010	12.2	57.6	1.7	8.8	188483	97.1
2011	8.6	57.7	1.5	5.2	194105	97.4
2012	7.7	59.4	1.5	4.5	230032	96.7
2013	8.5	59.5	1.5	5.2	264324	95.7
2014	7.4	59.7	1.4	5.2	266789	94.9
2015	5.7	57.3	1.3	4.8	268182	94.5
2016	6.4	55.7	1.3	6.0	277240	96.0
2017	7.2	53.0	1.4	6.6	294393	97.3
2018	7.3	54.5	1.3	6.8		96.2

12-8 规模以上工业企业主要经济指标（2018年）

单位：万元

分　组	Classify	企业单位数（个） Number of Enterprises (unit)	亏损企业 Loss Making Enterprises	工业总产值（当年价格） Gross Industrial Output Value (At Current Prices)
总计	**Total**	**1474**	**236**	**63962836**
#亏损企业	Deficit Enterprises	236	236	3871695
按隶属关系分	**Grouped by Jurisdiction of Management**			
#中央企业	Central Enterprises	104	13	12259975
地方企业	Local Enterprises	166	36	20002832
按登记注册类型分组	**Grouped by Registion Status**			
内资企业	Domestic Investment Enterprises	1365	219	51284411
国有	State-owned Enterprises	25	2	3226054
集体	Collective-owned Enterprises	5		50536
股份合作	Share-holding Corperative	4	1	13224
联营	Joint Ownership Enterprises			
有限责任公司	Limited Liability Corporations	606	111	31333528
股份有限公司	Share-holding Corperation Ltd.	111	17	6190872
私营	Private Enterprises	613	88	10467855
其他	Other Domestic Funded Enterprises	1		2343
港澳台商投资	Enterprises with Funds from Hong Kong,Macao and Taiwan	21	2	3430578
外商投资	Foreign Funded Enterprises	88	15	9247848
按轻重工业分	**Grouped by Light Industry and Heavy Industry**			
轻工业	Light Industry	379	63	11798118
重工业	Heavy Industry	1095	173	52164718
按企业规模分	**Grouped by Size of Enterprises**			
大型企业	Large-size	63	7	35696721
中型企业	Medium-size	175	22	11211514
小型企业	Small-size	1236	207	17054602
按控股情况分	**Grouped by Cast strand**			
国有控股	State owned shares	283	53	30104092

Major Economic Indicators of Industrial Enterprises above Designated Size（2018）

(10 000yuan)

工业销售产值（当年价）Value of Industry Products Sales (At Current Prices)	出口交货值 Export Delivery Value	平均用工人数（人）Average Number of Employed Persons (person)	资产总计 Total Assets	流动资产合计 Total Working Capitals	固定资产原价 Origing Value of Fixed Assets	累计折旧 Accumulative Total Depreciation
61502394	**6469221**	**514006**	**82940788**	**48976155**	**38319557**	**18380888**
3658818	501820	49184	8530291	4354396	3755715	1786741
11962801	781798	158078	23115353	13935500	9801159	4962689
19226092	1198684	117492	23188882	13649374	10610663	4492828
50075163	2532800	438037	67223465	41335777	26647687	11682540
3117041	150797	51278	7261631	4357212	2849156	1372464
50846		629	12806	7863	16939	10961
11476		259	26870	23025	4889	2533
30679270	1498117	265725	40917707	25994185	15068038	7013410
5940064	513028	46466	11469142	5873127	6398600	2411576
10274124	370857	73638	7534817	5080069	2309426	871360
2343		42	492	296	640	236
3368642	272563	33629	2974663	1753224	1065535	457895
8058590	3663858	42340	12742660	5887154	10606336	6240454
11295953	671080	92412	10219138	5894510	4351670	1840010
50206442	5798140	421594	72721650	43081645	33967887	16540878
34213513	4869920	286685	49342953	28897087	26781287	13814943
10802877	869118	100960	16189825	9267608	5791269	2320733
16486004	730183	126361	17408010	10811460	5747001	2245212
29615227	1491222	276663	46018066	27774402	17811523	8642690

12-8 续表1

单位：万元

分 组	Classify	负债合计 Total Liabilites	流动负债合计 Total Working Liabilities	非流动负债合计 Total Non-Working Liabilities
总计	**Total**	**45226396**	**37633140**	**7502041**
#亏损企业	Deficit Enterprises	6473089	5311490	1134853
按隶属关系分	**Grouped by Jurisdiction of Management**			
#中央企业	Central Enterprises	12481368	10198773	2282594
地方企业	Local Enterprises	13866027	12049964	1811442
按登记注册类型分组	**Grouped by Registion Status**			
内资企业	Domestic Investment Enterprises	38261343	32296826	5891291
国有	State-owned Enterprises	4405042	3239144	1165898
集体	Collective-owned Enterprises	2607	1942	665
股份合作	Share-holding Corperative	7715	7715	
联营	Joint Ownership Enterprises			
有限责任公司	Limited Liability Corporations	24599168	21394444	3181565
股份有限公司	Share-holding Corperation Ltd.	4989757	3924750	1065006
私营	Private Enterprises	4256904	3728692	478146
其他	Other Domestic Funded Enterprises	151	140	12
港澳台商投资	Enterprises with Funds from Hong Kong,Macao and Taiwan	2063508	1929192	134316
外商投资	Foreign Funded Enterprises	4901545	3407122	1476435
按轻重工业分	**Grouped by Light Industry and Heavy Industry**			
轻工业	Light Industry	6141647	4980140	1125968
重工业	Heavy Industry	39084748	32653000	6376074
按企业规模分	**Grouped by Size of Enterprises**			
大型企业	Large-size	26078155	21505757	4572398
中型企业	Medium-size	9445426	7965578	1479847
小型企业	Small-size	9702814	8161805	1449797
按控股情况分	**Grouped by Cast strand**			
国有控股	State owned shares	26724608	22673656	4050951

continued1

(10 000yuan)

所有者权益合计 Total Owners' Equities	实收资本 Total Capital Hold	营业收入 Total Revenue	主营业务收入 Revenue from Principal Business	营业成本 Total Cost	主营业务成本 Cost of Principal Business	税金及附加 Taxs and Other Changes	主营业务税金及附加 Taxes and Other Charges on Principal Business
37714377	**15875024**	**61439746**	**60211155**	**53214524**	**51865575**	**452164**	**442611**
2057199	2137358	3888480	3838974	3512075	3484484	38754	37393
10633984	4110359	12624884	12288840	11089056	10469919	78463	75824
9322852	3322543	19275093	18779039	17051020	16650360	87583	83788
28962107	11482936	50218586	49218304	43274835	42108654	348205	338788
2856589	739896	3371319	3297682	2742419	2682958	16968	14151
10199	7843	48902	48902	43707	43707	105	105
19155	11874	15585	15585	12908	12908	92	92
16318533	7326791	31676598	30845806	27689592	26651142	247766	242673
6479384	1868111	5308193	5268271	4405623	4380667	30635	29595
3277906	1528292	9795646	9739903	8379037	8335805	52614	52147
341	129	2343	2156	1549	1467	25	25
911155	257232	3117762	3003295	3362329	3263669	54328	54328
7841115	4134856	8103397	7989556	6577359	6493251	49631	49496
4077486	1815827	11197869	11114058	8746792	8679467	88108	85763
33636891	14059197	50241877	49097097	44467732	43186107	364056	356849
23264798	8655639	33814306	32931825	30312327	29237366	220385	216209
6744398	2898477	11300257	11102050	9225469	9065914	63737	60692
7705182	4320907	16325184	16177280	13675728	13562294	168042	165710
19293456	7707109	30814448	29963989	27293459	26263112	228115	220262

12-8 续表2

单位：万元

分组	Classify	销售费用 Expenses for Sales	管理费用 Expenses for Management	财务费用 Financial cost
总计	**Total**	**2353134**	**3365710**	**289372**
#亏损企业	Deficit Enterprises	202784	274703	110643
按隶属关系分	**Grouped by Jurisdiction of Management**			
#中央企业	Central Enterprises	272611	976308	81281
地方企业	Local Enterprises	717056	774832	63226
按登记注册类型分组	**Grouped by Registion Status**			
内资企业	Domestic Investment Enterprises	1848750	2714703	249115
国有	State-owned Enterprises	50093	320095	37090
集体	Collective-owned Enterprises	1661	3997	157
股份合作	Share-holding Corperative	518	1411	43
联营	Joint Ownership Enterprises			
有限责任公司	Limited Liability Corporations	1177176	1616186	114107
股份有限公司	Share-holding Corperation Ltd.	244812	331913	51725
私营	Private Enterprises	374390	441008	45911
其他	Other Domestic Funded Enterprises	101	93	83
港澳台商投资	Enterprises with Funds from Hong Kong,Macao and Taiwan	82135	107993	21222
外商投资	Foreign Funded Enterprises	422250	543013	19036
按轻重工业分	**Grouped by Light Industry and Heavy Industry**			
轻工业	Light Industry	1161422	598932	95304
重工业	Heavy Industry	1191712	2766778	194069
按企业规模分	**Grouped by Size of Enterprises**			
大型企业	Large-size	1004442	1808999	57248
中型企业	Medium-size	685812	637667	102444
小型企业	Small-size	662880	919044	129681
按控股情况分	**Grouped by Cast strand**			
国有控股	State owned shares	708958	1694128	136258

continued2

(10 000yuan)

营业利润 Operating Profit	利润总额 Total Profits	亏损企业亏损额 Total Loss of Deficit Enterprises	利税总额 Total Pre-tax Profits	应付职工薪酬 Salary Payable	本年应交增值税 Value Added Tax Payable
3902542	**4024412**	**249470**	**5708086**	**6562208**	**1231510**
-255153	-249470	249470	-123456	424377	87260
614115	648317	31208	946567	2266290	219787
814315	820362	93910	1341228	1997333	433284
2545781	2635190	197670	3984246	5575271	1000850
216991	224021	5645	304925	642362	63936
2249	2485		3173	2264	582
613	650	21	1509	1083	767
1450127	1503923	141573	2371204	3786661	619515
384791	401512	29473	539335	537799	107187
490518	502107	20959	763562	604750	208841
492	492		539	353	22
161648	165559	2155	229250	298616	9363
1195113	1223663	49645	1494591	688321	221297
542687	580581	72540	1109508	967948	440819
3359855	3443831	176930	4598579	5594260	790691
2365964	2418523	28022	3182766	4375255	543859
650340	667288	89452	1039795	1149838	308770
886239	938602	131996	1485525	1037115	378881
1340878	1383792	130175	2163466	4151369	551559

12-8 续表3

单位：万元

分组	Classify	企业单位数（个）Number of Enterprises (unit)	亏损企业 Loss Making Enterprises	工业总产值（当年价格）Gross Industrial Output Value (At Current Prices)
集体控股	Collective shares	20	3	466276
私人控股	Private holdings	1044	159	23644252
港澳台控股	Hong Kong and Macao Holdings	14	1	511918
外商投资	Foreign Investment	54	7	7821164
其他	Others	59	13	1415135
按工业行业大类分	**Grouped by Sector**			
煤炭开采和洗选业	Mining and Washing of Coal			
石油和天然气开采业	Extraction of Petroleum and Natural Gas			
黑色金属矿采选业	Mining and Processing of Ferrous Metal Ores			
有色金属矿采选业	Mining and Processing of Non-ferrous Metal Ores			
非金属矿采选业	Mining and Processing of Nonmetal Ores			
开采专业及辅助性活动	Mining Professional and Auxiliary Activity	5	2	856314
其他采矿业	Mining of other Ores			
农副食品加工业	Processing of Food from Agricultural Porducts	52	8	1596820
食品制造业	Manufacture of Foods	53	9	1707463
酒、饮料和精制茶制造业	Manufacture of Alcohol,Beverages and Tea	25	3	919561
烟草制品业	Manufacture of Tobacco	1		7463
纺织业	Manufacture of Textile	16	3	204831
纺织服装、服饰业	Textile, apparel industry	4	1	63180
皮革、毛皮、羽毛及其制品和制鞋业	Manufacture of Leather, Fur, Feather and Related Products, and Shoes	2		35553
木材加工和木、竹、藤、棕、草制品业	Processing of Timber, Manufacture of Wood,Plam and Straw Products	5	2	33788
家具制造业	Manufacture of Furniture	15		155055
造纸和纸制品业	Manufacture of Paper and Paper Products	24	2	313182
印刷和记录媒介复制业	Printing,Reproduction of Recording Media	33	7	959053

continued3

(10 000yuan)

工业销售产值（当年价） Value of Industry Products Sales (At Current Prices)	出口交货值 Export Delivery Value	平均用二人数（人） Average Number of Employed Persons (person)	资产总计 Tctal Assets	流动资产合计 Total Working Capitals	固定资产原价 Origing Value of Fixed Assets	累计折旧 Accumulative Total Depreciation
406225	71427	3562	462638	325050	142340	75299
22917458	926299	185012	23186197	14632073	9448922	3328861
516715	231670	3678	328428	191844	182339	97705
6691471	3554669	32806	11121318	4981396	9919355	5951452
1355298	193934	12285	1824141	1071390	815078	284882
856979		13625	1246851	918778	705246	479564
1530758	1229	7500	1020541	670241	410965	197814
1634529	9717	15669	820026	383774	529608	245924
1074689	128831	8533	1405969	626931	757750	322730
7463		475	40826	23556	32030	14861
192409	13242	7229	333995	129829	239287	83073
56524		1446	104278	84782	18577	4711
48848	2292	851	63209	41717	9202	4881
29488		420	130752	63553	58154	25654
143789		2243	131587	71722	43718	8841
303966	2035	2541	158689	88922	57252	18167
927450	1722	7459	793329	469786	514953	311203

12-8 续表4

单位：万元

分组	Classify	负债合计 Total Liabilites	流动负债合计 Total Working Liabilities	非流动负债合计 Total Non-Working Liabilities
集体控股	Collective shares	202001	176326	25676
私人控股	Private holdings	13197076	11315427	1808423
港澳台控股	Hong Kong and Macao Holdings	151189	127179	24011
外商投资	Foreign Investment	3999178	2555662	1425528
其他	Others	952344	784891	167453
按工业行业大类分	**Grouped by Sector**			
煤炭开采和洗选业	Mining and Washing of Coal			
石油和天然气开采业	Extraction of Petroleum and Natural Gas			
黑色金属矿采选业	Mining and Processing of Ferrous Metal Ores			
有色金属矿采选业	Mining and Processing of Non-ferrous Metal Ores			
非金属矿采选业	Mining and Processing of Nonmetal Ores			
开采专业及辅助性活动	Mining Professional and Auxiliary Activity	488284	473472	14813
其他采矿业	Mining of other Ores			
农副食品加工业	Processing of Food from Agricultural Porducts	740379	676577	57647
食品制造业	Manufacture of Foods	418084	373831	44252
酒、饮料和精制茶制造业	Manufacture of Alcohol,Beverages and Tea	818511	649961	150563
烟草制品业	Manufacture of Tobacco	6868	6868	
纺织业	Manufacture of Textile	218250	129517	88733
纺织服装、服饰业	Textile, apparel industry	60161	59399	762
皮革、毛皮、羽毛及其制品和制鞋业	Manufacture of Leather, Fur, Feather and Related Products, and Shoes	23829	16566	7263
木材加工和木、竹、藤、棕、草制品业	Processing of Timber, Manufacture of Wood,Plam and Straw Products	64744	28291	36453
家具制造业	Manufacture of Furniture	56246	47062	9183
造纸和纸制品业	Manufacture of Paper and Paper Products	86550	80626	5924
印刷和记录媒介复制业	Printing,Reproduction of Recording Media	312035	288016	19399

continued4

(10 000yuan)

所有者权益合计 Total Owners' Equities	实收资本 Total Capital Hold	营业收入 Total Revenue	主营业务收入 Revenue from Principal Business	营业成本 Total Cost	主营业务成本 Cost of Principal Business	税金及附加 Taxs and Other Changes	主营业务税金及附加 Taxes and Other Charges on Principal Business
260636	107223	395251	386613	310228	304847	2125	2119
9989108	3774569	21705394	21405425	18674088	18423063	170580	169314
177238	122707	532241	526114	451745	446601	1966	1966
7122140	3676492	6698246	6654705	5354466	5319417	43035	42968
871798	486924	1294166	1274310	1125538	1108535	6342	5981
758566	471681	779266	769150	702534	692004	5780	5746
280162	136405	1540684	1533461	1373396	1370165	4591	4528
401943	206023	1586171	1575771	1266946	1255967	7450	7375
587458	218003	1077390	1060878	751468	736534	21538	21535
33958	27400	9792	9792	5214	5214	442	442
115745	44984	161604	157563	157566	154703	1653	710
44117	33158	51846	51100	41134	40214	492	483
39380	21500	62600	47246	54367	43466	444	444
66008	15444	22282	21905	21116	21116	106	86
75341	26804	136751	135530	118377	117399	715	705
72139	36779	304314	303741	284263	282909	591	591
481294	242830	923525	915892	756384	751944	5577	5505

12-8 续表5

单位：万元

分　组	Classify	销售费用 Expenses for Sales	管理费用 Expenses for Management	财务费用 Financial cost
集体控股	Collective shares	19751	34389	1523
私人控股	Private holdings	1170585	1084664	133072
港澳台控股	Hong Kong and Macao Holdings	39468	15186	1574
外商投资	Foreign Investment	384493	472935	14766
其他	Others	29880	64407	2180
按工业行业大类分	**Grouped by Sector**			
煤炭开采和洗选业	Mining and Washing of Coal			
石油和天然气开采业	Extraction of Petroleum and Natural Gas			
黑色金属矿采选业	Mining and Processing of Ferrous Metal Ores			
有色金属矿采选业	Mining and Processing of Non-ferrous Metal Ores			
非金属矿采选业	Mining and Processing of Nonmetal Ores			
开采专业及辅助性活动	Mining Professional and Auxiliary Activity	4452	38692	-6069
其他采矿业	Mining of other Ores			
农副食品加工业	Processing of Food from Agricultural Porducts	53249	42036	7675
食品制造业	Manufacture of Foods	147911	62759	2328
酒、饮料和精制茶制造业	Manufacture of Alcohol,Beverages and Tea	170185	56480	9867
烟草制品业	Manufacture of Tobacco	823	2525	-255
纺织业	Manufacture of Textile	4107	11178	615
纺织服装、服饰业	Textile, apparel industry	3728	5007	928
皮革、毛皮、羽毛及其制品和制鞋业	Manufacture of Leather, Fur, Feather and Related Products, and Shoes	1767	2128	252
木材加工和木、竹、藤、棕、草制品业	Processing of Timber, Manufacture of Wood,Plam and Straw Products	834	2831	2358
家具制造业	Manufacture of Furniture	4299	5258	437
造纸和纸制品业	Manufacture of Paper and Paper Products	4497	5428	2175
印刷和记录媒介复制业	Printing,Reproduction of Recording Media	30908	75596	2131

continued5

(10 000yuan)

营业利润 Operating Profit	利润总额 Total Profits	亏损企业亏损额 Total Loss of Deficit Enterprises	利税总额 Total Pre-tax Profits	应付职工薪酬 Salary Payable	本年应交增值税 Value Added Tax Payable
29669	32988	1970	46552	31454	11440
1335907	1382435	63563	2005918	1662229	452903
22231	23050	2044	33581	46500	8565
1100910	1127262	41873	1365365	569903	195068
72947	74886	9845	93202	100754	11975
35558	33667	1728	45012	263241	5565
62230	63613	2199	82922	68676	14718
103091	103702	3126	153770	177780	42619
77380	98060	1049	154295	116578	34698
1042	478		2349	3862	1429
-12856	-10793	15086	-6885	37956	2256
1880	2345	23	5382	6553	2545
3688	4017		4478	6403	17
-583	-143	391	665	2318	703
7639	7361		9628	13215	1551
9161	11545	213	16447	19065	4311
51591	52072	1837	90511	114251	32862

12-8 续表6

单位：万元

分 组	Classify	企业单位数（个） Number of Enterprises (unit)	亏损企业 Loss Making Enterprises	工业总产值（当年价格） Gross Industrial Output Value (At Current Prices)
文教、工美、体育和娱乐用品制造业	Manufacture of Articles For Cultural,Educational and Sports Activities	12	3	444727
石油、炼焦及其他燃料加工业	Processing of Petroleum, Cokeing,Processing of Nuclear and Nuclear Fuel	7	4	41172
化学原料和化学制品制造业	Manufacture of Raw Chemical Materials and Chemical Products	86	9	2348920
医药制造业	Manufacture of Medicines	62	13	2439050
化学纤维制造业	Manufacture of Chemical Fibers	3		195314
橡胶和塑料制品业	Manufacture of Rubber and Plastics	38	5	978595
非金属矿物制品业	Manufacture of Non-metallic Mineral Products	157	25	2547040
黑色金属冶炼和压延加工业	Smelting and Pressing of Ferrous Metals	10	2	189206
有色金属冶炼和压延加工业	Smelting and Pressing of Non-ferrous Metals	44	6	1211073
金属制品业	Manufacture of Metal Products	97	16	1752315
通用设备制造业	Manufacture of General Purpose Machinery	92	13	1744067
专用设备制造业	Manufacture of Special Equipment	127	24	2474122
汽车制造业	Manufacture of Motor Vehicle	59	4	13748806
铁路、船舶、航空航天和其他运输设备制造业	Railways,Shipbuilding,Aerospace and Other Transportation Equipment Manufacturing Industry	85	7	5929348
电气机械和器材制造业	Manufacture of Electric Equipment and Machinery	142	30	7267488
计算机、通讯和其他电子设备制造业	Manufacture of Communication Equipment, Computers and other Electronic Equipment	93	12	9306024
仪器仪表制造业	Manufacture of Measuring Instruments and Machinery	60	6	1751304
其他制造业	Manufacture of Other Manufacturing	8	1	46267
废弃资源综合利用业	Recycling and Disposal of Waste	4	1	9879
金属制品、机械和设备修理业	Metal Products,Machinery and Equipment Repair Industry	6	3	41380
电力、热力的生产和供应业	Production and Supply of Electric Power and Heat Power	22	9	875708
燃气生产和供应业	Gas Mining and Supplying Industry	15	3	1617551
水的生产和供应业	Production and Supply of Water	10	3	151218

continued6

(10 000yuan)

工业销售产值（当年价）Value of Industry Products Sales (At Current Prices)	出口交货值 Export Delivery Value	平均用工人数（人）Average Number of Employed Persons (person)	资产总计 Total Assets	流动资产合计 Total Working Capitals	固定资产原价 Origing Value of Fixed Assets	累计折旧 Accumulative Total Depreciation
416366	158237	1216	48517	33759	14318	4897
40925		2638	92100	50117	61717	8378
2221388	204841	19091	3203396	1849912	1440939	746991
2128133	2321	19275	2386182	1441299	644883	275726
204486		724	169718	91680	157087	74032
960951	84184	10173	1989346	1218887	608437	192811
2588256	2604	17535	3500735	1624858	1248172	490276
191373		1064	128642	97633	32718	12724
1079230	197402	7110	2504369	1146656	528168	203429
1670602	80840	23992	2442277	1538482	1075884	468825
1994210	59503	20158	3991746	3040709	908095	451460
2382176	95479	26819	4787370	3201773	1112748	420612
13584963	453430	75497	9782950	7236666	2600297	1312498
5728906	459833	74941	10584101	6334158	3217392	1457772
6995867	897820	49951	9232519	6379605	2954357	1142653
8104327	3551997	57756	13483207	6379018	12602528	6807279
1664681	54992	16325	2507241	1670049	735423	324108
47362	274	978	81969	51359	25934	7688
9553		132	10476	3167	7778	1031
39307	6397	479	75141	31628	17107	6025
873906		9329	2991254	1167446	3050382	1532153
1615557		7198	2126762	523127	1517596	504052
152979		3634	570722	290576	380854	218046

12-8 续表7

单位：万元

分组	Classify	负债合计 Total Liabilites	流动负债合计 Total Working Liabilities	非流动负债合计 Total Non-Working Liabilities
文教、工美、体育和娱乐用品制造业	Manufacture of Articles For Cultural,Educational and Sports Activities	20737	19037	1700
石油、炼焦及其他燃料加工业	Processing of Petroleum, Cokeing,Processing of Nuclear and Nuclear Fuel	56992	45504	11488
化学原料和化学制品制造业	Manufacture of Raw Chemical Materials and Chemical Products	2002433	1487480	514953
医药制造业	Manufacture of Medicines	1233645	1063760	169885
化学纤维制造业	Manufacture of Chemical Fibers	86827	66708	20119
橡胶和塑料制品业	Manufacture of Rubber and Plastics	1342696	1087850	248068
非金属矿物制品业	Manufacture of Non-metallic Mineral Products	2514054	2205408	265347
黑色金属冶炼和压延加工业	Smelting and Pressing of Ferrous Metals	72329	68088	4242
有色金属冶炼和压延加工业	Smelting and Pressing of Non-ferrous Metals	715252	527965	187286
金属制品业	Manufacture of Metal Products	1631694	1247293	382353
通用设备制造业	Manufacture of General Purpose Machinery	2279569	2130518	141292
专用设备制造业	Manufacture of Special Equipment	2421029	2138546	282482
汽车制造业	Manufacture of Motor Vehicle	6340463	6036420	304043
铁路、船舶、航空航天和其他运输设备制造业	Railways,Shipbuilding,Aerospace and Other Transportation Equipment Manufacturing Industry	6068749	5019316	1049432
电气机械和器材制造业	Manufacture of Electric Equipment and Machinery	4808430	4225044	580820
计算机、通讯和其他电子设备制造业	Manufacture of Communication Equipment, Computers and other Electronic Equipment	4892938	3236328	1656610
仪器仪表制造业	Manufacture of Measuring Instruments and Machinery	1281024	1188455	92569
其他制造业	Manufacture of Other Manufacturing	44053	37367	6686
废弃资源综合利用业	Recycling and Disposal of Waste	7279	6458	821
金属制品、机械和设备修理业	Metal Products,Machinery and Equipment Repair Industry	16572	15365	1207
电力、热力的生产和供应业	Production and Supply of Electric Power and Heat Power	2473811	1658737	815074
燃气生产和供应业	Gas Mining and Supplying Industry	1229861	1086437	143424
水的生产和供应业	Production and Supply of Water	392023	204872	187151

continued7

(10 000yuan)

所有者权益合计 Total Owners' Equities	实收资本 Total Capital Hold	营业收入 Total Revenue	主营业务收入 Revenue from Principal Business	营业成本 Total Cost	主营业务成本 Cost of Principal Business	税金及附加 Taxs and Other Changes	主营业务税金及附加 Taxes and Other Charges on Principal Business
27780	15591	432606	432589	422813	422774	602	602
35107	22170	57025	55180	50890	49937	404	372
1200962	646027	2371264	2343415	1840331	1820517	71607	71580
1152536	301700	2116718	2115267	1081455	1080741	23953	23937
82891	85052	198779	198779	169184	169184	1106	1106
646649	459973	972144	952277	829791	812251	4540	3445
986678	679311	2831569	2748694	2512243	2430301	13719	13391
56312	26984	471244	471243	457074	457074	871	871
1789117	527490	1056982	1028924	898072	888251	5582	5368
810582	485848	1738036	1723595	1480461	1473403	18114	17664
1712177	384214	1702802	1652312	1410447	1365965	12379	12258
2366340	985535	2397925	2360726	1913941	1892611	16812	16260
3442486	1010026	13148973	12712720	12558754	12176594	92760	91953
4515352	1853772	6146287	6028332	5353985	5278639	25429	24659
4424087	1694408	6669661	6512857	6031006	5535558	51550	51484
8590269	3913163	7803209	7754929	6722977	6686862	35768	35552
1226216	397748	1673951	1659502	1316037	1292340	7680	5550
37916	21405	45719	44592	34890	34283	434	312
3197	1808	10496	10366	7716	7658	128	116
58569	58600	41983	39571	30578	28167	271	265
517443	385618	1043846	1019625	905419	893920	10189	9128
896901	358759	1681609	1609638	1515048	1467094	6317	6305
178699	78814	170697	153995	138649	129817	2572	2284

12-8 续表8

单位：万元

分组	Classify	销售费用 Expenses for Sales	管理费用 Expenses for Management	财务费用 Financial cost
文教、工美、体育和娱乐用品制造业	Manufacture of Articles For Cultural,Educational and Sports Activities	2398	3754	744
石油、炼焦及其他燃料加工业	Processing of Petroleum, Cokeing,Processing of Nuclear and Nuclear Fuel	1642	3430	386
化学原料和化学制品制造业	Manufacture of Raw Chemical Materials and Chemical Products	72271	168029	24515
医药制造业	Manufacture of Medicines	627806	216521	15671
化学纤维制造业	Manufacture of Chemical Fibers	1223	6396	2233
橡胶和塑料制品业	Manufacture of Rubber and Plastics	35877	43617	20725
非金属矿物制品业	Manufacture of Non-metallic Mineral Products	67603	97583	23783
黑色金属冶炼和压延加工业	Smelting and Pressing of Ferrous Metals	3159	4152	1773
有色金属冶炼和压延加工业	Smelting and Pressing of Non-ferrous Metals	17410	75854	7552
金属制品业	Manufacture of Metal Products	32609	136836	16644
通用设备制造业	Manufacture of General Purpose Machinery	61629	147503	9977
专用设备制造业	Manufacture of Special Equipment	123597	202682	21904
汽车制造业	Manufacture of Motor Vehicle	303737	367094	-19116
铁路、船舶、航空航天和其他运输设备制造业	Railways,Shipbuilding,Aerospace and Other Transportation Equipment Manufacturing Industry	81076	372252	38552
电气机械和器材制造业	Manufacture of Electric Equipment and Machinery	330403	421248	44964
计算机、通讯和其他电子设备制造业	Manufacture of Communication Equipment, Computers and other Electronic Equipment	63803	522358	-7459
仪器仪表制造业	Manufacture of Measuring Instruments and Machinery	45265	155727	1431
其他制造业	Manufacture of Other Manufacturing	1876	6301	1686
废弃资源综合利用业	Recycling and Disposal of Waste	881	691	46
金属制品、机械和设备修理业	Metal Products,Machinery and Equipment Repair Industry	2083	7194	-157
电力、热力的生产和供应业	Production and Supply of Electric Power and Heat Power	9438	43527	39331
燃气生产和供应业	Gas Mining and Supplying Industry	34462	37229	17716
水的生产和供应业	Production and Supply of Water	6128	15817	4032

continued8

(10 000yuan)

营业利润 Operating Profit	利润总额 Total Profits	亏损企业亏损额 Total Loss of Deficit Enterprises	利税总额 Total Pre-tax Profits	应付职工薪酬 Salary Payable	本年应交增值税 Value Added Tax Payable
2296	2410	208	19938	16333	16927
630	638	368	1930	23158	889
200343	196532	7944	333942	201951	65803
151965	158406	2935	421086	270239	238727
16030	16215		23231	8963	5910
36445	39837	2452	60195	68093	15819
116287	120280	14597	200539	121974	66540
3365	3401	597	6313	6873	2041
71387	73590	11184	105075	87051	25903
53946	59599	12094	112728	233630	35016
89435	94403	9208	158064	203916	51283
115251	132963	35514	217497	285069	67722
541918	551456	3208	799578	1351494	155362
361364	366484	7099	475276	1045784	83362
184750	213294	56697	384439	580175	119594
1275576	1279420	11070	1362620	713060	47431
162231	167464	3668	210119	234063	34975
775	2133	107	4014	6948	1447
1034	1216	163	1364	748	21
2336	2485	735	4259	5537	1503
80947	80871	38769	119017	118318	27957
90131	90439	3938	116243	104738	19487
4279	4954	1266	12046	44197	4520

12-9 规模以上国有及国有控股工业企业主要经济指标（2018年）

单位：万元

分 组	Classify	企业单位数（个） Number of Enterprises (unit)	亏损企业 Loss Making Enterprises	工业总产值（当年价格） Gross Industrial Output Value (At Current Prices)
总计	**Total**	**283**	**53**	**30104092**
#亏损企业	Deficit Enterprises	53	53	1388679
按隶属关系分	**Grouped by Jurisdiction of Management**			
#中央企业	Central Enterprises	15		2422196
地方企业	Local Enterprises	10	2	803858
按轻重工业分	**Grouped by Light Industry and Heavy Industry**			
轻工业	Light Industry	33	7	1626732
重工业	Heavy Industry	250	46	28477359
按企业规模分	**Grouped by Size of Enterprises**			
大型企业	Large-size	45	6	22093211
中型企业	Medium-size	82	10	4969789
小型企业	Small-size	156	37	3041092
按工业行业大类分	**Grouped by Sector**			
煤炭开采和洗选业	Mining and Washing of Coal			
石油和天然气开采业	Extraction of Petroleum and Natural Gas			
黑色金属矿采选业	Mining and Processing of Ferrous Metal Ores			
有色金属矿采选业	Mining and Processing of Non-ferrous Metal Ores			
非金属矿采选业	Mining and Processing of Nonmetal Ores			
开采专业及辅助性活动	Mining Professional and Auxiliary Activity	2		812193
其他采矿业	Mining of Other Ores			
农副食品加工业	Processing of Food from Agricultural Porducts	3	2	18790
食品制造业	Manufacture of Foods	8	1	230600
酒、饮料和精制茶制造业	Manufacture of Alcohol,Beverages and Tea	1		117576
烟草制品业	Manufacture of Tobacco	1		7463
纺织业	Manufacture of Textile	4	1	100523
纺织服装、服饰业	Textile, apparel industry			
皮革、毛皮、羽毛及其制品和制鞋业	Leather fur feathers and its products and footwear	1		32652
木材加工和木、竹、藤、棕、草制品业	Processing of Timber, Manufacture of Wood,Plato and Straw Products			

Major Economic Indicators of State-owned and State-holding Share Industrial Enterprises above Designated Size (2018)

(10 000yuan)

工业销售产值（当年价） Value of Industry Products Sales (At Current Prices)	出口交货值 Export Delivery Value	平均用工人数（人） Average Number of Employed Persons (person)	资产总计 Total Assets	流动资产合计 Total Working Capitals	固定资产原价 Origing Value of Fixed Assets	累计折旧 Accumulative Total Depreciation
29615227	**1491222**	**276663**	**46018066**	**27774402**	**17811523**	**8642690**
1369929	89594	24869	4612467	1887160	2410300	1254802
2294270	147212	37998	4966362	2870319	2170736	1120749
822771	3585	13280	2295269	1486893	678420	251714
1784477	10992	22974	2647528	1667607	1303495	623547
27830750	1480230	253689	43370539	26106795	16508028	8019143
21977406	1163340	204477	33065162	20929977	13160696	6669489
4710470	228544	51830	9205519	4675524	3292295	1403062
2927351	99338	20356	3747386	2168901	1358531	570139
812857		12952	1164126	857317	676091	461070
17651	1229	513	57105	36875	39391	20561
229656		3088	113462	73893	72076	37218
274732		1287	194541	132908	49450	33587
7463		475	40826	23556	32030	14861
96369	4804	5956	261563	84413	216656	74117
45422	2292	694	55680	34617	8599	4653

12-9 续表1

单位：万元

分组	Classify	负债合计 Total Liabilites	流动负债合计 Total Working Liabilities	非流动负债合计 Total Non-Working Liabilities
总计	**Total**	**26724608**	**22673656**	**4050951**
#亏损企业	Deficit Enterprises	3565575	2910824	654751
按隶属关系分	**Grouped by Jurisdiction of Management**			
#中央企业	Central Enterprises	2535489	1802278	733210
地方企业	Local Enterprises	1869553	1436865	432688
按轻重工业分	**Grouped by Light Industry and Heavy Industry**			
轻工业	Light Industry	1657475	1356201	301274
重工业	Heavy Industry	25067133	21317454	3749677
按企业规模分	**Grouped by Size of Enterprises**			
大型企业	Large-size	19022968	16196445	2826523
中型企业	Medium-size	5320385	4570600	749785
小型企业	Small-size	2381255	1906611	474643
按工业行业大类分	**Grouped by Sector**			
煤炭开采和洗选业	Mining and Washing of Coal			
石油和天然气开采业	Extraction of Petroleum and Natural Gas			
黑色金属矿采选业	Mining and Processing of Ferrous Metal Ores			
有色金属矿采选业	Mining and Processing of Non-ferrous Metal Ores			
非金属矿采选业	Mining and Processing of Nonmetal Ores			
开采专业及辅助性活动	Mining Professional and Auxiliary Activity	474696	459986	14710
其他采矿业	Mining of Other Ores			
农副食品加工业	Processing of Food from Agricultural Porducts	90747	90747	
食品制造业	Manufacture of Foods	54970	54614	356
酒、饮料和精制茶制造业	Manufacture of Alcohol,Beverages and Tea	101647	100893	755
烟草制品业	Manufacture of Tobacco	6868	6868	
纺织业	Manufacture of Textile	181325	94797	86529
纺织服装、服饰业	Textile, apparel industry			
皮革、毛皮、羽毛及其制品和制鞋业	Leather fur feathers and its products and footwear	22498	15235	7263
木材加工和木、竹、藤、棕、草制品业	Processing of Timber, Manufacture of Wood,Plato and Straw Products			

continued1

(10 000yuan)

所有者权益合计 Total Owners' Equities	实收资本 Total Capital Hold	营业收入 Total Revenue	主营业务收入 Revenue from Principal Business	营业成本 Total Cost	主营业务成本 Cost of Principal Business	税金及附加 Taxs and Other Changes	主营业务税金及附加 Taxes and Other Charges on Principal Business
19293456	**7707109**	**30814448**	**29963989**	**27298459**	**26263112**	**228115**	**220262**
1046891	1236008	1664475	1642635	1539055	1528625	13578	12404
2430873	607243	2413264	2361960	1949018	1907630	11001	11001
425716	132653	958056	935722	793401	775328	5967	4909
990052	567678	1847527	1802988	1492907	1459118	21003	18992
18303404	7139430	28966921	28161001	25805551	24803993	207112	201270
14042194	4887377	22273904	21542690	19840851	18892466	125392	121216
3885133	1768015	5347970	5248939	4654595	4583649	29402	26826
1366130	1051717	3192574	3172360	2803013	2786997	73321	72220
689430	457771	735367	726818	665366	655819	5314	5281
-33642	9600	20559	20341	16965	16883	49	49
58492	30100	236031	230097	194702	189442	1322	1322
92894	92894	274550	274395	198550	198392	9370	9370
33958	27400	9792	9792	5214	5214	442	442
80237	18696	103396	99356	105844	102982	1483	541
33182	15000	58766	43412	51196	40295	441	441

12-9 续表2

单位：万元

分组	Classify	销售费用 Expenses for Sales	管理费用 Expenses for Management	财务费用 Financial cost
总计	**Total**	**708958**	**1694128**	**136258**
#亏损企业	Deficit Enterprises	46993	122738	47609
按隶属关系分	**Grouped by Jurisdiction of Management**			
#中央企业	Central Enterprises	29418	243772	6722
地方企业	Local Enterprises	20675	76323	30367
按轻重工业分	**Grouped by Light Industry and Heavy Industry**			
轻工业	Light Industry	82750	107697	13889
重工业	Heavy Industry	626208	1586432	122368
按企业规模分	**Grouped by Size of Enterprises**			
大型企业	Large-size	552871	1230895	56513
中型企业	Medium-size	105883	297964	51732
小型企业	Small-size	50204	165269	28013
按工业行业大类分	**Grouped by Sector**			
煤炭开采和洗选业	Mining and Washing of Coal			
石油和天然气开采业	Extraction of Petroleum and Natural Gas			
黑色金属矿采选业	Mining and Processing of Ferrous Metal Ores			
有色金属矿采选业	Mining and Processing of Non-ferrous Metal Ores			
非金属矿采选业	Mining and Processing of Nonmetal Ores			
开采专业及辅助性活动	Mining Professional and Auxiliary Activity	4021	35689	-6120
其他采矿业	Mining of Other Ores			
农副食品加工业	Processing of Food from Agricultural Porducts	4096	2441	271
食品制造业	Manufacture of Foods	10726	12931	-152
酒、饮料和精制茶制造业	Manufacture of Alcohol,Beverages and Tea	29403	2206	-2183
烟草制品业	Manufacture of Tobacco	823	2525	-255
纺织业	Manufacture of Textile	1447	9039	337
纺织服装、服饰业	Textile, apparel industry			
皮革、毛皮、羽毛及其制品和制鞋业	Leather fur feathers and its products and footwear	1442	1905	148
木材加工和木、竹、藤、棕、草制品业	Processing of Timber, Manufacture of Wood,Plato and Straw Products			

continued2

(10 000yuan)

营业利润 Operating Profit	利润总额 Total Profits	亏损企业亏损额 Total Loss of Deficit Enterprises	利税总额 Total Pre-tax Profits	应付职工薪酬 Salary Payable	本年应交增值税 Value Added Tax Payable
1340878	**1383792**	**130175**	**2163466**	**4151369**	**551559**
-124021	-130175	130175	-85459	220248	31138
188885	193078		246746	547447	42667
28107	30943	5645	58179	94915	21269
141370	145402	21063	227242	227577	60837
1199509	1238390	109112	1936224	3923793	490722
971529	1001751	27794	1490182	3326541	363038
251857	254924	37931	403281	615903	118954
117492	127116	64450	270004	208925	69566
34537	32503		41730	252744	3912
-2106	-1968	1977	-1855	2499	64
16782	16732	204	23640	36307	5586
46948	46995		68538	18101	12173
1042	478		2349	3862	1429
-14097	-12413	14762	-9663	33108	1268
3679	4004		4415	5730	-31

12-9 续表3

单位：万元

分组	Classify	企业单位数（个）Number of Enterprises (unit)	亏损企业 Loss Making Enterprises	工业总产值（当年价格）Gross Industrial Output Value (At Current Prices)
家具制造业	Manufacture of Furniture			
造纸和纸制品业	Manufacture of Paper and Paper Products			
印刷和记录媒介复制业	Printing,Reproduction of Recording Media	4	1	319827
文教、工美、体育和娱乐用品制造业	Manufacture of Articles For Cultural,Educational and Sports Activities			
石油、炼焦及其他燃料加工业	Processing of Petroleum, Cokeing,Processing of Nuclear and Nuclear Fuel			
化学原料及化学制品制造业	Manufacture of Raw Chemical Materials and Chemical Products	22	2	1169761
医药制造业	Manufacture of Medicines	4	1	69970
化学纤维制造业	Manufacture of Chemical Fibers	2		123226
橡胶和塑料制品业	Manufacture of Rubber and Plastics	5	1	752814
非金属矿物制品业	Manufacture of Non-metallic Mineral Products	14	3	358594
黑色金属冶炼和压延加工业	Smelting and Pressing of Ferrous Metals	2		83916
有色金属冶炼和压延加工业	Smelting and Pressing of Non-ferrous Metals	14	3	783802
金属制品业	Manufacture of Metal Products	13	3	761578
通用设备制造业	Manufacture of General Purpose Machinery	17	2	1124264
专用设备制造业	Manufacture of Special Equipment	29	7	947350
汽车制造业	Manufacture of Motor Vehicle	18	2	10214706
铁路、船舶、航空航天和其他运输设备制造业	Railways,Shipbuilding,Aerospace and Other Transportation Equipment Manufacturing Industry	35	1	5146042
电气机械和器材制造业	Manufacture of Electric Equipment and Machinery	21	7	2897118
计算机、通讯和其他电子设备制造业	Manufacture of Communication Equipment, Computers and other Electronic Equipment	23	3	868710
仪器仪表制造业	Manufacture of Measuring Instruments and Machinery	11	1	934657
其他制造业	Manufacture of Other Manufacturing			
废弃资源综合利用业	Recycling and Disposal of Waste			
金属制品、机械和设备修理业	Metal Products,Machinery and Equipment Repair Industry	2	1	10681
电力、热力的生产和供应业	Production and Supply of Electric Power and Heat Power	13	6	669926
燃气生产和供应业	Gas Mining and Supplying Industry	7	3	1406326
水的生产和供应业	Production and Supply of Water	7	2	141029

continued3

(10 000yuan)

工业销售产值（当年价） Value of Industry Products Sales (At Current Prices)	出口交货值 Export Delivery Value	平均用工人数（人） Average Number of Employed Persons (person)	资产总计 Total Assets	流动资产合计 Total Working Capitals	固定资产原价 Origing Value of Fixed Assets	累计折旧 Accumulative Total Depreciation
314576	1722	3492	453132	280319	350631	225783
1120357	124642	13159	1563269	773809	1074417	591437
68209		1010	90794	52663	48959	15874
129192		520	75146	53168	81986	52618
743865	83583	7448	1789194	1084777	543937	166126
356731	2604	3619	1591274	398368	368751	89381
84225		175	74993	56746	18241	8894
660230	32915	4019	2131842	885934	408018	154210
754502	76038	15834	1687510	1006391	839731	381151
1130423	30158	10992	3235274	2481110	688907	332441
854211	39964	13324	2319682	1534833	658730	269441
10145671	412423	39654	6463218	5207305	1538845	894398
5003097	436126	68902	9594429	5725161	2970833	1380017
2824894	176276	26230	5014114	3490197	1667552	798736
833605	60813	15440	2056572	1221548	553770	242024
881095	5634	9778	1561810	925110	529154	242290
10681		201	33774	14524	4871	2630
669316		8209	1877668	587931	2532964	1454340
1405169		6292	2004832	479260	1457457	476889
141029		3400	512239	271670	379478	217945

12-9 续表4

单位：万元

分 组	Classify	负债合计 Total Liabilites	流动负债合计 Total Working Liabilities	非流动负债合计 Total Non-Working Liabilities
家具制造业	Manufacture of Furniture			
造纸和纸制品业	Manufacture of Paper and Paper Products			
印刷和记录媒介复制业	Printing,Reproduction of Recording Media	121387	116347	5040
文教、工美、体育和娱乐用品制造业	Manufacture of Articles For Cultural,Educational and Sports Activities			
石油、炼焦及其他燃料加工业	Processing of Petroleum, Cokeing,Processing of Nuclear and Nuclear Fuel			
化学原料及化学制品制造业	Manufacture of Raw Chemical Materials and Chemical Products	1089929	856307	233622
医药制造业	Manufacture of Medicines	37133	37047	86
化学纤维制造业	Manufacture of Chemical Fibers	10139	9909	230
橡胶和塑料制品业	Manufacture of Rubber and Plastics	1248949	1011206	237743
非金属矿物制品业	Manufacture of Non-metallic Mineral Products	1281578	1138143	143435
黑色金属冶炼和压延加工业	Smelting and Pressing of Ferrous Metals	51060	48686	2374
有色金属冶炼和压延加工业	Smelting and Pressing of Non-ferrous Metals	510107	389769	120338
金属制品业	Manufacture of Metal Products	1109064	762776	346288
通用设备制造业	Manufacture of General Purpose Machinery	1904117	1790254	113863
专用设备制造业	Manufacture of Special Equipment	1048529	940086	108442
汽车制造业	Manufacture of Motor Vehicle	4082624	3939994	142630
铁路、船舶、航空航天和其他运输设备制造业	Railways,Shipbuilding,Aerospace and Other Transportation Equipment Manufacturing Industry	5776551	4760181	1016370
电气机械和器材制造业	Manufacture of Electric Equipment and Machinery	2125144	1897069	228074
计算机、通讯和其他电子设备制造业	Manufacture of Communication Equipment, Computers and other Electronic Equipment	1448571	1109962	338608
仪器仪表制造业	Manufacture of Measuring Instruments and Machinery	810879	731306	79572
其他制造业	Manufacture of Other Manufacturing			
废弃资源综合利用业	Recycling and Disposal of Waste			
金属制品、机械和设备修理业	Metal Products,Machinery and Equipment Repair Industry	6674	6417	257
电力、热力的生产和供应业	Production and Supply of Electric Power and Heat Power	1606830	1077739	529091
燃气生产和供应业	Gas Mining and Supplying Industry	1174717	1036996	137721
水的生产和供应业	Production and Supply of Water	347879	190324	157555

continued4

(10 000yuan)

所有者权益合计 Total Owners' Equities	实收资本 Total Capital Hold	营业收入 Total Revenue	主营业务收入 Revenue from Principal Business	营业成本 Total Cost	主营业务成本 Cost of Principal Business	税金及附加 Taxs and Other Changes	主营业务税金及附加 Taxes and Other Charges on Principal Business
331745	170362	324467	322243	233403	232858	3572	3561
473341	314784	1190265	1166570	905580	888121	65679	65652
53662	11078	68286	68209	42302	42299	712	712
65007	64052	124729	124729	105393	105393	766	766
540245	397461	774433	755034	668510	651423	3486	2429
309695	317753	578616	573748	549167	545232	1926	1715
23933	15500	362235	362234	354103	354103	638	638
1621735	448383	619649	599570	529205	526381	4012	4012
578447	324327	812926	802285	662759	657497	3909	3760
1331157	136752	1122236	1075765	941462	898950	8099	8099
1271153	557084	945110	935900	797379	793497	7396	6916
2380594	724773	9976187	9666551	9162082	8887535	36959	36171
3817877	1620302	5530212	5418532	4880786	4808449	21864	21358
2888970	812777	2563821	2418986	2452233	1966022	24427	24381
608002	268326	959940	954742	754679	750710	5447	5316
750931	201584	917986	906591	756414	734397	3223	1100
27100	24204	10681	10681	8041	8041	43	43
270838	261822	869668	845538	809784	798303	8967	7906
830115	321437	1467965	1411952	1321843	1288212	6043	6038
164360	62886	156577	139919	125496	116664	2525	2245

12-9 续表5

单位：万元

分组	Classify	销售费用 Expenses for Sales	管理费用 Expenses for Management	财务费用 Financial cost
家具制造业	Manufacture of Furniture			
造纸和纸制品业	Manufacture of Paper and Paper Products			
印刷和记录媒介复制业	Printing,Reproduction of Recording Media	8435	41165	-1034
文教、工美、体育和娱乐用品制造业	Manufacture of Articles For Cultural,Educational and Sports Activities			
石油、炼焦及其他燃料加工业	Processing of Petroleum, Cokeing,Processing of Nuclear and Nuclear Fuel			
化学原料及化学制品制造业	Manufacture of Raw Chemical Materials and Chemical Products	26390	89677	22639
医药制造业	Manufacture of Medicines	8760	6161	26
化学纤维制造业	Manufacture of Chemical Fibers	575	4082	-82
橡胶和塑料制品业	Manufacture of Rubber and Plastics	26443	29283	18557
非金属矿物制品业	Manufacture of Non-metallic Mineral Products	2993	14976	8544
黑色金属冶炼和压延加工业	Smelting and Pressing of Ferrous Metals	790	1455	1302
有色金属冶炼和压延加工业	Smelting and Pressing of Non-ferrous Metals	5117	52094	2172
金属制品业	Manufacture of Metal Products	16358	92782	11892
通用设备制造业	Manufacture of General Purpose Machinery	33184	95482	3709
专用设备制造业	Manufacture of Special Equipment	35437	82997	6665
汽车制造业	Manufacture of Motor Vehicle	229621	238374	-40814
铁路、船舶、航空航天和其他运输设备制造业	Railways,Shipbuilding,Aerospace and Other Transportation Equipment Manufacturing Industry	63548	323661	30932
电气机械和器材制造业	Manufacture of Electric Equipment and Machinery	135922	253179	9957
计算机、通讯和其他电子设备制造业	Manufacture of Communication Equipment, Computers and other Electronic Equipment	18510	128073	23154
仪器仪表制造业	Manufacture of Measuring Instruments and Machinery	8975	102097	-551
其他制造业	Manufacture of Other Manufacturing			
废弃资源综合利用业	Recycling and Disposal of Waste			
金属制品、机械和设备修理业	Metal Products,Machinery and Equipment Repair Indust	211	2241	-19
电力、热力的生产和供应业	Production and Supply of Electric Power and Heat Power	283	22546	27295
燃气生产和供应业	Gas Mining and Supplying Industry	29547	32264	16537
水的生产和供应业	Production and Supply of Water	5902	14806	3333

continued5

(10 000yuan)

营业利润 Operating Profit	利润总额 Total Profits	亏损企业亏损额 Total Loss of Deficit Enterprises	利税总额 Total Pre-tax Profits	应付职工薪酬 Salary Payable	本年应交增值税 Value Added Tax Payable
39700	39654	493	63851	66307	20625
89567	84951	5024	196882	121749	46252
10182	10302	96	14564	9169	3550
14068	14163		19918	6171	4989
27128	29827	863	45160	57032	11846
-564	1215	8640	9417	25742	6277
3126	3101		4861	2119	1122
37286	38134	9156	60040	65303	17894
26509	30986	6476	48578	174133	13682
68086	70144	1051	110052	140822	31808
13137	18980	22209	53841	157676	27466
372954	377012	3122	550602	1056091	136631
285173	288682	5693	376498	987072	65951
80305	103509	5240	194832	383888	66897
34646	36127	7470	60038	146671	18463
61841	63526	1381	75630	157386	8881
375	409	330	626	2255	174
5761	1056	31488	32063	102876	22040
80043	80242	3938	104576	93277	18290
4769	5442	563	12286	43281	4319

12-10 规模以上外商及港澳台商投资工业企业主要经济指标（2018年）

单位：万元

分 组	Classify	企业单位数（个）Number of Enterprises (unit)	亏损企业 Loss Making Enterprises	工业总产值（当年价格）Gross Industrial Output Value (At Current Prices)
总计	**Total**	**109**	**17**	**12678426**
#亏损企业	Deficit Enterprises	17	17	840033
按登记注册类型分组	**Grouped by Type of Registration**			
港澳台商投资	Enterprises with Funds from Hong Kong, Macao &Taiwan	21	2	3430578
与港澳台商合资经营	Cooperative Enterprises	12	1	2989660
与港澳台商合作经营	Joint-venture Enterprises	1		2360
港澳台商独资	Enterprises with Sole Investment	7		426325
港澳台商投资股份有限公司	Share-holding Corporations Ltd. With their Investment			
其他港澳台投资	Other	1	1	12232
外商投资	Foreign Funded Enterprises	88	15	9247848
中外合资经营	Joint-venture Enterprises	48	9	2640149
中外合作经营	Cooperation Enterprises			
外资企业	Foreign Funded Enterprises	38	6	5706467
外商投资股份有限公司	Share-holding Corporations Ltd. With Foreign Funds	1		893918
其他外商投资	Other	1		7315
按轻重工业分	**Grouped by Light Industry and Heavy Industry**			
轻工业	Light Industry	27	5	3084513
重工业	Heavy Industry	82	12	9593913
按企业规模分	**Grouped by Size of Enterprises**			
大型企业	Large-size	11	1	8782251
中型企业	Medium-size	29	3	2094515
小型企业	Small-size	69	13	1801660
按工业行业大类分	**Grouped by Sector**			
煤炭开采和洗选业	Mining and Washing of Coal			
石油和天然气开采业	Extraction of Petroleum and Natural Gas			
黑色金属矿采选业	Mining and Processing of Ferrous Metal Ores			
有色金属矿采选业	Mining and Processing of Non-ferrous Metal Ores			
非金属矿采选业	Mining and Processing of Nonmetal Ores			
开采专业及辅助性活动	Mining Professional and Auxiliary Activity			
其他采矿业	Mining of Other Ores			

Major Economic Indicators of Foreign,Hong Kong,Macao and Taiwan Invested Industrial Enterprises above Designated Size（2018）

(10 000 yuan)

工业销售产值（当年价）Value of Industry Products Sales (At Current Prices)	出口交货值 Export Delivery Value	平均用工人数（人）Average Number of Employed Persons (person)	资产总计 Total Assets	流动资产合计 Total Working Capitals	固定资产原价 Origing Value of Fixed Assets	累计折旧 Accumulative Total Depreciation
11427231	**3936421**	**75969**	**15717323**	**7640378**	**11671870**	**6698348**
745831	371753	5347	952130	481315	567783	194467
3368642	272563	33629	2974663	1753224	1065535	457895
2921217	46605	30605	2749624	1632872	913782	374620
2189		73	26066	2381	943	718
433945	225958	2695	185925	100677	129225	70278
11291		256	36508	17294	21584	12279
8058590	3663858	42340	12742660	5887154	10606336	6240454
2491148	630604	19411	3522956	1927457	1668704	624783
4845394	3032226	19893	8573003	3576276	8811863	5543327
715010	15	2950	622635	367390	116254	70389
7038	1014	86	24066	16031	9515	1954
2840004	610731	17383	2982151	1412703	1543688	608308
8587227	3325690	58586	12735172	6227675	10128182	6090041
7570111	2877206	50273	11851847	5278026	9755260	5846871
1975366	615980	17106	2151669	1395426	1061895	446243
1881755	443235	8590	1713806	966926	854716	405235

12-10 续表1

单位：万元

分 组	Classify	负债合计 Total Liabilites	流动负债合计 Total Working Liabilities	非流动负债合计 Total Non-Working Liabilities
总计	**Total**	**6965052**	**5336315**	**1610750**
#亏损企业	Deficit Enterprises	741578	590114	151464
按登记注册类型分组	**Grouped by Type of Registration**			
港澳台商投资	Enterprises with Funds from Hong Kong, Macao &Taiwan	2063508	1929192	134316
与港澳台商合资经营	Cooperative Enterprises	1964004	1850983	113021
与港澳台商合作经营	Joint-venture Enterprises	150	150	
港澳台商独资	Enterprises with Sole Investment	90795	69501	21295
港澳台商投资股份有限公司	Share-holding Corporations Ltd. With their Investment			
其他港澳台投资	Other	8558	8558	
外商投资	Foreign Funded Enterprises	4901545	3407122	1476435
中外合资经营	Joint-venture Enterprises	2200660	1853879	346781
中外合作经营	Cooperation Enterprises			
外资企业	Foreign Funded Enterprises	2318020	1217672	1082360
外商投资股份有限公司	Share-holding Corporations Ltd. With Foreign Funds	373868	326575	47294
其他外商投资	Other	8996	8996	
按轻重工业分	**Grouped by Light Industry and Heavy Industry**			
轻工业	Light Industry	2057834	1598035	441811
重工业	Heavy Industry	4907219	3738280	1168939
按企业规模分	**Grouped by Size of Enterprises**			
大型企业	Large-size	4899474	3599149	1300325
中型企业	Medium-size	1239704	1041109	198595
小型企业	Small-size	825875	696056	111831
按工业行业大类分	**Grouped by Sector**			
煤炭开采和洗选业	Mining and Washing of Coal			
石油和天然气开采业	Extraction of Petroleum and Natural Gas			
黑色金属矿采选业	Mining and Processing of Ferrous Metal Ores			
有色金属矿采选业	Mining and Processing of Non-ferrous Metal Ores			
非金属矿采选业	Mining and Processing of Nonmetal Ores			
开采专业及辅助性活动	Mining Professional and Auxiliary Activity			
其他采矿业	Mining of Other Ores			

continued 1

(10 000 yuan)

所有者权益合计 Total Owners' Equities	实收资本 Total Capital Hold	营业收入 Total Revenue	主营业务收入 Revenue from Principal Business	营业成本 Total Cost	主营业务收入 Cost of Principal Business	税金及附加 Taxs and Other Changes	主营业务税金及附加 Taxes and Other Charges on Principal Business
8752271	**4392088**	**11221160**	**10992851**	**9939689**	**9756921**	**103959**	**103824**
210553	391985	735036	731033	668479	664913	2762	2714
911155	257232	3117762	3003295	3362329	3263669	54328	54328
785620	173226	2648689	2539450	2966666	2872435	52780	52780
2456	714	2189	2179	1836	1832	18	18
95130	54395	456911	451692	384252	379828	1326	1326
27950	28897	9973	9973	9576	9576	204	204
7841115	4134856	8103397	7989556	6577359	6493251	49631	49496
1322296	713712	2571583	2474142	2136613	2065868	13637	13544
6254983	3390218	4743222	4726822	3930525	3917163	30610	30568
248766	28432	781554	781554	506413	506413	5381	5381
15070	2495	7038	7038	3808	3808	4	4
924317	435886	2926959	2906091	2274293	2256623	20392	20351
7827954	3956202	8294201	8086760	7665395	7500298	83567	83473
6952374	3219942	7401602	7226239	6759396	6620924	82458	82458
911966	544117	1967096	1944192	1619807	1601289	9538	9513
887931	628029	1852462	1822420	1560486	1534708	11963	11853

12-10 续表2

单位：万元

分　组	Classify	销售费用 Expenses for Sales	管理费用 Expenses for Management	财务费用 Financial cost
总计	**Total**	**504384**	**651007**	**40258**
#亏损企业	Deficit Enterprises	73313	37419	27136
按登记注册类型分组	**Grouped by Type of Registration**			
港澳台商投资	Enterprises with Funds from Hong Kong, Macao &Taiwan	82135	107993	21222
与港澳台商合资经营	Cooperative Enterprises	44191	95395	19672
与港澳台商合作经营	Joint-venture Enterprises	130	215	-17
港澳台商独资	Enterprises with Sole Investment	37235	11283	897
港澳台商投资股份有限公司	Share-holding Corporations Ltd. With their Investment			
其他港澳台投资	Other	578	1100	670
外商投资	Foreign Funded Enterprises	422250	543013	19036
中外合资经营	Joint-venture Enterprises	168287	136198	35073
中外合作经营	Cooperation Enterprises			
外资企业	Foreign Funded Enterprises	119760	323264	-24234
外商投资股份有限公司	Share-holding Corporations Ltd. With Foreign Funds	134204	82269	8129
其他外商投资	Other		1282	68
按轻重工业分	**Grouped by Light Industry and Heavy Industry**			
轻工业	Light Industry	358726	167946	47325
重工业	Heavy Industry	145658	483060	-7067
按企业规模分	**Grouped by Size of Enterprises**			
大型企业	Large-size	307221	469631	6966
中型企业	Medium-size	124445	104241	21778
小型企业	Small-size	72718	77135	11514
按工业行业大类分	**Grouped by Sector**			
煤炭开采和洗选业	Mining and Washing of Coal			
石油和天然气开采业	Extraction of Petroleum and Natural Gas			
黑色金属矿采选业	Mining and Processing of Ferrous Metal Ores			
有色金属矿采选业	Mining and Processing of Non-ferrous Metal Ores			
非金属矿采选业	Mining and Processing of Nonmetal Ores			
开采专业及辅助性活动	Mining Professional and Auxiliary Activity			
其他采矿业	Mining of Other Ores			

continued 2

(10 000 yuan)

营业利润 Operating Profit	利润总额 Total Profits	亏损企业亏损额 Total Loss of Deficit Enterprises	利税总额 Total Pre-tax Profits	应付职工薪酬 Salary Payable	本年应交增值税 Value Added Tax Payable
1356761	**1389222**	**51800**	**1723840**	**986937**	**230660**
-52443	-51800	51800	-40882	76733	8157
161648	165559	2155	229250	298616	9363
141997	145289	111	201305	256726	3237
8	8		171	478	146
21799	22306		29145	38671	5512
-2155	-2044	2044	-1371	2741	469
1195113	1223663	49645	1494591	688321	221297
133917	157175	40467	226714	247576	55902
1019535	1025507	9178	1095561	322928	39444
39772	39060		170254	117199	125813
1888	1920		2061	618	137
75319	96633	35435	292009	312678	174984
1281442	1292589	16365	1431831	674260	55676
1123285	1145433	228	1382870	670149	154979
113822	116758	37305	167415	209282	41118
119654	127031	14267	173555	107506	34563

12-10 续表3

单位：万元

分 组	Classify	企业单位数（个） Number of Enterprises (unit)	亏损企业 Loss Making Enterprises	工业总产值（当年价格） Gross Industrial Output Value (At Current Prices)
农副食品加工业	Processing of Food from Agricultural Porducts			
食品制造业	Manufacture of Foods	7	2	689134
酒、饮料和精制茶制造业	Manufacture of Alcohol,Beverages and Tea	7	1	575127
烟草制品业	Manufacture of Tobacco			
纺织业	Manufacture of Textile			
纺织服装、服饰业	Textile, apparel industry			
皮革、毛皮、羽毛及其制品和制鞋业	Leather fur feathers and its products and footwear			
木材加工和木、竹、藤、棕、草制品业	Processing of Timber,Manufacture of Wood,Plam and Straw Products			
家具制造业	Manufacture of Furniture			
造纸和纸制品业	Manufacture of Paper and Paper Products	2		112977
印刷和记录媒介复制业	Printing,Reproduction of Recording Media	1		3505
文教、工美、体育和娱乐用品制造业	Manufacture of Articles For Cultural,Educational and Sports Activities	1		142216
石油、炼焦及其他燃料加工业	Processing of Petroleum, Cokeing,Processing of Nuclear and Nuclear Fuel	1		7258
化学原料和化学制品制造业	Manufacture of Raw Chemical Materials and Chemical Products	8		159918
医药制造业	Manufacture of Medicines	4		963609
化学纤维制造业	Manufacture of Chemical Fibers	2		126611
橡胶和塑料制品业	Manufacture of Rubber and Plastics	1	1	1685
非金属矿物制品业	Manufacture of Non-metallic Mineral Products	6	1	191209
黑色金属冶炼和压延加工业	Smelting and Pressing of Ferrous Metals	1		3269
有色金属冶炼和压延加工业	Smelting and Pressing of Non-ferrous Metals	4	2	138515
金属制品业	Manufacture of Metal Products	4	1	55840
通用设备制造业	Manufacture of General Purpose Machinery	7	2	155329
专用设备制造业	Manufacture of Special Equipment	8		229301
汽车制造业	Manufacture of Motor Vehicle	10		3294347
铁路、船舶、航空航天和其他运输设备制造业	Railways,Shipbuilding,Aerospace and Other Transportation Equipment Manufacturing Industry	9	1	196950
电气机械和器材制造业	Manufacture of Electric Equipment and Machinery	9	4	851078
计算机、通讯和其他电子设备制造业	Manufacture of Communication Equipment, Computers and other Electronic Equipment	11	1	4296451
仪器仪表制造业	Manufacture of Measuring Instruments and Machinery	3		112991
其他制造业	Manufacture of Other Manufacturing	1		2360
废弃资源综合利用业	Recycling and Disposal of Waste			
金属制品、机械和设备修理业	Metal Products,Machinery and Equipment Repair Industry	1	1	6397
电力、热力的生产和供应业	Production and Supply of Electric Power and Heat Power			
燃气生产和供应业	Gas Mining and Supplying Industry	1		362349
水的生产和供应业	Production and Supply of Water			

continued 3

(10 000 yuan)

工业销售产值（当年价） Value of Industry Products Sales (At Current Prices)	出口交货值 Export Delivery Value	平均用工人数（人） Average Number of Employed Persons (person)	资产总计 Total Assets	流动资产合计 Total Working Capitals	固定资产原价 Origing Value of Fixed Assets	累计折旧 Accumulative Total Depreciation
671744		4969	351360	153116	219740	89532
588745	124574	5176	981338	383479	615097	259667
109086		281	37064	10479	19948	7005
3505		29	3033	2628	364	75
142216	142216	144	358	62	381	157
7258		2310	45796	15897	45796	2478
158148	58538	434	351032	113652	219328	89516
794979	504	5227	850393	464136	201946	104054
135783		394	137676	71452	135146	71502
1517		165	5993	2308	2202	1414
189053		1316	270201	166308	174476	94181
3269		10	4123	4088	61	29
137167	111352	435	61726	34497	26595	9165
54915	4283	771	64167	28416	55435	23355
146670	18054	1474	173674	123311	83466	53867
348738	48524	1933	276708	208196	97181	48754
3219367	50516	32109	2986720	1776950	1015358	407194
189645	38360	1741	284538	247557	58147	40911
721756	373079	2986	920841	566614	411251	116931
3321153	2918862	10381	7114736	2889460	7962474	5174220
111582	41162	808	159347	145857	32645	21064
2189		73	2606	2381	943	718
6397	6397	72	11779	7232	3721	1313
362349		2731	622118	222304	290168	81245

12-10 续表4

单位：万元

分组	Classify	负债合计 Total Liabilites	流动负债合计 Total Working Liabilities	非流动负债合计 Total Non-Working Liabilities
农副食品加工业	Processing of Food from Agricultural Porducts			
食品制造业	Manufacture of Foods	215867	187826	28041
酒、饮料和精制茶制造业	Manufacture of Alcohol,Beverages and Tea	638073	475893	144192
烟草制品业	Manufacture of Tobacco			
纺织业	Manufacture of Textile			
纺织服装、服饰业	Textile, apparel industry			
皮革、毛皮、羽毛及其制品和制鞋业	Leather fur feathers and its products and footwear			
木材加工和木、竹、藤、棕、草制品业	Processing of Timber,Manufacture of Wood,Plam and Straw Products			
家具制造业	Manufacture of Furniture			
造纸和纸制品业	Manufacture of Paper and Paper Products	23494	23494	
印刷和记录媒介复制业	Printing,Reproduction of Recording Media	1687	1687	
文教、工美、体育和娱乐用品制造业	Manufacture of Articles For Cultural,Educational and Sports Activities	269	269	
石油、炼焦及其他燃料加工业	Processing of Petroleum, Cokeing,Processing of Nuclear and Nuclear Fuel	27385	15897	11488
化学原料和化学制品制造业	Manufacture of Raw Chemical Materials and Chemical Products	153919	99069	54850
医药制造业	Manufacture of Medicines	520003	404145	115857
化学纤维制造业	Manufacture of Chemical Fibers	84627	64738	19889
橡胶和塑料制品业	Manufacture of Rubber and Plastics	4206	4018	187
非金属矿物制品业	Manufacture of Non-metallic Mineral Products	165166	137203	27963
黑色金属冶炼和压延加工业	Smelting and Pressing of Ferrous Metals	2213	2213	
有色金属冶炼和压延加工业	Smelting and Pressing of Non-ferrous Metals	39459	28336	11122
金属制品业	Manufacture of Metal Products	42361	42287	75
通用设备制造业	Manufacture of General Purpose Machinery	49888	49524	364
专用设备制造业	Manufacture of Special Equipment	86950	81545	5405
汽车制造业	Manufacture of Motor Vehicle	2078778	1953670	125108
铁路、船舶、航空航天和其他运输设备制造业	Railways,Shipbuilding,Aerospace and Other Transportation Equipment Manufacturing Industry	85434	82567	2868
电气机械和器材制造业	Manufacture of Electric Equipment and Machinery	701873	560812	141061
计算机、通讯和其他电子设备制造业	Manufacture of Communication Equipment, Computers and other Electronic Equipment	1505148	595762	909386
仪器仪表制造业	Manufacture of Measuring Instruments and Machinery	59419	58919	500
其他制造业	Manufacture of Other Manufacturing	150	150	
废弃资源综合利用业	Recycling and Disposal of Waste			
金属制品、机械和设备修理业	Metal Products,Machinery and Equipment Repair Industry	2693	2693	
电力、热力的生产和供应业	Production and Supply of Electric Power and Heat Power			
燃气生产和供应业	Gas Mining and Supplying Industry	475991	463598	12393
水的生产和供应业	Production and Supply of Water			

continued 4

(10 000 yuan)

所有者权益合计 Total Owners' Equities	实收资本 Total Capital Hold	营业收入 Total Revenue	主营业务收入 Revenue from Principal Business	营业成本 Total Cost	主营业务收入 Cost of Principal Business	税金及附加 Taxs and Other Changes	主营业务税金及附加 Taxes and Other Charges on Principal Business
135493	82817	640650	637437	517727	514862	3895	3853
343265	84486	632785	617026	460808	447287	8036	8036
13570	6540	107930	107687	104152	103988	112	112
1346	120	3505	3505	2819	2819	17	17
88	176	140193	140193	139450	139450	1	1
18412	3300	4579	4287	3698	3452	238	212
197113	172642	183895	183152	153616	153485	570	570
330390	76747	853140	852680	538675	538507	6932	6932
53049	45800	135076	135076	111317	111317	878	878
1787	1030	2908	2908	2191	2191	27	27
105035	45255	190015	182881	162485	152908	1374	1374
1909	1266	3270	3269	2996	2996	2	2
22267	20324	137458	137457	123960	123960	238	238
21805	22137	68814	67161	61178	59856	717	717
123786	93282	161541	160792	143865	143703	839	839
189758	60127	254174	252353	196516	195488	2065	2004
907942	258550	2953204	2828424	3201910	3096430	54603	54603
199104	64608	189903	189617	141134	141111	1632	1632
218968	307887	705184	698889	635114	629910	1851	1851
5609588	2910975	3325085	3316605	2792600	2785249	17320	17320
99928	14538	112871	112323	67477	67477	1192	1192
2456	714	2189	2179	1836	1832	18	18
9086	18769	9073	6662	8262	5851	6	
146127	100000	403719	350289	365904	332796	1398	1398

12-10 续表5

单位：万元

分 组	Classify	销售费用 Expenses for Sales	管理费用 Expenses for Management	财务费用 Financial cost
农副食品加工业	Processing of Food from Agricultural Porducts			
食品制造业	Manufacture of Foods	63576	19483	20
酒、饮料和精制茶制造业	Manufacture of Alcohol,Beverages and Tea	106733	34480	11584
烟草制品业	Manufacture of Tobacco			
纺织业	Manufacture of Textile			
纺织服装、服饰业	Textile, apparel industry			
皮革、毛皮、羽毛及其制品和制鞋业	Leather fur feathers and its products and footwear			
木材加工和木、竹、藤、棕、草制品业	Processing of Timber,Manufacture of Wood,Plam and Straw Products			
家具制造业	Manufacture of Furniture			
造纸和纸制品业	Manufacture of Paper and Paper Products	1189	1051	978
印刷和记录媒介复制业	Printing,Reproduction of Recording Media	262	60	8
文教、工美、体育和娱乐用品制造业	Manufacture of Articles For Cultural,Educational and Sports Activities		416	-7
石油、炼焦及其他燃料加工业	Processing of Petroleum, Cokeing,Processing of Nuclear and Nuclear Fuel	70	76	31
化学原料和化学制品制造业	Manufacture of Raw Chemical Materials and Chemical Products	4384	8162	3095
医药制造业	Manufacture of Medicines	152935	95636	9843
化学纤维制造业	Manufacture of Chemical Fibers	1007	4730	2234
橡胶和塑料制品业	Manufacture of Rubber and Plastics	172	436	121
非金属矿物制品业	Manufacture of Non-metallic Mineral Products	1350	7104	526
黑色金属冶炼和压延加工业	Smelting and Pressing of Ferrous Metals	71	107	66
有色金属冶炼和压延加工业	Smelting and Pressing of Non-ferrous Metals	1796	4191	1432
金属制品业	Manufacture of Metal Products	857	4691	973
通用设备制造业	Manufacture of General Purpose Machinery	7239	7567	513
专用设备制造业	Manufacture of Special Equipment	9292	19189	-913
汽车制造业	Manufacture of Motor Vehicle	68121	111302	21332
铁路、船舶、航空航天和其他运输设备制造业	Railways,Shipbuilding,Aerospace and Other Transportation Equipment Manufacturing Industry	6166	17800	1686
电气机械和器材制造业	Manufacture of Electric Equipment and Machinery	48757	34620	23598
计算机、通讯和其他电子设备制造业	Manufacture of Communication Equipment, Computers and other Electronic Equipment	6631	256125	-34474
仪器仪表制造业	Manufacture of Measuring Instruments and Machinery	6675	5817	-1189
其他制造业	Manufacture of Other Manufacturing	130	215	-17
废弃资源综合利用业	Recycling and Disposal of Waste			
金属制品、机械和设备修理业	Metal Products,Machinery and Equipment Repair Industry		1515	-232
电力、热力的生产和供应业	Production and Supply of Electric Power and Heat Power			
燃气生产和供应业	Gas Mining and Supplying Industry	16972	16237	-951
水的生产和供应业	Production and Supply of Water			

continued 5

(10 000 yuan)

营业利润 Operating Profit	利润总额 Total Profits	亏损企业亏损额 Total Loss of Deficit Enterprises	利税总额 Total Pre-tax Profits	应付职工薪酬 Salary Payable	本年应交增值税 Value Added Tax Payable
37076	37196	264	59837	73964	18747
10775	30699	111	56205	80674	17471
2251	3677		4683	4444	894
340	340		490	145	134
333	392		392	4507	
466	425		735	21031	72
14290	14404		14333	9942	-642
44805	44177		182933	131231	131824
12231	12287		18072	4853	4907
-39	-69	69	67	187	110
18770	21622	1940	33042	8652	10046
28	27		30	58	
5614	5471	2425	9867	3931	4158
386	359	2364	2594	7411	1519
1780	3844	4023	7006	17139	2324
31401	31328		38004	24130	4611
167164	172163		237469	273719	10703
22861	22981	499	29636	28152	5023
-17225	-16218	39562	-6180	47079	8187
938528	938613	210	956307	195393	374
32897	33376		38450	11308	3883
8	8		171	478	146
-380	-331	331	-325	1143	
32404	32455		40025	37367	6172

12-11 规模以上大中型工业企业主要经济指标（2018年）

单位：万元

分 组	Classify	企业单位数（个） Number of Enterprises (unit)	亏损企业 Loss Making Enterprises	工业总产值（当年价格） Gross Industrial Output Value (At Current Prices)
总计	**Total**	**238**	**29**	**46908234**
#亏损企业	Deficit Enterprises	29	29	1982054
按隶属关系分	**Grouped by Jurisdiction of Management**			
#中央企业	Central Enterprises	59	3	11425329
地方企业	Local Enterprises	179	26	35482906
按登记注册类型分组	**Grouped by Registion Status**			
内资企业	Domestic Investment Enterprises	198	25	36031469
国有	State-owned Enterprises	19	1	3189463
集体	Collective-owned Enterprises			
股份合作	Share-holding Corperative			
联营	Joint Ownership Enterprises			
有限责任公司	Limited Liability Corporations	122	19	24580663
股份有限公司	Share-holding Corperation Ltd.	34	4	4749017
私营	Private Enterprises	23	1	3512325
其他	Other Domestic Funded Enterprises			
港澳台商投资	Enterprises with Funds from Hong Kong,Macao and Taiwan	7		3177920
外商投资	Foreign Funded Enterprises	33	4	7698846
按轻重工业分	**Grouped by Light Industry and Heavy Industry**			
轻工业	Light Industry	60	6	6020445
重工业	Heavy Industry	178	23	40887790
按企业规模分	**Grouped by Size of Enterprises**			
大型企业	Large-size	63	7	35696721
中型企业	Medium-size	175	22	11211514

Major Economic Indicators of Large and Medium-sized Industrial Enterprises above Designated Size（2018）

(10 000 yuan)

工业销售产值（当年价）Value of Industry Products Sales (At Current Prices)	出口交货值 Export Delivery Value	平均用工人数（人）Average Number of Employed Persons (person)	资产总计 Total Assets	流动资产合计 Total Working Capitals	固定资产原价 Origing Value of Fixed Assets	累计折旧 Accumulative Total Depreciation
45016390	**5739037**	**387645**	**65532778**	**38164695**	**32572556**	**16135676**
1845676	439690	28333	4720948	2092027	2686706	1349258
11128152	763787	152544	21779857	13211257	9384385	4735516
33888238	4975251	235101	43752920	24953439	23188171	11400160
35470914	2245852	320266	51529261	31491243	21755402	9842563
3079614	150797	50190	7158961	4299626	2799487	1352579
24124801	1401948	215266	33120365	21153980	12390773	6018494
4633771	428623	35200	8493249	4054170	5802764	2190674
3632728	264484	19610	2756686	1983467	762377	280816
3117505	113297	32221	2804625	1632900	1002165	425552
6427971	3379889	35158	11198892	5040552	9814990	5867562
5730754	477210	54706	7015422	4084729	2981025	1280375
39285637	5261828	332939	58517356	34079967	29591531	14855301
34213513	4869920	286685	49342953	28897087	26781287	13814943
10802877	869118	100960	16189825	9267608	5791269	2320733

12-11 续表1

单位：万元

分 组	Classify	负债合计 Total Liabilites	流动负债合计 Total Working Liabilities	非流动负债合计 Total Non-Working Liabilities
总计	**Total**	**35523581**	**29471335**	**6052245**
#亏损企业	Deficit Enterprises	3737660	3034664	702997
按隶属关系分	**Grouped by Jurisdiction of Management**			
#中央企业	Central Enterprises	11868988	9672540	2196447
地方企业	Local Enterprises	23654593	19798795	3855798
按登记注册类型分组	**Grouped by Registion Status**			
内资企业	Domestic Investment Enterprises	29384404	24831077	4553325
国有	State-owned Enterprises	4343830	3204289	1139541
集体	Collective-owned Enterprises			
股份合作	Share-holding Corperative			
联营	Joint Ownership Enterprises			
有限责任公司	Limited Liability Corporations	19745858	17370745	2375113
股份有限公司	Share-holding Corperation Ltd.	3612515	2695578	916936
私营	Private Enterprises	1682201	1560466	121735
其他	Other Domestic Funded Enterprises			
港澳台商投资	Enterprises with Funds from Hong Kong,Macao and Taiwan	1983847	1850039	133808
外商投资	Foreign Funded Enterprises	4155331	2790219	1365111
按轻重工业分	**Grouped by Light Industry and Heavy Industry**			
轻工业	Light Industry	4456408	3474844	981565
重工业	Heavy Industry	31067173	25996492	5070680
按企业规模分	**Grouped by Size of Enterprises**			
大型企业	Large-size	26078155	21505757	4572398
中型企业	Medium-size	9445426	7965578	1479847

continued 1

(10 000 yuan)

所有者权益合计 Total Owners' Equities	实收资本 Total Capital Hold	营业收入 Total Revenue	主营业务收入 Revenue from Principal Business	营业成本 Total Cost	主营业务成本 Cost of Principal Business	税金及附加 Taxs and Other Changes	主营业务税金及附加 Taxes and Other Charges on Principal Business
30009196	**11554117**	**45114563**	**44033876**	**39537796**	**38303281**	**284122**	**276901**
983287	1232819	2062993	2033590	1852843	1835410	14334	14022
9910870	3654572	11538122	11208028	10104929	9489264	72689	70429
20098326	7899545	33576441	32825848	29432867	28814016	211433	206472
22144856	7790057	35745865	34863445	31158593	30081068	192126	184931
2815131	732894	3332541	3260432	2712738	2653730	16573	13756
13374506	5469948	25062324	24281210	22168239	21166099	142912	138764
4880734	1226903	4032836	4007639	3426238	3411361	21372	21198
1074485	360313	3318164	3314164	2851378	2849878	11269	11213
820778	188370	2856351	2742560	3120236	3021998	53581	53581
7043561	3575690	6512347	6427871	5258967	5200215	38415	38390
2559014	1020110	5865050	5800579	4295878	4243518	48559	46485
27450182	10534007	39249513	38233296	35241918	34059763	235563	230416
23264798	8655639	33814306	32931825	30312327	29237366	220385	216209
6744398	2898477	11300257	11102050	9225469	9065914	63737	60692

12-11 续表2

单位：万元

分　组	Classify	销售费用 Expenses for Sales	管理费用 Expenses for Management	财务费用 Financial cost
总计	**Total**	**1690254**	**2446666**	**159692**
#亏损企业	Deficit Enterprises	120949	124362	75272
按隶属关系分	**Grouped by Jurisdiction of Management**			
#中央企业	Central Enterprises	261618	915972	74288
地方企业	Local Enterprises	1428636	1530694	85404
按登记注册类型分组	**Grouped by Registion Status**			
内资企业	Domestic Investment Enterprises	1258588	1872794	130948
国有	State-owned Enterprises	48935	313755	37076
集体	Collective-owned Enterprises			
股份合作	Share-holding Corperative			
联营	Joint Ownership Enterprises			
有限责任公司	Limited Liability Corporations	905048	1214406	59162
股份有限公司	Share-holding Corperation Ltd.	170551	225478	36854
私营	Private Enterprises	134054	119154	-2144
其他	Other Domestic Funded Enterprises			
港澳台商投资	Enterprises with Funds from Hong Kong,Macao and Taiwan	78530	101340	18810
外商投资	Foreign Funded Enterprises	353136	472532	9934
按轻重工业分	**Grouped by Light Industry and Heavy Industry**			
轻工业	Light Industry	830011	363864	64116
重工业	Heavy Industry	860243	2082802	95576
按企业规模分	**Grouped by Size of Enterprises**			
大型企业	Large-size	1004442	1808999	57248
中型企业	Medium-size	685812	637667	102444

continued 2

(10 000 yuan)

营业利润 Operating Profit	利润总额 Total Profits	亏损企业亏损额 Total Loss of Deficit Enterprises	利税总额 Total Pre-tax Profits	应付职工薪酬 Salary Payable	本年应交增值税 Value Added Tax Payable
3016303	**3085810**	**117474**	**4222561**	**5525093**	**852629**
-109671	-117474	117474	-63326	267479	39813
547776	577577	10261	850152	2202612	199886
2468527	2508234	107212	3372409	3322481	652742
1779196	1823619	79941	2672277	4645663	656531
216098	222357	5300	301672	634727	62741
1090338	1121623	63634	1726689	3328804	462154
292049	298140	10904	393625	434052	74113
180711	181499	102	250291	248080	57523
155797	158936		219580	284879	7063
1081310	1103255	37533	1330705	594552	189035
295380	324653	52759	694491	690489	321279
2720923	2761157	64715	3528070	4834604	531350
2365964	2418523	28022	3182766	4375255	543859
650340	667288	89452	1039795	1149838	308770

12-11 续表3

单位：万元

分组	Classify	企业单位数（个） Number of Enterprises (unit)	亏损企业 Loss Making Enterprises	工业总产值（当年价格） Gross Industrial Output Value (At Current Prices)
按控股情况分	**Grouped by Cast strand**			
国有控股	State owned shares	127	16	27063000
集体控股	Collective shares	3		275202
私人控股	Private holdings	74	7	11967191
港澳台控股	Hong Kong and Macao Holdings	4		270270
外商投资	Foreign Investment	23	4	6767995
其他	Others	7	2	564577
按工业行业大类分	**Grouped by Sector**			
煤炭开采和洗选业	Mining and Washing of Coal			
石油和天然气开采业	Extraction of Petroleum and Natural Gas			
黑色金属矿采选业	Mining and Processing of Ferrous Metal Ores			
有色金属矿采选业	Mining and Processing of Non-ferrous Metal Ores			
非金属矿采选业	Mining and Processing of Nonmetal Ores			
开采专业及辅助性活动	Mining Professional and Auxiliary Activity	2		836898
其他采矿业	Mining of other Ores			
农副食品加工业	Processing of Food from Agricultural Porducts	7		673651
食品制造业	Manufacture of Foods	14	2	981177
酒、饮料和精制茶制造业	Manufacture of Alcohol,Beverages and Tea	6		567638
烟草制品业	Manufacture of Tobacco	1		7463
纺织业	Manufacture of Textile	2	1	82815
纺织服装、服饰业	Textile, apparel industry	1		36184
皮革、毛皮、羽毛及其制品和制鞋业	Manufacture of Leather, Fur, Feather and Related Products, and Shoes	1		32652
木材加工和木、竹、藤、棕、草制品业	Processing of Timber, Manufacture of Wood,Plam and Straw Products			
家具制造业	Manufacture of Furniture	1		17695
造纸和纸制品业	Manufacture of Paper and Paper Products	1	1	7071
印刷和记录媒介复制业	Printing,Reproduction of Recording Media	7		516544

continued 3

(10 000 yuan)

工业销售产值（当年价）Value of Industry Products Sales (At Current Prices)	出口交货值 Export Delivery Value	平均用工人数（人）Average Number of Employed Persons (person)	资产总计 Total Assets	流动资产合计 Total Working Capitals	固定资产原价 Origing Value of Fixed Assets	累计折旧 Accumulative Total Depreciation
26687876	1391884	256307	42270680	25605501	16452991	8072551
222516	71427	1428	233595	180086	61979	33572
11738027	742251	91656	12158076	7547215	6224395	2162260
277896	73178	2513	171999	91186	123110	67532
5549445	3298591	28555	10059007	4428115	9333729	5683435
540631	161706	7186	639421	312594	376352	116327
836816		13441	1219137	903104	696889	476775
626928	1229	3622	619780	432059	219399	105403
934801		11162	523741	245793	334432	145929
737207	124574	6302	1128281	532581	626416	284971
7463		475	40826	23556	32030	14861
81420	2507	5554	227503	60994	210069	69470
30749		1065	67056	54495	11677	2659
45422	2292	694	55680	34617	8599	4653
17118		471	20974	5834	8825	3365
7071		325	13456	9426	1188	543
501710	1722	4720	511066	305834	369566	238397

12-11 续表4

单位：万元

分　组	Classify	负债合计 Total Liabilites	流动负债合计 Total Working Liabilities	非流动负债合计 Total Non-Working Liabilities
按控股情况分	**Grouped by Cast strand**			
国有控股	State owned shares	24343353	20767045	3576308
集体控股	Collective shares	118161	108068	10093
私人控股	Private holdings	7220189	6157282	1062907
港澳台控股	Hong Kong and Macao Holdings	84750	63456	21295
外商投资	Foreign Investment	3434513	2095144	1339370
其他	Others	322614	280342	42273
按工业行业大类分	**Grouped by Sector**			
煤炭开采和洗选业	Mining and Washing of Coal			
石油和天然气开采业	Extraction of Petroleum and Natural Gas			
黑色金属矿采选业	Mining and Processing of Ferrous Metal Ores			
有色金属矿采选业	Mining and Processing of Non-ferrous Metal Ores			
非金属矿采选业	Mining and Processing of Nonmetal Ores			
开采专业及辅助性活动	Mining Professional and Auxiliary Activity	482085	467273	14813
其他采矿业	Mining of other Ores			
农副食品加工业	Processing of Food from Agricultural Porducts	493172	441845	51327
食品制造业	Manufacture of Foods	277944	246933	31011
酒、饮料和精制茶制造业	Manufacture of Alcohol,Beverages and Tea	687420	542474	144947
烟草制品业	Manufacture of Tobacco	6868	6868	
纺织业	Manufacture of Textile	159545	79078	80467
纺织服装、服饰业	Textile, apparel industry	46627	46327	300
皮革、毛皮、羽毛及其制品和制鞋业	Manufacture of Leather, Fur, Feather and Related Products, and Shoes	22498	15235	7263
木材加工和木、竹、藤、棕、草制品业	Processing of Timber, Manufacture of Wood,Plam and Straw Products			
家具制造业	Manufacture of Furniture	12693	11648	1045
造纸和纸制品业	Manufacture of Paper and Paper Products	8676	7604	1073
印刷和记录媒介复制业	Printing,Reproduction of Recording Media	169209	166126	3083

continued 4

(10 000 yuan)

所有者权益合计 Total Owners' Equities	实收资本 Total Capital Hold	营业收入 Total Revenue	主营业务收入 Revenue from Principal Business	营业成本 Total Cost	主营业务成本 Cost of Principal Business	税金及附加 Taxs and Other Changes	主营业务税金及附加 Taxes and Other Charges on Principal Business
17927326	6655392	27621874	26791629	24495446	23476114	154795	148042
115434	37989	209023	202986	155617	150821	1146	1146
4937887	1307949	10846005	10637918	9719272	9538645	90485	90184
87249	49359	290759	285542	221470	217045	1323	1323
6624494	3332486	5607366	5584526	4472858	4453832	33952	33926
316807	170943	539537	531275	473133	466824	2422	2279
737052	458881	759103	749654	685606	675767	5636	5603
126608	54517	677066	676104	620016	619541	1351	1351
245797	104029	908149	898226	674407	664854	5913	5913
440861	177264	780362	765833	556284	543806	13478	13478
33958	27400	9792	9792	5214	5214	442	442
67958	10506	87774	84787	93787	91036	1305	363
20429	7500	28984	28239	21394	20474	377	367
33182	15000	58766	43412	51196	40295	441	441
8282	6000	21027	21027	17120	17120	70	70
4780	5000	5024	5024	4603	4603	7	7
341857	172398	513400	510706	407204	406099	3960	3896

12-11 续表5

单位：万元

分 组	Classify	销售费用 Expenses for Sales	管理费用 Expenses for Management	财务费用 Financial cost
按控股情况分	**Grouped by Cast strand**			
国有控股	State owned shares	658754	1528859	108244
集体控股	Collective shares	10453	19471	1195
私人控股	Private holdings	647381	430278	44320
港澳台控股	Hong Kong and Macao Holdings	37165	9828	708
外商投资	Foreign Investment	324728	427916	6891
其他	Others	11773	30315	-1667
按工业行业大类分	**Grouped by Sector**			
煤炭开采和洗选业	Mining and Washing of Coal			
石油和天然气开采业	Extraction of Petroleum and Natural Gas			
黑色金属矿采选业	Mining and Processing of Ferrous Metal Ores			
有色金属矿采选业	Mining and Processing of Non-ferrous Metal Ores			
非金属矿采选业	Mining and Processing of Nonmetal Ores			
开采专业及辅助性活动	Mining Professional and Auxiliary Activity	3977	37695	-6110
其他采矿业	Mining of other Ores			
农副食品加工业	Processing of Food from Agricultural Porducts	18917	12559	5284
食品制造业	Manufacture of Foods	127085	40529	294
酒、饮料和精制茶制造业	Manufacture of Alcohol,Beverages and Tea	118248	33680	8682
烟草制品业	Manufacture of Tobacco	823	2525	-255
纺织业	Manufacture of Textile	537	6358	190
纺织服装、服饰业	Textile, apparel industry	2765	3631	784
皮革、毛皮、羽毛及其制品和制鞋业	Manufacture of Leather, Fur, Feather and Related Products, and Shoes	1442	1905	148
木材加工和木、竹、藤、棕、草制品业	Processing of Timber, Manufacture of Wood,Plam and Straw Products			
家具制造业	Manufacture of Furniture	1873	1248	238
造纸和纸制品业	Manufacture of Paper and Paper Products	151	196	213
印刷和记录媒介复制业	Printing,Reproduction of Recording Media	12327	45467	-438

continued 5

(10 000 yuan)

营业利润 Operating Profit	利润总额 Total Profits	亏损企业亏损额 Total Loss of Deficit Enterprises	利税总额 Total Pre-tax Profits	应付职工薪酬 Salary Payable	本年应交增值税 Value Added Tax Payable
1223386	1256676	65725	1893463	3942444	481993
19935	20159		27614	17910	6309
711563	725510	11932	999038	968351	183043
20147	20595		27430	33563	5512
1014382	1036081	37533	1243595	505140	173563
26889	26790	2284	31421	57685	2210
35767	33880		44533	260158	5016
19424	21182		29180	30990	6647
60742	60817	1606	98660	141576	31930
59474	79599		122900	90531	29822
1042	478		2349	3862	1429
-13678	-13959	14762	-11567	30261	1087
1359	1628		3888	4825	1883
3679	4004		4415	5730	-31
480	624		1275	1810	582
-147	-164	164	-152	1608	6
45654	45657		75021	87602	25404

12-11 续表6

单位：万元

分组	Classify	企业单位数（个） Number of Enterprises (unit)	亏损企业 Loss Making Enterprises	工业总产值（当年价格） Gross Industrial Output Value (At Current Prices)
文教、工美、体育和娱乐用品制造业	Manufacture of Articles For Cultural,Educational and Sports Activities			
石油、炼焦及其他核燃料加工业	Processing of Petroleum, Cokeing,Processing of Nuclear and Nuclear Fuel	1		7258
化学原料和化学制品制造业	Manufacture of Raw Chemical Materials and Chemical Products	11	1	893018
医药制造业	Manufacture of Medicines	13		1943329
化学纤维制造业	Manufacture of Chemical Fibers	1		68703
橡胶和塑料制品业	Manufacture of Rubber and Plastics	3	1	739560
非金属矿物制品业	Manufacture of Non-metallic Mineral Products	9	1	427292
黑色金属冶炼和压延加工业	Smelting and Pressing of Ferrous Metals			
有色金属冶炼和压延加工业	Smelting and Pressing of Non-ferrous Metals	5		634412
金属制品业	Manufacture of Metal Products	8	2	775569
通用设备制造业	Manufacture of General Purpose Machinery	10	2	1002035
专用设备制造业	Manufacture of Special Equipment	22	4	1496715
汽车制造业	Manufacture of Motor Vehicle	17		13211274
铁路、船舶、航空航天和其他运输设备制造业	Railways,Shipbuilding,Aerospace and Other Transportation Equipment Manufacturing Industry	26	1	4737763
电气机械和器材制造业	Manufacture of Electric Equipment and Machinery	19	6	5252822
计算机、通讯和其他电子设备制造业	Manufacture of Communication Equipment, Computers and other Electronic Equipment	29	2	8574923
仪器仪表制造业	Manufacture of Measuring Instruments and Machinery	7		1342094
其他制造业	Manufacture of Other Manufacturing			
废弃资源综合利用业	Recycling and Disposal of Waste			
金属制品、机械和设备修理业	Metal Products,Machinery and Equipment Repair Industry			
电力、热力的生产和供应业	Production and Supply of Electric Power and Heat Power	8	3	615837
燃气生产和供应业	Gas Mining and Supplying Industry	5	2	1313111
水的生产和供应业	Production and Supply of Water	1		112733

continued 6

(10 000 yuan)

工业销售产值（当年价）Value of Industry Products Sales (At Current Prices)	出口交货值 Export Delivery Value	平均用工人数（人）Average Number of Employed Persons (person)	资产总计 Total Assets	流动资产合计 Total Working Capitals	固定资产原价 Origing Value of Fixed Assets	累计折旧 Accumulative Total Depreciation
7258		2310	45796	15897	45796	2478
813402	67151	12856	1715050	928302	973644	552938
1671666	504	12902	1698542	1027142	420573	194990
68703		330	32042	20228	21941	2530
731794	83583	7352	1782896	1079029	543121	165782
482072		4482	1691871	470903	387123	114608
535533	45544	3560	1930590	777450	342513	140469
781297	75502	15459	1670638	1022460	817743	371688
1287298	37928	12133	3125757	2392176	646758	292331
1371290	83914	16639	2660859	1872530	822355	318436
13049405	451639	70112	9151867	6752326	2462692	1260148
4604452	420444	68589	9492789	5719832	2924891	1351321
5046465	862844	35801	7850947	5408189	2627586	1016619
7420514	3435546	50294	12513138	5742108	12387839	6701075
1277017	42115	10503	1792130	1145886	597250	264870
615837		7779	1582355	491839	2290092	1381063
1312951		6084	1966040	462404	1446679	474146
112733		2629	401973	227704	294871	183160

12-11 续表7

单位：万元

分 组	Classify	负债合计 Total Liabilites	流动负债合计 Total Working Liabilities	非流动负债合计 Total Non-Working Liabilities
文教、工美、体育和娱乐用品制造业	Manufacture of Articles For Cultural,Educational and Sports Activities			
石油、炼焦及其他核燃料加工业	Processing of Petroleum, Cokeing,Processing of Nuclear and Nuclear Fuel	27385	15897	11488
化学原料和化学制品制造业	Manufacture of Raw Chemical Materials and Chemical Products	1153303	767843	385461
医药制造业	Manufacture of Medicines	835524	692942	142582
化学纤维制造业	Manufacture of Chemical Fibers	2200	1970	230
橡胶和塑料制品业	Manufacture of Rubber and Plastics	1245063	1007320	237743
非金属矿物制品业	Manufacture of Non-metallic Mineral Products	1324367	1177294	147072
黑色金属冶炼和压延加工业	Smelting and Pressing of Ferrous Metals			
有色金属冶炼和压延加工业	Smelting and Pressing of Non-ferrous Metals	363766	275395	88371
金属制品业	Manufacture of Metal Products	1124905	792745	332161
通用设备制造业	Manufacture of General Purpose Machinery	1831191	1720961	110230
专用设备制造业	Manufacture of Special Equipment	1300903	1143571	157332
汽车制造业	Manufacture of Motor Vehicle	5977687	5711197	266490
铁路、船舶、航空航天和其他运输设备制造业	Railways,Shipbuilding,Aerospace and Other Transportation Equipment Manufacturing Industry	5719533	4698576	1020957
电气机械和器材制造业	Manufacture of Electric Equipment and Machinery	4196000	3643434	552565
计算机、通讯和其他电子设备制造业	Manufacture of Communication Equipment, Computers and other Electronic Equipment	4432276	2873213	1559063
仪器仪表制造业	Manufacture of Measuring Instruments and Machinery	888369	835021	53348
其他制造业	Manufacture of Other Manufacturing			
废弃资源综合利用业	Recycling and Disposal of Waste			
金属制品、机械和设备修理业	Metal Products,Machinery and Equipment Repair Industry			
电力、热力的生产和供应业	Production and Supply of Electric Power and Heat Power	1302405	897784	404621
燃气生产和供应业	Gas Mining and Supplying Industry	1144766	1021046	123721
水的生产和供应业	Production and Supply of Water	287203	163720	123483

continued 7

(10 000 yuan)

所有者权益合计 Total Owners' Equities	实收资本 Total Capital Hold	营业收入 Total Revenue	主营业务收入 Revenue from Principal Business	营业成本 Total Cost	主营业务成本 Cost of Principal Business	税金及附加 Taxs and Other Changes	主营业务税金及附加 Taxes and Other Charges on Principal Business
18412	3300	4579	4287	3698	3452	238	212
561747	284200	848820	825594	626548	610831	7931	7931
863018	151056	1677748	1677007	855613	855413	18051	18051
29842	39252	63703	63703	57867	57867	228	228
537833	396661	759444	740296	654806	637958	3469	2411
367504	292006	762080	715103	685413	638201	3163	3163
1566824	397868	508436	481775	426925	418217	3051	2842
545733	296867	857117	845279	705897	700649	3610	3319
1294566	112586	1039794	994585	859892	819391	7847	7845
1359956	556769	1494220	1471667	1211339	1195320	10148	10111
3174180	874009	12603161	12187025	12109135	11742062	89190	88407
3773256	1523105	5115018	5000927	4464341	4392152	21859	21326
3654947	1195742	4774672	4622956	4383903	3892592	30531	30485
8080862	3589681	7168931	7127778	6232995	6200385	31513	31385
903761	228363	1285408	1275725	1045771	1024410	4457	2744
279950	229822	798616	774888	742445	732708	8202	7140
821274	305337	1375747	1319747	1229528	1195898	5947	5941
114770	39000	127626	112733	104838	96966	1709	1429

12-11 续表8

单位：万元

分组	Classify	销售费用 Expenses for Sales	管理费用 Expenses for Management	财务费用 Financial cost
文教、工美、体育和娱乐用品制造业	Manufacture of Articles For Cultural,Educational and Sports Activities			
石油、炼焦及其他核燃料加工业	Processing of Petroleum, Cokeing,Processing of Nuclear and Nuclear Fuel	70	76	31
化学原料和化学制品制造业	Manufacture of Raw Chemical Materials and Chemical Products	29649	84847	16966
医药制造业	Manufacture of Medicines	496091	177125	10616
化学纤维制造业	Manufacture of Chemical Fibers	216	1666	-1
橡胶和塑料制品业	Manufacture of Rubber and Plastics	25921	28656	18542
非金属矿物制品业	Manufacture of Non-metallic Mineral Products	21845	20648	6202
黑色金属冶炼和压延加工业	Smelting and Pressing of Ferrous Metals			
有色金属冶炼和压延加工业	Smelting and Pressing of Non-ferrous Metals	4047	40945	2008
金属制品业	Manufacture of Metal Products	17196	92607	9530
通用设备制造业	Manufacture of General Purpose Machinery	38612	96318	4328
专用设备制造业	Manufacture of Special Equipment	70713	104145	13593
汽车制造业	Manufacture of Motor Vehicle	271611	333979	-21443
铁路、船舶、航空航天和其他运输设备制造业	Railways,Shipbuilding,Aerospace and Other Transportation Equipment Manufacturing Industry	62562	322975	31671
电气机械和器材制造业	Manufacture of Electric Equipment and Machinery	269283	329239	31071
计算机、通讯和其他电子设备制造业	Manufacture of Communication Equipment, Computers and other Electronic Equipment	40786	460978	-11095
仪器仪表制造业	Manufacture of Measuring Instruments and Machinery	19168	105195	-3523
其他制造业	Manufacture of Other Manufacturing			
废弃资源综合利用业	Recycling and Disposal of Waste			
金属制品、机械和设备修理业	Metal Products,Machinery and Equipment Repair Industry			
电力、热力的生产和供应业	Production and Supply of Electric Power and Heat Power	215	19889	23703
燃气生产和供应业	Gas Mining and Supplying Industry	29153	31366	15829
水的生产和供应业	Production and Supply of Water	4975	10219	2637

continued 8

(10 000 yuan)

营业利润 Operating Profit	利润总额 Total Profits	亏损企业亏损额 Total Loss of Deficit Enterprises	利税总额 Total Pre-tax Profits	应付职工薪酬 Salary Payable	本年应交增值税 Value Added Tax Payable
466	425		735	21031	72
87054	83575	3531	127932	111685	36426
121097	125942		354218	229780	210225
3799	3928		5160	4110	1004
27083	29752	863	44897	56171	11676
24053	24306	7773	41848	40396	14379
40299	40256		59002	58661	15694
29450	33337	4461	48906	171470	11959
59811	61059	2082	100197	148523	31291
84379	87829	11469	142086	198304	44110
515134	524076		754010	1307436	140745
240473	244318	5693	320889	983771	54713
121744	146327	43306	254428	493747	77570
1213066	1214961	6671	1279905	639061	33432
128328	130076		156568	177041	22035
20977	16231	13494	46349	97022	21916
82267	82469	1597	106642	91079	18227
3029	3197		8288	36852	3382

12-12 规模以上高技术产业工业企业主要经济指标（2018年）

单位：万元

行 业	Sector	企业单位数（个）Number of Enterprises (unit)	亏损企业 Loss Making Enterprises
总计	**Total**	**296**	**44**
一、医药制造业	**Pharmaceutical Manufacturing**	**62**	**13**
（一）化学药品制造	Chemical manufacturing	22	3
化学药品原料药制造	Chemical raw materials Medicine manufacturing	6	1
化学药品制剂制造	Chemical preparations manufacturing	16	2
（二）中药饮片加工	Chinese medicine Pieces processing	1	
（三）中成药生产	Chinese medicine production	24	6
（四）兽用药品制造	Veterinary pharmaceutical manufacturing	4	2
（五）生物药品制造	Biopharmaceutical manufacturing	6	1
（六）卫生材料及医药用品制造	Sanitary materials and medical supplies manufacturing	1	
（七）药用辅料及包装材料	Pharmaceutical Excipients and Packaging Materials	4	1
二、航空、航天及设备制造业	**Aviation, Aerospace and Equipment Manufacturing Industry**	**57**	**6**
（一）飞机制造	Aircraft Manufacturing	14	2
（二）航天器及运载火箭制造	Spacecraft and Launch Vehicles Manufacturing	2	
（三）航空、航天相关设备制造	Aviation and aerospace-related equipment manufacturing	32	2
（四）其他航空航天器制造	Other aerospace manufacturing	5	
（五）航空航天器修理	Aerospace vehicle repair	4	2
三、电子及通讯设备制造业	**Electronic and communication equipment manufacturing**	**96**	**14**
（一）电子工业专用设备制造	Electronic equipment manufacturing	5	1
（二）光纤、光缆及锂离子电池制造	Optical Fiber, Cable and Lithium-ion Battery Manufacturing	3	1
（三）通信设备、雷达及配套设备制造	Communications Equipment, Radar and Ancillary Equipments Manufacturing	21	3
（四）广播电视设备制造	Broadcasting and TV Equipment	2	1
（五）非专业视听设备制造	Non-professional audiovisual equipment manufacturing	1	
（六）电子器件制造	Electronic device manufacturing	29	2
（七）电子元件及电子专用材料制造	Electronic components and electronic materials manufacturing	27	4
（八）智能消费设备制造	Smart consumer device manufacturing		
（九）其他电子设备制造	Other electronic equipment manufacturing	8	2
四、计算机及办公设备制造业	**Computer and office equipment manufacturing**	**5**	
（一）计算机整机制造	Computer machine manufacturing		
（二）计算机零部件制造	Computer parts manufacturing		
（三）计算机外围设备制造	Computer peripheral equipment manufacturing	1	
（四）工业控制计算机及系统制造造	Industrial Control Computer and System Manufacturing	2	
（五）信息安全设备制造	Information Security Equipment Manufacturing		
（六）其他计算机制造	Other computer manufacturing	2	
（七）办公设备制造	Office Equipment manufacturing		
五、医疗设备及仪器仪表制造业	**Medical equipment and instrumentation manufacturing**	**74**	**10**
（一）医疗仪器设备及器械制造	Medical equipment and device manufacturing	16	4
（二）通用仪器仪表制造	General Measuring Instruments and Machinery Manufacturing	33	5
（三）专用仪器仪表制造	Special Measuring Instruments and Machinery Manufacturing	16	1
（四）光学仪器制造	Optical Instruments Manufacturing	4	
（五）其他仪器仪表制造业	Other instrumentation manufacturing	5	
六、信息化学品制造业	**Information chemicals manufacturing**	**2**	**1**
信息化学品制造	Information Chemical Manufacturing	2	1

Major Economic Indicators of High Technology Industry Industrial Enterprises above Designated Size (2018)

(10 000 yuan)

工业总产值（当年价格）Gross Industrial Output Value (At Current Prices)	工业销售产值（当年价）Value of Industry Products Sales (At Current Prices)	出口交货值 Export Delivery Value	平均用工人数（人）Average Number of Employed Persons (person)	资产总计 Total Assets	流动资产合计 Total Working Capitals	固定资产原价 Origing Value of Fixed Assets	累计折旧 Accumulative Total Depreciation
19284818	**17368441**	**4481490**	**163451**	**28628672**	**15519527**	**17289156**	**8841836**
2439050	**2128133**	**2321**	**19275**	**2386182**	**1441299**	**644883**	**275726**
1502991	1272546	1758	8711	1294409	777131	350022	156151
50868	34353	1260	586	55080	29203	27054	6588
1452123	1238193	498	8125	1239329	747929	322968	149563
3339	2323		80	9417	6420	972	147
709084	648697	6	8093	696948	438858	159204	60964
9110	7636		416	71066	57788	10366	4717
186312	170391	80	1527	284961	145897	113641	49425
3420	3469		13	1706	1286	467	180
24795	23071	477	435	27675	13919	10212	4142
4920685	**4738473**	**457038**	**66220**	**9307570**	**5450533**	**2909284**	**1325142**
3369041	3282287	422458	51448	6914623	4022720	2199854	1005657
439309	438357	6641	4930	1084040	572009	335369	158516
1019317	927210	21542	8642	1064003	705587	332323	149431
59533	59207		875	194019	126922	28945	7777
33486	31413	6397	325	50885	23295	12793	3762
9906704	**8539350**	**3885060**	**59404**	**14119920**	**6738023**	**12963369**	**6896074**
32818	35936	51	517	71257	57636	16050	4669
616602	490149	343437	1564	642026	364090	347638	85745
2032121	1846610	174890	19050	2069531	1390550	663199	288258
16655	16399	11659	272	22317	19912	2365	1566
29758	26471	226	128	7695	1722	5792	3961
4880850	3825919	2993518	17931	7958483	3255026	8331396	5269416
2262507	2258566	360966	19217	3262008	1585011	3587229	1237807
35394	39302	313	725	86604	64077	9699	4651
48739	**91061**	**10425**	**433**	**76570**	**62720**	**2847**	**1619**
27435	70571	10425	206	60566	50525	2019	1240
13065	12512		152	9574	9049	132	64
8240	7979		75	6430	3147	696	316
1824300	**1735011**	**60641**	**17736**	**2632576**	**1771466**	**750848**	**334239**
109977	106089	6472	1769	163579	121764	35081	14096
671407	632780	6384	4347	619650	464151	144739	58928
248361	251506	42094	3071	470390	379092	62974	36249
737648	688949	5692	7758	1291287	757765	488118	216852
56907	55686		791	87669	48695	19936	8113
145340	**136412**	**66005**	**383**	**105855**	**55485**	**17926**	**9036**
145340	136412	66005	383	105855	55485	17926	9036

12-12 续表1

单位：万元

行业	Sector	负债合计 Total Liabilites	流动负债合计 Total Working Liabilities
总计	**Total**	**13667517**	**10571295**
一、医药制造业	**Pharmaceutical Manufacturing**	**1233645**	**1063760**
（一）化学药品制造	Chemical manufacturing	676761	548474
化学药品原料药制造	Chemical raw materials Medicine manufacturing	32390	30515
化学药品制剂制造	Chemical preparations manufacturing	644371	517959
（二）中药饮片加工	Chinese medicine Pieces processing	4976	4976
（三）中成药生产	Chinese medicine production	447145	410418
（四）兽用药品制造	Veterinary pharmaceutical manufacturing	27418	24651
（五）生物药品制造	Biopharmaceutical manufacturing	60729	60207
（六）卫生材料及医药用品制造	Sanitary materials and medical supplies manufacturing	1815	1815
（七）药用辅料及包装材料	Pharmaceutical Excipients and Packaging Materials	14801	13219
二、航空、航天及设备制造业	**Aviation, Aerospace and Equipment Manufacturing Industry**	**5505769**	**4488935**
（一）飞机制造	Aircraft Manufacturing	4287096	3552513
（二）航天器及运载火箭制造	Spacecraft and Launch Vehicles Manufacturing	599552	373333
（三）航空、航天相关设备制造	Aviation and aerospace-related equipment manufacturing	548126	496799
（四）其他航空航天器制造	Other aerospace manufacturing	59065	55310
（五）航空航天器修理	Aerospace vehicle repair	11930	10980
三、电子及通讯设备制造业	**Electronic and communication equipment manufacturing**	**5483053**	**3689443**
（一）电子工业专用设备制造	Electronic equipment manufacturing	36967	33900
（二）光纤、光缆及锂离子电池制造	Optical Fiber, Cable and Lithium-ion Battery Manufacturing	570487	436154
（三）通信设备、雷达及配套设备制造	Communications Equipment, Radar and Ancillary Equipments Manufacturing	1095146	881237
（四）广播电视设备制造	Broadcasting and TV Equipment	16937	16937
（五）非专业视听设备制造	Non-professional audiovisual equipment manufacturing	3069	3069
（六）电子器件制造	Electronic device manufacturing	1894159	925362
（七）电子元件及电子专用材料制造	Electronic components and electronic materials manufacturing	1838363	1365358
（八）智能消费设备制造	Smart consumer device manufacturing		
（九）其他电子设备制造	Other electronic equipment manufacturing	27926	27426
四、计算机及办公设备制造业	**Computer and office equipment manufacturing**	**17339**	**16939**
（一）计算机整机制造	Computer machine manufacturing		
（二）计算机零部件制造	Computer parts manufacturing		
（三）计算机外围设备制造	Computer peripheral equipment manufacturing	9182	9082
（四）工业控制计算机及系统制造造	Industrial Control Computer and System Manufacturing	6591	6291
（五）信息安全设备制造	Information Security Equipment Manufacturing		
（六）其他计算机制造	Other computer manufacturing	1565	1565
（七）办公设备制造	Office Equipment manufacturing		
五、医疗设备及仪器仪表制造业	**Medical equipment and instrumentation manufacturing**	**1327360**	**1222867**
（一）医疗仪器设备及器械制造	Medical equipment and device manufacturing	66771	54766
（二）通用仪器仪表制造	General Measuring Instruments and Machinery Manufacturing	415444	379462
（三）专用仪器仪表制造	Special Measuring Instruments and Machinery Manufacturing	193948	183672
（四）光学仪器制造	Optical Instruments Manufacturing	618103	572621
（五）其他仪器仪表制造业	Other instrumentation manufacturing	33095	32347
六、信息化学品制造业	**Information chemicals manufacturing**	**100352**	**89352**
信息化学品制造	Information Chemical Manufacturing	100352	89352

continued 1

(10 000 yuan)

非流动负债合计 Total Non-Working Liabilities	所有者权益合计 Total Owners' Equities	实收资本 Total Capital Hold	营业收入 Total Revenue	主营业务收入 Revenue from Principal Business	营业成本 Total Cost	主营业务成本 Cost of Principal Business	税金及附加 Taxs and Other Changes	主营业务税金及附加 Taxes and Other Charges on Principal Business
3096220	**14961153**	**6346532**	**17503987**	**17319954**	**14330622**	**14192058**	**88210**	**85093**
169885	**1152536**	**301700**	**2116718**	**2115267**	**1081455**	**1080741**	**23953**	**23937**
128288	617648	143241	1347023	1346453	742911	742482	14249	14249
1876	22689	12350	33699	33699	19510	19510	356	356
126412	594958	130891	1313324	1312754	723401	722972	13893	13893
	4442	3000	2323	2323	1601	1601	3	3
36727	249803	77701	617983	617271	270431	270177	7450	7449
2767	43647	14208	7207	7207	5219	5219	74	74
522	224231	52607	117474	117307	41756	41724	1972	1957
	-109	63	3469	3469	3420	3420	1	1
1582	12875	10880	21237	21237	16118	16118	204	204
1016833	**3801801**	**1541389**	**5132634**	**5021067**	**4539998**	**4468227**	**17720**	**16970**
734583	2627527	1180318	3713928	3615718	3364385	3299693	13318	13272
226219	484488	70000	442108	434867	356792	354320	641	641
51327	515876	221377	871381	867855	747484	745292	2820	2151
3755	134955	32048	71129	70949	45899	45894	726	697
950	38955	37647	34089	31677	25439	23028	216	210
1793610	**8636867**	**4035497**	**8261398**	**8206034**	**7162795**	**7121200**	**36563**	**36342**
3068	34290	14920	34568	31995	26923	25624	364	360
134332	71539	138825	478950	473691	448845	444303	734	734
213909	974385	331586	2144318	2126930	1914859	1905274	9161	9083
	5381	3600	16492	16361	11879	11879	149	149
	4626	4626	22825	22820	21341	21337	103	103
968797	6064324	3123818	3815884	3802062	3194135	3182209	19685	19549
473005	1423645	380893	1703392	1688345	1517442	1503701	5902	5900
500	58678	37229	44970	43831	27371	26875	466	466
400	**59231**	**31411**	**55328**	**54581**	**35950**	**35589**	**303**	**303**
100	51383	27600	35191	34536	20995	20668	207	207
300	2983	2311	12283	12283	9518	9518	44	44
	4865	1500	7855	7763	5438	5404	52	52
104493	**1305215**	**423535**	**1737655**	**1723031**	**1328545**	**1304513**	**8633**	**6502**
12005	96808	39287	99464	99290	40837	40503	1021	1021
35982	204206	166313	603018	598512	494832	492567	2754	2337
10276	276442	55880	258718	256523	160675	143269	2716	2716
45482	673185	142985	723582	716168	590420	586519	1855	141
748	54575	19070	52873	52538	41780	41655	287	287
11000	**5503**	**13000**	**200254**	**199974**	**181878**	**181788**	**1039**	**1039**
11000	5503	13000	200254	199974	181878	181788	1039	1039

12-12 续表2

单位：万元

行 业	Sector	销售费用 Expenses for Sales	管理费用 Expenses for Management
总计	**Total**	**849932**	**1218530**
一、医药制造业	**Pharmaceutical Manufacturing**	**627806**	**216521**
（一）化学药品制造	Chemical manufacturing	334654	138370
化学药品原料药制造	Chemical raw materials Medicine manufacturing	5711	5189
化学药品制剂制造	Chemical preparations manufacturing	328943	133181
（二）中药饮片加工	Chinese medicine Pieces processing	366	227
（三）中成药生产	Chinese medicine production	239825	61725
（四）兽用药品制造	Veterinary pharmaceutical manufacturing	455	512
（五）生物药品制造	Biopharmaceutical manufacturing	50938	13013
（六）卫生材料及医药用品制造	Sanitary materials and medical supplies manufacturing	1	47
（七）药用辅料及包装材料	Pharmaceutical Excipients and Packaging Materials	1567	2627
二、航空、航天及设备制造业	**Aviation, Aerospace and Equipment Manufacturing Industry**	**56651**	**289284**
（一）飞机制造	Aircraft Manufacturing	44218	181447
（二）航天器及运载火箭制造	Spacecraft and Launch Vehicles Manufacturing	1796	38573
（三）航空、航天相关设备制造	Aviation and aerospace-related equipment manufacturing	6635	54613
（四）其他航空航天器制造	Other aerospace manufacturing	2194	9254
（五）航空航天器修理	Aerospace vehicle repair	1809	5399
三、电子及通讯设备制造业	**Electronic and communication equipment manufacturing**	**100788**	**535980**
（一）电子工业专用设备制造	Electronic equipment manufacturing	2328	4147
（二）光纤、光缆及锂离子电池制造	Optical Fiber, Cable and Lithium-ion Battery Manufacturing	36107	14429
（三）通信设备、雷达及配套设备制造	Communications Equipment, Radar and Ancillary Equipments Manufacturing	13545	92725
（四）广播电视设备制造	Broadcasting and TV Equipment	1654	2214
（五）非专业视听设备制造	Non-professional audiovisual equipment manufacturing	719	315
（六）电子器件制造	Electronic device manufacturing	11773	303606
（七）电子元件及电子专用材料制造	Electronic components and electronic materials manufacturing	30364	109874
（八）智能消费设备制造	Smart consumer device manufacturing		
（九）其他电子设备制造	Other electronic equipment manufacturing	4299	8670
四、计算机及办公设备制造业	**Computer and office equipment manufacturing**	**1449**	**4955**
（一）计算机整机制造	Computer machine manufacturing		
（二）计算机零部件制造	Computer parts manufacturing		
（三）计算机外围设备制造	Computer peripheral equipment manufacturing	585	2551
（四）工业控制计算机及系统制造造	Industrial Control Computer and System Manufacturing	658	1623
（五）信息安全设备制造	Information Security Equipment Manufacturing		
（六）其他计算机制造	Other computer manufacturing	206	782
（七）办公设备制造	Office Equipment manufacturing		
五、医疗设备及仪器仪表制造业	**Medical equipment and instrumentation manufacturing**	**61246**	**169552**
（一）医疗仪器设备及器械制造	Medical equipment and device manufacturing	18353	16744
（二）通用仪器仪表制造	General Measuring Instruments and Machinery Manufacturing	20412	31077
（三）专用仪器仪表制造	Special Measuring Instruments and Machinery Manufacturing	15970	26651
（四）光学仪器制造	Optical Instruments Manufacturing	2508	90150
（五）其他仪器仪表制造业	Other instrumentation manufacturing	4004	4929
六、信息化学品制造业	**Information chemicals manufacturing**	**1991**	**2239**
信息化学品制造	Information Chemical Manufacturing	1991	2239

continued 2

(10 000 yuan)

财务费用 Financial cost	营业利润 Operating Profit	利润总额 Total Profits	亏损企业亏损额 Total Loss of Deficit Enterprises	利税总额 Total Pre-tax Profits	应付职工薪酬 Salary Payable	本年应交增值税 Value Added Tax Payable
63801	**1831216**	**1851173**	**62817**	**2321264**	**2174796**	**381880**
15671	**151965**	**158406**	**2935**	**421086**	**270239**	**238727**
12206	101471	101874	1060	292285	162755	176162
386	2507	2712	47	5173	2921	2104
11820	98964	99162	1013	287112	159834	174057
115	12	24		79	241	52
2024	39309	44691	1580	105184	89464	53042
450	498	598	148	790	1448	119
614	10217	10431	89	20784	13009	8380
				3	87	1
261	459	788	58	1962	3235	970
30189	**232313**	**238426**	**6973**	**304724**	**919877**	**48577**
23632	105724	110684	768	139698	733001	15696
1628	47230	46261		50288	74002	3386
3957	62751	63877	5800	91390	98197	24693
1159	14444	15341		19653	11331	3586
-187	2163	2264	405	3696	3346	1216
15862	**1241970**	**1246521**	**44473**	**1334243**	**731609**	**51159**
490	981	1306	708	3206	4485	1536
23110	-23072	-22445	32696	-17728	18035	3984
2581	129596	129810	2500	162569	196122	23598
126	64	117	264	537	2386	271
29	308	328		470	438	39
-29671	973595	975110	232	994254	253550	-540
18744	155317	156954	6834	182185	249583	19328
454	5180	5341	1239	8750	7010	2944
278	**11517**	**11760**		**13854**	**3971**	**1792**
154	9811	9998		11344	2299	1139
124	317	438		784	1239	302
1	1389	1324		1726	433	351
742	**182122**	**187575**	**6943**	**236230**	**242562**	**40022**
20	21675	21923	3275	29122	13421	6179
1953	52286	53740	3382	74413	50895	17919
310	59997	61678	286	75045	41029	10652
-2064	46385	48033		54454	130737	4566
523	1778	2202		3196	6480	707
1058	**11329**	**8485**	**1492**	**11127**	**6539**	**1603**
1058	11329	8485	1492	11127	6539	1603

12-13 规模以上工业企业主要经济效益指标（2018年）

行　业	Sector	总资产贡献率（%） Ratio of Total Assets to Industrial Output Value (%)	资产负债率（%） Assets-Liability Ratio (%)
总计	**Total**	**7.3**	**54.5**
按工业行业大类分	**Grouped by Sector**		
煤炭开采和洗选业	Mining and Washing of Coal		
石油和天然气开采业	Extraction of Petroleum and Natural Gas		
黑色金属矿采选业	Mining and Processing of Ferrous Metal Ores		
有色金属矿采选业	Mining and Processing of Non-ferrous Metal Ores		
非金属矿采选业	Mining and Processing of Nonmetal Ores		
开采专业及辅助性活动	Mining Professional and Auxiliary Activity	3.2	39.2
其他采矿业	Mining of Other Ores		
农副食品加工业	Processing of Food from Agricultural Porducts	8.8	72.6
食品制造业	Manufacture of Foods	19.1	51.0
酒、饮料和精制茶制造业	Manufacture of Alcohol,Beverages and Tea	11.4	58.2
烟草制品业	Manufacture of Tobacco	5.1	16.8
纺织业	Manufacture of Textile	-1.8	65.4
纺织服装、服饰业	Textile, Garments industry	5.9	57.7
皮革、毛皮、羽毛及其制品和制鞋业	Manufacture of Leather, Fur, Feather and Related Products	7.4	37.7
木材加工和木、竹、藤、棕、草制品业	Processing of Timber, Manufacture of Wood,Plam and Straw Products	2.2	49.5
家具制造业	Manufacture of Furniture	7.6	42.7
造纸和纸制品业	Manufacture of Paper and Paper Products	11.6	54.5
印刷和记录媒介复制业	Printing,Reproduction of Recording Media	11.8	39.3
文教、工美、体育和娱乐用品制造业	Manufacture of Articles For Cultural,Educational and Sports Activities	41.7	42.7

Major Indicators of Economic Performance of Industrial Enterprises above Designated Size （2018）

流动资产周转率（次）Rate of Annual Turnover Working Capitals (times)	成本费用利润率（%）Ratio of Profits to Cost (%)	工业产品销售率（%）Proportion of Industrial Products Sold (%)	产值利税率（%）Ratio of Output Value to Profits and Tax (%)	每百元固定资产实现利税（元）Profit and Tax per 100 yuan of Fixed Assets (yuan)	每百元销售收入实现利税（元）Profit and Tax per 100 yuan of Sales Revenue (yuan)
1.3	**6.8**	**96.2**	**8.9**	**14.9**	**9.5**
0.9	4.6	100.1	6.6	24.9	9.1
2.3	4.3	95.9	3.8	30.4	4.3
4.1	7.0	95.7	8.7	47.1	9.6
1.7	9.9	116.9	24.9	43.7	21.2
0.4	5.8	100.0	36.7	35.0	30.7
1.2	-6.2	93.9	3.9	4.5	4.0
0.6	4.6	89.5	4.4	18.2	6.4
1.5	6.9	137.4	11.1	104.8	11.3
0.4	-0.5	87.3	10.4	9.8	12.3
1.9	5.7	92.7	7.0	22.1	8.6
3.4	3.9	97.1	6.1	50.0	6.3
2.0	6.0	96.7	10.7	39.0	11.3
12.8	0.6	93.6	1.0	34.1	0.9

12-13 续表1

行　业	Sector	总资产贡献率（%） Ratio of Total Assets to Industrial Output Value (%)	资产负债率（%） Assets-Liability Ratio (%)
石油、炼焦及其他燃料加工业	Processing of Petroleum, Cokeing,Processing of Nuclear and Nuclear Fuel	2.2	61.9
化学原料和化学制品制造业	Manufacture of Raw Chemical Materials and Chemical Products	11.2	62.5
医药制造业	Manufacture of Medicines	18.1	51.7
化学纤维制造业	Manufacture of Chemical Fibers	15.1	51.2
橡胶和塑料制品业	Manufacture of Rubber and Plastics	4.0	67.5
非金属矿物制品业	Manufacture of Non-metallic Mineral Products	6.3	71.8
黑色金属冶炼和压延加工业	Smelting and Pressing of Ferrous Metals	5.9	56.2
有色金属冶炼和压延加工业	Smelting and Pressing of Non-ferrous Metals	4.5	28.6
金属制品业	Manufacture of Metal Products	5.2	66.8
通用设备制造业	Manufacture of General Purpose Machinery	4.1	57.1
专用设备制造业	Manufacture of Special Equipment	4.9	50.6
汽车制造业	Manufacture of Motor Vehicle	8.1	64.8
铁路、船舶、航空航天和其他运输设备制造业	Railways, Shipbuilding,Aerospace and Other Transportation Equipment Manufacturing Industry	4.8	57.3
电气机械和器材制造业	Manufacture of Electric Equipment and Machinery	4.6	52.1
计算机、通讯和其他电子设备制造业	Manufacture of Communication Equipment, Computers and other Electronic Equipment	10.6	36.3
仪器仪表制造业	Manufacture of Measuring Instruments and Machinery	8.5	51.1
其他制造业	Manufacture of Other Manufacturing	6.1	53.7
废弃资源综合利用业	Recycling and Disposal of Waste	13.2	69.5
金属制品、机械和设备修理业	Metal Products,Machinery and Equipment Repair Industry	5.8	22.1
电力、热力的生产和供应业	Production and Supply of Electric Power and Heat Power	5.1	82.7
燃气生产和供应业	Gas Mining and Supplying Industry	6.4	57.8
水的生产和供应业	Production and Supply of Water	2.8	68.7

continued 1

流动资产周转率（次） Rate of Annual Turnover Working Capitals (times)	成本费用利润率（%） Ratio of Profits to Cost (%)	工业产品销售率（%） Proportion of Industrial Products Sold (%)	产值利税率（%） Ratio of Output Value to Profits and Tax (%)	每百元固定资产实现利税（元） Profit and Tax per 100 yuan of Fixed Assets (yuan)	每百元销售收入实现利税（元） Profit and Tax per 100 yuan of Sales Revenue (yuan)
1.1	1.1	99.4	8.6	7.4	7.9
1.3	9.3	94.6	12.2	33.4	13.5
1.5	8.2	87.3	14.3	59.6	17.4
2.2	9.1	104.7	5.7	9.6	5.6
0.8	4.3	98.2	4.4	8.7	4.4
1.7	4.5	101.6	7.3	26.5	7.4
4.8	0.7	101.2	2.8	24.6	2.8
0.9	7.4	89.1	5.0	26.5	5.1
1.1	3.6	95.3	4.7	10.9	4.6
0.6	5.8	114.3	8.2	33.1	9.0
0.8	5.9	96.3	10.9	34.3	11.6
1.8	4.2	98.8	4.5	29.8	4.7
1.0	6.3	96.6	8.5	25.6	8.0
1.1	3.1	96.3	7.7	25.9	8.6
1.2	17.5	87.1	15.4	26.2	17.2
1.0	11.0	95.1	10.7	32.9	11.0
0.9	4.8	102.4	6.6	26.2	6.5
3.3	13.0	96.7	2.4	5.2	2.2
1.3	6.3	95.0	-1.0	-3.4	-1.1
0.9	8.1	99.8	7.9	6.0	7.3
3.2	5.6	99.9	8.3	12.0	8.2
0.6	3.0	101.2	8.7	7.4	8.4

12-14 规模以上大中型工业企业主要经济效益指标（2018年）

行 业	Sector	总资产贡献率（%）Ratio of Total Assets to Industrial Output Value (%)	资产负债率（%）Assets-Liability Ratio (%)
总计	**Total**	**6.8**	**54.2**
按国民经济行业分	**Grouped by Sector**		
煤炭开采和洗选业	Mining and Washing of Coal		
石油和天然气开采业	Extraction of Petroleum and Natural Gas		
黑色金属矿采选业	Mining and Processing of Ferrous Metal Ores		
有色金属矿采选业	Mining and Processing of Non-ferrous Metal Ores		
非金属矿采选业	Mining and Processing of Nonmetal Ores		
开采专业及辅助性活动	Mining Professional and Auxiliary Activity	3.2	39.5
其他采矿业	Mining of other Ores		
农副食品加工业	Processing of Food from Agricultural Porducts	5.5	79.6
食品制造业	Manufacture of Foods	19.1	53.1
酒、饮料和精制茶制造业	Manufacture of Alcohol,Beverages and Tea	11.4	60.9
烟草制品业	Manufacture of Tobacco	5.1	16.8
纺织业	Manufacture of Textile	-4.9	70.1
纺织服装、服饰业	Textile, apparel industry	7.0	69.5
皮革、毛皮、羽毛及其制品和制鞋业	Leather fur feathers and its products and footwear	8.2	40.4
木材加工和木、竹、藤、棕、草制品业	Processing of Timber,Manufacture of Wood,Plam and Straw Products		
家具制造业	Manufacture of Furniture	7.2	60.5
造纸和纸制品业	Manufacture of Paper and Paper Products	0.5	64.5
印刷和记录媒介复制业	Printing,Reproduction of Recording Media	14.9	33.1
文教、工美、体育和娱乐用品制造业	Manufacture of Articles For Cultural,Educational and Sports Activities		

Major Economic Indicators of Large and Medium-sized Industrial Enterprises above Designated Size（2018）

流动资产周转率（次）Rate of Annual Turnover Working Capitals (times)	成本费用利润率（%）Ratio of Profits to Cost (%)	工业产品销售率（%）Proportion of Industrial Products Sold (%)	产值利税率（%）Ratio of Output Value to Profits and Tax (%)	每百元固定资产实现利税（元）Profit and Tax per 100 yuan of Fixed Assets (yuan)	每百元销售收入实现利税（元）Profit and Tax per 100 yuan of Sales Revenue (yuan)
1.2	**7.0**	**96.0**	**9.0**	**13.0**	**9.6**
0.8	4.7	100.0	5.3	6.4	5.9
1.6	3.2	93.1	4.3	13.3	4.3
3.7	7.2	95.3	10.1	29.5	11.0
1.5	11.1	129.9	21.7	19.6	16.0
0.4	5.8	100.0	31.5	7.3	24.0
1.4	-13.8	98.3	-14.0	-5.5	-13.6
0.5	5.7	85.0	10.7	33.3	13.8
1.7	7.3	139.1	13.5	51.3	10.2
3.6	3.1	96.7	7.2	14.5	6.1
0.5	-3.2	100.0	-2.1	-12.8	-3.0
1.7	9.8	97.1	14.5	20.3	14.7

12-14 续表1

行　业	Sector	总资产贡献率（%） Ratio of Total Assets to Industrial Output Value (%)	资产负债率（%） Assets-Liability Ratio (%)
石油、炼焦及其他燃料加工业	Processing of Petroleum, Cokeing,Processing of Nuclear and Nuclear Fuel	1.6	59.8
化学原料和化学制品制造业	Manufacture of Raw Chemical Materials and Chemical Products	8.6	67.3
医药制造业	Manufacture of Medicines	21.3	49.2
化学纤维制造业	Manufacture of Chemical Fibers	16.1	6.9
橡胶和塑料制品业	Manufacture of Rubber and Plastics	3.5	69.8
非金属矿物制品业	Manufacture of Non-metallic Mineral Products	2.9	78.3
黑色金属冶炼和压延加工业	Smelting and Pressing of Ferrous Metals		
有色金属冶炼和压延加工业	Smelting and Pressing of Non-ferrous Metals	3.2	18.8
金属制品业	Manufacture of Metal Products	3.5	67.3
通用设备制造业	Manufacture of General Purpose Machinery	3.3	58.6
专用设备制造业	Manufacture of Special Equipment	5.8	48.9
汽车制造业	Manufacture of Motor Vehicle	8.1	65.3
铁路、船舶、航空航天和其他运输设备制造业	Railways,Shipbuilding,Aerospace and Other Transportation Equipment Manufacturing Industry	3.7	60.3
电气机械和器材制造业	Manufacture of Electric Equipment and Machinery	3.6	53.5
计算机、通信和其他电子设备制造业	Manufacture of Communication Equipment, Computers and other Electronic Equipment	10.8	35.4
仪器仪表制造业	Manufacture of Measuring Instruments and Machinery	8.6	49.6
其他制造业	Manufacture of Other Manufacturing		
废弃资源综合利用	Recycling and Disposal of Waste		
金属制品、机械和设备修理业	Metal Products,Machinery and Equipment Repair Industry		
电力、热力生产和供应业	Production and Supply of Electric Power and Heat Power	4.4	82.3
燃气生产和供应业	Gas Mining and Supplying Industry	6.4	58.2
水的生产和供应业	Production and Supply of Water	2.7	71.5

continued 1

流动资产周转率（次）Rate of Annual Turnover Working Capitals (times)	成本费用利润率（%）Ratio of Profits to Cost (%)	工业产品销售率（%）Proportion of Industrial Products Sold (%)	产值利税率（%）Ratio of Output Value to Profits and Tax (%)	每百元固定资产实现利税（元）Profit and Tax per 100 yuan of Fixed Assets (yuan)	每百元销售收入实现利税（元）Profit and Tax per 100 yuan of Sales Revenue (yuan)
0.3	11.0	100.0	10.1	1.6	17.1
0.9	11.0	91.1	14.3	13.1	15.5
1.6	8.2	86.0	18.2	84.2	21.1
3.2	6.6	100.0	7.5	23.5	8.1
0.7	4.1	99.0	6.1	8.3	6.1
1.6	3.3	112.8	9.8	10.8	5.9
0.7	8.5	84.4	9.3	17.2	12.2
0.8	4.0	100.7	6.3	6.0	5.8
0.4	6.1	128.5	10.0	15.5	10.1
0.8	6.3	91.6	9.5	17.3	9.7
1.9	4.1	98.8	5.7	30.6	6.2
0.9	5.0	97.2	6.8	11.0	6.4
0.9	2.9	96.1	4.8	9.7	5.5
1.3	18.1	86.5	14.9	10.3	18.0
1.1	11.2	95.2	11.7	26.2	12.3
1.6	2.1	100.0	7.5	2.0	6.0
3.0	6.3	100.0	8.1	7.4	8.1
0.6	2.6	100.0	7.4	2.8	7.4

12-15 规模以上工业主要产品生产能力（2018年）

Production Capacity of Major Products of Industrial Enterprises above Designated Size（2018）

指 标	Item	2018
棉纺锭/纺纱量（锭/吨）	Cotton spindles / spinning volume(ingot/ton)	300180
气流纺锭/纺纱量（头/吨）	Rotor spinning / spinning volume(head/ton)	2256
棉布织机/布（台/万米）	Cotton loom / cloth (unit/10000 meter)	3319
化学纤维（吨）	Chemical Fibre (ton)	48000
硅酸盐水泥熟料（吨）	Portland Cement Clinker (ton)	830000
水泥（吨）	Cement(ton)	2700000
平板玻璃（重量箱）	Plate Glass(weight case)	6370000
钢材（吨）	Rolled Steel (ton)	767600
铁合金（吨）	Ferroalloy (ton)	
金属切削机床（台）	Metal-cutting Machine Tools（unit）	8800
汽车（辆）	Motor Vehicles（unit）	543000
其中：乘用车（辆）	Passenger Vehicles（unit）	303000
新能源乘用车（辆）	New energy passenger car(unit)	133000
商用汽车（辆）	Commercial vehicle(unit)	240000
太阳能电池（千瓦）	Solar cell （KW)	7450000
微型计算机设备（台）	Micro Computer Equipment（unit）	
移动通信手持机（台）	Mobile Handset（unit）	20017000
彩色电视机（台）	Color TV Set（unit）	28512
发电设备容量总计/发电量（万千瓦/万千瓦小时）	Total capacity of power generation equipment / generation capacity (10000 KW/10000 KWh)	353
其中：火电设备容量（万千瓦）	Thermal Power（10 000kw）	351
水电设备容量（万千瓦）	Hydropower（10 000kw）	2

主要统计指标解释

工业 指从事自然资源的开采，对采掘品和农产品进行加工和再加工的物质生产部门。具体包括：（1）对自然资源的开采，如采矿、晒盐等（但不包括禽兽捕猎和水产捕捞）；（2）对农副产品的加工、再加工，如粮油加工、食品加工、缫丝、纺织、制革等；（3）对采掘品的加工、再加工，如炼铁、炼钢、化工生产、石油加工、机器制造、木材加工等，以及电力、自来水、煤气的生产和供应等；（4）对工业品的修理、翻新，如机器设备的修理、交通运输工具（如汽车）的修理等。

工业统计调查单位为独立核算法人工业企业。

独立核算法人工业企业指从事工业生产经营活动的单位。独立核算法人工业企业应同时具备以下条件：①依法成立，有自己的名称、组织机构和场所，能够承担民事责任；②独立拥有和使用资产，承担负债，有权与其他单位签订合同；③独立核算盈亏，并能够编制资产负债表。

国有及国有控股企业 指国有企业加上国有控股企业。国有企业（即原全民所有制工业或国营工业）指企业全部资产归国家所有，并按《中华人民共和国企业法人登记管理条例》规定登记注册的非公司制的经济组织。包括国有企业、国有独资公司和国有联营企业。1957年以前的公私合营和私营工业，后均改造为国营工业，1992年改为国有工业，这部分工业的资料不单独分列时，均包括在国有企业内。国有控股企业是对混合所有制经济的企业进行的“国有控股”分类。它是指这些企业的全部资产中国有资产（股份）相对其他所有者中的任何一个所有者占资（股）最多的企业。该分组反映了国有经济控股情况。

本篇涉及的其他企业登记注册类型的解释详见综合篇。

轻工业 指主要提供生活消费品和制作手工工具的工业。按其所使用的原料不同，可分为两大类：（1）以农产品为原料的轻工业，是指直接或间接以农产品为基本原料的轻工业。主要包括食品制造、饮料制造、烟草加工、纺织、缝纫、皮革和毛皮制作、造纸以及印刷等工业；（2）以非农产品为原料的轻工业，是指以工业品为原料的轻工业。主要包括文教体育用品、化学药品制造、合成纤维制造、日用化学制品、日用玻璃制品、日用金属制品、手工工具制造、医疗器械制造、文化和办公用机械制造等工业。

重工业 指为国民经济各部门提供物质技术基础的主要生产资料的工业。按其生产性质和产品用途，可以分为下列三类：（1）采掘（伐）工业，是指对自然资源的开采，包括石油开采、煤炭开采、金属矿开采、非金属矿开采等工业；（2）原材料工业，指向国民经济各部门提供基本材料、动力和燃料的工业。包括金属冶炼及加工、炼焦及焦炭、化学、化工原料、水泥、人造板以及电力、石油和煤炭加工等工业；（3）加工工业，是指对工业原材料进行再加工制造的工业。包括装备国民经济各部门的机械设备制造工业、金属结构、水泥制品等工业，以及为农业提供的生产资料如化肥、农药等工业。

根据上述划分原则，修理业中以重工业产品为修理作业对象的划为重工业，反之划为轻工业。

工业总产值

（1）定义：

工业总产值是工业企业在一定时期内生产的以货币形式表现的工业最终产品和提供工业性劳务活动的总价值量。它反映一定时间内工业生产的总规模和总水平。

（2）计算原则：

工业生产的原则，即凡是企业在报告期生产的经检验合格的产品，不管是否在报告期销售，均包括在内。

最终产品的原则，即凡是计入工业总产值的产品，必须是本企业生产的经检验合格的，不需要再进行任何加工的最终产品。如果企业有中间产品（半成品）对外销售，则对外销售的中间产品应视为企业的最终产品。

工厂法原则，即工业总产值是以工业企业作为基本计算（核算）单位，即按企业的最终产品计算工业总产值。按这种方法计算的工业总产值，不允许同一产品价值在企业内部重复计算，不能把企业内部各个车间（分厂）生产的成果相加，但允许企业间的重复计算。

（3）内容及计算方法：

1995年全国工业普查对工业总产值（原规定）的内容及计算原则和方法做了某些修订，修订后的工业总产值（新规定）包括三项内容：即本期生产成品价值、对外加工费收入、在制品半成品期末期初差额价值三部分。

本期生产成品价值指企业本期生产，并在报告期内不再进行加工，经检验、包装入库的全部工业成品（半成品）价值合计，包括企业生产的自制设备及提供给本企业在建工程、其他非工业部门和福利部门等单位使用的成品价值。本期生产成品价值为按自备原材料生产的产品的数量乘以本期不含增值税（销项税额）的产品实际销售平均单价计算；会计核算中按成本价格转账的自制设备和自产自用的成品，按成本价格计算生产成品价值。生产成品价值中不包括用订货者来料加工的成品（半成品）价值。

对外加工费收入指企业在报告期内完成的对外承接的工业品加工（包括用订货者来料加工生产）的加工费收入和对外工业修理作业所取得的加工费收入。对外加工费收入按不含增值税（销项税额）的价格计算，可根据会计“产品销售收入”科目的有关资料取得。

对于本企业对内非工业部门提供的加工修理、设备安装的劳务收入，如果企业会计核算基础较好，能取得这部分资料，而且这部分价值所占比重较大，应包括在对外加工费收入中。

自制半成品在制品期末期初差额价值指企业报告期自制半成品在制品期末减期初的差额价值，本指标一般可以从会计核算资料中取得。如果会计产品成本核算中不计算半成品、在制品的成本，则总产值中也不包括这部分价值,反之则包括。

（4）工业总产值统计范围变化和计算方法修订情况：

1984年以前工业总产值不包括村办工业，村办工业总产值划归农业。1984年以后工业总产值包括村办工业。

1995年工业普查对工业总产值计算方法做了修订，即从1995年始按新修订（新规定）方法计算工业总产值。新规定与原规定的区别如下：

全价与加工费的计算原则不同：新规定为凡自备原材料，不论其生产繁简程度如何，一律按全价计算工业总产值；凡来料加工，允许按加工费计算工业总产值。原规定则视生产加工的繁简程度不同，规定哪些行业按全价，哪些行业按加工费计算工业总产值。

自制半成品、在产品期末期初差额价值的计算原则不同：新规定要求，凡会计产品成本核算时计算了成本的差额价值，总产值中就应包括，否则可不包括；原规定则按生产周期六个月的界限区分，凡生产周期六个月以上的企业，总产值计算中应包括这部分差额价值，否则可不包括。

计算价格不同：新规定按不含增值税（销项税额）的价格计算；原规定则按含增值税（销项税额）的价格计算。

工业增加值 指工业企业在报告期内以货币表现的工业生产活动的最终成果。

工业增加值有两种计算方法：一是生产法，即工业总产出减去工业中间投入加上应交增值税；二是收入法，即从收入的角度出发，根据生产要素在生产过程中应得到的收入份额计算，具体构成项目有固定资产折旧、劳动者报酬、生产税净额、营业盈余，这种方法也称要素分配法。本年鉴中的工业增加值是以收入法计算的。

生产法工业增加值的计算方法为：

工业增加值＝工业总产出–工业中间投入+应交增值税

（1）工业总产出：指工业企业在一定时期内工业生产活动的总成果。工业总产出包括：成品生产价值，对外加工费收入，自制半成品、在产品期末期初差额价值。1995年后用新规定计算的工业总产值代替。

（2）工业中间投入：指工业企业在工业生产活动中消耗的外购物质产品和对外支付的服务费用。服务费用包括支付给物质生产部门（工业、农业、批发零售贸易业、建筑业、运输邮电业）的服务费用和支付给非物质生产部门（如保险、金融、文化教育、科学研究、医疗卫生、行政管理等）的服务费用。工业中间投入的确定须遵循以下原则：必须从外部购入的，并已计入工业总产出的产品和服务价值；必须是本期投入生产，并一次性消耗掉（包括本期摊销的低值易耗品等）的产品和服务价值。

工业中间投入包括直接材料费用、制造费用中的工业中间投入、管理费用中的工业中间投入、销售费用中的工业中间投入和利息支出五部分。

资产总计 指企业拥有或控制的能以货币计量的经济资源，包括各种财产、债权和其他权利。资产按流动性分为流动资产、长期投资、固定资产、无形资产、递延资产和其他资产。该指标根据企业会计“资产负债表”中“资产总计”项目的期末数增列。

流动资产 指企业可以在一年内或者超过一年的一个生产周期内变现或者耗用的资产，包括现金及各种存款、短期投资，应收及预付款项、存货等。

固定资产原价 指企业在建造、购置、安装、改建、扩建、技术改造某项固定资产时所支出的全部货币总额。它一般包括买价、包装费、运杂费和安装费等。

固定资产净值 指固定资产原价减去历年已提折旧额后的净额。计算公式为：

固定资产净值=固定资产原价-累计折旧

负债合计 指企业所承担的能以货币计量，将以资产或劳务偿付的债务，偿还形式包括货币、资产或提供劳务。负债一般按偿还期长短分为流动负债和长期负债。根据会计“资产负债表”中“负债合计”的年末数填列。

所有者权益合计 指企业投资人对企业净资产的所有权。企业净资产为企业全部资产与企业全部负债的差额，包括实收资本、资本公积、盈余公积、未分配利润等。根据会计“资产负债表”中“所有者权益”项的期末数填列。

主营业务收入 指会计“利润表”中对应指标的本年累计数。未执行2001年《企业会计制度》的企业，用“产品销售收入”的本期累计数代替。

主营业务成本 指会计“利润表”中对应指标的本年累计数。未执行2001年《企业会计制度》的企业，用“产品销售成本”的本期累计数代替。

主营业务税金及附加 指会计“利润表”中对应指标的本年累计数。未执行2001年《企业会计制度》的企业，用“产品销售税金及附加”的本期累计数代替。

利润总额 指企业在生产经营过程中各种收入扣除各种耗费后的盈余，反映企业在报告期内实现的盈亏总额，包括营业利润、补贴收入、投资净收益和营业外收支净额。根据会计“利润表”中的对应指标的本期累计数填列。

本年应交增值税 指企业按税法规定，从事货物销售或提供加工、修理修配劳务等增加货物价值的活动本期应交纳的税金。指企业在报告期应交增值税额。计算公式为：

本年应交增值税=销项税额-（进项税额-进项税额转出）-出口抵减内销产品应纳税额-减免税款+出口退税

本年进项税额 指工业企业在报告期内购入货物或接受应税劳务而支付的、准予从销项税额中抵扣的增值税额。

本年销项税额 指工业企业在报告期内销售货物或提供应税劳务应收取的增值税额。

总资产贡献率 反映企业全部资产的获利能力，是企业经营业绩和管理水平的集中体现，是评价和考核企业盈利能力的核心指标。计算公式为：

总资产贡献率（%）=（利润总额+税金总额+利息支出）/平均资产总额×100%

公式中：税金总额为产品销售税金及附加与应交增值税之和；平均资产总额为期初期末资产之和的算术平均值。

资产负债率 该指标既反映企业经营风险的大小，也反映企业利用债权人提供的资金从事经营活动的能力。计算公式为：

资产负债率（%）=负债总额/资产总额×100%

资产与负债均为报告期期末数。

流动资产周转次数 指一定时期内流动资产完成的周转次数，反映投入工业企业流动资金的周转速度。计算公式为：

流动资产周转次数=产品销售收入/全部流动资产平均余额

公式中：全部流动资产平均余额为期初和期末的流动资产之和的算术平均值。

成本费用利润率 反映企业投入的生产成本及费用的经济效益，同时也反映企业降低成本所取得的经济效益。计算公式为：

成本费用利润率（%）=利润总额/成本费用总额×100%

公式中：成本费用总额为产品销售成本、销售费用、管理费用、财务费用之和。

产品销售率 该指标反映工业产品已实现销售的程度，是分析工业产销衔接情况，研究工业产品满足社会需求的指标。计算公式为：

产品销售率（%）=工业销售产值/工业总产值（现价）×100%

Explanatory Notes on Main Statistical Indicators

Industry refers to the material production sector which is engaged in the extraction of natural resources and processing and reprocessing of minerals and agricultural products, including (1) extraction of natural resources, such as mining, salt production (but not including hunting and fishing); (2) processing and reprocessing of farm and sideline produces, such as rice husking, flour milling, wine making, oil pressing, silk reeling, spinning and weaving, and leather making; (3) manufacture of industrial products, such as steel making, iron smelting, chemicals manufacturing, petroleum processing, machine building, timber processing; water and gas production and electricity generation and supply; (4)repairing of industrial products such as the repairing of machinery and means of transport (including cars).

In industrial statistics surveys, the units of enquiry are corporate industrial enterprises with independent accounting systems.

Corporate industrial enterprises with independent accounting systems refer to enterprises engaging in industrial production activities, which meet the following requirements: (1) They are established legally, having their own names, organizations, location and able to take civil liability; (2) They possess and use their assets independently, assume liabilities and are entitled to sign contracts with other units; (3) They are financially independent and compile their own balance sheets.

State-owned and State-holding Enterprises refer to state-owned enterprises plus State-holding enterprises. State-owned enterprises (originally known as State-run enterprises with ownership by the whole society) are non-corporate economic entities registered in accordance with the Regulation of the People's Republic of China on the Management of Registration of Legal Enterprises, where all assets are owned by the State. Included in this category are State-owned enterprises, State-funded corporations and State-owned joint-operation enterprises. Joint State- private industries and private industries, which existed before 1957, were transformed into state-run industries since 1957, and into State-owned industries after 1992. Statistics on those enterprises are included in the State- owned industries instead of being grouped them separately. State-holding enterprises are a sub- classification of enterprises with mixed ownership, referring to enterprises where the percentage of State assets (or shares by the State) is larger than any other single share holder of the same enterprise. This sub- classification illustrates the control of the State over a particular industry.

For explanation of enterprises of other types of registration covered in this chapter, please refer to General Survey.

Light Industry refers to the industry that produces consumer goods and hand tools. It consists of two categories, depending on the materials used:

(1) Industries using farm products as raw materials. These are the branches of light industry which directly or indirectly use farm products as basic raw materials, including the manufacture of food and beverages, tobacco processing, textile, clothing, fur and leather manufacturing, paper making, printing, etc.

(2) Industries using non-farm products as raw materials. These are the branches of light industry which use manufactured goods as raw materials, including the manufacture of cultural, educational articles and sports goods, chemicals, synthetic fibre, chemical products for daily use, glass products for daily use, metal products for daily use, hand tools, medical apparatus and instruments, and the manufacture of cultural and office machinery.

Heavy Industry refers to the industry which produces capital goods, and provides various sectors of the national economy with necessary material and technical basis for production. It consists of the following three branches according to the purpose of production or the use of products:

(1) Mining, quarrying and logging industry, which refers to the industry that extracts natural resources, including extraction of petroleum, coal, metal and non-metal ores.

(2) Raw materials industry refers to the industry that provides various sectors of the national economy with raw materials, fuels and power. It includes smelting and processing of metals, coking and coke chemistry, chemical materials and building materials such as cement, plywood, and power, petroleum refining and coal dressing

(3) Manufacturing industry which refers to the industry that processes raw materials. It includes machine-building industries which equip sectors of the national economy; industries producing metal structure and cement products; and industries producing means of agricultural production, such as chemical fertilizers and pesticides.

In accordance with the above principles of classification, the repairing trades, which are engaged primarily in repairing products of heavy industry, are classified as heavy industry while those which are engaged in repairing products of light industry are classified as light industry.

Gross Industrial Output Value

(1) Definition: Gross industrial output value is the total volume of final industrial products produced and industrial services provided during a given period in monetary terms. It reflects the total achievements and overall scale of industrial production during a given period.

(2) Principles for calculation:

Statistics on industrial production follow the principle that all products produced by the enterprises and accepted through quality check during the reference period are to be included no matter whether they are sold or not during the reference period.

Determination of final products follows the principle that all products that are included in the calculation of gross industrial output value are the final products of the enterprise which have been accepted through quality check and require no further processing. If an enterprise has intermediate (semi-finished) products to sell, these intermediate products are considered as the final products of the enterprise.

Gross industrial output value is calculated following the principle of factory approach, i.e. industrial enterprise is used as the basic accounting unit in calculating the gross industrial output value. By this approach, value of the same product is not to be double-counted, and the output value of different workshops (branch factories) within the enterprise should not be added. However, this approach allows the possibility of double counting between enterprises.

(3) Content and method of calculation: The old definition of gross industrial output value was modified during the 1995 National Industrial Census. The revised (new) definition of gross industrial output value consists of 3 components: value of the finished products during the reference period, income from processing for external parties, and value of change in semi-finished products between the end and the beginning of the reference period.

Value of finished products during the reference period: refers to the value of all finished (semi-finished) industrial products that are produced during the reference period without the need for further processing, checked for acceptance, packed and put into the warehouse of the enterprise, including the value of own-produced equipment and the value of products provided to the projects under construction of the enterprise, and to other non-industrial or welfare units. Value of finished products during the reference period is calculated by the quantity of products produced using own materials multiplied by the average unit prices at which products are sold (excluding value-added tax). Own-produced equipment and products produced for own use are valued at cost prices as in the case of enterprise accounting. Value of finished products does not include the value of finished products (semi-finished products) that are produced using the materials from the clients who place the orders.

Income from external processing: refers to income from contracted external processing of industrial products (including processing of industrial products using materials from the clients), and the income from industrial repairing work provided to other parties. Income from external processing is calculated using information from the item "products sales income" in the enterprise accounting at the prices with value-added tax excluded.

For income from services such as processing, repairing and installation of equipment provided to non- industrial units within the enterprise, if the accounting work of the enterprise is good enough to separate it from other records, and the share of such services is significant, it should also be included in the income from external processing.

Value of change in semi-finished products between the end and the beginning of the reference period: refers to the value of change in semi-finished products between the end and the beginning of the reference period, which generally can be obtained from accounting records of enterprises. If the enterprise accounting excludes the cost of semi-finished products, then it should not be included in the gross industrial output value, and the reverse if otherwise.

(4) Changes in the scope and method of calculation of the gross industrial output value

Prior to 1984, the value of rural industry run by villages was classified into agriculture instead of industry Since 1984, it has been included in the gross industrial output value. Method of calculation for the gross industrial output value was modified in the industrial census in 1995. The difference in the new method as compared with the old one is outlined below:

Principle in using full value vs. processing fee: The new method stipulates that all products produced using own materials are to be calculated with full value in reporting the gross industrial output value irrespective of the complexity of production, and for external processing, it allows calculation using processing fee. In the old method, however, the use of full value or processing fee was determined by the degree of complexity of production in different branches of industries.

Principle in determining the value of change in semi-finished products: The new method requires that value of change in semi-finished products should be included in the gross industrial output value if it is included in the accounting record of the enterprise, otherwise it should not be included. In the old method, it is determined by the type of enterprises in terms of production cycle. If the production cycle is over 6 months, the value of change in semi-finished products is included in the gross industrial output value, otherwise it is not.

Difference in prices: The new method uses prices excluding value-added tax in the calculation of gross industrial output value, while the old method used prices including value-added tax.

Value–added of Industry refers to the final results of industrial production of industrial enterprises in money terms during the reference period.

Industrial value-added can be calculated by two approaches: the production approach, i.e. gross industrial output value minus intermediate input plus value-added tax, and the income approach, i.e. income for various factors used in the course of production, including depreciation of fixed assets, remuneration of labourers, net of production tax, and operating surplus. Value-added of industry in the Yearbook is calculated by the income approach as follows:

Value-added of industry = gross industrial output - industrial intermediate input + value-added tax

(1) Gross industrial output: refers to the total achievements of industrial production activities during a given period. Gross industrial output includes value of finished products, income from external processing, and value of change in semi-finished products between the end and the beginning of the reference period. Since 1995, the gross industrial output value obtained by the new method is used in the calculation.

(2) Industrial intermediate input: refers to purchased goods and paid services consumed during the industrial production of enterprises. Fees paid for services include fees paid for the services provided by material production sectors (industry, agriculture, wholesale and retail trade, construction, transport, post and telecommunications) and by non-material production sectors (insurance, banking, culture, education, scientific research, health and medical care, public administration, etc.). The determination of industrial intermediate input follows the principle that the goods and services must be purchased from outside and included in the gross industrial output, and that the goods and services are inputted into production and consumed (include low-value consumables) during the reference period.

Industrial intermediate input includes 5 components, namely direct consumption of materials, industrial intermediate input in manufacturing cost, industrial intermediate input in management cost, industrial intermediate input in marketing cost and expenditure on interest.

Total Assets refer to all economic resources, in monetary term, these are owned or controlled by enterprises, including properties, creditor's equity and other economic rights of all forms. Classified by the degree of liquidity, total assets include working capitals, long-term investment, fixed assets, intangible assets, deferred assets and other assets. Data on this indicator can be obtained by the year-end figures of total assets in the Assets and Liability Table of accounting records of enterprises.

Working Capital refers to capital that an enterprise can cash or use during one year or one production cycle that may exceed one year, including cash and savings deposits of various forms, short-term investment, money receivable and prepaid money, inventories, etc.

Original Value of Fixed Assets refers to the total value, in monetary terms, that an enterprise spent on fixed assets, through construction, purchase, installation, transformation, expansion or technical upgrading. Generally, it covers cost of purchase, packing, transportation and installation, etc.

Net Value of Fixed Assets refers to the original value of fixed assets minus depreciation over the years, i.e.:

Net value of fixed assets = original value of fixed assets - cumulative depreciation

Total Liabilities refer to payable liabilities of enterprises that have to be repaid in terms of money, assets or labour services. In terms of payment, it can be divided into liquid liabilities and long-term liabilities. Data on this item is obtained from the ending figures on total liabilities from the Assets and Liability Table from the enterprises.

Total Equity refers to the ownership of net assets of enterprise by its investors. Net assets equal total assets minus total liabilities of the enterprise, including the paid-in capital, accumulation of capital and operating surplus and non-distributed profits. Data are obtained from the ending figures on "total equity" from the "balance sheets".

Revenue from Principal Business refers to the annual accumulation of the corresponding item in the "profit table" of the accountant. For enterprises that do not follow the 2001 Enterprise Accounting Standards, the year-end accumulation of revenue from the sales of products is used as a substitute.

Cost of Principal Business refers to the annual accumulation of the corresponding item in the "profit table" of the accountant. For enterprises that do not follow the 2001 Enterprise Accounting Standards, theyear-end accumulation of cost for the sales of products is used as a substitute.

Tax and Extra Charges from Principal Bosiness refer to the annual accumulation of the corresponding item in the "profit table" of the accountant. For enterprises that do not follow the 2001 Enterprise Accounting Standards, the year-end accumulation of tax and extra charges from the sales of products is used as a substitute.

Total Profits refers to the balance of various incomes minus various spendings in the course of operation, reflecting the total profits and losses of enterprises in reporting period. It includes: operating profits, income from subsidies, net investment income and net income from activities other than operation. Data are obtained from the annual accumulation of the corresponding item in the "profit table" of the accountant.

Value-added Tax Payable in the Current Year refers to the payable tax of enterprises which engaged in selling of goods or providing services that bring added value to the goods, such as processing, repairing, fitting and other activities should be paid according to Tax Law. It refers to the amount of the value-added tax which should be paid by the enterprises during the reference period. The formula is as tollows:

Value-added Tax Payable in the Current Year = tax on sales-(tax on purchase-transferred tax on purchase)- exports deduct tax payable on domestic sales-tax relief+the export tax rebate.

Tax on Purchase in Current Year refers to goods purchased by industrial enterprises or value added tax that should be paid but being granted the right to deduct from the tax on sales.

Tax on Sales in Current Year refers to value added tax on industrial enterprises from sales of goods or taxable services that should be charged value added tax.

Ratio of Profits, Taxes and Interests to Average Assets reflects the profit-making capability of all assets of the enterprise and is a key indicator manifesting the performance and management and evaluating the profit-making potential of the enterprise. It is calculated as

$$\text{Ratio of Profits, Taxes and Interests to Average Assets}(\%) = \frac{\text{otal profits+ total taxes+ interest payment}}{\text{average assets}} \times 100\%$$

In the above formula, total taxes is the sum of tax and extra charges on the sales of products and value-added tax payable; and average assets is the arithmetic mean of the sum of beginning assets and ending assets.

Ratio of Debts to Assets reflects both the operation risk and the capability of the enterprise in making use of the capital from the creditors. It is calculated as follows:

$$\text{Ratio of Debts to Assets}(\%) = \frac{\text{total debts}}{\text{total assets}} \times 100\%$$

Both assets and debts are figures at the end of the reference period.

Turnover of Working Capital refers to the number of times of turnover of working capital in a given period of time, which reflects the speed of the turnover of working capital of industrial enterprises, and is calculated as follows:

$$\text{Turnover of Working Capital} = \frac{\text{sales revenue of products}}{\text{average balance of total working capital}}$$

In the above formula, average balance of total working capital refers to the arithmetic mean of the sum of working capital at the beginning and at the end of the reference period.

Ratio of Profits to Total Industrial Costs refers to the ratio of profits realized in a given period to the total costs in the same period, which reflects the economic efficiency of input cost and is calculated as follows:

$$\text{Ratio of Profits to Total Industrial Cost}(\%) = \frac{\text{total profits}}{\text{total costs}} \times 100\%$$

Total costs in the above formula are the sum of cost of products sold, marketing cost, management cost and financial cost.

Sales Ratio of Products is an indicator reflecting the actual sale of industrial products, analyzing the production-selling and supply-demand relations. It is calculated as:

$$\text{Sales Ratio of Products (\%)} = \frac{\text{value of industrial sales}}{\text{gross industrial output value (current prices)}} \times 100\%$$

13 能 源

ENERGY

资料整理：于元英　张　育　李　婷
Data management：Yu Yuanying　Zhang Yu　Li Ting
数据审核：马建华
Data audit：Ma Jianhua

第十三部分　能源

一、简要说明

1.本章资料包括规模以上工业能源购销存情况、全市单位GDP能耗、规模以上工业企业用水情况等，由西安市统计局能源与环境处提供。

2.2018年数据口径与往年相同。

二、主要指标

规模以上工业综合能源消费量（万吨标准煤）	674.69	比上年下降	3.4%
单位GDP能耗（吨标准煤/万元）	0.370	比上年下降	5.99%

13　ENERGY

Ⅰ.Brief Introduction

1.Data in this chapter reflects energy purchases consumption and inventory of industrial enterprises above designated size,energy consumption per unit of GDP in whole city, and statistics on water use of industrial enterprises above designated size. data in this chapter are provided and compiled by Energy and Environment Division of the Xi'an Bureau of Statistics.

2.The data caliber of 2018 is same as the previous years.

Ⅱ.Major Indicators

		Increase over Preceding Year
Comprehensive Energy Consumption Above Designated Size(10 000 Tons of Standard Coal)	674.69	-3.4%
Energy Consumption of GDP per Unit (Tons of Standard Coal /10 000 yuan)	0.370	-5.99%

13-1 全市及各区县单位GDP能耗

Energy Consumption per Unit of GDP by Region

单位：吨标准煤 / 万元 (ton of SCE/10 000 yuan)

地 区 Region	单位GDP能耗 Energy Consumption Per Unit of GDP															
	GDP按2005年价格计算 GDP are calculated at 2005 constant prices						GDP按2010年价格计算 GDP are calculated at 2010 constant prices						GDP按2015年价格计算 GDP are calculated at 2015 constant prices			
	2005	2006	2007	2008	2009	2010	2010	2011	2012	2013	2014	2015	2015	2016	2017	2018
西安市 Xi'an	**0.911**	**0.873**	**0.823**	**0.768**	**0.726**	**0.711**	**0.575**	**0.555**	**0.535**	**0.516**	**0.486**	**0.470**	**0.410**	**0.394**	**0.384**	**0.370**
新城区 Xincheng	0.783	0.751	0.708	0.667	0.629	0.621	0.563	0.544	0.525	0.506	0.479	0.463	0.416	0.401	0.378	0.353
碑林区 Beilin	0.640	0.613	0.580	0.547	0.514	0.510	0.438	0.421	0.406	0.392	0.368	0.356	0.287	0.277	0.258	0.250
莲湖区 Lianhu	0.766	0.735	0.701	0.646	0.609	0.587	0.521	0.501	0.483	0.466	0.430	0.416	0.372	0.359	0.330	0.314
灞桥区 Baqiao	1.194	1.163	1.091	1.023	0.964	0.923	0.663	0.638	0.615	0.592	0.562	0.543	0.517	0.497	0.426	0.419
未央区 Weiyang	1.122	1.078	1.019	0.951	0.894	0.882	0.680	0.655	0.632	0.609	0.563	0.539	0.444	0.427	0.376	0.369
雁塔区 Yanta	0.884	0.842	0.795	0.749	0.703	0.674	0.512	0.494	0.476	0.459	0.441	0.425	0.362	0.349	0.313	0.299
阎良区 Yanliang	0.825	0.778	0.740	0.695	0.656	0.652	0.533	0.515	0.497	0.480	0.444	0.430	0.364	0.352	0.311	0.326
临潼区 Lintong	0.940	0.912	0.860	0.790	0.753	0.717	0.676	0.652	0.629	0.607	0.558	0.541	0.502	0.484	0.427	0.378
长安区 Chang'an	1.059	0.994	0.939	0.890	0.841	0.824	0.642	0.619	0.596	0.575	0.555	0.532	0.460	0.443	0.345	0.334
高陵区 Gaoling	0.892	0.848	0.790	0.747	0.704	0.677	0.487	0.467	0.451	0.435	0.403	0.391	0.345	0.333	0.310	0.333
鄠邑区 Huyi	1.411	1.367	1.287	1.188	1.123	1.089	0.978	0.940	0.906	0.873	0.844	0.811	0.791	0.761	0.657	0.640
蓝田县 Lantian	1.727	1.673	1.606	1.517	1.444	1.414	1.083	1.047	1.011	0.978	0.924	0.895	0.771	0.742	0.680	0.669
周至县 Zhouzhi	1.502	1.465	1.386	1.309	1.237	1.212	0.959	0.928	0.897	0.867	0.801	0.778	0.649	0.626	0.567	0.545
西咸新区 Xixian																0.862

13-1 续表 continude

地 区 Region	比上年增长(%) Growth Rates over Preceding Year(%)												
	2006	2007	2008	2009	2010	2011	2012	2013	2014	2015	2016	2017	2018
西安市 Xi'an	**-4.15**	**-5.75**	**-6.65**	**-5.56**	**-2.06**	**-3.56**	**-3.51**	**-3.57**	**-5.89**	**-3.20**	**-3.83**	**-4.61**	**-5.99**
新城区 Xincheng	-4.15	-5.67	-5.79	-5.80	-1.15	-3.51	-3.50	-3.50	-5.39	-3.27	-3.58	-3.27	-4.72
碑林区 Beilin	-4.18	-5.44	-5.65	-5.95	-0.91	-3.89	-3.50	-3.50	-6.06	-3.20	-3.66	-3.65	-5.42
莲湖区 Lianhu	-4.07	-4.60	-7.93	-5.65	-3.58	-3.84	-3.60	-3.61	-7.76	-3.14	-3.58	-5.93	-6.12
灞桥区 Baqiao	-2.54	-6.20	-6.24	-5.80	-4.20	-3.81	-3.62	-3.64	-5.20	-3.30	-3.75	-6.95	-8.25
未央区 Weiyang	-3.97	-5.44	-6.63	-6.05	-1.31	-3.60	-3.60	-3.60	-7.60	-4.16	-3.86	-4.49	-4.48
雁塔区 Yanta	-4.71	-5.64	-5.80	-6.08	-4.18	-3.61	-3.61	-3.60	-3.89	-3.58	-3.55	-6.36	-6.54
阎良区 Yanliang	-5.77	-4.80	-6.08	-5.62	-0.61	-3.38	-3.50	-3.50	-7.59	-3.00	-3.46	-3.99	-4.32
临潼区 Lintong	-3.03	-5.73	-8.16	-4.58	-4.81	-3.52	-3.51	-3.51	-8.07	-3.00	-3.46	-6.29	-5.71
长安区 Chang'an	-6.15	-5.53	-5.22	-5.50	-2.08	-3.60	-3.63	-3.63	-3.40	-4.10	-3.56	-5.10	-4.56
高陵区 Gaoling	-4.85	-6.85	-5.50	-5.70	-3.82	-3.93	-3.52	-3.54	-7.32	-3.00	-3.52	-4.00	-5.88
鄠邑区 Huyi	-3.07	-5.85	-7.70	-5.50	-2.99	-3.85	-3.60	-3.62	-3.40	-3.82	-3.84	-3.89	-5.86
蓝田县 Lantian	-3.13	-4.01	-5.50	-4.84	-2.06	-3.39	-3.40	-3.30	-5.48	-3.17	-3.84	-3.27	-5.21
周至县 Zhouzhi	-2.46	-5.43	-5.51	-5.50	-2.06	-3.30	-3.30	-3.30	-7.63	-2.90	-3.50	-3.64	-5.59
西咸新区 Xixian													-12.51

注：能源消耗按等价值计算；2013年以前数据，根据第三次经济普查结果进行了调整。

13-2　主要年份全社会用电量

单位：万千瓦时

行　业	Sector	2000	2007	2008
总　计	**Total**	**732373**	**1482896**	**1605089**
#行业用电量合计	Total of Industry of Electricity	599855	1215799	1293574
1. 第一产业	Primary Industry	77579	120134	127054
2. 第二产业	Secondary Industry	354245	700026	724852
3. 第三产业	Tertiary Industry	168031	395639	441668
一、农、林、牧、渔、水利业	Agriculture ,Forestry,Animal Husbandry and Fishery	77579	120134	127054
二、工业	Industry	345175	674990	696291
1. 轻工业	Light Industry	152125	187323	182176
2. 重工业	Heavy Industry	193050	487667	514115
三、建筑业	Construction	9070	25036	28561
四、交通运输、仓储及邮政业	Traffic,Transport, Storage and Post	22904	53825	56614
五、信息传输、计算机服务和软件业	Information Transmission,Computer Service and Software		21938	26680
六、商业、住宿和餐饮业	Commercial,Hotels and Catering Services		107343	111676
七、金融、房地产、商务及居民服务业	Finance,Real Estate,Business Affairs and Households Services		67674	81674
八、公共事业及管理组织	Public Utilities and Management Organization		144859	165024
九、城乡居民生活用电	Electricity Consumption of Urban and Rural Residents	132518	267097	311515
1. 乡村	Rural	31281	38395	63072
2. 城市	City	101237	228702	248443

注：1.本表数据来源于国网陕西省供电公司西安供电公司和国网陕西电力公司西咸供电公司。
2.2017年及以后为包含西咸新区数据。

Electricity Consumption of the Whole Society in Representative Years

(10 000 kw. h)

2009	2010	2011	2012	2013	2014	2015	2016	2017	2018
1724067	**1993751**	**2167453**	**2352571**	**2554679**	**2753213**	**2844836**	**3120582**	**3613693**	**3967465**
1358483	1499903	1590486	1706859	1854696	2002503	2049492	2216797	2586468	2821250
99083	103720	117984	109086	110405	95997	89970	87825	102033	28998
766029	883259	910360	932622	991202	1086105	1088866	1147294	1388903	1430389
493371	507924	562142	665151	753089	820401	870656	981678	1095531	1361863
99083	103720	117984	109086	110405	95997	89970	87825	102033	100432
724920	838317	859796	875018	920024	998132	997115	1062188	1287836	1326060
167144	177362	183766	175392	170246	165933	165290	170735	183582	
557776	660955	676030	699626	749778	832199	831826	891453	1104254	
41108	44942	50564	57605	71179	87973	91750	85106	101068	110600
62031	58509	66684	69633	78722	88805	90914	109911	128970	149353
29328	30760	33191	37444	39551	42662	46203	61950	77104	90433
122203	148418	166558	199970	228117	253199	277248	301414	334387	396284
102400	116163	131236	150832	165833	180824	185329	212666	232317	220400
177409	154074	164473	207271	240866	254911	270962	295737	322753	427688
365585	493848	576966	645713	699982	750710	795344	903785	1027226	1146216
99941	142059	169898	197937	216148	235938	241920	263871	288571	321715
265644	351789	407068	447776	483834	514773	553424	639914	738655	824501

13-3 规模以上工业企业能源购进、消费及库存（2018年）

能源名称	Name	年初库存量 Stock (year-beginning)	购进量 /实物量 Purchases	其中： 购自省外 Wherein: purchased from outside the province
原煤(吨)	Raw Coal (ton)	**904905**	**11389780**	**16435**
洗精煤(吨)	Washed Coal(ton)			
其他洗煤(吨)	Other Washed Coals(ton)	66968	295946	
煤制品（吨）	Briquettes(ton)	22		
焦炭(吨)	Coke(ton)	1	620	620
其他焦化产品(吨)	Other Coking Products(ton)			
焦炉煤气(万立方米)	Coke Oven Gas(10000 cu.m)			
高炉煤气(万立方米)	Blast Furnace Gas(10000 cu.m)			
转炉煤气(万立方米)	Converter Gas(10000 cu.m)			
发生炉煤气(万立方米)	Producer Gas(10000 cu.m)			
天然气（气态）（万立方米）	Natural Gas(10 000cu.m)	1206	62099	
液化天然气（液态）（吨）	Liquefied Natural Gas (Liquid)(ton)	15	2796	
煤层气(万立方米)	Voalbed Gas(10000 cu.m)			
原油(吨)	Crude Oil(ton)			
汽油(吨)	Gasoline(ton)	80	18918	692
煤油(吨)	Kerosene(ton)	45	173	
柴油(吨)	Diesel Oil(ton)	1360	81939	921
燃料油(吨)	Fuel Oil(ton)	12	465	
液化石油气(吨)	LPG(ton)		567	
炼厂干气(吨)	Refinery Gas(ton)			
石脑油(吨)	Naphtha(ton)			
润滑油（吨）	Lubricating Oil (ton)	1	751	
石蜡(吨)	Paraffin(ton)			
溶剂油（吨）	Solvent Oil (ton)	2	390	
石油焦(吨)	Petrol Coke(ton)			
石油沥青(吨)	Petroleum Asphalt(ton)	12	11926	5346
其它石油制品(吨)	Other Petroleum Products(ton)	71	2083	
热力(百万千焦)	Heat (1 million kilo-joule)		3799865	
电力(万千瓦时)	Electricity(10 000kwh)		803543	
煤矸石(用于燃料)(吨)	Coal Gangue(used for fuel)(ton)	15	2967	
城市生活垃圾(用于燃料)(吨)	City Domestic Waste(used for fuel)(ton)			
生物燃料（吨标准煤）	Biofuel(tons of SCE)	66	8725	
余热余压（百万千焦）	Residual Heat and Pressure(million of KJ)		194151	
工业废料(用于燃料)（吨）	Industrial Waste(used for fuel)(ton)			
其他燃料（吨标准煤）	Other Fuels(ton of SCE)		1276	
能源合计(吨标准煤)	Total Energy(ton of SCE)			

Energy Purchases, Consumption and Inventory of Industrial Enterprises above Designated Size (2018)

消费量 合计 Consumption Total	工业 生产消费 Industrial Production Consume	用于 原材料 as Raw Material	非工业 生产消费 Non-industrial Production Consume	期末库存量 Stock (year-end)
11507273	**11506445**	**1091156**	**828**	**778527**
241515	241515			114230
621	621			
62585	61822	946	763	817
2900	2896		4	40
18760	15588	175	3172	44
158	158			40
81986	78477	511	3509	1081
478	466		12	
566	491		75	
773	773			
391	391	386		1
11167	11167	11167		402
2083	2083			72
5569850	5533566		36284	
954474	946760		7714	
2034	2034			948
8735	8607		128	49
194151	194151			
1130	1130			148
10572819	10541480		31339	

13-4 规模以上工业企业分行业主要能源品种消费量（2018年）

Major Energy Consumption above Designated Size by Industry（2018）

行 业	Sector	原煤（吨） Raw Coal (ton)	天然气（万立方米） Natural Gas(10 000 cu.m)
总 计	**Total**	**11507273**	**62585**
煤炭开采和洗选业	Coal Mining and Dressing		
石油和天然气开采业	Petroleum and Natural Gas Extraction		
黑色金属矿采选业	Ferrous Metals Mining and Dressing		
有色金属矿采选业	Nonferrous Metals Mining and Dressing		
非金属矿采选业	Nonmetal Minerals Mining and Dressing		
开采辅助活动	Ancillary activities for mining		369
其他采矿业	Other Mining Industry		
农副食品加工业	Agricultural Products and Non-stable Food Processing Industry	227122	729
食品制造业	Food Production	1539	4089
酒、饮料和精制茶制造业	Wine, soft drinks and refined tea industry	7234	4502
烟草制品业	Tobacco Processing		21
纺织业	Textile Industry		299
纺织服装、服饰业	Textile, apparel industry		46
皮革、毛皮、羽毛及其制品和制鞋业	Leather, Fur, Feather (eiderdown) and Their Products Industry		
木材加工和木、竹、藤、棕、草制品业	Timber Processing,Bamboo,Cane,Palm Fiber and Straw Products		
家具制造业	Furniture Manufacturing		32
造纸及纸制品业	Papermaking and Paper products	556	625
印刷和记录媒介复制业	Printing,Record Medium Reproduction		569
文教、工美、体育和娱乐用品制造业	Culture, education, Craft art, sports and entertainment goods manufacturing industry		
石油加工、炼焦和核燃料加工业	Petroleum Refining, Ccoke Making and Nuclear Fuel Processing Industry		339
化学原料和化学制品制造业	Raw Chemical Materials and Chemical Products	1390745	3231
医药制造业	Medical and Pharmaceutical Products	432	2294
化学纤维制造业	Chemical Fiber		
橡胶和塑料制品业	Rubber and plastic products industry	44584	316
非金属矿物制品业	Nonmetal Mineral Products	112157	1762
黑色金属冶炼和压延加工业	Smelting and Pressing of Ferrous Metals	2883	174
有色金属冶炼和压延加工业	Smelting and Pressing of Nonferrou Metals		848
金属制品业	Metal Products		382
通用设备制造业	General Equipment Manufacturing Industry		669
专用设备制造业	Special Purpose Equipment		443
汽车制造业	Automotive Manufacturing		4777
铁路、船舶、航空航天和其他运输设备制造业	Railroad, marine, aerospace and other transportation equipment manufacturing		90
电气机械和器材制造业	Electric Equipment and Machinery		2948
计算机、通信和其他电子设备制造业	Communication Equipment, Computer and Other Electronic Equipment Manufacturing Industry		3097
仪器仪表制造业	Instrument manufacturing industry		31
其他制造业	Other manufacturing		31
废弃资源综合利用	Comprehensive utilization of waste resources		
金属制品、机械和设备修理业	Metal products, machinery and equipment repair industry		7
电力、热力生产和供应业	Electric Power, Heating Power Generating and Supplying Industry	9720021	27466
燃气生产和供应业	Gas Mining and Supplying Industry		2135
水的生产和供应业	Water Processing and Supplying Industry		263

13-4 续表 continued

行 业	Sector	汽油 (吨) Gasoline (ton)	柴油 (吨) Diesel Oil (ton)	热力 (百万千焦) Heat (million kilo joule)	电力 (万千瓦时) Electricity (10 000 kwh)
总 计	**Total**	**18760**	**81986**	**5569850**	**954474**
煤炭开采和洗选业	Coal Mining and Dressing				
石油和天然气开采业	Petroleum and Natural Gas Extraction				
黑色金属矿采选业	Ferrous Metals Mining and Dressing				
有色金属矿采选业	Nonferrous Metals Mining and Dressing				
非金属矿采选业	Nonmetal Minerals Mining and Dressing				
开采辅助活动	Ancillary activities for mining	1439	13192		3620
其他采矿业	Other Mining Industry				
农副食品加工业	Agricultural Products and Non-stable Food Processing Industry	828	670	1716239	19684
食品制造业	Food Production	683	1658	439149	19262
酒、饮料和精制茶制造业	Wine, soft drinks and refined tea industry	451	1135	142005	13109
烟草制品业	Tobacco Processing	31	37	93396	602
纺织业	Textile Industry	75	9	115514	21621
纺织服装、服饰业	Textile, apparel industry	63	9		149
皮革、毛皮、羽毛及其制品和制鞋业	Leather, Fur, Feather (eiderdown) and Their Products Industry	36		11149	276
木材加工和木、竹、藤、棕、草制品业	Timber Processing,Bamboo,Cane,Palm Fiber and Straw Products	18	13		1760
家具制造业	Furniture Manufacturing	197	182		2597
造纸及纸制品业	Papermaking and Paper products	83	159		3680
印刷和记录媒介复制业	Printing,Record Medium Reproduction	351	238	110486	11546
文教、工美、体育和娱乐用品制造业	Culture, education, Craft art, sports and entertainment goods manufacturing industry	185	962		1389
石油加工、炼焦和核燃料加工业	Petroleum Refining, Ccoke Making and Nuclear Fuel Processing Industry	772	246		2459
化学原料和化学制品制造业	Raw Chemical Materials and Chemical Products	518	1946	56440	84521
医药制造业	Medical and Pharmaceutical Products	754	129	155028	12460
化学纤维制造业	Chemical Fiber	10	4	1224067	5798
橡胶和塑料制品业	Rubber and plastic products industry	60	65	2205	19352
非金属矿物制品业	Nonmetal Mineral Products	993	47407	624	71205
黑色金属冶炼和压延加工业	Smelting and Pressing of Ferrous Metals	4	39		3088
有色金属冶炼和压延加工业	Smelting and Pressing of Nonferrou Metals	567	114	22225	28285
金属制品业	Metal Products	748	364	8620	15312
通用设备制造业	General Equipment Manufacturing Industry	1125	173	382	11483
专用设备制造业	Special Purpose Equipment	2248	1419	38236	15454
汽车制造业	Automotive Manufacturing	2250	6175	345632	116620
铁路、船舶、航空航天和其他运输设备制造业	Railroad, marine, aerospace and other transportation equipment manufacturing	636	333	58226	12017
电气机械和器材制造业	Electric Equipment and Machinery	1372	582	761230	61009
计算机、通信和其他电子设备制造业	Communication Equipment, Computer and Other Electronic Equipment Manufacturing Industry	415	51	210388	209622
仪器仪表制造业	Instrument manufacturing industry	689	26	4659	2568
其他制造业	Other manufacturing	99	73		610
废弃资源综合利用	Comprehensive utilization of waste resources	3	168		121
金属制品、机械和设备修理业	Metal products, machinery and equipment repair	14	5		107
电力、热力生产和供应业	Electric Power, Heating Power Generating and Supplying Industry	203	4299	53950	164818
燃气生产和供应业	Gas Mining and Supplying Industry	518	84		7337
水的生产和供应业	Water Processing and Supplying Industry	317	22		10878

13-5 规模以上工业企业分行业综合能源消费量（2018年）

Comprehensive Energy Consumption by Sector above Designated Size（2018）

单位：吨标准煤 (ton of SCE)

行　业	Scetor	2018	比上年增长(%) Increase over Preceding Year (%)
总　计	**Total**	**6746859**	**-3.4**
煤炭开采和洗选业	Coal Mining and Dressing		
石油和天然气开采业	Petroleum and Natural Gas Extraction		
黑色金属矿采选业	Ferrous Metals Mining and Dressing		
有色金属矿采选业	Nonferrous Metals Mining and Dressing		
非金属矿采选业	Nonmetal Minerals Mining and Dressing		
开采专业及辅助性活动	Mining Professional and Auxiliary Activity	30716	63.2
其他采矿业	Other Mining Industry		
农副食品加工业	Agricultural Products and Non-stable Food Processing Industry	175748	-6.0
食品制造业	Food Production	95651	0.3
酒、饮料和精制茶制造业	Wine, soft drinks and refined tea industry	79340	-0.8
烟草制品业	Tobacco Processing	4258	-15.5
纺织业	Textile Industry	31690	-1.1
纺织服装、服饰业	Textile, apparel industry	863	3.6
皮革、毛皮、羽毛及其制品和制鞋业	Leather, Fur, Feather (eiderdown) and Their Products Industry	772	-1.6
木材加工和木、竹、藤、棕、草制品业	Timber Processing,Bamboo,Cane,Palm Fiber and Straw Products	4994	-47.1
家具制造业	Furniture Manufacturing	4096	24.6
造纸和纸制品业	Papermaking and Paper products	16105	-6.1
印刷和记录媒介复制业	Printing,Record Medium Reproduction	26147	-0.3
文教、工美、体育和娱乐用品制造业	Culture, education, Craft art, sports and entertainment goods manufacturing industry	2799	101.6
石油煤炭及其他燃料加工业	Petroleum，Coking and Other Fuel	16504	-14.2
化学原料和化学制品制造业	Raw Chemical Materials and Chemical Products	1106998	-3.3
医药制造业	Medical and Pharmaceutical Products	51991	-0.4
化学纤维制造业	Chemical Fiber	48887	4.6
橡胶和塑料制品业	Rubber and plastic products industry	59528	4.3
非金属矿物制品业	Nonmetal Mineral Products	352337	-8.8
黑色金属冶炼和压延加工业	Smelting and Pressing of Ferrous Metals	8574	40.6
有色金属冶炼和压延加工业	Smelting and Pressing of Nonferrou Metals	48012	-8.4
金属制品业	Metal Products	26258	-0.1
通用设备制造业	General Equipment Manufacturing Industry	20665	0.5
专用设备制造业	Special Purpose Equipment	28283	-1.2
汽车制造业	Automotive Manufacturing	200276	-1.6
铁路、船舶、航空航天和其他运输设备制造业	Railroad, marine, aerospace and other transportation equipment manufacturing	16491	-6.7
电气机械和器材制造业	Electric Equipment and Machinery	142423	-1.2
计算机、通信和其他电子设备制造业	Communication Equipment, Computer and Other Electronic Equipment Manufacturing Industry	305104	4.7
仪器仪表制造业	Instrument manufacturing industry	4506	14.6
其他制造业	Other manufacturing	1392	42.1
废弃资源综合利用	Comprehensive utilization of waste resources	367	5.2
金属制品、机械和设备修理业	Metal products, machinery and equipment repair industry	234	-10.1
电力、热力生产和供应业	Electric Power, Heating Power Generating and Supplying Industry	3786083	-4.6
燃气生产和供应业	Gas Mining and Supplying Industry	33884	38.8
水的生产和供应业	Water Processing and Supplying Industry	14885	4.2

13-6 规模以上工业企业用水情况（2018年）

Statistics on Water Use of Industrial Enterprises above Designated Size（2018）

指　标	Item	取水量（万立方米）Water Use (10 000 cu.m)	外供水量（万立方米）Outward Water Supply (10 000 cu.m)
合　计	**Total**	**78962**	**66106**
地表淡水	Surface fresh water	51649	3131
地下淡水	Underground fresh water	14205	1180
自来水	Tap Water	11876	61795
陆地苦咸水	Land lake Salt water	2	
矿井水	Mine Water	72	
雨水	Rain Water	22	
再生水	Reclaimed Water	1134	
其他水	Other Water	2	
外排水量	Efflux capacity	5347	
重复用水量	Repeated water consumption	140022	

13-7 规模以上工业企业分行业用水情况（2018年）

Volume of Water Use of Industrial Enterprises above Designated Size by Industry (2018)

行业	Sector	取水量（万立方米）Water Use (10 000 cu.m)
总计	**Total**	**78962**
煤炭开采和洗选业	Coal Mining and Dressing	
石油和天然气开采业	Petroleum and Natural Gas Extraction	
黑色金属矿采选业	Ferrous Metals Mining and Dressing	
有色金属矿采选业	Nonferrous Metals Mining and Dressing	
非金属矿采选业	Nonmetal Minerals Mining and Dressing	
开采专业及辅助性活动	Mining Professional and Auxiliary Activity	166
其他采矿业	Other Mining Industry	
农副食品加工业	Agricultural Products and Non-stable Food Processing Industry	244
食品制造业	Food Production	443
酒、饮料和精制茶制造业	Wine, soft drinks and refined tea industry	659
烟草制品业	Tobacco Processing	3
纺织业	Textile Industry	84
纺织服装、服饰业	Textile, apparel industry	17
皮革、毛皮、羽毛及其制品和制鞋业	Leather, Fur, Feather (eiderdown) and Their Products Industry	1
木材加工和木、竹、藤、棕、草制品业	Timber Processing,Bamboo,Cane,Palm Fiber and Straw Products	2
家具制造业	Furniture Manufacturing	12
造纸和纸制品业	Papermaking and Paper products	17
印刷和记录媒介复制业	Printing,Record Medium Reproduction	64
文教、工美、体育和娱乐用品制造业	Culture, education, Craft art, sports and entertainment goods manufacturing industry	5
石油煤炭及其他燃料加工业	Petroleum，Coking and Other Fuel	79
化学原料和化学制品制造业	Raw Chemical Materials and Chemical Products	1142
医药制造业	Medical and Pharmaceutical Products	298
化学纤维制造业	Chemical Fiber	51
橡胶和塑料制品业	Rubber and plastic products industry	209
非金属矿物制品业	Nonmetal Mineral Products	635
黑色金属冶炼和压延加工业	Smelting and Pressing of Ferrous Metals	3
有色金属冶炼和压延加工业	Smelting and Pressing of Nonferrou Metals	135
金属制品业	Metal Products	57
通用设备制造业	General Equipment Manufacturing Industry	65
专用设备制造业	Special Purpose Equipment	137
汽车制造业	Automotive Manufacturing	796
铁路、船舶、航空航天和其他运输设备制造业	Railroad, marine, aerospace and other transportation equipment manufacturing	106
电气机械和器材制造业	Electric Equipment and Machinery	581
计算机、通信和其他电子设备制造业	Communication Equipment, Computer and Other Electronic Equipment Manufacturing Industry	1419
仪器仪表制造业	Instrument manufacturing industry	38
其他制造业	Other manufacturing	5
废弃资源综合利用	Comprehensive utilization of waste resources	
金属制品、机械和设备修理业	Metal products, machinery and equipment repair industry	3
电力、热力生产和供应业	Electric Power, Heating Power Generating and Supplying Industry	4614
燃气生产和供应业	Gas Mining and Supplying Industry	32
水的生产和供应业	Water Processing and Supplying Industry	66840

13-7 续表 continude

行 业	Sector	外供水量（万立方米）Outward Water Supply (10 000 cu.m)
总 计	**Total**	**66106**
煤炭开采和洗选业	Coal Mining and Dressing	
石油和天然气开采业	Petroleum and Natural Gas Extraction	
黑色金属矿采选业	Ferrous Metals Mining and Dressing	
有色金属矿采选业	Nonferrous Metals Mining and Dressing	
非金属矿采选业	Nonmetal Minerals Mining and Dressing	
开采专业及辅助性活动	Mining Professional and Auxiliary Activity	
其他采矿业	Other Mining Industry	
农副食品加工业	Agricultural Products and Non-stable Food Processing Industry	
食品制造业	Food Production	
酒、饮料和精制茶制造业	Wine, soft drinks and refined tea industry	
烟草制品业	Tobacco Processing	
纺织业	Textile Industry	
纺织服装、服饰业	Textile, apparel industry	
皮革、毛皮、羽毛及其制品和制鞋业	Leather, Fur, Feather (eiderdown) and Their Products Industry	
木材加工和木、竹、藤、棕、草制品业	Timber Processing,Bamboo,Cane,Palm Fiber and Straw Products	
家具制造业	Furniture Manufacturing	
造纸和纸制品业	Papermaking and Paper products	
印刷和记录媒介复制业	Printing,Record Medium Reproduction	
文教、工美、体育和娱乐用品制造业	Culture, education, Craft art, sports and entertainment goods manufacturing industry	
石油煤炭及其他燃料加工业	Petroleum，Coking and Other Fuel	
化学原料和化学制品制造业	Raw Chemical Materials and Chemical Products	
医药制造业	Medical and Pharmaceutical Products	
化学纤维制造业	Chemical Fiber	
橡胶和塑料制品业	Rubber and plastic products industry	
非金属矿物制品业	Nonmetal Mineral Products	
黑色金属冶炼和压延加工业	Smelting and Pressing of Ferrous Metals	
有色金属冶炼和压延加工业	Smelting and Pressing of Nonferrou Metals	
金属制品业	Metal Products	
通用设备制造业	General Equipment Manufacturing Industry	
专用设备制造业	Special Purpose Equipment	3
汽车制造业	Automotive Manufacturing	
铁路、船舶、航空航天和其他运输设备制造业	Railroad, marine, aerospace and other transportation equipment manufacturing	
电气机械和器材制造业	Electric Equipment and Machinery	
计算机、通信和其他电子设备制造业	Communication Equipment, Computer and Other Electronic Equipment Manufacturing Industry	
仪器仪表制造业	Instrument manufacturing industry	
其他制造业	Other manufacturing	
废弃资源综合利用	Comprehensive utilization of waste resources	
金属制品、机械和设备修理业	Metal products, machinery and equipment repair industry	
电力、热力生产和供应业	Electric Power, Heating Power Generating and Supplying Industry	
燃气生产和供应业	Gas Mining and Supplying Industry	
水的生产和供应业	Water Processing and Supplying Industry	66103

13-8 分区县规模以上工业企业综合能源消费量（2018年）

Comprehensive Energy Consumption above Designated Size by Region（2018）

单位：吨标准煤 (ton of SCE)

区 县	Region	综合能源消费量 Comprehensive Energy Consumption	增速（%） Growth Rate (%)
全 市	**Total**	**6746859**	**-3.4**
新城区	Xincheng	363633	4.1
碑林区	Beilin	77406	62.3
莲湖区	Lianhu	173078	-3.3
灞桥区	Baqiao	819114	-5.9
未央区	Weiyang	251475	0.9
雁塔区	Yanta	251789	6.1
阎良区	Yanliang	38015	-4.9
临潼区	Lintong	74258	-8.5
长安区	Chang'an	494088	8.0
高陵区	Gaoling	176355	-6.4
鄠邑区	Huyi	831486	-8.9
蓝田县	Lantian	108966	-6.5
周至县	Zhouzhi	15988	-3.5
西咸新区	Xixian	3071208	-5.2

主要统计指标解释

单位生产总值能耗 指一定时期内，一个国家或地区每生产一个单位的生产总值所消耗的能源。计算公式为：

单位生产总值能耗=能源消费总量/生产总值

工业企业能源消费量 指工业企业在工业生产活动和非工业生产活动中消费的能源，包括工业生产活动中作为燃料、动力、原料、辅助材料使用的能源，生产工艺中使用的能源，用于能源加工转换的能源；非工业生产活动中使用的能源。具体包括：

（1）用于本企业产品生产、工业性作业和其他生产性活动的能源；

（2）用于技术更新改造措施、新技术研究和新产品试制以及科学试验等方面的能源；

（3）用于经营维修、建筑及设备大修理、机电设备和交通运输工具等方面的能源；

（4）用于劳动保护的能源；

（5）生产交通运输工具的企业（如造船厂、汽车制造厂），向成品轮船、汽车中添加动力用油，应算作企业的能源消费，但不作为工业生产消费，应作为非工业生产消费和交通运输工具消费。

（6）其他非生产消费的能源。

工业生产能源消费量 指工业企业为进行工业生产活动所消费的能源。主要包括：

（1）用于本企业产品生产、工业性作业的能源，包括用作原料、材料、燃料、动力的能源；作为能源加工转换企业，还包括用作加工转换的能源（这部分能源不能理解为用作原材料，用作原材料的概念见后面的解释）；

（2）产品生产过程中作为辅助材料使用的能源；

（3）生产工艺过程使用的能源；

（4）新技术研究、新产品试制、科学试验使用的能源；

（5）为了工业生产活动而在进行的各种修理过程中使用的能源；

（6）生产区内的劳动保护用能等。

用于原材料的能源消费量 指能源产品不作能源使用，即不作燃料、动力使用，而作为生产另外一种产品（非能源产品）的原料或作为辅助材料使用，作原料使用时通常构成这种产品的实体。它与用作加工转换的区别是：用作加工转换，投入的是能源，产出的主要产品还是能源（或产出的产品属于加工转换过程中产生的不作能源使用的其他副产品和联产品）。而用作原材料时，投入的是能源，产出的主要产品是能源范畴以外的产品，包括产出的某种产品在广义上可以用作能源（比如可以燃烧以提供热量），但通常意义上不作能源使用的产品。

非工业生产能源消费量 指在工业企业能源消费中，除“工业生产能源消费”以外的能源消费，即非工业生产用能和工业企业附属的不从事工业生产活动的非独立核算单位用能。比如本企业施工单位进行技术更新改造、维修等过程用能，非生产区的劳动保护用能，科研单位、农场、车队、学校、医院、食堂、托儿所等单位用能。但是必须注意，上述单位如果是独立核算的，其用能既不能包括在“工业企业能源消费”中，亦不能包括在“非工业生产能源消费”中。

生产交通运输工具的企业（如造船厂、汽车制造厂），向成品轮船、汽车中添加动力用油，应算作企业的非工业生产消费。

综合能源消费量 指企业（单位）在报告期内工业生产实际消费的各种能源（扣除能源加工转换和能源回收利用等重复因素）的总和。计算综合能源消费量时，需要将各种能源品种的消费量换算成按照标准计量单位（如：吨标准煤）计量的消费量。

取水量 指企业从各种水源直接提取或者从市场购买的用于厂区、办公区内工业生产活动的水量，以实际获得的新水量为准。

外供水量 指企业外供给其他单位的水或水产品的量，以离厂水量为准。包括外供给其他企业或市场的原水、自来水、海水淡化水、矿泉水、纯净水等。不包括直流冷却水量、再生水（中水）、未利用直接排放的矿井水和雨水量、北方地区供暖企业供给城镇热力网内循环的热水量、进入城镇污水管网和直接排到自然环境中的水量。

Explanatory Notes on Main Statistical Indicators

Energy Consumption per Unit of GDP refers to the energy consumption per unit of Gross Domestic Product in a country or the Gross Regional Product in a region in the same reference period. The formula is:

Energy Consumption per Unit of GDP= Total Energy Consumption/Gross Domestic Product

Energy Consumption of Industrial Enterprises refers to the energy consumed by industrial enterprises in industrial production activities and non-industrial production activities, including energy used as fuel, power, raw materials and auxiliary materials in industrial production activities, energy used in production processes, energy for processing and conversion, and energy in the course of use of non-industrial production activities. Specifically, it includes:

(1)Energy used for the production, industrial operation and other productive activities of the enterprise;

(2)Energy for technological upgrading, new technology research and trial production of new products and scientific experiments.

(3) Energy for maintenance, construction and equipment repair, electrical and mechanical equipment and transportation.

(4) Energy for labor protection;

(5)Enterprises manufactured means of conveyance (such as making shipyards and automobile manufacturers), adding power oil to the finished product ships and cars, should be used as the energy consumption of the enterprises, but not as industrial production and consumption, it should be included in the consumption of non-industrial production and transportation means.

(6)Other non-productive energy sources.

Energy Consumption of Industrial Production refers to the energy consumed by industrial enterprises in industrial production activities. It mainly includes:

(1)Energy for the production and industrial operation of the products of the enterprise, including energy for raw materials, materials, fuel and power; as energy processing and conversion enterprises, including energy for processing and conversion (this part of the energy cannot be understood as raw materials, the concept of raw material is explained later)

(2)Energy used as auxiliary material during the production of products;

(3)Energy used in the production process;

(4)Energy for new technology research, trial production of new products and scientific test;

(5)Energy used in various repair processes for industrial production activities;

(6)Labor protection energy in the production area.

Energy Consumption for Raw Materials refers the energy products are not used for energy use, that is, not to be used as fuel and power, but as raw materials for the production of another product (non-energy products) or as auxiliary materials, which usually constitute the entity of this product when used as a raw material. The difference between it and the conversion of processing is that it is used as a process conversion, which is invested in energy, the main product of the output still is energy (or the produced product belongs to other by-products and associated products that are not used for energy use in the process of processing and conversion). When used as raw materials, energy is invested, and the main product is beyond the energy category, including a product that can be used as a source of energy in the broad sense (for example, to be burned to provide heat), but in general, it is not used for energy use.

Non–industry Consumption Energy refers to the energy consumed by industrial enterprises except for industrial production activities, means that energy consumed by non-industry production and it is not independent accounting units which was engaged in industrial production activities affiliated to industrial enterprises. For example, the energy consumption of technical renovation, maintenance and other processes carried out by construction units of this enterprise, labor protection for non-production areas, energy consumption of scientific research units, farms, motorcade, schools, hospitals, canteens, nursery schools and other units. However, it must be noted that if the above-mentioned units are independently accounted, their use can neither be included in the "industrial energy consumption" nor in the "non-industrial production energy consumption".

Enterprises manufactured means of conveyance(such as making shipyards and automobile manufacturers) adding power oil to finished ships and cars, should be regarded as non-industrial production and consumption of enterprises.

Comprehensive Energy Consumption refers to the sum of the various energy sources for the actual consumption of industrial production during the reporting period (the repeating factors of the conversion of energy processing and energy recovery and utilizationhave been deducted). When calculating the comprehensive energy consumption, it is necessary to convert the consumption of various types of energy into the consumption measured in accordance with the standard unit of measurement (e.g. tons of standard coal).

Water Intake refers to the amount of water directly extracted from a variety of water sources or purchased from the market for industrial production activities in the factory and office areas, which is based on the actual new amount of water.

External Water Supply refers to the quantity of water or aquatic products supplied to other units by the enterprises, taking the quantity of water away from the plant as the criterion. It includes raw water, tap water, desalination water, mineral water, purified water, etc., which are supplied to other enterprises or markets. Direct current cooling water, reclaimed water (water), unused mine water and rain water, the hot water in the urban heat network supplied by the heating enterprises in the north are not included.

14 建筑业

CONSTRUCTION

资料整理：杨雪峰
Data management: Yang Xuefeng
数据审核：陈　英
Data audit: Chen Ying

第十四部分　建筑业

一、简要说明

1.本章资料反映我市建筑业概况和发展情况。包括建筑业企业基本情况和生产经营情况。主要指标有企业个数、签订合同额、本年新签合同额、建筑业总产值、从事建筑业活动的平均人数、房屋施工面积、营业利润、应交增值税、劳动生产率等。

2.本章资料统计范围，根据建筑业发展的实际情况，建筑业统计范围从2002年年报起由原具有建筑业资质等级四级及四级以上的独立核算的建筑业企业调整为具有建筑业资质的独立核算建筑业企业。

3.本章建筑业企业统计数据是根据国家统计局制定的《建筑业统计报表制度》整理汇总的。资质以内建筑业统计报表由国家统计局根据企业实际情况采取全面调查的方法布置、收集，2011年年报开始由资质内建筑业企业通过联网直报系统上报。

4.2018年资质以内建筑业数据为四经普一套表单位上报数据。

二、主要指标

企业个数（个）	1209	比上年增长	14.6%
#国有及国有控股企业	168	比上年增长	9.8%
建筑业总产值（亿元）	3925.72	比上年增长	18.8%
#国有及国有控股企业	3083.48	比上年增长	16.4%
房屋建筑竣工面积（万平方米）	2755.17	比上年增长	7.9%
房屋建筑面积竣工率（%）	17.4	比上年下降	1.5个百分点

14 CONSTRUCTION

I. Brief Introduction

1.Main Contents:Data in this chapter show the general situation and the development of the construction industry in Xi'an. They cover the situation of production and management of the construction enterprises, including the number of enterprises; total contract value; newly signed contract value; gross output value of the construction industry; the average number of employed persons engage in the activities of construction enterprises; floor space of building completed in construction enterprises; profits of construction enterprises; value–added tax payable; labour productivity and etc.

2.Scope of Statistics:In view of the development of the construction industry, starting from 2002 the scope of construction statistics has been adjusted to include all the construction enterprises of various types of ownership with qualification certificates and independent accounting systems, replacing the previous criteria that required construction enterprises of various types of ownership to have qualification certificates at or above Class 4 with independent accounting systems.

3.Sources of Data and Methods of Survey:Data on construction enterprises are collected in accordance with the Statistical Reporting System of Constructionby the National Bureau of Statistics. The construction statistical reports are deployed and collected through comprehensive survey by National Bureau of Statistics in accordance with the real conditions of the enterprises. Since 2011,construction enterprises with qualification certificates reported through internet.

4.The construction industry data within the 2018 qualification shall be reported as a set of forms for the fourth economic census.

Ⅱ.Major Indicators.

		Increase over Preceding Year
Number of Enterprises(item)	1209	14.6%
#State–owned or State Holding Majority Shares	168	9.8%
Total Output Value of Construction(100 mil. yuan)	3925.72	18.8%
State–owned or State Holding Majority Shares	3083.48	16.4%
Floor Space of Buildings Completed(10 000 sq.m)	2755.17	7.9%
Rate of Floor Space of Buildings Completed(%)	17.4	–1.5 percentage points

14-1 主要年份建筑业总产值

Total Output Value of Construction in Representative Years

单位：亿元 (100 million yuan)

年份 Year	单位数（个） Number of Enterprises (unit)	建筑业总产值 Total Output Value of Construction	国有及国有控股 State-owned or State Holding Majority Shares	集体企业 Collective-owned Enterprises
2000	184	105.93	78.87	14.87
2001	205	114.81	91.82	15.47
2002	223	133.47	85.03	15.35
2003	204	177.11	119.99	13.40
2004	244	244.42	201.68	16.59
2005	235	326.65	276.68	19.61
2006	217	416.48	348.20	23.65
2007	279	604.75	432.63	32.67
2008	328	915.12	676.12	460.14
2009	326	1074.55	875.19	47.15
2010	324	1334.00	1034.04	58.39
2011	336	1619.09	1278.33	79.42
2012	396	1874.23	1364.70	96.83
2013	420	2228.41	1702.08	154.87
2014	539	2586.33	1981.24	95.02
2015	706	2650.41	2044.05	69.73
2016	893	2897.55	2288.23	63.35
2017	1055	3304.54	2588.18	70.56
2018	1209	3925.72	3083.48	52.99

注：1、1996年以后建筑业年报统计范围由往年的县及县以上（含县级建制镇）各种经济类型的建筑企业，改为具有建筑业资质等级三级及三级以上的各种经济类型的建筑施工企业；2002年改为具有建筑业资质等级的各种经济类型的建筑施工企业。
2、本表资料含劳务分包企业。
3、由于统计口径变化，对部分年份建筑业总产值相关数据进行了修订。

14-2 全市建筑施工总承包企业基本情况（2018年）

Basic Situation of Construction General Contracting Contractors in Whole City（2018）

指标	Item	合计 Total	国有及国有控股 State-owned or State Holding Majority Shares
企业单位数（个）	Number of Enterprises (unit)	771	131
#二级以上企业	Special and First and Second Class Enterprise	623	113
计算劳动生产率的平均人数（万人）	Average Number of Employed Persons in Calculation of Labor Productivity (10 000 persons)	77.95	58.65
#二级以上企业	Special and First and Second Class Enterprise	74.92	57.31
建筑业总产值（亿元）	Total Output Value of Construction(100 million yuan)	3560.84	2872.37
#二级以上企业	Special and First and Second Class Enterprise	3412.80	2798.72
全员劳动生产率	Overall Labor Productivity	45.68	48.97
按总产值计算(万元/人)	Calculated by Total Output Value(10 000yuan/person)		

14-3 施工总承包和专业承包建筑企业生产情况（2018年）

分 组	Classify	签订的合同额（万元）Contract Value (10 000 yuan)	上年结转合同额（万元）Contract Value Carried Over from 2017 (10 000 yuan)	本年新签合同额（万元）Contract Value Signed in 2018 (10 000 yuan)
总计	**Total**	**101669161**	**50237622**	**51431539**
#国有及国有控股	State-owned and State Holding Majority Shares	85329176	43963900	41365276
一、按登记注册类型分	**Grouped by Registion Status**			
内资	Domestic Investment Enterprises	101273295	50099877	51173419
国有企业	State-owned Enterprises	2874312	1608583	1265729
集体企业	Collective-owned Enterprises	760616	225132	535485
股份合作企业	Share-holding Corperative Enterprises	4579		4579
联营企业	Joint Ownership Enterprises	33034	6722	26312
国有独资公司	State-owned Company	16230213	6985585	9244628
其他有限责任公司	Limited Liability Corporations	69168350	36609831	32558519
股份有限公司	Share-holding Corperation Ltd.	1519240	597369	921872
私营企业	Private Enterprises	10682951	4066655	6616296
其他企业	Others			
港澳台商投资企业	Enterprises with Funds from Hong Kong,Macao and Taiwan			
外商投资企业	Enterprises with Foreign Investment	395866	137745	258121
二、按国民经济行业分	**Grouped by Sector**			
房屋建筑业	Building Engineering Construction	36564368	14086432	22477936
土木工程建筑业	Civil Engineering Construction	60243914	35069636	25174278
建筑安装业	Installation of Construction	3348609	688403	2660207
建筑装饰、装修和其他建筑业	Architectural Decoration and Other Construction	1512270	393151	1119119
三、按隶属关系分	**Grouped by Administrative Relationship**			
中央	Central	58299694	35817805	22481889
地方	Region	43369467	14419817	28949650
四、按企业资质等级分	**Grouped by Class of Enterprises**			
1. 施工总承包	Overall Contractor for Construction	95164986	48328314	46836671
#特级	Special Class	59773205	32234275	27538930
一级	First Class	23969927	11399629	12570298
二级	Second Class	8541983	3231738	5310244
2. 专业承包	Special Contractor	6504175	1909308	4594868
#一级以上	First Class	5326406	1541649	3784758
二级	Second Class	689958	230643	459315

Main Indicators on General Constructing Contractors and Professional Contractors（2018）

建筑业总产值（万元）Total Output Value of Constrution (10 000 yuan)					竣工产值（万元）Completed Output Value (10 000 yuan)	房屋建筑施工面积（平方米）Number of Projects under Construction (sq.m)	
	在外省完成的产值 Output Value in Other Provinces	建筑工程产值 Output Value of Constrution	安装工程产值 Output Value of Installation	其他产值 Others			本年新开工 Beginning Projects in This Year
39257185	**17409890**	**34851747**	**3069649**	**1335790**	**12749334**	**158553917**	**49096122**
30834757	16204498	28457356	1547750	829650	10080757	127550551	37367488
39132015	17409890	34727405	3068821	1335790	12748834	158124072	49096122
1423894	688836	1216645	171143	36106	442863	491270	284693
529907	1530	452687	55117	22103	343970	3049574	1735399
4480		4480			3346		
28913		28913			23461	250783	220964
7160451	3237346	6738941	184906	236604	3475816	26575580	7074734
23356795	12231667	21231256	1566812	558727	5723344	98506730	30748600
521550	258905	493680	27829	41	694277	8808833	1281354
6106025	991606	4560803	1063014	482209	2041757	20441302	7750378
125170		124342	828		500	429845	
14812799	3264501	13297788	1133578	381433	6223155	144855344	46316751
21527879	13282530	20001497	714673	811710	5505358	10057707	1869443
1914242	610161	757963	1092519	63760	561353	3018913	740301
1002265	252698	794499	128879	78887	459468	621953	169627
19081024	13859700	18181495	498929	400600	5340197	45821014	11424292
20176161	3550190	16670252	2570720	935190	7409137	112732903	37671830
35608445	16490712	32154738	2301137	1152569	11179981	156194059	47590589
19133830	10439556	18048959	875868	209004	5193969	92499745	27714072
11177397	5123168	10015060	733925	428412	4253544	42214723	8775299
3816778	549045	3042160	554046	220572	1226327	19890427	10501842
3648740	919178	2697009	768512	183221	1569353	2359858	1505533
2769844	803707	2081284	563169	125391	1299347	942300	608189
557644	61284	393563	131033	33048	198312	677794	290072

14-3 续表

分　组	Classify	房屋建筑竣工面积（平方米）Floor Space of Buildings Completed (sq.m)	房屋竣工价值（万元）Housing Completion Value (10 000 yuan)
总计	**Total**	**27551666**	**5575155**
#国有及国有控股	State-owned and State Holding Majority Shares	19556518	4431792
一、按登记注册类型分	**Grouped by Registion Status**		
内资	Domestic Investment Enterprises	27551666	5575155
国有企业	State-owned Enterprises	68801	12933
集体企业	Collective-owned Enterprises	2080502	271483
股份合作企业	Share-holding Corperative Enterprises		
联营企业	Joint Ownership Enterprises	14784	1042
国有独资公司	State-owned Company	4098832	1151806
其他有限责任公司	Limited Liability Corporations	13650229	2762259
股份有限公司	Share-holding Corperation Ltd.	1807925	512411
私营企业	Private Enterprises	5830593	863221
其他企业	Others		
港澳台商投资企业	Enterprises with Funds from Hong Kong,Macao and Taiwan		
外商投资企业	Enterprises with Foreign Investment		
二、按国民经济行业分	**Grouped by Sector**		
房屋建筑业	Building Engineering Construction	26191977	5343671
土木工程建筑业	Civil Engineering Construction	905436	165605
建筑安装业	Installation of Construction	377228	59994
建筑装饰、装修和其他建筑业	Architectural Decoration and Other Construction	77025	5885
三、按隶属关系分	**Grouped by Administrative Relationship**		
中央	Central	5562608	1290492
地方	Region	21989058	4284663
四、按企业资质等级分	**Grouped by Class of Enterprises**		
1. 施工总承包	Overall Contractor for Construction	26486399	5496108
#特级	Special Class	13580833	3145006
一级	First Class	9714409	1844877
二级	Second Class	2714829	429586
2. 专业承包	Special Contractor	1065267	79047
#一级以上	First Class	732181	51569
二级	Second Class	146016	21958

continued

从事建筑业活动的平均人数（人） Average Number of Employed Persons in Construction Enterprises Productivity(person)	建筑业企业期末从业人员数（人） The Number of Employees in Construction Enterprises at the end of Period (person)	工程技术人员 Technical Personnel	自有机械设备年末净值（万元） The Net Value of Machinery and Equipment Owned at the end of the Year (10 000 yuan)	自有机械设备年末总台数（台） The Total Number of Machinery and Equipment Owned owned (stand)	自有机械设备年末总功率（千瓦） Total Power of Machinery and Equipment Owned at the end of the Year (kw)	企业总产值（万元） Gross Output Value of Enterprises (10 000 yuan)
857651	**740351**	**115101**	**740713**	**77160**	**3495433**	**43236623**
623488	532869	74479	553094	43545	2828988	34262120
856825	739381	114652	740413	76935	3495133	43110978
51247	52389	4710	16785	4563	93812	1423894
20542	18711	3334	13860	4825	29327	543982
203	197	33	1285	46	4460	4480
990	995	282	6477	34	2039	28913
129568	94580	23322	138501	11554	633252	7447691
456358	384251	48969	414245	31081	2199983	26514942
19226	19962	1170	2758	3031	24163	524550
178691	168296	32832	146502	21801	508097	6622526
826	970	449	300	225	300	125645
359910	301685	45745	134362	22552	602910	15178372
433684	386305	58160	577046	44087	2725682	24864854
35794	25518	6365	8739	5140	85113	2068157
28263	26843	4831	20566	5381	81728	1125240
411285	371732	45274	489257	31227	2461075	22110833
446366	368619	69827	251456	45933	1034358	21125790
779533	675077	100782	684136	67995	3236055	39399279
338968	255244	36739	307752	24949	1853928	21952449
295489	284962	35587	236483	22001	915139	11833336
114739	105757	19922	105041	17072	374347	4078071
78118	65274	14319	56577	9165	259378	3837344
53853	42894	9222	40825	5640	181103	2903073
14328	14142	3665	11458	2359	62388	599063

14-4 施工总承包和专业承包建筑业企业主要指标（2018年）

指　标	Item	企业数（个）Number of Enterprises (unit)	总产值（万元）Total Output Value (10 000 yuan)	从事建筑业活动的平均人数（人）Average Number of Employed Persons in Construction Enterprises (person)
总计	**Total**	**1198**	**39257185**	**857651**
#国有及国有控股	State-owned and State Holding Majority Shares	168	30834757	623488
一、按登记注册类型分	**Grouped by Registion Status**			
内资	Domestic Investment Enterprises	1192	39132015	856825
国有企业	State-owned Enterprises	21	1423894	51247
集体企业	Collective-owned Enterprises	42	529907	20542
股份合作企业	Share-holding Corperative Enterprises	1	4480	203
联营企业	Joint Ownership Enterprises	2	28913	990
国有独资公司	State-owned Company	48	7160451	129568
其他有限责任公司	Limited Liability Corporations	136	23356795	456358
股份有限公司	Share-holding Corperation Ltd.	8	521550	19226
私营企业	Private Enterprises	934	6106025	178691
其他企业	Others			
港澳台商投资企业	Enterprises with Funds from Hong Kong,Macao and Taiwan			
外商投资企业	Enterprises with Foreign Investment	6	125170	826
二、按国民经济行业分	**Grouped by Sector**			
房屋建筑业	Building Engineering Construction	465	14812799	359910
土木工程建筑业	Civil Engineering Construction	360	21527879	433684
建筑安装业	Installation of Construction	180	1914242	35794
建筑装饰、装修和其他建筑业	Architectural Decoration and Other Construction	193	1002265	28263
三、按隶属关系分	**Grouped by Administrative Relationship**			
中央	Central	56	19081024	411285
地方	Region	1142	20176161	446366
四、按企业资质等级分	**Grouped by Class of Enterprises**			
1. 施工总承包	Overall Contractor for Construction	771	35608445	779533
#特级	Special Class	24	19133830	338968
一级	First Class	163	11177397	295489
二级	Second Class	436	3816778	114739
2. 专业承包	Special Contractor	427	3648740	78118
#一级以上	First Class	161	2769844	53853
二级	Second Class	185	557644	14328

Major Indicators of General Construction Contractors and Professional Contractors (2018)

建筑业企业期末从业人员数（人）The Number of Employees in Construction Enterprises at the End of Period (person)	利润总额（万元）Total Profit (10000 yuan)	利税总额（万元）Total Profits and Taxes (10000 yuan)	按总产值计算劳动生产率（万元/人）Productivity by Gross Output Value (10000 yuan/person)	产值利润率（%）Profit Rate of Output Value (%)	产值利税率（%）Profit and Tax Rate of Output Value (%)	资产总计（万元）Total Assets (10000 yuan)	负债总计（万元）Total Liabilities (10000 yuan)	资产负债率（%）Asset Liability Ratio (%)
740351	**1163645**	**2055601**	**45.77**	**3.0**	**5.2**	**50238094**	**38392820**	**76.4**
532869	834825	1377793	49.46	2.7	4.5	38077786	31074936	81.6
739381	1101859	1987777	45.67	2.8	5.1	50036421	38250809	76.4
52389	46107	93241	27.78	3.2	6.5	1334826	1043807	78.2
18711	32323	61242	25.80	6.1	11.6	490804	254367	51.8
197	87	388	22.07	1.9	8.7	8362	6975	83.4
995	2147	3249	29.21	7.4	11.2	32218	7688	23.9
94580	197632	304964	55.26	2.8	4.3	8866050	6713802	75.7
384251	617212	1042049	51.18	2.6	4.5	29437680	24651132	83.7
19962	12733	38118	27.13	2.4	7.3	620218	472267	76.1
168296	193618	444526	34.17	3.2	7.3	9246263	5100772	55.2
970	61786	67824	151.54	49.4	54.2	201673	142011	70.4
301685	372805	758280	41.16	2.5	5.1	16247145	11929031	73.4
386305	674063	1088440	49.64	3.1	5.1	30362953	23959966	78.9
25518	80576	131200	53.48	4.2	6.9	2470635	1757614	71.1
26843	36201	77681	35.46	3.6	7.8	1157361	746209	64.5
371732	599508	850237	46.39	3.1	4.5	25229004	21046665	83.4
368619	564137	1205364	45.20	2.8	6.0	25009090	17346155	69.4
675077	1033629	1797545	45.68	2.9	5.0	45802895	35235310	76.9
255244	571289	832149	56.45	3.0	4.3	25385865	20646758	81.3
284962	203522	489516	37.83	1.8	4.4	12742981	9962536	78.2
105757	136780	306049	33.26	3.6	8.0	5811309	3486119	60.0
65274	130016	258056	46.71	3.6	7.1	4435199	3157510	71.2
42894	94100	179128	51.43	3.4	6.5	2885671	2145482	74.3
14142	21600	47625	38.92	3.9	8.5	1003381	646949	64.5

14-5 施工总承包和专业承包建筑业企业财务状况（2018年）

单位：万元

指 标	Item	资产总计 Total Assets	流动资产合计 Total Current Assets
总计	**Total**	**50238094**	**40846157**
#国有及国有控股	State-owned and State Holding Majority Shares	38077786	30351070
一、按登记注册类型分	**Grouped by Registion Status**		
内资	Domestic Investment Enterprises	50036421	40645317
国有企业	State-owned Enterprises	1334826	1000412
集体企业	Collective-owned Enterprises	490804	406871
股份合作企业	Share-holding Corperative Enterprises	8362	8002
联营企业	Joint Ownership Enterprises	32218	29222
国有独资公司	State-owned Company	8866050	6969139
其他有限责任公司	Limited Liability Corporations	29437680	23848943
股份有限公司	Share-holding Corperation Ltd.	620218	488092
私营企业	Private Enterprises	9246263	7894636
其他企业	Others		
港澳台商投资企业	Enterprises with Funds from Hong Kong, Macao and Taiwan		
外商投资企业	Enterprises with Foreign Investment	201673	200840
二、按国民经济行业分	**Grouped by Sector**		
房屋建筑业	Building Engineering Construction	16247145	14151213
土木工程建筑业	Civil Engineering Construction	30362953	23529583
建筑安装业	Installation of Construction	2470635	2188228
建筑装饰、装修和其他建筑业	Architectural Decoration and Other Construction	1157361	977133
三、按隶属关系分	**Grouped by Administrative Relationship**		
中央	Central	25229004	19303196
地方	Region	25009090	21542961
四、按企业资质等级分	**Grouped by Class of Enterprises**		
1. 施工总承包	Overall Contractor for Construction	45802895	36897649
#特级	Special Class	25385865	19466891
一级	First Class	12742981	11103065
二级	Second Class	5811309	4982549
2. 专业承包	Special Contractor	4435199	3948508
#一级	First Class	2885671	2651627
二级	Second Class	1003381	848195

Financial Status of General Constructing Contractors and Professional Contractors (2018)

(10 000yuan)

固定资产原价 Original Value of Fixed Assets	累计折旧 Accumulated Depreciation	本年折旧 Depreciation of This Year	负债合计 Total Liabilities	流动负债合计 Total Current Liabilities	非流动负债 Non Current Liabilities	所有者权益合计 Total Owners' Equity	实收资本 Paid in Capital
4063210	**2198059**	**407629**	**38392820**	**36089302**	**1989550**	**11847499**	**7813649**
3048770	1746081	335941	31074936	29241750	1790591	7002850	4206711
4062448	2197907	407564	38250809	35947291	1989550	11787837	7808849
187881	90686	21426	1043807	995893	47914	291019	181619
70443	27374	4989	254367	224144	18026	236437	224834
1378	1218	11	6975	6757		1387	847
1422	1375	162	7688	6449	78	24530	13847
1019414	661919	119543	6713802	6187131	491701	2152248	1170053
1935261	1049065	198718	24651132	23416122	1224737	4786548	3049651
22956	8186	1190	472267	429827	42440	147951	65946
823693	358084	61525	5100771	4680968	164654	4147717	3102052
762	152	65	142011	142011		59662	4800
847029	376841	66994	11929031	11247382	538933	4318339	2761012
2982619	1709159	325637	23959966	22471904	1351321	6404987	4220280
119298	64678	8125	1757614	1666409	76102	713021	512093
114264	47381	6873	746209	703607	23194	411152	320264
2465680	1528886	303961	21046665	19953311	1061285	4182339	2586362
1597530	669173	103668	17346155	16135991	928265	7665160	5227287
3730574	2030838	382621	35235310	33136309	1867365	10569810	6904377
1618865	959762	184603	20646758	19344995	1301763	4739107	2478376
1184600	657629	128253	9962536	9624530	267422	2780445	2037032
621458	284980	50393	3486119	3107866	240168	2327415	1952979
332636	167221	25003	3157510	2952993	122185	1277689	909272
218279	120115	15003	2145482	2093407	39743	740189	526709
79139	37414	7949	646949	583605	28306	356433	265930

14-5 续表

单位：万元

指　标	Item	营业收入 Total Revenue	主营业务收入 Main Business Income
总计	**Total**	**45663742**	**45393644**
#国有及国有控股	State-owned and State Holding Majority Shares	35831690	35625313
一、按登记注册类型分	**Grouped by Registion Status**		
内资	Domestic Investment Enterprises	45210733	44940635
国有企业	State-owned Enterprises	1358537	1351091
集体企业	Collective-owned Enterprises	577439	577148
股份合作企业	Share-holding Corperative Enterprises	3555	3555
联营企业	Joint Ownership Enterprises	19677	19677
国有独资公司	State-owned Company	7421913	7367148
其他有限责任公司	Limited Liability Corporations	28185241	28021313
股份有限公司	Share-holding Corperation Ltd.	513930	513519
私营企业	Private Enterprises	7130443	7087184
其他企业	Others		
港澳台商投资企业	Enterprises with Funds from Hong Kong, Macao and Taiwan		
外商投资企业	Enterprises with Foreign Investment	453009	453009
二、按国民经济行业分	**Grouped by Sector**		
房屋建筑业	Building Engineering Construction	15792022	15682090
土木工程建筑业	Civil Engineering Construction	26440887	26293177
建筑安装业	Installation of Construction	2247375	2242275
建筑装饰、装修和其他建筑业	Architectural Decoration and Other Construction	1183459	1176102
三、按隶属关系分	**Grouped by Administrative Relationship**		
中央	Central	23311542	23182942
地方	Region	22352200	22210702
四、按企业资质等级分	**Grouped by Class of Enterprises**		
1. 施工总承包	Overall Contractor for Construction	41673680	41415498
#特级	Special Class	23849949	23748651
一级	First Class	11589168	11537911
二级	Second Class	4471486	4369319
2. 专业承包	Special Contractor	3990063	3978146
#一级	First Class	2885118	2880674
二级	Second Class	635520	630171

continued 1

(10 000yuan)

营业成本 Total Cost	主营业务成本 Main Business Costs	税金及附加 Taxs and Other Charges	主营业务税金及附加 The Main Business Tax and Surcharges	管理费用 Management Costs	营业利润 Operating Profit	利润总额 Total Profit	应付职工薪酬 Payable to Employees	应交增值税 Value Added Tax Payable
42665359	**41999000**	**194372**	**190084**	**1373816**	**1191294**	**1163645**	**6401609**	**697584**
33704025	33522558	112958	110591	984136	875891	834825	5026175	430010
42277838	41611479	193153	188865	1371112	1129500	1101859	6365124	692764
1243252	1233327	8503	8480	68167	45221	46107	293590	38632
506256	505779	12698	12659	19098	32895	32323	113376	16221
3283	3283	34	34	151	87	87	983	268
16227	16227	278	210	1058	2143	2147	5907	824
6886149	6839291	36900	36091	225537	202264	197632	1309264	70432
26645709	26129669	74671	73111	749527	640278	617212	3553638	350166
470132	468254	1266	1266	17559	14536	12733	105043	24118
6506832	6415649	58804	57014	290015	192076	193618	983323	192105
387521	387521	1219	1219	2704	61794	61786	36485	4820
14844706	14315894	90567	88053	292458	386706	372805	2684071	294908
24703883	24579563	88336	86706	923466	687195	674063	3302509	326041
2039705	2034785	8022	7960	104290	81963	80576	245754	42602
1077065	1068758	7448	7365	53602	35430	36201	169275	34033
21850510	21750680	60599	59052	762972	633758	599508	3135150	190130
20814849	20248320	133773	131032	610844	557536	564137	3266459	507454
39046356	38393997	172398	168145	1205971	1064450	1033629	5950718	591519
22561569	22111199	52203	51457	586065	587377	571289	3142258	208657
10865294	10760192	59600	58561	364095	219517	203522	1919169	226394
4060214	3974270	43850	41511	184516	133945	136780	653639	125419
3619003	3605003	21974	21939	167845	126844	130016	450891	106065
2643961	2633762	14743	14729	99290	94915	94100	306873	70285
555029	551484	3934	3914	46326	21251	21600	85111	22091

14-6 劳务分包建筑业企业生产经营情况（2018年）

单位：万元

指 标	Item	固定资产原价 Original Value of Fixed Assets	本年折旧 Depreciation of this year
总计	**Total**	**382**	**148**
#国有及国有控股	State-owned and State Holding Majority Shares		
一、按登记注册类型分	**Grouped by Registion Status**		
内资	Domestic Investment Enterprises	382	148
国有企业	State-owned Enterprises		
集体企业	Collective-owned Enterprises		
股份合作企业	Share-holding Corperative Enterprises		
联营企业	Joint Ownership Enterprises		
国有独资公司	State-owned Company		
其他有限责任公司	Limited Liability Corporations		
股份有限公司	Share-holding Corperation Ltd.		
私营企业	Private Enterprises	382	148
其他企业	Others		
港澳台商投资企业	Enterprises with Funds from Hong Kong,Macao and Taiwan		
外商投资企业	Enterprises with Foreign Investment		
二、按国民经济行业分	**Grouped by Sector**		
房屋建筑业	Building Engineering Construction	143	20
土木工程建筑业	Civil Engineering Construction	56	18
建筑安装业	Installation of Construction		
建筑装饰、装修和其他建筑业	Architectural Decoration and Other Construction	183	110
三、按隶属关系分	**Grouped by Administrative Relationship**		
中央	Central		
地方	Region	382	148

Production and Management Situation of Subcontractor Construction Enterprises (2018)

(10 000yuan)

资产总计 Total Assets	负债合计 Total Liabilities	实收资本 Paid in Capital	营业收入 Total Revenue	主营业务收入 Main Business Income	营业成本 Total Cost	主营业务成本 Main Business Cost
62643	**54075**	**4022**	**89478**	**89478**	**82261**	**82254**
62643	54075	4022	89478	89478	82261	82254
62643	54075	4022	89478	89478	82261	82254
9325	7188	1261	20912	20912	20063	20063
4609	3159	501	5667	5667	5352	5352
48709	43728	2260	62899	62899	56846	56839
62643	54075	4022	89478	89478	82261	82254

14-6 续表

单位：万元

指标	Item	营业税金及附加 Taxs and Other Charges	主营业务税金及附加 Taxs and Other Charges on Principal Business
总计	**Total**	**473**	**473**
#国有及国有控股	State-owned and State Holding Majority Shares		
一、按登记注册类型分	**Grouped by Registion Status**		
内资	Domestic Investment Enterprises	473	473
国有企业	State-owned Enterprises		
集体企业	Collective-owned Enterprises		
股份合作企业	Share-holding Corperative Enterprises		
联营企业	Joint Ownership Enterprises		
国有独资公司	State-owned Company		
其他有限责任公司	Limited Liability Corporations		
股份有限公司	Share-holding Corperation Ltd.		
私营企业	Private Enterprises	473	473
其他企业	Others		
港澳台商投资企业	Enterprises with Funds from Hong Kong,Macao and Taiwan		
外商投资企业	Enterprises with Foreign Investment		
二、按国民经济行业分	**Grouped by Sector**		
房屋建筑业	Building Engineering Construction	76	76
土木工程建筑业	Civil Engineering Construction	24	24
建筑安装业	Installation of Construction		
建筑装饰、装修和其他建筑业	Architectural Decoration and Other Construction	373	373
三、按隶属关系分	**Grouped by Administrative Relationship**		
中央	Central		
地方	Region	473	473

continued 1

(10 000yuan)

销售费用 Sale Expenses	管理费用 Management Costs	财务费用 Financial Expenses	营业利润 Operating Profit	利润总额 Total Profit	应付职工薪酬 Payable to Employees	应交增值税 Value Added Tax Payable
10	**5289**	**38**	**1415**	**1417**	**3271**	**3327**
10	5289	38	1415	1417	3271	3327
10	5289	38	1415	1417	3271	3327
	418	38	317	320	2853	546
	218		73	73	359	214
10	4653		1025	1024	59	2567
10	5289	38	1415	1417	3271	3327

14-7 各区县建筑业主要经济指标（2018年）

Major Indicators of Construction Enterprises by Region（2018）

区 县	Region	企业个数（个）Number of Enterprises (unit)	总产值（亿元）Total Output Value (100 million yuan)	从事建筑业活动的平均人数（万人）Average Number of Employed Persons in Construction Enterprises Labor Productivity(10 000person)	全员劳动生产率（万元/人）Overall Labor Productivity (10 000 yuan/person)	利税总额（亿元）Total Pre-tax Profits (100 million yuan)
全 市	**Total**	**1198**	**3925.72**	**85.77**	**45.77**	**205.56**
新城区	Xincheng	65	373.60	5.69	65.66	12.07
碑林区	Beilin	164	835.20	16.65	50.16	37.59
莲湖区	Lianhu	92	344.19	6.97	49.38	15.95
灞桥区	Baqiao	49	239.32	3.84	62.32	11.25
未央区	Weiyang	220	718.53	22.65	31.72	35.80
雁塔区	Yanta	379	1025.19	20.03	51.18	60.89
阎良区	Yanliang	29	17.20	0.66	26.06	1.42
临潼区	Lintong	34	13.86	0.68	20.38	0.94
长安区	Chang'an	55	207.22	3.51	59.04	13.55
高陵区	Gaoling	17	40.03	2.03	19.72	4.68
鄠邑区	Huyi	13	19.98	0.68	29.38	1.42
蓝田县	Lantian	13	18.17	0.47	38.66	2.13
周至县	Zhouzhi	15	9.50	0.38	25.00	0.83
西咸新区	Xixian	53	63.73	1.53	41.65	7.04

注：本表数据依据施工总承包和专业承包企业数据加工整理。

14-8 各区县建筑业房屋施工及竣工面积（2018年）

Floor Space of Buildings under Construction & Completed by Region（2018）

区 县	Region	房屋建筑施工面积（万平方米）Floor Space under Construction (10 000sq.m)	本年新开工面积 Newly Started This Year	房屋建筑竣工面积（万平方米）Floor Space of Buildings Completed (10 000sq.m)	竣工房屋价值（亿元）Value of Buildings Completed (100 million yuan)
全 市	**Total**	15855.39	4909.61	2755.17	557.52
新城区	Xincheng	1320.08	401.96	366.73	65.32
碑林区	Beilin	4511.33	1476.03	834.92	165.07
莲湖区	Lianhu	2139.47	579.67	397.50	117.86
灞桥区	Baqiao	493.34	259.36	21.36	1.52
未央区	Weiyang	2772.67	814.50	236.06	38.59
雁塔区	Yanta	3628.57	958.26	529.66	118.84
阎良区	Yanliang	37.95	17.34	15.56	2.00
临潼区	Lintong	80.79	49.61	17.72	2.86
长安区	Chang'an	252.23	54.19	70.78	9.10
高陵区	Gaoling	150.58	84.22	73.62	9.85
鄠邑区	Huyi	81.61	44.24	52.48	10.25
蓝田县	Lantian	110.00	83.73	84.48	9.81
周至县	Zhouzhi	48.70	16.28	15.00	2.62
西咸新区	Xixian	228.07	70.22	39.30	3.83

14-9 各区县建筑业企业主要经济效益指标（2018年）

Major Economic Performance Indicators on Construction Enterprises by Region（2018）

区县 Region		人均利润总额（元/人）Per Profit (yuan/person)	人均利税（元/人）Per Pre-Tax Profits (yuan/person)	人均竣工产值（元/人）Per Output Value of Buildings Completed (yuan/person)	人均施工面积（平方米/人）Per Floor Space of Buildings Under Construcyion (sq.m/person)	人均竣工面积（平方米/人）Per Floor Space of Buildings Completed (sq.m/person)
全　市	**Total**	**13568**	**23968**	**148654**	**185**	**32**
新城区	Xincheng	12130	21215	293511	232	64
碑林区	Beilin	12540	22571	169404	271	50
莲湖区	Lianhu	10046	22892	251686	307	57
灞桥区	Baqiao	17793	29300	301536	129	6
未央区	Weiyang	9998	15808	40195	122	10
雁塔区	Yanta	16630	30404	131477	181	26
阎良区	Yanliang	6066	21566	193405	58	24
临潼区	Lintong	3037	13865	85764	119	26
长安区	Chang'an	26192	38587	256034	72	20
高陵区	Gaoling	14279	23083	54142	74	36
鄠邑区	Huyi	6264	20957	240741	121	78
蓝田县	Lantian	25964	45210	248117	233	179
周至县	Zhouzhi	4995	21853	142723	128	39
西咸新区	Xixian	27810	45878	178937	149	26

14-9 续表 continued

区县 Region		产值利润率（%）Ratio of Profits to Output Value (%)	产值利税率（%）Ratio of Pre-tax Profits to Output Value (%)	资产利润率（%）Ratio of Profits to Assets (%)	资产利税率（%）Ratio of Pre-tax Profits to Assets (%)	资产负债率（%）Ratio of Debts to Assets (%)
全　市	**Total**	**3.0**	**5.2**	**2.3**	**4.1**	**76.4**
新城区	Xincheng	1.8	3.2	2.3	4.1	83.0
碑林区	Beilin	2.5	4.5	2.1	3.7	80.6
莲湖区	Lianhu	2.0	4.6	1.5	3.4	73.0
灞桥区	Baqiao	2.9	4.7	2.3	3.7	76.4
未央区	Weiyang	3.2	5.0	2.1	3.4	79.3
雁塔区	Yanta	3.2	5.9	2.3	4.1	76.4
阎良区	Yanliang	2.3	8.3	1.3	4.7	55.0
临潼区	Lintong	1.5	6.8	0.4	1.8	37.7
长安区	Chang'an	4.4	6.5	4.7	7.0	72.9
高陵区	Gaoling	7.2	11.7	5.1	8.2	28.0
鄠邑区	Huyi	2.1	7.1	3.5	11.7	61.0
蓝田县	Lantian	6.7	11.7	21.6	37.7	42.6
周至县	Zhouzhi	2.0	8.7	2.3	9.9	52.8
西咸新区	Xixian	6.7	11.0	7.7	12.7	61.4

主要统计指标解释

建筑业统计单位 指从事房屋、构筑物建造和设备安装活动的法人企业。建筑业法人企业应具有建筑业资质并能够独立核算，同时其应具备以下条件：①依法成立，有自己的名称、组织机构和场所，能够承担民事责任；②独立拥有和使用资产，承担负债，有权与其他单位签订合同；③独立核算盈亏，能够编制资产负债表。

建筑业总产值 是以货币形式表现的建筑业企业在一定时期内生产的建筑业产品和提供的服务的总和。建筑业总产值包括：

（1）建筑工程产值：指列入建筑工程预算内的各种工程价值。

（2）安装工程产值：指设备安装工程价值，不包括被安装设备本身的价值。

（3）其他产值：建筑业总产值中除建筑工程、安装工程以外的产值。包括房屋构筑物修理产值、非标准设备制造产值、总包企业向分包企业收取的管理费以及不能明确划分的施工活动所完成的产值。

a. 房屋构筑物修理产值：指房屋和构筑物修理所完成的产值，但不包括被修理房屋、构筑物本身价值和生产设备的修理价值。

b. 非标准设备制造产值：指加工制造没有定型的非标准生产设备的加工费和原材料价值（如化工厂、炼油厂用的各种罐、槽，矿井生产统一使用的各种漏斗、三角槽、阀门等）以及附属加工厂为本企业承建工程制作的非标准设备的价值。

建筑业增加值 指建筑业企业在报告期内以货币形式表现的建筑业生产经营活动的最终成果。

从2004年第一次全国经济普查开始，建筑业现价增加值按生产法和分配法（收入法）两种方法计算，以收入法的计算结果为准，即从收入的角度出发，根据生产要素在生产过程中应得的收入份额计算。具体计算方法：经济普查年度建筑业增加值按照《经济普查年度GDP核算方案》计算，非经济普查年度建筑业增加值按照非经济普查年度GDP核算方案》计算。

房屋建筑施工面积 指在报告期内施过工的全部房屋建筑面积，包括本期新开工的房屋面积、上期施工跨入本期继续施工的房屋面积、上期停缓建在本期恢复施工的房屋面积、本期竣工的房屋面积及本期施工后又停缓建的房屋面积。

房屋建筑竣工面积 指在报告期内房屋建筑按照设计要求全部完工，达到了使用条件，经验收鉴定合格，正式移交使用单位的房屋建筑面积。

Explanatory Notes on Main Statistical Indicators

Statistical Unit in the Construction Industry refers to a corporate enterprise engaged in the construction of buildings and structures and in the installation of equipment. A corporate construction enterprise should have qualification certificates with independent accounting system, and should meet the following 3 requirements: a) being set up in line with relevant legal basis, having its full name, organization and location, and capable of taking civil liabilities; b) independently possessing and using its assets and assuming its liabilities, and entitled to sign contracts with other institutions; and c) making independent accounts of its profits and losses, and capable of compiling its own balance sheet.

Gross Output Value of Construction refers to total of construction products and services, expressed in money terms, produced or rendered by construction and installation enterprises during a given period of time. It includes:

(1)Output value of construction projects: the value of projects covered by the project budgets;

(2) Output value of installation projects: the value of the installation of equipment, (excluding the value of the equipment to be installed);

(3)Other output values: the output value of construction industry apart from that of construction projects and installation projects. It includes: output value of repair of buildings and structures; output value of non-standard equipment manufacturing; overhead expenses received by contracted enterprises from the sub-contracted enterprises and the completed output value of construction activities for which there is no clear definition.

a. Output value of repair of buildings and structures: the value created through the repairs of buildings or structures. It does not include the value of buildings or structures being repaired and the value of the repair of production equipment;

b. Output value of manufactured non-standard equipment: the value of non-standard production equipment, including raw materials and manufacturing cost, made for the construction project (i.e., chemical plant; kettles or tanks used by refineries; various fillers, triangle tanks, valves used by mines). It also includes the output value of equipment manufactured by subsidiary workshops.

Value-added of Construction refers to the final result of the activities of production and operation of enterprises of the construction industry in monetary terms during the reference period.

Starting from the 2004 economic census, value-added of construction is calculated by both production approach and income approach, with the figures from the income approach as the final figures. Under the income approach, calculation starts from the perspective of income and is based on the share of income derived from the production process by the relevant factors of production. Specifically, value-added of construction for the Census years is calculated in accordance with the Programme of Compilation of GDP and National Accounts for the Year of Economic Census, and value-added of construction for other years is calculated in accordance with the Programme of Compilation of GDP and National Accounts for the Non Economic Census Years.

Floor Space of Buildings Under Construction refers to floor space of buildings under construction during the reference period, including the floor space of buildings for which construction has newly started; buildings for which construction has started earlier and is continuing during the reference period; and buildings for which construction has been suspended earlier but has restarted during the reference period; buildings completed during the reference period; and buildings under construction but construction has subsequently been during the reference period.

Floor Space of Buildings Completed refers to the floor space of buildings that are completed in the reference period in accordance with the requirements of the design, up to the standard for being put into use, and having been checked and accepted by departments concerned as qualified ones.

15 运输邮电和信息化

TRANSPORT,POSTAL TELECOMMUNICATION SERVICE AND INFORMATIZATION

资料整理：齐昆峰
Data management：Qi Kunfeng
数据审核：王金桂
Data audit：Wang Jingui

第十五部分　运输邮电和信息化

一、简要说明

本章资料包括交通运输业和邮电通信业的基本情况，主要是交通运输工具、货物和旅客运输量、邮电业务、邮政局所及服务点等基本情况，以及一套表单位信息化情况。运输邮电资料由西安市统计局服务业和社会科技处根据有关部门提供资料整理。信息化资料主要根据国家统计联网直报平台一套表单位的信息化统计数据整理。2017年起运输邮电数据为西安原口径数据，信息化数据为包含西咸新区数据。

二、主要指标

邮电业务总量（亿元）	739.53	比上年增长	68.1%
全社会车辆数（万辆）	325.63	比上年增长	12.8%
#民用小轿车	183.43	比上年增长	13.3%

15　TRANSPORT,POSTAL TELECOMMUNICATION SERVICES AND INFORMATIZATION

Ⅰ.Brief Introduction

Data in this chapter consists of primarily basic condition of transportation, postal service and communication, mainly including transportation facility amount of goods and passenger transportation, basic data of postal service, post offices and service establishments of Xi' an City. Data on transportation industry in this chapter is compiled by Tertiary Industry and Social&Science and Technology Division of the Xi' an Bureau of Statistics according to the data provided by department concerned of the municipal government. Data on informationization are obtained from data in "Five Top" Units of National Statistical Networking Platrform. Since 2017, the range of data on transportation, post and communication industry is the original range in Xi' an and data on informationization includes data in XiXian.

Ⅱ.Major Indicators

		Increase over Preceding Year
Amount of Postal and Telecommunication Service(100 mil. yuan)	739.53	68.1%
Number of Vehides in the whole Sciety(10 000 unit)	325.63	12.8%
Civil Car	183.43	13.3%

15-1 主要年份各种交通线路和桥梁

Transportation Routes and Bridges in Representative Years

年 份 Year	公路里程 （公里） Length of Highways (km)	桥 梁 （座） Bridges (seat)	桥梁长度 （米） Length of Bridge (m)
1989	2563		
1990	2586		
1991	2785		
1992	2786		
1993	2801		
1994	2830		
1995	2852		
1996	2877		
1997	3026		
1998	3047		
1999	2789		
2000	3010		
2001	3298		
2002	7862	629	29799
2003	8360	629	29799
2004	8360	629	29799
2005	8500	634	46973
2006	9530	634	46973
2007	9672	1319	91412
2008	11895	1710	151996
2009	12378	1856	154866
2010	12378	1856	154866
2011	12599	1863	149743
2012	13127	2190	214978
2013	13135	2213	224962
2014	13251	2213	224949
2015	13328	2323	250910
2016	13356	2423	256058
2017	13383	2435	286841
2018	14722	2460	293531

注：本表数据来自市交通局、民航通航里程2013年统计口径发生较大变化。
2017年起数据为西安原口径数据。

15-1 续表 continued

年 份 Year	永久式桥梁 （座） Permanent Bridges (seat)	永久式桥梁长度 （米） Length of Permanent Bridges (m)	民航通航里程 （重复航线）（公里） Length of Total Civil Aviation Routes(km)
1989			
1990			
1991			
1992			65007
1993			83215
1994			100800
1995			119753
1996			126433
1997			173010
1998			180000
1999			141284
2000			139764
2001			154614
2002	629	29799	211000
2003	629	29799	381800
2004	629	29799	386953
2005	632	46915	485749
2006	632	46915	418852
2007	1275	90716	553355
2008	1657	150980	515524
2009	1803	153850	587904
2010	1803	153850	742375
2011	1811	148810	898628
2012	2138	213985	981450
2013	2161	223970	70643568
2014	2171	224165	78626210
2015	2286	250175	93375419
2016	2386	255322	92561215
2017	2399	286164	113501600
2018	2438	292960	

15-2 各种交通线路里程和桥梁数（2018年）

Length of Transportation Routes and Number of Bridges (2018)

指　标	Item	2018
公路里程（公里）	**Length of Highways (km)**	**14722**
等级公路	Expressways and Class I to IV Highways	13992
高速	Expressway	573
一级	First Class	328
二级	Second Class	1466
三级	Third Class	1422
四级	Forth Class	10203
等外公路	Highways below Class IV	730
桥梁	**Bridges**	
永久式桥梁	Permanent	
座（座）	Seat (seat)	2438
长度（米）	Length (m)	292960
民航通航里程（公里）（重复航线）	**Length of Total Civil Aviation Routes(km)**	
国际航线（公里）	International routes(km)	
民航航线条数（条）	**Length of Civil Aviation routes(Article)**	**345**
国际航线（条）	International routes(Article)	64

注：本表数据来自市交通局。
本表数据为西安原口径数据。
民航通航里程因航空公司系统升级，数据暂缺。

15-3 主要年份全社会车辆数

Possession of Civil Vehicles in Representative Years

单位：辆、台 (unit)

年 份 Year	合计 Total	汽车 Motor	载客汽车 Passenget Vehicles	载货汽车 Ordinary Trucks	摩托车 Motorcycles	拖拉机 Tractors
1999	**279335**	133192	63772	44348		38023
2000	**310252**	138318	89783	44974		37177
2001	**369988**	172436	110744	55453		31355
2002	**454998**	206653	134527	64623	176960	36083
2003	**516719**	242599	163872	70781	191834	34733
2004	**512802**	276012	195524	74557	156709	34755
2005	**544586**	377628	240923	82463	131440	34741
2006	**608155**	393778	296078	89772	131449	33236
2007	**840376**	522616	360081	97614	284594	32028
2008	**875005**	595735	430472	89093	247079	30176
2009	**1012937**	754803	567326	113430	224121	31347
2010	**1253461**	961283	739038	145740	259239	29151
2011	**1445811**	1174874	928669	171649	241132	25600
2012	**1633257**	1380125	1123105	186412	224279	24458
2013	**1862063**	1634885	1372371	207058	200419	21898
2014	**2139024**	1926012	1658714	224409	190625	17484
2015	**2394052**	2191023	1929195	224322	179619	18099
2016	**2588479**	2444000	2191862	226915	119771	19352
2017	**2885557**	2716361	2451906	243998	145207	17776
2018	**3256344**	3098008	2804240	272474	134264	16808

注：本表数据来自市车管所。
2017年起数据为西安原口径数据。

15-4 全社会车辆数（2018年）

Possession of Civil Vehicles（2018）

指 标	Item	2018
合计（辆）	**Total (unit)**	**3256344**
民用汽车（辆）	Motor(unit)	3098008
#私人汽车拥有量	Possession of Private Vehicles	2795224
载客汽车	Passenger Vehicles	2804240
#大 型	Large	20051
轿 车	Car	1834314
普通载货汽车	Ordinary Trucks	272474
#重、中型	Heavy and Medium	71181
其他汽车	Others	21294
#三 轮	Three Wheelers	3720
拖拉机（台）	Tractors(unit)	16808
# 大中型	Large and Medium	
小 型	Small-sized	
摩托车（辆）	Motorcycle (unit)	134264
普通摩托车	Bicycle Motor	131673
挂车（辆）	Articulated Trailers (unit)	7264
其他类型车（辆）	Others (unit)	

注：本表数据来自市车管所。
　　本表数据为西安原口径数据。

15-5 主要年份交通运输量及周转量

Passenger Traffic and Kilometers and Freight Traffic and Ton-kilometers in Representative Years

年 份 Year	客运量 （万人次） Passenger Traffic (10 000 person-times)	旅客周转量 （万人公里） Passenger-Km (10 000 person-Km)	货运量 （万吨） Freight Traffic (10 000 tons)	货物周转量 （万吨公里） Freight Ton-Km (10 000 ton-Km)
1978	1334		3723	
1979	1420		3919	
1980	1508		3655	
1981	1839		3379	
1982	2340		4067	
1983	3054		4225	
1984	2899		4966	
1985	2404		5681	
1986	2186		5409	
1987	3781		6294	
1988	5721		6968	
1989	6092		8742	
1990	5748		6980	
1991	4193		3389	
1992	4368		8233	
1993	8036		8406	
1994	8321		8754	
1995	9069		9590	
1996	9854		10577	
1997	8922		9358	
1998	9223		9429	
1999	10311	2130383	9766	3452383
2000	8068	2507896	6999	3691963
2001	9078	2658037	7728	4229430
2002	12399	2524444	9482	4544040
2003	11413	2596402	9392	5037684
2004	10832	3112374	14845	5850029
2005	10479	1607568	12051	1249525
2006	11245	1721217	11832	1354318
2007	12466	1753464	15124	1473182
2008	26501	2529007	27560	3490707
2009	28693	2582025	30606	3766806
2010	30294	2942957	34323	4301680
2011	33375	3223544	39239	5212010
2012	36154	3387448	44924	5958742
2013	38289	3634915	50119	6471497
2014	25719	3091147	42039	6234128
2015	26904	3241463	46270	6430083
2016	23671	2909172	23888	5521252
2017	24287	3267158	25497	5979131
2018	25543	3545241	26892	6382177

注：本表数据由市交通局、西安铁路局、咸阳机场、长安航空公司、东方航空公司西北分公司提供。
2016年陕西省公路运输统计计算系数变化，因此与往年数据不可比。
2017年起数据为西安原口径数据。

15-6 交通运输量及运输周转量

Passenger Traffic and Kilometers and Freight Traffic and Ton-kilometers

指 标	Item	2017	2018
一、客运量合计（万人次）	**Passenger Traffic(10 000 person-times)**	**24287**	**25543**
铁路	Railway	4500	5523
公路	Highway	15601	15555
民航	Civil Aviation	4186	4465
二、旅客周转量合计（万人公里）	**Passenger-Km (10 000 person-Km)**	**3267158**	**3545241**
铁路	Railway	680961	708536
公路	Highway	900328	899071
民航	Civil Aviation	1685869	1937634
三、货运量合计（万吨）	**Freight Traffic(10 000 tons)**	**25497**	**26892**
铁路	Railway	994	1170
公路	Highway	24477	25691
民航	Civil Aviation	26	31
四、货物周转量（万吨公里）	**Freight Ton-Kin (10 000 ton-Km)**	**5979131**	**6382177**
铁路	Railway	2459206	2565134
公路	Highway	3509694	3805312
民航	Civil Aviation	10232	11731

注：本表数据由市交通局、西安铁路局、咸阳机场、长安航空公司、东方航空公司西北分公司提供。
2017年起数据为西安原口径数据。

15-7 主要年份邮政电信情况

年份 Year	邮电业务总量（万元） Business Volume of Postal and Telecommunication Services(10 000 yuan)	电信业务总量 Business Volume of Telecommunication Services	邮政业务总量 Business Volume of Postal Services
1978	1420		
1979	1616		
1980	1640		
1981	1713		
1982	2154		
1983	2250		
1984	2484		
1985	2972		
1986	3244		
1987	3911		
1988	5327		
1989	5973		
1990	7843		
1991	5700		
1992	6610		
1993	36581		
1994	54034		
1995	76450		
1996	104566		
1997	124601		
1998	204927		
1999	306457		
2000	461628		
2001	367620		
2002	515259	470492	44767
2003	820943	770673	50270
2004	1027415	975045	52370
2005	1320447	1261033	59414
2006	1867560	1796533	71027
2007	2267633	2191250	76383
2008	2646662	2564524	82138
2009	2989246	2900836	88410
2010	3231059	3167750	63309
2011	2005025	1944329	60696
2012	2162035	2098273	63762
2013	2479430	2313630	165800
2014	2922011	2695332	226679
2015	3315324	2983024	332300
2016	3831119	3299859	531260
2017	4398547	3728783	669764
2018	7395253	6621776	773477

注：2002年及以后，邮政电信机构分离；2001－2010年邮电业务总量按2000年不变价格计算；2011年后邮电业务总量按2010年不变价格计算，故与以往年份不可比。
2017年起数据为西安原口径数据。

Basic Statistic on Postal and Telecommunication Service in Representative Years

固定电话年末用户数（户） Number of Immobile Telephone at Year-end (subscriber)	农村电话用户数 Number of Telephone in Rural Areas at Year-end	移动电话用户年末数（户） Number of Mobile Phone at Year-end (subscriber)	互联网年末宽带用户数（户） Number of Broad Band Net User (subscriber)
12828	1062		
13487	1052		
14024	1086		
14497	1125		
15357	1129		
16922	1156		
18611	1203		
21624	1239		
26373	1235		
30200	1290		
34265	1357		
39506	1498		
45267	1668		
49516	2479		
60727	2613		
101327	2671		
197398	5067		
299485	8386		
430270	13654		
573244	21202		
736998	37863		
874586	74761		
1242637	170199		
1711500	259374	1277400	17183
2095230	358803	1964200	35230
2538393	415593	2412392	160900
2934424	480276	3500900	243448
3214806	500847	4199570	339280
3159639	467526	5510720	508775
3145819	419446	6645863	586213
3068807	383869	7377575	813987
2891009	358238	11200566	1167916
2617691	335048	14230800	1461804
2703640	320189	16141463	1841027
3110176	335864	18035397	2023059
3191112	330602	21606662	2670473
3066575	372823	20253157	2779458
2920773	306336	17669953	2899714
2843336	314457	17395026	3358343
2732174	294055	18542137	3467859
2622787	244984	18580879	3924786

注：本表数据由市邮政管理局、市邮政局，中国联通、中国电信、中国移动等西安分公司提供。

15-8 邮政业务及服务网点

Postal Service and Branch Post Office

指 标	Item	2010	2011	2012	2013	2014	2015	2016	2017	2018
一、邮政业务总量（万元）	**Business Volume of Postal Services(10 000 yuan)**	**63309**	**60696**	**63077**	**165800**	**226679**	**332300**	**531260**	**669764**	**773477**
二、邮政业务收入（万元）	**Gross Income of Post Services (10 000 yuan)**	**58831**	**65174**	**71778**	**177100**	**213893**	**307008**	**439867**	**544555**	**616823**
其中：快递业务收入（万元）	Express Delivery Business Income (10 000 yuan)				97100	134306	207451	331605	413699	475783
三、函件（万件）	**Number of Letters (10 000 pcs)**	**8176**	**3061**	**2769**	**2856**	**2112**	**1707**	**1367**	**1360**	**1081**
四、包件（万件）	**Parcels (10 000 pcs)**	**59**	**91**	**50**	**89**	**71**	**69**	**51**	**48**	**49**
五、汇票（万张）	**Money Order (10 000 pcs)**	**123**	**112**	**90**	**148**	**81**	**48**	**17**	**15**	**11**
六、报纸订销累计份数（万份）	**Accumulated Newspaper Prescribing and Sales Volume (10 000 pcs)**	**11724**	**12603**	**13052**	**14495**	**14338**	**14457**	**14395**	**14744**	**14915**
七、杂志订销累计份数（万份）	**Accumulated Magazine Prescribing and Sales Volume (10 000 pcs)**	**550**	**564**	**613**	**1628**	**1572**	**1285**	**1155**	**956**	**1059**
八、特快专递类业务（万件）	**Express Mail Service Volume (10 000 pcs)**	**582**	**1901**	**129**	**138**	**107**	**61**	**63**	**63**	**63**
九、集邮业务量（万枚）	**Stamps For Collection (10 000 pcs)**	**860**	**1060**	**2312**	**1431**	**1477**	**1920**	**1607**	**1687**	**1135**
十、邮政营销网点（处）	**Number of Post Office Branch Establishments (unit)**	**305**	**277**	**279**	**269**	**280**	**299**	**297**	**297**	**297**
#设在农村的局所	In it: Number of Post Offices in Rural Area	20	50	115	110	123	140	149	149	148
十一、邮政信筒信箱（个）	**Number of Mailboxes(unit)**	**1108**	**1108**	**1108**	**1108**	**1170**	**1170**	**422**	**422**	**290**

注：本表数据来自市邮政管理局和邮政局，2013年邮政数据统计口径变化。
本表2017年起数据未包含西咸新区。

15-9 电信业务情况

Telecommunication Service

指 标	Item	2010	2011	2012	2013	2014	2015	2016	2017	2018
一、电信业务总量（万元）	**Business Volume of Telecommunication Services (10 000 yuan)**	**3167750**	**1944329**	**2098273**	**2313630**	**2695332**	**2983024**	**3299859**	**3728783**	**6621776**
二、电信业务总收入（万元）	**Gross Income of Telecommunication Services (10 000 yuan)**	**1038865**	**1029629**	**1162257**	**1316435**	**1356705**	**1338203**	**1420708**	**1451625**	**1495207**
三、固定电话年末用户数（万户）	**Number of Immobile Telephone at Year-end(10 000 subscribers)**	**261.77**	**270.36**	**311.02**	**319.11**	**306.66**	**292.08**	**284.33**	**273.22**	**262.28**
#农村电话年末户数	Number of Telephone in Rural Areas at Year-end	33.50	32.02	33.59	33.06	37.28	30.63	31.45	29.41	24.50
四、电话交换机总容量（万门）	**Capacity (number) of Telephone Switchboard (10 000 lines)**	**449.05**	**441.49**	**420.38**	**378.02**	**230.01**	**145.08**	**75.92**		
五、移动电话用户年末数（万户）	**Number of Mobile Phone at Year-end (10 000 subscribers)**	**1423.08**	**1614.15**	**1803.54**	**2160.67**	**2025.32**	**1767.00**	**1739.50**	**1854.21**	**1858.09**
#4G电话用户数	4G Mobile Phone Subscribers							1113.03	1369.00	1499.18
六、互联网年末用户数（万户）	**Number of Broad Band Net User (10 000 subscribers)**	**146.18**	**184.10**	**202.31**	**267.05**	**277.95**	**289.97**	**335.83**	**346.79**	**392.48**

注：本表数据由中国联通、中国电信、中国移动等西安分公司提供。
2017年起数据为西安原口径数据。

15-10 一套表单位信息化基本情况（2018年）

单位：个

指 标	Item	企业数 Number of Enterprises	使用计算机的企业 Computer-used Enterprise
总计	**Total**	**7408**	**7386**
按国民经济门类分	**According To the Categories of National Economy**		
采矿业	Mining Industry	5	5
制造业	Manufacturing Industry	1373	1371
电力、热力、燃气及水生产和供应业	Electricity, Heat, Gas and Water Production and Supply	47	47
建筑业	Construction Business	1203	1199
批发和零售业	Wholesale and Retail Trade	1378	1377
交通运输、仓储和邮政业	Transportation, Warehousing and Postal Services	205	203
住宿和餐饮业	Accommodation and Catering Industry	677	677
信息传输、软件和信息技术服务业	Information Transmission, Software and Information Technology	250	250
房地产业	Estate	1275	1264
租赁和商务服务业	Leasing and Business Services	308	307
科学研究和技术服务业	Scientific Eesearch and Eechnical Services	274	274
水利、环境和公共设施管理业	Management of Water Wonservancy, Environment and Public Facilities	65	65
居民服务、修理和其他服务业	Services of Households, Repairs and Other Services	62	62
教育	Education	18	18
卫生和社会工作	Health and Social Service	66	66
文化、体育和娱乐业	Culture, Sports and Entertainment	202	201

注：一套表单位包括规模以上工业企业、限额以上批零住餐企业、资质以内建筑业企业、规模以上服务业企业、房地产开发经营企业。

Basic Statistics on Informatization of “One Sheet” Units（2018）

(unit)

有信息技术人员的企业 Enterprises with Information Technology Personnel	有局域网的企业 LAN Enterprises	使用信息化管理的企业 Enterprises Managed by Information Technology	有信息化 投入的企业 Enterprises with Informatization Input	使用互联网的企业 Enterprises Using the Internet
5459	**5696**	**7168**	**6411**	**7379**
3	5	5	5	5
1201	1170	1343	1287	1369
36	40	47	41	47
864	843	1145	1040	1199
959	1060	1330	1156	1375
123	143	199	158	203
500	507	656	609	677
242	231	246	241	250
773	915	1225	997	1261
216	231	302	267	307
225	227	270	250	274
48	52	63	56	65
43	43	61	55	62
18	15	18	18	18
63	59	66	62	66
145	155	192	169	201

15-11 一套表单位信息化设施及投入情况（2018年）

指　标	Item	期末使用计算机数量（台）Computers Used at the End of Period（unit）
总计	**Total**	**643482**
按国民经济门类分	**According To the Categories of National Economy**	
采矿业	Mining Industry	9058
制造业	Manufacturing Industry	144282
电力、热力、燃气及水生产和供应业	Electricity, Heat, Gas and Water Production and Supply	7370
建筑业	Construction Business	81500
批发和零售业	Wholesale and Retail Trade	61746
交通运输、仓储和邮政业	Transportation, Warehousing and Postal Services	26855
住宿和餐饮业	Accommodation and Catering Industry	16703
信息传输、软件和信息技术服务业	Information Transmission, Software and Information Technology	160154
房地产业	Estate	38635
租赁和商务服务业	Leasing and Business Services	15375
科学研究和技术服务业	Scientific Eesearch and Eechnical Services	52588
水利、环境和公共设施管理业	Management of Water Wonservancy, Environment and Public Facilities	5817
居民服务、修理和其他服务业	Services of Households, Repairs and Other Services	1841
教育	Education	2684
卫生和社会工作	Health and Social Service	9579
文化、体育和娱乐业	Culture, Sports and Entertainment	9295

注：一套表单位包括规模以上工业企业、限额以上批零住餐企业、资质以内建筑业企业、规模以上服务业企业、房地产开发经营企业。

Information Technology Facilities and Investment of "One Sheet" Units (2018)

信息技术人员（人） Information Technology Personnel（Person）	拥有网站个数（个） Number of Websites Owned（unit）	信息化投入（万元） Informatization Input (10 000 yuan)	一次性投入（万元） Disposable Input (10 000 yuan)	运营维护投入（万元） Operation and Maintenance Input (10 000 yuan)
29137	**5004**	**465111**	**266645**	**198465**
36	2	512	203	309
6257	1315	115958	78495	37463
192	29	6476	6046	430
3476	753	24669	17509	7160
3033	758	75157	22142	53015
863	106	60217	45983	14234
1090	311	7230	3636	3594
8862	294	88576	57218	31358
1708	641	24195	12222	11973
704	228	35919	4145	31774
1945	248	18279	14006	4273
139	48	1154	632	522
82	39	479	240	239
105	15	894	474	420
218	75	2638	1837	801
427	142	2758	1857	901

15-12 一套表单位信息化管理情况（2018年）

单位：个

指 标	Item	企业数 Number of Enterprises	使用信息化管理的企业 Number of Enterprises Managed by Information Technology
总计	**Total**	**7408**	**7168**
按国民经济门类分	**According To the Categories of National Economy**		
采矿业	Mining Industry	5	5
制造业	Manufacturing Industry	1373	1343
电力、燃气及水的生产供应业	Electricity, Heat, Gas and Water Production and Supply	47	47
建筑业	Construction Business	1203	1145
批发和零售业	Wholesale and Retail Trade	1378	1330
交通运输、仓储和邮政业	Transportation, Warehousing and Postal Services	205	199
住宿和餐饮业	Accommodation and Catering Industry	677	656
信息传输、软件和信息技术服务业	Information Transmission, Software and Information Technology	250	246
房地产业	Estate	1275	1225
租赁和商务服务业	Leasing and Business Services	308	302
科学研究和技术服务业	Scientific Eesearch and Eechnical Services	274	270
水利、环境和公共设施管理业	Management of Water Wonservancy, Environment and Public Facilities	65	63
居民服务、修理和其他服务业	Services of Households, Repairs and Other Services	62	61
教育	Education	18	18
卫生和社会工作	Health and Social Service	66	66
文化、体育和娱乐业	Culture, Sports and Entertainment	202	192

注：一套表单位包括规模以上工业企业、限额以上批零住餐企业、资质以内建筑业企业、规模以上服务业企业、房地产开发经营企业。

Information Management Situation of "One Sheet" Units (2018)

(unit)

财务管理 Financial Management	购销存管理 Purchase and Sale Management	生产制造管理 Manufacturing Management	物流配送管理 Logistics Distribution Management	客户关系管理 Customer Relationship Management	人力资源管理 Human Resource Management	其他 Others
6411	**2935**	**1009**	**660**	**2121**	**2783**	**1295**
5	2	1		1	2	1
1235	829	628	234	431	506	170
45	20	22	[illegible]	12	25	9
1028	202	92	32	239	473	229
1152	916	74	248	499	400	175
182	46	15	52	35	69	48
536	295	25	28	189	180	150
235	90	26	15	99	135	55
1109	262	58	13	334	545	246
279	54	9	12	104	141	54
244	68	35	7	64	137	70
56	16	3	3	8	24	13
53	23	4	4	26	26	14
15	2			5	6	6
60	40	1	2	21	26	16
177	70	16	9	54	88	39

15-13 一套表单位电子商务交易情况（2018年）

指 标	Item	企业数（个） Number of Enterprises (unit)
总计	**Total**	**7408**
按国民经济门类分	**According To the Categories of National Economy**	
采矿业	Mining Industry	5
制造业	Manufacturing Industry	1373
电力、燃气及水的生产供应业	Electricity, Heat, Gas and Water Production and Supply	47
建筑业	Construction Business	1203
批发和零售业	Wholesale and Retail Trade	1378
交通运输、仓储和邮政业	Transportation, Warehousing and Postal Services	205
住宿和餐饮业	Accommodation and Catering Industry	677
信息传输、软件和信息技术服务业	Information Transmission, Software and Information Technology	250
房地产业	Estate	1275
租赁和商务服务业	Leasing and Business Services	308
科学研究和技术服务业	Scientific Eesearch and Eechnical Services	274
水利、环境和公共设施管理业	Management of Water Wonservancy, Environment and Public Facilities	65
居民服务、修理和其他服务业	Services of Households, Repairs and Other Services	62
教育	Education	18
卫生和社会工作	Health and Social Service	66
文化、体育和娱乐业	Culture, Sports and Entertainment	202

注：一套表单位包括规模以上工业企业、限额以上批零住餐企业、资质以内建筑业企业、规模以上服务业企业、房地产开发经营企业。

E-commerce Transactions of "One Sheet" Units (2018)

有电子商务交易的企业（个） Enterprises with Ecommerce Transactions (unit)			拥有电子商务交易平台的企业（个） With Ecommerce Trading Platform Enterprises (unit)	全年电子商务销售金额（万元） Sales of Ecommerce (10 000 yuan)	全年电子商务采购金额（万元） Purchases of Ecommerce (10 000 yuan)
	有电子商务销售的企业 Ecommerce Sales Enterprises	有电子商务采购的企业 E-Commerce Purchases Enterprises			
875	**669**	**382**	**98**	**6692328**	**3345227**
139	91	83	21	209607	239335
2		2	1		4
58	4	55		183	1048156
204	184	76	40	5818868	1970813
15	8	9	4	94288	640
280	273	59	3	146477	881
51	25	31	15	215971	8527
24	2	22	1	800	2058
33	27	16	7	159495	72336
9	4	6		253	1013
10	9	5	1	4808	188
7	4	3	2	247	45
2	1	2		11346	473
6	4	3		1258	61
35	33	10	3	28727	695

主要统计指标解释

公路里程 指在一定时期内实际达到《公路工程技术标准JTJ01-88》规定的等级公路，并经公路主管部门正式验收交付使用的公路里程数。包括大中城市的郊区公路以及通过小城镇街道部分的公路里程和桥梁、隧道渡口的长度，不包括大中城市的街道、厂矿、林区生产用道和农业生产用道的里程。两条或多条公路共同经由同一路段，只计算一次，不得重复计算里程长度。它是反映公路建设发展规模的重要指标，也是计算运输网密度等指标的基础资料。

民用航空航线里程 指民航运输定期班机飞行的航线长度的总和。航线长度按机场之间的距离计算，通常有两种计算方法：一是将每条航线长度相加称为重复计算航线里程；一是将两线或两条以上航线经过同一区段里程，只计算一次航线长度称为不重复计算航线里程。一般常用的是后者，它能确切反映民航运输网的规模，是表明民航事业为国民经济服务和方便人民生活程度的主要指标。

货（客）运量 指在一定时期内，各种运输工具实际运送的货物（旅客）数量。它是反映运输业为国民经济和人民生活服务的数量指标，也是制定和检查运输生产计划、研究运输发展规模和速度的重要指标。货运按吨计算，客运按人计算。货物不论运输距离长短、货物类别，均按实际重量统计。旅客不论行程远近或票价多少，均按一人一次客运量统计；半价票、小孩票也按一人统计。

货物（旅客）周转量 指在一定时期内，由各种运输工具运送的货物（旅客）数量与其相应运输距离的乘积之总和。它是反映运输业生产总成果的重要指标，也是编制和检查运输生产计划，计算运输效率、劳动生产率以及核算运输单位成本的主要基础资料。计算货物周转量通常按发出站与到达站之间的最短距离，也就是计费距离计算。计算公式为：

货物（旅客）周转量=Σ货物（旅客）运输量×运输距离

民用汽车拥有量 指报告期末，在公安交通管理部门按照《机动车注册登记工作规范》，已注册登记领有民用车辆牌照的全部汽车数量。汽车拥有量统计的主要分类：根据汽车结构分为载客汽车、载货汽车及其他汽车；根据汽车所有者不同分为个人（私人）汽车、单位汽车；根据汽车的使用性质分为营运汽车、非营运汽车；根据汽车大小规格不同载客汽车分为大型、中型、小型和微型，载货汽车分为重型、中型、轻型和微型。

邮电业务总量 指以价值量形式表现的邮电通信企业为社会提供各类邮电通信服务的总数量。邮电业务量按专业分类包括函件、包件、汇票、报刊发行、邮政快件、特快专递、邮政储蓄、集邮、公众电报、用户电报、传真、长途电话、出租电路、无线寻呼、移动电话、分组交换数据通信、出租代维等。计算方法为各类产品乘以相应的平均单价（不变价）之和，再加上出租电路和设备、代用户维护电话交换机和线路等的服务收入。它综合反映了一定时期邮电业务发展的总成果，是研究邮电业务量构成和发展趋势的重要指标。计算公式为：

邮电业务总量=Σ（各类邮电业务量×不变单价）+出租代维及其他业务收入

移动电话用户 是指通过移动电话交换机进入移动电话网、占用移动电话号码的电话用户。用户数量以报告期末在移动电话营业部门实际办理登记手续进入移动电话网的户数进行计算，一部移动电话统计为一户。

电话用户 指接入国家公众固定电话网，并按固定电话业务进行经营管理的电话用户。1997年以前，电话用户分为市内电话用户和农村电话用户。“市内电话用户”是指接入县城及县以上城市的电话网上的电话用户；“农村电话用户”是指接入县邮电局农话台及县以下农村电话交换点，以县城为中心（除市活用户外）联通县、乡（镇）、行政村、村民小组的用户。从1997年起，电话用户数分组调整为以用户所在区域划分为“城市电话用户”和“乡村电话用户”，与过去的按市内电话和农村电话划分方法不同。而电话用户总数、电话机总部数统计范围不变。

农村电话用户 指县城关区以下的集镇和农村接入局用交换机的电话用户数。

局用交换机容量 是指安装在本地电信运营商内用于接续本地固定电话的电话交换机容量，有倍增设备按倍增后的数量计数。包括现用和备用的人工或自动交换机的全部容量。

计算机数 指报告期末企业（单位）使用的计算机数量，包括台式机、笔记本电脑和平板电脑。

信息技术人员 指专职从事信息技术系统的制定、设计、开发、安装、操作、维护、管理和评估的人员。

信息化投入 包括企业（单位）一次性投入和运

营维护投入。

一次性投入 包括企业（单位）购置各类硬件和软件的实际支出。

运营维护投入 包括企业（单位）更新维护各类信息通信硬件和软件的实际支出。

互联网 指在世界范围内的公共计算机网络。它提供一系列通信服务（包括万维网）的接入，并传送电子邮件、新闻、娱乐和数据文件等。

全年电子商务销售金额 指报告期内企业（单位）借助网络订单而销售的商品和服务总额。借助网络订单指通过网络接受订单，付款和配送可以不借助于网络。

全年电子商务采购金额 指报告期内企业（单位）借助网络订单而采购的商品和服务总额。借助网络订单指通过网络发送订单，付款和配送可以不借助于网络。

Explanatory Notes on Main Statistical Indicators

Length of Highways refers to the length of highways which are built in conformity with the grades specified by the highway engineering standard formulated by the Ministry of Communications, and have been formally checked and accepted by the departments of highways and put into use. The length of highways includes that of the suburb highways at large and medium- sized cities,highways passing through streets at small cities and towns,and also the length of bridges, tunnel and ferries. It does not include the length of streets in big and medium-sized cities and highways built for the production purpose at factories, mines, forest areas and agricultural areas. If two or more highways go the same section of the way, the length of the section is only calculated for once and no duplication is allowed. The length of highways is an important indicator to show the development of the highway construction and to provide essential information to calculate the transport network density.

Length of Civil Aviation Routes refers to the length of all routes for regular civil aviation flights. There are usually two ways to calculate the distance between airports connected by the route length: one is to put the length of all air routes together, called duplicated calculation of the length of the routes; the other is not to allow the duplication in calculation when two or more routes passing the same section of aviation routes. The latter is usually used, as it can precisely show the size of the civil aviation network and indicate the extent of civil aviation serving the national economy and the people.

Freight (Passenger) Traffic refers to the volume of freight (passenger) transported with various means. Freight transport is calculated in tons and passenger traffic is calculated in the number of persons. Despite the type of freight and travelling distance, the freight transport is calculated in the actual weight of the goods: and despite the travelling distance and ticket price, the passenger traffic is calculated by the principle that one person can be counted only once in one travel. The passenger who travel with a half price ticket or a child ticket is also calculated as one person. The freight (passenger) traffic provides a quantitative measure to show how the transport industry serves the national economy and people, and is also an important indicator for planning the transport industry and for studying the development scale and speed of the transport industry.

Freight Ton-kilometers(Passenger-kilometers) refer to the sum of the products of the volume of transported cargo (passengers) multiplying by the transport distance, usually using ton-kilometer and passenger-kilometer as units for measurement. Normally, the shortest distance between the departure station and the destination station (i.e., the payable distance) is the basis to calculate the freight ton-kilometers. This is an important indicator to show the total results of the transport industry, to prepare and examine the transport plan and to measure the efficiency, the labour productivity and the unit cost of transport.

The formula is as follows:

Freight Ton-kilometers(Passenger-kilometers)=Σ {Freight (Passenger) Traffic × Distance of Transportation }

Measuring unit: ton-kilometer (person-kilometer)

Possession of Civil Motor Vehicles refer to the total numbers of vehicles that are registered and received vehicles license tags according to the Work Standard for Motor Vehicles Registration formulated by the Transport Management Office under the department of public security at the end of the reference period. They are divided into categories. According to the structure of motor vehicles, they are divided into passenger vehicles, trucks and others; according to ownership into private vehicles and vehicles for the unit' s use; according to kind of usage into working vehicles and non-working vehicles; and according to size of vehicles into large passenger vehicles, medium-sized passenger vehicles, small passenger vehicles and mini passenger vehicles, heavytrucks, light-heavy trucks, light trucks and mini-trucks.

Business Volume of Post and Telecommunications refers to the total amount of post and telecommunications services, expressed in value terms, provided by the post and telecommunications departments for the society. Post and telecommunication services can be classified asletters, parcels, remittance, issue of newspapers and magazines, fast mail service, express mail service, savings deposits, stamps for collection, public and individual telegraph service, facsimiles, long-distance telephone service,leasing of telephone lines, urban paging service, mobile telephone service, data transfer

and transmission, etc. The accounting approach is to multiply the service products of all types with their average unit price (constant price) to get sum of business value, plus income from other services such as leasing of telephone lines and equipment, maintenance of telephone switchboards and lines on behalf of customers. This indicator reflects the overall results of post and telecommunications service during a given period, and is important to study the composition of business service and the development of post and telecommunications service.

The formula is as follows:

Business Volume of Post and Telecommunications=Σ (Transaction of Post and Telecommunication Service x Constant Price) + Income from Leasing, Maintenance and other Services

Mobile Telephone Subscribers refer to the persons who own mobile telephone numbers and are connected with the mobile telephone communication network through the mobile telephone switchboards. The number of subscribers is calculated by the subscribers who have completed registration at mobile communication business centers and entered into the mobile telephone network. One mobile telephone is taken as a subscriber.

Telephone Subscribers refer to subscribers that are connected to the public line telephone network provided with telephone services. Before 1997, telephone subscribers were classified as city subscribers and village subscribers. City subscribers referred to those connected

to city telephone networks in county towns and cities, while village subscribers referred to those connected to village telephone stations at and below counties. Since 1997, the classification of telephone subscribers was modified on the basis of physical location of the subscribers as Urban telephone subscribers and rural telephone subscribers , which is different from the previous classification of categorizing local telephones and rural telephones , while the definition of total subscribers and total number of telephones remain unchanged.

Rural Telephone Subscribers refer to telephone subscribers, located at towns under county town and country, that are connected to the public line telephone network.

Capacity of Office Telephone Exchanges refers to the capacity (measured in gate) of telephone exchanges installed in the offices of local telecommunication service providers for communication between fixed telephones. It includes the capacity of both manual and automatic exchanges in use and for stand-by purpose. Equipment with expansion function is to be counted by the expanded capacity.

The number of computer srefers to the number of computers used in an enterprise or a company at the end of the reporting period, including desktops, laptops, and tablet computers.

Information technology personnel refers topeople who is engaged in the formulation, design, development, installation, operation, maintenance, management and evaluation of an information technology system.

Informatization Input includes the One-time investment input and operation maintenance investment of an enterprise or a company.

One-time Investment Input includes the actual expenditure in purchasing all kinds of hardware and software of an enterprise or a company.

Operation and Maintenance Input includesthe actual expenditure inupdating and maintenance of all kinds of information communication hardware and software of anenterprise or a company.

The Internet refers to the public computer network around the world. It provides access to a range of communications services including the world wide web, and transmits e-mail, news, entertainment, and data files,etc.

The amount of E-commerce sales during the whole year the total amount of goods and services sold by means of network orders of an enterprise or a company during the reporting period.By means of network ordersmeans that the orders are received over the network, but the payment and distribution can be made without the network.

The amount of E-commerce purchases during the whole year refers to the total amount of goods and services purchased by means of network orders of an enterprise or a company during the reporting period.

By means of network orders means that the orders are sent over the network, but the payment and distribution can be made without the network.

16 国内贸易

DOMESTIC TRADE

资料整理：马晓庆　杨　骏　左　宇　赵琳瑛　胡树建
Data management: Ma Xiaoqing　Yang Jun　Zuo Yu　Zhao Linying　Hu Shujian
数据审核：黄小丹
Data audit:Huang Xiaodan

第十六部分　国内贸易

一、简要说明

1.本章资料反映西安市批发和零售业、住宿和餐饮业的发展与经营状况，主要内容包括：社会消费品零售总额，限额以上批发和零售业、住宿和餐饮业基本情况、连锁经营情况，重点交易市场情况等。

2.限额以上企业指年主营业务收入2000万元及以上的批发企业（单位）；500万元及以上的零售业企业（单位）；200万元及以上的住宿和餐饮业企业（单位）。

3.批发业、零售业、住宿业、餐饮业大中小微型企业划分按照《统计上大中小微型企业划分办法（2017）》标准执行。

4.2018年数据口径与往年相同。

二、主要指标

社会消费品零售总额（亿元）	4658.72	比上年增长	9.6%

16　DOMESTIC TRADE

I.Brief Introduction

1.This chapter reflects the management and development of wholesale and retail trades, hotels and catering services in Xi' an, mainly including: total retail sales of consumer goods, the basic conditions enterprises above designated size in wholesale and retail trades, hotels and catering services, the conditions of chain stores,focus on transaction markets, etc.

2.Enterprises above designated size cover wholesale enterprises with revenue from principal business over 20 million yuan, retail enterprises with revenue from principal business over 5 million yuan, hotel and catering services enterprises with revenue from principal business over 2 million yuan.

3.The division standard of large/medium/small/mini sized enterprises of wholesale, retail trades, hotels and catering services is based on the division standard of large/medium/small/mini sized enterprises in 2017.

4.The data cabliber of 2018 is same as the previous years.

Ⅱ .Maior Indicators

		Increase over Preceding Year
Total Retail Sales of Consumer Goods (100 mil. yuan)	4658.72	9.6%

16-1 主要年份社会消费品零售额

Total Retail Sales of Consumer Goods in Representative Years

单位：亿元 (100 million yuan)

年 份 Year	社会消费品零售总额 Total Retail Sales of Consumer Goods	城镇 Urban	乡村 Village	批发和零售业 Wholesale Trades and Retail Trades	住宿和餐饮业 Accommodation and Catering Trade	其他行业 Others
1978	12.70	8.82	3.88	11.01	0.53	0.21
1980	15.88	11.53	4.35	13.05	0.80	0.20
1985	32.92	26.09	6.83	25.04	1.69	0.48
1986	37.50	29.25	8.25	28.88	1.97	0.64
1987	43.86	34.62	9.24	33.32	2.50	0.49
1988	59.65	47.74	11.91	44.84	2.97	0.78
1989	68.05	54.60	13.45	54.41	2.98	0.76
1990	72.77	59.42	13.35	57.46	3.79	0.90
1991	81.04	66.93	14.11	60.35	4.43	1.26
1992	100.84	89.17	11.67	71.86	6.13	2.30
1993	115.38	104.41	10.97	75.99	7.49	2.71
1994	144.64	131.56	13.08	89.79	9.12	3.43
1995	186.60	165.98	20.62	115.46	11.97	3.73
1996	222.94	198.19	24.75	145.05	15.83	4.02
1997	264.47	238.17	26.30	169.08	22.12	4.17
1998	291.45	257.39	34.06	183.43	30.97	4.27
1999	323.37	283.32	40.05	207.96	34.78	4.85
2000	360.42	317.12	43.30	232.89	41.42	5.43
2001	406.21	358.97	47.24	265.25	48.87	5.86
2002	459.76	409.86	49.90	309.36	51.42	6.45
2003	502.65	449.62	53.03	440.28	53.30	9.07
2004	578.55	520.89	57.66	509.55	56.87	12.13
2005	670.56	604.63	65.93	592.77	63.59	14.20
2006	784.95	708.31	76.64	694.03	74.77	16.15
2007	936.21	845.59	90.62	828.63	89.32	18.26
2008	1176.58	1063.93	112.65	1033.00	122.90	20.68
2009	1398.37	1336.41	61.96	1250.41	147.96	
2010	1678.01	1610.88	67.13	1497.71	180.30	
2011	2039.24	1968.41	70.83	1825.79	213.45	
2012	2400.67	2326.84	73.83	2156.49	244.18	

年 份 Year	社会消费品零售总额 Total Retail Sales of Consumer Goods	按销售单位所在地分 By Location of Establishments			按消费形态分By Consumption Patterns	
		城镇零售额 Urban Areas	城区 Urban District	乡村零售额 Rural Areas	商品零售 Retail Sales	餐饮收入 Catering income
2013	2742.89	2657.49	2124.72	85.40	2526.10	216.79
2014	3093.89	2996.43	2596.00	97.46	2865.07	228.82
2015	3405.38	3292.83	2832.66	112.55	3146.45	258.93
2016	3767.20	3639.32	3266.69	127.88	3486.21	280.99
2017	4249.81	4098.00	3524.33	151.81	3916.20	333.61
2018	4658.72	4489.78	3900.88	168.94	4288.32	370.40

注：依据2008年第二次经济普查数据，对2005-2007年数据进行调整。
依据2013年第三次经济普查数据，对2009-2013年数据进行调整。
2009年以前按经营单位所在地分为市和县及县以下。
2002年以前按行业分组中不包括制造业零售额和农业对非农业居民零售额。
2016年数据根据第三次农业普查结果及有关制度规定进行了修订。

16-2 社会消费品零售总额

Total Retail Sales of Consumer Goods

单位：亿元 (100 million yuan)

分　类	Classify	2017	2018
社会消费品零售总额	**Total Retail Sales of Consumer Goods**	**4249.81**	**4658.72**
（一）按销售单位所在地分	Grouped by Region		
（1）城镇	Urban	4098.00	4489.78
#城区	District	3524.33	3900.88
（2）乡村	Village	151.81	168.94
（二）按消费形态分	Grouped by Consumption Patterns		
（1）商品零售	Retail Sales	3916.20	4288.32
（2）餐饮收入	Catering Income	333.61	370.40

注：2016年数据根据第三次农业普查结果及有关制度规定进行了修订。

16-3 各区县社会消费品零售总额

Total Retail Sales of Consumer Goods by Region

单位：亿元 (100 million yuan)

区　县	Region	2005	2008	2009	2010	2011	2012	2013	2014	2015	2016	2017	2018
全　市	**Toatl**	**670.56**	**1176.58**	**1398.37**	**1678.01**	**2039.24**	**2400.67**	**2742.89**	**3093.89**	**3405.38**	**3767.20**	**4249.81**	**4658.72**
新城区	Xincheng	129.00	207.01	241.56	285.41	342.48	397.08	446.06	499.78	557.59	607.98	667.03	739.79
碑林区	Beilin	131.09	206.80	241.48	285.45	342.56	395.07	445.11	505.87	561.46	610.53	625.92	670.40
莲湖区	Lianhu	116.34	169.62	198.10	234.84	282.08	325.93	368.62	413.00	451.82	491.72	503.68	544.95
灞桥区	Baqiao	17.89	27.01	36.26	50.18	68.02	95.43	132.26	154.28	173.26	200.82	232.31	260.53
未央区	Weiyang	64.38	164.14	200.54	245.41	301.10	361.75	423.72	480.79	515.21	586.17	558.35	615.17
雁塔区	Yanta	104.87	225.95	272.35	327.95	401.56	472.92	534.30	596.50	656.47	714.37	782.59	847.50
阎良区	Yanliang	8.25	13.85	16.41	19.67	23.91	27.87	31.37	34.93	37.90	41.22	45.59	49.94
临潼区	Lintong	20.37	29.02	34.29	40.95	49.72	57.75	64.08	72.63	77.99	84.66	96.47	107.75
长安区	Chang'an	37.36	64.67	76.80	91.86	111.41	130.09	144.94	164.00	183.37	202.49	231.40	258.60
高陵区	Gaoling	4.75	9.48	11.51	14.09	17.53	22.43	25.01	28.40	31.73	44.54	51.78	59.15
鄠邑区	Huyi	14.18	23.21	27.31	32.63	39.38	45.49	50.97	57.52	63.71	69.98	77.75	86.61
蓝田县	Lantian	13.53	21.44	25.00	29.70	35.64	41.18	45.74	51.57	56.40	62.08	70.42	81.10
周至县	Zhouzhi	8.54	14.38	16.75	19.86	23.84	27.68	30.71	34.63	38.47	50.64	57.08	62.84
西咸新区	Xixian												274.39

注：2016年数据根据第三次农业普查结果及有关制度规定进行了修订。

16–4 限额以上批发零售贸易企业财务状况（2018年）

单位：万元

分 类	Classify	单位数（个）Number (unit)	资产总计 Total Assets	流动资产合计 Circulating Funds	固定资产合计 Total Fixed Assets
总计	**Total**	**1388**	**27697649.5**	**21031085.2**	**1609875.9**
一、批发企业	**Wholesale Enterprises**	**595**	**15655932.7**	**12806363.1**	**501282.3**
1. 按登记注册类型分组	Grouped by Category of Commodities				
内资企业	Domestic Funded Enterprises	574	13554522.0	11427948.1	351060.4
国有	State-owned Enterprises	16	1142829.2	959006.0	78641.7
集体	Collective-owned Enterprises	4	75499.7	33734.3	12513.7
股份合作	Corperative Enterprises				
联营	Joint Ownership Enterprises				
国有联营	State Joint Ownership Enterprises				
集体联营	Collective Joint Ownership Enterprises				
国有与集体联营	Joint State-collective Enterprises				
其他联营	Others Joint Ownership Enterprises				
有限责任公司	Limited Liability Corporations	247	8597424.7	7084072.7	157393.9
国有独资公司	State Funded Corporations	17	1461839.4	1279010.7	13195.3
其他有限责任公司	Other Limited Liability Corporations	230	7135585.3	5805062.0	144198.6
股份有限公司	Share-holding Corporations Ltd.	17	1384896.5	1136850.9	50435.5
私营	Private Enterprises	287	2352133.7	2213751.1	50925.5
私营独资	Private-funded Enterprises	1	873.9	786.0	87.9
私营合伙	Private Partnership Enterprises				
私营有限责任公司	Private Limited Liability Corporations	278	2197156.9	2081144.5	49092.2
私营股份有限公司	Private Share-holding Corporations Ltd.	8	154102.9	131820.6	1745.4
其他	Other Enterprises	3	1738.2	533.1	1150.1
港澳台商投资	Enterprises with Funds from Hong Kong, Macao &Taiwan	4	83860.7	77179.1	6288.3
外商投资	Foreign Funded Enterprises	17	2017550.0	1301235.9	143933.6
2. 按国民经济行业分组	Grouped by Sector				

Financial Status of Wholesale and Retail Enterprises above Designated Size (2018)

(10 000 yuan)

固定资产原价 Original Value of Fixed Assets	累计折旧 Accumulated Depreciation	负债合计 Total Liabilities	流动负债合计 Circulating Liabilities	非流动负债合计 Non-Circulating Liabilities	所有者权益合计 Total Owners' Equities	实收资本 Paid in Capital	营业收入 Total Revenue	主营业务收入 Revenue from Principal Business
2563711.7	**950223.8**	**20043775.5**	**18705764.6**	**1348599.7**	**7653874.0**	**4859895.4**	**68356471.2**	**67791042.6**
796519.7	**294792.9**	**11596023.4**	**10805821.7**	**801739.0**	**4059909.3**	**2758866.6**	**48422784.6**	**48216244.5**
626424.7	274936.0	9988795.1	9602414.7	397917.7	3565726.9	2469956.2	39095231.1	38911468.9
151849.2	73114.2	663213.2	652994.0	10219.2	479616.0	79187.9	2441716.2	2432084.5
17765.1	5129.9	67753.2	39416.7	28336.5	7746.5	12401.4	45100.7	44274.6
260882.9	103467.7	6322540.8	6060682.9	271848.0	2274883.9	1750912.7	23971854.3	23869930.5
26425.2	13229.9	1232868.0	1225610.7	7257.3	228971.4	146710.6	4404686.8	4393502.5
234457.7	90237.8	5089672.8	4835072.2	264590.7	2045912.5	1604202.1	19567167.5	19476428.0
97145.7	46559.9	1148552.7	1104998.3	43554.4	236343.8	195155.7	5185532.5	5150600.7
96829.4	45862.0	1786406.1	1743993.7	43959.6	565727.6	431131.0	7429798.3	7393349.5
201.5	113.6	937.8	919.0	18.8	-63.9	50.0	3955.5	3955.0
92140.1	43007.0	1668853.3	1629903.0	40497.5	528303.6	407109.8	6741580.5	6705448.1
4487.8	2741.4	116615.0	113171.7	3443.3	37487.9	23971.2	684262.3	683946.4
1952.4	802.3	329.1	329.1		1409.1	1167.5	21229.1	21229.1
10875.1	4586.8	68524.8	68524.8		15335.9	5635.7	138882.0	138700.7
159219.9	15270.1	1538703.5	1134882.2	403821.3	478846.5	283274.7	9188671.5	9166074.9

单位：万元

分 类	Classify	营业成本 Total Cost	主营业务成本 Cost of Principal Business	税金及附加 Taxs and Other Changes	主营业务税金及附加 Taxs and Other Changes on Principal
总计	**Total**	**63861685.6**	**63589853.1**	**308372.9**	**294396.6**
一、批发企业	**Wholesale Enterprises**	**46561464.4**	**46419517.2**	**215727.7**	**209085.0**
1. 按登记注册类型分组	Grouped by Category of Commodities				
内资企业	Domestic Funded Enterprises	37462584.4	37330709.2	211831.8	205189.1
国有	State-owned Enterprises	2042138.6	2036693.8	169421.4	167830.3
集体	Collective-owned Enterprises	41356.7	41356.2	60.2	60.2
股份合作	Corperative Enterprises				
联营	Joint Ownership Enterprises				
国有联营	State Joint Ownership Enterprises				
集体联营	Collective Joint Ownership Enterprises				
国有与集体联营	Joint State-collective Enterprises				
其他联营	Others Joint Ownership Enterprises				
有限责任公司	Limited Liability Corporations	23224544.0	23158658.1	27615.9	23526.5
国有独资公司	State Funded Corporations	4311382.9	4309160.4	4747.4	2080.3
其他有限责任公司	Other Limited Liability Corporations	18913161.1	18849497.7	22868.5	21446.2
股份有限公司	Share-holding Corporations Ltd.	5103166.3	5073247.1	3870.6	3085.9
私营	Private Enterprises	7033504.6	7002879.8	10863.7	10686.2
私营独资	Private-funded Enterprises	3928.6	3928.0	1.2	1.2
私营合伙	Private Partnership Enterprises				
私营有限责任公司	Private Limited Liability Corporations	6380647.2	6350066.9	8835.6	8658.1
私营股份有限公司	Private Share-holding Corporations Ltd.	648928.8	648884.9	2026.9	2026.9
其他	Other Enterprises	17874.2	17874.2		
港澳台商投资	Enterprises with Funds from Hong Kong, Macao &Taiwan	104555.8	104555.1	792.8	792.8
外商投资	Foreign Funded Enterprises	8994324.2	8984252.9	3103.1	3103.1
2. 按国民经济行业分组	Grouped by Sector				

continued 1

(10 000 yuan)

销售费用 Sale Expenses	管理费用 Management Expenses	财务费用 Financial Expenses	营业利润 Business Profits	利润总额 Total Profits	应付职工薪酬 Salary Payable	所得税费用 Income Tax Expenses	应交增值税 Value Added Tax Payable
2172966.0	**915793.8**	**239034.1**	**855418.5**	**877683.2**	**1083806.4**	**209210.8**	**524901.5**
695499.6	**325378.7**	**136978.3**	**466896.6**	**472279.2**	**389996.5**	**123766.8**	**251006.1**
637436.8	287987.0	63339.5	412667.5	413989.7	331553.9	113283.1	237452.3
65879.3	37880.1	1144.3	124678.6	118640.1	57519.2	35121.0	64485.1
1254.7	1875.3	212.3	341.5	342.8	1781.1	4.0	195.7
286362.8	161296.0	53575.7	219934.2	224406.5	154917.4	56609.9	96795.0
52809.7	22618.2	5965.3	15266.1	15337.3	22330.1	5921.4	12111.8
233553.1	138677.8	47610.4	204668.1	209069.2	132587.3	50688.5	84683.2
101805.0	5327.5	-7182.2	-23178.6	-23733.5	44706.3	1004.4	16070.7
181956.1	81466.2	15514.0	87933.1	90901.1	71953.1	20543.8	59905.8
101.6	10.2	25.1	-111.2	-111.2	51.2		12.2
174856.0	76531.0	14167.2	68494.4	71376.5	58814.0	20170.4	57489.2
6998.5	4925.0	1321.7	19549.9	19635.8	13087.9	373.4	2404.4
178.9	141.9	75.4	2958.7	3432.7	676.8		
23256.4	9094.8	17.0	1165.1	1151.5	16370.1	266.8	5668.8
34806.4	28296.9	73621.8	53064.0	57138.0	42072.5	10216.9	7885.0

16-4 续表2

单位：万元

分 类	Classify	单位数（个） Number (unit)	资产总计 Total Assets	流动资产合计 Circulating Funds	固定资产合计 Total Fixed Assets
农、林、牧产品批发	Wholesale of Agricultural,Forestry and Animal Husbandry Products	4	73839.2	31755.5	12459.0
食品、饮料及烟草制品批发	Wholesale of food Beverages and Tobaccos	70	1550034.7	1106112.4	196570.7
纺织、服装及家庭服务器批发	Wholesale of Textiles, Garments and Daily Articles	32	652120.0	614808.2	12641.6
文化、体育用品及器材批发	Wholesale of Culture, Sports Appliances and Equipments	30	342602.7	269282.7	9778.1
医药及医疗器材批发	Wholesale of Medicines and Medical Appliances	115	2601802.3	2453238.9	55126.2
矿产品、建材及化工产品批发	Wholesale of Mineral Products, Building Materials and Chemical Products	213	8874531.8	6835965.5	190910.4
机械设备、五金产品及电子产品批发	Wholesale of Machinery, Hardware, and Electronic Equipment	120	1451851.4	1395754.6	20296.8
贸易经纪与代理	Trade Broker and Agency	5	85996.7	83805.2	961.1
其他批发	Other wholesale not Classified Elsewhere	6	23153.9	15640.1	2538.4
二、零售企业	**Retail Trade**	**793**	**12041716.8**	**8224722.1**	**1108593.6**
1. 按登记注册类型分组	Grouped by Category of Commodities				
内资	Domestic Funded Enterprises	742	8102454.8	5602745.8	760949.7
国有	State-owned Enterprises	7	383299.2	330054.0	34904.5
集体	Collective-owned Enterprises	18	11628.0	3941.1	6155.4
股份合作	Corperative Enterprises				
联营	Joint Ownership Enterprises				
国有联营	State Joint Ownership Enterprises				
集体联营	Collective Joint Ownership Enterprises				
国有与集体联营	Joint State-collective Enterprises				
其他联营	Others Joint Ownership Enterprises				
有限责任公司	Limited Liability Corporations	300	4463752.9	2765639.6	503739.4
国有独资公司	State Funded Corporations	11	217472.6	133793.1	53988.3

continued 2

(10 000 yuan)

固定资产原价 Original Value of Fixed Assets	累计折旧 Accumulated Depreciation	负债合计 Total Liabilities	流动负债合计 Circulating Liabilities	非流动负债合计 Non-Circulating Liabilities	所有者权益合计 Total Owners' Equities	实收资本 Paid in Capital	营业收入 Total Revenue	主营业务收入 Revenue from Principal Business
17711.6	5131.1	63864.7	36105.5	27759.2	9974.5	13857.0	40973.4	40147.3
274109.9	77539.2	708565.0	596652.8	111912.2	841469.7	189768.6	3038387.5	3016075.0
26200.1	13558.5	559728.9	559328.9	400.0	92391.1	50148.0	1234353.6	1209561.9
20628.3	10850.2	217984.3	210303.0	7681.3	124618.4	66149.0	655533.6	653869.6
85272.0	30104.9	2230698.1	1985327.5	246917.9	371104.2	313674.0	4035088.3	4025516.3
319119.6	127956.5	6517138.3	6129439.6	397688.7	2357393.5	1988538.2	35066966.5	34932713.2
45941.3	25615.1	1206556.8	1198068.7	8488.1	245294.6	124249.5	4161686.3	4148712.2
1509.9	548.8	78039.6	77709.4	330.2	7957.1	5481.3	170174.9	170035.3
6027.0	3488.6	13447.7	12886.3	561.4	9706.2	7001.0	19620.5	19613.7
1767192.0	**655430.9**	**8447752.1**	**7899942.9**	**546860.7**	**3593964.7**	**2101028.8**	**19933686.6**	**19574798.1**
1227990.8	464872.0	5732594.0	5348778.6	382866.9	2369860.8	1561311.3	12846733.5	12595026.3
54457.7	19553.2	268383.4	265227.6	3155.8	114915.8	3372.3	664231.4	659742.4
7299.4	1144.0	8598.3	8021.0	577.3	3029.7	1783.9	31826.1	31826.1
759630.7	254800.5	3164470.0	2903229.8	260297.3	1299282.9	869313.9	6341931.5	6205731.1
76049.9	21542.8	149751.0	136702.7	13048.3	67721.6	29515.9	283979.0	279559.1

16-4 续表3

单位：万元

分 类	Classify	营业成本 Total Cost	主营业务成本 Cost of Principal Business	税金及附加 Taxs and Other Changes	主营业务税金及附加 Taxs and Other Changes on Principal
农、林、牧产品批发	Wholesale of Agricultural,Forestry and Animal Husbandry Products	38023.8	38023.3	35.8	26.7
食品、饮料及烟草制品批发	Wholesale of food Beverages and Tobaccos	2517409.9	2508141.3	170517.6	168802.1
纺织、服装及家庭服务器批发	Wholesale of Textiles, Garments and Daily Articles	1124767.3	1103148.3	2273.9	1910.8
文化、体育用品及器材批发	Wholesale of Culture, Sports Appliances and Equipments	602863.9	601932.6	718.1	674.0
医药及医疗器材批发	Wholesale of Medicines and Medical Appliances	3696504.6	3696275.0	7772.4	7008.6
矿产品、建材及化工产品批发	Wholesale of Mineral Products, Building Materials and Chemical Products	34419331.8	34321418.0	29518.0	25945.6
机械设备、五金产品及电子产品批发	Wholesale of Machinery, Hardware, and Electronic Equipment	3987870.9	3975917.7	4736.5	4646.7
贸易经纪与代理	Trade Broker and Agency	156977.3	156946.1	99.5	14.6
其他批发	Other wholesale not Classified Elsewhere	17714.9	17714.9	55.9	55.9
二、零售企业	**Retail Trade**	**17300221.2**	**17170335.9**	**92645.2**	**85311.6**
1. 按登记注册类型分组	Grouped by Category of Commodities				
内资	Domestic Funded Enterprises	11220166.9	11152438.5	62383.2	60115.3
国有	State-owned Enterprises	592964.4	592783.5	971.0	971.0
集体	Collective-owned Enterprises	26198.3	26198.3	380.1	377.5
股份合作	Corperative Enterprises				
联营	Joint Ownership Enterprises				
国有联营	State Joint Ownership Enterprises				
集体联营	Collective Joint Ownership Enterprises				
国有与集体联营	Joint State-collective Enterprises				
其他联营	Others Joint Ownership Enterprises				
有限责任公司	Limited Liability Corporations	5584168.2	5549058.9	23265.9	22479.1
国有独资公司	State Funded Corporations	245725.3	243860.3	801.9	796.5

continued 3

(10 000 yuan)

销售费用 Sale Expenses	管理费用 Management Expenses	财务费用 Financial Expenses	营业利润 Business Profits	利润总额 Total Profits	应付职工薪酬 Salary Payable	所得税费用 Income Tax Expenses	应交增值税 Value Added Tax Payable
1317.5	1330.3	211.5	51.6	56.6	1932.6	3.4	53.5
104665.4	64481.1	-3251.0	188268.8	187679.6	98896.5	41371.1	75992.9
60723.0	21329.6	227.8	25000.7	25187.1	33057.8	6566.7	16655.0
22395.7	18510.8	273.3	7181.7	8035.3	17102.8	1198.7	1508.7
115112.5	71072.3	40113.1	98672.4	99031.2	74969.9	25141.7	50301.4
318304.5	98873.4	97225.2	87774.4	90986.0	122744.2	33865.1	88872.1
65143.6	46044.2	1884.2	56609.9	57547.0	39052.5	15222.1	15783.3
6994.5	3205.1	265.7	2862.0	3260.4	1518.1	267.3	1553.3
842.9	531.9	28.5	475.1	496.0	722.1	130.7	285.9
1477466.4	**590415.1**	**102055.8**	**388521.9**	**405404.0**	**693809.9**	**85444.0**	**273895.4**
809405.5	439917.8	81432.4	228021.2	239890.7	454622.8	44286.8	158574.8
28228.7	19526.4	1690.3	17940.7	18289.0	20483.0	3581.9	10023.6
1213.1	2846.4	124.3	877.7	952.9	2037.4	48.9	227.9
409422.8	195388.5	38136.3	92236.0	100629.5	246725.0	19979.0	80371.3
19323.1	10226.0	860.8	6637.7	7676.5	22181.0	1000.5	1025.4

16-4 续表4

单位：万元

分 类	Classify	单位数（个）Number (unit)	资产总计 Total Assets	流动资产合计 Circulating Funds	固定资产合计 Total Fixed Assets
其他有限责任公司	Other Limited Liability Corporations	289	4246280.3	2631846.5	449751.1
股份有限公司	Share-holding Corporations Ltd.	11	840222.4	470958.3	65113.3
私营	Private Enterprises	402	2399643.3	2030863.6	149680.5
私营独资	Private-funded Enterprises	11	4712.6	2399.7	1786.4
私营合伙	Private Partnership Enterprises	2	438.6	306.3	106.4
私营有限责任公司	Private Limited Liability Corporations	384	2379762.3	2018120.1	143147.7
私营股份有限公司	Private Share-holding Corporations Ltd.	5	14729.8	10037.5	4640.0
其他	Other Enterprises	4	3909.0	1289.2	1356.6
港澳台商投资	Enterprises with Funds from Hong Kong, Macao &Taiwan	26	2026700.7	1366659.5	129136.8
外商投资	Foreign Funded Enterprises	25	1912561.3	1255316.8	218507.1
2. 按国民经济行业分组	Grouped by Sector				
综合零售	Integrated Retail	121	4088369.2	2145528.7	492398.3
食品、饮料及烟草制品专门零售	Food, Beverages and Tobaccos Special Retail Trade	70	150274.3	119155.7	17711.8
纺织、服装及日用品专门零售	Special Retail of Textiles,Garments and Daily Consumer Articles	54	439010.2	312286.9	24350.8
文化、体育用品及器材专门零售	Retail of Culture,Sports Appliances and Equipments	52	760010.0	627200.5	77785.2
医药及医疗器材专门零售	Retail of Medicines and Medical Appliances	31	349697.0	298416.6	17199.2
汽车、摩托车、燃料及零配件专门零售	Retail of Motor Vehicles,Motorcycles, Fuel and Parts	304	4028186.7	2836063.0	369634.4
家用电器及电子产品专门零售	Special Retail of Household Electric Appliances and Electronic Products	70	548996.0	530232.2	3718.9
五金、家具及室内装饰材料专门零售	Special Retail of Hardware,Furniture and Decoration Materials	43	531837.5	400161.8	50366.7
货摊、无店铺及其他零售业	Non-shop and Other Retail	48	1145335.9	955676.7	55428.3

continued 4

(10 000 yuan)

固定资产原价 Original Value of Fixed Assets	累计折旧 Accumulated Depreciation	负债合计 Total Liabilities	流动负债合计 Circulating Liabilities	非流动负债合计 Non-Circulating Liabilities	所有者权益合计 Total Owners' Equities	实收资本 Paid in Capital	营业收入 Total Revenue	主营业务收入 Revenue from Principal Business
683580.8	233257.7	3014719.0	2766527.1	247249.0	1231561.3	839798.0	6057952.5	5926172.0
120594.5	54695.0	385468.4	357064.4	28404.0	454754.0	359144.0	452728.1	427527.7
284139.1	134166.5	1904034.7	1814006.7	90022.4	495608.6	325484.2	5342729.1	5256911.7
2228.7	442.3	1106.8	1104.8		3605.8	2260.0	44522.1	44522.0
229.9	79.7	318.3	212.5	105.8	120.3	101.0	10705.6	10705.6
274669.1	131273.1	1892050.0	1802735.8	89310.6	487712.3	320769.5	5227600.5	5141874.8
7011.4	2371.4	10559.6	9953.6	606.0	4170.2	2353.7	59900.9	59809.3
1869.4	512.8	1639.2	1229.1	410.1	2269.8	2213.0	13287.3	13287.3
229970.5	100833.7	1274656.9	1243181.8	31475.1	752043.8	230048.2	2514862.7	2431555.2
309230.7	89725.2	1440501.2	1307982.5	132518.7	472060.1	309669.3	4572090.4	4548216.6
780905.7	286966.2	2574770.7	2417179.8	157588.9	1513598.5	900988.3	3818788.9	3615407.8
27620.4	9826.0	109903.5	91890.3	18013.2	40370.8	54067.0	255672.6	243357.1
60563.5	35209.1	214016.4	201707.1	12309.3	224993.8	112266.9	640807.3	626178.0
100201.4	22396.5	548042.4	469646.2	78396.2	211967.6	86024.9	761948.8	756417.3
26811.9	9612.7	262276.1	261270.9	62.3	87420.9	35167.7	473865.9	470253.4
596002.3	224859.6	2966750.6	2775483.1	191267.4	1061436.1	723325.8	8573621.0	8502796.6
10524.7	6793.7	390094.7	388330.6	1764.1	158901.3	69326.5	1310711.6	1294058.5
96437.3	46070.6	396938.1	331163.5	65771.1	134899.4	42732.1	1254768.9	1223017.3
68124.8	12696.5	984959.6	963271.4	21688.2	160376.3	77129.6	2843501.6	2843312.1

16-4 续表5

单位：万元

分 类	Classify	营业成本 Total Cost	主营业务成本 Cost of Principal Business	税金及附加 Taxs and Other Changes	主营业务税金及附加 Taxs and Other Changes on Principal
其他有限责任公司	Other Limited Liability Corporations	5338442.9	5305198.6	22464.0	21682.6
股份有限公司	Share-holding Corporations Ltd.	392970.8	389379.4	870.3	823.1
私营	Private Enterprises	4612005.1	4583158.3	36823.7	35392.4
私营独资	Private-funded Enterprises	41493.5	41493.1	175.2	175.1
私营合伙	Private Partnership Enterprises	9112.3	9112.3	34.7	34.7
私营有限责任公司	Private Limited Liability Corporations	4505596.0	4476831.9	36464.4	35033.2
私营股份有限公司	Private Share-holding Corporations Ltd.	55803.3	55721.0	149.4	149.4
其他	Other Enterprises	11860.1	11860.1	72.2	72.2
港澳台商投资	Enterprises with Funds from Hong Kong, Macao &Taiwan	2098241.1	2036660.8	12657.8	12150.1
外商投资	Foreign Funded Enterprises	3981813.2	3981236.6	17604.2	13046.2
2.按国民经济行业分组	Grouped by Sector				
综合零售	Integrated Retail	3102028.5	3089830.3	23548.5	22167.6
食品、饮料及烟草制品专门零售	Food, Beverages and Tobaccos Special Retail Trade	208763.7	194429.8	1031.8	997.9
纺织、服装及日用品专门零售	Special Retail of Textiles,Garments and Daily Consumer Articles	491735.9	474374.2	2904.5	2899.1
文化、体育用品及器材专门零售	Retail of Culture,Sports Appliances and Equipments	601547.3	598949.8	6242.3	5772.0
医药及医疗器材专门零售	Retail of Medicines and Medical Appliances	340942.8	339746.6	2496.7	2479.7
汽车、摩托车、燃料及零配件专门零售	Retail of Motor Vehicles,Motorcycles, Fuel and Parts	7877969.4	7809636.5	19871.9	19201.5
家用电器及电子产品专门零售	Special Retail of Household Electric Appliances and Electronic Products	1165465.9	1161355.9	2966.0	2799.1
五金、家具及室内装饰材料专门零售	Special Retail of Hardware,Furniture and Decoration Materials	949932.0	940177.6	26640.4	26072.5
货摊、无店铺及其他零售业	Non-shop and Other Retail	2561835.7	2561835.2	6943.1	2922.2

continued 5

(10 000 yuan)

销售费用 Sale Expenses	管理费用 Management Expenses	财务费用 Financial Expenses	营业利润 Business Profits	利润总额 Total Profits	应付职工薪酬 Salary Payable	所得税费用 Income Tax Expenses	应交增值税 Value Added Tax Payable
390099.7	185162.5	37275.5	85598.3	92953.0	224544.0	18978.5	79345.9
43906.3	23040.8	3937.5	5439.1	5308.6	22594.9	1019.9	2448.3
326080.7	198680.1	37370.5	111336.3	114499.8	162466.6	19656.6	65502.4
1201.9	1406.0	19.2	263.0	246.2	813.6	35.7	348.0
909.5	608.8	0.1	40.2	14.8	391.9	8.4	77.0
321513.3	194881.1	36673.3	112201.5	115447.9	160211.2	19612.5	64951.1
2456.0	1784.2	677.9	-1168.4	-1209.1	1049.9		126.3
553.9	435.6	173.5	191.4	210.9	315.9	0.5	1.3
255424.3	84033.4	11676.6	72380.6	76047.8	113467.2	15997.4	37451.9
412636.6	66463.9	8946.8	88120.1	89465.5	125719.9	25159.8	77868.7
449942.4	175377.8	22653.4	85896.3	92507.0	212576.8	16629.5	59121.3
27296.0	17282.6	1080.6	-2261.1	-1348.2	19745.3	657.0	2648.3
92040.1	29071.9	2694.0	24761.0	24702.5	51679.3	4898.4	26872.8
90588.2	42365.5	3557.2	17619.3	20877.0	36502.1	4219.2	5570.0
98963.8	18401.7	2939.4	10056.7	10417.8	59502.4	1404.0	5653.0
317489.7	147739.3	44357.9	132104.6	134006.3	193333.0	39546.0	105586.1
93953.3	40294.3	3119.2	4557.1	5132.9	38430.5	985.1	15489.2
66104.5	89801.0	20774.9	109793.9	110011.8	15323.5	15599.9	22208.9
241088.4	30081.0	879.2	5994.1	9096.9	66717.0	1504.9	30745.8

16-5 限额以上住宿和餐饮企业财务状况（2018年）

单位：万元

分　类	Classify	单位数（个） Number (unit)	资产总计 Total Assets	流动资产合　计 Circulating Funds	固定资产合　计 Total Fixed Assets
总计	**Total**	**696**	**3141425.1**	**1266337.4**	**1179022.5**
一、住宿业	**Hotel Services**	**335**	**2416327.2**	**879943.2**	**1043740.2**
1.按登记注册类型分组	Grouped by Type of Registration				
内资	Domestic Funded Enterprises	321	2149701.0	767847.4	919546.1
国有	State-owned Enterprises	17	61550.2	16123.0	35122.6
集体	Collective-owned Enterprises	1	107.4	107.4	
股份合作	Cooperative Enterprises				
联营	Joint Ownership Enterprises				
国有联营	State Joint Ownership Enterprises				
集体联营	Collective Joint Ownership Enterprises				
国有与集体联营	Joint State-collective Enterprises				
其他联营	Others Joint Ownership Enterprises				
有限责任公司	Limited Liability Corporations	128	1651056.0	538855.0	781496.9
国有独资公司	State Sole Funded Corporations	6	102917.6	18135.7	69298.4
其他有限责任公司	Other Limited Liability Corporations	122	1548138.4	520719.3	712198.5
股份有限公司	Share-holding Corporations Ltd.	3	11139.5	1083.3	10051.2
私营	Private Enterprises	172	425847.9	211678.7	92875.4
私营独资	Private-funded Enterprises	4	2326.6	1485.1	443.0
私营合伙	Private Partnership Enterprises				
私营有限责任公司	Private Limited Liability Corporations	165	408297.6	201102.9	86613.2
私营股份有限公司	Private Share-holding Corporations Ltd.	3	15223.7	9090.7	5819.2
其他	Other Enterprises				
港澳台商投资	Enterprises with Funds from Hong Kong, Macao &Taiwan	6	135181.8	58144.6	56639.5
外商投资	Foreign Funded Enterprises	8	131444.4	53951.2	67554.6
2.按国民经济行业分组	Grouped by Sector				
旅游饭店	Tourist Hotel	171	2025723.9	700460.7	962844.2
一般旅馆	Normal Hotel	149	322905.3	167573.2	52940.2
民宿服务	Home and Lodging Services	2	3351.5	637.2	2610.6
其他住宿业	Others	13	64346.5	11272.1	25345.2

注：本表统计范围为法人单位。

Finacial Status of Hotels and Catering Enterprises above Designated Size (2018)

(10 000 yuan)

固定资产原价 Original Value of Fixed Assets	累计折旧 Accumulated Depreciation	负债合计 Total Liabilities	流动负债合计 Circulating Liabilities	非流动负债合计 Non-Circulating Liabilities	所有者权益合计 Total Owners' Equities	实收资本 Paid in Capital	营业收入 Total Revenue	主营业务收入 Revenue from Principal Business
2063732.0	**850226.8**	**2454339.7**	**1896618.3**	**558194.4**	**687085.4**	**1154394.3**	**1407537.1**	**1384845.8**
1803996.9	**727324.2**	**1928218.2**	**1425477.7**	**502740.5**	**488109.0**	**917644.6**	**675826.7**	**662251.2**
1540208.8	595117.9	1707758.2	1313458.7	394299.5	441942.8	761889.8	585608.1	579036.6
65206.2	30081.3	43165.8	35417.7	7748.1	18384.4	29640.4	29967.0	28805.4
		85.8	65.8	20.0	21.6	15.0	334.7	334.7
1256213.1	464561.2	1301564.8	966413.8	335151.0	349491.2	568905.2	340681.4	338200.2
116634.5	45063.8	97422.9	41884.6	55538.3	5494.7	79240.0	28618.9	28611.6
1139578.6	419497.4	1204141.9	924529.2	279612.7	343996.5	489665.2	312062.5	309588.6
17287.9	7236.7	5706.3	5625.3	81.0	5433.2	5433.2	3772.5	3772.5
201501.6	93238.7	357235.5	305936.1	51299.4	68612.4	157896.0	210852.5	207923.8
919.3	476.3	1843.9	1843.9		482.7	855.5	1327.0	1316.2
190517.4	88516.7	326863.8	289364.4	37499.4	81433.8	151840.5	203746.8	200828.9
10064.9	4245.7	28527.8	14727.8	13800.0	-13304.1	5200.0	5778.7	5778.7
133851.5	77212.0	152356.0	53563.6	98792.4	-17174.2	74873.6	42190.8	36984.2
129936.6	54994.3	68104.0	58455.4	9648.6	63340.4	80881.2	48027.8	46230.4
1673539.6	677762.9	1669302.8	1202618.4	466684.4	356421.1	760695.7	505622.1	495399.9
93994.9	41054.7	227650.3	192084.2	35566.1	95255.0	143858.9	143352.9	140302.2
3008.8	398.2	2115.3	2115.3		1236.2	4000.0	975.9	975.9
33453.6	8108.4	29149.8	28659.8	490.0	35196.7	9090.0	25875.8	25573.2

16-5 续表1

单位：万元

分类	Classify	营业成本 Total Cost	主营业务成本 Cost of Principal Business
总计	**Total**	**598227.3**	**586978.3**
一、住宿业	**Hotel Services**	**242664.9**	**234822.0**
1.按登记注册类型分组	Grouped by Type of Registration		
内资	Domestic Funded Enterprises	210072.0	206427.9
国有	State-owned Enterprises	12404.7	12227.5
集体	Collective-owned Enterprises	258.0	258.0
股份合作	Cooperative Enterprises		
联营	Joint Ownership Enterprises		
国有联营	State Joint Ownership Enterprises		
集体联营	Collective Joint Ownership Enterprises		
国有与集体联营	Joint State-collective Enterprises		
其他联营	Others Joint Ownership Enterprises		
有限责任公司	Limited Liability Corporations	130182.9	129717.3
国有独资公司	State Sole Funded Corporations	7626.8	7626.8
其他有限责任公司	Other Limited Liability Corporations	122556.1	122090.5
股份有限公司	Share-holding Corporations Ltd.	2085.3	2085.3
私营	Private Enterprises	65141.1	62139.8
私营独资	Private-funded Enterprises	476.2	465.4
私营合伙	Private Partnership Enterprises		
私营有限责任公司	Private Limited Liability Corporations	62868.1	59877.6
私营股份有限公司	Private Share-holding Corporations Ltd.	1796.8	1796.8
其他	Other Enterprises		
港澳台商投资	Enterprises with Funds from Hong Kong, Macao &Taiwan	14479.1	10704.4
外商投资	Foreign Funded Enterprises	18113.8	17689.7
2.按国民经济行业分组	Grouped by Sector		
旅游饭店	Tourist Hotel	187991.8	183419.8
一般旅馆	Normal Hotel	49610.0	46339.1
民宿服务	Home and Lodging Services	321.1	321.1
其他住宿业	Others	4742.0	4742.0

continued 1

(10 000 yuan)

税金及附加 Taxs and Other Changes	主营业务税金及附加 Taxs and Other Changes on Principal Business	销售费用 Sale Expenses	管理费用 Management Expenses	财务费用 Financial Expenses	营业利润 Business Profits	利润总额 Total Profits	应付职工薪酬 Salary Payable	所得税费用 Income Tax Expenses	应交增值税 Value Added Tax Payable
15349.1	**12491.1**	**458807.6**	**290638.3**	**27458.5**	**16437.2**	**15504.4**	**408470.2**	**14422.6**	**28955.6**
10634.7	**7971.6**	**207604.3**	**209744.5**	**21173.4**	**-19268.1**	**-19388.6**	**199929.4**	**4865.6**	**19173.9**
8286.2	5790.8	185408.1	187029.9	13318.6	-25893.2	-25675.4	177044.4	2224.6	16133.2
627.0	491.8	9410.2	7276.5	446.0	-99.4	-108.9	9787.9	351.5	966.0
1.3	1.3	39.2	31.6	-0.1	4.7	4.7	144.0	0.5	10.3
5986.5	3798.9	101257.7	112497.5	12547.3	-23067.0	-23247.9	112646.6	1016.3	9049.9
295.7	191.5	9925.8	5579.4	338.0	4487.8	4656.1	8890.1		369.9
5690.8	3607.4	91331.9	106918.1	12209.3	-27554.8	-27904.0	103756.5	1016.3	8680.0
263.1	263.1	1334.9	5.2	1.4	69.4	-11.8	1780.0		165.1
1408.3	1235.7	73366.1	67219.1	5324.0	-2800.9	-2311.5	52685.9	856.3	5941.9
18.7	18.7	621.2	346.9	3.3	-139.3	-139.4	577.8	1.8	30.3
1365.8	1193.2	71587.8	64514.5	4300.4	-2084.6	-1594.3	51043.2	854.5	5465.7
23.8	23.8	1157.1	2357.7	1020.3	-577.0	-577.8	1064.9		445.9
960.8	793.7	11340.6	13097.4	2775.2	-480.9	-680.1	11178.7	500.0	1156.0
1387.7	1387.1	10855.6	9617.2	79.6	7106.0	6966.9	11706.3	2141.0	1884.7
9200.1	7109.5	148149.2	159400.0	18573.1	-18997.4	-18813.1	154784.8	3815.1	14615.8
1071.6	750.2	49242.5	39742.7	2392.1	-671.8	-601.1	38943.1	1047.3	3253.3
		458.0	393.8	3.5	-200.5	-591.4	198.7		0.1
363.0	111.9	9754.6	10208.0	204.7	601.6	617.0	6002.8	3.2	1304.7

16-5 续表2

单位：万元

分类	Classify	单位数（个） Number (unit)	资产总计 Total Assets	流动资产合计 Circulating Funds	固定资产合计 Total Fixed Assets
二、餐饮业	**Catering Trade**	**361**	**725097.9**	**386394.2**	**135282.3**
1.按登记注册类型分组	Grouped by Type of Registration				
内资	Domestic Funded Enterprises	349	605414.9	330860.5	112226.4
国有	State-owned Enterprises	3	4222.9	1166.4	2956.5
集体	Collective-owned Enterprises				
股份合作	Cooperative Enterprises				
联营	Joint Ownership Enterprises				
国有联营	State Joint Ownership Enterprises				
集体联营	Collective Joint Ownership Enterprises				
国有与集体联营	Joint State-collective Enterprises				
其他联营	Others Joint Ownership Enterprises				
有限责任公司	Limited Liability Corporations	129	206289.6	121727.5	45861.3
国有独资公司	State Sole Funded Corporations	4	14477.5	4894.4	9024.0
其他有限责任公司	Other Limited Liability Corporations	125	191812.1	116833.1	36837.3
股份有限公司	Share-holding Corporations Ltd.	4	199413.7	89946.0	23407.0
私营	Private Enterprises	213	195488.7	118020.6	40001.6
私营独资	Private-funded Enterprises	11	4093.2	2036.8	1546.9
私营合伙	Private Partnership Enterprises				
私营有限责任公司	Private Limited Liability Corporations	201	191064.5	115671.5	38436.0
私营股份有限公司	Private Share-holding Corporations Ltd.	1	331.0	312.3	18.7
其他	Other Enterprises				
港澳台商投资	Enterprises with Funds from Hong Kong, Macao &Taiwan	6	56369.1	26985.0	10733.0
外商投资	Foreign Funded Enterprises	6	63313.9	28548.7	12322.9
2.按国民经济行业分	Grouped by Sdctor				
正餐服务	Dinner	341	595619.2	325798.6	110358.9
快餐服务	Fast Food	11	80235.7	32201.3	18727.8
饮料及冷饮服务	Beverages and Cold Drinks	4	36628.3	23437.8	3355.7
餐饮配送及外卖送餐服务	Catering Distribution and Takeaway Servic	1	8751.3	3767.5	410.9
其他餐饮业	Other Catering Services	4	3863.4	1189.0	2429.0

continued 2

(10 000 yuan)

固定资产原价 Original Value of Fixed Assets	累计折旧 Accumulated Depreciation	负债合计 Total Liabilities	流动负债合　计 Circulating Liabilities	非流动负债合　计 Non-Circulating Liabilities	所有者权益合计 Total Owners' Equities	实收资本 Paid in Capital	营业收入 Total Revenue	主营业务收入 Revenue from Principal Business
259735.1	**122902.6**	**526121.5**	**471140.6**	**55453.9**	**198976.4**	**236749.7**	**731710.4**	**722594.6**
210308.7	97630.6	464546.8	416199.5	48820.3	140868.1	212604.0	528345.5	526973.1
4652.1	1695.6	3360.1	735.8	2624.3	862.8	2067.0	6832.4	6832.4
92276.2	46389.4	183062.7	172529.0	10533.7	23226.9	89239.8	179911.7	179174.6
16053.6	7005.1	15263.8	14944.9	318.9	-786.3	6641.2	12394.9	12161.2
76222.6	39384.3	167798.9	157584.1	10214.8	24013.2	82598.6	167516.8	167013.4
41499.4	18091.4	91949.6	65438.8	26510.8	107464.1	61005.6	89394.2	89309.2
71881.0	31454.2	186174.4	177495.9	9151.5	9314.3	60291.6	252207.2	251656.9
2269.0	722.1	2368.1	2247.6	120.5	1725.1	1398.4	6199.7	6181.0
69420.7	30559.5	183506.4	174948.4	9031.0	7558.1	58793.2	245457.7	244926.1
191.3	172.6	299.9	299.9		31.1	100.0	549.8	549.8
20938.8	10205.8	31252.5	30478.6	773.9	25116.6	9998.1	71895.3	71895.3
28487.6	15066.2	30322.2	24462.5	5859.7	32991.7	14147.6	131469.6	123726.2
210803.6	99993.0	466944.9	420214.1	47203.8	128674.3	209822.5	525055.8	523523.9
39697.8	19871.5	42713.7	36850.7	5863.0	37522.0	18030.8	164846.5	157270.8
5827.3	2471.6	8517.0	8360.0	157.0	28111.3	2797.2	35833.9	35833.9
476.5	65.6	5149.0	3009.0	2140.0	3602.3	5000.0	1809.2	1809.2
2929.9	500.9	2796.9	2706.8	90.1	1066.5	1099.2	4165.0	4156.8

16-5 续表3

单位：万元

分 类	Classify	营业成本 Total Cost	主营业务成本 Cost of Principal Business
二、餐饮业	**Catering Trade**	**355562.4**	**352156.3**
1.按登记注册类型分组	Grouped by Type of Registration		
内资	Domestic Funded Enterprises	265264.8	264791.0
国有	State-owned Enterprises	5704.6	5704.6
集体	Collective-owned Enterprises		
股份合作	Cooperative Enterprises		
联营	Joint Ownership Enterprises		
国有联营	State Joint Ownership Enterprises		
集体联营	Collective Joint Ownership Enterprises		
国有与集体联营	Joint State-collective Enterprises		
其他联营	Others Joint Ownership Enterprises		
有限责任公司	Limited Liability Corporations	90166.1	89869.9
国有独资公司	State Sole Funded Corporations	7773.1	7613.5
其他有限责任公司	Other Limited Liability Corporations	82393.0	82256.4
股份有限公司	Share-holding Corporations Ltd.	41299.7	41255.2
私营	Private Enterprises	128094.4	127961.3
私营独资	Private-funded Enterprises	3989.4	3939.4
私营合伙	Private Partnership Enterprises		
私营有限责任公司	Private Limited Liability Corporations	123894.1	123811.0
私营股份有限公司	Private Share-holding Corporations Ltd.	210.9	210.9
其他	Other Enterprises		
港澳台商投资	Enterprises with Funds from Hong Kong, Macao &Taiwan	21933.4	21933.4
外商投资	Foreign Funded Enterprises	68364.2	65431.9
2.按国民经济行业分	Grouped by Sdctor		
正餐服务	Dinner	259087.9	258577.4
快餐服务	Fast Food	83196.7	80309.3
饮料及冷饮服务	Beverages and Cold Drinks	8658.7	8658.7
餐饮配送及外卖送餐服务	Catering Distribution and Takeaway Servic	1957.9	1957.9
其他餐饮业	Other Catering Services	2661.2	2653.0

continued 3

(10 000 yuan)

税金及附加 Taxs and Other Changes	主营业务税金及附加 Taxs and Other Changes on Principal Business	销售费用 Sale Expenses	管理费用 Management Expenses	财务费用 Financial Expenses	营业利润 Business Profits	利润总额 Total Profits	应付职工薪酬 Salary Payable	所得税费用 Income Tax Expenses	应交增值税 Value Added Tax Payable
4714.4	**4519.5**	**251203.3**	**80893.8**	**6285.1**	**35705.3**	**34893.0**	**208540.8**	**9557.0**	**9781.7**
4495.0	4300.1	179508.2	62551.2	6035.5	12972.8	12548.4	169333.3	4025.7	9180.5
321.4	321.4	786.3	441.6	2.9	-424.6	-423.9	712.8	0.0	326.2
1502.1	1406.5	61240.7	24681.1	2294.1	-162.1	40.3	53022.5	1087.8	3273.4
270.7	269.5	1505.9	2120.2	103.0	626.3	635.5	3870.9	162.1	469.4
1231.4	1137.0	59734.8	22560.9	2191.1	-788.4	-595.2	49151.6	925.7	2804.0
584.8	584.8	34488.6	8103.2	172.9	8724.1	7756.8	45974.7	1660.2	882.6
2086.7	1987.4	82992.6	29325.3	3565.6	4835.4	5175.2	69623.3	1277.7	4698.3
98.7	66.2	1085.9	735.2	18.1	272.1	289.6	1430.0	17.7	147.9
1984.7	1917.9	81622.9	28538.0	3545.6	4565.5	4887.7	68061.2	1259.1	4517.5
3.3	3.3	283.8	52.1	1.9	-2.2	-2.1	132.1	0.9	32.9
81.8	81.8	35907.5	2566.5	578.9	10822.9	10672.9	16051.2	2596.4	131.9
137.6	137.6	35787.6	15776.1	-329.3	11909.6	11671.7	23156.3	2934.9	469.3
4410.5	4221.3	185003.6	61542.0	6057.8	11433.1	11027.5	170939.2	4005.2	8833.5
211.5	207.8	49932.0	17565.5	115.8	14001.3	13713.6	31385.2	2942.4	782.0
37.8	37.8	15677.6	1001.1	-83.5	10540.7	10421.9	5576.4	2596.8	41.0
24.3	24.3	64.3	202.9	170.1	-610.3	-614.1	203.6		
30.3	28.3	525.8	582.3	24.9	340.5	344.1	436.4	12.6	125.2

16-6 限额以上批发零售贸易业商品购进、销售、库存总额（2018年）

单位：万元

分 类	Classify	单位数（个）Number unit	商品购进额 Total Purchases	进口 Imports
总计	**Total**	**1409**	**70060728.6**	**7246154.4**
一、批发企业	**Wholesale Enterprises**	**596**	**53970343.9**	**6929283.6**
1.按登记注册类型分组	Grouped by Type of Registration			
内资企业	Domestic Funded Enterprises	575	44949710.5	634748.6
国有	State-owned Enterprises	16	2359485.6	
集体	Collective-owned Enterprises	4	46240.5	
有限责任公司	Limited Liability Corporations	247	25685163.1	499987.6
国有独资公司	State Sole Funded Corporations	17	4418697.9	
其他有限责任公司	Other Limited Liability Corporations	230	21266465.2	499987.6
股份有限公司	Share-holding Corporations Ltd.	18	9546444.2	23923.5
私营	Private Enterprises	287	7296225.0	110837.5
私营独资	Private-funded Enterprises	1	3213.9	
私营合伙	Private Partnership Enterprises			
私营有限责任公司	Private Limited Liability Corporations	278	6608937.2	110837.5
私营股份有限公司	Private Share-holding Corporations Ltd.	8	684073.9	
其他	Other Enterprises	54	7306192.7	23587.1
港澳台商投资	Enterprises with Funds from Hong Kong, Macao &Taiwan	4	108222.2	
外商投资	Foreign Funded Enterprises	17	8912411.2	6294535.0
个体经营户	Individusl Enterprises			
2.按国民经济行业分组	Grouped by Economic Sector			
农、林、牧产品批发	Wholesale of Agricultural,Forestry and Animal Husbandry Products	4	38510.4	
食品、饮料及烟草制品批发	Wholesale of Food, Beverages and Tobacco Products	70	2401459.0	8077.8
纺织、服装及家庭服务器批发	Wholesale of Textiles, Garments and Daily Articles	33	1177298.0	
文化、体育用品及器材批发	Wholesale of Culture, Sports Articles and Equipments	30	676709.7	
医药及医疗器材批发	Wholesale of Medicines and Medical Appliances	115	4220662.4	5740.3
矿产品、建材及化工产品批发	Wholesale of Mineral Products, Building Materials and Chemical Products	213	41158846.9	4640579.3

Total Purchases,Sales and Inventories of Wholesale and Retail Enterprises above Designated Size (2018)

(10 000 yuan)

商品销售额 Sales Value	公共网络商品销售额 Public Network Sales	批发额 Wholesale Trade	出口 Exports	零售额 Retail Trade	期末商品库存额 Value of Stock at Final goods
80174033.1	**9249769.2**	**56487896.0**	**7248170.1**	**23685208.8**	**2958406.5**
57471385.0	**5579430.7**	**55797196.8**	**7244988.5**	**1673259.9**	**1310878.7**
47803595.5	5579015.6	46291270.7	784000.0	1511396.5	1188810.2
2825951.3	1390673.6	2726235.7	34706.0	99715.6	79091.5
47427.6		45987.4		1440.2	4238.0
26852262.0	395312.5	26383163.4	387021.9	468170.3	643744.2
4617242.3		4432908.6		184333.7	65420.4
22235019.7	395312.5	21950254.8	387021.9	283836.6	578323.8
9736558.4	3752117.5	9150959.6	259488.3	585598.8	53521.7
8319425.1	40912.0	7965711.1	102783.8	353714.0	408155.1
3955.1		3955.1			221.6
7599521.8	39633.7	7354810.2	102783.8	244711.6	378853.8
715948.2	1278.3	606945.8		109002.4	29079.7
7748906.1	3753579.0	7666182.8	441.3	82723.3	142766.2
161384.4		88356.5		73027.9	32529.8
9506405.1	415.1	9417517.0	6460988.5	88888.1	89538.7
40655.6		40655.6			1661.0
3321785.4	1402705.5	3083409.5	6416.0	238375.9	142118.5
1381614.9	1518.6	1327790.4	155668.2	53824.5	170535.1
726642.8	8409.9	709090.7	4826.9	17552.1	66972.3
4631007.8	34207.6	4419492.6	5887.3	211515.2	366276.1
42812179.2	4102970.9	41858167.7	4360881.7	954011.5	425214.4

16-6 续表1

单位：万元

分　类	Classify	单位数（个） Number unit	商品购进额 Total Purchases	进口 Imports
机械设备、五金产品及电子产品批发	Wholesale of Machinery, Hardwares, Transport Means and Electronic Products	120	4142732.9	2260765.1
贸易经纪与代理	Trade Manage and Agent	5	136298.9	14121.1
其他批发	Other Wholesales	6	17825.7	
3.按经营形式分组	Grouped by Means of Operation			
独立门店	Independent Shop	385	30333380.8	6847589.5
连锁总店	Headquarter of Chain Store	1	71179.7	
连锁门店	Chain Store			
其他	Other	209	23561914.9	81694.1
二、零售企业	**Retail Trade**	**813**	**16090384.7**	**316870.8**
1.按登记注册类型分组	Grouped by Registration Status			
内资	Domestic Funded Enterprises	746	11208070.9	242707.0
国有	State-owned Enterprises	8	691799.0	
集体	Collective-owned Enterprises	18	32509.2	824.9
有限责任公司	Limited Liability Corporations	302	5170797.1	123011.8
国有独资公司	State Sole Funded Corporations	11	271476.0	2082.9
其他有限责任公司	Other Limited Liability Corporations	291	4899321.1	120928.9
股份有限公司	Share-holding Corporations Ltd.	11	329188.8	
私营	Private Enterprises	403	4973681.9	118870.3
私营独资	Private-funded Enterprises	11	47897.3	
私营合伙	Private Partnership Enterprises	2	11480.8	
私营有限责任公司	Private Limited Liability Corporations	385	4864697.3	99318.0
私营股份有限公司	Private Share-holding Corporations Ltd.	5	49606.5	19552.3
其他	Other Enterprises	6	13948.1	
港澳台商投资	Enterprises with Funds from Hong Kong, Macao &Taiwan	26	2296496.9	74163.8
外商投资	Foreign Funded Enterprises	25	2443018.9	
个体经营户	Individusl Enterprises	15	142488.0	
2.按国民经济行业分组	Grouped by Registered Kind			
综合零售	General Retail Sales Trade	129	2909831.8	203.6
食品、饮料及烟草制品专门零售	Retail of Food, Beverage and Tobaccos	72	253540.8	536.2
纺织、服装及日用品专门零售	Retail of Textiles, Garments and Daily Articles	56	599819.3	1067.6

continued 1

(10 000 yuan)

商品销售额 Sales Value	公共网络商品销售额 Public Network Sales	批发额 Wholesale Trade	出口 Exports	零售额 Retail Trade	期末商品库存额 Value of Stock at Final goods
4363158.8	29618.2	4261393.7	2676602.4	100836.8	121875.7
171560.2		78750.8	34706.0	92809.4	12833.0
22780.3		18445.8		4334.5	3392.6
32526852.7	78500.0	31080680.7	6933208.4	1445243.7	744521.3
71793.3		71212.2		581.1	347.7
24868575.1	5500930.7	24642204.2	311780.1	226370.9	565845.0
22702648.1	**3670338.5**	**690699.2**	**3181.6**	**22011948.9**	**1647527.8**
14682391.2	823173.2	429364.4	3181.6	14253026.8	1184218.9
701177.9	67.7	169903.9		531274.0	91500.9
33367.6		1258.8		32108.8	2918.5
7396611.9	114857.0	95894.5	1000.4	7300717.4	601044.2
306227.4	24.5	3021.9	1000.4	303205.5	55629.3
7090384.5	114832.5	92872.6		6997511.9	545414.9
541873.8	64241.7	3493.1		538380.7	23536.7
5996054.8	644006.8	158814.1	2181.2	5837240.7	465174.5
50264.8	6870.5			50264.8	583.0
12454.0				12454.0	137.6
5864069.0	637128.4	158814.1	2181.2	5705254.9	460718.5
69267.0	7.9			69267.0	3735.4
17460.0	512.0			17460.0	178.7
2816399.3	74926.9	219881.4		2596517.9	381259.6
5063914.1	2771726.4	41425.7		5022488.4	76699.0
139656.5	512.0	27.7		139628.8	5322.3
4551200.8	39485.7	23434.7		4527766.1	254305.5
311894.7	10612.3	51565.7		260329.0	28897.4
813165.8	26672.8	2884.2		810281.6	131505.7

16-6 续表2

单位：万元

分 类	Classify	单位数（个）Number unit	商品购进额 Total Purchases	进口 Imports
文化、体育用品及器材专门零售	Retail of Culture, Sports Articles and Equipments	53	649609.4	2082.9
医药及医疗器材专门零售	Retail of Medicines and Medical Appliances	31	439610.8	
汽车、摩托车、燃料及零配件专门零售	Retail of Motor Vehicles, Motorcycles, Feuls and Parts	308	8457778.0	308889.9
家用电器及电子产品专门零售	Retail of Household Electronic Equipments and Products	70	909227.8	2752.0
五金、家具及室内装饰材料专门零售	retail of Hardwares, Furniture and Room Decorative Building	46	1098911.9	824.9
货摊、无店铺及其他零售业	No Fixed Stores and Other Retails	48	772054.9	513.7
3.按经营形式分组	Grouped by Means of Operation			
独立门店	Independent Shop	656	12946276.1	315861.3
连锁总店	Headquarter of Chain Store	38	1032343.1	
连锁门店	Chain Store	12	152795.9	
其他	Other	107	1958969.6	1009.5
4.按零售业态分组	Grouped by Retail Size			
有店铺	Retail of Shop	700	14477791.7	283321.0
食杂店	Grocery Store	18	47749.7	
便利店	Convenience Store	25	1763796.0	
折扣店	Dime Store	5	19639.3	
超市	Supermarket	66	265664.6	
大型超市	Larget Supermarket	14	1720968.0	
仓储会员店	Warehouse Club	2	22977.2	
百货店	Department Store	58	976625.7	203.6
专业店	Special Store	194	3858019.5	67518.6
专卖店	Monopoly Store	257	4293920.5	196046.5
家居建材商店	Home-building Material Store	19	975780.1	
购物中心	Shopping Center	25	283440.5	
厂家直销中心	Factory Outlet Center	17	249210.6	19552.3
无店铺零售	Retail of No-shop	109	1587007.9	33549.8
电视购物	TV Shopping	1	44149.4	
邮购	Mail Order	2	9245.5	4834.9
网上商店	Online Stores	40	730736.5	554.1
自动售货亭	Vending Machine	1	2957.2	

continued 2

(10 000 yuan)

商品销售额 Sales Value	公共网络商品销售额 Public Network Sales	批发额 Wholesale Trade	出口 Exports	零售额 Retail Trade	期末商品库存额 Value of Stock at Final goods
898696.2	5117.3	266445.5	1000.4	632250.7	252081.8
521853.6	11370.0	2277.5		519576.1	88560.7
9456815.7	115230.9	255185.2		9201630.5	795558.8
1497251.4	294840.1	67124.2		1430127.2	39275.6
1411953.0	80618.0	2974.9	2181.2	1408978.1	32250.1
3239816.9	3086391.4	18807.3		3221009.6	25092.2
15889280.3	574109.4	306622.9	1000.4	15582657.4	1173931.5
1432935.9	46812.5	22312.3		1410623.6	172598.2
701784.9	33676.2	4351.7		697433.2	17183.8
4678647.0	3015740.4	357412.3	2181.2	4321234.7	283814.3
18410105.9	485614.3	638062.7		17772043.2	1511886.3
59901.3	6920.1	457.3		59444.0	8435.4
1701552.7	5596.9	2963.1		1698589.6	30281.8
26854.5				26854.5	5605.0
407062.1	4061.0	14924.2		392137.9	20973.4
1857391.1	15518.5	18052.2		1839338.9	194816.6
25583.6		15802.5		9781.1	190.1
1750807.9	20904.4	18195.2		1732612.7	97571.0
4975233.1	337918.0	433218.3		4542014.8	557915.3
5133623.3	16071.5	82097.6		5051525.7	525722.8
1274390.8	78623.9			1274390.8	25473.0
924589.6		2389.7		922199.9	22471.4
273115.9		49952.6		223153.3	22430.5
4267366.7	3184668.0	52450.1	3181.6	4214916.6	133116.1
78906.6				78906.6	1088.0
12075.9	24.5	3021.9	1000.4	9054.0	1208.9
3158270.5	3148231.9	7731.1		3150539.4	23932.2
3512.2				3512.2	285.9

16-7 限额以上住宿和餐饮业经营情况（2018年）

单位：万元

分 类	Classify	单位数（个）Number (unit)	营业额 Business Revenue
总计	**Total**	**742**	**1666404.0**
一、住宿业	**Lodging Services**	**353**	**815270.8**
1. 按国民经济行业分组	Grouped by Economic Sector		
旅游饭店	Tour Restaurant	184	619698.1
一般旅馆	Common Hotel	154	167699.6
民宿服务	Home and Lodging Services	2	1034.6
其他住宿业	Others	13	26838.5
2. 按登记注册类型分组	Grouped by Registration Status		
内资企业	Domestic Funded Enterprises	337	708324.6
国有	State-owned Enterprises	21	50688.3
集体	Collective-owned Enterprises	1	334.7
有限责任公司	Limited Liability Corporations	134	400280.1
国有独资公司	State-funded Corporations	6	30120.2
其他有限责任公司	Other Limited Liability Corporations	128	370159.9
股份有限公司	Stock Limited Corporation	5	22366.9
私营	Private Enterprises	175	232988.6
私营独资	Private-funded Enterprises	4	1349.2
私营合伙	Private Partnership Enterprises		
私营有限责任公司	Private Limited Liability Corporations	168	225348.7
私营股份有限公司	Private Share Holding Corporations	3	6290.7
其他	Others	1	1666.0
港澳台商投资	Enterprises Funded by Hong Kong, Macao and Taiwan	7	56203.4

Statistic on Hotel Services and Catering Services above Designed Size (2018)

(10 000 yuan)

客房收入 From Hotel Room	公共网络客房收入 Public Network Room Revenue	餐费收入 From Meals	公共网络餐费收入 Public Network Catering Revenue	商品销售收入 From Commodities
490275.5	**69297.4**	**1024968.2**	**60060.9**	**61136.5**
447760.3	**63403.5**	**285793.6**	**10393.9**	**20422.4**
312813.0	41113.6	234804.4	9302.0	17953.9
119891.2	22016.9	39359.9	1091.9	2137.6
222.5	2.3	649.0		29.5
14833.6	270.7	10980.3		301.4
392821.1	57369.1	247459.5	9849.0	18819.8
23081.1	2209.5	20869.1	125.3	1541.9
237.7		50.0		47.0
199631.2	20817.9	159877.2	5612.5	5661.8
14909.8	750.1	13945.7		342.6
184721.4	20067.8	145931.5	5612.5	5319.2
5107.8	66.7	5226.7		9782.2
163545.1	34275.0	61011.2	4111.2	1764.4
887.4	19.5	204.2	5.6	30.5
158304.0	33334.3	58988.3	4103.2	1733.9
4353.7	921.2	1818.7	2.4	
1218.2		425.3		22.5
29557.4	4018.9	18692.9	269.4	540.0

16-7 续表1

单位：万元

分　类	Classify	单位数（个）Number (unit)	营业额 Business Revenue
外商投资	Foreign Funded Enterprises	8	50506.8
个体经营	Individual Enterprises	1	236.0
二、餐饮业	**Catering Trade**	**389**	**851133.2**
1. 按国民经济行业分	Grouped by Economic Sector		
正餐服务	Dinner Services	369	631658.8
快餐服务	Fast Food Services	11	174270.5
饮料及冷饮服务	Beverages and Cold Drinks	4	38341.0
餐饮配送及外卖送餐服务	Catering Distribution and Takeaway Servic	1	2572.7
其他餐饮业	Other Catering Services	4	4290.2
2. 按登记注册类型分	Grouped by Registration Status		
内资	Domestic Funded Enterprises	360	611552.9
国有	State-owned Enterprises	6	13054.1
集体	Collective-owned Enterprises		
有限责任公司	Limited Liability Corporations	136	224771.3
国有独资公司	State-funded Corporations	4	13164.9
其他有限责任公司	Other Limited Liability Corporations	132	211606.4
股份有限公司	Stock Limited Corporation	4	94844.7
私营	Private Enterprises	213	266712.3
私营独资	Private-funded Enterprises	11	6425.1
私营合伙	Private Partnership Enterprises		
私营有限责任公司	Private Limited Liability Corporations	201	259704.5
私营股份有限公司	Private Share Holding Corporations	1	582.7
其他	Others	1	12170.5
港澳台商投资	Enterprises Funded by Hong Kong, Macao and Taiwan	6	76602.9
外商投资	Foreign Funded Enterprises	6	139301.9
个体经营	Individual Enterprises	17	23675.5

continued 1

(10 000 yuan)

客房收入 From Hotel Room	公共网络客房收入 Public Network Room Revenue	餐费收入 From Meals	公共网络餐费收入 Public Network Catering Revenue	商品销售收入 From Commodities
25145.8	1889.5	19641.2	275.5	1062.6
236.0	126.0			
42515.2	**5893.9**	**739174.6**	**49667.0**	**40714.1**
42515.2	5893.9	532739.0	42334.4	35960.5
		165627.3	7325.9	377.1
		34569.9	6.7	3752.0
		2572.7		
		3665.7		624.5
42108.4	5893.9	514468.5	39864.2	35176.6
1211.5		9429.5		1644.6
26053.1	4121.6	181944.5	4322.9	6212.1
454.3	66.1	8350.2	860.0	1297.0
25598.8	4055.5	173594.3	3462.9	4915.1
3949.8	1312.7	64662.6	12277.8	20787.4
4316.0	459.6	253207.1	23263.5	6532.5
92.7		6221.5		110.9
4223.3	459.6	246432.9	23263.5	6391.6
		552.7		30.0
6578.0		5224.8		
406.8		71569.4	7749.6	3805.0
		131129.5	1887.0	91.9
		22007.2	166.2	1640.6

16-8 限额以上批发和零售业主要商品分类销售额（2018年）

Sale Values of Wholesale and Retail Enterprises above Designated Size by Category of Main Commodities（2018）

单位：万元 (10 000 yuan)

分类	Classify	销售合计 Total Sales Value	批发 Wholesale Value	零售 Retail Value
总计	**Total**	**83047853.3**	**57429055.1**	**25618798.2**
其中：通过公共网络实现的商品销售	Sales Achieved through the Public Network	8746394.5	5329109.3	3417285.2
粮油、食品类	Cereals, Oils and Foodstuffs	3249395.2	1689848.0	1559547.2
粮油类	Grain and Oil	696680.6	92952.7	603727.9
肉禽蛋类	Meat, Poultry and Eggs	310074.4	107929.6	202144.8
水产品类	Aquatic Products	57237.6	15831.6	41406.0
蔬菜类	Vegetables	898375.0	829780.3	68594.7
干鲜果品类	Fresh and Dried Fruit Category	757271.0	553819.2	203451.8
饮料类	Beverages	387927.9	193679.2	194248.7
烟酒类	Tobacco and Liquor	2237537.7	1846034.9	391502.8
服装、鞋帽、针、纺织品类	Clothing, Shoes, Hats and Textiles	6508668.6	4019236.7	2489431.9
#服装类	Clothing	5667841.2	3855679.2	1812162.0
鞋帽类	Shoes and Hats	553074.0	132581.6	420492.4
针、纺织品类	Knitwear and Textiles	287753.4	30975.9	256777.5
化妆品类	Cosmetics	689041.5	56346.6	632694.9
金银珠宝类	Gold,Silver and Jewelry	693846.0	258280.0	435566.0
日用品类	Articles for Daily Use	1105771.3	113373.9	992397.4
#儿童玩具类	Children's Toys	110050.9		110050.9
五金、电料类	Hardwear and Electrical Materials	323769.0	103454.7	220314.3
体育、娱乐用品类	Sports and Recreation Articles	993218.2	13888.9	979329.3
#照相器材类	Photography Equipment	153145.3		153145.3
书报杂志类	Newspapers and Magazines	297861.0	174095.3	123765.7
电子出版物及音像制品类	E-journal and Video Products	31663.5	3942.9	27720.6
家用电器和音像器材类	Household Appliances and Video Products	2820431.2	902931.2	1917500.0
中西药品类	Traditional Chinese and Western Medicine	4639898.2	4141656.6	498241.6
#西药	Western Medicine	3739823.8	3404377.6	335446.2
中草药及中成药	Chinese Herbal Medicine and Traditional Chinese Medicine	207552.0	135544.2	72007.8
文化办公用品类	Cultural and Official Goods	1141147.5	253785.1	887362.4
#计算机及其配套产品	Among Them： Computers and Ancillary Products	393859.7	111170.2	282689.5
家具类	Furniture	1120723.7		1120723.7
通讯器材类	Communication Appliances	1486916.7	324139.8	1162776.9
煤炭及制品类	Coal and Related Products	4354274.6	4354274.6	
木材及制品类	Wood and Wooden Products	55077.9	55077.9	
石油及制品类	Petroleum and Related Products	14295974.0	11585298.2	2710675.8
化工材料及制品类	Raw Chemical Materials	4366352.7	4366352.7	
#化肥类	Chemical Fertilizers	145647.4	145647.4	
金属材料类	Metal Materials	19266809.7	19266809.7	
建筑及装潢材料类	Buildings and Decoration Materials	1264217.2	349716.6	914500.6
机电产品及设备类	Mechanical and Electrical Products	1188058.0	1184592.3	3465.7
#农机类	Agricultural Machinery			
汽车类	Automobile	8785432.5	890720.0	7894712.5
种子饲料类	Seeds and Feedstuff	12196.6	12196.6	
棉麻类	Cotton,Hemp	22223.0	22223.0	
其他类	Others	1709419.9	1247099.7	462320.2

注：本表为定期季度报表数据。

16-9 亿元以上商品交易市场成交情况（2018年）

Basic Statistics on Commodity Exchange Markets of Transaction Value over 100 Million Yuan (2018)

分 类	Classify	年末出租摊位数（个）Number of Rental Booths at Year-end (unit)	成交额（万元）Turnover (10 000 yuan)
1. 粮油、食品类	Cereals, Oils and Foodstuffs	6252	3051490
#粮油类	Grain and Oil	368	366084
肉禽蛋类	Meat, Poultry and Eggs	774	266114
水产品类	Aquatic Products	464	75524
蔬菜类	Vegetables	2206	975771
干鲜果品类	Fresh and Dried Fruit Category	2422	1367582
2. 饮料类	Beverages	343	14211
3. 烟酒类	Tobacco and Liquor	177	12394
4. 服装、鞋帽、针纺织品类	Clothing, Shoes, Hats and Textiles	6892	3796366
#服装类	Clothing	3861	1988803
鞋帽类	Shoes and Hats	1823	1703483
针纺织品类	Knitwear and Textiles	1208	104080
5. 化妆品类	Cosmetics	22	764
6. 金银珠宝类	Gold,Silver and Jewelry		
7. 日用品类	Articles for Daily Use	544	36970
#洗涤用品类	Bathing and Washing		
儿童玩具类	Children's Toys		
8. 五金、电料类	Hardwear and Electrical Materials	769	101806
9. 体育、娱乐用品类	Sports and Recreation Articles	187	105604
10. 书报杂志类	Newspapers and Magazines		
11. 电子出版物及音像制品类	E-journal and Video Products		
12. 家用电器和音像器材类	Household Appliances and Video Products	195	66848
13. 中西药品类	Traditional Chinese and Western Medicine	135	1485
#西药	Western Medicine		
中草药及中成药	Chinese Herbal Medicine and Traditional Chinese Medicine		
14. 文化办公用品类	Cultural and Official Goods	742	196691
#计算机及其配套产品	Computer and Related Products	532	169726
15. 家具类	Furniture	2586	1081162
16. 通讯器材类	Communication Appliances	1001	307180
17. 煤炭及制品类	Coal and Related Products		
18. 木材及制品类	Wood and Wooden Products		
19. 石油及制品类	Petroleum and Related Products		
20. 化工材料及制品类	Raw Chemical Materials	191	461272
#化肥类	Chemical Fertilizers	160	13800
21. 金属材料类	Metal Materials	87	57560
22. 建筑及装潢材料类	Buildings and Decoration Materials	6778	1163701
23. 机电产品及设备类	Mechanical and Electrical Products	590	107000
#农机类	Agricultural Machinery		
24. 汽车类	Automobile	1530	259000
25. 种子饲料类	Seeds and Feedstuff		
26. 棉麻类	Cotton,Hemp		
27. 其他类	Others	40	8165

16-10 批发和零售业连锁经营情况（2018年）

Basic Statistics on Chain Business of Wholesale and Retail Trades（2018）

指　标	Item	本年合计 Total	上年合计 Total Last Year	本年直营店 Regular Chain
一、门店总数（个）	**Number of Stores(unit)**	**2373**	**1531**	**2175**
二、年末从业人员数（人）	**Employees at Year-end(person)**	**26186**	**19943**	**25285**
三、年末零售营业面积（平方米）	**Operating Area of Retail at Year-end(sq.m)**	**1048297**	**1031689**	**1037327**
四、连锁门店商品购进额（万元）	**Purchases Value of Chain Stores(10 000 yuan)**	**3233337**	**2817682**	**3211654**
其中：统一配送商品购进额	Centralized Purchases and Delivery	2846913	2374033	2825230
其中：自有配送中心配送商品购进额	Self Centralized Purchases and Delivery	2590012	2156716	2584782
非自有配送中心配送商品购进额	Non-self Centralized Purchases and Delivery	51914	59612	51914
五、连锁门店商品销售额（万元）	**Sales Value of Chain Store(10 000 yuan)**	**3930298**	**3554952**	**3901758**
其中：零售额	Retail Value	1663978	1494483	1635438

16-10 续表 continued

指　标	Item	上年直营店 Regular Chain Last Year	本年加盟店 Franchise	上年加盟店 Franchise Last Year
一、门店总数（个）	**Number of Stores(unit)**	**1288**	**198**	**243**
二、年末从业人员数（人）	**Employees at Year-end(person)**	**18932**	**901**	**1011**
三、年末零售营业面积（平方米）	**Operating Area of Retail at Year-end(sq.m)**	**1011479**	**10970**	**20210**
四、连锁门店商品购进额（万元）	**Purchases Value of Chain Stores(10 000 yuan)**	**2772903**	**21683**	**44779**
其中：统一配送商品购进额	Centralized Purchases and Delivery	2329254	21683	44779
其中：自有配送中心配送商品购进额	Self Centralized Purchases and Delivery	2126617	5230	30099
非自有配送中心配送商品购进额	Non-self Centralized Purchases and Delivery	59612		
五、连锁门店商品销售额（万元）	**Sales Value of Chain Store(10 000 yuan)**	**3508069**	**28540**	**46883**
其中：零售额	Retail Value	1447600	28540	46883

注：上年同期数为本年在库企业加报数据。

16-11 住宿和餐饮业连锁经营情况（2018年）

Basic Statistics on Chain Business of Hotels and Catering Services（2018）

指　标	Item	本年合计 Total	上年合计 Total Last Year
一、门店总数（个）	**Number of Stores(unit)**	**413**	**354**
二、年末从业人员数（人）	**Employees at Year-end(person)**	**13303**	**12672**
三、年末餐饮营业面积（平方米）	**Operating Area of Retail at Year-end(sq.m)**	**146570**	**137952**
四、客房总数（间）	**Guest Rooms(room)**		
五、床位数（张）	**Guest Beds(bed)**		
六、餐位数（位）	**Dining Seats(set)**	**84987**	**80487**
七、连锁门店商品购进额（万元）	**Operating Area of Catering Services at Year end(room)(10 000yuan)**	**97068**	**81236**
其中：统一配送商品购进额	Centralized Purchases and Delivery	92719	77844
其中：自有配送中心配送商品购进额	Self Centralized Purchases and Delivery	65328	53602
非自有配送中心配送商品购进额	Non-self Centralized Purchases and Delivery	16261	14191
八、连锁门店商品营业额（万元）	**Sales Value of Chain Store(10 000 yuan)**	**262999**	**222037**
其中：餐费收入	Catering Revenues	257930	218131
商品销售额	Sales Value	5019	3869

16-11 续表 continued

指　标	Item	本年直营店 Regular Chain	上年直营店 Regular Chain Last Year
一、门店总数（个）	**Number of Stores(unit)**	**406**	**349**
二、年末从业人员数（人）	**Employees at Year-end(person)**	**13136**	**12349**
三、年末餐饮营业面积（平方米）	**Operating Area of Retail at Year-end(sq.m)**	**145220**	**137252**
四、客房总数（间）	**Guest Rooms(room)**		
五、床位数（张）	**Guest Beds(bed)**		
六、餐位数（位）	**Dining Seats(set)**	**84719**	**80321**
七、连锁门店商品购进额（万元）	**Operating Area of Catering Services at Year end(room)(10 000yuan)**	**95770**	**80212**
其中：统一配送商品购进额	Centralized Purchases and Delivery	92719	77844
其中：自有配送中心配送商品购进额	Self Centralized Purchases and Delivery	65328	53602
非自有配送中心配送商品购进额	Non-self Centralized Purchases and Delivery	16261	14191
八、连锁门店商品营业额（万元）	**Sales Value of Chain Store(10 000 yuan)**	**259766**	**220404**
其中：餐费收入	Catering Revenues	254696	216499
商品销售额	Sales Value	5019	3869

16-12 限额以上住宿和餐饮业经营情况（2018年）

单位：个、亿元

分 类	Classify	2015 单位数 Number of Enterprises	2015 营业额 Business Revenue
总计	**Total**	**567**	**127.75**
一、住宿业	**Lodging Services**	**239**	**57.99**
1. 按登记注册类型分组	Grouped by Registration Status		
内资企业	Domestic Funded Enterprises	221	47.30
国有	State-owned Enterprises	29	6.48
集体	Collective-owned Enterprises	2	0.18
股份合作	Cooperative Enterprises		
联营	Joint Ownership Enterprises		
国有联营	State Joint Ownership Enterprises		
集体联营	Collective Joint Ownership Enterprises		
国有与集体联营	Joint State-collective Ownership Enterprises		
其他联营	Other Joint Ownership Enterprises		
有限责任公司	Limited Liability Corporations	119	30.21
国有独资公司	State-funded Corporations	4	1.32
其他有限责任公司	Other Limited Liability Corporations	115	28.89
股份有限公司	Stock Limited Corporation	5	1.74
私营	Private Enterprises	66	8.69
私营独资	Private-funded Enterprises	3	0.12
私营合伙	Private Partnership Enterprises		
私营有限责任公司	Private Limited Liability Corporations	62	8.54
私营股份有限公司	Private Share Holding Corporations	1	0.03
其他	Others		
港澳台商投资	Enterprises Funded by Hong Kong, Macao and Taiwan	8	5.17
外商投资	Foreign Funded Enterprises	10	5.52
个体经营	Individual Enterprises		
2. 按国民经济行业分组	Grouped by Economic Sector		
旅游饭店	Tour Restaurant	176	50.12
一般旅馆	Common Hotel	56	6.15
民宿服务	Home and Lodging Services		
其他住宿业	Others	7	1.72

注：本表统计范围为法人、个体及产业活动单位。

Statistic on Hotel Services and Catering Services above Designed Size（2018）

(100 million yuan)

2016		2017		2018	
单位数 Number of Enterprises	营业额 Business Revenue	单位数 Number of Enterprises	营业额 Business Revenue	单位数 Number of Enterprises	营业额 Business Revenue
604	**127.52**	**716**	**142.38**	**742**	**166.64**
258	**60.07**	**319**	**68.04**	**353**	**81.53**
242	50.55	301	57.61	337	70.84
30	6.45	25	5.77	21	5.07
1	0.04	1	0.04	1	0.03
126	31.67	138	35.02	134	40.03
7	2.84	8	3.87	6	3.01
119	28.83	130	31.15	128	37.02
4	1.72	4	1.92	5	2.24
81	10.67	133	14.86	175	23.30
3	0.18	2	0.10	4	0.13
77	10.45	129	14.68	168	22.53
1	0.04	2	0.08	3	0.64
				1	0.17
7	4.25	7	5.21	7	5.62
9	5.27	9	5.14	8	5.05
		2	0.08	1	0.02
184	50.88	193	54.26	184	61.97
65	7.34	116	11.61	154	16.78
				2	0.10
9	1.85	10	2.17	13	2.68

16-12 续表1

单位：个、亿元

分 类	Classify	2015 单位数 Number of Enterprises	2015 营业额 Business Revenue
二、餐饮业	**Catering Trade**	**328**	**69.76**
1. 按登记注册类型分	Grouped by Registration Status		
内资	Domestic Funded Enterprises	284	50.46
国有	State-owned Enterprises	4	1.10
集体	Collective-owned Enterprises		
股份合作	Cooperative Enterprises		
联营	Joint Ownership Enterprises		
国有联营	State Joint Ownership Enterprises		
集体联营	Collective Joint Ownership Enterprises		
国有与集体联营	Joint State-collective Ownership Enterprises		
其他联营	Other Joint Ownership Enterprises		
有限责任公司	Limited Liability Corporations	167	31.89
国有独资公司	State-funded Corporations	1	0.12
其他有限责任公司	Other Limited Liability Corporations	166	31.77
股份有限公司	Stock Limited Corporation	1	3.53
私营	Private Enterprises	108	12.58
私营独资	Private-funded Enterprises	9	0.46
私营合伙	Private Partnership Enterprises		
私营有限责任公司	Private Limited Liability Corporations	97	11.97
私营股份有限公司	Private Share Holding Corporations	2	0.15
其他	Others	4	1.36
港澳台商投资	Enterprises Funded by Hong Kong, Macao and Taiwan	7	4.28
外商投资	Foreign Funded Enterprises	6	9.94
个体经营	Individual Enterprises	31	5.08
2. 按国民经济行业分	Grouped by Economic Sector		
正餐服务	Dinner Services	315	63.80
快餐服务	Fast Food Services	7	4.71
饮料及冷饮服务	Beverage and Cold Beverage Services		
餐饮配送及外卖送餐服务	Catering Distribution and Takeaway Servic		
其他餐饮业	Other Catering Services	6	1.25

continued 1

(100 million yuan)

2016		2017		2018	
单位数 Number of Enterprises	营业额 Business Revenue	单位数 Number of Enterprises	营业额 Business Revenue	单位数 Number of Enterprises	营业额 Business Revenue
346	**67.45**	**397**	**74.34**	**389**	**85.11**
321	49.87	364	56.40	360	61.16
4	1.06	4	1.03	6	1.31
166	26.02	144	22.36	136	22.48
1	0.11	2	0.67	4	1.32
165	25.91	142	21.69	132	21.16
2	6.22	5	8.58	4	9.48
146	15.49	208	23.31	213	26.67
12	0.56	13	0.65	11	0.64
131	14.73	192	22.49	201	25.97
3	0.20	3	0.17	1	0.06
3	1.08	3	1.12	1	1.22
6	3.97	7	3.97	6	7.65
5	10.13	5	11.66	6	13.93
14	3.48	21	2.31	17	2.37
335	61.68	384	58.74	369	63.17
8	4.82	10	15.25	11	17.43
				4	3.83
				1	0.26
3	0.95	3	0.35	4	0.42

主要统计指标解释

批发业 指批发商向批发、零售单位及其他企事业、机关单位批量销售生活用品和生产资料的活动，以及从事进出口贸易和贸易经纪与代理的活动。批发商可以对所批发的货物拥有所有权，并以本单位、公司的名义进行交易活动；也可以不拥有货物的所有权，而以中介身份做代理销售商。还包括各类商品批发市场中固定摊位的批发活动。

零售业 指百货商店、超级市场、专门零售商店、品牌专卖店、售货摊等主要面向最终消费者（如居民等）的销售活动。包括以互联网、邮政、电话、售货机等方式的销售活动，还包括在同地点，后面加工生产，前面销售的店铺（如前店后厂的面包房）。不包括：谷物、种子、饲料、牲畜、矿产品、生产用原料、化工原料、农用化工产品、机械设备(乘用车、计算机及通信设备等除外）等生产资料的销售（批发业）；非零售单位附带的零售活动（如汽车修理单位销售汽车零件）；商业零售单位所在商厦的物业管理（物业管理）；商业零售单位所在的商品市场、商业大厦的市场管理活动（市场管理）。

住宿业 指有偿为顾客提供临时住宿的服务活动，不包括提供长期住宿场所的活动（如出租房屋、公寓等）。

餐饮业 指在一定场所，对食物进行现场烹饪、调制，并出售给顾客主要供现场消费的服务活动。

社会消费品零售总额 指批发和零售业、餐饮业、新闻出版业、邮政业和其他服务业等，售予城乡居民用于生活消费的商品和社会集团用于公共消费的商品之总量。社会消费品零售总额包括：

一、批发和零售业企业（单位）售予城乡居民用于生活消费和社会集团用于公共消费的商品。包括：

1. 售予城乡居民的各种生活消费品；

2. 售予入境旅游的外国人、华侨、港澳台同胞的各类商品；

3. 售予行政事业单位、社会团体、军队和武警等机构的商品，以及以零售方式售予各类企业的商品。具体包括：用于非生产和社会交往的办公用品，如通讯设备、计算器具和设备、电讯网络设备、文印设备、音像视听器材和设备、纸张、本册、文具及装订文印材料、家具、日用电器、针纺织品、清洁卫生用品、文体用品、奖品、纪念品、礼品等；供内部人员乘坐的交通工具和燃料；用于办公设施修缮的各类配件、材料、工具等；用于取暖和防暑降温的设备、燃料、材料及食品等；专用于教学的用品和设备；非营利医疗机构的中、西药品、中药材和医疗设备器材；非专用的劳动保护用品；不对外营业的内部食堂用的餐具、炊具、设备、清洁卫生工具和食品、燃料等；军队、武警用于其人员生活的衣着品和个人用品；其他各类非生产性设备和用品。

二、餐饮业出售的主食、菜肴、烟酒饮料和其他商品。

三、新闻出版业、邮政业售予城乡居民、企事业单位、军队和武警等机构的书报杂志、音像制品、邮品等。

四、其他服务业出售的食品、烟酒饮料、服装鞋帽、日常生活用品、医药保健用品、艺术品、工艺美术品、玩具、殡葬用品以及其他消费品。

批发和零售业商品购进、销售、库存总额 指各种登记注册类型的批发和零售业企业（单位）以本企业（单位）为总体的，从国内、国外市场购进的商品总量，销售和出口的商品总量，库存的商品总量等情况。该指标可以反映商品流转过程中商品的购进、销售、库存之间的比例关系和存在的问题。

购进总额 指从本企业（单位）以外的单位和个人购进（包括从境外直接进口）作为转卖或加工后转卖的商品总额。它反映批发和零售业从国内、国外市场上购进商品的总量。商品购进包括：（1）从工农业生产者购进的商品；（2）从出版社、报社的出版发行部门购进的图书、杂志和报纸；（3）从各种登记注册类型的批发和零售业企业（单位）购进的商品；（4）从其他单位购进的商品，如从机关、团体、企业等单位购进的剩余物资，从住宿和餐饮业、其他服务业购进的商品，从海关、市场管理部门购进的缉私和没收的商品，从居民手中收购的废旧商品等；（5）从国（境）外直接进口的商品。不包括企业（单位）为自身经营用和未通过买卖行为而收入的商品以及销售退回、商品升溢等。

销售总额 指对本企业（单位）以外的单位和个人出售（包括对境外直接出口）的商品总额。它反映批发和零售业在国内市场上销售商品以及出口商品的总量。商品销售包括：（1）售给城乡居民和社会集团消费用的商品；（2）售给工业、农业、建筑业、运输邮电业、批发和零售业、住宿和餐饮业、其他服务业等作为生产、经营使用的商品；（3）售给批发和零售业作为转卖或加工后转卖的商品；（4）对国（境）外直接出口的商品。不包括出售本企业（单位）自用的废旧包装用品，未通过买卖行为付出的商品，经本单位介绍、由买卖双方直接结算、本单位只收取手续费的业务，购货退出的商品以及商品损耗和损失等。

库存总额 指报告期末各种登记注册类型的批发和零售业企业（单位）已取得所有权的商品。它反映批发和零售业企业（单位）的商品库存情况和对市场商品供应的保证程度。商品库存包括：（1）存放在批发和零售业经营单位（如门市部、批发站、经营处）仓库、货场、货柜和货架中的商品；（2）挑选、整理、包装中的商品；（3）已记入购进而尚未运到本单位的商品，即发货单或银行承兑凭证已到而货未到的商品；（4）寄放他处的商品，如因购货方拒绝承付而暂时存放在购货方的商品和已办完加工成品收回手续而未提回的商品；（5）委托其他单位代销（未做销售货调出）尚未售出的商品；（6）代其他单位购进尚未交付的商品。不包括所有权不属于本单位的商品、委托外单位加工生产尚未收回成品的商品、外贸企业代理其他单位从国外进口尚未付给订货单位的商品、代国家物资储备部门保管的商品等。

住宿和餐饮业营业额 指住宿和餐饮业法人企业（单位）在经营活动中因提供服务或销售商品等取得的收入。包括：客房收入、餐费收入、商品销售额和其他收入。客房收入指住宿和餐饮业法人企业（单位）在经营活动中因提供住宿服务取得的收入。餐费收入指住宿和餐饮业法人企业（单位）因为顾客提供就餐服务取得的收入，包括经烹饪、调制加工后出售的各种食品，如主食、炒菜、凉拌菜等的收入。商品销售额指住宿和餐饮业法人企业（单位）伴随服务而出售商品所取得的收入（含增值税）。其他收入指营业收入中除客房收入、餐费收入、商品销售额以外的其他收入，包括娱乐、健身和商务服务等。

连锁企业（或称连锁店、连锁公司） 指在核心企业或总店的领导下，由分散的、经营同类商品或服务的企业或活动单位，采取共同方针，实行集中采购和分散销售的有机结合，通过规范化经营，实现规模效益的经济联合组织形式。一般连锁店应由若干个分店组成。其经营特征：（1）经营同类商品；（2）使用统一商号；（3）统一采购配送，采购与销售相分离（部分商品可根据物流合理和保质保鲜原则，由供应商直接送货到门店，其余均由总部统一配送）。

连锁门店的形式分为直营连锁和加盟连锁。

直营连锁也叫正规连锁。指连锁门店均由总部独资或控股开设，在总部的直接领导下统一经营。总部采取纵深式的管理方式，直接下令掌管所有的零售门店，零售门店也必须完全接受总部指挥。这是大型垄断商业资本通过吞并、兼并或独资、控股等途径，发展壮大自身实力和规模的一种形式。

加盟连锁包括特许连锁和自由连锁两种形式。

特许连锁指各连锁门店（被特许人）通过合同形式，取得使用总部（特许人）商标、商号、经营技术和销售总部开发的商品的特许权，各加盟连锁门店为独立法人，在总部指导下统一经营。

自由连锁也称自愿连锁。指连锁公司的门店均为独立法人，各自的资产所有权关系不变，在公司总部的指导下共同经营。各成员店使用共同的店名，与总部订阅有关购、销、宣传等方面的合同，并按合同开展经营活动。在合同规定的范围之外，各成员店可以自由活动。根据自愿原则，各成员店可自由加入连锁体系，也可自由退出。

Explanatory Notes on Main Statistical Indicators

Wholesale Trade refers to the activities of wholesaler selling at wholesale commodities for daily use and capital goods to enterprises of wholesale and retail trades and other enterprises, institutions and government offices, including the activities of wholesaler engaged in import and export and acting as a trade agent. The wholesaler may have the right of ownership over the commodities of wholesale and trade in the name of its own or a company, the wholesaler may not have the right of ownership, only acts an agent. The wholesale trade also include the activities of wholesaler at the fixed stalls of the wholesale market of different commodities.

Retail Trade refers to the activities of department store,supermarket, franchised store, brand store, retail stall and on-the-spot-making-selling store selling commodities to the final consumers (citizens) by any means including internet, post, telephone, sales machine. Retail trade excludes the activities of sales of capital goods such a grain, seed, feed, livestock, mineral products, raw material for production, industrial chemicals, chemical products for farm, machine and equipment (vehicle, computer and communication equipment), and the activities of supplementary sales of non-retailer such as the sales of spare parts of car repair business

Hotel Services refer to the activities of enterprises providing paid services of lodging to the customer, excluding the activities of providing long period of services of lodging (such as leased house and apartments).

Catering Services refer to the activities of enterprises providing on-the-spot services of selling food cooked and prepared to the customer in certain sites

Total Retail Sales of Consumer Goods refer to the sum of retail sales of commodities sold by wholesale and retail trades, catering services, publishing, post and telecommunications and other service industries to urban and rural households for household consumption and to social institutions for public consumption. Retail sales of consumer goods include:

1) Sales sold by wholesale and retail trades to urban~thA and rural households for household consumption and to social institutions for public consumption.

a) of commodities to urban and rural households;

b) of commodities to foreigners, overseas Chinese and Chinese compatriots from Hong Kong, Macao and Taiwan visiting China;

c) of commodities to government agencies, institutions, social organizations, military and armed police units, and commodities to enterprises in the form of retail sales. More specifically, they include: office facilities and articles for non-production purposes such as communications equipment, computing equipment and instruments, TV and network equipment, printing and copying equipment, audio-visual equipment and instruments, paper, notebooks, stationeries, furniture, electric appliances, knitwear, sanitation and cleaning articles, cultural and sport articles, articles for prizes, souvenirs, etc.; transport vehicles and fuels for employees; materials, spare parts and tools for the maintenance of office facilities; equipment, fuels, materials and food for winter heating or summer cooling purposes; articles and equipment for teaching purpose; Chinese and western medicines and medical equipment and facilities purchased by non profit-making medical institutes; non- specialized work safety articles; cooking utensils, tableware, equipment, cleaning articles, food and fuels purchased by in-house cafeterias; clothes and personal articles purchased by military or armed police units for their officials and soldiers; and other equipment and articles for non-production purposes.

2) Sales of stable food, cooked dishes, beverages, tobaccos and other articles by catering units.

3) Sales of books, newspapers, magazines, audio-visual products and post products by publishing, post and telecommunications departments to urban and rural households and to enterprises, institutions, military and armed police units.

4) Sales of food, beverages, tobaccos, clothing, hats, footwear, articles for daily use, medicines, medical and health articles, work of art, handicrafts, toys, funeral articles and other articles by other service industries.

Purchase, Sales and Stock of Commodities by Wholesale and Retail Trades refer to the total volume of commodities purchased, total volume of sales and exports, and the stock of commodities by wholesale and retail enterprises (establishments) of different status of registration from domestic and overseas markets. This indicator reflects the relationship among purchase, sales and stock of commodities in the circulation of goods and reveals the existing problems.

Total Purchases of Commodities refer to the total value of purchases of commodities by enterprises (establishments)from other establishments or individuals (including direct import from abroad) for the purpose of re-selling, either with or without further processing of the commodities purchased. The commodities include: (1) commodities purchased from agricultural and industrial producer, wholesaler, retailer, publishing house and other service business; (2) commodities purchased from institutions and government departments; (3) confiscated goods purchased from the customs authorities or market management agencies; (4) second-hand goods and wastes purchased from residents; The commodities exclude 1 commodities purchased by enterprises (establishments) for use in their own business operation, commodities obtained without buying or selling procedures such as materials, consumable goods of low value, office appliances, etc. 2 received goods without trading, such as goods handed over from others, borrowed goods, preserved goods for others, donated goods from others, processed and retrieved goods, etc. 3. goods of direct settlement between buyer and seller with handling fees introduced by others, 4. goods returned or refused to pay by the buyer, 5. excessive goods.

Total Sales of Commodities refer to value of commodities sold by the establishments to other establishments and individuals (including goods sold for self consumption, including the value-added tax). The commodities include: (1) commodities sold to urban and rural residents and social groups for their consumption; (2) commodities sold to establishments in all industries for their production and operation, including agriculture, industry, construction, transportation, post and telecommunications, catering services, and public utility including commodities sold to wholesale and retail establishments for re-selling, with or without further processing; and (3) commodities for direct export to abroad.Excluded are (1) extended commodities without trading, such as goods handed over to other enterprises and institutions because of the change of organizations, lent goods, returned goods preserved for others, extended processing materials and samples donated to others, (2) goods of direct settlement between buyer and seller with handling fees introduced by others, (3)goods returned after purchase, (4) damaged and spoiled goods, (5) waste and used goods of selfuse,

Total Stock of Commodities refers to total commodities possessed by wholesaler and retailer of various types of registration status at the end of the reference period, reflecting the commodity stock level of various wholesaler and retailer and the potential for market supply. It includes: (1) commodities located in storage, garages, counters, and shelves of operating places (such as sale stores, wholesale centres, and operating offices) ; (2) commodities in the process of being selected, sorted, and packed; (3) commodities not arrived but recorded as purchase in the account, i.e. commodities not arrived but payment receipts for the commodities from the sellers or the banks arrived; (4) commodities deposited in other places rather than places mentioned above, for instance: commodities in the hold of purchasers temporarily due to the refusal of payment and commodities not taken back after going through the formalities; (5) commodities entrusted to other units to sell but not sold yet; (6) commodities purchased for other units but not delivered yet. Commodities not included as stock are those not owned by the enterprises (units), commodities on commission for processing but not yet delivered, imported commodities of agency of foreign trade enterprise but not yet delivered to ordering units and finally those put in stock on behalf of the state material reserves units.

Business Revenue of Hotels and Catering Services refers to revenue received from providing services or selling commodities by corporate enterprises and establishments engaged in hotels and catering services, including income from hotels, from catering services, from selling of commodities and from other services. Income from hotels refers to income of corporate enterprises and establishments engaged in hotels and catering services by providing lodging services. Income from catering services refers to income of corporate enterprises and establishments engaged in hotels and catering services by providing catering services, including selling of cooked or prepared foods such as staple food, cooked dishes or cold dishes. Income from selling of commodities refers to income of corporate enterprises and establishments engaged in hotels and catering services by selling commodities (including value-added tax) that accompany the services they provide. Income from other activities refers to income received other than income from hotels, catering services or selling of commodities, such as income from providing recreation, fitness or business services.

Chain Head Stores (headquarter) refer to the core leading stores responsible for development, allocation, administration and utilization of resources (name of stores, brand of stores, operation model, service standard, management way, ect.) of chain stores. Chain stores refers to the stores engaged in providing homogeneous commodities or services, with the central leadership of head store and guided by common policies, conduct centralized purchase and distributed selling of commodities, in order to gain better efficiency through standardized operation. The chain stores include regular chain stores, franchise chain stores and voluntary chain stores.

Regular Chain store refers to chain stores that are invested or controlled by the headquarters. They operate under direct and unified management from the headquarters.

Franchise chain store refers to the chain stores (franchisees) which are franchised with operation resources such as trade marks, names, patent and operation know-how by the franchisors in form of contract and pay the operation fees to the franchisors.

Voluntary chain store refers the stores operate jointly on the voluntary bases while maintaining their status of independent legal entities with full ownership of their assets. They sell goods of same brand from same channel of resource to the consumers.

17 对外经济贸易和旅游

FOREIGN TRADE AND ECONOMIC COOPERATION TOURISM

资料整理：马晓庆
Data management: Ma Xiaoqing
数据审核：黄小丹
Data audit: Huang Xiaodan

第十七部分　对外经济贸易和旅游

一、简要说明

本章资料包括对外经济贸易、利用外资和旅游等方面资料，由西安市统计局贸易外经处根据西安市商务局、投资合作局、西安海关和文旅局提供资料整理。

二、主要指标

进出口总值（亿元）	3303.24	比上年增长	29.6%
#出　口	1957.17	比上年增长	26.1%
实际利用外资（亿美元）	63.54	比上年增长	14.9%

17 FOREIGN TRADE AND ECONOMIC COOPERATION,TOURISM

Ⅰ.Brief Introduction

Data in this chapter consists of data on foreign trade, using of foreign capital and fund and tourism. Data on foreign economy and trade and tourism are compiled and provided by Foreign Economy Division of the Xi'an Bureau of Statistics according to the data from Xi'an Bureau of Commerce, Xi'an Investment Committee, Xi'an Custom Office and Xi'an Tourism Development Committee.

Ⅱ.Major Indicators

		Increase over Preceding Year
Total Imports and Exports (100 mil.yuan)	3303.24	29.6%
#Exports	1957.17	26.1%
Actual Utilized Foreign Investments (USD 100 mil.)	63.54	14.9%

17-1 主要年份外资、外贸基本情况

Main Indicators on Foreign Investments and International Trading in Representative Years

指　标	Item	1990	1995	2000	2005	2010	2012
一、利用外资签定协议项目(个)	**Number of Projects of Foreign Capital Used through the Signed Agreements and Contracts (unit)**	**11**	**184**	**135**	**157**	**82**	**87**
合同外资（万美元）	Contracted Foreign Investments (USD 10 000)	415	28956	54123	121499	119689	360264
实际利用外资（万美元）	Actual Utilized Foreign Investments (USD 10 000)	1154	18653	15633	57113	156653	247800
二、进出口总值（万美元）	**Total Imports and Exports (USD 10 000)**	**38229**	**137510**	**173696**	**390146**	**1039273**	**1301446**
#进口总值	Total Imports	9939	27347	67634	126705	507544	571568
出口总值	Total Exports	28290	110163	106062	263441	531729	729878
进出口差额(出口-进口)	Balance of Imports and Exports	18351	82816	38428	136736	24185	158310
三、国际旅游者人数总计（万人次）	**Total Number of International Tourists (10 000 person-times)**	**25.88**	**41.35**	**65.03**	**77.56**	**84.18**	**115.35**
#外国人	Foreigners	15.40	37.11	54.65	65.86	73.21	101.40
港、澳、台同胞	Chinese Compatriot From Hong Kong, Macao and Taiwan	10.07	4.16	10.38	11.70	10.97	13.95
四、国际旅游者人天数总计（万人天）	**Total Number of Days of International Tourists (10 000 person/day)**	**55.03**	**84.44**	**162.69**	**224.93**	**241.67**	**334.44**
#外国人	Foreigners	33.48	75.71	131.44	190.99	211.48	294.90
港、澳、台同胞	Chinese Compatriot From Hong Kong, Macao and Taiwan	21.55	8.56	31.15	33.94	30.19	39.54
五、国际旅游收入（亿元）	**Earning of International Tourism (100 millon**	**1.96**	**10.38**	**22.41**	**33.54**	**42.40**	**59.89**
#商品收入	Income from Mercantile	0.44	2.57	7.71	11.25	11.87	14.19
劳务收入	Income from Labour Service	1.52	7.81	14.70	22.29	30.53	45.70
六、国际旅游者在西安人均停留天数（天）	**Number of Days of Average Tourists Staying in Xi'an (day)**	**2.1**	**2.0**	**2.5**	**2.9**	**2.9**	**2.9**

注：1.2014年起市文化和旅游局未发布国际旅游统计数据。
2.本表来源于市商务局、西安海关、市文化和旅游局、市投资合作局。2018年利用外资包含西咸新区、进出口总值为西安原口径数据。
3.合同外资2016年前名称为“利用外资签订协议金额”，实际利用外资2016年前名称为“外商实际直接投资额”。下同。

17-1 续表 continued

指 标	Item	2013	2014*	2015*	2016*	2017*	2018*
一、利用外资签定协议项目(个)	**Number of Projects of Foreign Capital Used through the Signed Agreements and Contracts (unit)**	**152**	**103**	**73**	**72**	**143**	**219**
合同外资（万美元）	Contracted Foreign Investments (USD 10 000)	251874	255321	193684	102103	464954	475508
实际利用外资（万美元）	Actual Utilized Foreign Investments (USD 10 000)	312994	370310	400833	450466	530680	635370
二、进出口总值（万美元）	**Total Imports and Exports (USD 10 000)**	**1798534**	**15321514**	**17616896**	**18299476**	**25450843**	**33032389**
#进口总值	Total Imports	950715	7974693	9418142	8826392	9928641	13460734
出口总值	Total Exports	847819	7346822	8198754	9473084	15522202	19571655
进出口差额(出口-进口)	Balance of Imports and Exports	-102896	-627871	-1219388	646692	5593561	6110921
三、国际旅游者人数总计（万人次）	**Total Number of International Tourists (10 000 person-times)**	**121.11**					
#外国人	Foreigners	106.90					
港、澳、台同胞	Chinese Compatriot From Hong Kong, Macao and Taiwan	14.21					
四、国际旅游者人天数总计（万人天）	**Total Number of Days of International Tourists (10 000 person/day)**	**351.11**					
#外国人	Foreigners	310.26					
港、澳、台同胞	Chinese Compatriot From Hong Kong, Macao and Taiwan	40.85					
五、国际旅游收入（亿元）	**Earning of International Tourism (100 millon**	**64.16**					
#商品收入	Income from Mercantile	14.69					
劳务收入	Income from Labour Service	49.47					
六、国际旅游者在西安人均停留天数（天）	**Number of Days of Average Tourists Staying in Xi'an (day)**	**2.9**					

注：2014年以后进出口数据计量单位为万元。

17-2　主要年份利用外资情况

Utilization of Foreign Capital in Representative Years

单位：万美元　　　　(USD 10 000)

年　份 Year	合同外资 Contracted Foreign Investments	实际利用外资 Actual Utilized Foreign Investments
1983	3500	800
1985	8361	1106
1986	19919	4010
1987	3218	5552
1988	2423	6758
1989	1645	11632
1990	415	1154
1991	591	1094
1992	24165	5200
1993	57289	8996
1994	20321	15240
1995	28956	18653
1996	35978	20510
1997	27214	22057
1998	40034	22286
1999	40390	13801
2000	54123	15633
2001	60736	17687
2002	70692	20281
2003	96380	25557
2004	78312	27595
2005	121499	57113
2006	182525	82463
2007	143978	111567
2008	118230	114738
2009	60027	121872
2010	119689	156653
2011	120083	200522
2012	360264	247800
2013	251874	312994
2014	255321	370310
2015	193684	400833
2016	102103	450466
2017	464954	530680
2018	475508	635370

注：本表数据来源于市投资合作局。2018年数据包含西咸新区。

17–3 外国和港澳台地区在西安投资情况（2018年）

Foreign, Hong Kong, Macao and Taiwan Investment Situation in Xi'an (2018)

单位：万美元 (USD 10 000)

指 标	Item	项目数（个）Number of Projects(unit)	合同外资 Contracted Foreign Investments	实际利用外资 Actual Utilized Foreign Investments
合计数	**Total**	**219**	**475508.00**	**635370.00**
一、按企业类别分组	By Enterprise Category			
1. 中外合资经营企业	Joint-venture Enterprises	85	220947.80	44361.00
2. 中外合作经营企业	Cooperation Enterprises	4	1659.70	
3. 外资企业	Wholly Foreign-owned Enterprises	129	251606.03	144608.00
4. 外商投资股份制	FDI Shareholding Inc.	1		
5. 外方股东留存收益	Retained earnings of foreign shareholders		500.00	208785.00
6. 境外融资	Overseas Financing		794.47	237616.00
二、按国民经济行业分组	Grouped by Sector			
（一）农、林、牧、渔业	Agriculture, Forestry, Animal Husbandry and Fishery	4	348.22	
（二）采矿业	Mining			157163.00
（三）制造业	Manufacturing	23	115221.07	234469.00
（四）电力、燃气及水的生产供应业	Generation and Supply of Electricity, Production and Supply of Gas and Water	2	6444.95	5507.00
（五）建筑业	Construction	5	1101.80	39690.00
（六）批发和零售业	Wholesale and Retail Trades	56	84801.23	55967.00
（七）交通运输、仓储和邮政业	Transportation, Storage and Post	9	32765.64	36093.00
（八）住宿和餐饮业	Hotels and Catering Services	10	632.25	1160.00
（九）信息传输、软件和信息技术服务业	Information Transmission, Computer Service and Software	26	35446.09	3545.00
（十）金融业	Financial Intermediation	21	44917.90	30757.00
（十一）房地产业	Real Estate	15	55915.51	67179.00
（十二） 租赁和商务服务业	Leasing and Business Services	28	17538.70	2169.00
（十三）科学研究和技术服务业	Scientific Research and Technical Service	14	79745.29	817.00
（十四）水利、环境和公共设施管理业	Management of Water Conservancy, Environment and Public Facilities	2	288.59	

注：本表数据来源于市投资合作局。本表数据包含西咸新区。

17-3 续表1

单位：万美元 (USD 10 000)

指　标	Item	项目数（个） Number of Projects(unit)	合同外资 Contracted Foreign Investments	实际利用外资 Actual Utilized Foreign Investments
（十五）居民服务、修理和其他服务业	Services to Households, repairs and other services	3	239.32	393.00
（十六）教育	Education			
（十七）卫生和社会工作	Health and social work			461.00
（十八）文化、体育和娱乐业	Culture, Sports and Entertainment	1	101.44	
（十九）公共管理、社会保障和社会组织	Public administration, social security and social organizations			
（二十）国际组织	International Organizations			
三、按投资国别、地区分组	By Country(Region)			
香港	Hong Kong,China	90	309370.42	227295.00
澳门	Macao,China			
台湾省	Taiwan,China	6	4237.76	15418.00
日本	Japan	9	876.91	71876.00
马来西亚	Malaysia	3	473.55	3.00
新加坡	Singapore	10	18433.41	34020.00
韩国	Korea Rep.	28	9425.77	207502.00
德国	Germany	3	4629.42	7803.00
意大利	Italy			22.00
法国	France	1	4.76	809.00
英国	United Kingdom	3	301.29	332.00
瑞士	Switzerland			
丹麦	Denmark			
加拿大	Canada	3	53.19	162.00
美国	United States	11	6924.70	15449.00
澳大利亚	Australia	3	226.86	12622.00
维尔京群岛	Virgin Is.(E)	4	74123.61	6059.00
其它	Others	45	46426.35	35998.00

17-4 各区县、开发区实际利用外资

Actual Utilized Investment by Foreign Entrepreneurs by Region and Development Zone

单位：万美元 (USD 10 000)

区县及开发区	Region and Economic Zone	2010	2011	2012	2013	2014	2015	2016	2017	2018
区县合计	**Sum of Region**	**38855**	**49726**	**58119**	**45164**	**51423**	**59765**	**67874**	**72527**	**119635**
新城区	Xincheng	4900	6765	7800	5012	6500	7775	8768	10340	11947
碑林区	Beilin	5150	6273	7800	5103	5871	6873	9360	9941	10570
莲湖区	Lianhu	5471	7405	7800	5100	5843	6873	7532	8656	9392
灞桥区	Baqiao	5215	6001	7397	6124	6933	8148	9056	9601	10570
未央区	Weiyang	5023	6202	7800	6000	6834	7870	8614	9433	10380
雁塔区	Yanta	5488	6912	8190	6179	6847	8074	8907	9843	10772
阎良区	Yanliang	1208	2070	2200	2200	2346	2555	2801	3000	3200
临潼区	Lintong	1200	2000	2400	2400	2504	2765	3031	1102	4094
长安区	Chang'an	1680	2300	2768	3003	3360	3961	4440	4762	5200
高陵区	Gaoling	950	1089	1100	1100	1182	1478	1621	1740	1860
鄠邑区	Huyi	1050	1060	1115	1173	1288	1339	1479	1700	1666
蓝田县	Lantian	550	600	650	660	707	1283	1401	1490	1862
周至县	Zhouzhi	970	1050	1100	1110	1210	773	864	920	920
西咸新区	Xixian									37202
开发区合计	**Sum of Development Zones**	**117798**	**150797**	**189681**	**267830**	**318887**	**311265**	**381023**	**458153**	**515513**
高新区	GaoXin	51130	64935	81776	132632	149387	167112	203870	260293	287000
经开区	JingKai	42608	54201	68202	81423	103009	114538	129186	145000	167000
曲江新区	Qujiang	17187	21002	26433	33870	41436	0	20588	24212	26500
浐灞生态区	Chanba Eco-District	3070	3856	4837	7266	8453	9800	10833	12402	13600
航空基地	Aviation Industry Base	1239	1701	2072	2640	3082	3636	4186	2045	5250
航天基地	Aerospace Base	1554	2030	2403	3000	3501	3980	4567	5117	6100
国际港务区	International Trade&Logistic Park	1010	1571	2082	3469	5050	6429	7793	9083	10063
其它	Others									222

注：本表数据来源于市投资合作局。2018年数据包含西咸新区。

17-5 主要年份进出口总值

Total Imports and Exports in Representative Years

单位：万美元 (USD 10 000)

年份 Year	进出口总值 Total Imports and Exports	出口总值 Total Exports	进口总值 Total Imports
1987	13596	7540	6056
1990	38229	28290	9939
1991	55356	41511	13845
1992	70467	53060	17407
1993	93330	62393	30937
1994	104752	76897	27855
1995	137510	110163	27347
1996	143187	91745	51442
1997	150668	107753	42915
1998	180589	100492	80097
1999	172919	94495	78424
2000	173696	106062	67634
2001	169914	87948	81966
2002	186966	112479	74487
2003	230932	140327	90605
2004	309295	203539	105756
2005	390146	263441	126705
2006	415403	272862	142541
2007	536162	347133	189029
2008	704029	447113	256916
2009	724618	333114	391504
2010	1039273	531729	507544
2011	1260179	582662	677517
2012	1301446	729878	571568
2013	1798534	847819	950715
2014*	15321514	7346822	7974693
2015*	17616896	8198754	9418142
2016*	18299476	9473084	8826392
2017*	25450843	15522202	9928641
2018*	33032390	19571656	13460734

注：本表数据来源于西安海关。2014年及以后数据计量单位为万元。2018年数据为西安原口径数据。

17-6 外贸商品进出口总值分国别和地区（2018年）

Total Value of Imports and Exports by Country and Region（2018）

单位：万元 (10 000 yuan)

国别和地区	Country and Region	进出口总值 Total Imports and Exports	出口 Exports
亚洲	**Asia**	**23889144**	**13253475**
#香港	Hong kong	6073578	6068555
台湾省	Taiwan	6689148	925520
日本	Japan	1485733	489577
菲律宾	Phiilippines	102765	76878
马来西亚	Malaysia	543402	475748
韩国	Korea	6592029	3206597
非洲	**Africa**	**449063**	**332296**
#埃及	Egypt	103135	102980
突尼斯	Tunisia	3268	3093
埃塞俄比亚	Ethiopia	2301	2145
博茨瓦纳	Botswana	13	13
南非	South Africa	132411	33849
欧洲	**Europe**	**3377781**	**2342044**
#德意志联邦国	Germany	663600	393285
法国	France	689980	634669
意大利	Italy	128625	59348
荷兰	Netherland	474382	305269
英国	England	325172	267004
瑞士	Switzerland	54685	9263
西班牙	Spain	32441	24869
俄罗斯联邦	Russia	175703	115672
拉丁美洲	**Latin America**	**739354**	**370989**
#哥伦比亚	Colombia	9225	9218
巴西	Brazil	57181	38884
阿根廷	Argentina	8227	8081
北美洲	**North America**	**4072206**	**3139188**
加拿大	Canada	160496	71065
美国	America	3911710	3068123
大洋洲及太平洋岛屿	**Oceanic and Pacific Islands**	**504799**	**133662**
#澳大利亚	Australia	490003	124303
新西兰	New Zealand	10562	5982

注：本表数据来源于西安海关，为西安原口径数据。

17-7 主要商品分大类出口金额

Export Value of Major Merchandise by Type

单位：万美元 (USD 10 000)

商品分类	HS Section and Division	2000	2005
食用蔬菜、根及块茎	Edible Vegetables, Certain,Roots amd Tubers	1095	1190
蔬菜、水果、坚果或植物其他部分的制品	Vegetables, Fruits, Nuts, or Products Made of Other Parts of Plants	2076	10531
矿砂、矿渣及矿灰	Ores,Slags and Ash	4083	63247
无机化学品；贵金属、稀土金属、放射性元素及其同位素的有机及无机化合物	Inorganic Chemicals,Organic or Inorganic Compounds of Precious Metals,of Rare Earth Metals,of Radioactive Elements or of Isotopes	3714	10997
有机化学品	Organic Chemicals	2367	8569
羊毛、动物细毛或粗毛、马毛纱线及其机织物	Wool ,Fine or Coarse Animal Hair; Horsehair Yarn and Woven Fabric	810	903
棉花	Cotton	3197	3240
化学纤维短纤	Short Staple Chemical' Fibers	5061	1471
针织或钩编的服装及衣着附件	Articles of Apparel and Clothing Accessories, Knitted or Crocheted	6753	5736
非针织或非钩编的服装及衣着附件	Articles of Apparel and Clothing Accessories, not Knitted or Crocheted	7269	5068
其它纺织制成品；成套物品；旧衣着及旧纺织品	Other Made Up Textile Articles;Sets;Worn Clothing and Worn Textile Articles;Rags Articles	1649	3000
鞋靴、护膝和类似品及其零件	Footwear,Gaiters and The Like,Parts of Such Articles Headgear and Parts Thereof	1347	1368
玻璃及其制品	Glass and Glassware	3376	8576
钢铁	Iron and Steel	3534	5314
钢铁制品	Articles of Iron or Steel	5535	13959
铅及制品	Lead Areticles Thereof	1371	12
锌及制品	Zinc Areticles Thereof	4031	135
其他贱金属、金属陶瓷及其制品	Other Base Metals,Germets;Areticles Thereof	1066	11233
贱金属工具、器具、利口器、餐匙、餐叉及其零件	Tools,Implements,Cutlery,Spoons and Forks, of Base Metal;Parts Thereof of Base Metal	2933	3052
核反应堆、锅炉、机器、机械器具及其零件	Nuclear Reactors ,Boilers, Machinery and Mechanical Appliances; and Parts Thereof	10915	30832
电机、电气设备及其零件；录音机及放声机、电视图象、声音的录制和重放设备及其零件、附件	Electrical Machinery and Equipment and Parts Thereof;Sound Recorders and Repreducers, Television Image and Sound Recordes and Repreducers, and Parts and Accessories of Such Articles	8339	23605
光学、照相、电影、计量、检验、医疗或外科仪器及设备、精密仪器及设备；上述物品的零配件、附件	Optical,Photographic,Cinematographic,Measuring, Checking,Precision Medical or Surgical Instruments and Apparatus;Parts and Accessories Thereof	2020	2341
家具、寝具、褥垫、弹簧床垫、软床垫及类似的填充制品；未列名灯具及照明装置；发光标志、发光名牌及类似品；活动房屋	Mattresses,Mattress Supports,Cushions and Similar Stuffed Furnishings;Lamps and Lighting Fittings, not Elsewhere Spcified or Included;Illumihated Signs,Illuminated	2587	4773

注：本表数据来源于西安海关。2014年及以后数据计量单位为万元。2018年数据为西安原口径数据。

17-7 续表1

单位：万美元

商品分类	HS Section and Division	2006	2007
食用蔬菜、根及块茎	Edible Vegetables, Certain,Roots amd Tubers	1136	1232
蔬菜、水果、坚果或植物其他部分的制品	Vegetables, Fruits, Nuts, or Products Made of Other Parts of Plants	15374	37426
矿砂、矿渣及矿灰	Ores,Slags and Ash	52046	47378
无机化学品；贵金属、稀土金属、放射性元素及其同位素的有机及无机化合物	Inorganic Chemicals,Organic or Inorganic Compounds of Precious Metals,of Rare Earth Metals,of Radioactive Elements or of Isotopes	10916	16508
有机化学品	Organic Chemicals	11923	11182
羊毛、动物细毛或粗毛、马毛纱线及其机织物	Wool ,Fine or Coarse Animal Hair; Horsehair Yarn and Woven Fabric	1400	1065
棉花	Cotton	3808	3255
化学纤维短纤	Short Staple Chemical' Fibers	1556	1767
针织或钩编的服装及衣着附件	Articles of Apparel and Clothing Accessories, Knitted or Crocheted	5332	5345
非针织或非钩编的服装及衣着附件	Articles of Apparel and Clothing Accessories, not Knitted or Crocheted	4078	3875
其它纺织制成品；成套物品；旧衣着及旧纺织品	Other Made Up Textile Articles;Sets;Worn Clothing and Worn Textile Articles;Rags Articles	3342	3090
鞋靴、护膝和类似品及其零件	Footwear,Gaiters and The Like;Parts of Such Articles Headgear and Parts Thereof	216	348
玻璃及其制品	Glass and Glassware	8272	6246
钢铁	Iron and Steel	4900	11366
钢铁制品	Articles of Iron or Steel	16903	17329
铅及制品	Lead Areticles Thereof	158	1650
锌及制品	Zinc Areticles Thereof	4119	2470
其他贱金属、金属陶瓷及其制品	Other Base Metals,Germets;Areticles Thereof	17695	23414
贱金属工具、器具、利口器、餐匙、餐叉及其零件	Tools,Implements,Cutlery,Spons and Forks, of Base Metal;Parts Thereof of Base Metal	3607	3917
核反应堆、锅炉、机器、机械器具及其零件	Nuclear Reactors ,Boilers, Machinery and Mechanical Appliances; and Parts Thereof	36174	47381
电机、电气设备及其零件；录音机及放声机、电视图象、声音的录制和重放设备及其零件、附件	Electrical Machinery and Equipment and Parts Thereof;Sound Recorders and Repreducers, Television Image and Sound Recordes and Repreducers, and Parts and Accessories of Such Articles	22801	33393
光学、照相、电影、计量、检验、医疗或外科仪器及设备、精密仪器及设备；上述物品的零配件、附件	Optical,Photographic,Cinematographic,Measuring, Checking,Precision Medical or Surgical Instruments and Apparatus;Parts and Accessories Thereof	3521	4230
家具、寝具、褥垫、弹簧床垫、软床垫及类似的填充制品；未列名灯具及照明装置；发光标志、发光名牌及类似品；活动房屋	Mattresses,Mattress Supports,Cushions and Similar Stuffed Furnishings;Lamps and Lighting Fittings, not Elsewhere Spcified or Included;Illumihated Signs,Illuminated	5086	8301

continued 1

(USD 10 000)

2008	2009	2010	2011	2012	2013	2014*	2015*	2016*	2017*	2018*
1374	803	4740	2016	1961	2699	2686	2039	2555	1129	659
29270	21920	41289	36763	2576	49361	132663	112701	102768	149311	131711
40502	6141	325	4709	1679	1686	14977	96	178	346	25
15882	9774	24875	11735	8911	12588	67764	44508	49950	52192	52289
13954	16294	982	20067	17890	28694	109986	109654	117162	148719	176287
720	460	10133	796	562	2433	15782	3005	5648	3153	5680
3213	2346	98	2628	2185	5827	9252	14309	6429	5301	5531
1181	2217	479	2586	2375	8245	13685	11581	11178	14502	12923
4371	3617	3209	3366	12316	6491	29551	37030	31646	36441	30570
3623	2919	3394	3262	7050	4861	33872	23610	19393	40633	52971
3187	2813	544	2838	4412	4471	18906	15677	15187	26219	19425
380	367	150	1003	5252	6293	20186	5032	2292	18614	18514
6538	5574	928	8073	10995	13856	54453	45991	46764	46059	49904
11966	4254	18549	16681	8407	6730	31854	20390	27589	28467	34424
26568	11943	5998	25319	24259	33546	102720	88740	100956	164963	151403
2	1	10	2	4913	16	3		26	19	1
46	78	28545	10	11	59	109	93	20	334	48
27576	11276	3556	28092	21397	24030	106691	95442	83309	103608	115801
4083	2777	2893	3641	5176	5992	30653	25321	24868	33582	41004
75911	52372	130296	99631	127795	211009	1929864	2744726	3431041	6147739	8252801
56758	53355	136	137105	183536	327931	3113155	3625079	4264312	7044093	8971300
6348	5255	196	11066	14908	17879	112646	119117	107892	108613	149348
8296	4769	5328	3860	25644	23595	52352	42140	40142	77439	83975

17-8 主要商品分大类进口金额

Import Value of Major Merchandise by Type

单位：万美元 (USD 10 000)

商品分类	HS Section and Division	2000	2005	2009	2010	2011	2012
无机化学品；贵金属、稀土金属、放射性元素及其同位素的有机及无机化合物	Inorganic Chemicals,Organic or Inorganic Compounds of Precious Metals,of Rare Earth Metals,of Radioactive Elements or of Isotopes	1467	317	5040	7513	19766	13329
有机化学品	Organic Chemicals	7257	15237	14186	13949	18100	12331
塑料及其制品	Plastic and Articles Thereof	2559	4317	3134	4091	3250	3107
钢铁	Iron and Steel	2467	752	2537	10949	10643	5928
铜及制品	Copper and Articles Thereof	2367	689	41195	43343	78482	11857
铝及制品	Aluminium and Articles Thereof	2652	3627	6505	3116	5913	8649
核反应堆、锅炉、机器、机械器具及其零件	Nuclear Reactors ,Boilers, Machinery and Mechanical Appliances; and Parts Thereof	12990	38050	87493	134753	135240	98802
电机、电气设备及其零件；录音机及放声机、电视图象、声音的录制和重放设备及其零件、附件	Electrical Machinery and Equipment and Parts Thereof;Sound Recorders and Repreducers, Television Image and Sound Recordes and Repreducers,and Parts and Accessories of Such Articles	5911	23337	113034	207937	230957	257444
车辆及其零件、附件、铁道及电车道车辆除外	Vehicles Other Than Railway or Tramway Rolling- and Rarts and Accessories Thereof	1530	1387	1798	3109	1527	2222
航空器、航天器及其零配件	Aircraft, Spacecraft and Parts Thereof	10443	8800	13057	3620	4654	8516
光学、照相、电影、计量、检验、医疗或外科仪器及设备、精密仪器及设备；上述物品的零配件、附件	Optical,Photographic,Cinematographic,Measuring, Checking,Precision Medical or Surgical	3673	10424	24210	37414	39317	48206

17-8 续表 continued

单位：万美元 (USD 10 000)

商品分类	HS Section and Division	2013	2014*	2015*	2016*	2017*	2018*
无机化学品；贵金属、稀土金属、放射性元素及其同位素的有机及无机化合物	Inorganic Chemicals,Organic or Inorganic Compounds of Precious Metals,of Rare Earth Metals,of Radioactive Elements or of Isotopes	11869	166549	185175	299328	246352	371885
有机化学品	Organic Chemicals	12504	98293	86359	154656	123439	148022
塑料及其制品	Plastic and Articles Thereof	8014	37082	54103	76182	103008	157809
钢铁	Iron and Steel	1802	11893	17403	16093	16567	18717
铜及制品	Copper and Articles Thereof	65170	169061	484480	224287	240188	571455
铝及制品	Aluminium and Articles Thereof	11758	45295	43935	34384	32032	71631
核反应堆、锅炉、机器、机械器具及其零件	Nuclear Reactors ,Boilers, Machinery and Mechanical Appliances; and Parts Thereof	186974	2017587	2021311	990108	926081	1056642
电机、电气设备及其零件；录音机及放声机、电视图象、声音的录制和重放设备及其零件、附件	Electrical Machinery and Equipment and Parts Thereof;Sound Recorders and Repreducers, Television Image and Sound Recordes and Repreducers,and Parts and Accessories of Such Articles	444407	3919650	5011437	5272203	6510729	9406713
车辆及其零件、附件、铁道及电车道车辆除外	Vehicles Other Than Railway or Tramway Rolling- and Rarts and Accessories Thereof	2966	17521	19700	22697	26662	22430
航空器、航天器及其零配件	Aircraft, Spacecraft and Parts Thereof	9179	43191	35164	31933	101247	31940
光学、照相、电影、计量、检验、医疗或外科仪器及设备、精密仪器及设备；上述物品的零配件、附件	Optical,Photographic,Cinematographic,Measuring, Checking,Precision Medical or Surgical	61727	452559	542812	521411	307404	341141

注：本表数据来源于西安海关。2014年以后数据计量单位为万元。2018年数据为西安原口径数据。

17-9 按贸易方式分外贸出口总值

Total Value of Exports in Foreign Trade by Type of Trade

单位：万元 (10 000 yuan)

指 标	Item	2018	2018年比2017年增长（%） Growth Rate in 2018 over 2017(%)
出口总值	**Total Exports**	**19571656**	**26.1**
1.一般贸易	General Trade	3486269	16.8
2.国家间、国际组织无偿援助	Between Countries, International Organizations	7290	46.9
和赠送的物资	Aid and Donated Materials		
3.来料加工装配贸易	Assembly Processing Trade	9621968	28602.9
4.进料加工贸易	Processing With Imported Trade	2831311	-72.9
5.对外承包工程出口货物	Exports Contracted Projects	278711	-29.1
6.租赁贸易	Lease Trade	32	
7.易货贸易	Barter		
8.出料加工贸易	Material Processing	60	141774.2
9.保税监管场所进出境货物	Inward and Outward Goods of Free	112	0.6
（保税仓库进出境货物）	(Trade Storehouse)		
10.海关特殊监管区域物流货物	Re-export Goods of Free Trade Zone	3337282	100.3
11.其他	Others	8621	74.1

注：本表数据来源于西安海关。本表数据为西安原口径数据。

17-10 按贸易方式分外贸进口总值

Total Value of Imports in Foreign Trade by Type of Trade

单位：万元 (10 000 yuan)

指标名称	Item	2018	2018年比2017年增长（%）Growth Rate in 2018 over 2017(%)
进口总值	**Total Imports**	**13460734**	**35.0**
1.一般贸易	General Trade	2547940	8.6
2.国家间、国际组织无偿援助和赠送的物资	Between Countries, Internationals Organization Aid and Donated Materials		
3.华侨、港澳台同胞、外籍华人捐赠物资	The overseas Chinese, Hong Kong, Macao, Taiwan,Chinese of foreign Donated Materials		
4.来料加工装配贸易	Assembly Processing Trade	6291353	20522.7
5.进料加工贸易	Processing With Imported Trade	3268404	-50.7
6.来料加工装配进口的设备	Assembly Processing Trade Equipment	817	24.4
7.租赁贸易	Lease Trade		
8.外商投资企业作为投资进口的设备、物品	Foreign-invested Enterprises as the Import Investment of Equipment, Goods	14572	-31.0
9.出料加工贸易	Material Processing	158	69680.5
10.易货贸易	Barter		
11.保税监管场所进出境货物（保税仓库进出境货物）	Inward and Outward Goods of Free (Trade Storehouse)	35970	14.3
12.海关特殊监管区域物流货物（保税区仓储转口货物）	Re-export Goods of Free Trade Zone (Re-exports)	322479	-0.4
13.海关特殊监管区域进口设备（出口加工区进口设备）	Export Processing Zones Imported (Equipment)	957236	87.0
14.其他	Other	21805	95.8

注：本表数据来源于西安海关。本表数据为西安原口径数据。

17-11 主要年份旅游人数及收入

Number of Tourists and Tourism Earnings in Representative Years

年 份 Year	接待旅游者人数（万人次） Number of Tourists (10 000 person-times)	国际旅游人数 Number of International Tourists	旅游总收入（万元） Total Tourism Earnings (10 000 yuan)	国际旅游收入 Earning of International Tourists	国际旅游者在西安人均停留天数（天） Number of Days of Average International Tourists Staying in Xi'an(day)
1980	4.00	4.00	1757	1757	3.8
1985	21.15	21.15	7029	7029	2.2
1990	25.88	25.88	19628	19628	2.1
1995	791.35	41.35	440000	103818	2
1997	1010.53	48.53	510000	166359	2.6
1998	1105.80	47.98	560000	160244	2.6
1999	1260.40	55.41	830000	186282	2.5
2000	1567.00	65.03	1050000	224100	2.5
2001	1752.20	67.20	1130000	240700	2.4
2002	1984.13	74.13	1310000	260000	2.2
2003	1647.67	33.66	1064200	121200	2.5
2004	2149.03	65.03	1544000	273900	2.9
2005	2423.60	77.56	1785000	335380	2.9
2006	2738.70	86.73	2043000	378270	2.9
2007	3118.01	100.01	2372000	424263	2.9
2008	3232.20	63.20	2435200	287200	2.6
2009	3929.29	67.29	2974000	310500	2.9
2010	5285.18	84.18	4051800	424000	2.9
2011	6653.23	100.23	5301500	512800	2.9
2012	7978.35	115.35	6543900	598900	2.9
2013	10130.00	121.11	8114400	641600	2.9
2014	12000.00		9500000		
2015	13600.80		10736900		
2016	15012.56		12138100		
2017	18093.14		16333000		
2018	24738.75		25548100		

注：本表数据来源于市文化和旅游局。2014年以后市文化和旅游局未发布国际旅游统计数据。2018年数据包含西咸新区。

17-12 主要年份旅行社及A级景点

Statistics of Travel Agencies and Level-A Scenic Spots in Representative Years

项 目	Item	2005	2010	2012	2013	2014	2015	2016	2017	2018
旅行社数（个）	Number of Travel Agencies (unit)	221	334	344	360	385	353	410	452	583
旅行社营业收入（亿元）	Revenue of Travel Agencies (100 million yuan)	17.82	31.22	49.49	57.93	45.70	59.54	66.68	79.39	93.93
旅游A级景点数（个）	Number of Level-A Scenic Spots(unit)	18	34	55	61	67	74	72	77	77
旅游A级景点年接待游客人次（万人次）	Number of Tourists Received at Level-A Scenic Spots (10 000 person times)	930	2726	5306	7163	7462	8553	10454	18120	24506

注：本表数据来源市文化和旅游局。2018年数据包含西咸新区。2018年旅行社数、旅行社管理收入来源于第四次经济普查583家有营业收入的企业数据。2018年旅游A级景点数及接待游客不包含西咸新区。

主要统计指标解释

进出口总额 指实际进出我国国境的货物总金额。包括对外贸易实际进出口货物，来料加工装配进出口货物，国家间、联合国及国际组织无偿援助物资和赠送品，华侨、港澳台同胞和外籍华人捐赠品，租赁期满归承租人所有的租赁货物，进料加工进出口货物，边境地方贸易及边境地区小额贸易进出口货物（边民互市贸易除外），中外合资企业、中外合作经营企业、外商独资经营企业进出口货物和公用物品，到、离岸价格在规定限额以上的进出口货样和广告品（无商业价值、无使用价值和免费提供出口的除外），从保税仓库提取在中国境内销售的进口货物，以及其他进出口货物。该指标可以观察一个国家在对外贸易方面的总规模。我国规定出口货物按离岸价格统计，进口货物按到岸价格统计。

商品经营单位所在地进、出口额 指在所在地海关注册登记的有进出口经营权的企业实际进、出口额。

商品目的地进口额和商品货源地出口额 目的地进口额指进口货物的消费、使用或最终抵运地的实际进口额；货源地出口额指出口货物的产地或原始发货地的实际出口额。

利用外资 指我国各级政府、部门、企业和其他经济组织通过对外借款、吸收外商直接投资以及用其他方式筹措的境外现汇、设备、技术等。

外商直接投资 指外国企业和经济组织或个人（包括华侨、港澳台胞以及我国在境外注册的企业）按我国有关政策、法规，用现汇、实物、技术等在我国境内开办外商独资企业、与我国境内的企业或经济组织共同举办中外合资经营企业、合作经营企业或合作开发资源的投资（包括外商投资收益的再投资），以及经政府有关部门批准的项目投资总额内企业从境外借入的资金。

旅游人数：

（1）入境旅游人数：指报告期内来我国观光、度假、探亲访友、就医疗养、购物、参加会议或从事经济、文化、体育、宗教活动的外国人、港澳台同胞、入境游客。统计时，外国人、港澳台同胞每入境一次统计1人次。

（2）出境人数：指中国（大陆）居民因公或因私出境前往其他国家、中国香港特别行政区、澳门特别行政区和台湾省观光、度假、探亲访友、就医疗养、购物、参加会议或从事经济、文化、体育、宗教活动的人数，即出境游客。统计时，按每出境一次统计1人次。

（3）国内旅游人数：指在报告期内在中国（大陆）观光游览、度假、探亲访友、就医疗养、购物、参加会议或从事经济、文化、体育、宗教活动的中国（大陆）居民人数，其出游的目的不是通过所从事的活动谋取报酬。统计时，国内游客按每出游一次统计1人次。

国际旅游（外汇）收入 指入境游客在中国（大陆）境内旅行、游览过程中用于交通、参观游览、住宿、餐饮、购物、娱乐等全部花费。

国内旅游收入 又称旅游总花费指国内游客在国内旅行、游览过程中用于交通、参观游览、住宿、餐饮、购物、娱乐等全部花费。

国际旅行社 指经营业务范围包括入境旅游业务、出境旅游业务和国内旅游业务的旅行社。

国内旅行社 指经营范围仅限于国内旅游业务的旅行社。

星级饭店 指设备、设施、服务符合《旅游饭店星级的划分与评定》（GB/T14308—2003），通过相关旅游管理部门评定，并取得星级饭店称号的饭店（含预备星级饭店）。

Explanatory Notes on Main Statistical Indicators

Total Imports and Exports at Customs refer to the real value of commodities imported and exported across the border of China. They include the actual imports and exports through foreign trade, imported and exported goods under the processing and assembling trades and materials, supplies and gifts as aid given gratis between governments and by the United Nations and other international organizations, and contributions donated by overseas Chinese, compatriots in Hong Kong and Macao and Chinese with foreign citizenship, leasing commodities owned by tenant at the expiration of leasing period, the imported and exported commodities processed with imported materials, commodities trading in border areas (excluding mutual exchange goods), the imported and exported commodities and articles for public use of the Sino-foreign joint ventures, cooperative enterprises and ventures with sole foreign investment. Also included is import or export of samples and advertising goods for which CIF or FOB value are beyond the permitted ceiling (excluding goods of no trading or use value and free commodities for export), imported goods sold in China from bonded warehouses and other imported or exported goods. The indicator of the total imports and exports at customs can be used to observe the total size of external trade in a country. In accordance with the stipulation of the Chinese government, imports are calculated at CIF, while exports are calculated at FOB.

Import Export Value by Location of China's Foreign Trade Managing Units refers to actual value of imports and exports carried out by corporations which have been registered by the local Customs house and are vested with right to run import export business.

Import Value of Commodities by Place of Destination and Export Value of Commodities by Place of Origin in China The former indicator refers to the value of import commodities of the places of their consumption, utilization or the places of their final destination. The latter indicator refers to the value of export commodities of the places of their origin or the places of the commodities dispatched.

Utilization of Foreign Capitals refers to remittance, equipment and technology financed from abroad, by loans, foreign direct investment and other forms undertaken by the Chinese governments at all levels, by various departments, enterprises and other economic units.

Foreign Borrowings refer to funds borrowed from abroad through formal signing of borrowing agreements with foreign institutions, including loans of foreign governments, loans of international financial institutions, commercial loans of foreign banks, export credit, and funds raised by Chinese bonds (and shares before 1996) issued abroad. It is an important part of China's utilization of foreign capitals.

Foreign Direct Investment refers to the investments inside China by foreign enterprises and economic organizations or individuals (including overseas Chinese, compatriots from Hong Kong, Macao and Taiwan, and Chinese enterprises registered abroad), following the relevant policies and laws of China, for the establishment of ventures exclusively with foreign own investment, Sino-foreign joint ventures and cooperative enterprises or for co-operative exploration of resources with enterprises or economic organizations in China.

Number of Tourists

(1) Visitor arrivals refer to the number of foreigners,Chinese compatriots from Hong Kong, Macao and Taiwan Chinese (mainland) who come to China (mainland) for sight-seeing,vacation,visiting relatives, medical treatment, shopping, attending conference, or to engage in economic, cultural, sports and religious activities. In compiling statistics, each time of entering China is counted as one person-time.

(2) Number of Chinese residents going abroad refer to the number of Chinese (mainland) residents going to other countries, Hong Kong Special Administrative region, Macao Special Administrative region and Taiwan for on official or private purposes, for sight-seeing, vacation, visiting relatives, medical treatment, shopping, attending conference, or to engage in economic, cultural, sports and religious

activities. In compiling statistics, each time of leaving is counted as one person-time.

(3) Number of domestic tourists refers to the number of Chinese (mainland) residents who travel within China (mainland) for sight-seeing, vacation, visiting relatives, medical treatment, shopping, attending conference, or to engage in economic, cultural, sports and religious activities. In compiling statistics, each time of travelling is counted as one person-time.

Foreign Exchange Earnings from International Tourism refer to the total expenditure of foreigners, overseas Chinese,Chinese compatriots from Hong Kong,Macao and Taiwan during their stay in the mainland of China on transportation,sighting,accommodation, food,shopping and entertainment.

Income from Domestic Tourism refer to expenditure of domestic tourists on transportation,sighting, accommodation, food, shopping and entertainment while they travel.

International Travel Agencies refer to travel agencies engaged in tourism entering China, Chinese residents going abroad and domestic tourism.

Domestic Travel Agencies refer to travel agencies only engaged in domestic tourism.

Star–rated Hotels refer to hotels rated with stars as assessed by the relevant tourism authorities according to GB/T14308-2003 standard with reference to their infrastructure, facilities and service levels.

18 规模以上服务业

SERVICE INDUSTRY OBOVE DESIGNATED SIZE

资料整理：王家峰
Data management：Wang Jiafeng
数据审核：王金桂
Data audit：Wang Jingui

第十八部分　规模以上服务业

一、简要说明

1.本章主要包括规模以上服务业（九个门类、四个中类）单位个数及主要经济指标，由西安市统计局服务业和社科处提供。

2.统计范围：辖区内年营业收入1000万元及以上，或年末从业人员50人及以上服务业法人单位。包括：交通运输、仓储和邮政业，信息传输、软件和信息技术服务业，租赁和商务服务业，科学研究和技术服务业，水利、环境和公共设施管理业，教育，卫生和社会工作；以及物业管理、房地产中介服务、房地产租赁经营和其他房地产业等行业。

辖区内年营业收入500万元及以上，或年末从业人员50人及以上服务业法人单位。包括：居民服务、修理和其他服务业，文化、体育和娱乐业。

二、主要指标

规模以上服务业单位个数（个）	1670		
规模以上服务业资产总计（亿元）	8359.00	比上年增长	6.4%
规模以上服务业营业收入（亿元）	2588.75	比上年增长	20.4%
规模以上服务业利润总额（亿元）	158.29	比上年增长	-2.8%

18 SERVICE INDUSTRY OBOVE DESIGNATED SIZE

Ⅰ.Brief Introduction

1.The data in this chapter consists of the number of service units and main economic indicators of Service enterprises above designated size (Including nine categories, four Class) , data in this chapter is provided by Tertiary Industry and Social Science&Technology Division of Xi'an Bureau of Statistice.

2.Scope of statistics:Service Industry unit with business revenue over 10 million yuan per year or number of employed persons over 50 at year–end, including transport, storage and post, information transmission, software and information technology, leasing and business services, scientific research and technical services, water conservancy, environment and public facilities administration, education, health and social services, own real estate business activities and other real estate services.

Services industry activity unit with business revenue over 5 million yuan per year or number of employed persons over 50 at year–end, including services to households, repair and other services, culture, sports and entertainment.

II. Major Indicators

		Increase over Preceding Year
Number of Units for services and Enterprises above the Designated Size(units)	1670	
Total Assets for services and Enterprises above the Designated Size(100 mil.yuan)	8359.00	6.4%
Operating Income for services and Enterprises above the Designated Size(100 mil.yuan)	2588.75	20.4%
The total Profit for services and Enterprises above the Designated Size(100 mil.yuan)	158.29	–2.8%

18-1 规模以上服务业按登记注册类型分主要经济指标（2018年）

Main Economic Indicators for Services above the Designated Size grouped by Registration Type（2018）

单位：万元 （10 000 yuan）

指 标	Item	企业单位数（个）Number of Enterprises (unit)	资产总计 Total Assets	固定资产原价 Original Value of Fixed Assets
总计	**Total**	**1670**	**83589990.5**	**47715297.2**
按登记注册类型分组	**Grouped by Registration Type**			
内资企业	Domestic Funded Enterprises	1604	82251335.4	46451924.4
国有	State-owned Enterprises	70	2726810.4	1350583.0
集体	Collective-owned Enterprises	13	67349.1	10640.1
股份合作	Corperative Enterprises	4	12276.0	3452.3
联营	Joint Ownership Enterprises	1	3648.8	542.5
国有联营	State Joint Ownership Enterprises			
集体联营	Collective Joint Ownership Enterprises			
国有与集体联营	Joint State-collective Enterprises			
其他联营	Others Joint Ownership Enterprises	1	3648.8	542.5
有限责任公司	Limited Liability Corporrations	815	69428747.9	40901712.4
国有独资公司	State Funded Corporations	109	34846029.0	20865985.0
其他有限责任公司	Other Limited Liability Corporrations	706	34582718.9	20035727.4
股份有限公司	Other Limited Liability Corporrations	52	4960244.9	3119225.8
私营	Other Limited Liability Corporrations	632	4847558.5	1026822.4
私营独资	Private-funded Enterprises	13	14091.4	5180.6
私营合伙	Private Partnership Enterprises	6	59946.4	42033.2
私营有限责任公司	Private Limited Liability Corporations	581	4359424.2	942331.4
私营股份有限公司	Private Share-holding Corporations Ltd.	32	414096.5	37277.2
其他	Other Enterprises	17	204699.8	38945.9
港澳台商投资	Enterprises with Funds from Hong Kong, Macao &Taiwan	24	723657.3	929688.0
与港澳台商合资经营	Joint Ventures	8	224174.6	141456.0
与港澳台商合作经营	Cooperation Enterprises	1	28524.6	2822.0
港澳台商独资	Enterprises with Sole Investment from Hong Kong Macau and Taiwan	14	466258.1	784836.4
港澳台商投资股份有限公司	Share-holding Corporations Ltd. with funds from Hong Kong, Macao & Taiwan			
其他港澳台投资	Other Hong Kong, Macao and Taiwan Investment	1	4700.0	573.6
外商投资	Foreign Funded Enterprises	42	614997.8	333684.8
中外合资经营	Sino-foreign Joint Ventures Enterprises	12	284084.8	187515.0
中外合作经营	Sino-Foreign Cooperation Enterprises	1	4320.1	4320.9
外资企业	Foreign Owned Enterprises	23	308148.5	138679.1
外商投资股份有限公司	Limited Company Funded by Foreign Investment	1	655.0	368.6
其他外商投资	Other Foreign Funded Enterprises	5	17789.4	2801.2

18-1 续表1

单位：万元

指 标	Item	负债合计 Total Liabilities	所有者权益合计 Total Owners' Equities	营业收入 Paid in Capital
总计	**Total**	**49777084.0**	**33812906.5**	**25887537.8**
按登记注册类型分组	**Grouped by Registration Type**			
内资企业	Domestic Funded Enterprises	48985538.7	33265796.7	25076613.1
国有	State-owned Enterprises	2012793.1	714017.3	2072752.2
集体	Collective-owned Enterprises	53078.0	14271.1	47111.3
股份合作	Corperative Enterprises	7060.9	5215.1	4085.8
联营	Joint Ownership Enterprises	3955.8	-307.0	1.8
国有联营	State Joint Ownership Enterprises			
集体联营	Collective Joint Ownership Enterprises			
国有与集体联营	Joint State-collective Enterprises			
其他联营	Others Joint Ownership Enterprises	3955.8	-307.0	1.8
有限责任公司	Limited Liability Corporrations	42372300.2	27056447.7	16831906.4
国有独资公司	State Funded Corporations	21207740.1	13638288.9	3401365.5
其他有限责任公司	Other Limited Liability Corporrations	21164560.1	13418158.8	13430540.9
股份有限公司	Other Limited Liability Corporrations	1511078.9	3449166.0	2136909.2
私营	Other Limited Liability Corporrations	2890240.5	1957318.0	3816313.8
私营独资	Private-funded Enterprises	10588.7	3502.7	15023.1
私营合伙	Private Partnership Enterprises	37008.6	22937.8	74349.6
私营有限责任公司	Private Limited Liability Corporations	2575453.3	1783970.9	3582845.9
私营股份有限公司	Private Share-holding Corporations Ltd.	267189.9	146906.6	144095.2
其他	Other Enterprises	135031.3	69668.5	167532.6
港澳台商投资	Enterprises with Funds from Hong Kong, Macao &Taiwan	506712.2	216945.1	467052.7
与港澳台商合资经营	Joint Ventures	77349.7	146824.9	89610.7
与港澳台商合作经营	Cooperation Enterprises	18753.2	9771.4	1759.0
港澳台商独资	Enterprises with Sole Investment from Hong Kong Macau and Taiwan	410265.7	55992.4	372699.5
港澳台商投资股份有限公司	Share-holding Corporations Ltd. with funds from Hong Kong, Macao & Taiwan			
其他港澳台投资	Other Hong Kong, Macao and Taiwan Investment	343.6	4356.4	2983.5
外商投资	Foreign Funded Enterprises	284833.1	330164.7	343872.0
中外合资经营	Sino-foreign Joint Ventures Enterprises	145596.8	138488.0	72575.0
中外合作经营	Sino-Foreign Cooperation Enterprises	261.7	4058.4	2400.3
外资企业	Foreign Owned Enterprises	131753.9	176394.6	241095.8
外商投资股份有限公司	Limited Company Funded by Foreign Investment	33.4	621.6	872.5
其他外商投资	Other Foreign Funded Enterprises	7187.3	10602.1	26928.4

continued1

(10 000 yuan)

主营业务收入 Revenue from Principal Business	营业成本 Total Cost	主营业务成本 Cost of Principal Business	销售费用 Sale Expenses
25461070.3	**19661919.2**	**19388622.1**	**1258937.1**
24663575.9	19163269.7	18905513.5	1204932.2
1996706.9	1955688.2	1911944.8	29468.5
46955.8	18912.9	18912.9	8789.1
3802.8	499.8	493.7	107.3
1.8	92.8	92.8	
1.8	92.8	92.8	
16573166.8	12800039.7	12613109.3	795726.1
3363044.6	2278051.3	2243412.0	76644.9
13210122.2	10521988.4	10369697.3	719081.2
2111524.7	1377530.7	1370834.7	161999.7
3764177.5	2880086.2	2860795.3	201706.0
15023.1	10771.2	10771.2	1781.8
74113.4	42848.5	42848.5	1854.2
3532664.3	2741749.3	2722467.4	187116.2
142376.7	84717.2	84708.2	10953.8
167239.6	130419.4	129330.0	7135.5
454492.1	268420.9	254586.3	42037.3
88771.1	57469.3	57446.3	1969.7
1740.9			
360996.6	210126.9	196315.3	38518.1
2983.5	824.7	824.7	1549.5
343002.3	230228.6	228522.3	11967.6
71709.6	46073.0	46066.5	4956.5
2400.3	591.4	591.4	
241095.8	163310.8	163310.8	6422.7
872.5	8.6	8.6	
26924.1	20244.8	18545.0	588.4

18-1 续表2

单位：万元

指　标	Item	管理费用 Management Expenses	财务费用 Financial Expenses	投资收益 Investment Income
总计	**Total**	**2485578.9**	**1256296.0**	**223023.6**
按登记注册类型分组	**Grouped by Registration Type**			
内资企业	Domestic Funded Enterprises	2373019.3	1237348.6	222503.5
国有	State-owned Enterprises	228383.8	17503.6	10068.4
集体	Collective-owned Enterprises	17911.8	-105.2	122.1
股份合作	Corperative Enterprises	3564.1	-76.1	252.5
联营	Joint Ownership Enterprises	279.3	318.8	
国有联营	State Joint Ownership Enterprises			
集体联营	Collective Joint Ownership Enterprises			
国有与集体联营	Joint State-collective Enterprises			
其他联营	Others Joint Ownership Enterprises	279.3	318.8	
有限责任公司	Limited Liability Corporrations	1454933.2	1155476.7	189958.9
国有独资公司	State Funded Corporations	205518.2	859415.0	59266.6
其他有限责任公司	Other Limited Liability Corporrations	1249415.0	296061.7	130692.3
股份有限公司	Other Limited Liability Corporrations	148407.6	33917.9	14226.2
私营	Other Limited Liability Corporrations	498684.4	29015.2	7875.4
私营独资	Private-funded Enterprises	3233.8	48.5	
私营合伙	Private Partnership Enterprises	17031.5	869.9	22.8
私营有限责任公司	Private Limited Liability Corporations	452421.9	23536.2	7598.8
私营股份有限公司	Private Share-holding Corporations Ltd.	25997.2	4560.6	253.8
其他	Other Enterprises	20855.1	1297.7	
港澳台商投资	Enterprises with Funds from Hong Kong, Macao &Taiwan	48383.6	13596.3	424.3
与港澳台商合资经营	Joint Ventures	13994.7	68.7	414.5
与港澳台商合作经营	Cooperation Enterprises	826.4	737.2	
港澳台商独资	Enterprises with Sole Investment from Hong Kong Macau and Taiwan	33225.5	12765.1	9.8
港澳台商投资股份有限公司	Share-holding Corporations Ltd. with funds from Hong Kong, Macao & Taiwan			
其他港澳台投资	Other Hong Kong, Macao and Taiwan Investment	337.0	25.3	
外商投资	Foreign Funded Enterprises	64176.0	5351.1	95.8
中外合资经营	Sino-foreign Joint Ventures Enterprises	13335.2	6106.8	21.1
中外合作经营	Sino-Foreign Cooperation Enterprises	258.9	-26.3	
外资企业	Foreign Owned Enterprises	47710.4	-637.6	74.7
外商投资股份有限公司	Limited Company Funded by Foreign Investment	460.1	8.3	
其他外商投资	Other Foreign Funded Enterprises	2411.4	-100.1	

continued2

(10 000 yuan)

营业利润 Business Profits	利润总额 Total Profits	应付职工薪酬 Salary Payable	从业人员平均人数（人） Annual Average Employed Persons (person)
1588474.9	**1582864.5**	**5114155.7**	**478344**
1473480.9	1466094.3	4925704.3	464883
11960.0	17429.4	522087.6	49674
1544.8	1459.9	25919.6	5846
135.5	307.7	1445.1	293
-689.1	-748.8	233.8	51
-689.1	-748.8	233.8	51
829493.5	809479.4	3329537.6	270657
47182.6	66721.5	505627.6	44657
782310.9	742757.9	2823910.0	226000
398503.4	395247.2	326967.2	27445
224114.9	233985.9	680379.5	105599
-825.3	-826.9	5512.1	1214
11613.3	11590.4	19238.8	2038
196388.7	205040.6	615189.3	97621
16938.2	18181.8	40439.3	4726
8417.9	8933.6	39133.9	5318
84202.1	84948.8	65508.4	5606
16150.1	16469.6	18566.1	1975
183.7	182.3	114.2	8
67628.0	67997.3	45438.3	3438
240.3	299.6	1389.8	185
30791.9	31821.4	122943.0	7855
419.6	797.4	16205.9	1205
1585.4	1585.4	483.7	65
24578.1	25061.5	92980.0	5640
398.6	460.5	164.4	6
3810.2	3916.6	13109.0	939

18-2 规模以上服务业按规模分主要经济指标（2018年）

单位：万元

指标	Item	企业单位数（个）Number of Enterprises (unit)	资产总计 Total Assets	固定资产原价 Original Value of Fixed Assets
总计	**Total**	**1670**	**83589990.5**	**47715297.2**
按企业规模分组	**Grouped by Size of Enterprises**			
大型企业	Large-size	167	49539254.0	41645103.7
中型企业	Medium-size	352	15108335.0	3156669.1
小型企业	Small-size	947	17104944.8	2418167.2
微型企业	Microenterprise	204	1837456.7	495357.2

18-2 续表1

单位：万元

指标	Item	销售费用 Sale Expenses	管理费用 Managenment Expenses	财务费用 Financial Expenses
总计	**Total**	**1258937.1**	**2485578.9**	**1256296.0**
按企业规模分组	**Grouped by Size of Enterprises**			
大型企业	Large-size	813088.1	1372238.4	964991.0
中型企业	Medium-size	253714.4	549377.3	108182.3
小型企业	Small-size	183017.6	512139.9	160092.2
微型企业	Microenterprise	9117.0	51823.3	23030.5

Main Economic Indicators for Services above the Designated Size grouped by Size of Enterprises（2018）

（10 000 yuan)

负债合计 Total Liabilities	所有者权益合计 Total Owners' Equities	营业收入 Paid in Capital	主营业务收入 Revenue from Principal Business	营业成本 Total Cost	主营业务成本 Cost of Principal Business
49777084.0	**33812906.5**	**25887537.8**	**25461070.3**	**19661919.2**	**19388622.1**
29022434.6	20516819.4	15037991.8	14806011.2	11005278.9	10855087.7
8976254.0	6132081.0	5127458.7	5031587.8	4033998.4	3975925.3
10840892.9	6264051.9	5195583.6	5119188.4	4207379.5	4159771.4
937502.5	899954.2	526503.7	504282.9	415262.4	397837.7

continued 1

（10 000 yuan)

投资收益 Investment Income	营业利润 Business Profits	利润总额 Total Profits	应付职工薪酬 Salary Payable	从业人员平均人数（人） Annual Average Employed Persons (person)
223023.6	**1588474.9**	**1582864.5**	**5114155.7**	**478344**
83379.6	1052816.6	1028086.4	3539710.2	261769
49693.0	253430.2	265128.5	868397.2	99113
80443.6	246102.7	252599.0	670633.9	111953
9507.4	36125.4	37050.6	35414.4	5509

18-3 规模以上服务业按行业分主要经济指标（2018年）

单位：万元

指　标	Item	企业单位数（个）Number of Enterprises (unit)	资产总计 Total Assets	固定资产原价 Original Value of Fixed Assets
总计	**Total**	**1670**	**83589990.5**	**47715297.2**
按国民经济行业大类分组	**Grouped by sector categories**			
铁路运输业	Railway transport industry	4	4626400.4	4828161.0
道路运输业	The road transport industry	126	27173024.2	20406176.1
水上运输业	Water transportation			
航空运输业	The air transport industry	13	3826194.8	3786739.2
管道运输业	Pipeline transportation	1	126427.4	16920.7
多式联运和运输代理业	Multimodal Transport and Transport Agent Industry	21	166518.8	50357.0
装卸搬运和仓储业	Loading, Unloading, Forwarding and Storage Industry	33	941163.1	231983.8
邮政业	The postal service	9	680288.3	490161.5
电信、广播电视和卫星传输服务业	Telecommunication, broadcasting and satellite transmission services	17	7841872.9	12697821.5
互联网和相关服务	The Internet and related services	45	431556.8	31271.0
软件和信息技术服务业	Software and information technology services	191	3626987.6	631246.9
物业管理	Property management	161	1258756.9	358624.2
房地产中介服务	Real estate intermediary service	8	24588.2	3722.0
其他房地产业	Other Real Estate	1	2044.8	543.9
房地产租赁经营	Owned Real Estate Business Activities	24	867254.7	260143.5
租赁业	Leasing industry	6	53565.2	37408.8
商务服务业	Business services	307	11910910.1	968371.0
研究和试验发展	Research and development	29	1182971.3	400511.0
专业技术服务业	Professional and technical services	232	6616770.9	737125.7
科技推广和应用服务业	Promotion and application of science and technology services	20	476946.6	127996.2
水利管理业	Water resources management industry	4	5760.1	1437.3
生态保护和环境治理业	Ecological protection and environmental control industries	8	185030.0	81339.2
公共设施管理业	Public facilities management industry	50	1536689.5	324107.2
土地管理业	Land Administration Industry	4	4361028.7	125179.3
居民服务业	Resident services	28	183388.6	87524.1
机动车、电子产品和日用产品修理业	Motor vehicles, electronics and household goods-repairing	18	177362.7	21568.9
其他服务业	Other service industries	18	26496.2	6220.7
教育	Education	18	99319.6	22149.5
卫生	Health	68	621217.4	318764.6
社会工作	Social work	1	307.9	6.5
新闻出版业	Press and publishing industry	30	480927.1	84216.7
广播、电视、电影和影视录音制作业	Radio, television, film and video recordings	84	739279.1	85704.2
文化艺术业	Culture and arts	45	2588941.2	306185.8
体育	Physical education	11	266621.8	37631.2
娱乐业	The entertainment industry	35	483377.6	147977.0

Main Economic Indicators for Services above the Designated Size grouped by Industry（2018）

（10 000 yuan）

负债合计 Total Liabilities	所有者权益合计 Total Owners' Equities	营业收入 Paid in Capital	主营业务收入 Revenue from Principal Business	营业成本 Total Cost	主营业务成本 Cost of Principal Business
49777084.0	**33812906.5**	**25887537.8**	**25461070.3**	**19661919.2**	**19388622.1**
3156519.9	1469880.5	750253.3	748206.5	661430.3	661260.4
16589802.6	10583221.6	2369889.5	2338279.7	1730563.2	1714364.9
1135328.1	2690866.7	501197.6	450048.9	444351.4	420101.6
107493.5	18933.9	127062.7	120865.5	125069.5	120535.6
91492.7	75026.1	238884.0	238884.0	198872.8	198853.7
762571.2	178591.9	632191.2	625017.0	596753.9	593948.0
478966.1	201322.2	756688.4	735863.0	631718.1	629763.2
3062455.9	4779417.0	4539839.0	4464135.0	3078658.6	2991545.5
162147.5	269409.3	715382.9	714665.0	531206.3	531050.6
2003741.1	1623246.5	3575542.5	3538048.3	2499322.2	2492971.1
930862.2	327894.7	681991.9	637078.2	531588.8	500579.8
13530.6	11057.6	21483.6	21483.6	8261.3	8261.3
1072.0	972.8	4305.2	3766.0	2037.1	1749.6
673022.8	194231.9	116066.4	104111.0	37286.9	36347.1
40177.9	13387.3	20547.7	20240.4	15218.5	14909.4
7869784.3	4041125.8	2801736.3	2780992.2	2302622.9	2277513.9
421843.1	761128.2	595850.7	560342.2	447841.4	418479.1
4259082.5	2357688.4	4609947.1	4584357.7	3789310.4	3773681.1
255841.4	221105.2	83723.0	82807.6	46479.2	46456.2
4169.3	1590.8	8357.1	8152.3	6341.1	6165.7
107252.1	77777.9	49290.6	47944.3	26625.8	26269.2
1005227.1	531462.4	489425.6	483804.7	360562.2	358419.9
3219778.2	1141250.5	442890.2	442292.5	333816.3	333816.3
188562.3	-5173.7	91565.3	91427.7	68660.6	68660.6
152185.2	25177.5	45771.3	45187.6	36772.5	36661.1
12104.5	14391.7	54000.7	53968.8	47062.6	47062.6
71312.2	28007.4	121320.6	120924.5	85248.0	83490.7
375623.8	245593.6	460370.6	456688.4	319126.7	313019.8
1898.8	-1590.9	553.1	553.1	587.1	587.1
234590.7	246336.4	299858.7	290566.5	227138.0	220593.3
482506.0	256773.1	397714.7	386008.0	304092.4	295728.7
1416409.7	1172531.5	169948.2	152690.0	81137.6	80845.4
100262.5	166359.3	44796.7	43962.1	35659.4	35384.4
389466.2	93911.4	69091.4	67708.0	50496.1	49545.2

18-3 续表1

单位：万元

指 标	Item	销售费用 Sale Expenses	管理费用 Managenment Expenses	财务费用 Financial Expenses
总计	**Total**	**1258937.1**	**2485578.9**	**1256296.0**
按国民经济行业大类分组	**Grouped by sector categories**			
铁路运输业	Railway transport industry	73.6	8512.2	135527.3
道路运输业	The road transport industry	14694.1	139909.9	751820.1
水上运输业	Water transportation			
航空运输业	The air transport industry	9585.0	52248.3	17959.8
管道运输业	Pipeline transportation	165.8	1994.7	-71.2
多式联运和运输代理业	Multimodal Transport and Transport Agent Industry	2108.3	16142.6	-56.1
装卸搬运和仓储业	Loading, Unloading, Forwarding and Storage Industry	15567.2	23000.5	14752.2
邮政业	The postal service	2742.4	114011.9	1934.9
电信、广播电视和卫星传输服务业	Telecommunication, broadcasting and satellite transmission services	595192.1	252797.7	49968.4
互联网和相关服务	The Internet and related services	36260.6	51738.4	-610.7
软件和信息技术服务业	Software and information technology services	111846.6	694564.6	16554.7
物业管理	Property management	16417.4	80633.7	12118.2
房地产中介服务	Real estate intermediary service	1414.8	7154.0	-34.2
其他房地产业	Other Real Estate		1633.1	-4.9
房地产租赁经营	Owned Real Estate Business Activities	4049.3	24543.5	15122.6
租赁业	Leasing industry	1638.5	2615.4	1233.7
商务服务业	Business services	119244.3	214656.9	150273.7
研究和试验发展	Research and development	13382.8	76952.4	1441.2
专业技术服务业	Professional and technical services	90673.6	367964.2	-2574.4
科技推广和应用服务业	Promotion and application of science and technology services	3806.8	36637.9	3697.9
水利管理业	Water resources management industry	65.4	1304.0	3.4
生态保护和环境治理业	Ecological protection and environmental control industries	7578.9	7576.1	1793.8
公共设施管理业	Public facilities management industry	21291.2	51118.6	2175.0
土地管理业	Land Administration Industry	5531.3	16532.9	37232.9
居民服务业	Resident services	12712.6	11883.9	248.9
机动车、电子产品和日用产品修理业	Motor vehicles, electronics and household goods-repairing	2469.1	4195.2	1781.1
其他服务业	Other service industries	1463.7	3856.2	2.3
教育	Education	8783.8	17564.4	274.3
卫生	Health	40606.4	70150.9	4912.6
社会工作	Social work		334.6	0.6
新闻出版业	Press and publishing industry	24083.5	40347.8	-1080.1
广播、电视、电影和影视录音制作业	Radio, television, film and video recordings	33219.2	39526.8	7567.8
文化艺术业	Culture and arts	47033.6	36371.0	17586.4
体育	Physical education	4985.3	5347.7	-346.6
娱乐业	The entertainment industry	10249.9	11756.9	15090.4

continued 1

(10 000 yuan)

投资收益 Investment Income	营业利润 Business Profits	利润总额 Total Profits	应付职工薪酬 Salary Payable	从业人员平均人数（人） Annual Average Employed Persons (person)
223023.6	**1588474.9**	**1582864.5**	**5114155.7**	**478344**
	-56582.1	-61815.7	5209.4	376
19013.9	-35990.9	-23918.3	595981.0	67582
14308.8	10593.4	10326.9	160291.3	9233
	-919.2	-761.6	9821.1	635
-121.5	34126.5	33359.0	26390.4	2839
1294.1	-4551.4	3616.3	24169.9	3294
	-869.2	-5032.0	225590.5	28399
7551.2	491597.3	478390.3	640709.7	43016
998.2	97620.1	99895.1	52334.0	5072
12590.9	291853.6	298651.5	1424488.1	70498
2002.9	43376.2	43739.1	214962.2	45015
515.5	4900.2	4879.5	8941.4	942
	610.3	-58.6	535.0	40
8126.6	39153.1	23282.7	11671.5	1715
	-306.4	-402.8	2770.0	301
92859.4	107073.6	106676.9	362929.9	65448
15741.9	63886.0	66954.6	160836.9	8330
17847.0	345821.3	325394.0	652397.6	55406
100.1	13269.1	13344.4	15780.0	1206
	607.4	610.2	953.6	157
1.8	6146.0	7220.0	11191.6	1079
2520.2	47490.6	47456.1	112002.1	17110
991.5	31364.1	30887.7	12248.0	879
276.3	-2307.6	-2531.0	25438.6	4984
1082.9	932.3	1993.2	5896.2	948
-320.9	702.8	519.3	28159.4	5369
15.5	9079.3	8921.6	33259.4	4624
3110.3	27211.9	28676.7	127209.3	16270
	-370.7	-379.7	415.2	81
769.6	11168.5	17306.4	53526.6	4295
2516.3	13306.3	16787.2	34633.5	4047
19030.5	15820.8	24907.4	52087.0	6049
	-1338.2	-1190.2	8182.5	1109
190.6	-16000.1	-14841.7	13142.8	1996

18-4 规模以上服务业按隶属关系分主要经济指标（2018年）

单位：万元

指标	Item	企业单位数（个）Number of Enterprises (unit)	资产总计 Total Assets	固定资产原价 Original Value of Fixed Assets
总计	**Total**	**1670**	**83589990.5**	**47715297.2**
按隶属关系分	**Grouped by affiliation**			
中央	Central	89	17653890.8	17313387.8
地方	Region	242	41329052.8	22952700.1
其他	Others	1339	24607046.9	7449209.3

18-4 续表1

单位：万元

指标	Item	销售费用 Sale Expenses	管理费用 Management Expenses	财务费用 Financial Expenses
总计	**Total**	**1258937.1**	**2485578.9**	**1256296.0**
按隶属关系分	**Grouped by affiliation**			
中央	Central	617882.4	577605.3	153612.8
地方	Region	161613.9	415192.1	878982.3
其他	Others	479440.8	1492781.5	223700.9

Main Economic Indicators for Services above the Designated Size grouped by Affiliation（2018）

（10 000 yuan)

负债合计 Total Liabilities	所有者权益合计 Total Owners' Equities	营业收入 Paid in Capital	主营业务收入 Revenue from Principal Business	营业成本 Total Cost	主营业务成本 Cost of Principal Business
49777084.0	**33812906.5**	**25887537.8**	**25461070.3**	**19661919.2**	**19388622.1**
9276390.4	8377500.4	9510944.0	9381881.0	7415031.1	7314796.0
24612521.5	16716531.3	4502104.5	4405110.5	3246583.5	3187868.4
15888172.1	8718874.8	11874489.3	11674078.8	9000304.6	8885957.7

continued 1

（10 000 yuan)

投资收益 Investment Income	营业利润 Business Profits	利润总额 Total Profits	应付职工薪酬 Salary Payable	从业人员平均人数（人） Annual Average Employed Persons (person)
223023.6	**1588474.9**	**1582864.5**	**5114155.7**	**478344**
30210.3	679121.2	627031.9	1346090.1	101370
89174.2	114004.2	131127.9	1075456.7	111183
103639.1	795349.5	824704.7	2692608.9	265791

主 要 统 计 指 标 解 释

国家统计局规模以上服务业单位统计标准：辖区内年营业收入1000万元及以上，或年末从业人员50人及以上服务业法人单位。包括：交通运输、仓储和邮政业，信息传输、软件和信息技术服务业，租赁和商务服务业，科学研究和技术服务业，水利、环境和公共设施管理业，教育，卫生和社会工作；以及物业管理、房地产中介服务、自有房地产经营活动和其他房地产业等行业。

辖区内年营业收入500万元及以上，或年末从业人员50人及以上服务业法人单位。包括：居民服务、修理和其他服务业，文化、体育和娱乐业。

固定资产原价 指固定资产的成本，包括企业在购置、自行建造、安装、改建、扩建、技术改造某项固定资产时所发生的全部支出总额。根据会计“固定资产”科目的期末借方余额填报。

资产总计 指企业过去的交易或者事项形成的、由企业拥有或者控制的、预期会给企业带来经济利益的资源。资产一般按流动性（资产的变现或耗用时间长短）分为流动资产和非流动资产。其中流动资产可分为货币资金、交易性金融资产、应收票据、应收账款、预付款项、其他应收款、存货等；非流动资产可分为长期股权投资、固定资产、无形资产及其他非流动资产等。根据会计“资产负债表”中“资产总计”项目的期末余额数填报。

执行《企业会计准则》或《小企业会计准则》的企业：资产总计=流动资产合计+非流动资产合计；执行其他企业会计制度的企业资产包括流动资产、长期投资、固定资产、无形资产和其他资产等。

负债合计 指企业过去的交易或者事项形成的，预期会导致经济利益流出企业的现时义务。负债一般按偿还期长短分为流动负债和非流动负债。根据会计“资产负债表”中“负债合计”项目的期末余额数填报。

执行《企业会计准则》或《小企业会计准则》的企业：负债合计=流动负债合计+非流动负债合计；执行其他企业会计制度的企业负债包括流动负债和长期负债。

所有者权益合计 指企业资产扣除负债后由所有者享有的剩余权益。公司的所有者权益又称股东权益。包括实收资本、资本公积、盈余公积、未分配利润等。根据会计“资产负债表”中“所有者权益合计”项目的期末余额数填报。

营业收入 指企业经营主要业务和其他业务所确认的收入总额。营业收入合计包括“主营业务收入”和“其他业务收入”。根据会计“利润表”中“营业收入”项目的本期金额数填报。

主营业务收入 指企业确认的销售商品、提供劳务等主营业务的收入。根据会计“主营业务收入”科目的期末贷方余额（结转前）填报。执行《企业会计准则》或《小企业会计准则》的企业，如未设置该科目，以“营业收入”代替填报。

营业成本 指企业经营主要业务和其他业务所发生的成本总额。包括企业（单位）在报告期内从事销售商品、提供劳务等日常活动发生的各种耗费。包括“主营业务成本”和“其他业务成本”。根据会计“利润表”中“营业成本”项目的本期金额数填报。

主营业务成本 指企业经营主要业务所发生的成本总额。根据会计“主营业务成本”科目的期末借方余额（结转前）填报。执行《企业会计准则》或《小企业会计准则》的企业，如未设置该科目，以“营业成本”代替填报。

销售费用 指企业在销售商品和材料、提供劳务的过程中发生的各种费用，包括保险费、包装费、展览费和广告费、商品维修费、预计产品质量保证损失、运输费、装卸费等以及为销售本企业商品而专设的销售机构（含销售网点、售后服务网点等）的职工薪酬、业务费、折旧费等经营费用。建筑业企业销售费用指企业从事施工生产活动过程中发生的各项费用，包括应由企业负担的运输费、装卸费、包装费、保险费、维修费、展览费、差旅费、广告费和其他经费。房地产企业销售费用指企业在从事主要经营业务过程中所发生的各项销售费用，包括转让、销售、结算和出租开发产品等。执行《企业会计准则》或《小企业会计准则》的企业，根据会计“利润表”中“销售费用”项目的本期金额数填报。执行其他企业会计制度的企业，根据会计“利润表”中“营业费用（或经营费用）”项目的本期金额数填报。

管理费用 指企业为组织和管理企业生产经营所发生的费用，包括企业在筹建期间内发生的开办费、董事会和行政管理部门在企业经营管理中发生的，或者应当由企业统一负担的公司经费等。根据会计“利润表”中“管理费用”项目的本期金额数填报。

财务费用 指企业为筹集生产经营所需资金等而发生的筹资费用，包括企业生产经营期间发生的利息支出（减利息收入）、汇兑损失（减汇兑收益）以及相关的手续费等。根据会计“利润表”中“财务费用”项目的本期金额数填报。

投资收益 指企业确认的投资收益或投资损失，反映企业以各种方式对外投资所取得的收益。根据会计

"利润表"中"投资收益"项目的本期金额数填报。如为投资损失以"-"号记。

营业利润 指企业从事生产经营活动所取得的利润。执行《企业会计准则》的企业，营业利润为营业收入减去营业成本、营业税金及附加、销售费用、管理费用、财务费用、资产减值损失，再加上公允价值变动收益和投资收益。执行《小企业会计准则》的企业，营业利润为营业收入减去营业成本，营业税金及附加、销售费用、管理费用、财务费用，再加上投资收益后的金额；执行其他企业会计制度的企业，营业利润为主营业务收入减去主营业务成本、主营业务税金及附加，加上其他业务利润后，再减去销售费用、管理费用、财务费用后的金额。根据会计"利润表"中"营业利润"项目的本期金额数填报。

利润总额 指企业在一定会计期间的经营成果，是生产经营过程中各种收入扣除各种耗费后的盈余，反映企业在报告期内实现的盈亏总额。根据会计"利润表"中"利润总额"项目的本期金额数填报。执行《企业会计准则》或《小企业会计准则》的企业，利润总额为营业利润加上营业外收入，减去营业外支出后的金额；执行其他企业会计制度的企业，利润总额为营业利润加上投资收益、政府补助、营业外收入，再减去营业外支出后的金额。

应付职工薪酬 指企业为获得职工提供的服务而给予各种形式的报酬以及其他相关支出。包括职工工资、奖金、津贴和补贴，职工福利费，医疗保险费、养老保险费、失业保险费、工伤保险费和生育保险费等社会保险费，住房公积金，工会经费和职工教育经费，非货币性福利，因解除与职工的劳动关系给予的补偿，其他与获得职工提供的服务相关的支出。执行《企业会计准则》或《小企业会计准则》的企业，根据会计科目"应付职工薪酬"的本年贷方累计发生额填报；执行其他企业会计制度的企业，应将本年上述职工薪酬包含的科目归并填报。

从业人员平均人数 指报告期内（年度、月度）平均拥有的人员数。按"谁用工，谁统计"的原则，包括正式人员，劳务派遣人员和临时聘用人员。

Explanatory Notes on Main Statistical Indicators

Statistical standard of the services unit above the designated size of the National Bureau of Statistics: The legal entities of the area whoseannual revenues are10 million yuan and above, or at the end of the service sector whose employees are more than 50 people.Including: transportation, storage and postal services, information transmission, software and information technology services, leasing and business services, scientific research and technological services, water conservancy, environment and public facilities management industry, education, health and social work as well as property management and real estate services industries.The legal entitiesof the area whoseannual revenues are 5 million yuan and above, or at the end of the service sector whose employees are more than 50 people.Including: service, repair and other services, cultural, sports and entertainment.

Original value of fixed assets: It refers to the cost of fixed assets, including the enterprise itself costs on the acquisition, construction, installation, alteration, expansion, technological innovation of an asset for all expenditure. Depending on the "fixed assets" account debit balance at the end of filling.

Total assets: It refers to the resourcesformed by past transactions or events, that the enterprise owns or controls, is expected to bring economic benefits to the enterprise. Asset is classified into current assets and non-current assets by its liquidity (realization of assets or spent time). Current assets can be divided into currency, tradable financial assets, notes receivable, accounts receivable, prepayments, other receivables and inventory; and non-current assets can be classified as equity investments, fixed assets, intangible assets and other non-current assets. It depends on the "balance sheet" of "total assets" closing balance number of items.

For business enterprisesthat implemented the 2006 accounting standard: total assets= total current assets +total non-current assets; for those who didn't implement the accounting standards, assets for business enterprises include current assets, long-term investments, fixed assets, intangible assets and other assets.

Total liabilities: It refers tothe present obligations of the enterprise that formed by past transactions or events and are expected to lead to an outflow of economic benefits. Liability is divided into current and non-current liabilities according to the length of the repayment period. It depends onthe "balance sheets" in the "total" closing balance number of items.

For business enterprises that implemented the 2006 accounting standard: total liabilities = total current liabilities+ total non-current liabilities; for those who didn't implement the accounting standards, liabilities include current liabilities and long-term liabilities.

Totalowners ' equity: It refers to the residual rights and interests enjoyed by the owner after deducting the liabilities of an enterprise. The owner of the company is also called the shareholder's right. It includes the paid in capital, capital reserves, surplus reserves, undistributed profit and so on. According to the accounting "balance sheet", "the owner's equity total", the final balance of the project is reported.

Operating income: It refers to the total revenue recognized by the business and other business operations of the enterprise. Total operating income includes "main business income" and "other business income". It's reported according to the "business income" project of the "business income" in the accounting "profit statement".

The main business income: It refers to the income of the business of the main business, such as the sale of goods, services, etc..It's reported in accordance with the final credit balance of the accounts of the subject's "main business income" (before the transfer). For business enterprises that didn't implement the accounting standard, if not set up the subject, should fill the forms instead of the "operating income".

Operating cost: It refers to the total cost incurred by the business and other business of the enterprise. It includes a variety of costs of enterprises (units) in the reporting period to engage in sales of goods, services and other daily activities provided.It includes"the main business costs" and "other business costs". According to the "operating cost" of the "business cost" of the project in accordance with the accounting statement.

The main business cost: It refers to the total cost of the main business. It's reported in accordance with the final debit balance of the subject of accounting "main business cost". For business enterprises that didn't implement the accounting standard, if not set up the subject, should fill the forms instead of the "operating costs".

Selling expenses: It refers to the expenses of the enterprisein sales of goods and materials and providing services, including insurance, packing, exhibition fees and advertising fees, maintenance of commodity, expected to ensure product quality loss, transportation, loading and unloading charges and sales of the enterprise products and dedicated sales organizations (including sales network and after-sales service network) employee compensation, business expenses, depreciation charges and operating expenses. Construction enterprises selling expenses refers to expenses occurring in the process of production enterprises engaged in construction activities, including transportation fee shall be borne by the enterprise, handling, packing, insurance, maintenance, exhibition fees, poor travel costs, advertising costs and other expenses. Real estate enterprise sales cost refers to the business in the main business process of the sales costs, including transfer, sales, settlement and rental development products, etc.. According to the "sales expense" in accounting "profit statement", the amount of the item in this period of the project is reported. For business enterprises that didn't implement the 2006 accounting standard, according to the number of "operating expenses (or operating expenses)" of the project in accordance with the "profit statement".

Management expenses: It refers to the expenses for the organization and management of enterprise production and management of the enterprises, including costs in construction occurred during the start-up costs, the board of directors and administrative departments in enterprise management, or shall be made by the enterprise unified burden of company funds. According to the "management fee" in the accounting "profit table", the amount of this period of the project is reported.

Financial expenses: It refers to the costs of the enterprise to raise the production and business operation required capital and funding, including occurred during the production and operation of enterprises interest payments (a reduction in interest income), exchange loss (less exchange gains) and related fees. It is reported according to the amount of the "financial expense" in the project of "financial expense" in the accounting "profit statement".

Investment income: It refers to the enterprise confirming the investment income or investment losses, reflecting the foreign investment income of the enterprise in various ways. According to the "investment income" in the accounting "profit statement", the amount of this period of the project is reported. Such as investment losses to "-".

Operating profit: It refers tothe profits made by the enterprises in the production and operation activities. For business enterprises that implemented the 2006 accounting standard, operating profit is revenues minus operating costs, business taxes and surcharges, sales, management costs, financial costs, asset impairment loss and plus fair value changes in income and investment income. Without executing the "accounting standards for business enterprises" enterprises, operating profit equals the main business income minus the cost of major business, main business tax and surcharges, and plus profit from other operations, then minus the cost of sales and management costs, financial costs. It is reported according to the number of "operating profit" items in the accounting "profit table".

Total profit: It refers to the business results of the enterprise in a certain accounting period, and it is the production and operation of various kinds of income after deducting the cost of earnings, reflecting the enterprise in the reporting period to achieve total profit and loss. According to the amount of the total amount of the total profit of the project in accordance with the accounting profit table. For business enterprises that implemented the 2006 accounting standard, the total profit is operating profit plus operating income, andminus operating expenses; while who didn't execute the " accounting standards for business enterprises", a total profit is operating profit plus return on investment, income subsidies, camp outside the industry income, andminus operating expenses.

Employee compensation: It refers tovarious forms of remuneration and other related expenses paid by the company for the services provided by the staff and workers. It includes wages, bonuses, allowances and subsidies, employee welfare benefit expenses, medical insurance, endowment insurance, unemployment insurance, work-related injury insurance premiums and maternity insurance fees social insurance, housing provident fund, the trade union funds and employee education funds, non-monetary benefits, for the solution in addition to give labor relations and workers compensation, and obtain a worker to provide other services related expenditure. For business enterprises that implemented the accounting standard, according to accounting subjects "to deal with workers' compensation" this year, the accumulated credits is filled; those who didn't execute the "accounting standards for business enterprises", it should be the employee compensation including the amalgamative course reportingthis year.

Average number of persons engaged in service

activities: It refers to the number of persons engaged in the service industry in the reporting period (annual, monthly). The principles of statistics is implemented according to the principle that "who labor, who statistics," including the official personnel, labor sent contingent personnel and temporaryemployeeswho take part in the enterprise service activities. And it don't include employees who receive wages, dividends, bonusas well as not participate in the service activities of the enterprise.

19 金融业

FINANCIAL INTERMEDIATION

资料整理：罗延庆
Data management:Luo Yanqing
数据审核：刘　婷
Data audit：Liu Ting

第十九部分　金融业

一、简要说明

本章资料包括金融、证券和保险业情况，由西安市统计局综合处根据人民银行西安分行营业管理部和市金融工作局提供资料整理。本部分为西安原口径数据。

二、主要指标

金融机构人民币（含外资）存款余额（亿元）	20948.18	比上年增长	4.5%
金融机构人民币（含外资）贷款余额（亿元）	19729.82	比上年增长	16.4%
保费收入（亿元）	478.56	比上年增长	13.6%

19　FINANCIAL INTERMEDIATION

Ⅰ.Brief Introduction

This chapter includes information of the financial, securities and insurance, compiled by Integration Division of the Xi'an Bureau of Statistics, according to data from Xi'an Branch Management Department of the People's Bank of China, Provincial Banking Bureau and Xi'an Financial Office. Data in this chapter is based on original range.

Ⅱ.Major Indicators

		Increase over Preceding Year
Deposits in Financial Institution(100 mil. yuan)	20948.18	4.5%
Loans in Financial Institutions(100 mil. yuan)	19729.82	16.4%
Premiums(100 mil. yuan)	478.56	13.6%

19-1 西安银行系统机构、人员数

Number of Institution and Employed Person in Finance System in Xi'an

机构名称	Name of Institution	2017 机构数（个）Number of Institution (unit)	2017 年末人数（人）Number of Staff and Workers (person)	2018 机构数（个）Number of Institution (unit)	2018 年末人数（人）Number of Staff and Workers (person)
合计	**Total**	**2132**	**39628**	**2111**	**39172**
1. 人民银行西安分行营业管理部	Management Department of the People's Bank of China Xi'an Branch	1	360	1	355
2. 国家开发银行	National Development Bank	1	193	1	205
3. 中国进出口银行	Export Import Bank of China	1	71	1	77
4. 中国工商银行	Industrial and Commercial Bank of China	184	4727	183	4562
5. 中国农业银行	Agricultural Bank of China	176	3134	166	3093
6. 中国银行	Bank of China	133	3525	129	3438
7. 中国建设银行	Construction Bank of China	204	4332	204	4374
8. 交通银行	Bank of Communication	58	1212	59	1191
9. 中国邮政储蓄银行	The Postal Savings Bank of China	275	858	270	866
10. 中国农业发展银行	Agricultural Development Bank of China	11	283	11	280
11. 中信银行	CITIC Bank	29	883	29	852
12. 中国光大银行	China Everbright Bank	44	920	45	915
13. 华夏银行	China Huaxia Bank	20	857	24	797
14. 广发银行	China Guangfa Bank	2	192	9	206
15. 平安银行	Pingan Bank	12	384	12	404
16. 招商银行	China Merchants Bank	55	1571	55	1535
17. 上海浦东发展银行	Pufa Bank	39	684	35	665
18. 兴业银行	Fujian Industrial Bank	70	837	60	825
19. 中国民生银行	China Minsheng Banking	21	1008	22	1086
20. 恒丰银行	Evergrowing Bank	17	441	17	417
21. 浙商银行	China Zheshang Bank	8	456	10	490
22. 渤海银行	China Bohai Bank	1	124	2	133
23. 北京银行	Bank of Beijing	22	836	24	813
24. 齐商银行	Qi Commercial Bank	8	229	8	221
25. 成都银行	Bank of Chengdu	6	184	6	177
26. 重庆银行	Bank of Chongqing	6	275	6	290
27. 宁夏银行	Bank of Ningxia	7	236	7	230
28. 昆仑银行	Bank of Kunlun	15	436	15	447
29. 西安银行	Bank of Xi'an	145	2586	144	2596
30. 长安银行	Bank of Changan	59	761	59	710
31. 农村商业银行	Rural Commercial Bank	343	4632	406	5503
其中：秦农银行	Qinnong Bank	235	3448	298	4380
32. 农村信用社	Rural Credit Cooperatives	136	1808	67	841
33. 村镇银行	Village Bank	11	266	11	248
34. 香港汇丰银行	Huifeng Bank of Hong Kong	3	41	3	40
35. 香港东亚银行	Dongya Bank of Hong Kong	6	217	6	177
36. 新加坡星展银行	DBS Bank	1	13	1	15
37. 英国标准渣打银行	British Standard Chartered Bank	1	22	1	34
38. 韩亚银行	Hana Bank	1	34	1	37
39. 富邦华一银行	Fubon Bank			1	27

注：本表数据来源于人民银行西安分行营管部。

19-2 金融机构（含外资）本外币存贷款年末余额（2018年）

Deposits and Loans of Local Currency and Foreign Currency in Financial Institution (Including Foreign-Funded Institution)at Year-end（2018）

单位：万元 (10 000 yuan)

指 标	Item	2018	比年初增减额 Increase or Decrease Compared with The Beginning of The Year
一、各项存款	**All Deposits**	**212667159**	**8886151**
（一）境内存款	Domestic Deposits	212417473	8905550
1. 住户存款	Household Deposits	84654980	8672362
（1）活期存款	Demand Deposits	32660353	2502787
（2）定期及其他存款	Time and Other Deposits	51994627	6169575
2. 非金融企业存款	Non Financial Enterprises Deposits	83183098	-879074
（1）活期存款	Demand Deposits	44137408	240597
（2）定期及其他存款	Time and Other Deposits	39045690	-1119671
3. 广义政府存款	General Government Deposits	37250732	1065255
（1）财政性存款	Fiscal Deposits	1511425	-1637425
（2）机关团体存款	Institution Deposits	35739307	2702680
4. 非银行业金融机构存款	Non Banking Financial Institution Deposits	7328663	47007
（二）境外存款	Foreign Deposits	249686	-19399
二、各项贷款	**All Loans**	**198915956**	**27097453**
（一）境内贷款	Domestic Loans	198709839	27036670
1. 住户贷款	Household loans	52094087	11891387
（1）短期贷款	Short-term Loans	5901844	1564179
消费贷款	Consumer loans	3710606	1327999
经营贷款	Business loans	2191237	236180
（2）中长期贷款	Medium-term and Long-term loans	46192243	10327208
消费贷款	Consumer loans	42544090	9787947
经营贷款	Business loans	3648154	539261
2. 非金融企业及机关团体贷款	Non Financial Enterprises and Institution Loans	146613895	15145382
（1）短期贷款	Short-term Loans	28389919	1238684
（2）中长期贷款	Medium-term and Long-term loans	107834866	9211345
（3）票据融资	Bill Financing	10128745	4589252
（4）融资租赁	Financial Leasing	7096	-7389
（5）各项垫款	Various Advance Funds	253269	113490
3. 非银行业金融机构贷款	Non Banking Financial Institution Loans	1857	-98
（二）境外贷款	Foreign Loans	206117	60783

注：本表数据来源于人民银行西安分行营管部。

19-3 金融机构（不含外资）本外币存贷款年末余额（2018年）

Deposits and Loans Domestic Funded Financial Institution of Local Currency and Foreign Currency at Year-end（2018）

单位：万元 （10 000 yuan）

指 标	Item	2018	比年初增减额 Increase or Decrease Compared with The Beginning of The Year
一、各项存款	**All Deposits**	**211101151**	**8524569**
（一）境内存款	Domestic Deposits	210877760	8541172
1. 住户存款	Household Deposits	84448815	8671031
（1）活期存款	Demand Deposits	32603017	2504453
（2）定期及其他存款	Time and Other Deposits	51845798	6166578
2. 非金融企业存款	Non Financial Enterprises Deposits	81872664	-1348404
（1）活期存款	Demand Deposits	43844317	195747
（2）定期及其他存款	Time and Other Deposits	38028347	-1544151
3. 广义政府存款	General Government Deposits	37247619	1121539
（1）财政性存款	Fiscal Deposits	1511425	-1637425
（2）机关团体存款	Institution Deposits	35736193	2758964
4. 非银行业金融机构存款	Non Banking Financial Institution Deposits	7308662	97006
（二）境外存款	Foreign Deposits	223390	-16603
二、各项贷款	**All Loans**	**197693090**	**27115694**
（一）境内贷款	Domestic Loans	197514590	27079154
1. 住户贷款	Household loans	52009574	11905933
（1）短期贷款	Short-term Loans	5901844	1564544
消费贷款	Consumer loans	3710606	1327999
经营贷款	Business loans	2191237	236545
（2）中长期贷款	Medium-term and Long-term loans	46107730	10341389
消费贷款	Consumer loans	42475066	9793663
经营贷款	Business loans	3632664	547726
2. 非金融企业及机关团体贷款	Non Financial Enterprises and Institution Loans	145503159	15173319
（1）短期贷款	Short-term Loans	28185581	1187214
（2）中长期贷款	Medium-term and Long-term loans	106946615	9300366
（3）票据融资	Bill Financing	10110620	4579638
（4）融资租赁	Financial Leasing	7096	-7389
（5）各项垫款	Various Advance Funds	253247	113490
3. 非银行业金融机构贷款	Non Banking Financial Institution Loans	1857	-98
（二）境外贷款	Foreign Loans	178500	36540

注：本表数据来源于人民银行西安分行营管部。

19-4 主要年份金融机构（含外资）人民币存贷款年末余额

Deposits and Loans in Financial Institutions (Including Foreign-funded) in Representative Years

单位：亿元 (100million yuan)

年 份 Year	存款年末余额（亿元） Balance of Deposit at Year-end	非金融企业存款 Non Financial Enterprises Deposits	住户存款 Household Deposits	贷款年末余额 Balance of Loan at Year-end
1978	11.66		2.57	21.72
1980	17.02		4.22	23.08
1985	40.64		14.26	49.08
1990	146.17	31.10	77.09	152.77
1995	471.89	114.54	291.46	403.16
1996	619.98	199.85	394.02	477.97
1997	686.72	227.61	433.56	503.32
1998	799.54	245.44	499.68	597.34
1999	1014.27	347.49	586.40	786.20
2000	1335.63	540.19	675.83	972.51
2001	1629.72	674.49	800.86	1185.97
2002	2191.47	884.69	988.04	1598.42
2003	2665.87	1041.43	1210.56	1954.18
2004	3061.66	1159.98	1432.86	2052.33
2005	3599.70	1237.37	1716.76	2158.10
2006	4066.16	1374.91	1950.53	2344.77
2007	4582.71	1702.12	2002.38	2683.77
2008	5749.37	2213.67	2513.70	3275.12
2009	7522.08	3077.99	3084.20	4482.63
2010	8933.23	3556.78	3641.09	6482.28
2011	10430.27	5997.60	4155.65	7564.93
2012	12125.53	6927.84	4787.03	8635.22
2013	13763.19	7759.61	5357.05	10023.63
2014	15166.78	8604.03	5698.15	11668.14
2015	17796.38	7031.75	6571.18	13714.02
2016	19073.96	7788.07	7035.81	15282.65
2017	20047.62	8203.27	7497.30	16954.81
2018	20948.18	8125.23	8360.33	19729.82

注：本表数据来源于人民银行西安分行营管部，对部分历史年份数据进行了修订。

19-5 金融机构（含外资）人民币存贷款年末余额（2018年）

Year-end Balance of RMB Deposits and Loans in Financial Institutions（Including Foreign-funded）（2018）

单位：万元 (10 000 yuan)

指 标	Item	2018	比年初增减额 Increase or Decrease Compared with The Beginning of The Year
一、各项存款	**All Deposits**	**209481810**	**9005748**
（一）境内存款	Domestic Deposits	209355980	8981666
1. 住户存款	Household Deposits	83603290	8618303
（1）活期存款	Demand Deposits	32102938	2465451
（2）定期及其他存款	Time and Other Deposits	51500352	6152852
2. 非金融企业存款	Non Financial Enterprises Deposits	81252346	-755306
（1）活期存款	Demand Deposits	43222289	457990
（2）定期及其他存款	Time and Other Deposits	38030057	-1213296
3. 广义政府存款	General Government Deposits	37224704	1070392
（1）财政性存款	Fiscal Deposits	1511425	-1637424
（2）机关团体存款	Institution Deposits	35713279	2707816
4. 非银行业金融机构存款	Non Banking Financial Institution Deposits	7275640	48277
（二）境外存款	Foreign Deposits	125830	24082
二、各项贷款	**All Loans**	**197298208**	**27539215**
（一）境内贷款	Domestic Loans	197285671	27535526
1. 住户贷款	Household loans	52092418	11891339
（1）短期贷款	Short-term Loans	5900206	1564112
消费贷款	Consumer loans	3708969	1327932
经营贷款	Business loans	2191237	236180
（2）中长期贷款	Medium-term and Long-term loans	46192212	10327227
消费贷款	Consumer loans	42544058	9787966
经营贷款	Business loans	3648154	539261
2. 非金融企业及机关团体贷款	Non Financial Enterprises and Institution Loans	145191396	15644285
（1）短期贷款	Short-term Loans	27581620	1364259
（2）中长期贷款	Medium-term and Long-term loans	107221641	9580949
（3）票据融资	Bill Financing	10128745	4589252
（4）融资租赁	Financial Leasing	7096	-7389
（5）各项垫款	Various Advance Funds	252293	117214
3. 非银行业金融机构贷款	Non Banking Financial Institution Loans	1857	-98
（二）境外贷款	Foreign Loans	12537	3689

注：本表数据来源于人民银行西安分行营管部。

19-6 金融机构（不含外资）人民币存贷款年末余额（2018年）

Year-end Balance of RMB Deposits and Loans in Financial Institutions (Not Including Foreign-funded) (2018)

单位：万元 (10 000 yuan)

指 标	Item	2018	比年初增减额 Increase or Decrease Compared with The Beginning of The Year
一、各项存款	**All Deposits**	**208119543**	**8685532**
（一）境内存款	Domestic Deposits	208001474	8663469
1. 住户存款	Household Deposits	83446125	8629103
（1）活期存款	Demand Deposits	32063855	2470384
（2）定期及其他存款	Time and Other Deposits	51382270	6158719
2. 非金融企业存款	Non Financial Enterprises Deposits	80078119	-1190585
（1）活期存款	Demand Deposits	43041794	447833
（2）定期及其他存款	Time and Other Deposits	37036325	-1638418
3. 广义政府存款	General Government Deposits	37221591	1126675
（1）财政性存款	Fiscal Deposits	1511426	-1637425
（2）机关团体存款	Institution Deposits	35710165	2764100
4. 非银行业金融机构存款	Non Banking Financial Institution Deposits	7255639	98276
（二）境外存款	Foreign Deposits	118069	22063
二、各项贷款	**All Loans**	**196108758**	**27583074**
（一）境内贷款	Domestic Loans	196096907	27579217
1. 住户贷款	Household loans	52007905	11905885
（1）短期贷款	Short-term Loans	5900206	1564477
消费贷款	Consumer loans	3708969	1327932
经营贷款	Business loans	2191237	236545
（2）中长期贷款	Medium-term and Long-term loans	46107699	10341408
消费贷款	Consumer loans	42475035	9793682
经营贷款	Business loans	3632664	547726
2. 非金融企业及机关团体贷款	Non Financial Enterprises and Institution Loans	144087145	15673430
（1）短期贷款	Short-term Loans	27383767	1313998
（2）中长期贷款	Medium-term and Long-term loans	106333390	9669970
（3）票据融资	Bill Financing	10110620	4579638
（4）融资租赁	Financial Leasing	7096	-7389
（5）各项垫款	Various Advance Funds	252272	117213
3. 非银行业金融机构贷款	Non Banking Financial Institution Loans	1857	-98
（二）境外贷款	Foreign Loans	11851	3857

注：本表数据来源于人民银行西安分行营管部。

19-7 保险业务情况

Indicators of Insurance Business

指　标	Item	2014	2015	2016	2017	2018
保险金额（亿元）	**Amount Insured(100 million yuan)**	**51454**	**62319**	**108296**	**151617**	**191547**
保费收入（万元）	**Premiums(10 000 yuan)**	**2194924**	**2630158**	**3458459**	**4211039**	**4785554**
一、财产险（万元）	**Property Insurance(10 000 yuan)**	**741762**	**835526**	**933181**	**1037060**	**1125618**
（一）财产保险	Property Insurance	668574	746317	833296	916524	959618
1. 机动车辆及第三者责任	Motor Vehicle and Outside Person Liability	602904	674555	738965	821186	862137
2. 企业财产险	Enterprise Property Insurance	41996	49949	64568	62226	65716
3. 货物运输险	Freight Transport Insurance	4427	5497	4814	5314	6777
4. 家庭财产险	Family Property Insurance	584	754	981	1385	1772
5. 建工及安工保险及其责任险	Construction and Installation Projects Insurance and Related Liability Insurance	16893	12325	18368	20001	17174
6. 其他	Others	1770	3237	5600	6412	6042
（二）责任保险	Liability Insurance	16328	23096	26922	32136	38508
（三）信用保险	Export Credit Insurance	8401	10449	17563	14733	10114
（四）保证保险	Guarantee Insurance	36868	45472	42665	60814	100393
（五）农业保险	Agriculture Insurance	11591	10192	12735	12853	16985
二、人身险（万元）	**Personnel Insurance(10 000 yuan)**	**1453162**	**1794632**	**2525278**	**3173979**	**3659936**
（一）人寿保险	Life Insurance	1238142	1506062	2158260	2625509	3023129
1. 非分红保险	Non Dividend Insurance	444520	681952	1261138	1554807	1355990
2. 分红保险	Dividend Insurance	780652	810889	882110	1055099	1651416
3. 投资连接保险	Insurance Connection Insurance	316	286	236	217	212
4. 万能保险	Universal Insurance	12654	12935	14776	15386	15512
（二）意外伤害险	Unforeseen Injury Insurance	52963	63450	71888	84603	112382
（三）健康保险	Health Insurance	162057	225120	295130	463867	524426
赔款支出和各项给付	**Indemnity and Other Expenditure**	**807652**	**876182**	**1159143**	**1187057**	**1308241**
一、财产险（万元）	**Property Insurance(10 000 yuan)**	**372906**	**406530**	**422765**	**489353**	**553641**
（一）财产保险	Property Insurance	360385	375449	393905	452892	497773
1. 机动车辆及第三者责任	Motor Vehicle and Outside Person Liability	327319	348185	359288	393011	459840
2. 企业财产险	Enterprise Property Insurance	22257	16753	22038	30811	20020
3. 家庭财产保险	Family Property Insurance	107	112	324	757	4565
4. 货物运输保险	Freight Transport Insurance	2429	999	1341	2427	1376
5. 建工及安工保险及其责任险	Construction and Installation Projects Insurance and Related Liability Insurance	6719	8023	9741	12471	9683
6. 其他	Others	1554	1377	1173	13414	2309
（二）责任保险	Liability Insurance	5695	6300	11030	12703	14948
（三）信用保险	Export Credit Insurance	1668	7884	3287	3346	5273
（四）保证保险	Guarantee Insurance	2752	13129	10690	11597	23608
（五）农业保险	Agriculture Insurance	2406	3768	3853	8816	12039
二、人身险（万元）	**Personnel Insurance(10 000 yuan)**	**434746**	**469652**	**736378**	**697704**	**754600**
（一）人寿保险	Life Insurance	360895	379370	637444	557798	581062
1. 非分红保险	Non Dividend Insurance	44359	56908	82635	136279	138591
2. 分红保险	Dividend Insurance	313706	318993	551206	418013	438997
3. 投资连接保险	Insurance Connection Insurance	33	48	485	162	35
4. 万能保险	Universal Insurance	2797	3421	3118	3344	3438
（二）意外伤害险	Unforeseen Injury Insurance	11438	16796	15577	19939	23621
（三）健康保险	Health Insurance	62413	73486	83357	119967	149917
退保金（万元）	**Withdrawal(10 000 yuan)**	**405676**	**433227**	**482983**	**682534**	**762277**
#人寿保险	Life Insurance	403099	414260	459733	659965	751597
1. 非分红保险	Non Dividend Insurance	20818	195551	276544	524211	582955
2. 分红保险	Dividend Insurance	382274	218693	183191	135723	168632
3. 投资连接保险	Insurance Connection Insurance					
4. 万能保险	Universal Insurance	7	16	-2	31	11

注：本表数据来源于市金融工作局。

19-8 西安地区证券期货系统机构、人员数

Number of Institution and Employed Person in Securities and Futures System in Xi'an

机构名称	Name of Institution	2017		2018	
		机构数（个）Number of Institution (unit)	年末人数（人）Number of Staff and Workers (person)	机构数（个）Number of Institution (unit)	年末人数（人）Number of Staff and Workers (person)
证券经营机构	**Securities Company and the Sales Department**	**376**	**8961**	**403**	**8718**
一、证券公司	**Securities Company**	**209**	**5238**	**225**	**5102**
西部证券股份有限公司	Western Securities Company Ltd.	116	2693	116	2568
陕西开源证券经纪有限责任公司	KaiYuan Securities Company Ltd.	67	1883	75	1838
中邮证券有限公司	China Post Securities	26	662	34	696
二、证券营业部（含外地公司在西安营业部）	**Sales Department (include Xi'an departments of nonlocal companies.)**	**167**	**3723**	**178**	**3616**
期货经纪公司	**Futures Company**	**30**	**526**	**34**	**552**
迈科期货经纪有限公司	Maike Futures Company Ltd.	10	211	11	214
陕西长安期货经纪有限公司	Shanxi ChangAn Futures Company Ltd.	11	128	11	193
西部期货经纪有限公司	Western Futures Brokerage Co., Ltd.	9	187	12	145

注：1.本表数据来源于市金融工作局。
2.证券公司包括三家公司及其在西安和外地的营业部。
3.中邮证券有限公司原为西安华弘证券经纪有限责任公司。

19-9 证券期货市场基本情况（2018年）

Basic Facts on Securities and Futures Markets（2018）

指 标	Item	2018
一、上市公司情况	**Listed Securities Companies**	
拥有上市股份公司（个）	Number of Listed Share-holding Companies(unit)	34
上市股份公司总股本（亿股）	Total Capital of Listed Share-holding Companies (100 millon shares)	550.02
#流通股(亿股)	Negotiable Shares(100 million shares)	482.08
总市值（亿元）	Total Market Capitalization(100 million yuan)	3838.09
本期证券市场筹措资金（亿元）	Financing in the Current Stock Marke (100 millon yuan)	238.50
二、证券经营机构情况	**Securities Trading Organizations**	
拥有证券公司（个）	Number of Securities Companies(unit)	3
证券营业部（个）（含外地公司在西安营业部）	Number of Securities Business Departments(unit)	188
投资者开户数（万户）	Number of Investors Who have Opened an Account(10 000 accounts)	366.66
证券交易总额（亿元）	Total Turnover(100 million yuan)	32892.35
三、期货市场情况	**Futures Market**	
拥有期货经纪公司（个）	Number of Futures Business Management Companies(unit)	3
期货分支机构（个）	Number of Branches(unit)	30
期货代理交易额（亿元）	Total Transaction Value in Futures Commissioning (100 million yuan)	22408.17
每个经纪公司平均拥有注册资金（万元）	Average Registered Capital of Each Business Management Company(10 000 yuan)	39300

注：本表数据来源于市金融工作局；期货分支机构、代理交易额数据为西安本市和外地公司在西安市口径数据。

主 要 统 计 指 标 解 释

存款 指企业、机关、团体或居民根据资金必须收回的原则，把货币资金存入银行或其他信贷机构保管并取得一定利息的一种信用活动形式。根据存款对象或性质的不同可划分为企业存款、财政存款、机关团体存款、住户存款、信托及委托类存款、其他存款等科目。它是银行信贷资金的主要来源。

贷款 指银行或其他信贷机构根据资金必须归还的原则，按一定利率，为企业、个人等提供资金的一种信用活动形式。我国银行贷款分为短期贷款、中长期贷款、融资租凭、票据融资等。

保险金额 指保险人承担赔偿或者给付保险金责任的最高限额。

保费 指投保人为取得保险人在约定范围内所承担赔偿责任而支付给保险人的费用。

赔款 指保险人根据保险合同的规定，向被保险人支付的赔偿保险责任损失的金额。

给付 包括死伤医疗给付和满期给付。死伤医疗给付是指保险人根据人寿保险及长期健康保险合同的规定，因被保险人在保险期内发生保险责任范围内的保险事故支付给被保险人（或受益人）的金额。满期给付是指被保险人生存期满，保险人按人寿保险合同规定支付给被保险人的满期保险金额。

Explanatory Notes on Main Statistical Indicators

Deposit is a form of credit by which enterprises, institutions, organizations or households can put money into banks and other credit institutions for safekeeping and interest earning under the principle of free withdrawal. According to different depositors, deposits are divided into enterprise deposits, fiscal deposits, deposits of government agencies and organizations, savings deposits of rural and household deposits, agricultural savings deposits, entrusted deposits and other deposits. Deposits are major sources of the credit funds of banks.

Loan is a form of credit by which banks and other credit institutions provide funds at certain interest rate to enterprises and individuals in the light of the principle of unconditional repayment. Loans from Chinese banks include short-term loan, medium and long term loans, finance lease and other bill finance.

Amount Insured refers to the maximum that the insurant will get for the claim of the case insured.

Premium is the fee paid by the insurant to the insurer to obtain the obligation of compensation from the insurance within the agreed terms.

Settled Claim is the compensation paid by the insurer to the insurant in accordance with the insurance contract.

Payment includes payment for death, injury or medical treatment and payment at maturity. Payment for death, injury or medical treatment refers to the money paid to the insurant (or the beneficiary) in accordance with the life or health insurance contract when the insurant encounters accidents within the insured period covered in the contract. Payment at maturity refers to the payment to the insurant in accordance with the life insurance contract at the end of the insured period.

20 教育和科技

EDUCATION,SCIENCE AND TECHNOLOGY

资料整理：郝　静　陈春光
Data management：Hao Jing Chen Chunguang
数据审核：王金桂
Data audit：Wang Jingui

第二十部分　教育和科技

一、简要说明

本章资料包括教育事业、科技事业基本情况，由西安市统计局服务业和社会科技处根据西安市教育局等有关部门提供资料整理。本章资料数据口径见表下备注。科技部分因数据来源较晚，故从2018年起错年使用。

二、主要指标

普通高等学校数（所）	63	与上年	持平
普通高等学校（本专科）在校学生（万人）	71.28	比上年减少	1.40万人
高等学校研究生在校人数（万人）	11.16	比上年增加	0.81万人

20　EDUCATION,SCIENCE AND TECHNOLOGY

Ⅰ.Brief Introduction

Data in this chapter consists of primarily data of educational undertakings, science and technology activities of Xi'an city, compiled by Tertiary Industry and Social & Science and Technology Division of the Xi'an Bureau of Statistics according to data from Xi'an Bureau of Education concerned. Field and range of data are Listed in the explanatory notes below the chart, because of their large differences. Data of science and technology.

Ⅱ Major Indicators

		Increase over Preceding Year
Number of Regular Institutions of Higher Education(unit)	63	essentially on a par with last year's
Student Enrollment of Regular Institutions of Higher Education (Universities and colleges) (10 000 persons)	71.28	−1.40（10 000 persons）
Postgraduates Enrollment of Regular Institutions of Higher Education (10 000 persons)	11.16	0.81（10 000 persons）

20-1 主要年份各类普通教育基本情况

Basic Statistics on Regular Eduction in Representative Years

指 标	Item	2010	2012	2013	2014	2015	2016	2017	2018
学校数（所）	**Number of Schools (units)**								
普通高等学校	Regular Institutions of Higher Education	50	62	63	63	63	63	63	63
普通中等专业学校	Regular Specialized Secondary Schools	28	24	22	22	20	20	16	15
普通中学	Regular Secondary School	436	419	418	421	422	422	448	456
小学	Primary Schools	1531	1322	1291	1257	1234	1190	1125	1130
幼儿园	Kindergarten	1004	1239	1295	1343	1417	1475	1605	1780
毕业生人数（万人）	**Graduates (10 000 persons)**								
普通高等学校	Regular Institutions of Higher Education	18.3	20.9	20.17	21.27	23.23	24.06	23.07	23.21
普通中等专业学校	Regular Specialized Secondary Schools	2.5	2.1	1.93	1.76	1.32	1.25	1.06	0.84
普通中学	Regular Secondary School	17.0	15.6	15.24	14.54	13.92	13.96	13.89	13.50
小学	Primary Schools	9.6	8.9	8.51	8.29	7.85	8.46	9.06	9.32
幼儿园	Kindergarten	5.4	7.6	8.42	8.90	10.01	9.81	10.79	11.41
招生数（万人）	**New Enrollment (10 000 persons)**								
普通高等学校	Regular Institutions of Higher Education	21.7	25.2	23.88	23.58	23.41	23.08	23.70	23.67
普通中等专业学校	Regular Specialized Secondary Schools	2.1	1.7	1.35	1.25	0.95	0.88	0.96	0.83
普通中学	Regular Secondary School	16.2	15.0	14.47	13.97	13.41	13.72	14.08	14.37
小学	Primary Schools	8.6	8.9	9.56	10.13	10.51	11.65	13.13	15.16
幼儿园	Kindergarten	8.4	11.6	11.00	9.55	11.96	13.65	13.98	13.03
在校学生数（万人）	**Total Enrollment (10 000 persons)**								
普通高等学校	Regular Institutions of Higher Education	73.3	80.7	83.83	85.42	84.83	83.10	83.02	82.44
普通中等专业学校	Regular Specialized Secondary Schools	6.8	5.4	4.66	4.07	3.47	3.11	2.74	2.48
普通中学	Regular Secondary School	48.9	45.3	43.73	42.57	41.37	40.70	41.74	42.46
小学	Primary Schools	51.6	50.9	51.95	53.79	56.62	59.79	66.68	73.09
幼儿园	Kindergarten	18.4	27.1	28.56	28.95	30.90	31.80	34.81	35.40
教职工数（人）	**Staff and Teachers (persons)**								
普通高等学校	Regular Institutions of Higher Education	72247	74041	74993	74954	74857	73686	74218	75609
普通中等专业学校	Regular Specialized Secondary Schools	3249	2733	2599	2315	1991	1917	1556	1529
普通中学	Regular Secondary School	39207	41197	41003	40576	40689	41352	44546	45390
小学	Primary Schools	34118	32208	31863	32162	32585	34646	38494	41122
幼儿园	Kindergarten	18710	27735	31989	33062	36004	39753	44895	49604
专任教师（人）	**Number of Full-time Teachers (persons)**								
普通高等学校	Regular Institutions of Higher Education	42098	44487	46436	46766	47768	47158	47917	49018
普通中等专业学校	Regular Specialized Secondary Schools	1845	1595	1474	1346	1228	1210	998	958
普通中学	Regular Secondary School	31506	31526	31419	32615	33014	33962	36565	37539
小学	Primary Schools	29944	29651	29421	28395	28748	30941	34163	36878
幼儿园	Kindergarten	10638	14293	16238	17337	19096	21395	23789	25823

注：1.本表数据来源于市教育局。

2.本表中普通高等学校毕业生、招生、在校生数含普通高等学校研究生及普通高等学校本、专科学生。

3.本表中小学的学校数是指独立小学个数，其在校生、教职工等指标均为普通初等教育；幼儿园的校数是指独立的幼儿园个数，其在校生、教职工等指标均为学前教育。（下表同）

4.本表中普通中学学生数据为普通中等教育口径，小学学生数为普通初等教育口径，幼儿园学生数为学前教育口径。

5.本表2017年及以后年份数据含西咸新区。

20-2 各级各类学校、教职工情况（2018年）

Situation of All Kinds of Schools and Staff Members at All Levels （2018）

指　标	Item	学校数（所）Number of Schools (units)	教职工数（人）Number of Staff and Teachers (persons)	专任教师数（人）Full-time Teachers (persons)
一、高等教育	**Higher education**	**75**	**77946**	**50188**
（一）研究生培养机构	Postgraduate training institutions	(44)		
1、普通高校	Institutions of Higher Schools	(23)		
2、科研机构	Scientific Research Institution	(21)		
（二）普通高等学校	Regular Institutions of Higher Schools	63	75609	49018
1、本科院校	Universities and Colleges of Undergraduate Course	42	65268	41934
其中：独立学院	Non-university Tertiary	11	5848	3824
2、专科院校	Higher Vocational Colleges	21	10341	7084
其中：高等职业学校	Higher Vocational College	19	8928	6310
（三）成人高等学校	Adult Higher Schools	12	2337	1170
二、中等职业教育	**Secondary Occupation Education**	**147**	**11581**	**8721**
(一)普通中等专业学校	Regular Specialized Secondary Schools	15	1529	958
(二)成人中等专业学校	Adult Secondary Specialized Schools	2	153	72
其中：市属	Municipal schools			
(三)职业高中学校	Vocational Hight Schools	60	3499	2584
其中：市属	Municipal schools	60	3499	2584
(四)技工学校	Technical Schools	70	6400	5107
其中：市属	Municipal schools	30	2244	1881
三、基础教育	**Elementary Education**	**3376**	**136537**	**100543**
（一）普通中等教育	Regular Institutions Education	456	45390	37539
1、高中	Senior High Schools	166		20487
完全中学	Complete Secondary Schools	102	14146	11791
高级中学	Senior Secondary Schools	50	7688	6309
十二年一贯制学校	Twelve-year Consistency Schools	14	2954	2387
2、初中	Junior Middle Schools	290		17052
初级中学	Junior Middle Schools	237	15677	12956
九年一贯制学校	Nine-year Consistency Schools	53	4925	4096
完全中学	Complete Secondary school	(102)		
十二年一贯制学校	Twelve-year Consistency schools	(14)		
附设普通初中班的学校	Senior Secondary Schools with Regular Junior Secondary Classes	(1)		
（二）普通初等教育	Regular Primary Education	1130	41122	36878
独立小学	Independent Primary Schools	1130		35307
教学点	Teaching Points	(286)		1571
九年一贯制学校	Nine-year Consistency schools	(53)		
十二年一贯制学校	Twelve-year Consistency schools	(14)		
附设小学班的学校	Schools with Primary Classes	(4)		
（三）特殊教育	Special Education Schools	9	379	271
特殊教育学校	Special Education Schools	9	379	271
附设特教班的学校	Schools with Special Edution Classes	(1)		
（四）工读学校	Reformatory Schools	1	42	32
（五）学前教育	Preschool Education	1780	49604	25823
幼儿园	Kindergarten	1780	49604	25758
附设幼儿班的学校	Schools with Nursery Classes	(67)		65
另有：职业技术培训机构	Technique Training Institution	2072	21259	15145

注：1.本表数据来源于市教育局。
2.本表为西安市行政区划内各级各类学校全口径数据（不含军事院校、党校）。
3.技工学校数据由西安市人力资源和社会保障局提供。
4.按照事业统计主体校原则，完全中学、十二年一贯制学校的学校数计入普通高中，九年一贯制学校的校数计入普通初中。
5.教职工数和专任教师按照办学类型划分。
6.( ) 内数据不计入总计，下表同。
7.本表数据包含西咸新区。

20-3 各级各类教育学生情况（2018年）

Basic Facts on Education Student by School Type（2018）

单位：人 (person)

指　标	Item	毕业生数 Number of Graduates	招生数 New Enrollment	在校学生数 Total Enrollment	女生 Female Students
一、高等教育	**Higher education**	**379696**	**498176**	**1302383**	**619514**
(一)研究生	Postgraduates	27276	38582	112250	52773
1、高等学校	Institutions of Higher Schools	27088	38399	111626	52596
2、科研机构	Scientific Research Institution	188	183	624	177
（二）普通高等教育	Regular Institutions of Higher Schools	205014	198260	712810	348797
1、本科	Universities Course Schools	126163	130682	502486	253686
2、专科	Junior Colleges	78851	67578	210324	95111
（三）成人高等教育	Higher Vocational Colleges	46765	66220	131468	64692
其中：成人高等学校	Contains:Adult Higher Education	4232	12628	25716	10751
（四）网络本专科生	Network Undergraduate and clooege students	100641	195114	345855	153252
1、本科	Universities Course Schools	39203	67173	129396	58141
2、专科	Junior Colleges	61438	127941	216459	95111
二、中等职业教育	**Secondary Occupation Education**	**39965**	**61256**	**181220**	**69819**
1、普通中等专业学校	Regular Specialized Secondary Schools	8392	8291	24842	10367
2、成人中等专业学校	Adult Secondary Specialized Schools	89	128	313	135
3、职业高中学校	Vocational high Schools	14064	17295	46380	20875
其中：市属	Municipal schools	14064	17295	46380	20875
4、技工学校	Technical Schools	17420	35542	109685	38442
其中：市属	Municipal schools	6190	12968	34762	14561
三、基础教育	**Elementary Education**	**342577**	**425975**	**1512081**	**716073**
(一)普通中等教育	Regular Institutions Education	134956	143650	424615	200707
1、高中	Senior High Schools	53783	50666	154399	75427
完全中学	Complete Secondary Schools	25535	25359	76219	37452
高级中学	Senior Secondary Schools	25990	23138	71551	34802
十二年一贯制学校	Twelve-year Consistency schools	2258	2169	6629	3173
2、初中	Junior Middle Schools	81173	92984	270216	125280
初级中学	Junior Middle Schools	43051	47197	137916	63311
九年一贯制学校	Nine-year Consistency Schools	6023	7717	21522	10034
十二年一贯制学校	Twelve-year Consistency Schools	3379	5751	14534	6580
完全中学	Complete Secondary school	28720	32319	96244	45355
(二)普通初等教育	Regular Primary Education	93154	151606	730898	344617
小学	Pricmary Schools	85873	138245	669067	315815
九年一贯制学校	Nine-year Consistency schools	5141	10584	47549	22305
十二年一贯制学校	Twelve-year Consistency Schools	2140	2777	14282	6497
（三）特殊教育	Special Education Schools	352	461	2615	991
1、特殊教育学校	Special Education Schools	124	133	1058	392
2、小学附设特教班	Primary Schools with Special Education Classes		3	5	
3、小学随班就读	Elementary Inclusive	122	162	972	390
4、初中随班就读	Junior Mainstreaming	102	127	365	130
5、小学送教上门	Primary School Delivery	4	29	174	63
6、初中送教上门	Junior High School Delivery		7	41	16
（四）工读学校	Reformatory Schools	21	12	18	
（五）学前教育	Preschool Education	114094	130246	353935	169758
1、独立幼儿园	Independent Kindergartens	112889	129362	352533	169072
2、附设幼儿园	Attached Kindergartens	1205	884	1402	686
另有：职业技术培训机构	Vocational and Technical Institutions	492750		637563	337381

注：1.本表数据来源于市教育局。

2.本表数据包含西咸新区。

20-4 主要年份普通高等学校和科研机构研究生情况

Basic Statistics of Postgraduates on Regular Institutions of Higher Education and Scientific Research Institution in Representative Years

单位：人 (person)

年 份 Year	毕业生数 Number of Graduates	高等学校 Higher Schools	招生数 New Enrollment	高等学校 Higher Schools	在校学生数 Total Enrollment	高等学校 Higher Schools
1978			232	232	232	232
1980			127	127	651	651
1985	754	754	2819	2819	4799	4799
1990	2051	2051	1662	1662	5275	5275
1995	1769	1769	2712	2712	7974	7974
2000	3236	3236	6924	6924	16620	16620
2001	3881	3770	9274	8966	22564	21855
2002	4103	3952	11282	10882	28446	27471
2003	5971	5765	14322	13882	36936	35790
2004	8384	8127	17310	16871	45402	44169
2005	10416	10127	18583	18106	52699	51310
2006	12914	12552	19581	19105	58433	56951
2007	15506	15124	20570	20167	64137	62801
2008	17234	16788	21892	21443	67296	65834
2009	19025	18574	24879	24400	72366	70908
2010	19526	19129	25971	25477	76993	75483
2011	20965	20605	26686	26256	81696	80332
2012	22963	22578	28065	27618	84712	83306
2013	24778	24385	28786	28333	87002	85570
2014	24092	23881	28636	28436	88518	87826
2015	25322	25104	29487	29293	91448	90790
2016	24779	24562	30263	30079	94720	94102
2017	25808	25616	36296	36084	104092	103458
2018	27276	27088	38582	38399	112250	111626

注：1.本表数据来源于市教育局。
2.本表2017年及以后年份数据包含西咸新区。

20–5 主要年份普通高等学校基本情况（本专科）

Basic Statistics on Regular Institution of Higher Education in Representative Years

单位：所、万人　　　　(units 10 000 persons)

年 份 Year	学校数 Number of Schools	毕业生数 Number of Graduates	招生数 New Enrollment	在校学生数 Total Enrollment	教职工数 Number of Staff and Teachers	专任教师数 Full-time Teachers
1978	21	0.60	1.31	2.88	2.24	0.87
1980	24	0.21	1.08	4.17	2.55	0.97
1985	28	1.17	2.28	6.49	3.40	1.28
1990	31	2.11	2.00	7.50	4.15	1.56
1995	32	2.87	3.13	10.07	4.21	1.59
2000	25	2.71	6.79	17.75	3.81	1.57
2001	32	3.31	8.31	23.24	4.30	1.75
2002	35	3.82	10.75	30.15	4.67	2.06
2003	37	5.89	12.21	36.42	4.92	2.21
2004	41	7.66	13.17	40.29	5.45	2.69
2005	44	10.08	14.68	47.79	5.73	2.95
2006	47	11.75	15.15	51.40	6.14	3.29
2007	48	14.33	16.96	56.03	6.56	3.67
2008	48	15.82	19.31	60.10	6.90	3.89
2009	49	15.04	18.84	63.22	7.08	4.06
2010	50	16.33	19.16	65.74	7.22	4.21
2011	61	17.68	20.52	68.52	7.27	4.27
2012	62	18.64	22.46	72.40	7.40	4.45
2013	63	17.73	21.05	75.27	7.50	4.64
2014	63	18.88	20.74	76.64	7.50	4.68
2015	63	20.72	20.49	75.75	7.49	4.78
2016	63	21.60	20.07	73.68	7.37	4.72
2017	63	20.50	20.10	72.68	7.42	4.79
2018	63	20.50	19.83	71.28	7.56	4.90

注：1.本表数据来源于市教育局。
2.本表2017年及以后年份数据包含西咸新区。

20-6 主要年份普通中等专业学校基本情况

Basic Statistics on Regular Specialized Secondary Schools in Representative Years

年 份 Year	学校数（所） Number of Schools (units)	毕业生数（万人） Number of Graduates (10 000 persons)	招生数（万人） New Enrollment (10 000 persons)	在校学生数（万人） Total Enrollment (10 000 persons)	教职工数（人） Number of Staff and Teachers(person)	专任教师数（人） Full-time Teachers(person)
1978	19	0.19	0.45	0.82	3937	1110
1980	31	0.18	0.42	1.50	3895	1474
1985	37	0.43	0.76	1.70	6071	2363
1990	44	0.56	0.68	2.09	7136	2891
1995	46	0.97	1.37	3.74	5903	2533
2000	47	1.63	1.90	6.02	6964	3172
2001	47	1.70	1.58	5.63	5252	2467
2002	46	1.60	1.69	5.57	5170	2508
2003	34	1.62	1.80	5.28	4562	2302
2004	35	1.40	2.09	5.71	4676	2388
2005	32	1.44	2.26	6.16	3924	2130
2006	31	1.84	2.61	7.30	3621	2014
2007	30	2.03	2.91	7.97	3548	2011
2008	29	2.58	2.55	8.06	3278	1814
2009	28	2.70	2.15	7.44	2965	1720
2010	28	2.45	2.08	6.75	3249	1845
2011	24	2.34	1.96	6.11	2868	1723
2012	24	2.15	1.67	5.43	2733	1595
2013	22	1.93	1.35	4.66	2599	1474
2014	22	1.76	1.25	4.07	2315	1346
2015	20	1.32	0.95	3.47	1991	1228
2016	20	1.25	0.88	3.11	1917	1210
2017	16	1.06	0.96	2.74	1556	998
2018	15	0.84	0.83	2.48	1529	958

注：1.本表数据来源于市教育局。
2.本表2017年及以后年份数据包含西咸新区。

20-7 主要年份普通中等教育基本情况

Basic Situation of General Secondary Education in Major Years

年 份 Year	学校数（所） Number of Schools (units)	毕业生数（万人） Number of Graduates (10 000 persons)	招生数（万人） New Enrollment (10 000 persons)	在校学生数（万人） Total Enrollment (10 000 persons)	教职工数（人） Number of Staff and Teachers(person)	专任教师数（人） Full-time Teachers(person)
1978	962	10.85		44.16	27380	20660
1980	1002	12.33	14.03	44.08	29867	22530
1985	563	10.72	13.05	38.24	30063	22050
1990	518	9.11	10.49	30.03	30739	22386
1995	485	8.13	12.40	32.32	30423	21984
2000	466	12.01	17.88	48.31	34385	26230
2001	470	13.85	18.98	52.50	35442	27190
2002	467	15.76	19.68	55.36	36706	28335
2003	467	16.76	18.78	56.44	38252	29887
2004	461	18.01	18.85	56.54	39121	30600
2005	460	18.82	18.83	55.74	39456	31094
2006	457	18.04	18.61	56.11	39341	31203
2007	453	18.37	17.96	54.68	39171	31373
2008	442	17.99	17.16	52.83	39088	31425
2009	439	17.80	16.57	50.63	39002	31415
2010	436	17.01	16.15	48.89	39207	31506
2011	423	16.44	15.42	47.20	41135	31675
2012	419	15.64	14.98	45.33	41197	31526
2013	418	15.24	14.47	43.73	41003	31419
2014	421	14.54	13.97	42.57	40576	32615
2015	422	13.92	13.41	41.37	40689	33014
2016	422	13.96	13.72	40.70	41352	33962
2017	448	13.89	14.08	41.74	44546	36565
2018	456	13.50	14.37	42.46	45390	37539

注：1.本表数据来源于市教育局。
2.本表2017年及以后年份数据包含西咸新区。

20-8 各区县普通中等教育基本情况（2018年）

Basic Situation of Ordinary Secondary Education in Various Districts and Counties（2018）

单位：所、人 (unit, person)

区县	Region	学校数 Number of Schools	毕业生数 Number of Graduates	高中 Senior	招生数 New Enrollment	高中 Senior	在校学生数 Total Enrollment	女生 Female Students	高中 Senior	教职工数 Number of Staff and Teachers	专任教师数 Full-time Teachers
合计	**Total**	**456**	**134956**	**53783**	**143650**	**50666**	**424615**	**200707**	**154399**	**45390**	**37539**
新城区	Xincheng	25	10739	3903	10670	3890	32606	15718	11609	2765	2351
碑林区	Beilin	36	15904	6785	16624	6767	51024	23232	20362	4003	3146
莲湖区	Lianhu	20	10314	3644	10869	3677	32676	15653	11088	2884	2357
灞桥区	Baqiao	26	7453	2092	8881	2496	24936	11894	6836	2832	2300
未央区	Weiyang	33	10325	4328	12877	4177	35658	17148	12411	4144	3431
雁塔区	Yanta	48	15820	5814	18865	5911	53550	25516	17481	5783	4840
阎良区	Yanliang	12	3306	1344	3133	1083	9657	4903	3517	1121	997
临潼区	Lintong	33	9842	4359	8486	3155	26845	13313	10706	3269	2765
长安区	Chang'an	50	12715	5549	13831	5351	40454	19313	16210	4153	3716
高陵区	Gaoling	15	3360	1280	3925	1291	11076	5563	3747	1010	835
鄠邑区	Huyi	34	8793	4296	7842	3457	24156	11021	11011	2901	2467
蓝田县	Lantian	45	9167	3794	8487	3588	25929	12705	10972	3294	2558
周至县	Zhouzhi	35	9691	4393	8666	3310	27671	11810	11245	3087	2248
西咸新区	Xixian	44	7527	2202	10494	2513	28377	12918	7204	4144	3528

注：本表数据来源于市教育局。

20–9 主要年份职业高中基本情况

Basic Statistics on Vocational Secondary Schools in Representative Years

单位：所、人　　(unit, person)

年　份 Year	学校数 Number of Schools	毕业生数 Number of Graduates	招生数 New Enrollment	在校学生数 Total Enrollment	教职工数 Number of Staff and Teachers	专任教师数 Full-time Teachers
1985	40	1661	8346	17621	1375	868
1990	58	5936	8095	20151	2674	1574
1995	71	8976	12490	32673	2394	1877
2000	95	9949	13903	32188	3311	1997
2001	85	10300	15591	34336	3517	2113
2002	78	8659	17231	39428	3461	2192
2003	87	10755	17310	44033	4036	2458
2004	83	12177	17865	46358	4101	2515
2005	91	15092	20603	51766	4750	2892
2006	96	14887	21158	53828	5193	3126
2007	86	14881	24434	56012	4899	3064
2008	84	15813	30201	62963	4878	3008
2009	84	14691	31042	72388	5129	3179
2010	84	18100	30042	78244	5222	3178
2011	78	22493	27641	75108	4849	3173
2012	77	24048	24995	67969	4775	3148
2013	74	21243	23043	61968	4699	3085
2014	81	19156	19508	60024	4860	3186
2015	80	18565	15060	49092	3239	2214
2016	64	17773	14305	43576	3126	2275
2017	62	14325	17080	45145	3318	2405
2018	60	14064	17295	46380	3499	2584

注：1.本表数据来源于市教育局。
　　2.本表2017年及以后年份数据包含西咸新区。

20-10 各区县职业高中基本情况（2018年）

Basic Statistics on Vocational Secondary Schools by Region（2018）

单位：所、人 (unit, person)

区 县	Region	学校数 Number of Schools	毕业生数 Number of Graduates	招生数 New Enrollment	在校学生数 Total Enrollment	女生 Female Students	教职工数 Number of Staff and Teachers	专任教师数 Full-time Teachers
合 计	**Total**	**60**	**14064**	**17295**	**46380**	**20875**	**3499**	**2584**
新城区	Xincheng	8	4806	5003	13646	5791	639	406
碑林区	Beilin	7	417	2272	6691	2426	353	186
莲湖区	Lianhu	5	1891	1310	3975	2420	284	210
灞桥区	Baqiao	6	517	544	1699	1168	159	126
未央区	Weiyang	3	621	785	1748	812	154	115
雁塔区	Yanta	10	1416	2697	5065	2311	460	360
阎良区	Yanliang	2	690	1154	2453	1328	215	154
临潼区	Lintong	5	726	662	2319	919	185	149
长安区	Chang'an	4	1174	952	3657	1722	461	381
高陵区	Gaoling	1	442	317	917	289	86	79
鄠邑区	Huyi	2	426	498	1162	414	217	191
蓝田县	Lantian	1	484	486	1476	554	152	128
周至县	Zhouzhi	3	454	378	1238	583	89	64
西咸新区	Xixian	3		237	334	138	45	35

注：本表数据来源于市教育局。

20-11 主要年份普通初等教育基本情况

Basic Situation of General Primary Education in Major Years

年 份 Year	学校数（所） Number of Schools (units)	毕业生数 （万人） Number of Graduates (10 000 persons)	招生数 （万人） New Enrollment (10 000 persons)	在校学生数 （万人） Total Enrollment (10 000 persons)	教职工数（人） Number of Staff and Teachers(person)	专任教师数 （人） Full-time Teachers(person)
1978	2667	13.07	14.10	74.03	29744	26428
1980	2337	11.91	12.57	73.36	31770	28360
1985	2337	11.21	9.57	62.16	31075	26430
1990	2343	8.67	10.85	61.87	33788	29090
1995	2360	9.93	14.09	79.36	35568	30270
2000	2323	13.83	11.51	77.81	35336	30215
2001	2277	14.20	11.07	74.51	34257	29281
2002	2137	13.89	10.13	70.78	34143	29428
2003	2084	12.97	9.28	66.78	34080	29531
2004	2016	12.37	9.12	63.75	33794	29367
2005	1980	11.92	8.47	60.47	33907	29674
2006	1929	11.53	9.16	59.33	34460	30018
2007	1872	11.38	8.67	56.83	34901	30533
2008	1781	10.58	8.33	54.66	34653	30382
2009	1666	9.96	7.84	52.52	34389	30334
2010	1531	9.61	8.64	51.56	34118	29944
2011	1424	8.92	8.77	51.39	32457	29900
2012	1322	8.88	8.88	50.85	32208	29651
2013	1291	8.51	9.56	51.95	31863	29421
2014	1257	8.29	10.13	53.79	32162	28395
2015	1234	7.85	10.51	56.62	32585	28748
2016	1190	8.46	11.65	59.79	34646	30941
2017	1125	9.06	13.13	66.68	38494	34163
2018	1130	9.32	15.16	73.09	41122	36878

注：1.本表数据来源于市教育局。
　　2.本表2017年及以后年份数据包含西咸新区。

20-12 各区县普通初等教育基本情况（2018年）

Basic Situation of General Primary Education in Various Districts and Counties（2018）

单位：所、人 (unit, person)

区 县	Region	学校数 Number of Schools	毕业生数 Number of Graduates	招生数 New Enrollment	在校学生数 Total Enrollment	女生 Female Students	教职工数 Number of Staff and Teachers	专任教师数 Full-time Teachers
合 计	**Total**	**1130**	**93154**	**151606**	**730898**	**344617**	**41122**	**36878**
新城区	Xincheng	35	5811	6656	37291	17552	2213	2007
碑林区	Beilin	42	6793	8981	47821	22398	2719	2274
莲湖区	Lianhu	48	8149	11034	57551	27299	2643	2385
灞桥区	Baqiao	79	6500	12809	58758	28036	3032	2732
未央区	Weiyang	70	9759	22474	97944	45660	4311	3832
雁塔区	Yanta	80	13059	24956	114832	53986	5585	5036
阎良区	Yanliang	23	2340	3257	16607	8052	1023	948
临潼区	Lintong	105	5926	7628	40585	19435	2772	2546
长安区	Chang'an	133	8128	16339	73025	34478	4253	3803
高陵区	Gaoling	71	2845	4674	23027	11227	1556	1339
鄠邑区	Huyi	101	4793	5446	29156	13521	2021	1772
蓝田县	Lantian	84	4983	4959	27855	13249	2537	2335
周至县	Zhouzhi	123	5419	6473	35283	16185	2429	2174
西咸新区	Xixian	136	8649	15920	71163	33539	4028	3695

注：本表数据来源于市教育局。

20-13 主要年份学前教育基本情况

Basic Conditions of Pre-school Education in Representative Years

年 份 Year	幼儿园（个） Number of Kindergartens (unit)	班数（个） Number of Class (unit)	在园幼儿数（万人） Student Enrollment (10000 persons)	教职工数（人） Number of Staff and Teachers(person)	专任教师数（人） Full-time Teachers(person)
1978	191		4.44	3568	1315
1980	186		9.61	5525	2657
1985	310	3135	9.71	6887	2770
1990	256	3816	14.04	6123	2058
1995	257	4464	16.40	6173	2659
2000	367	4142	12.85	6346	2995
2001	366	4306	11.97	6224	3069
2002	378	4186	11.53	6541	3397
2003	610	4470	12.39	8959	4853
2004	660	4507	12.16	9870	5577
2005	737	4712	12.75	10528	5959
2006	863	5037	13.00	12335	7106
2007	830	5081	14.00	13468	7951
2008	905	5506	15.00	14932	8704
2009	896	5710	16.00	15928	9240
2010	1004	6420	18.00	18710	10638
2011	1122	8010	24.00	23680	12577
2012	1239	8729	27.10	27735	14293
2013	1295	9408	28.56	31989	16238
2014	1343	9782	28.95	33062	17337
2015	1417	10457	30.90	36004	19096
2016	1475	11090	31.80	39753	21395
2017	1605	12234	34.81	44895	23789
2018	1780	12970	35.39	49604	25823

注：1.本表数据来源于市教育局。
2.幼儿园在园人数中包括学前班。
3.本表2017年及以后年份数据包含西咸新区。

20-14 主要年份特殊教育基本情况

Basic Statistics on Special Education in Representative Years

单位：所、人 (unit, person)

年 份 Year	学校数 Number of Schools	毕业生数 Number of Graduates	招生数 New Enrollment	在校学生数 Total Enrollment	教职工数 Number of Staff and Teachers	专任教师数 Full-time Teachers
1980	1	48	64	315	66	43
1985	2	14	36	318	94	59
1990	5	35	111	451	142	96
1995	5	27	147	1363	204	141
2000	5	269	145	1880	230	156
2001	5	237	209	1915	238	162
2002	5	216	148	1661	232	157
2003	5	156	161	1380	237	166
2004	5	137	142	1290	236	167
2005	5	184	182	1445	240	169
2006	6	171	143	1425	254	178
2007	6	169	114	1342	259	190
2008	6	83	96	1286	259	190
2009	7	311	202	1523	335	234
2010	8	214	402	1529	340	235
2011	8	280	222	1393	343	231
2012	8	197	220	1392	352	248
2013	8	194	212	1174	338	243
2014	8	172	222	1225	345	238
2015	8	168	338	1373	352	240
2016	8	214	327	1604	359	246
2017	9	237	774	2498	386	272
2018	9	352	461	2615	379	271

注：1.本表数据来源于市教育局。
2.包括盲、聋、哑、弱智儿童教育。
3.本表2017年及以后年份数据包含西咸新区。

20-15 基础教育监测评价情况（2018年）

Monitoring and Evaluation of Basic Education（2018）

指 标	Item	2018
入学率(%)	Enrollment Rate(%)	
小学	Primary Schools	99.99
初中	Junior Middle Schools	99.98
巩固率(%)	The Consolidation Rate (%)	
小学(六年)	Primary Schools (six years)	101.73
初中(三年)	Junior Middle Schools (three years)	98.74
毕业率(%)	The Graduate Rate(%)	
小学	Primary school	99.99
初中	Junior middle school	99.24
专任教师学历合格率(%)	Qualified Rate Of Full-time Teacher Education (%)	
小学	Primary Schools	100.00
初中	Junior Middle Schools	99.99
高中	Senior Middle Schools	99.00
幼儿园	Kindergartens	99.27
小学教师专科以上学历达到率(%)	Rate of Primary School Teachers with College degree or Above (%)	99.09
初中教师本科以上学历达到率(%)	Rate of Junior Middle SchoolTeachers with Bachelor degree or Above (%)	93.59
高中教师研究生以上学历达到率(%)	Rate of Senior Middle School Teachers with Postgraduate degree or Above (%)	18.45

注：1.本表数据来源于市教育局。
2.本表数据包含西咸新区。

20-16 主要年份平均每万人口在校学生数及构成

单位：人、%

年 份 Year	平均每万人 高等学校在校学生 Per 10000 people on average Hight Education Students in the school	平均每万人 高中阶段在校学生 Per 10000 people on average Number of Senior high School Students in the school	平均每万人 初中在校学生 Per 10000 people on average Number of Junior Secondary School Students in the school	平均每万人 小学在校学生 Per 10000 people on average Number of Primary School Students in the school
1978	58			1486
1980	84			1434
1985	117			1124
1990	123			1016
1995	168			1224
2000	282			1131
2001	366			1072
2002	470			1007
2003	560			932
2004	618	463	517	879
2005	715	492	489	815
2006	760	534	484	788
2007	817	543	466	744
2008	863	571	444	708
2009	901	619	413	672
2010	939	635	361	660
2011	1090	576	337	604
2012	1132	541	319	595
2013	1146	448	307	605
2014	1157	414	301	626
2015	1125	374	286	650
2016	1080	360	280	641
2017	982	363	270	693
2018	956	335	270	731

注：1.本表数据来源于市教育局。
2.2011年起，表中三个比重指标数据参与计算的学生总数含成人教育及网络教育数据。
3.本表2017年及以后年份数据含西咸新区。

The Average Number of Students in the School every 10000 Individuals in Representative Years

(persons,%)

平均每万人 学前教育在校学生 Average Number of Pre-school Students per 10,000 people	普通高等学校在校学生 占学生总数比重 Senior high School Students in the school in accounting for the proportion of the total number of students	中等学校在校学生 占学生总数比重 Junior Secondary School students in the school in accounting for the proportion of the total number of students	小学在校学生 占学生总数比重 Primary School students in the school in accounting for the proportion of the total number of students
	2.3	34.9	58.6
	3.1	33.2	55.3
	5.3	31.3	50.9
	6.7	25.1	51.7
	7.3	28.0	53.6
	11.5	34.8	46.0
	14.6	35.9	42.6
	18.2	36.4	39.0
	20.1	33.8	33.5
	22.2	35.2	31.6
	26.4	36.2	30.1
	27.7	37.1	28.7
	29.3	36.3	26.7
	30.8	36.1	25.2
	31.8	36.5	23.7
217	33.0	35.0	23.2
282	29.8	30.1	19.9
317	31.0	28.2	19.5
333	32.6	25.3	20.2
336	33.2	23.8	20.9
355	32.8	22.2	21.9
360	31.4	21.4	22.6
362	29.1	21.3	23.4
354	27.5	20.2	24.4

20–17　民办教育情况（2018年）

单位：所、人

指　标	Item	学校数 Number of Schools	毕业生数 Number of Graduates
一、民办高等教育(民办高校)	**Private higher Education (Institutions)**	**16**	**79146**
二、民办中等教育	**Private Secondary Education**	**97**	**38299**
民办普通高中	Ordinary High School	31	6330
民办普通中等专业学校	Civilian run ordinary secondary vocational school	1	1187
民办职业高中	Vocational high school	36	8505
民办普通初中	Ordinary Junior middle school	29	20233
民办的附设中职班	Private primary school class		2044
三、民办普通小学	**Private Primary School**	**84**	**11500**
四、民办幼儿园	**Private kindergarten**	**1141**	**80431**
另有：民办培训机构	Private Training Institutions	786	272551

注：1.本表数据来源于市教育局。
2.毕业生数中幼儿园为离园人数。
3.民办高等教育在校生为民办高校普通、成人本专科学生数。
4.聘请校外教师中，小学、中学、幼儿园为代课教师和兼任教师之和。
5.按照教育报表制度，民办的附设中职班教职工计入基础教育主体校教职工总数，专任教师为中职层次，故单独统计。
6.本表数据含西咸新区。

Private Education Situation（2018）

(unit, person)

招生数 New Enrollment	在校学生数 Total Enrollment	教职工数 Number of Teachers and Staff	专任教师 Full-time Teachers	聘请外校教师 Teachers hired from Outside Schools
74814	**247984**	**19527**	**13073**	
46940	**126152**	**11044**	**8633**	**37**
7227	20305	5399	4346	
660	1726	215	145	
12207	30032	1611	1014	37
25451	69526	3819	3128	
1395	4563			
28184	**120821**	**5623**	**4787**	
96358	**256924**	**35611**	**17401**	**4**
	417587	13822	10138	5712

20-18 全市研究与试验发展（R&D）活动情况（2017年）

Scientific and Technological Activities in the Whole City （2017）

指　标	Item	2017
一、单位数（个）	**Number of Units(unit)**	**2320**
#有R&D活动单位数	The Number of R&D active units	680
二、R&D人员（人）	**Personnel Eagaged in R&D（person）**	**107874**
三、R&D人员折合全时当量（人年）	**R&D Stuff Equivalent to Full Time equivalent （person year）**	**74423.8**
四、R&D经费内部支出（万元）	**R&D Internal Expenditure（10000 yuan）**	**3601731.2**
五、R&D项目(课题)（项）	**R&D Project（Issue）**	**42577**

注：本表数据来源于省统计局反馈。

20-19 规模以上重点行业企业研究与试验发展（R&D）情况（2017年）

R&D Project Status of Key Enterprises above Designated Size（2017）

指　标	Item	2017
一、企业数（个）	**Number of Enterprises(unit)**	**2093**
工业	Industry	1404
非工业	Non-industry	689
#有R&D活动的单位数	The number of R&D active units	506
工业	Industry	435
非工业	Non-industry	71
二、R&D人员（人）	**Personnel Eagaged in R&D (person)**	**53282**
工业	Industry	39953
非工业	Non-industry	13329
三、R&D人员折合全时当量（人年）	**R&D Stuff Equivalent to Full Time equivalent (person year)**	**35003**
工业	Industry	27259
非工业	Non-industry	7744
四、R&D经费内部支出（万元）	**R&D Internal Expenditure (10000 yuan)**	**1477649**
工业	Industry	1104702
非工业	Non-industry	372947
五、R&D项目（课题）（项）	**R&D Project (issue)**	**3369**
工业	Industry	2690
非工业	Non-industry	679

20-20 规模以上工业企业研究与试验发展（R&D）基本情况（2017年）

R&D Project Status of Industrial Enterprises above Designated Size（2017）

指　标	Item	企业数（个）Number of enterprises (unit)	有R&D活动的企业数 The Number of R&D enterprises
总计	**Total**	**1404**	**435**
按企业规模分	**Grouped by Size of Enterprises**		
大型企业	Large-size	68	49
中型企业	Medium-size	186	97
小型企业	Small-size	1110	284
微型企业	Microenterprise	40	5
按登记注册类型分	**Grouped by Registered Status**		
内资企业	Domestic Investment Enterprises	1289	403
国有企业	State-owned Enterprises	35	25
集体企业	Collective-owned Enterprise	7	
股份合作企业	Stock Cooperative Enterprises	5	
联营企业	Affiliated Enterprise		
有限责任公司	Limited Liability Corporations	637	211
股份有限公司	Share-holding Corporation Ltd	115	75
私营企业	Private Enterprise	488	92
其他	Other Domestic Funded Enterprises	2	
港、澳、台商投资企业	Enterprises with Funds from Hong Kong, Macao And Taiwan	26	5
外商投资企业	Foreign Funded Enterprises	89	27
按国民经济行业分	**Grouped by Sector**		
采矿业	Mining	7	2
煤炭开采和洗选业	Mining and Washing of Coal		
石油和天然气开采业	Extraction of Petroleum and Natural Gas	1	1

20-20 续表1 continued 1

指 标	Item	企业数（个）Number of enterprises (unit)	有R&D活动的企业数 The Number of R&D enterprises
黑色金属矿采选业	Mining of Ferrous Metal Ores		
有色金属矿采选业	Mining of Non-ferrous Metal Ores		
非金属矿采选业	Mining and Processing of Nonmetal Ores		
开采辅助活动	Mining Other Ores	6	1
制造业	Manufacturing Industry	1354	430
农副食品加工业	Processing of Food from Agriculture Products	51	1
食品制造业	Manufacture of Food	46	7
酒、饮料和精制茶制造业	Manufacture of Beverages	24	5
烟草制品业	Manufacture of Tobacco	3	1
纺织业	Manufacture of Textile	16	3
纺织服装、服饰业	Manufacture of Textile Wearing, Apparel	4	
皮革、毛皮、羽毛及其制品和制鞋业	Manufacture of Leather, Furs, Feather, Related Products and Footware	2	1
木材加工和木、竹、藤、棕、草制品业	Processing of Timber,Manufacture of Wood, Bamboo, Rattan, Palm and Straw Products	6	
家具制造业	Manufacture of Furniture	14	
造纸及纸制品业	Manufacture of Paper And Paper Products	24	
印刷和记录媒介复制业	Printing and Reproduction of Recording Media	31	5
文教、工美、体育和娱乐用品制造业	Education, Art, Sports And Entertainment Products Manufacturing	12	
石油加工、炼焦和核燃料加工业	Processing of Petroleum,Coking and Processing of Nuclear Fuel	8	
化学原料和化学制品制造业	Manufacture of Raw Chemical Materials and Chemical Products	84	37

20-20 续表2 continued 2

指 标	Item	企业数（个）Number of enterprises (unit)	有R&D活动的企业数 The Number of R&D enterprises
医药制造业	Manufacture of Medicines	59	32
化学纤维制造业	Manufacture of Chemical Fiber	3	1
橡胶和塑料制品业	Manufacture of Rubber and Manufacture of Plastic	37	6
非金属矿物制品业	Manufacture of Non-metallic Mineral Products	147	5
黑色金属冶炼和压延加工业	Smelting and Pressing of Ferrous Metals	16	1
有色金属冶炼和压延加工业	Smelting and Pressing of Non-ferrous Metals	40	20
金属制品业	Manufacture of Metal Products	82	18
通用设备制造业	Manufacture of General Purpose Machinery	84	23
专用设备制造业	Manufacture of Special Equipment	122	62
汽车制造业	Manufacture of Motor Vehicle	53	18
铁路、船舶、航空航天和其他运输设备制造业	Railways, Ships, Aerospace And Other Transportation Equipment Manufacturing Industry	80	41
电气机械和器材制造业	Manufacture of Electric Equipment and Machinery	142	50
计算机、通信和其他电子设备制造业	Manufacture of Communication Equipment, Computers and Other Electronic Equipment	91	51
仪器仪表制造业	Manufacture of Measuring Instruments and Machinery	56	35
其他制造业	Other Manufacturing	9	5
废弃资源综合利用业	Comprehensive Utilization Of Waste Resources	4	1
金属制品、机械和设备修理业	Metal Products, Machinery and Equipment Repair Industry	4	1
电力、热力、燃气及水的生产供应业	Production and Supply of Electric Power,Heat,Gas and Water	43	3
电力、热力生产和供应业	Production and Supply of Electric Power and Heat Power	21	3
燃气生产和供应业	Production and Supply of Gas	15	
水的生产和供应业	Production and Supply of Water	7	

20-21 规模以上工业企业研究与试验发展（R&D）人员和经费支出情况（2017年）

指标	Item	R&D人员（人）R&D personnel（person）	研究人员 Researchers
总计	**Total**	**39953**	**17153**
按企业规模分	**Grouped by Size of Enterprises**		
大型企业	Large-size	26674	11129
中型企业	Medium-size	7477	3399
小型企业	Small-size	5761	2606
微型企业	microenterprise	41	19
按登记注册类型分	**Grouped by Registion Status**		
内资企业	Domestic Investment Enterprises	36092	15556
国有企业	State-owned Enterprises	10636	4542
集体企业	Collective-owned Enterprises		
股份合作企业	Stock cooperative enterprises		
联营企业	Affiliated companies		
有限责任公司	Limited Liability Corporations	19583	8296
股份有限公司	Share-holding Corperation Ltd.	3869	1783
私营企业	Private Enterprises	2004	935
其他	Other Domestic Funded Enterprises		
港、澳、台商投资企业	Enterprises with Funds from Hong Kong,Macao and Taiwan	1437	457
外商投资企业	Foreign Funded Enterprises	2424	1140
按国民经济行业分	**Grouped by Sector**		
采矿业	Mining	1466	777
煤炭开采和洗选业	Mining and Washing of Coal		
石油和天然气开采业	Extraction of Petroleum and Natural Gas	879	466
黑色金属矿采选业	Mining of Ferrous Metal Ores		
有色金属矿采选业	Mining of Non-ferrous Metal Ores		
非金属矿采选业	Mining and Processing of Nonmetal Ores		
开采辅助活动	Mining of Other Ores	587	311
制造业	Mannfacturing Industry	37223	15844
农副食品加工业	Processing of Food from Agricultural Products	15	6
食品制造业	Manufacture of Foods	122	28
酒、饮料和精制茶制造业	Manufacture of Beverages	109	58
烟草制品业	Manufacture of Tobacco	50	20
纺织业	Manufacture of Textile	183	90
纺织服装、服饰业	Manufacture of Textile Wearing Apparel		
皮革、毛皮、羽毛及其制品和制鞋业	Manufacture of Leather, Fur, Feather and Related Products and Footwear	51	10

R&D Personnel and Expenditure Conditions of Industrial Enterprises above Designated Size（2017）

R&D经费内部支出（万元） R&D Intramural Expenditure (10000 yuan)	政府资金 Government funds	企业资金 Enterprise funds	境外资金 Foreign funds
1104702	**306292**	**790980**	**1491**
832146	284371	546442	666
156801	13524	138673	465
115124	8387	105244	360
631	10	621	
929142	305844	617198	824
312687	112565	199113	530
484619	181665	301437	283
100345	9351	88174	11
31491	2263	28474	
22445	205	22240	
153115	243	151542	667
19196	3967	15229	
5958	3806	2152	
13238	161	13077	
1081869	302225	772214	1491
56		56	
1104	1	937	
1037		1037	
584		584	
4135	30	4105	
1882		1882	

20-21 续表1

指标	Item	R&D人员（人）R&D personnel（person）	研究人员 Researchers
木材加工和木、竹、藤、棕、草制品业	Processing of Timber,Manufacture of Wood, Bamboo,Rattan,aplam and Straw Products		
家具制造业	Manufacture of Furniture		
造纸及纸制品业	Manufacture of Paper and Paper Products		
印刷和记录媒介复制业	Printing,Reproduction of Recording Media	366	122
文教、工美、体育和娱乐用品制造业	Manufacture of Articles For Culture, Education and Sport Activities		
石油加工业、炼焦和核燃料加工业	Processing of Petroleum, Coking, Processing of Nuclear Fuel		
化学原料及化学制品制造业	Manufacture of Raw Chemical Materials and Chemical Products	2523	1152
医药制造业	Manufacture of Medicines	1263	596
化学纤维制造业	Manufacture of Chemical Fibers	18	7
橡胶和塑料制品业	Manufacture of Rubber and Manufacture of Plastics	301	136
非金属矿物制品业	Manufacture of Non-metallic Mineral Products	171	86
黑色金属冶炼和压延加工业	Smelting and Pressing of Ferrous Metals	12	6
有色金属冶炼和压延加工业	Smelting and Pressing of Non-ferrous Metals	967	304
金属制品业	Manufacture of Metal Products	2230	765
通用设备制造业	Manufacture of General Purpose Machinery	915	441
专用设备制造业	Manufacture of Special Equipment	2484	1210
汽车制造业	Manufacture of Motor Vehicle	3774	1232
铁路、船舶、航空航天和其他运输设备制造业	Railways,Shipbuilding,Aerospace and Other Transportation Equipment Manufacturing Industry	11796	4923
电气机械和器材制造业	Manufacture of Electric Equipment and Machinery	3062	1301
计算机、通讯和其他电子设备制造业	Manufacture of Communication Equipment, Computers and other Electronic Equipment	4786	2335
仪器仪表制造业	Manufacture of Measuring Instruments and Machinery	1913	963
其他制造业	Other Manufacturing	101	48
废弃资源综合利用业	Comprehensive Utilization Of Waste Resources	3	1
金属制品、机械和设备修理业	Metal Products,Machinery and Equipment Repair Industry	8	4
电力、热力、燃气及水生产和供应业	Production and Distribution of Electricity,Heat,Gas and Water	1264	532
电力、热力的生产和供应业	Production and Supply of Electric Power and Heat Power	1264	532
燃气生产和供应业	Gas mining and supplying industry		
水的生产和供应业	Production and Supply of Water		

continued 1

R&D经费内部支出（万元） R&D Intramural Expenditure (10000 yuan)	政府资金 Government funds	企业资金 Enterprise funds	境外资金 Foreign funds
2481		2481	
71558	8678	62593	
39390	164	38897	
620		620	
11757	1504	10182	
4369	56	4314	
310	6	304	
20392	3452	16810	
44524	10322	34041	146
22367	1229	20641	350
44655	6671	37740	12
123927	1368	120240	16
334144	252017	82127	
101822	3512	96317	967
186677	11792	174697	
62684	1320	60319	
1059	102	956	
4		4	
332		332	
3637	100	3537	
3637	100	3537	

20-22 规模以上工业企业研究和试验发展（R&D）项目情况（2017年）

指标	Item	项目数（项）The number of items（item）
总计	**Total**	**2690**
按企业规模分	**Grouped by Size of Enterprises**	
大型企业	Large-size	1118
中型企业	Medium-size	739
小型企业	Small-size	821
微型企业	microenterprise	12
按登记注册类型分	**Grouped by Registion Status**	
内资企业	Domestic Investment Enterprises	2565
国有企业	State-owned Enterprises	599
集体企业	Collective-owned Enterprises	
股份合作企业	Stock cooperative enterprises	
联营企业	Affiliated companies	
有限责任公司	Limited Liability Corporations	1208
股份有限公司	Share-holding Corperation Ltd.	492
私营企业	Private Enterprises	266
其他	Other Domestic Funded Enterprises	
港澳台商投资	Enterprises with Funds from Hong Kong,Macao and Taiwan	10
外商投资企业	Foreign Funded Enterprises	115
按国民经济行业分	**Grouped by Sector**	
采矿业	Mining	142
煤炭开采和洗选业	Mining and Washing of Coal	
石油和天然气开采业	Extraction of Petroleum and Natural Gas	67
黑色金属矿采选业	Mining of Ferrous Metal Ores	
有色金属矿采选业	Mining of Non-ferrous Metal Ores	
非金属矿采选业	Mining and Processing of Nonmetal Ores	
开采辅助活动	Mining of Other Ores	75
制造业	Mannfacturing Industry	2462
农副食品加工业	Processing of Food from Agricultural Products	1
食品制造业	Manufacture of Foods	12
酒、饮料和精制茶制造业	Manufacture of Beverages	11
烟草制品业	Manufacture of Tobacco	8
纺织业	Manufacture of Textile	14
纺织服装、服饰业	Manufacture of Textile Wearing Apparel	
皮革、毛皮、羽毛及其制品和制鞋业	Manufacture of Leather, Fur, Feather and Related Products and Footwear	17

R&D Project Status of Industrial Enterprises above Designated Size（2017）

参加项目人员（人） Personnel participating in the project（person）	项目经费内部支出（万元） Intramural Expenditure（10 000 yuan）
34506	**1099864**
23268	827724
6162	156472
5038	115037
38	631
30730	924540
9219	309386
16653	483433
3113	100257
1745	31464
1437	22445
2339	152879
1039	19196
578	5958
461	13238
32418	1077040
15	56
117	1103
106	1036
50	573
110	4135
48	1882

20-22 续表1

指标	Item	项目数（项）The number of items（item）
木材加工和木、竹、藤、棕、草制品业	Processing of Timber,Manufacture of Wood, Bamboo,Rattan,aplam and Straw Products	
家具制造业	Manufacture of Furniture	
造纸及纸制品业	Manufacture of Paper and Paper Products	
印刷和记录媒介复制业	Printing,Reproduction of Recording Media	17
文教、工美、体育和娱乐用品制造业	Manufacture of Articles For Culture, Education and Sport Activities	
石油加工业、炼焦和核燃料加工业	Processing of Petroleum, Coking, Processing of Nuclear Fuel	
化学原料及化学制品制造业	Manufacture of Raw Chemical Materials and Chemical Products	354
医药制造业	Manufacture of Medicines	170
化学纤维制造业	Manufacture of Chemical Fibers	1
橡胶和塑料制品业	Manufacture of Rubber and Manufacture of Plastics	26
非金属矿物制品业	Manufacture of Non-metallic Mineral Products	19
黑色金属冶炼和压延加工业	Smelting and Pressing of Ferrous Metals	1
有色金属冶炼和压延加工业	Smelting and Pressing of Non-ferrous Metals	142
金属制品业	Manufacture of Metal Products	113
通用设备制造业	Manufacture of General Purpose Machinery	108
专用设备制造业	Manufacture of Special Equipment	276
汽车制造业	Manufacture of Motor Vehicle	122
铁路、船舶、航空航天和其他运输设备制造业	Railways,Shipbuilding,Aerospace and Other Transportation Equipment Manufacturing Industry	348
电气机械和器材制造业	Manufacture of Electric Equipment and Machinery	392
计算机、通讯和其他电子设备制造业	Manufacture of Communication Equipment, Computers and other Electronic Equipment	177
仪器仪表制造业	Manufacture of Measuring Instruments and Machinery	116
其他制造业	Other Manufacturing	15
废弃资源综合利用业	Comprehensive Utilization Of Waste Resources	1
金属制品、机械和设备修理业	Metal Products,Machinery and Equipment Repair Industry	1
电力、热力、燃气及水生产和供应业	Production and Distribution of Electricity,Heat,Gas and Water	86
电力、热力的生产和供应业	Production and Supply of Electric Power and Heat Power	86
燃气生产和供应业	Gas mining and supplying industry	
水的生产和供应业	Production and Supply of Water	

continued 1

参加项目人员（人） Personnel participating in the project（person）	项目经费内部支出 （万元） Intramural Expenditure （10 000 yuan）
148	2479
2164	71493
1143	39332
15	620
233	11744
149	4369
6	310
927	20392
2077	44524
744	22359
2055	44642
3650	123246
10033	333015
2780	101481
4216	186614
1541	60239
80	1059
3	4
8	332
1049	3628
1049	3628

20-23 规模以上工业企业新产品开发、生产及销售情况（2017年）

指标	Item	新产品开发项目数（项）Number of new product development projects（item）
总计	**Total**	**2713**
按企业规模分	**Grouped by Size of Enterprises**	
大型企业	Large-size	987
中型企业	Medium-size	777
小型企业	Small-size	927
微型企业	microenterprise	22
按登记注册类型分	**Grouped by Registion Status**	
内资企业	Domestic Investment Enterprises	2556
国有企业	State-owned Enterprises	613
集体企业	Collective-owned Enterprises	
股份合作企业	Stock cooperative enterprises	
联营企业	Affiliated companies	
有限责任公司	Limited Liability Corporations	1184
股份有限公司	Share-holding Corperation Ltd.	460
私营企业	Private Enterprises	299
其他	Other Domestic Funded Enterprises	
港、澳、台商投资企业	Enterprises with Funds from Hong Kong,Macao and Taiwan	16
外商投资企业	Foreign Funded Enterprises	141
按国民经济行业分	**Grouped by Sector**	
采矿业	Mining	36
煤炭开采和洗选业	Mining and Washing of Coal	
石油和天然气开采业	Extraction of Petroleum and Natural Gas	1
黑色金属矿采选业	Mining of Ferrous Metal Ores	
有色金属矿采选业	Mining of Non-ferrous Metal Ores	
非金属矿采选业	Mining and Processing of Nonmetal Ores	
开采辅助活动	Mining of Other Ores	35
制造业	Mannfacturing Industry	2654
农副食品加工业	Processing of Food from Agricultural Products	4
食品制造业	Manufacture of Foods	21
酒、饮料和精制茶制造业	Manufacture of Beverages	12
烟草制品业	Manufacture of Tobacco	18
纺织业	Manufacture of Textile	20
纺织服装、服饰业	Manufacture of Textile Wearing Apparel	
皮革、毛皮、羽毛及其制品和制鞋业	Manufacture of Leather, Fur, Feather and Related Products and Footwear	19

New Product Development, Production and Sales of Above-scale Industrial Enterprises（2017）

新产品开发经费支出（万元） New Product Development Expenditure （10 000 yuan）	新产品产值 （万元） New product output value （10 000 yuan）	新产品销售收入 （万元） Sales of new products （10 000 yuan）
1194082	**11257678**	**8827778**
879340	9450455	7117592
175294	1010014	922065
138073	794980	786081
1375	2229	2040
1017323	10423365	8218086
364036	1271383	1331512
	3320	2302
533375	8466762	6180878
81219	559238	574195
38693	122662	129199
3054	596080	412561
173705	238233	197131
7719	2400	2235
260		
7460	2400	2235
1185148	11252755	8817013
643	346	482
3446	14321	22677
1347	2967	2629
2808	157377	118966
4964	15793	15780
2305	9264	17816

20-23 续表1

指标	Item	新产品开发项目数（项）Number of new product development projects（item）
木材加工和木、竹、藤、棕、草制品业	Processing of Timber,Manufacture of Wood, Bamboo,Rattan,aplam and Straw Products	
家具制造业	Manufacture of Furniture	
造纸及纸制品业	Manufacture of Paper and Paper Products	
印刷和记录媒介复制业	Printing,Reproduction of Recording Media	16
文教、工美、体育和娱乐用品制造业	Manufacture of Articles For Culture, Education and Sport Activities	
石油加工业、炼焦和核燃料加工业	Processing of Petroleum, Coking, Processing of Nuclear Fuel	
化学原料及化学制品制造业	Manufacture of Raw Chemical Materials and Chemical Products	328
医药制造业	Manufacture of Medicines	142
化学纤维制造业	Manufacture of Chemical Fibers	1
橡胶和塑料制品业	Manufacture of Rubber and Manufacture of Plastics	24
非金属矿物制品业	Manufacture of Non-metallic Mineral Products	13
黑色金属冶炼和压延加工业	Smelting and Pressing of Ferrous Metals	1
有色金属冶炼和压延加工业	Smelting and Pressing of Non-ferrous Metals	127
金属制品业	Manufacture of Metal Products	104
通用设备制造业	Manufacture of General Purpose Machinery	102
专用设备制造业	Manufacture of Special Equipment	298
汽车制造业	Manufacture of Motor Vehicle	148
铁路、船舶、航空航天和其他运输设备制造业	Railways,Shipbuilding,Aerospace and Other Transportation Equipment Manufacturing Industry	348
电气机械和器材制造业	Manufacture of Electric Equipment and Machinery	541
计算机、通讯和其他电子设备制造业	Manufacture of Communication Equipment, Computers and other Electronic Equipment	205
仪器仪表制造业	Manufacture of Measuring Instruments and Machinery	149
其他制造业	Other Manufacturing	11
废弃资源综合利用业	Comprehensive Utilization Of Waste Resources	
金属制品、机械和设备修理业	Metal Products,Machinery and Equipment Repair Industry	2
电力、热力、燃气及水生产和供应业	Production and Distribution of Electricity,Heat,Gas and Water	23
电力、热力的生产和供应业	Production and Supply of Electric Power and Heat Power	23
燃气生产和供应业	Gas mining and supplying industry	
水的生产和供应业	Production and Supply of Water	

continued 1

新产品开发经费支出（万元） New Product Development Expenditure （10 000 yuan）	新产品产值 （万元） New product output value （10 000 yuan）	新产品销售收入 （万元） Sales of new products （10 000 yuan）
3740	2590	2590
57736	339130	325399
48153	415891	306407
1125		
10515	54800	48871
3917	5332	5565
313	980	980
22909	141170	229798
43435	208105	205293
25983	101266	145634
54369	314044	299927
118135	6448362	3670146
369845	1376485	1771614
133025	892741	916124
202646	542002	495546
72402	206727	207957
1141	3050	6805
	12	8
248		
1215	2523	8530
1215	2523	8530

20–24 规模以上非工业重点行业企业研究与试验发展（R&D）基本情况（2017）

R&D Project Status of Non-Industrial Key Enterprises above Designated Size（2017）

指标	Item	单位数（个）Number of Units (unit）	#有R&D活动单位数（个）The Number of R&D active units (unit）
总计	**Total**	**689**	**71**
按企业规模分	**Grouped by Size of Enterprises**		
大型企业	Large-size	157	43
中型企业	Medium-size	399	27
小型企业	Small-size	124	1
微型企业	Microenterprise	9	
按登记注册类型分	**Grouped by Registered Status**		
内资企业	Domestic Investment Enterprises	662	66
港、澳、台商投资企业	Enterprises with Funds from Hong Kong, Macao And Taiwan	7	
外商投资企业	Foreign Funded Enterprises	20	5
按国民经济行业分	**Grouped by Sector**		
建筑业	Construction	332	27
交通运输、仓储和邮政业	Traffic, Transport, Storage and Post	40	1
信息传输、软件和信息技术服务业	Information Transmission, Computer Services and Software	93	15
租赁和商务服务业	Leasing and Business Services	37	2
科学研究和技术服务业	Scientific Research, Technical Sevice	115	25
水利、环境和公共设施管理业	Management of Water Conservancy, Environment and Public Facilities	31	
卫生和社会工作	Health, Social Security		
文化、体育和娱乐业	Culture, Sports and Entertainment	41	1

20-25 规模以上非工业重点行业企业研究与试验发展（R&D）人员和经费支出情况（2017年）

R&D Personnel and Expenditure of Non-Industrial Key Enterprises above Designated Size (2017)

指标	Item	R&D人员（人）R&D personnel (person)	#研究人员 #Researchers
总计	**Total**	13329	6124
按企业规模分	**Grouped by Size of Enterprises**		
大型企业	Large-size	12200	5612
中型企业	Medium-size	1117	506
小型企业	Small-size	12	6
微型企业	Microenterprise		
按登记注册类型分	**Grouped by Registered Status**		
内资企业	Domestic Investment Enterprises	12666	5793
港、澳、台商投资企业	Enterprises with Funds from Hong Kong, Macao And Taiwan		
外商投资企业	Foreign Funded Enterprises	663	331
按国民经济行业分	**Grouped by Sector**		
建筑业	Construction	4767	1771
交通运输、仓储和邮政业	Traffic, Transport, Storage and Post	43	23
信息传输、软件和信息技术服务业	Information Transmission Computer Services and Software	4470	2248
租赁和商务服务业	Leasing and Business Services	33	18
科学研究和技术服务业	Scientific Research, Technical Sevice	3992	2053
水利、环境和公共设施管理业	Management of Water Conservancy, Environment and Public Facilities		
卫生和社会工作	Health, Social Security		
文化、体育和娱乐业	Culture, Sports and Entertainment	24	11

20-25 续表1 continued 1

指标	Item	R&D经费内部支出（万元）R&D Intramural Expenditure (10000 yuan)	#政府资金 # Government funds
总计	**Total**	372947	7154
按企业规模分	**Grouped by Size of Enterprises**		
大型企业	Large-size	328206	6843
中型企业	Medium-size	44686	256
小型企业	Small-size	55	55
微型企业	Microenterprise		
按登记注册类型分	**Grouped by Registered Status**		
内资企业	Domestic Investment Enterprises	334811	7038
港、澳、台商投资企业	Enterprises with Funds from Hong Kong, Macao And Taiwan		
外商投资企业	Foreign Funded Enterprises	38136	116
按国民经济行业分	**Grouped by Sector**		
建筑业	Construction	139630	242
交通运输、仓储和邮政业	Traffic, Transport, Storage and Post	87	40
信息传输、软件和信息技术服务业	Information Transmission, Computer Services and Software	176199	1000
租赁和商务服务业	Leasing and Business Services	4287	
科学研究和技术服务业	Scientific Research, Technical Sevice	52447	5872
水利、环境和公共设施管理业	Management of Water Conservancy, Environment and Public Facilities		
卫生和社会工作	Health, Social Security		
文化、体育和娱乐业	Culture, Sports and Entertainment	297	

20-25 续表2 continued 2

指标	Item	#企业资金 # Enterprise funds	#境外资金 # Foreign funds
总计	**Total**	360945	3112
按企业规模分	**Grouped by Size of Enterprises**		
大型企业	Large-size	319702	135
中型企业	Medium-size	41243	2977
小型企业	Small-size		
微型企业	Microenterprise		
按登记注册类型分	**Grouped by Registered Status**		
内资企业	Domestic Investment Enterprises	326036	
港、澳、台商投资企业	Enterprises with Funds from Hong Kong, Macao And Taiwan		
外商投资企业	Foreign Funded Enterprises	34909	3112
按国民经济行业分	**Grouped by Sector**		
建筑业	Construction	139384	
交通运输、仓储和邮政业	Traffic, Transport, Storage and Post	47	
信息传输、软件和信息技术服务业	Information Transmission, Computer Services and Software	175003	
租赁和商务服务业	Leasing and Business Services	1301	2977
科学研究和技术服务业	Scientific Research, Technical Sevice	44914	135
水利、环境和公共设施管理业	Management of Water Conservancy, Environment and Public Facilities		
卫生和社会工作	Health, Social Security		
文化、体育和娱乐业	Culture, Sports and Entertainment	297	

20–26 规模以上非工业重点行业企业研究与试验发展（R&D）项目情况（2017年）

The Situation of Non-Industrial Key Enterprises above Designated Size Projects（2017）

指标	Item	合计 Total	参加项目人员（人） Personnel participating in the project（person）	项目经费内部支出（万元） Intramural Expenditure（10 000 yuan）
总计	**Total**	679	11546	372771
按企业规模分	**Grouped by Size of Enterprises**			
大型企业	Large-size	587	10476	328079
中型企业	Medium-size	91	1060	44637
小型企业	Small-size	1	10	55
微型企业	Microenterprise			
按登记注册类型分	**Grouped by Registered Status**			
内资企业	Domestic Investment Enterprises	655	10899	334723
港、澳、台商投资企业	Enterprises with Funds from Hong Kong, Macao And Taiwan			
外商投资企业	Foreign Funded Enterprises	24	647	38048
按国民经济行业分	**Grouped by Sector**			
建筑业	Construction	222	4392	139548
交通运输、仓储和邮政业	Traffic, Transport, Storage and Post	2	19	87
信息传输、软件和信息技术服务业	Information Transmission, Computer Services and Software	56	3863	176152
租赁和商务服务业	Leasing and Business Services	2	31	4287
科学研究和技术服务业	Scientific Research, Technical Sevice	391	3217	52400
水利、环境和公共设施管理业	Management of Water Conservancy, Environment and Public Facilities			
卫生和社会工作	Health, Social Security			
文化、体育和娱乐业	Culture, Sports and Entertainment	6	24	297

20-27 主要年份知识产权情况

Intellectual Property Rights in Major Years

指 标	Item	2015	2016	2017	2018
一、专利申请合计数（件）	**Patents Application Accepted(unit)**	60986	46103	81110	56408
发明专利	Inventions	14024	18569	40439	24074
实用新型专利	Utility Models	15735	18369	22461	24313
外观专利	Designs	31227	9165	18210	8021
二、授权专利合计（件）	**Patents Application Granted(unit)**	25103	38279	25042	31640
发明专利	Inventions	5873	6686	7902	8025
实用新型专利	Utility Models	12030	12344	11595	17070
外观专利	Designs	7200	19249	5545	6545
三、注册商标（件）	**Registered Trade Mark(unit)**	9600	35391	28448	34500

注：1.本表数据由市场监管局提供。
2.本表数据为西安原口径数据。

20-28 主要年份民事知识产权维权情况

Protection of Civil Intellectual Property Rights in Major Years

指 标	Item	2015	2016	2017	2018
1、专利纠纷	Patent controversies	130	95	112	449
2、商标纠纷	Trade mark controversies	277	353	404	892
3、著作权纠纷	Copyright controversies	327	404	190	520
4、技术合同纠纷	Technological contract controversies	12	10	36	47
5、其他知识产权纠纷	Others IPR controversies	67	25	110	182

注：1.本表数据由市二级人民法院提供。
2.本表数据为西安原口径数据。

20–29 规模以上工业企业自主知识产权情况（2017年）

The Independent Intellectual Property Rights of Industrial Enterprises above Designated Size（2017）

指　标	Item	专利申请数（件）Number of Patent Applications (piece)	#发明专利 Invention Patent of	期末有效发明专利数（件）Number of Valid Invention Patents At the End of the Term (piece)
总计	**Total**	**5686**	**2575**	**10551**
按企业规模分	**Grouped by Size of Enterprises**			
大型企业	Large-size	2855	1539	4163
中型企业	Medium-size	1059	370	2426
小型企业	Small-size	1730	640	3891
微型企业	Microenterprise	42	26	71
按登记注册类型分	**Grouped by Registered Status**			
内资企业	Domestic Investment Enterprises	5522	2506	9960
国有企业	State-owned Enterprises	1182	680	2002
集体企业	Collective-owned Enterprise			
股份合作企业	Stock Cooperative Enterprises			6
联营企业	Affiliated Enterprise			
有限责任公司	Limited Liability Corporations	2546	1186	4478
股份有限公司	Share-holding Corporation Ltd	1124	424	2551
私营企业	Private Enterprise	670	216	923
其他	Other Domestic Funded Enterprises			
港、澳、台商投资企业	Enterprises with Funds from Hong Kong, Macao And Taiwan	13	9	63
外商投资企业	Foreign Funded Enterprises	151	60	528
按国民经济行业大类分	**Grouped by Sector**			
采矿业	Mining	337	207	379
煤炭开采和洗选业	Mining and Washing of Coal			
石油和天然气开采业	Extraction of Petroleum and Natural Gas	303	182	274
黑色金属矿采选业	Mining of Ferrous Metal Ores			
有色金属矿采选业	Mining of Non-ferrous Metal Ores			
非金属矿采选业	Mining and Processing of Nonmetal Ores			
开采辅助活动	Mining Other Ores	34	25	105
制造业	Manufacturing Industry	5122	2234	9971
农副食品加工业	Processing of Food from Agriculture Products			
食品制造业	Manufacture of Food	2		29
酒、饮料和精制茶制造业	Manufacture of Beverages	11	5	32
烟草制品业	Manufacture of Tobacco	35	7	13
纺织业	Manufacture of Textile	15	4	15
纺织服装、服饰业	Manufacture of Textile Wearing, Apparel			
皮革、毛皮、羽毛及其制品和制鞋业	Manufacture of Leather, Furs, Feather, Related Products and Footware	16	4	3

20-29 续表1 continued 1

指 标	Item	专利申请数（件） Number of Patent Applications (piece)	#发明专利 Invention Patent of	期末有效发明专利数（件） Number of Valid Invention Patents At the End of the Term (piece)
木材加工和木、竹、藤、棕、草制品业	Processing of Timber,Manufacture of Wood, Bamboo, Rattan, Palm and Straw Products			
家具制造业	Manufacture of Furniture			
造纸及纸制品业	Manufacture of Paper And Paper Products			
印刷和记录媒介复制业	Printing and Reproduction of Recording Media	22	19	99
文教、工美、体育和娱乐用品制造业	Education, Art, Sports And Entertainment Products Manufacturing			
石油加工、炼焦和核燃料加工业	Processing of Petroleum,Coking and Processing of Nuclear Fuel			
化学原料和化学制品制造业	Manufacture of Raw Chemical Materials and Chemical Products	380	220	759
医药制造业	Manufacture of Medicines	83	34	350
化学纤维制造业	Manufacture of Chemical Fiber			
橡胶和塑料制品业	Manufacture of Rubber and Manufacture of Plastic	32	8	90
非金属矿物制品业	Manufacture of Non-metallic Mineral Products	39	9	148
黑色金属冶炼和压延加工业	Smelting and Pressing of Ferrous Metals	10		15
有色金属冶炼和压延加工业	Smelting and Pressing of Non-ferrous Metals	168	118	605
金属制品业	Manufacture of Metal Products	205	121	395
通用设备制造业	Manufacture of General Purpose Machinery	218	84	593
专用设备制造业	Manufacture of Special Equipment	824	260	1065
汽车制造业	Manufacture of Motor Vehicle	646	157	532
铁路、船舶、航空航天和其他运输设备制造业	Railways, Ships, Aerospace And Other Transportation Equipment Manufacturing Industry	870	629	2023
电气机械和器材制造业	Manufacture of Electric Equipment and Machinery	590	183	1146
计算机、通信和其他电子设备制造业	Manufacture of Communication Equipment, Computers and Other Electronic Equipment	627	262	1142
仪器仪表制造业	Manufacture of Measuring Instruments and Machinery	285	106	769
其他制造业	Other Manufacturing	44	4	148
废弃资源综合利用业	Comprehensive Utilization Of Waste Resources			
金属制品、机械和设备修理业	Metal Products, Machinery and Equipment Repair Industry			
电力、燃气及水的生产供应业	Production and Supply of Electric Power,Gas and Water	227	134	201
电力、热力生产和供应业	Production and Supply of Electric Power and Heat Power	222	134	201
燃气生产和供应业	Production and Supply of Gas	2		
水的生产和供应业	Production and Supply of Water	3		

20-30 规模以上非工业重点行业企业知识产权（2017年）

Intellectual Property Rights of Non-Industrial Key Enterprises above Designated Size（2017）

指 标	Item	专利申请数（件）Number of Patent Applications (piece)	#发明专利 Invention Patent of	有效发明专利数（件）Number of Valid Invention Patents At the End of the Term (piece)
总计	**Total**	**2233**	**834**	**3231**
按企业规模分	**Grouped by Size of Enterprises**			
大型企业	Large-size	2040	750	3011
中型企业	Medium-size	185	79	219
小型企业	Small-size	8	5	1
微型企业	Microenterprise			
按登记注册类型分	**Grouped by Registered Status**			
内资企业	Domestic Investment Enterprises	2220	833	3187
港、澳、台商投资企业	Enterprises with Funds from Hong Kong, Macao And Taiwan			
外商投资企业	Foreign Funded Enterprises	13	1	44
按国民经济行业分	**Grouped by Sector**			
建筑业	Construction	579	159	671
交通运输、仓储和邮政业	Traffic, Transport, Storage and Post			
信息传输、软件和信息技术服务业	Information Transmission, Computer Services and Software	670	245	335
租赁和商务服务业	Leasing and Business Services	1	1	1
科学研究和技术服务业	Scientific Research, Technical Sevice	983	429	2211
水利、环境和公共设施管理业	Management of Water Conservancy, Environment and Public Facilities			
卫生和社会工作	Health, Social Security			
文化、体育和娱乐业	Culture, Sports and Entertainment			13

主要统计指标解释

普通高等学校 指按国家规定的设置标准和审批程序批准举办的，通过全国普通高等学校统一招生考试，招收高中毕业生为主要培养对象，实施高等学历教育的全日制大学、独立设置的学院和高等专科学校、高等职业学校及其他机构（独立学院和分校、大专班）。

大学、独立设置的学院主要实施本科层次以上教育。高等专科学校、高等职业学校实施专科层次教育。其他机构是承担国家普通招生计划任务不计校数的机构，包括独立学院、普通高等学校分校、大专班和批准筹建的普通高等学校等。独立学院指由普通本科高校按新机制、新模式举办的本科层次的二级学院，一些普通本科高校按公办机制和模式建立的二级学院，“分校”或其他类似的二级办学机构不属此范畴。

成人高等学校 指按照国家规定的设置标准和审批程序批准举办的，通过全国成人高等教育统一招生考试，招收具有高中毕业或同等学历的人员为主要培养对象，利用函授、业余、脱产等多种形式对其实施高等学历教育的学校。包括职工高等学校、农民高等学校、管理干部学院、教育学院、独立函授学院、广播电视大学、其他机构等。其他机构是承担国家成人招生计划任务不计校数的机构。

小学学龄儿童净入学率 指调查范围内已入小学学习的学龄儿童占校内外学龄儿童总数（包括弱智儿童，不包括盲聋哑儿童）的比重。计算公式为：

小学学龄儿童净入学率（%）=已入学的小学学龄儿童数／校内外小学学龄儿童总数×100%

研究与试验发展（R&D） 指在科学技术领域，为增加知识总量，以及运用这些知识去创造新的应用进行的系统的创造性的活动，包括基础研究、应用研究、试验发展三类活动。国际上通常采用R&D活动的规模和强度指标反映一国的科技实力和核心竞争力。

基础研究 指为了获得关于现象和可观察事实的基本原理的新知识（揭示客观事物的本质、运动规律，获得新发现、新学说）而进行的实验性或理论性研究，它不以任何专门或特定的应用或使用为目的。其成果以科学论文和科学著作为主要形式。用来反映知识的原始创新能力。

应用研究 指为获得新知识而进行的创造性研究，主要针对某一特定的目的或目标。应用研究是为了确定基础研究成果可能的用途，或是为达到预定的目标探索应采取的新方法（原理性）或新途径。其成果形式以科学论文、专著、原理性模型或发明专利为主。用来反映对基础研究成果应用途径的探索。

试验发展 指利用从基础研究、应用研究和实际经验所获得的现有知识，为产生新的产品、材料和装置，建立新的工艺、系统和服务，以及对已产生和建立的上述各项作实质性的改进而进行的系统性工作。其成果形式主要是专利、专有技术、具有新产品基本特征的产品原型或具有新装置基本特征的原始样机等。在社会科学领域，试验发展是指把通过基础研究、应用研究获得的知识转变成可以实施的计划（包括为进行检验和评估实施示范项目）的过程。人文科学领域没有对应的试验发展活动。主要反映将科研成果转化为技术和产品的能力，是科技推动经济社会发展的物化成果。

R&D人员 指参与研究与试验发展项目研究、管理和辅助工作的人员，包括项目（课题）组人员，企业科技行政管理人员和直接为项目（课题）活动提供服务的辅助人员。反映投入从事拥有自主知识产权的研究开发活动的人力规模。

R&D人员全时当量 指全时人员数加非全时人员按工作量折算为全时人员数的总和。例如：有两个全时人员和三个非全时人员（工作时间分别为20%、30%和70%），则全时当量为2+0.2+0.3+0.7=3.2人年。为国际上比较科技人力投入而制定的可比指标。

R&D经费内部支出 合计指调查单位用于内部开展R&D活动（基础研究、应用研究和试验发展）的实际支出。包括用于R&D项目（课题）活动的直接支出，以及间接用于R&D活动的管理费、服务费、与R&D有关的基本建设支出以及外协加工费等。不包括生产性活动支出、归还贷款支出以及与外单位合作或委托外单位进行R&D活动而转拨给对方的经费支出。

R&D经费内部支出中政府资金 指R&D经费内部支出中来自各级政府部门的各类资金，包括财政科学技术拨款、科学基金、教育等部门事业费以及政府部门预算外资金的实际支出。

R&D经费内部支出中企业资金 指R&D经费内部支出中来自本企业的自有资金和接受其他企业委托而获得的经费，以及科研院所、高校等事业单位从企业获得的资金的实际支出。

R&D项目（课题）数 指在当年立项并开展研究工作、以前年份立项仍继续进行研究的研发项目（课题）数，包括当年完成和年内研究：工作已告失败的研发项目（课题），但不包括委托外单位进行的研发项目（课题）数。

R&D项目（课题）人员全时当量 指实际参加研发项目（课题）活动人员折合的全时当量。

R&D项目（课题）经费内部支出 指调查单位内部在报告年度进行研发项目（课题）研究和试制等的实际支出。包括劳务费、其他日常支出、固定资产购建费、外协加工费等，不包括委托或与外单位合作进行项目（课题）研究而拨付给对方使用的经费。

新产品产值 指报告期企业生产的新产品的产值。新产品是指采用新技术原理、新设计构思研制、生产的全新产品，或在结构、材质、工艺等某一方面比原有产品有明显改进，从而显著提高了产品性能或扩大了使用功能的产品。新产品产值、新产品销售收入既包括经政府有关部门认定并在有效期内的新产品，也包括企业自行研制开发，未经政府有关部门认定，从投产之日起一年之内的新产品。

新产品销售收入 指报告期企业销售新产品实现的销售收入。

专利 是专利权的简称，是对发明人的发明创造经审查合格后，由专利局依据专利法授予发明人和设计人对该项发明创造享有的专有权。包括发明、实用新型和外观设计。反映拥有自主知识产权的科技和设计成果情况。

发明（专利） 指对产品、方法或者其改进所提出的新的技术方案。是国际通行的反映拥有自主知识产权技术的核心指标。

Explanatory Notes on Main Statistical Indicators

Regular Institutions of Higher Education refer to educational establishments set up according to the government evaluation and approval procedures, recruiting graduates from senior secondary schools as the main target by National Matriculation TEST. They include full-time universities, colleges, institutions of higher professional education, institutions of higher vocational education, institutions of higher vocational education and others (non-university tertiary, branch schools and undergraduate classes) .

Universities and colleges primarily provide undergraduate courses; institutions of higher professional education and institutions of higher vocational education primarily provide professional trainings; and others refer to educational establishments, which are responsible for enrolling higher education students under the State Plan but not enumerated in the total number of schools, including: branch schools of universities and colleges, and universities and colleges that have been approved and under plan for construction. Non-university tertiary refers to the regular undergraduate branch college which is running in new mechanism and mode, excluding the branch schools and other similar branches of educational institutions.

Institutions of Higher Education for Adults refer to educational establishments, set up in line with relevant rules approved by the government, enrolling staff and workers with senior secondary school or equivalent education, and providing higher education courses in many forms of correspondence, spare time, or full time for adults. Professionals thus trained receive a qualification equivalent to graduates studying regular courses at regular universities, colleges and professional colleges. Institutions of higher learning for adults include schools of higher education for staff and workers, schools of higher education for peasants, colleges for management cadres, pedagogical colleges, independent correspondence colleges, Radio and TV universities and other educational establishments. Other educational establishments have undertakings to enrol adult students but not enumerated in the schools under the State Plan.

Net Enrolment Ratio of Primary Schools refers to the proportion of school age children enrolled at schools to the total number of school age children both in and outside schools (including retarded children, but excluding blind, deaf and mute children) . The formula is:

$$\text{Net Enrolment Ratio Of Primary Schools} = \frac{\text{Total Primary School-age Children at Schools}}{\text{Total Primary School-age WnerdlihChether or Not Attending School}} \times 100\%$$

Research and Development (R&D) refers to systematic and creative activities in the field of science and technology aiming at increasing the knowledge and using the knowledge for new application. R&D includes 3 categories of activities: basic research, applied research and experimentation for development. The scale and intensity of R&D are widely used internationally to reflect the strength of S&T and the core competitiveness of a country in the world.

Basic Research refers to empirical or theoretical research aiming at obtaining new knowledge on the fundamental principles regarding phenomena or observable facts to reveal the intrinsic nature and underlying laws and to acquire new discoveries or new theories. Basic research takes no specific or designated application as the aim of the research. Results of basic research are mainly released or disseminated in the form of scientific papers or monographs. This indicator reflects the innovation capacity for original knowledge.

Applied Research refers to creative research aiming at obtaining new knowledge on a specific objective or target. Purpose of the applied research is to identify the possible uses of results from basic research, or to explore new (fundamental) methods or new approaches. Results of applied research are expressed in the form of scientific papers, monographs, fundamental models or invention patents. This indicator reflects the exploration of ways to apply the results of basic research.

Experiments and Development refer to systematic activities aiming at using the knowledge from basic and applied researches or from practical experience to develop new products, materials and equipment, to establish new production process, systems and services, or to make substantial improvement on the existing products, process or services. Results of experiment and development activities are embodied in patents, exclusive technology, and monotype of new products or equipment. In social sciences, experiment and development activities refer to the process of converting the knowledge from basic or applied researches into feasible programmes (including conduct of demonstration projects for assessment and evaluation) . There are no experiment and development activities in the science of humanities. This indicator reflects the capability of transferring the results of S&T into technique and products, and measures the realization of S&T in spearheading the economic and social development.

R&D Personnel refer to persons engaged in research, management and supporting activities of R&D, including persons in the project teams, persons engaged in the management of S&T activities of enterprises and supporting staff providing direct service to the research projects. This indicator reflects the size of personnel engaged in R&D activities with independent intellectual property.

Full-time Equivalent of R&D Personnel refers to the sum of the full-time persons and the full-time equivalent of part-time persons converted by workload. For instance, if there are 2 full-time persons and 3 part-time workers (20%, 30% and 70% of working hours respectively on R&D activities) , the full-time equivalent are 2+0.2+0.3+0.7=3.2 person-years. This is an internationally comparable indicator of S&T manpower input.

Total Internal Expenditure of Funds on R&D refers to the real expenditure of surveyed units on their own R&D activities (basic research, application study, test and development) including direct expenditure on R&D activities, indirect expenditure of management and services on R&D activities, expenditure on capital construction and material processing by others. Excluding the expenditure on production activities, return of loan, and fees transferred to cooperated and entrusted agencies on R&D activities.

Internal Expenditure of Government Funds refersto the expenditure of funds on R&D activities from government agencies at different levels, including appropriate funds on science and technology from financial departments, scientific funds, operating expenses from education departments and the real expenditure of extra budgetary funds from government agencies.

Internal Expenditure of Funds of Enterprises refers to the expenditure of funds on R&D activities from self-raised funds of enterprises and funds from other enterprises through entrustment, and the expenditure of funds of institutions, such as institution of scientific research and universities, from enterprises.

Number of R&D Projects (subjects) refers to the number of R&D projects (subjects) set up and implemented at the reference year, and the number of R&D projects (subjects) set up in former years and under implementation, including the projects (subjects) finished and failed at the reference year, excluding the projects (subjects) implemented by others through entrustment.

Full-time Equivalent of R&D Personnel refers to the full-time equivalent of persons actually engaged in R&D projects. (subjects)

Internal Expenditure of Funds on R&D Projects (subjects) refers to the real expenditure of internal funds of the surveyed units on research and test of R&D projects (subjects) at the reference year, including service fee, other daily expenditure, cost for capital goods, cost of external process; excluding expenditure of funds transferred to other cooperated and entrusted units of the projects.

Output Value of New Products refers to the output value of new products during the reporting period. The new products refer to brand new products produced with new technology and new design, or product that represent noticeable improvement in terms of structure, material, or production process for improving significantly the character of function of the older versions. The output value and sales income of the new products include those of new products certified by relevant government agencies within the period of certification, as well as new products designed and produced by enterprises within a year without certification by government agencies.

Sales Income of New Products refers to the real sales income of new products of the enterprises at the reporting period.

Patent is an abbreviation for the patent right and refers to the exclusive right of ownership by the inventors or designers for the creation or inventions, given from the patent offices after due process of assessment and approval in accordance with the Patent Law. Patents are granted for inventions, utility models and designs. This indicator reflects the achievements of S&T and design with independent intellectual property.

Patented Inventions refer to new technical proposals to the products or methods or their modifications. This is universal core indicator reflecting the technologies with independent intellectual property.

21 文化、体育、卫生、社会福利和其他

CULTURE,SPORTS,PUBLIC HEALTH,SOCIAL WELFARE INSTITUTIONS AND OTHER SOCIAL ACTIVITIES

资料整理：郝　静
Data management：Hao Jing
数据审核：王金桂
Data audit：Wang Jingui

第二十一部分　文化、体育、卫生、社会福利和其他

一、简要说明

本章资料主要包括文化、卫生、民政、体育、计划生育、共青团、妇联以及公检法等方面的内容，由西安市统计局服务业和社会科技处根据西安市文广新局、卫计委、民政局、体育局、妇联、团市委以及公安局、检察院、法院等部门提供资料整理。本章资料数据口径见表下注释。

二、主要指标

公共图书馆藏量（千册件）	7711	比上年增加	371
医院数（个）	343	比上年增加	14
医院床位数（万张）	6.34	比上年增加	5146（张）

21　CULTURE,SPORTS,PUBLIC HEALTH,SOCIAL WELFARE INSTITUTIONS AND OTHER SOCIAL ACTIVITIES

Ⅰ.Brief Introduction

Data in this chapter primarily consists of data of culture, sanitation, civil administration, physical education, family planning, Communist Youth League, the Women's Federation, public security organs, procuratorial organs and people's court, compiled by Tertiary Industry and Social Science & Technology Division of Xi'an Bureau of Statistics according to data from Xi'an Bureau of Cuture, health and Family Planning Commision, Bureau of Civial Adnimistration, Bureau of PE, the Women's Federation, Municipal Committee of Communist Youth League, Bureau of Public Security, Procuratorate, People's Court and other department concerned. The field and range of data in this chapter are listed in the explanatory notes below the chare.

Ⅱ.Major Indicators

		Increase over Preceding Year
Number of Collections in Libraries（1000 volume-times）	7711	371
Number of Hospitals(unit)	343	14
Number of Beds(10 000 units)	6.34	5146（unit）

21-1 电影基本情况（2018年）

The Basic Situation of Film（2018）

指 标	Item	2018
电影制片厂（个）	Film Studio(unit)	1
电影制片厂从业人员（人）	Film Studio Employees(person)	898
电影发行放映管理机构（个）	Film Projection and Publication Administrating Institutions(unit)	2
电影发行放映管理机构从业人员（人）	Film Projection and Publication Administrating Institution Staff(person)	8
电影放映单位（个）	Unit of Film Shows(unit)	275
电影院	Cinema	118
影剧院	Theaters	5
放映队	File Projection Team	152
电影放映单位从业人员（人）	Staff of Unit of Film Shows(person)	3755
电影院	Cinema	3540
影剧院	Theaters	63
放映队	File Projection Team	152
电影放映场数（千场）	Number of Film Shows（1000 shows）	1606
电影观众人数（千人次）	Number of Spectators(1000 person-times)	31225
电影票房收入（万元）	Box-office Receipts(10 000yuan)	100617
平均每一放映场次的观众人次（人次）	Average Audience of Each Projection(person-times)	19
平均每一放映场次的放映收入（元）	Average Income of Each Projcetion(yuan)	627

注：本表数据来源于市文广新局。
　　本表数据含西咸新区。

21-2 图书馆基本情况（2018年）

The Basic Situation of Library（2018）

指　标	Item	2018
公共图书馆个数（个）	Number of Public Libraries(unit)	13
公共图书馆从业人员（人）	Public Library Practitioners (person)	473
公共图书馆藏量（千册件）	Public Library Reserves(1 000 volume-times)	7711
电子图书（千册）	E-books(1 000 volumes)	6354
阅览室坐席（个）	Number of Seatings in Reading Room(unit)	5123
书刊文献外借人次（千人次）	Number of Books and literature Borrowed by Readers (1 000 person-times)	1272
书刊文献外借册次（千册件）	Volumes of Books and literature Lent to Readers(1 000 volume-times)	3633
图书流通人次（千人次）	Book Circulation Person-time (1 000 person-times)	7184
县以上公共图书馆购书经费（万元）	Book-purchase Fund of Public Library above the County Level(10 000 yuan)	2024
公共图书馆建筑面积（万平方米）	Building Area of Public Library (10 000 sq.m)	9.44

注：本表数据来源于市文广新局。
　　本表数据含西咸新区。

21-3 艺术表演基本情况（2018年）

The Basic Situation of Art Performance（2018）

指　标	Item	2018
艺术表演团体机构数（个）	Number of Organization of Art Performance Troupes(unit)	18
艺术表演团体从业人员（人）	Art Performance Troupes Practitioners (person)	2361
艺术表演团体演出场次（场）	Number of Performances by Art Performance Troupes(show)	5153
#国内演出场次	Domestic Performance	4997
艺术表演观众人次（千人次）	Audience for the Art Performance(1 000 person-times)	6553
艺术表演团体本年创作首映剧目（个）	Art Performance Troupes Creative Premieres of the Year (unit)	13
艺术表演场馆数（个）	Number of Art Performance Places(unit)	16
艺术表演场馆从业人员（人）	Art Performance Place Practitioners (person)	858
艺术表演场馆坐席（个）	Art Performance Place Seatings(unit)	9981
艺术科研机构（个）	Art and Research Institutions(unit)	2
艺术科研机构从业人员（人）	Art and Research Institutions Practitioners(person)	52

注：本表数据来源于市文广新局。
　　本表数据含西咸新区。

21-4 主要年份群众艺术馆、文化馆（站）活动情况

Basic Statistics on Activities of Mass Art Centers and Cultural Centers in Representative Years

指　　标	Item	2010	2013	2014	2015	2016	2017	2018
机构数（个）	Number of Insititutions (unit)	197	198	199	199	190	202	202
举办展览个数（个）	Number of Exhibitions (unit)	705	658	627	606	562	649	632
举办展览参观人次（千人次）	Number of Exhibition Visitors(1 000 person-times)		301	326	289	287	418	392
组织文艺活动次数（次）	Art Performances and Story-telling Sessions (times)	3729	4114	3617	3811	4246	5498	6518
组织文艺活动参加人次（千人次）	Number of Culture Activities attendees (1 000 person-times)		1633	1576	1574	1688	2631	3322
举办训练班班次（个）	Number of Training Courses (unit)	3018	1616	1872	2126	1906	2597	3310
举办训练班结业人次（千人次）	Number of Certificate Trained Persons (1 000 person-times)	133	155	156	207	149	188	209
组织各类理论研讨和讲座次数（次）	Number of Theoretical Discussion and Seminars(times)		122	254	216	189	101	113
组织各类理论研讨和讲座参加人次（千人次）	Number of Persons in Theoretical Discussion and Seminars(1 000 person-times)		19	28	25	18	17	15
本年收入（千元）	Income of this year (1 000 yuan)	42937	101365	89520	102567	103706	133378	116324
本年支出（千元）	Expenditure of this year (1 000 yuan)	45160	93485	84827	100749	111942	141012	119354

注：本表数据来源于市文广新局。
　　本表2017年及以后年份数据含西咸新区。

21-5 文物保护业基本情况（2018年）

Basic Statistics on Cultural Relics Protection（2018）

指　　标	Item	机　构（个）Insititution (unit)	人　员（人）Personnel (person)	文物藏品 实际数量（件）Factual Number of Collections (piece)	一级品（件）Grade One (piece)	举办陈列展览次数(次) Times of exhibition (times)	参观人员（千人次）Number of Visitors (1000 person-times)
文物保护管理机构	Cultural Relics administrative Departments	26	532	29135	36	15	1437
其他文物机构	Other Agencies	5	146	40899			
博物馆	Museums	100	4715	1892772	3849	536	33053
#免费开放馆	Museums Open Free	96	3812	1877156	2588	487	23129
文物科研机构	Scientific Research of Historical Relics Preservation	3	247	37120	186		

注：本表数据来源于市文物局。
　　本表数据为西安原口径数据。

21-6 主要年份广播电台及节目制作情况

Basic Statistics of Broadcasting Stations and Program Production in Representative Years

指　标	Item	2010	2013	2014	2015	2016	2017	2018
省、地广播电台（座）	Broadcasting Stations at the Province and District Level(set)	2						
省、地广播电视台（座）	Broadcasting Station at Province and District Level(set)		2	2	2	2	2	2
县级广播电视台（座）	Number of Wire Broadcasting Stations and TV Relaying Stations(set)	6	6	6	6	6	6	6
中、短波转播发射台（座）	Medium and Short Wave Broadcast Transmitting Station (base)	55	57	57	13	13	13	13
节目套数（套）	Number of Programs(set)	18	20	20	20	20	20	20
全年播出时间(时：分)	Broadcasting Hours annually (houe:minute)	124100	138278	143873	137075	139159	132252	1E+05
广播节目综合人口覆盖率（%）	Broadcasts comprehensive population coverage (%)	99.4	99.47	99.49	99.55	99.62	99.65	100
制作广播节目(时：分)	Productions of Broadcasting (houe:minute)	110639	106554	104459	116603	119424	100169	1E+05
#新闻资讯类	News Programs	13786	14355	13208	12208	7590	6362	6761
专题服务类	Special Subject Programs	24451	30181	26884	21864	26957	26907	28463
综艺类	Variety Programs	37720	24516	27148	37885	39735	25793	41535
广播剧类	Literature Programs	2406	3083	3712	6674	3990	4680	5404
广告类	Advertisements	28339	20552	18465	15777	18363	15968	13627
其他类	Service Programs	3937	13867	15042	22195	22787	20459	21628

注：本表数据来源于市文广新局。
中、短波转播发射台2014年之前统计口径为中短波、调频发射台及转播台。数据变化因指标含义变化所致。
本表2017年及以后年份数据含西咸新区。

21-7 主要年份电视台及节目制作情况

Basic Statistics of TV Stations and Production of TV Program in Representative Years

指　标	Item	2010	2013	2014	2015	2016	2017	2018
调频电视转播发射台（座）	FM Television Relay Station (base)	10	11	11	48	48	47	48
无线电视节目（套）	Program Productions of Non-cable television Stations (set)	6	6	6	6	2	2	2
有线电视节目（套）	Program Productions of cable television Stations (set)	16	16	16	16	20	20	21
全年播出时间（时：分）	Broadcasting Hours annually (houe:minute)	141856	140927	143000	141839	140312	136960	128368
电视节目综合人口覆盖率（%）	TV shows comprehensive population coverage(%)	98.57	98.84	98.96	99.01	99.11	99.13	100
制作电视节目（时：分）	Earth Stations of Satellite TV (houe:minute)	29626	46614	35182	43563	54200	49001	45731
#新闻资讯类	News and Information Programs	8930	13360	11797	11839	12891	10517	9387
专题服务类	Special Subject Programs	7762	7751	8289	8073	9346	9769	10808
综艺类	Variety Programs	3942	6508	5014	6242	7883	9080	8789
影视剧类	Film and Television Drama	1729	1820	110	462	490	870	363
广告类	Advertisement	3313	8066	3491	7921	6198	6493	3981
其他类	Service Programs	3950	9109	6479	9026	17390	12272	12403

注：本表数据来源于市文广新局。
调频电视转播发射台2014年之前统计口径为发射台及转播台。数字变化因指标含义变化所致。
本表2017年及以后年份数据含西咸新区。

21-8 竞技体育情况（2018年）

The Situation of Competitive Sports（2018）

指　标	Item	2018
奥运会获得奖牌(枚)	Number of Medals Won in the Olympic Games(unit)	
金牌数	Gold	
银牌数	Silver	
铜牌数	Bronze	
全运会获得奖牌(枚)	Number of Medals Won in the National Games(unit)	
金牌数	Gold	
银牌数	Silver	
铜牌数	Bronze	
省运会获得奖牌(枚)	Number of Medals Won in the Provincial Games(unit)	
金牌数	Gold	521.5
银牌数	Silver	178
铜牌数	Bronze	17
其他国际、国内赛事	Other International and Domestic Events	
金牌数(枚)	Gold(unit)	8
银牌数(枚)	Silver(unit)	52
体育传统项目学校(个)	Sports Traditional Project School(unit)	128
体育传统项目学校在校训练学生数(人)	Number of Students in the Sports Traditional Project School (person)	5800
高水平体育后备人才基地(个)	High Level Sports Reserve Base(unit)	3
省级示范性体校(个)	Provincial Demonstration Sports School(unit)	3
等级教练员人数(人)	Number of Graded Coaches (person)	76
国家级	National Level	
高　级	Senior Level	14
一　级	One Level	28
二　级	Two Level	24
三　级	Three Level	10
二级运动员人数(人)	Second Grade Athletes (person)	236

注：本表数据来源于市体育局。
　　本表数据不含西咸新区，且仅包括市本级。

21-9 群众体育情况（2018年）

The Situation of Mass Sports（2018）

指 标	Item	2018
全年承办的县级以上群众性体育赛事（个）	Mass Sports Events Held throughout the Year(unit)	500
国家级	National Level	9
省 级	Provincial Level	3
市 级	City Level	51
县 级	County Level	437
全年举办的社会体育指导员培训班（期）	Training Course for Social Sports Instructors Held throughout the Year （time）	20
社会体育指导员人数（名）	Social Sports Instructor（person）	23129
体育先进社区（个）	Advanced Sports Community(unit)	
#国家级	National Level	
省 级	Provincial Level	
群众体育先进单位（个）	Advanced Unit of Mass Sports(unit)	11
#国家	National Level	
省 级	Provincial Level	11
晨晚健身站点（个）	Morning and Evening Fitness sites(unit)	1600
全民健身活动中心（个）	National Fitness Center(unit)	5
乡镇体育健身工程（个）	Township Sports Fitness Project(unit)	5
村级农民体育健身工程（个）	Village Level Farmers' Sports Fitness Project(unit)	90
体育人口（万人）	Sports Population(10 000 person)	460

注：本表数据来源于市体育局。
本表数据不含西咸新区。

21-10 体育产业情况（2018年）

The Situation of Sport Industry (2018)

指　标	Item	2018
全市县级标准公共体育场地建设情况	Construction of Standard Public Sports Venues in the County Level	
已建场地个数（个）	Number of Built Sites(units)	3
在建场地个数（个）	Number of Sites in Construction(units)	4
全市全民健身设施建设情况	Construction of National Fitness Facilities in the City	
全民健身长廊（个）	National Fitness Corridor(units)	3
全民健身园区（个）	National Fitness Park(units)	24
多功能运动场（个）	Multifunction Playground(units)	41
户外营地（个）	Outdoor Camps(units)	
全民健身室内健身房（个）	Fitness Indoor Gymnasium(units)	10
健身步道（千米）	Fitness Footpath(km)	22.2
自行车专用道（千米）	Bicycle Special Road(km)	50
全市体育彩票销售情况	Sales of Sports Lottery in the City	
体育彩票销售网点数量（个）	Number of Sales Outlets of Sports Lottery (units)	1418
体育彩票销售网点数量占全省的比重（%）	Proportion of Sports Lottery Sales Outlets Accounts for the Proportion of the Whole Province（%）	35
本年体育彩票销售金额（万元）	Sales Amount of Sports Lottery in this Year (10 000 yuan)	341400
本年体育彩票销售金额占全省的比重（%）	Sales Amount of Sports Lottery in this year Accounts for the Proportion of the Whole Province（%）	41.91
全市体育产业单位数量（个）	Number of Sports Industrial Units in the City (units)	583

注：本表数据来源于市体育局。
本表数据不含西咸新区。

21-11 主要年份医疗卫生机构、床位、人员情况

Number of Health Care Institutions, Beds and Personnel in Health Care Institutions in Representative Years

年份 Year	医疗卫生机构数（个） Number of Health Care Institutions (unit)	医院数（个） Number of Health Care Hospital (unit)	医疗卫生机构床位数（张） Number of Health Care Bed (unit)	医院床位数（张） Number of Hospital Bed (unit)	卫生技术人员数（人） Number of Medical Technical Personnel (person)
2009	5284	261	36849	32371	52620
2010	5632	258	39407	34274	57756
2011	5554	268	41010	35976	61281
2012	5576	276	44239	39213	66899
2013	5503	281	47867	42753	71134
2014	5554	281	51065	45561	76005
2015	5802	295	54708	49830	81462
2016	5869	292	56332	51508	86258
2017	6376	329	63942	58219	94221
2018	6638	343	68981	63365	101477

注：本表数据来源于市卫计委。
本表2017年及以后年份数据含西咸新区。

21-12 医疗卫生机构、床位及人员情况（2018年）

卫生机构	Health Care Institutions	机构数（个）Number of Institutions (unit)	床位数（张）Number of Beds (unit)
总计	**Total**	**6638**	**68981**
一、医院	**Hospitals**	**343**	**63365**
综合医院	General Hospitals	217	44665
中医医院	Hospitals Specialized in Traditional Chinese Medicine	51	6926
中西医结合医院	Hospitals Integrating Traditional Chinese Medicine with Western Therapeutics in Practice	4	1203
民族医院	Nationalities Hospitals		
专科医院	Specialized Hospitals	70	10472
护理院	Nursing centers	1	99
二、基层医疗卫生机构	**Commuting Health Hare Service Centre**	**6212**	**3864**
社区卫生服务中心(站)	Community Health Care Center(Station)	222	1647
社区卫生服务中心	Community Health Care Center	121	1636
社区卫生服务站	Community Health Care Station	101	11
卫生院	Health Center	119	2187
街道卫生院	Urban Health-center	2	119
乡镇卫生院	Rural Health-center	117	2068
村卫生室	Village Clinics	3337	
门诊部	Outpatient Department	292	30
诊所、卫生所、医务室	Clinic, Health Center, Infirmary	2242	
三、专业公共卫生机构	**College of Public Health Institutions**	**54**	**1522**
疾病预防控制中心	Center for Disease Control and Prevention	16	
专科疾病防治院（所、站）	Specialized Disease Prevention and Cure Center (Place, Station)	1	800
健康教育所（站、中心）	Health Education Institute (Station, Center)	2	
妇幼保健院（所、站）	Maternal and Child Health Hospital (Station)	15	722
急救中心（站）	Emergency Center	2	
采供血机构	Blood Collection Agencies	1	
卫生监督所（中心）	Health Supervision Agencies (Center)	14	
计划生育技术服务机构	Institutions of Technical Service for Family Planning	3	
四、其他卫生机构	**Other Health Institution**	**29**	**230**
疗养院	Nursing Centres	1	230
卫生监督检验(监测、检测)所(站)	Health Supervision and Inspection Agencies		
医学科学研究机构	Medical Scientific Research Institutions	3	
医学在职培训机构	Medical Training Institutions	5	
临床检验中心（所、站）	Clinical Testing Center (Place, Station)	4	
统计信息中心	Statistical Information Center	1	
其他	Other	15	

注：本表数据来源于市卫计委。
本表人员合计中包括乡村医生3210人和卫生员137人，不含乡镇卫生院在村卫生室工作的执业（助理）医师、注册护士。
本表数据含西咸新区。

Number of Health Care Institutions, Beds and Personnel in Health Care Institutions（2018）

人员合计（人） Total Number of Employed Persons (person)	卫生技术人员 Medical Technical Personnel	执业（助理）医师数 Licensed (Assistant) Doctors	#执业医师 Chartered Doctors
125179	**101477**	**33776**	**30322**
91385	**74944**	**22690**	**21658**
66901	55762	16923	16189
8855	7025	2129	1999
1424	1119	386	373
14156	10994	3242	3089
49	44	10	8
28135	**22452**	**9980**	**7693**
6212	5183	1584	1282
5139	4238	1235	971
1073	945	349	311
3980	3366	905	604
222	191	68	42
3758	3175	837	562
4593	1246	1086	376
4930	4475	2030	1706
8420	8182	4375	3725
4566	**3438**	**915**	**810**
1080	826	362	330
604	472	88	85
77	31		
1874	1457	404	342
135	73	37	35
139	86	10	8
569	430		
88	63	14	10
1093	**643**	**191**	**161**
79	44	17	14
137	94	51	50
188	78	6	6
251	118	7	5
5			
433	309	110	86

21-12 续表1

卫生机构	Health Care Institutions	人员合计（人）	
		卫生技术人员中	
		注册护士 Registered Nurses	药师（士） Junior Paramedics
总计	**Total**	**46450**	**4423**
一、医院	**Hospitals**	**37413**	**3141**
综合医院	General Hospitals	27921	2192
中医医院	Hospitals Specialized in Traditional Chinese Medicine	3187	455
中西医结合医院	Hospitals Integrating Traditional Chinese Medicine with Western Therapeutics in Practice	550	72
民族医院	Nationalities Hospitals		
专科医院	Specialized Hospitals	5727	419
护理院	Nursing centers	28	3
二、基层医疗卫生机构	**Commuting Health Hare Service Centre**	**7915**	**1159**
社区卫生服务中心(站)	Community Health Care Center(Station)	1872	392
社区卫生服务中心	Community Health Care Center	1459	317
社区卫生服务站	Community Health Care Station	413	75
卫生院	Health Center	984	215
街道卫生院	Urban Health-center	80	7
乡镇卫生院	Rural Health-center	904	208
村卫生室	Village Clinics	160	
门诊部	Outpatient Department	1755	219
诊所、卫生所、医务室	Clinic, Health Center, Infirmary	3144	333
三、专业公共卫生机构	**College of Public Health Institutions**	**964**	**112**
疾病预防控制中心	Center for Disease Control and Prevention	62	14
专科疾病防治院（所、站）	Specialized Disease Prevention and Cure Center (Place, Station)	251	24
健康教育所（站、中心）	Health Education Institute (Station, Center)		
妇幼保健院（所、站）	Maternal and Child Health Hospital (Station)	593	60
急救中心（站）	Emergency Center	18	2
采供血机构	Blood Collection Agencies	27	7
卫生监督所（中心）	Health Supervision Agencies (Center)		
计划生育技术服务机构	Institutions of Technical Service for Family Planning	13	5
四、其他卫生机构	**Other Health Institution**	**158**	**11**
疗养院	Nursing Centres	16	5
卫生监督检验(监测、检测)所(站)	Health Supervision and Inspection Agencies		
医学科学研究机构	Medical Scientific Research Institutions	7	3
医学在职培训机构	Medical Training Institutions	1	
临床检验中心（所、站）	Clinical Testing Center (Place, Station)	2	
统计信息中心	Statistical Information Center		
其他	Other	132	3

continued 1

Total Number of Employed Persons (person)				
Among:Medical Technical Personnel		其他技术人员	管理人员	工勤技能人员
技师（士） Technicians	其他 Others	Other Technical Personnel	Administrative Personnel	Logistics Technical Workers
6035	**10793**	**925**	**9723**	**9707**
4463	**7237**	**646**	**7931**	**7864**
3243	5483	468	5477	5194
412	842	85	796	949
72	39	6	189	110
733	873	87	1468	1607
3			1	4
1036	**2362**	**81**	**1078**	**1177**
413	922	45	470	514
361	866	32	386	483
52	56	13	84	31
308	954	8	278	328
10	26		6	25
298	928	8	272	303
268	203	16	261	178
47	283	12	69	157
420	**1027**	**101**	**546**	**481**
218	170	54	104	96
47	62	5	68	59
	31	30	16	
135	265	3	193	221
	16	1	35	26
15	27	1	47	5
	430	4	73	62
5	26	3	10	12
116	**167**	**97**	**168**	**185**
3	3		15	20
18	15	15	18	10
3	68	47	45	18
63	46	5	15	113
			5	
29	35	30	70	24

21-13 各区县医疗卫生机构、床位及人员情况（2018年）

Number of Health Care Institutions, Beds and Employed Persons in Health Care Institutions By Region (2018)

区 县	Region	机构（个） Number of Health Care Institutions (unit)	床位（张） Number of Beds (unit)	人员合计（人） Total Number of Employed Persons (person)	#卫生技术人员 Total Number of Medical Technical Personnel
合 计	**Total**	**6638**	**68981**	**125179**	**101477**
新城区	Xincheng	260	7657	14963	12122
碑林区	Beilin	425	9374	16471	13934
莲湖区	Lianhu	392	8223	15096	12324
灞桥区	Baqiao	415	3129	5358	4449
未央区	Weiyang	422	6795	12425	10456
雁塔区	Yanta	441	8992	18466	15201
阎良区	Yanliang	183	1605	3174	2542
临潼区	Lintong	507	2799	4133	3172
长安区	Chang'an	635	6692	9653	7560
高陵区	Gaoling	230	2202	3675	3071
鄠邑区	Huyi	461	2946	5208	4092
蓝田县	Lantian	626	1706	3167	2483
周至县	Zhouzhi	530	2353	4042	2862
西咸新区	Xixian	710	2644	4596	3447
高新区	Gaoxin	330	1796	4421	3513
国际港务区	International Trade&Logistic Park	71	68	331	249

注：本表数据来源于市卫计委。

21-14 各区县农村村级卫生组织情况（2018年）

Village Level Health Organization in the Rural Area by Region（2018）

区 县	Region	村卫生室（个） Village Health Room（unit）	乡村医生和卫生员（人） Rural Doctors and Health Workers（person）	#乡村医生 Rural Doctors	#卫生员 Health Workers
全 市	**Total**	3337	3347	3210	137
新城区	Xincheng				
碑林区	Beilin				
莲湖区	Lianhu				
灞桥区	Baqiao	171	187	186	1
未央区	Weiyang	57	33	33	
雁塔区	Yanta	30	42	42	
阎良区	Yanliang	80	106	106	
临潼区	Lintong	347	322	313	9
长安区	Chang'an	410	326	325	1
高陵区	Gaoling	121	161	159	2
鄠邑区	Huyi	366	331	326	5
蓝田县	Lantian	524	394	394	
周至县	Zhouzhi	456	637	524	113
西咸新区	Xixian	515	531	526	5
高新区	Gaoxin	214	222	221	1
国际港务区	International Trade&Logistic Park	46	55	55	

注：本表数据来源于市卫计委。

21-15 各区县社区卫生服务中心（站）情况（2018年）

Situations of Community Health Service Center (Station) by Region (2018)

区 县 Region	社区卫生服务中心（站）（个） Community Health Care Center(Station) (unit)	床位数（张） Number of Beds (unit)	人员数（人） Personnel Number (person)	卫生技术人员（人） Medical Technical Personnel (person)	执业（助理）医师 Licensed (Assistant) Doctors	注册护士 Registered Nurses
全 市 Total	**222**	**1647**	**6212**	**5183**	**1584**	**1872**
新城区 Xincheng	15	38	328	271	89	101
碑林区 Beilin	17	71	444	348	157	104
莲湖区 Lianhu	17	185	706	591	190	237
灞桥区 Baqiao	20	76	427	360	117	130
未央区 Weiyang	29	75	674	566	166	245
雁塔区 Yanta	34	30	945	811	266	301
阎良区 Yanliang	8	72	170	151	42	58
临潼区 Lintong	28	568	692	581	153	156
长安区 Chang'an	16	306	661	532	148	154
高陵区 Gaoling	8		111	102	21	49
鄠邑区 Huyi						
蓝田县 Lantian						
周至县 Zhouzhi						
西咸新区 Xixian	16	38	303	246	76	110
高新区 Gaoxin	11	120	570	469	132	166
国际港务区 International Trade& Logistic Park	3	68	181	155	27	61

注：本表数据来源于市卫计委。

21-16 主要年份医疗卫生机构各类人员情况

Number of Personnel in Health Care Institutions in Representative Years

单位：人 (person)

指 标	Item	2010	2013	2014	2015	2016	2017	2018
人员合计	**Total**	**71230**	**90129**	**95633**	**102684**	**107906**	**116939**	**125179**
卫生技术人员	Medical Technical Personnel	56579	71134	76005	81462	86258	94221	101477
执业（助理）医师	Licensed (Assistant) Doctors	18763	23885	24820	26626	27864	30820	33776
#执业医师	Chartered Doctors	16613	21205	22145	23818	25023	27683	30322
注册护士	Registered Nurses	22640	29967	32136	34819	37518	41603	46450
药师(士)	Junior Paramedics	3030	3551	3709	3957	4075	4280	4423
技师（士）	Technicians	4589	4089	4276	4690	5058	5593	6035
其他	Other	7557	9642	11064	11370	11743	11925	10793
其他技术人员	Other Technical Personnel	1156	590	621	816	835	839	925
管理人员	Administrative Personnel	6416	7160	7355	8248	8470	9003	9723
工勤技能人员	Logistics Technical Workers	7079	7437	7944	8326	8913	9179	9707

注：本表数据来源于市卫计委。
本表2011年及以后合计栏数据含乡村医生和卫生员。
本表2017年及以后年份数据含西咸新区。

21-17 医疗卫生机构门诊、住院及病床使用情况（2018年）

指　标	Item	总诊疗人次数 总计 Total
总计	**Total**	**63199317**
一、医院	**Hospitals**	**36959967**
综合医院	General Hospitals	27180664
中医医院	Hospitals Specialized in Traditional Chinese Medicine	3122748
中西医结合医院	Hospitals Integrating Traditional Chinese Medicine with Western Therapeutics in Practice	373126
民族医院	Nationalities Hospitals	
专科医院	Specialized Hospitals	6282716
护理院	Nursing Centers	713
二、基层医疗卫生机构	**Commuting Health Care Service Centre**	**25100378**
社区卫生服务中心（站）	Community Health Care Center(Station)	4638553
社区卫生服务中心	Community Health Care Center	3679469
社区卫生服务站	Community Health Care Station	959084
卫生院	Health Center	2129601
街道卫生院	Urban Health-center	75590
乡镇卫生院	Rural Health-center	2054011
村卫生室	Village Clinics	11238689
门诊部	Outpatient Department	1933081
诊所、卫生所、医务室	Clinic, Health Center, Infirmary	5160454
三、专业公共卫生机构	**College of Public Health Institutions**	**1108524**
专科疾病防治院（所、站）	Specialized Disease Prevention and Cure Center (Place, Station)	47986
妇幼保健院（所、站）	Maternal and Child Health Hospital (Place, Station)	899410
急救中心（站）	Emergency Center(Station)	161128
四、其他卫生机构	**Other Health Institution**	**30448**
疗养院	Sanatorium	30448

注：本表数据来源于市卫计委。
　　本表数据含西咸新区。

Medical and Health Institutions Outpatient, Inpatient and Utilization of Beds（2018）

Total Number of Clinics (person time)				观察室 Observation Room	
门、急诊人次数合计 Total Number of People In Outpatient and Emergency Department	门诊人次数(人次) Number of Outpatients (person time)	急诊人次数小计(人次) The Number of Emergency Subtotal (person time)	死亡人数（人）Number of Deaths (person)	留观病例数(人次) Number of Patients Receiving (person times)	死亡人数（人）Number of Deaths (persons)
62371928	**58779740**	**3592188**	**2960**	**32353**	**49**
36729543	**33461343**	**3268200**	**2954**	**32084**	**49**
26990421	24381346	2609075	2797	27265	49
3109813	3002654	107159	88	461	
372088	337584	34504	34	802	
6256508	5739046	517462	35	3556	
713	713				
24503413	**24438233**	**65180**	**6**	**52**	
4508957	4459865	49092	6		
3568307	3526841	41466	6		
940650	933024	7626			
2116351	2100263	16088		52	
75590	74492	1098			
2040761	2025771	14990		52	
10807611	10807611				
1925689	1925689				
5144805	5144805				
1108524	**849751**	**258773**		**217**	
47986	47363	623			
899410	802388	97022		217	
161128		161128			
30448	**30413**	**35**			
30448	30413	35			

21-17 续表1

指　标	Item	急诊死亡率（%） Emergency Mortality (%)	入院人数合计（人） Total Number of Admission Patients (person)
总计	**Total**	**0.08**	**2328412**
一、医院	**Hospitals**	**0.09**	**2229778**
综合医院	General Hospitals	0.11	1711220
中医医院	Hospitals Specialized in Traditional Chinese Medicine	0.08	191317
中西医结合医院	Hospitals Integrating Traditional Chinese Medicine with Western Therapeutics in Practice	0.1	40540
民族医院	Nationalities Hospitals		
专科医院	Specialized Hospitals	0.01	285338
护理院	Nursing Centers		1363
二、基层医疗卫生机构	**Commuting Health Care Service Centre**	**0.01**	**56584**
社区卫生服务中心（站）	Community Health Care Center(Station)	0.01	32091
社区卫生服务中心	Community Health Care Center	0.01	32091
社区卫生服务站	Community Health Care Station		
卫生院	Health Center		24226
街道卫生院	Urban Health-center		716
乡镇卫生院	Rural Health-center		23510
村卫生室	Village Clinics		
门诊部	Outpatient Department		267
诊所、卫生所、医务室	Clinic, Health Center, Infirmary		
三、专业公共卫生机构	**College of Public Health Institutions**		**39019**
专科疾病防治院（所、站）	Specialized Disease Prevention and Cure Center (Place, Station)		7144
妇幼保健院（所、站）	Maternal and Child Health Hospital (Place, Station)		31875
急救中心（站）	Emergency Center(Station)		
四、其他卫生机构	**Other Health Institution**		**3031**
疗养院	Sanatorium		3031

continued 1

出院人数合计 （人） Total Number of Discharge Patients (person)	死亡人数 （人） Number of Hospital Csualty (person)	病床周转次数 （次） Nnumber of Bed Remover (times)	病床使用率 （%） Bed occupancy rate (%)	出院者平均住院日 （天） Average Stay Days in Hospital (day)
2324262	**10109**	**35**	**83.73**	**8.7**
2225711	**10078**	**36.6**	**87.21**	**8.7**
1707189	8722	39.8	88.05	8
192449	455	28.5	83.71	11
40302	264	35.1	93.72	9.7
284503	564	28.9	85.69	10.6
1268	73	12.8	33.95	8.3
56215	**11**	**14.8**	**31.54**	**7.7**
31870	11	19.6	38.18	7.1
31870	11	19.7	38.39	7.1
24078		11.1	26.57	8.6
687		5.8	45.04	29
23391		11.4	25.5	8
267				
39308	**20**	**26**	**81.96**	**11.3**
7613	20	9.5	95.82	36.1
31695		44.5	66.4	5.4
3028		**13.2**	**40.88**	**11.1**
3028		13.2	40.88	11.1

21-18 提供住宿的社会服务机构（2018年）

Social Welfare Insititutions Providing Accommodation（2018）

指　标	Item	机构数（个）Number of Institutions	年末职工人数（人）Number of Staff and Workers at the End of Year	#女性 Female	床位数（张）Number of Beds	年末在院人数（人）Number of Persons Housed at the Year-end
1、养老服务机构	Pension Service Institutions	144	2916	1954	26577	17794
2、儿童福利院	Baby Welfare Homes	1	71	43	551	551
3、社会福利医院	Social Welfare Hospitals	1	146	60	750	423
4、救助站	Rescue Station	8	110	41	415	75
5、军事供应站	Military Supply Station	1	17		1	

注：本表数据来源于市民政局。
　　本表数据含西咸新区。

21-19 主要年份社会福利事业单位机构及人员情况

Number of Social Welfare Institutions and Personnel

单位：个、人　　(unit, person)

指　标	Item	2010	2013	2014	2015	2016	2017	2018
一、机构	**Insititutions**							
烈士纪念建筑物管理单位	Institutions Managing Memorial Buildings of Martyrs	2	2	2	2	2	2	2
救助类单位	Units Providing Assistance	8	8	9	9	9	9	9
殡仪服务单位	Funeral Service Units	22	25	26	26	25	27	25
殡仪馆	Funeral Homes	4	4	3	3	3	3	3
公墓	Cemeteries	14	15	16	16	16	19	18
殡葬管理单位	Funeral Management Units	4	6	7	7	6	5	4
二、人员	**Staff**							
烈士纪念建筑物管理单位	Institutions Managing Memorial Buildings of Martyrs	37	42	44	42	42	44	42
救助类单位	Units Providing Assistance	116	137	139	119	121	114	110
殡仪服务单位	Funeral Service Units	1371	1430	1392	1510	1510	1518	1337
殡仪馆	Funeral Homes	375	491	470	497	481	484	458
公墓	Cemeteries	939	855	838	929	953	959	824
殡葬管理单位	Funeral Management Units	57	84	84	84	76	75	55

注：本表数据来源于市民政局。
　　本表2017年及以后年份数据含西咸新区。

21-20 社会保障基本情况（2018年）

Basic Situation of Social Security（2018）

单位：万人、万户 （10 000 persons、10 000 households）

指 标	Item	2018
基本养老保险参保人数	Number of Basic Old-age Insurance	661.7
1. 城镇企业职工养老保险参保人数	Number of Town Enterprise Worker Old-age Insurance	389.28
其中：离退休人员	Retired Personnel	68.72
2. 机关事业单位养老保险参保人数	Number of Institution Old-age Insurance	28.29
其中：离退休人员	Retired Personnel	10.36
3. 城乡居民养老保险参保人数	Number of Rural Residents Old-age Insurance	244.13
城镇基本医疗保险参保人数	Number of urban basic medical insurance	527
失业保险参保人数	Number of unemployed insurance	167.54
生育保险参保人数	Number of Maternity insurance	213
工伤保险参保人数	Number of industrial injury insurance	229
城镇居民最低生活保障户数	The Number of Minimum Living Guarantee for Urban Resident Households	1.72
城镇居民最低生活保障人数	The Number of Minimum Living Guarantee for Urban Residents	2.63
农村居民最低生活保障户数	The Number of Minimum Living Guarantee for Rural Resident Households	2.59
农村居民最低生活保障人数	The Number of Minimum Living Guarantee for Rural Residents	7.26

注：本表数据来源于市人社局、市民政局。
本表中“基本养老保险参保人数”不含西咸新区，其他指标均含西咸新区。

21-21 全市及各区县新型农村合作医疗情况（2018年）

Situation of the New Rural Cooperative Medical Care of the Whole City and Area County（2018）

区 县	Region	参加新型农村合作医疗人数（万人） Participate in The New Rural Cooperative Medical Population （10 000 persons）
合 计	**Total**	**438.10**
新城区	Xincheng	
碑林区	Beilin	
莲湖区	Lianhu	
灞桥区	Baqiao	19.55
未央区	Weiyang	6.26
雁塔区	Yanta	4.35
阎良区	Yanliang	16.65
临潼区	Lintong	56.31
长安区	Chang'an	69.35
高陵区	Gaoling	23.84
鄠邑区	Huyi	44.98
蓝田县	Lantian	56.25
周至县	Zhouzhi	59.09
西咸新区	Xixian	71.56
高新区	Gaoxin	
国际港务区	International Trade&Logistic Park	9.91

注：本表数据来源于市卫计委。
本表数据含西咸新区。

21-22 全市及各区县优抚对象人员情况（2018年）

Statistics on Persons Enjoying Favoured Treatment by Region（2018）

单位：人 (person)

区 县	Region	伤残人员 Number of Disabled Veterans	烈军属人员 Number of Family Members of Martyrs and Soldiers	在乡复员军人 Demobilized Soldiers in Hometown	带病回乡退伍军人 Veterans Returning Home in Sick
合 计	**Total**	**5166**	**865**	**2380**	**1072**
市本级	City Level	45			
新城区	Xincheng	600	31	5	
碑林区	Beilin	622	47	5	1
莲湖区	Lianhu	719	47	21	2
灞桥区	Baqiao	269	50	147	154
未央区	Weiyang	225	58	77	3
雁塔区	Yanta	708	52	45	7
阎良区	Yanliang	110	51	160	59
临潼区	Lintong	270	77	434	226
长安区	Chang'an	357	84	275	105
高陵区	Gaoling	144	65	193	123
鄠邑区	Huyi	252	57	214	82
蓝田县	Lantian	213	67	287	165
周至县	Zhouzhi	320	92	227	100
西咸新区	Xixian	312	87	290	45

注：本表数据来源于市民政局。

21-23 全市及各区县计划生育和婚姻登记情况（2018年）

Conditions of Birth Control and Marriage Registration by Region（2018）

区 县	Region	计划生育率（%） Family Planning Rate(%)	节育率(%) Birth control Rate(%)
合 计	**Total**	**99.63**	**89.00**
新城区	Xincheng	99.98	85.00
碑林区	Beilin	100.00	87.66
莲湖区	Lianhu	99.99	90.20
灞桥区	Baqiao	99.85	87.23
未央区	Weiyang	99.98	86.57
雁塔区	Yanta	99.93	89.31
阎良区	Yanliang	98.80	87.93
临潼区	Lintong	99.38	90.45
长安区	Chang'an	99.72	84.59
高陵区	Gaoling	99.44	89.02
鄠邑区	Huyi	98.94	93.50
蓝田县	Lantian	98.82	90.27
周至县	Zhouzhi	99.14	88.60
西咸新区	Xixian	99.83	91.70

注：本表数据来源于市计生委、市民政局、市法院。
本表中计划生育率、节育率、结婚对数、再婚人数含西咸新区，离婚对数西咸包含不完全。

21-23 续表1 continued 1

区 县	Region	结婚对数（对） Marriages (couple)	再婚人数（人） Remarriages (person)	离婚对数（对） Divorced Couple (couple)
合 计	**Total**	**93007**	**43784**	**42034**
新城区	Xincheng	4593	2203	2561
碑林区	Beilin	7790	3093	3415
莲湖区	Lianhu	6451	3288	3495
灞桥区	Baqiao	6191	3457	2951
未央区	Weiyang	7622	3395	3774
雁塔区	Yanta	12921	5654	6061
阎良区	Yanliang	2425	1456	1216
临潼区	Lintong	5622	2601	2843
长安区	Chang'an	11791	6270	5531
高陵区	Gaoling	2680	1612	1390
鄠邑区	Huyi	4988	2059	1646
蓝田县	Lantian	4837	1693	1690
周至县	Zhouzhi	5787	1914	2223
西咸新区	Xixian	9309	5089	3238

21-24 全市及各区县妇幼卫生保健情况（2018年）

Care Health Conditions of Women and Child by Region（2018）

区　县	Region	5岁以下儿童死亡率（‰） Mortality rate of Children under 5-year-old（‰）	新生儿死亡率（‰） Infant Mortality Ratio in 2012（‰）	婴儿死亡率（‰） Neonatal Mortality Ratio（‰）
合　计	**Total**	**2.21**	**0.96**	**1.73**
新城区	Xincheng	1.59	1.14	1.59
碑林区	Beilin	1.36	0.54	1.09
莲湖区	Lianhu	2.09	1.2	2.09
灞桥区	Baqiao	1.81	0.69	1.39
未央区	Weiyang	1.31	0.56	1.03
雁塔区	Yanta	1.25	0.92	1.17
阎良区	Yanliang	3.16	0.79	1.97
临潼区	Lintong	2.21	0.92	2.03
长安区	Chang'an	3.48	1.32	2.28
高陵区	Gaoling	3.91	1.95	2.23
鄠邑区	Huyi	2.92	1.12	2.25
蓝田县	Lantian	5.06	2.17	3.86
周至县	Zhouzhi	2.84	1.11	2.37
西咸新区	Xixian	1.43	0.31	1.02

注：本表数据来源于市卫计委。
　　本表数据含西新区。

21-24 续表1 continued 1

区　县	Region	孕产妇死亡率（1/10万） Maternal Mortality Ratio (one in hundred thousandth)	产妇住院分娩比例（%） Proportion of maternal Hospital Births (%)
合　计	**Total**	**6.73**	**100**
新城区	Xincheng		100
碑林区	Beilin		100
莲湖区	Lianhu		100
灞桥区	Baqiao		100
未央区	Weiyang		100
雁塔区	Yanta		100
阎良区	Yanliang		100
临潼区	Lintong	18.45	100
长安区	Chang'an	12.01	100
高陵区	Gaoling	55.85	100
鄠邑区	Huyi		100
蓝田县	Lantian	24.11	100
周至县	Zhouzhi		100
西咸新区	Xixian	10.22	100

21-25 主要年份律师、公证及调解情况

Basic Statistics on Lawyer, Notaries and Mediation in Representative Years

指 标	Item	2010	2013	2014	2015	2016	2017	2018
一、律师工作	**Lawyers**							
律师事务所（个）	Number of Law Offices (unit)	95	116	122	149	176	200	224
律师（人）	Lawyers(person)	1202	1639	1846	2198	2462	2836	3796
#专职	Full-time	1139	1560	1738	2092	2337	2716	3476
兼职	Part-time	63	77	88	91	84	120	148
刑事诉讼辩护及代理（件）	Criminal Litigation Defense and Agency（case）		3267	3118	3524	3260	5872	5869
民事诉讼代理（件）	Civil Litigation Agency(case)		10754	9985	15308	16743	24593	28810
行政诉讼代理（件）	Administrative Litigation Agency(case）		319	374	532	601	1584	1256
非诉讼法律事务（件）	Nonlitigious Legal Matters（case）		2265	2352	2780	2840	4981	3900
二、公证工作	**Notarization**							
公证处（个）	Number of Notary Offices (unit)	14	14	14	14	14	14	14
公证人员（人）	Notarial Personnel (person)	202	222	298	307	293	285	296
#公证员	Notaries	112	115	118	121	115	116	116
办理公证件数（件）	Number of Notarized Documents Issued (case)	106491	136471	135413	135622	144662	150300	161932
国内	Domestic	72670	98572	90171	86589	95194	96085	110311
涉外	Foreign-related	33410	37444	44773	49033	49468	54215	51621
港澳台	Hong Kong. Macao and Taiwan related	411	455	469	373	512	641	1601
三、人民调解工作	**Number of People Mediations**							
已建调委会数（个）	Number of Mediation Committees (unit)	3911	4040	4059	4052	4062	3903	3589
调解人员数（人）	Number of Mediators (person)	15717	15240	15793	14838	14888	14295	14216
调解纠纷数（件）	Number of Civil Disputes Mediated (case)	22247	33651	33641	31696	27455	48690	24868
#调解成功数	Number of Cases Successfully Mediated	22164	32368	32537	30590	26426	47921	24364

注：本表数据来源于市司法局。

2015年开始统计上将港澳台并入国内，表中2015年以后办理公证件数中港澳台所列数据为其中数，2014年及以前年份港澳台数据与国内、涉外数据为并列关系。

本表2017年及以后年份数据含西咸新区。

21-26 主要年份共青团组织情况

Basic Facts on Communist Youth League in Representative Years

单位：个、人 (unit, person)

指　标	Item	2010	2013	2014	2015	2016	2017	2018
一、基层团组织	**Grass-root Youth League Organisations**	**7006**	**10770**	**10152**	**10074**	**10530**	**10237**	**9438**
二、共青团员	**Youth League Members**	**308141**	**344096**	**343121**	**331261**	**251706**	**201789**	**162527**
#女团员	Female Youth League Members	142379	158287	153212	146213	110092	88182	
三、专职团干部	**Full-time Youth League Cadre**	**311**	**737**	**659**	**496**	**165**	**158**	**96**

注：本表数据来源于共青团西安市委员会。
本表数据不含西咸新区。

21-27 妇联组织及工作情况（2018年）

The Basic Situation of Women's Federation（2018）

指　标	Item	2018
一、妇联组织	**Women's Organizations**	
市级妇联（个）	Municipal Women's Federation(unit)	1
街道妇联（个）	Street Women's Federation(unit)	105
社区妇联（个）	Community Women's Federation(unit)	873
县（区）妇联（个）	County (district) Women's Federation(unit)	13
乡（镇）妇联（个）	Township (town) Women's Federation(unit)	39
村妇联	Village Women's Representative Conference	1586
二、妇联工作	**Women's Work**	
巾帼建功标兵（个）	Women Business Model(unit)	138
巾帼建功集体（个）	Group of Women Business Model(unit)	39
巾帼文明岗（个）	Women's Civilized Model Post(unit)	89
三八红旗手标兵（人）	Models of "March 8 Red-Banner Holders" (person)	
三八红旗手（人）	March 8 Red-Banner Holders (person)	27
三八红旗集体（个）	March 8 Red-Banner Groups(unit)	15
五好家庭（户）	Five-virtue Family	181
本级最美家庭（户）	The Best Family at the Present Level	472
乡镇最美家庭（户）	The Best Family in the Town	132
街道最美家庭（户）	The Best Family in the Street	758
村最美家庭（户）	The Best Family in the Village	3225
社区最美家庭（户）	The Best Family in the Community	732

注：本表数据来源于市妇联。
本表数据为西安原口径数据。

21-28 主要年份交通、火灾及安全生产情况

Transportation, Fire and Safety Production in Representative Years

指 标	Item	2010	2013	2014	2015	2016	2017	2018
道路交通事故	**Road Accidents**							
事故数(起)	Number of Traffic Accident (case)	2323	2252	1970	2392	2943	2858	3153
死亡人数（人）	Number of Deaths (person)	531	460	483	481	476	453	430
受伤人数（人）	Number of Injuries (person)	2520	2217	1832	2318	3012	2856	3219
损失（万元）	Economic Loss (10 000 yuan)	736.6	1143.9	1264	1470.2	1653.7	1777.3	2190.9
火灾事故	**Fire Accidents**							
事故数(起)	Number of Cases (case)	1825	4062	3199	2590	3434	2353	2066
死亡人数（人）	Number of Deaths (person)	13	26	17	20	16	8	26
受伤人数（人）	Number of Injuries (person)	7	6	5	7	7	2	37
损失（万元）	Economic Loss (10 000 yuan)	2224.2	3011.9	4381.1	2401.5	1901.1	1659.1	1783.1
农机事故	**Farm Machinery Accidents**							
事故数(起)	Number of Cases (case)	5	1	24	47	4	2	4
死亡人数（人）	Number of Deaths (person)		1	1	1	1		2
工矿商贸事故	**Accidents in Industry, Mine,Business and Trade**							
事故数(起)	Number of Cases (case)	20	14	10	10	33	36	33
死亡人数（人）	Number of Deaths (person)	24	18	15	11	35	43	41

注：本表数据来源于市公安局及安监局。其中交通、火灾数据2011年及以前年份来自于市安监局，2012年以后数据来自于市公安局。2014年农机及工矿商贸事故发生起数统计口径变化，数据与以前年份不可比。
本表中交通火灾数据为西安原口径，农机和工矿商贸事故2017年及以后年份含西咸新区。工矿商贸事故2017年数据以此表为准。

21-29 主要年份刑事案件情况

Data on Criminal Cases in Representative Years

指 标	Item	2010	2013	2014	2015	2016	2017	2018
一、案件数情况	**Data on Number of Cases**							
立案数（起）	Number of Registered Cases(case)	48566	72611	77051	108955	98056	79828	70332
破案数（起）	Number of Cleared up Cases(case)	18906	26587	25830	28629	30730	33128	33616
破案率（%）	Percent of Cleared up Cases(%)	38.9	36.6	33.5	26.3	31.3	41.5	47.8
抓获作案成员(人)	Number of Criminals Caught(person)	13104	14255	14184	12827	11982	12848	11153
二、查获犯罪集团情况	**Data on Hunted down and Seized Criminal Gangs**							
查获犯罪集团个数（个）	Number of Hunted down and Seized Criminal Gangs (person)	186	695	359	153	119	97	75
查获犯罪集团人数（人）	Number of Members of Hunted down and Seized Criminal Gangs (person)	939	2632	1508	680	492	418	359
涉及案件（起）	Number of Cases Involved(case)	1172	2439	1111	291	242	303	180
三、涉枪案件情况	**Data on Cases with Guns Involved**							
立案数（起）	Number of Registered Cases(case)	16	17	13	9	21	22	13
破案数（起）	Number of Cleared up Cases(case)	11	16	8	6	17	17	7
破案率（%）	Percent of Cleared up Cases(%)	68.8	94.1	61.5	66.7	81	77.3	53.8

注：本表数据来源于市公安局。
本表数据为西安原口径数据。

21-30 主要年份治安案件情况

Data on Public Order Cases in Representative Years

指 标	Item	2010	2013	2014	2015	2016	2017	2018
受理数（起）	Number of Accepted Cases(case)	58968	94853	108780	104553	109124	95821	92927
查处数（起）	Number of Investigated and Prosecuted Cases(case)	57151	93546	106811	100954	106999	93634	90563
查处率（%）	Percent of Investigated and Prosecuted Cases(%)	96.9	98.6	98.2	96.6	98.1	97.7	97.5
查处违法人数（人）	Number of Investigated and Prosecuted Law-breakers and Crime Committer(person)	45856	46253	52922	40838	40126	34625	32185

注：本表数据来源于市公安局。
本表数据为西安原口径数据。

21-31 主要年份西安市人民检察院案件办理情况

Data on Acceptance of Cases of Xi'an People's Procuratorate

指　标	Item	2010	2013	2014	2015	2016	2017	2018
一、审查逮捕案件受理件数（件）	**Examination and Arresting(case)**	**4229**	**5748**	**6443**	**6545**	**7381**	**7184**	**7216**
二、逮捕各类案件人数（人）	**Arresting of Criminals of each kind(person)**	**6183**	**7177**	**7534**	**6692**	**7763**	**7511**	**7162**
决定逮捕贪污贿赂犯罪嫌疑人（人）	Suspects of Corporation and Bribery to be Arrested (person)	51	49	64	100	26	27	56
决定逮捕渎职、侵权犯罪嫌疑人（人）	Suspects of Misprision and Tortious to be Arrested (person)	2		18	4		22	2
批准逮捕刑事犯罪嫌疑人（人）	Suspects of Criminal to be Arrested (person)	6130	7128	7452	6588	7737	7462	7104
三、刑事立案监督、侦查活动监督（件）	**Supervision of Acceptance of Criminal** Cases and Investigation (case)	**623**	**368**	**284**	**162**	**118**	**79**	**56**
四、审查起诉案件受理件数（件）	**Examination and Prosecution (case)**	**4662**	**6371**	**7278**	**6922**	**8090**	**8933**	**9288**
五、起诉各类案件人数（人）	**Prosecution of Criminals of each kind(person)**	**5946**	**7615**	**8399**	**8018**	**9445**	**10365**	**10193**
起诉贪污贿赂犯罪被告人（人）	Prosecution of Criminals of Corruption and Bribery to be Defendants(person)	163	151	123	153	154	179	101
起诉渎职、侵权犯罪被告人（人）	Prosecution of Misprision and Tortious to be Defendants (person)	22	24	44	17	39	38	12
起诉刑事犯罪被告人（人）	Prosecution of Criminal to be Defendants (person)	5761	7440	8232	7848	9252	10148	10080

注：本表数据来源于市检察院。
　　本表数据为西安原口径数据。

21-32 西安市中级人民法院案件基本情况（2018年）

Law Cases Basic Data of Xi'an Intermediate People's Court（2018）

单位：件、万元　　(case,10 000 yuan)

指　标	Item	全市结案 the whole City	中级人民法院结案 the Intermediate People's Court	基层人民法院结案 the Basic People's Court
合　计	**Total**	**208345**	**27578**	**180767**
刑事	Criminal	11652	3579	8073
民事	Civil	129654	17356	112298
行政	Administration	1696	34	1662
执行	Execution	61527	5144	56383
其他类型	Other types	3816	1465	2351

注：本表数据来源于市中级人民法院。
　　本表数据为西安原口径数据。

主 要 统 计 指 标 解 释

艺术表演团体 指由文化部门主办或实行行业管理（经文化行政部门审批并领取营业性演出许可证），专门从事表演艺术等活动的各类专业艺术表演团体，含民间职业剧团。（不包括群众业余文艺表演团队）

艺术表演场馆 指由文化部门主办或实行行业管理（向文化行政部门备案或领取合资（合作）演出场所许可证），有观众席、舞台、灯光设备，公开售票、专供文艺团体演出的文化活动场所。附属于文化部门机构内非独立核算的剧场、排演场，公开营业的也应单独统计。

图书馆 指各类图书馆的管理与服务（对文献和信息的搜集、整理、存储、利用和管理，向社会公众开放并提供科学、文化等各种知识普及教育）。包括公共图书馆和各类机构内部举办的或单独举办的图书馆的管理与服务。不包括部队系统以及文化馆（文化中心、群众艺术馆）、文化站内设的图书室。

群众文化活动 指开展群众文化活动的场所的管理和组织活动。包括文化馆（含综合性文化中心、群众艺术馆）、文化站、文化宫、少年宫等群众文化活动。在本制度中，目前暂不统计文化部门以外的文化宫和少年宫。

文化馆 （含综合性文化中心、群众艺术馆）、文化站：指专门从事群众文化活动的群众文化场馆。不包括临时抽调人员组成、没有编制的农村和街道文化工作队、服务站等。

广播节目综合人口覆盖率 根据国家广电总局制定的《广播电视人口覆盖率统计技术标准和方法》进行统计调查的，分别反映中央、省级、地市级、县级广播节目在本行政区域的综合覆盖情况，反应以无线方式传输的广播节目综合覆盖情况，综合反映广播公共服务覆盖的规模、能力、水平。

电视节目综合人口覆盖率 根据国家广电总局制定的《广播电视人口覆盖率统计技术标准和方法》进行统计调查的，分别反映中央、省级、地市级、县级电视节目在本行政区域的综合覆盖情况，反应以无线方式传输的电视节目综合覆盖情况，综合反映广播公共服务覆盖的规模、能力、水平。

博物馆 指为了研究、教育、欣赏的目的，收藏、保护、展示人类活动和自然环境的见证物，向公众开放，非盈利性、永久性社会服务机构，包括以博物馆（院）、纪念馆（舍）科技馆、陈列馆等专有名称开展活动的单位。

等级运动员人数 指经考核正式批准授予等级运动员称号的人数。运动员等级分为国际级运动健将、运动健将、一级运动员、二级运动员、三级运动员、少年级运动员。

等级裁判员人数 指经考核正式批准授予等级裁判员称号的人数。裁判员等级分为国际裁判、国家级裁判、一级裁判、二级裁判、三级裁判。

医疗卫生机构 指从卫生（卫生计生）行政部门取得《医疗机构执业许可证》、《计划生育技术服务许可证》或从民政、工商行政、机构编制管理部门取得法人单位登记证书，为社会提供医疗服务、公共卫生服务或从事医学科研和学在职培训等工作的单位。包括医院、基层医疗卫生机构、专业公共卫生机构、其他医疗卫生机构。

医院 包括综合医院、中医医院、中西医结合医院、民族医院、各类专科医院和护理院，不包括专科疾病防治院、妇幼保健院和疗养院，包括医学院校附属医院。

基层医疗卫生机构 包括社区卫生服务中心（站）、乡镇(街道)卫生院、村卫生室、门诊部、诊所(医务室)。

专业公共卫生机构 包括疾病预防控制中心、专科疾病防治机构、妇幼保健机构（含妇幼保健计划生育服务中心）、健康教育机构、急救中心（站）、采供血机构、卫生监督机构、取得《医疗机构执业许可证》或《计划生育技术服务许可证》的计划生育技术服务机构。

其他医疗卫生机构 包括疗养院、临床检验中心、医学科研机构、医学在职教育机构、卫生监督（监测、检测）机构、医学考试中心、农村改水中心、人才交流中心、统计信息中心等卫生事业单位。

卫生技术人员 包括执业医师、执业助理医师、注册护士、药师(士)、检验及影像技师(士)、卫生监督员和见习医(药、护、技)师(士)等卫生专业人员。不包括从事管理工作的卫生技术人员(如院长、副院长、党委书记等)。

执业(助理)医师 指《医师执业证》"级别"为"执业（助理）医师"且实际从事医疗、预防保健工作的人员，不包括实际从事管理工作的执业（助理）医师。执业（助理）医师类别分为临床、中医、口腔和公共卫生四类。

提供住宿的社会服务机构 包括养老服务机构、精神疾病服务机构、儿童福利机构以及其他提供住宿机构。

烈士纪念建筑物管理机构 指民政部门管理的、独立核算的褒扬烈士的陵园、纪念馆等单位的总称。

殡葬服务机构 指为殡葬服务的单位总称。殡仪馆（含火葬场）、公墓、独立核算的骨灰堂、殡葬管理机构等。

公证人员 指在国家公证机关依法办理公证事务的司法人员，包括公证员、助理公证员和在公证处工作的其他人员。

办理公证文书 指公证处在一定时期内办结的公证文书件数。公证文书按司法部规定或批准的格式制作，包括国内公证和涉外公证两部分。国内公证分为经济合同公证和民事法律关系公证两大类。

调解人员 指在人民调解委员会担负调解民间一般民事纠纷和轻微违法行为引起纠纷的工作人员，包括调解委员会的委员和调解小组的调解员。

Explanatory Notes on Main Statistical Indicators

Arts Performance Troupes refer to the various professional performing arts groups, which sponsored by the cultural sectors or guided by the cultural society (Receive commercial performance license approved by the cultural administration authority),including non-governmental troupes. (The mass amateur arts performance troupes are not included.)

Arts Performance Places refer to the various sites for cultural activities, which sponsored by the cultural sectors or guided by the cultural society (approved by the cultural market administration, or receive joint/cooperative venues permit), with the facility of auditorium, stage and lighting, and selling tickets in public, including the opera halls and rehearse sites, etc. which are affiliated to the culture sectors without independent financial accounts and open to the public.

Library refers to all types of library management and services(collection, collation, storage, use and management of literature and information, open and provide scientific, cultural and other literacy education to the public). Including the management and services of public libraries and the libraries internally or separately organized by various sectors. Excluding the libraries in troops system and cultural palaces (cultural centers, mass art centers),cultural stations.

Mass Culture Center refers to the management and organization of the places where mass culture activities hold. Including cultural palace (cultural center ,mass art center), cultural stations, cultural palaces ,youth palaces and other mass cultural activities. In this system ,cultural palaces and youth palaces beyond cultural sectors are not counted at present.

Cultural Palaces (Cultural Centers, Mass Art Centers),Cultural Stations refers to the mass cultural venues specialized in mass cultural activities. Excluding rural and street cultural teams, service stations which made up by temporary without authorized strength.

Radio Coverage of Population refers to the comprehensive coverage which respectively reflected central, province, city, prefecture and county radio programs by wireless in the administrative region, and comprehensively reflect the size, capacity, level of the public broadcasting services, according to Statistical Standard and Method on Television and Radio Coverage of Population established by the State Administration of Broadcasting ,Film and Television

Television Coverage of Population refers to the comprehensive coverage which respectively reflected central, province, city, prefecture and county television programs by wireless in the administrative region, and comprehensively reflect the size, capacity, level of the public broadcasting services, according to Statistical Standard and Method on Television and Radio Coverage of Population established by the State Administration of Broadcasting , Film and Television

Museum refers to the non-profit, permanent society service sectors which collect ,protect ,show human activities and the witnesses of natural environment, including the units that organize activities with the proper name such as museum, memorial hall , science and technology museum, exhibition hall, etc.

Number of Athletes in Grades refers to the number of athletes who have been given titles through examination. The titles of athletes include international masters of sports, masters of sports, first-grade, second-grade and third-grade sportsmen and young athletes.

Number of Referees in Grades refers to the number of referees who have been given titles after examination. They are classified as international referees, national referees and referees of the first, second and third grades.

Medical and health institutions are the organizations that have got the practice license of medical institution and family planning technical services license from health administrative departments or have obtained legal entity registration certificate from civil, industrial and commercial administration, organization management departments, to provide medical services, public health services or engaged in medical research and medical job training. It includes hospitals, primary medical and health institutions, professional public health institutions, and other medical and health institutions.

Hospitals include general hospital, hospital of traditional Chinese medicine, hospital of integrated traditional Chinese and Western Medicine, National Hospital, various specialist hospitals and nursing homes, excluding specialized disease prevention and treatment centers , Maternity and child care centers and sanatorium, including hospitals affiliated to medical colleges and universities.

Primary medical and health institutions include community health service centers (stations), township (street) health centers, village clinics, outpatient department, clinics.

Professional public health institutions include the center for disease control and prevention, specialized disease prevention and treatment centers, maternity and child care centers (including maternal and child health family planning service center), health education institutions, first aid agencies,collecting and supplying agencies, health supervision institutions, andfamily planning technical service institutions which have got the practice license of medical institution and family planning technical services license.

Other medical and health institutions include sanatorium, clinical inspection center, medical research institutions, medical in-service education institutions, health supervision institutions, medical examination center, Rural change water quality center, personnel exchange center, statistical information center and other health institutions.

Health technical personnel include practicing physician, practicing assistant doctors, registered nurses, pharmacists, inspection and imaging technicians, health supervisors and clerksand other health professionals. It does not include health technical personnel engaged in management work such as Dean, vice president, Secretary of the Party committee, etc.

Practicing physician(assistant) refers to the practitioner who is a practitioner (assistant) doctor and actually engaged in medical care and preventive health care, and does not include the practitioner (assistant) practitioner who is actually engaged in the management work. Practitioners (assistants) are classified into four categories: clinical, Chinese traditional, oral and public health.

Social services providing accommodation include pension services, psychiatric care services, child welfare institutions, and other lodging establishments.

Martyr memorial buildings management organization refers to the floorboard of cemetery, memorial and other units which are independent accounting and managedby civil affairs department to praise the Martyrs

Funeral service agencies refer to the units that serve funeral services. It includes Funeral home (including crematorium), cemetery, independent accounting ashes hall, funeral and interment management organization, etc.

Notary Personnel refers to judicial workers of the state notary offices handling notarization work according to law. They include notaries, assistant notaries, and other people working for notary offices.

Notarized Documents refer to the documents settled by notary offices in a year. The notary documents are drawn up in accordance with the regulations of the Ministry of Justice, including domestic documents and foreign-related documents. Domestic documents are divided into two major categories, documents on economic contracts and documents on civil legal relations.

Mediators refer to workers on peoples mediation committees responsible for mediating in civil disputes and cases of slight infraction of the law. They include members of the mediation committees and mediators of mediation groups.

22 企业调查

ENTERPRISES INVESTIGATION

资料整理：薛　燕
Data management：Xue Yan
数据审核：黄雪冰
Data audit：Huang Xuebing

第二十二部分　企业调查

一、简要说明

1.本章资料主要包括各行业企业景气调查指数和企业家信心指数等，由西安市统计局社会经济调查中心提供。

2.本章资料调查范围：包括规模以上工业、资质内建筑业、限额以上批发和零售业、限额以上住宿和餐饮业、房地产开发业和规模以上服务业。

3.调查方法：采用非全面调查的方法进行统计。

二、主要指标

企业景气指数（第四季度）	125.2
企业家信心指数（第四季度）	125.5

22　ENTERPRISES INVESTIGATION

Ⅰ.Brief Introduction

1.Data in this chapter consists prosperity survey indices of various industries and Entrepreneur Expectation Indicator, provided by Xi'an Municipal Bureau of Statics .

2. The field of investigation and statistics range. The data in this chapter consists of industrial enterprises above designated size, construction enterprises which possess qualification grades, wholesaletrades and retail trades enterprises above designated size, hotels and catering services enterprises above designated size, real estate industry and services above designated size.

3. Methodology on survey. The survey is conducted bynon–overall investigation.

Ⅱ.Major Indicators

Business Climate Index（Fourth Quarter）	125.2
Entrepreneur Expectation Indicator（Fourth Quarter）	125.5

22-1 企业景气指数（2018年）

Business Climate Index（2018）

指　标	Item	一季度 First Quarter	二季度 Second Quarter	三季度 Third Quarter	四季度 Fourth Quarter
企业景气指数	**Business Climate Index**	**130.4**	**129.1**	**126.0**	**125.2**
按行业门类分	**Grouped by Sector**				
工业	Industry	145.7	141.4	132.8	136.7
建筑业	Construction	109.2	110.2	108.3	107.7
批发和零售业	Wholesale and Retail Sales	123.9	123.0	131.6	119.6
住宿和餐饮业	Hotels and Catering Services	131.2	120.4	126.7	115.5
房地产开发业	Real Estate Development	132.6	132.4	129.2	127.7
规模以上服务业	Services above the Designated Size	127.7	128.2	125.2	124.6

22-2 企业家信心指数（2018年）

Entrepreneur Expectation Indicator（2018）

指　标	Item	一季度 First Quarter	二季度 Second Quarter	三季度 Third Quarter	四季度 Fourth Quarter
企业家信心指数	**Entrepreneur Expectation Indicator**	**132.4**	**131.3**	**125.8**	**125.5**
按行业门类分	**Grouped by Sector**				
工业	Industry	144.5	142.5	131.6	135.8
建筑业	Construction	113.4	114.5	110.3	108.2
批发和零售业	Wholesale and Retail Sales	123.3	123.7	126.1	120.9
住宿和餐饮业	Hotels and Catering Services	130.2	126.0	129.1	123.8
房地产开发业	Real Estate Development	137.9	136.6	130.3	128.0
规模以上服务业	Services above the Designated Size	131.7	130.4	126.1	124.9

主 要 统 计 指 标 解 释

企业景气指数：是根据企业家对本企业综合生产经营情况所作的判断与预期（通常是对“良好”、“一般”、“不佳”的选择）而编制的指数，用以综合反映企业的生产经营状况。企业景气指数也称“企业综合生产经营景气指数”。

企业家信心指数：是根据企业家对企业外部市场经济环境与宏观政策的认识、看法判断和预期（通常是对“乐观”、“一般”、“不乐观”的选择）而编制的指数，用以综合反映企业家对宏观经济环境的感受与信心。企业家信心指数也称“宏观经济景气指数”。

景气指数的表示方式：景气指数的表示范围在0～200之间，其含义：100为景气指数的临界值，表明景气状况变化不大；100～200为景气区间，表明景气状况趋于上升或改善，越接近于200，状况越景气；0～100为不景气区间，表明经济状况趋于下降或恶化，越接近于0，状况越不景气。

Explanatory Notes on Main Statistical Indicators

Business Climate Index it is an index worked out according to the judgment and anticipation (normally a choice from good, ordinary, not good) of entrepreneurs made based on synthetic productive and operational situation of the enterprise. It is used to reflect synthetically the productive and operational situation of the enterprise. It is also referred to as synthetic and productive operational prosperity index of enterprise.

Confidence index of entrepreneur it is an index worked out according to the judgment and anticipation (normally a choice from optimistic , ordinary , not optimistic) of entrepreneurs made based on their understandings and views of the market and economic environment outside the enterprise and the macro policies. It is used to reflect synthetically the confidence and feelings of the entrepreneurs to the macro economic environment. It is also referred to as macro-economy prosperity index.

The way to express prosperity index the range of prosperity index is from 0 to 200; 100 is the critical value, and means economic situation didn't change largely; from 100 to 200 is the interval of prosperity; and from 0 to 100 is the interval of not prosperity, meaning economic situation is going down or worse, the closer to 0, the worse the economic situation.

中国统计出版社有限公司最新图书简目

（仅供参考，以实际出版为准）

统计资料

中国统计年鉴　中国统计摘要　中国第三产业统计年鉴
中国第三次全国农业普查综合资料　国际统计年鉴　金砖国家联合统计手册
中国-东盟国家统计手册　中国农村统计年鉴　中国县域统计年鉴
中国农产品价格调查年鉴　中国城市统计年鉴　中国价格统计年鉴
中国贸易外经统计年鉴　中国零售和餐饮连锁企业统计年鉴　中国商品交易市场统计年鉴
大中型批发零售和住宿餐饮企业统计年鉴　中国住户调查年鉴　中国工业统计年鉴
中国环境统计年鉴　中国能源统计年鉴　中国建筑业统计年鉴
中国房地产统计年鉴　中国固定资产投资统计年鉴　中国对外直接投资统计公报
中国人口和就业统计年鉴　中国劳动统计年鉴　中国社会统计年鉴
中国科技统计年鉴　中国高技术产业统计年鉴　全国企业创新调查年鉴
中国文化及相关产业统计年鉴　2018年时间利用调查资料　中国妇女儿童状况统计资料
中国基本单位统计年鉴　中国教育统计年鉴　中国教育经费统计年鉴
中国民族统计年鉴　中国残疾人事业统计年鉴　长江经济带发展统计年鉴

省级综合统计年鉴系列

北京 天津 河北 山西 内蒙古 辽宁 吉林 黑龙江 上海 江苏 浙江 安徽 福建 江西 山东 河南 湖北 湖南 广东 广西 海南 重庆 四川 贵州 云南 西藏 陕西 甘肃 青海 宁夏 新疆 新疆生产建设兵团

市(县)级综合统计年鉴系列

滨海新区 石家庄 唐山 邯郸 保定 沧州 邢台 廊坊 承德 衡水 秦皇岛 张家口 太原 大同 阳泉 长治 晋城 朔州 晋中 运城 忻州 临汾 吕梁 呼和浩特 鄂尔多斯 包头 沈阳 大连 长春 延吉 四平 白山 通化 哈尔滨 齐齐哈尔 黑龙江垦区 上海浦东新区 南京 无锡 徐州 常州 苏州 南通 连云港 淮安 盐城 扬州 镇江 泰州 宿迁 江阴 丹阳 海门 张家港 杭州 宁波 温州 嘉兴 湖州 绍兴 金华 衢州 舟山 台州 丽水 合肥 安庆 福州 厦门 宁德 漳州 龙岩 莆田 泉州 三明 南平 南昌 九江 上饶 新余 抚州 赣州 景德镇 济南 青岛 潍坊 枣庄 潍坊 聊城 郑州 洛阳 平顶山 三门峡 南阳 商丘 信阳 济源 汝州 武汉 十堰 荆州 宜昌 荆门 咸宁 黄冈 长沙 鹰潭 广州 深圳 惠州 东莞 汕尾 湛江 肇庆 南宁 柳州 桂林 贵港 梧州 来宾 河池 防城港 海口 三亚 儋州 成都 内江 贵阳 黔南 毕节 昆明 文山 德宏 西安 延安 安康 铜川 汉中 商洛 银川 兰州 庆阳 乌鲁木齐 昌吉 阿勒泰 兵团一师、二师、三师、四师、六师、七师、八师、十师、十三师、十四师

调查年鉴系列

天津 内蒙古 上海 河南 湖北 湖南 广东 广西 重庆 四川 云南 甘肃 宁夏 南宁 贵港 昆明

统计方法应用／实用手册

Python数据分析基础（第二版）　医用多元统计分析（第三版）　中华生物统计用表
中国国民经济核算体系（2016）基础知识　国民经济核算初级教程　医学统计学手册
全国统计专业技术资格考试系列考试用书：统计业务知识（第四版修订版）统计业务知识学习指导与习题
全国统计专业技术资格考试系列考试用书：统计相关知识（第四版）统计相关知识学习指导与习题

统计通俗读物／统计科普图书

领导干部统计知识问答　《防范和惩治统计造假、弄虚作假督察工作规定》辅导读本
统计新媒体运营指南　统计公文知识问答　理解国民账户　中国古代统计史简编

重点图书

新中国70年　第三次全国农业普查农作物面积遥感测量图集　中国第四次经济普查年鉴
新编英汉汉英统计大词典　中国国民经济核算体系2016　国民经济行业分类注释
挑大学选专业2019–考研择校指南　挑大学选专业2019–高考志愿填报指南　中华医学统计百科全书

发行部电话：(010)63376907　63376908　63376909　同样行书店电话：68783171　68783172
地址：北京市丰台区西三环南路甲6号　邮政编码:100073　网址：http: //www. zgtjcbs.com